PRINCIPLES AND PRACTICE OF
MANAGEMENT ACCOUNTING

PRINCIPLES AND PRACTICE OF MANAGEMENT ACCOUNTING

DR. N P SRINIVASAN
Former Professor and Head
Department of Commerce and School of Business
University of Madras, Chennai

DR. M SAKTHIVEL MURUGAN
Professor-Incharge
DB Jain College, Thoraipakkam
Chennai, Tamil Nadu

NEW AGE MANAGEMENT

An Imprint of

NEW AGE INTERNATIONAL (P) LIMITED, PUBLISHERS
LONDON • NEW DELHI • NAIROBI
Bangalore • Chennai • Cochin • Guwahati • Hyderabad • Kolkata • Lucknow • Mumbai
Visit us at **www.newagepublishers.com**

Published by New Age International (P) Ltd., Publishers
First Edition: 2019

GLOBAL OFFICES

- **New Delhi** **NEW AGE INTERNATIONAL (P) LIMITED, PUBLISHERS**
  7/30 A, Daryaganj, New Delhi-110002, (INDIA)
  Tel.: (011) 23253771, 23253472, **Telefax:** 23267437, 43551305
  E-mail: contactus@newagepublishers.com • Visit us at www.newagepublishers.com
- **London** **NEW AGE INTERNATIONAL (UK) LTD.**
  27 Old Gloucester Street, London, WC1N 3AX, UK
  E-mail: info@newacademicscience.co.uk • Visit us at www.newacademicscience.co.uk
- **Nairobi** **NEW AGE GOLDEN (EAST AFRICA) LTD.**
  Ground Floor, Westlands Arcade, Chiromo Road (Next to Naivas Supermarket)
  Westlands, Nairobi, KENYA, **Tel.:** 00-254-713848772, 00-254-725700286
  E-mail: kenya@newagepublishers.com

BRANCHES

- **Bangalore** 37/10, 8th Cross (Near Hanuman Temple), Azad Nagar, Chamarajpet, Bangalore- 560 018
  Tel.: (080) 26756823, **Telefax:** 26756820, **E-mail: bangalore@newagepublishers.com**
- **Chennai** 26, Damodaran Street, T. Nagar, Chennai-600 017, **Tel.:** (044) 24353401, **Telefax:** 24351463
  E-mail: chennai@newagepublishers.com
- **Cochin** CC-39/1016, Carrier Station Road, Ernakulam South, Cochin-682 016, **Tel.:** (0484) 2377303, **Telefax:** 4051304
  E-mail: cochin@newagepublishers.com
- **Guwahati** Hemsen Complex, Mohd. Shah Road, Paltan Bazar, Near Starline Hotel, Guwahati-781 008,
  Tel.: (0361) 2513881, **Telefax:** 2543669, **E-mail: guwahati@newagepublishers.com**
- **Hyderabad** 105, 1st Floor, Madhiray Kaveri Tower, 3-2-19, Azam Jahi Road, Near Kumar Theater, Nimboliadda Kachiguda, Hyderabad-500 027, **Tel.:** (040) 24652456, **Telefax:** 24652457
  E-mail: hyderabad@newagepublishers.com
- **Kolkata** RDB Chambers (Formerly Lotus Cinema) 106A, 1st Floor, S N Banerjee Road, Kolkata-700 014
  Tel.: (033) 22273773, **Telefax:** 22275247, **E-mail: kolkata@newagepublishers.com**
- **Lucknow** 16-A, Jopling Road, Lucknow-226 001, **Tel.:** (0522) 2209578, 4045297, **Telefax:** 2204098
  E-mail: lucknow@newagepublishers.com
- **Mumbai** 142C, Victor House, Ground Floor, N.M. Joshi Marg, Lower Parel, Mumbai-400 013
  Tel.: (022) 24927869, **Telefax:** 24915415, **E-mail: mumbai@newagepublishers.com**
- **New Delhi** 22, Golden House, Daryaganj, New Delhi-110 002, **Tel.:** (011) 23262368, 23262370, **Telefax:** 43551305
  E-mail: sales@newagepublishers.com

ISBN: 978-81-224-3078-3
C-17-12-10929

Printed in India at Print-o-Pack, Delhi.
Typeset at In-house, Delhi.

NEW AGE INTERNATIONAL (P) LIMITED, PUBLISHERS
7/30 A, Daryaganj, New Delhi-110002
Visit us at **www.newagepublishers.com**
(CIN: U74899DL1966PTC004618)

PREFACE

The large scale industrial production has resulted in widening the area of managerial supervision. The Management has to depend upon accounting information for taking various strategic decisions. Financial Accounting provides necessary accounting information which is made useful by analysis and interpretation of financial statements with the help of Management Accounting. Management Accounting, in the present day, has become an integral part of Business. It helps management in planning, coordinating, communicating and controlling.

Management Accounting is a wide and diverse subject. As a distinct accounting tool it has immense potentiality to meet the growing needs of decision makers and controllers of modern business and industry. Management Accounting includes modern techniques such as Break-even Analysis, Variance Analysis, Financial statement analysis and Budgetary control etc., which enable managers of modern business to plan and control their activities in an efficient way. Because of its increasing importance it has become a special subject of study in Commerce and Management courses of Undergraduate and Postgraduate level and other professional examinations like BCom., BBA, MCom., MBA, CA, ICWA, ACS, CAIIB etc.

This book entitled *Principles and Practices of Management Accounting*, provides a detailed coverage of the subject in a comprehensive way keeping the interests of undergraduate, postgraduate students of Commerce and Management in view. Each Chapter has been presented with a number of illustrations and review questions and problems based on past university questions. Theortical explanations have been made in a succinct but clear way in order to make the subject more easy and also comprehensive even for beginners.

We hope that both the students and teachers will find this book highly useful. We would be very much obliged to receive from the readers any constructive suggestions for improving the standard of the book.

We take this opportunity to offer our sincere thanks to New Age International (P)Ltd. Publishers for bringing out this book in its excellent form.

Dr. N.P. Srinivasan

Dr. M. Sakthivel Murugan

CONTENTS

1

Comparative Accounting Systems

Accounting refers to the discipline of recording and classifying the monetary effects of business transaction and events of an enterprise for the purpose of analyzing and finally reporting the results to a variety of interested parties. If transactions are mostly financial in nature, the accounting system is termed as financial accounting. On the other hand, if they relate to costing information, the system is known as cost accounting.

Financial accounting looks to the interests of external parties who have a financial stake in the concern's affairs, like shareholders, creditors, debenture-holders, employees, regulatory bodies, etc. And cost accounting is mainly concerned with the cost information, which is used by the management to ascertain and control the cost.

Accounting, which is primarily concerned with providing information related to the conduct of the various aspects of the business, like cost or profit associated with some portions of business operations, is called management accounting. However, in the broader sense, any accounting, which is useful to the management, may be termed as management accounting. All financial and cost information generated by accountants is of some interest to the management. But, in practice management accounting differs from financial accounting, cost accounting and budgetary control and financial planning in its emphasis upon 'purpose' rather than upon techniques. Some of the weaknesses of cost and financial accounting systems have also paved the way much for the development of the management accounting system.

FINANCIAL ACCOUNTING

Financial accounting is defined as the science and art of recording and classifying business transactions and making significant summaries for the determination of year end profit or loss and the effect on owner's capital, assets and liabilities. The American Institute of Certified Public Accountants has defined financial accounting as art of recording, classifying and summarizing in a significant manner and in terms of money transactions and events which are, in part at least, of a financial character, and interpreting results thereof. Financial accounting is thus concerned with the compilation and communication of financial information.

In the words of Smith and Ashburn, "Accounting is the science of recording and classifying business transactions and events, primarily of a financial character, and art of making significant summaries, analysis and interpretation of those transactions and events and communicating results to persons who must make decisions or form judgment."

Attributes of Accounting

The above definitions bring out the following as the attributes of accounting.

1. Accounting is both an art and science. Analysis, interpretations and communication of financial results are the art of accounting requiring special knowledge, experience and judgment. As a science, accounting is governed by certain principles, concepts, conventions and policies. But, it is not an exact science like other physical sciences; rather it is an exacting science.
2. It involves recording, classifying, and summarizing. Recording means systematically writing down in account books the transactions and events reasonably soon after their occurrence. Classifying is the process of grouping of transactions or entries of one nature at one place. This is done by opening accounts in a book called ledger. Summarizing involves the preparation of reports and statements from the classified data [i.e., ledger]. This involves the preparation of final accounts.
3. It records transactions in terms of money. This provides a common measure of recording and increases the understanding or the state of affairs of the business.
4. It records only those transactions and events, which are financial in character. Non-financial events, however important they may be for the business, are not recorded in accounting.
5. It is the art of interpreting the results of operations. It aids to determine the financial position of the enterprise, the progress it has made, and how well it is getting along.
6. It involves communication. The results of analysis and interpretation are communicated to the management and other interested parties.

Objectives of Financial Accounting

An analysis of the above definitions brings out clearly the objectives and functions of financial system. The following may be listed out as its main objectives.

1. To ascertain the operating results of enterprises
2. To reveal the financial position of the business
3. To enable control over the business operations as well as all resources made use for the business.

Functions of Financial Accounting

The following are the major functions of accounting:

1. **Keeping systematic records:** As a language of business, accounting is to report results of most of the business events. Hence, its main function is to keep a systematic record

of these events. This function embraces recording transactions in journal and subsidiary books like cashbook, sales book, etc., posting them to ledger accounts and ultimately preparing the financial statements (final accounts).

2. **Communicating the results:** The second main function of accounting is to communicate the financial facts of the enterprise to the various interested parties like owners, investors, creditors, employees, government, and research scholars, etc. The purpose of this function is to enable these parties to have better understanding of the business and take sound and realistic economic decisions.
3. **Meeting the legal requirements:** Accounting aims at fulfilling the legal requirements, especially of the tax authorities and regulators of the business.
4. **Protecting properties of the business:** Accounting helps protecting the property of the business. It discharges this function in accordance with certain fundamental truths and uniform enforcement of generally accepted accounting principles.
5. **Planning and controlling of the business activities:** Accounting also helps planning future activities of an enterprise and controlling its day-to-day operations. This function is done mainly to promote maximum operational efficiency.

Principles of Financial Accounting

Accounting is the language of business and information about business is communicated to outsiders through accounting statements. In order to make these statements easily understandable and meaningful, it is necessary that accounting should be based on certain uniform scientifically laid down norms, which are called as accounting principles. The accounting principles are rules of action or a body of doctrine universally adopted while recording the business transactions. Adopting uniform principles in recording transactions ensures uniformity, clarity and understanding. If accounting is to serve its purpose more effectively, it should be based on certain uniform and scientifically laid down principles or postulates, also termed as accounting standards. The accounting principles can be classified into two categories: (1) Accounting Concepts and (2) Accounting Conventions.

Basic Features of Accounting Principles

The general acceptance of an accounting principle depends on how well it meets the following criteria:

1. **Usefulness or Relevance:** A principle is said to be useful if it results in information that is meaningful and useful to its users.
2. **Objectivity:** A principle is said to be objective if it results in information, which is not influenced, by the personal bias or judgment of those who furnish it. Objectivity means reliability, trustworthiness and verifiability of accounting system.
3. **Feasibility:** A principle is said to be feasibility if it can be implemented without undue complexity or cost. Thus the time, labour and cost of generating accounting data should not exceed its probable uses and resulting benefits.

Meaning and Significance of Accounting Concepts

Accounting concepts are those basic assumptions or conditions upon which the accounting system is based. Some of the important accounting concepts are as follows:

1. **Business entity concept:** As per this concept, business is treated as a separate entity or unit distinct from that of the proprietor. The significance of this concept is that without such a distinction the affairs of the business will be mixed up with the private affairs of the proprietor and the true picture of the business will not be available. The transactions between the proprietor and the business are recorded in the business books separately and are shown separately under the heading 'capital account'. For example, when the proprietor invests ₹ 50,000 in his business, it is assumed that the owner has given that much money to the business and will be shown as a 'liability' for the business. When he withdraws, say ₹ 10,000 from the business, it is to charged to his capital account and the net amount due to him will be only ₹ 40,000.

   The concept of separate entity applies to all forms of business organization, viz., a sole trader, a partnership, or a company. The entity concept has two major implications for accounting:

   I All business transactions are recorded from the firm's point of view and not from the point of view of other parties, such as owners, managers or customers. For example, when a customer buys goods from the business it is recorded as sales by the firm and not as purchases by the customer.

   II It demarcates clearly the business transactions from the personal transactions of the owner. For example, the household expenses of the owner paid by the business are treated as drawings made by the owner and not treated as business expenses.

2. **Going concern concept:** As per this concept, it is assumed that a business unit has a perpetual succession or continued existence and transactions are recorded from this point of view. Hence, while valuing the business assets, the accountant does not take into account the realizable or market values of the assets. Assets are valued at cost at which they were originally purchased less depreciation till date, which is calculated on the basis of the original cost only.

   The concept presumes that the business will continue in operation long enough to charge the cost of fixed assets over their useful life against the business income. It is only on the basis of this concept that a distinction is made between capital expenditure and revenue expenditure. If it is expected that the business will exist only for a limited period, the accounting records are to be kept accordingly.

3. **Dual aspect concept:** Each business transaction has two aspects, i.e., the receiving of a benefit [debit] and giving of a benefit [credit]. For example, if a business purchases furniture, it must have given up cash or have incurred an obligation to pay for it in future. Technically speaking, 'for every debit, there is a credit'. This concept is the core of accountancy and upon this the whole superstructure of 'Double entry system of book keeping' has been raised. As each transaction involves giving account and receiving account

equally, the total assets of a business firm will always be equal to its total equities, i.e., liabilities. That is

External liabilities + Capital = Total Assets

Total Liabilities = Total Assets

This is called the Accounting or Balance Sheet equation.

4. **Cost concept:** This concept is based on the 'going concern concept'. According to this concept, assets purchased are normally entered in the accounting books at the cost at which they are purchased and this cost is the basis for all subsequent accounting purpose since the business is not going to be liquidated but is to be continued for a long time to come. This concept also prevents arbitrary values being used for recording purposes, mainly those resulting in the acquisition of assets.
5. **Money measurement concept:** According to this concept, accounting records only those transactions, which can be expressed in terms of money. Events or transactions, which cannot be expressed in terms of money cannot find place in accounts books, however important they may be. Qualitative or non-monetary transactions are either omitted or recorded separately. For example, a strained relationship between production manager and sales manager, which may affect directly the operating results of the business, does not find place in accounting records.
6. **Realization concept:** According to this concept, the revenue is recognized only when the sale is made. But the sale is a gradual process, which starts with the purchase of raw materials for production and ends with the sale. If no sale is effected, no revenue is recognized. This is important to stop business firms from inflating their profits. However, there are certain exceptions to this concept like hire purchase sale, or contract, etc.
7. **Accrual concept:** This concept is based on the economic premise that all transactions are settled in cash but even if cash settlement has not yet taken place, it is proper to bring the transaction or event concerned into books. Expenditure incurred during the year but not paid and income earned but not received is called as accrued items. According to this concept, these items are taken into consideration while arriving at profit or loss. This concept enables to define income and expense.
8. **Matching concept:** The matching concept provides guidelines as to how the expense be matched with revenues. In other words, costs are reported as expenses in the period in which the associated revenue is reported. Note that costs are matched with revenues, not the other way round. The expense shown in an income statement must refer to the same accounting period or production units, division or department of business unit to which revenue refers.

Meaning and Significance of Accounting Conventions

Accounting conventions are those customs, usage and traditions that are being followed by the accountants for a long time while preparing the accounting statements. The most important conventions are conservatism, consistency, and material disclosure.

1. **Convention of conservatism:** According to this convention, financial statements are usually drawn up on a conservative basis. While preparing accounts and statements, accountants are expected not to take into account 'anticipated profits' but to provide for all possible 'anticipated losses'. Window dressing in accounts is not permitted. This practice of accountants acts a guard against the 'personal judgment' in the preparation of financial statements. It is only on the basis of the convention, the inventory is valued at 'cost or market price, whichever is lower'. Similarly, provision for bad and doubtful debts is made in books before ascertaining profits.
2. **Convention of consistency:** According to this convention, accounting practices should remain unchanged for a fairly long time. And they should not be changed unless it becomes absolutely essential to change them. For example, if a particular method of charging depreciation on a particular asset is followed, it should be followed consistently. However, consistency does not prevent the introduction of improved accounting methods or techniques. If any change is required, such change and its effects should be stated clearly. The aim of this convention is to provide for continuity in accounting practices and methods and enable meaningful comparison practice of accounting statements over a period or between different firms.
3. **Convention of material disclosure:** Apart from the legal requirements, good accounting demands that all vital information should be disclosed. For example, in addition to asset values; the mode of valuation should also be disclosed. The practice of giving footnotes, references, and parentheses in statements is in accordance with this convention only. Accountants should report only material information and ignore insignificant details while preparing the accounting statements. If this is not done, the whole accounting process becomes highly cumbersome and meaningless. What is material depends upon the circumstances and the discretion of the accountant. Because of this convention only, the cost of asset and its written down value alone are shown in the balance sheet. Materiality depends on the amount involved in relation to the asset or to revenues and expenditure or to profit.

Limitations of Financial Accounting

Financial accounting was able to cope with the needs of business in the initial stages when business was not so complex. But the growth and complexities of modern business have made financial accounting highly inadequate. Most limitations are mainly due to the cumulative effect of recorded facts, accounting conventions and personal judgments on financial statements. The inadequacies or limitations of financial accounting are as follows:

1. **Financial information is incomplete and inexact:** The financial statements are essentially interim reports usually prepared for an accounting period. Hence, the financial information, as revealed by them, is neither complete nor exact. The true financial position or the ultimate gain or loss can be known only when the business is closed down.
2. **Qualitative information is ignored:** Financial accounting takes into account only the quantitative information, which is expressed in monetary terms. But a number of qualitative

factors, such as the reputation and image of the management with the public, cordial industrial relations and efficiency of workers, customer satisfaction, competitive strength etc., which cannot be expressed in monetary terms, are not considered by the financial accounting. However, these factors are essential for understanding the real financial condition and the operating efficiency of the business.

3. **Financial information is mainly historical in nature:** As the financial statements are compiled on the basis of historical costs, they fail to take into account such factors as the decrease in money value, or increase in the price level changes. Since these statements deal with past data, not with the future, they are of little value in decision-making.
4. **Financial information is based on accounting concepts and conventions:** Accounting concepts and conventions used for the preparation of financial statement make it unrealistic. For example, the value of fixed assets in the balance sheet is shown on the basis of going concern concept. This means that the value put on an asset rarely represents the amount of cash, which would be realized on liquidation. Similarly, the income statement prepared and based on the convention of conservatism fails to disclose true income, as it includes probable losses and ignores probable income.
5. **Personal judgments influence financial statements:** Many items in the financial statements are left to the personal judgment of the accountant. For example, the method of valuation of inventory, the method of depreciation, treatment of deferred is possibility of making improper assumptions either mistakenly or in order to distort the real picture. However, such indiscreet personal judgments are controlled to a certain extent by the convention of conservatism.

Users of the Accounting Information

Following are some of the groups of people who would like to make use of the accounting information:

1. **Owners:** The primary objective of accounting is to provide necessary information to owners relating to their business. For example, shareholders of a company are interested in the accounting information with a view to ascertain the profitability and financial strength of the company.
2. **Management:** In large business organizations, there is a separation of the ownership and management functions. The managements of such concerns are more concerned with the accounting information because of their accountability to the owners for better performance of their concerns.
3. **Creditors:** Trade creditors, debenture holders, bankers, and other lending institutions are interested in knowing the short-term as well as long-term position of the company. The financial statements provide the required information for ascertaining such a position.
4. **Regulatory agencies:** Various governments and other agencies use accounting reports not only as a basis for tax assessment but also in evaluating how well various business concerns are operating under regulatory framework.

5. **Government:** Government all over the world is using financial statements for compiling statistics concerning business units, which, in turn, help in compiling national accounts.
6. **Potential investors:** Investors use the information in accounting reports to a greater extent in order to determine the relative merits of various investment opportunities.
7. **Employees:** Employees are interested in the earnings of the enterprise because their pay hike and payment of bonus depend on the size of profits earned.
8. **Researchers:** The research scholars in their research in accounting theory as well as business affairs and practices also use accounting data.

In addition, those with indirect concern about business enterprise include financial analysts and advisors, financial press and reporting, trade associations, labour unions, consumers, and public at large. Thus, the list of actual and potential users of accounting information is large.

COST ACCOUNTING

Meaning of Cost, Costing and Cost Accounting

Cost is the amount of resources given up in exchange for some goods or services. The resources given up are money or money's worth expressed in monetary terms. Institute of Costs and Works Accountants of India defines costs as the amount of expenditure (actual or notional) incurred on or attributed to a specified thing or activity.

The costing technology of the Institute of Costs and Management Accountants, London, defines costing as the technique and process of ascertaining costs. These techniques consisting of principles and rules that govern the procedure of ascertaining cost of products or services.

The costing technology of ICMA, London, defines cost accounting as the process of accounting the cost from the point of view of which expenditure is incurred or committed to the establishment of its ultimate relationship with cost centres and cost units. In its widest usage, it embraces the preparation of statistical data, the application of cost control methods and the ascertainment of the profitability of activities carried out or planned. It is a formal mechanism by means of which costs of products or services are ascertained and controlled.

Objectives of Cost Accounting

The various objectives of cost accounting are as follows:

1. To record, analyze and classify costs of products and operations with a view to ascertain the cost per unit of production and also the cost of each element of expenditure.
2. To help the management in its task of cost minimization by facilitating cost control through standard costing and budgetary control, etc.
3. To provide information to enable management to make such tactical decisions of closing down of or continuance of a department, a product mix, make or buy, etc. and also on strategic investment decisions.

Functions of Cost Accounting

More specifically, the following may be listed as functions of cost accounting:

1. To ascertain the unit cost of the product or services or that of the department and estimate the net result on costs, profit or loss for each item of operations in production or services.
2. To help construction of budget, budgetary control and standard costing and to develop the control systems through analysis and exceptions.
3. To present and interpret data for managerial decision-making and control and suggest suitable criteria for choosing among the alternative investments, products, markets, etc.

Importance of Cost Accounting

1. Cost accounting is an aid to management. It enables management to maintain an effective control over inventory to maximize the efficiency and to minimize wastages and losses by providing detailed costing information. It facilitates delegation of responsibilities for important tasks and rating of employees. It helps price fixation and cost estimation.
2. It is an aid to creditors, investors, banks and other financial institutions. It benefits immensely by the installation of an efficient costing system. They can rely on costing records to form their judgment about the profitability and future prospects of the firm.
3. It is an aid to employees. They are benefited in a number of ways by the installation of an efficient costing system. For example, they are benefited through continuous employment and higher remuneration by way of incentives, bonus, etc.
4. It is an aid to the nation. Costing system boosts up the government revenue by bringing prosperity to the business firm. Cost reduction, cost control and elimination of wastes and inefficiencies lead to the progress of the industry and thus facilitates progress of a country as a whole.

Limitations of Cost Accounting

1. Cost accounting, despite its advantages to various parties, such as the management, creditors, employees, etc., has certain inherent deficiencies or limitations, which pave the way for the emergence of management accounting.
2. Any costing system needs to conform to the nature and character of the business firm and this damages the uniformity and universality of any such system.
3. Costing data are essentially post facto and historical in nature. Different forms of predetermined cost systems, such as estimation costing, standard costing, etc., rectify this limitation. But they are also notional costs that enhance the degree of approximation and therefore limit accuracy.
4. Cost accounting system is also based on conventions of treatments of certain items like depreciation, capital and revenue expenditure, fixed costs, wastes and tangibles, etc. This necessarily introduces subjective elements into the whole process.
5. Cost accounting depends heavily on interpretation rather than on actuality of the collected information. This is a part of its role in managerial assistance. However, this tends to make the system more imperative than factual.

EMERGENCE OF MANAGERIAL ACCOUNTING

The term management accounting came into existence when accountants added a third function to the following two existing functions. This concept was introduced

1. to determine the profit or loss of the firm for a period and evaluate its assets and liabilities.
2. to generate information for controlling operations to maximize efficiency.

The third function was that of assisting the management in planning and decision-making. The term became popular only after 1950, following the visit of the accounting team of the Anglo-American Council for Productivity Management of USA during the second quarter of 1950.

In its report, the team stated that management accounting is the presentation of accounting information in such a way to assist management in the creation of policy and in the day-to-day operations of an undertaking. It recommended that industrial accountants should make greater efforts to acquaint themselves with the problems of the management and the technical process in the industry and concentrate their efforts in producing information, which would serve as a guide to policy and actions. Since then the term has become quite popular in the USA and other countries.

Concept of Management Accounting

In ordinary language, any system of accounting which assists management in carrying out its functions more efficiently may be termed as management accounting. The Institute of Chartered Accountants of England and Wales stated that any form of accounting that enables a business to be conducted more efficiently could be regarded as management accounting.

On the same lines, **Robert N. Antony,** in his book *Management Accounting*, has stated that management accounting is concerned with accounting information, which is useful to management. However, these definitions are very general in nature. Some of the important definitions, which are specific, are given below:

The Institute of Cost and Management Accountants, London, has defined management accounting as the application of professional knowledge and skill in the preparation of accounting information in such a way as to assist management in the formation of policies, in the planning and control of operations of undertakings.

The definition given by the American Accounting Association is as follows:

Management accounting is the application of appropriate techniques and concepts in processing historical data of an entity to assist the management in establishing plans for reasonable economic objectives in the making of rational decisions towards these objectives.

In the words of Brown and Howard, management accounting may be defined broadly as that aspect of accounting, which is concerned with the efficient management of a business through the presentation to management of such information that will facilitate efficient and opportune planning and control.

The above definitions clearly indicate that the management accounting is concerned with the accounting information that is useful to the management. The common thread underlying these definitions is that the management accounting is concerned with the efficiency of the various phases of management.

However, it should be clearly understood that it does not supplant financial or cost accounting systems but it supplements them in order to serve the diverse requirements of modern management.

Functions of Management Accounting

The basic function of management accounting is to assist the management in performing its functions effectively. The manner in which management accounting satisfies the requirements of the management for arriving at appropriate business decisions may be described as follows:

1. **Modification of data:** Accounting data as such are not suitable for managerial decision-making and control process. However, they may be used as the basis for making future estimates and projections. In fact, management accounting modifies the available data by rearranging the same, by resorting to a process of classification and combination, which enables retention of similarities of data without eliminating dissimilarities.

   For example, sales figures for different months may be classified to know the total sales made during the period, productwise, salesmanwise, territorywise, etc.

2. **Analysis and interpretation of data:** The accounting data is analyzed and interpreted meaningfully for effective planning and decision-making. For this purpose, the data is presented in a comparative form.

   Analytical tools, such as comparative financial statements, common size statements, trend statements and ratio analysis are used and likely trends are projected.

3. **Facilitating management control:** Management accounting enables all accounting efforts to be directed towards the attainment of goals efficiently by controlling the operations of the company more effectively. Standards of performance are essential elements of any system of control. All this is made possible through standard costing and budgetary control systems, which are an integral part of management accounting.

4. **Use of qualitative information:** Mere financial data and its analysis and interpretation are not sufficient enough for decision-making process. The management may need qualitative information, which cannot be readily converted into monetary terms. Such information may be obtained from statistical compilations, engineering records, case studies, minutes of meetings, etc. Management accounting does not restrict itself to financial data for helping the management, it also uses such information.

5. **Satisfaction of information needs of different levels of management:** Different levels of management, such as top management, middle level management and lower level management need different types of information.

The top management needs concise information covering the entire field of the business activities at relatively long intervals. The middle level management requires technical data regularly and the lower level management is interested in detailed figures relating to the particular sphere of activity at short intervals. Hence, the main function of management accounting is to process the accounting and other data in such a way as to satisfy the needs of different levels of management.

Scope of Management Accounting

The main concern of management accounting is to provide necessary information quantitative and as well as qualitative to the management for planning and control. For this purpose, it draws out information from accounting as well as from non-accounting sources.

Hence, its scope is quite vast and it includes within its fold almost all aspects of business operations. However, the following areas may rightly be pointed out as lying within the ambit of management accounting:

1. **Financial accounting:** The major function of management accounting is the rearrangement or modification of data. The very basis for such a function is provided by financial accounting. Hence, management accounting cannot obtain full control and coordination of operations without a well-designed financial accounting system.
2. **Cost accounting:** Planning, decision-making and control are the basis of managerial functions. The cost accounting system provides the necessary tools, such as standard costing, budgetary control, inventory control, marginal costing, etc., for carrying out such functions efficiently. Hence, cost accounting is considered as a necessary adjunct of management accounting.
3. **Revaluation accounting:** Revaluation or replacement value accounting is mainly concerned with ensuring that capital is maintained in real terms and profit is calculated on this basis.
4. **Statistical methods:** Statistical tools, such as graphs, charts, diagrams and presentation index number, etc., make the information impressive and comprehensive. Other tools, such as time series, regression analysis, sampling techniques, etc. are highly useful for planning and forecasting.
5. **Operational research [O.R.]:** Modern managements are faced with highly complicated business problems in their decision-making processes. O.R. techniques, such as linear programming, queuing theory, decision theory, etc., enable management to find scientific solutions for the business problems.
6. **Taxation:** This includes computation of income tax as per tax laws and regulations, filing returns and making tax payments. In recent times, it also includes tax planning.
7. **Organization and methods [O.M.]:** This deals with the organizations reducing cost and improving the efficiency of accounting as also of office systems, procedures, and operations, etc.
8. **Office services:** This includes maintenance of proper data processing and other office management services, communication on best use of latest mechanical devices, etc.
9. **Law:** Most of the management decisions are taken in a legal environment, where the requirements of a number of statutory provisions or regulations have to be fulfilled. Some

of the statutes that have their influence on management decision, are as follows: The Companies Act, The Controller of Capital Issues Act, MRTP Act, FERA, etc.

10. **Internal audit:** This includes the development of a suitable system of internal audit for internal control.
11. **Interim reporting:** This includes the preparation of quarterly, half-yearly and other interim reports and income statements, cash flow and fund flow statements, scrap reports, etc.

Utility of Management Accounting

Management accounting provides all assistance to the management in all of its functions. By providing the accounting information in the required form and at the required time, it enables the management to perform its functions effectively. It makes available the relevant information after modifying the same suitably for effective planning and decision-making process. It helps to replace intuitive decision-making system with scientific decision-making ones.

Control refers to observing whether the actual results correspond to plans and taking suitable action if there is any deviation. Management accounting includes such tools as budgetary control, standard costing, etc. that greatly helps the management to exercise its control functions effectively.

The standard of performance enables the management to fix responsibilities and know the weak spots in the enterprise without much difficulty.

Coordination among the departmental managers is essential to avoid conflict of interests between them so as to achieve the company's overall objective as planned. Effective coordination could be achieved through departmental budgets and reports, which form an integral part of management accounting.

Organizing is another important function of the management. A sound organization entails delegation of authority and fixation of responsibility without much difficulty. This can be achieved by establishing cost centre or profit centre.

Management accounting assists considerably in establishing such profit centre as also in establishing a sound system of internal control and internal audit for these centres.

Communication is yet another function of management which involves transmission of data, information, results, etc. to both outsiders and insiders. While the decisions of the top management has to be communicated to the middle and low level employees, the results and the requirements of the lower level should be reported to the top management. Results are also to be reported to shareholders, creditors, prospective investors, etc., who wish to know about the company's financial position and progress.

Hence, a suitable reporting system is essential for effective communication of relevant facts. Management accounting helps the management in this regard. From these points it is clear that management accounting is useful to management in every field of activity and hence forms a part of management.

Limitations of Management Accounting

Management accounting is recent discipline and therefore it is still in the process of development. Hence, it suffers from all the limitations of a new discipline. Some of the limitations are

1. They are mainly with the rearrangement or modification of data for the purpose asked for. It derives information from the financial, cost accounting and other records. The accounting statements and records suffer from certain limitations, as they are prepared on the basis of certain accounting concepts and conventions.

   Management accounting adopts the information supplied by these statements and records as such for further processing. Hence, limitations of these statements and records may be transmitted to the management accounting system. This may limit its effectiveness and make the information a sub-standard one.

2. **Persistence of intuition decision-making:** Management accounting assists management in taking decisions scientifically. It includes decision tools, such as marginal costing, differential costing and operational research techniques, such as linear programming, decision theory, etc.

   It provides all types of information in time. Despite the facilities provided, the management mostly resorts to simple methods of decision-making by intuition or hunch. This makes the management accounting system a waste.

3. It has a very wide scope. Management requires information from both accounting and as well as non-accounting sources, quantitative and qualitative information. In an endeavour to provide such an information, management accounting includes many disciplines and deals with a wide range of subjects. This creates many problems and brings a degree of inexactness and subjectivity in the conclusions obtained through it.
4. It is very costly. The installation of a management accounting system needs a very elaborate organization and numerous rules and regulations. This results in heavy investments, which only very big concerns can afford.
5. It invites opposition from within the organization. Management accounting needs a radical change in the accounting organization. It demands rearrangement of personnel and their activities. This is strongly opposed by the people concerned.
6. It is comparatively a new discipline and still in the process of development. Hence, it has to face the same impediment, which a new discipline faces and requires improvements of techniques, fluidity of concepts, sharpening of analytical tools, etc. All this may create doubt about the very usefulness of management accounting.

Tools of Management Accounting

The following tools and techniques are used in management accounting to assist management:

1. Analysis of financial statements
2. Ratio analysis
3. Funds flow analysis

4. Cash flow analysis
5. Cost volume profit analysis
6. Differential cost analysis
7. Budgetary control and standard costing
8. Management reporting.

Financial Accounting vs. Management Accounting

Financial accounting and management accounting are closely inter-related since management draws out a major part of the information from financial accounting and modifies the same for managerial use. Despite such close relationships between the two, there are certain fundamental differences, which are as follows:

1. **Objectives:** The main objective of management accounting is to assist management in its task of planning and control. Hence, it is designed principally to provide information for internal use by the management. Financial accounting is designed to supply information through financial statements to external parties like shareholders, creditors, debenture holders, banks, regulatory bodies, etc. Thus, management accounting is primarily an internal reporting system while financial accounting is primarily an external reporting system.
2. **Subject matter:** Financial accounting deals with the position of the business as a whole, i.e. the financial statements report mostly the overall performance or position of the business. On the other hand, management accounting deals with the details of the various departments, divisions, products, types of inventory or other subdivisions of the enterprise. The reports of management accounting are concerned with the profitability or performance, etc. of each of the divisions or departments. In short, it provides detailed analytical data for managerial use.
3. **Nature of data:** Financial accounting is concerned with the monetary records of past events, whereas management accounting is concerned with future information. In other words, financial accounting makes use of data which is historical, quantitative, and monetary, while management accounting uses data which is descriptive, statistical and subjective and relates to the future.
4. **Periodicity of reporting:** The period of reporting is much longer in financial accounting as compared to management accounting. Normally, financial statements are prepared at the end of the accounting year, but the management requires information at frequent intervals. Hence, in management accounting greater emphasis is laid on furnishing information quickly and at short intervals.
5. **Precision:** As the information is meant for internal use, there is less emphasis on precision in the case of management accounting but the information provided in financial accounting is meant for use by external parties and therefore it has to be more precise as compared to management accounting.

6. **Element of compulsion:** Financial accounting has more or less become compulsory or statutory for every business. But a business is free to install or not to install a system of management accounting.

The above points of distinctions show that management accounting is highly flexible or less rigid in approach as compared to financial accounting.

COST ACCOUNTING *vs.* MANAGEMENT ACCOUNTING

Cost accounting is not merely a tool for cost ascertainment and cost recording, it is also a good tool for cost control, ascertainment of profitability and for management decision-making process. That is why most of the cost accounting concepts are used in management accounting for assisting the management. Although there appeared to be overlapping of areas between cost accounting and management accounting, the following distinctions between the two are listed below:

1. Cost accounting is mostly concerned with cost ascertainment and cost control-employing tools like budgetary control, standard costing, responsibility accounting, etc. for such purposes. Management accounting is concerned with all such matters in a wider perspective that assists the management in the formulation of policies, improvement of productivity, profitability and in guiding the management on the point of finance in the day-to-day operations.
2. Cost accounting deals primarily with cost data, while the management accounting involves considerations of both cost and revenue. Management accounting is an all-inclusive accounting information system that covers financial, cost accounting and all aspects of business finance. But it is not a substitute for other accounting functions.

However, one should not be very much concerned with the boundaries of cost and management accounting systems because both are complementary in nature. Without a well-established cost accounting system the management accounting system cannot function efficiently.

In the absence of cost accounting, details of cost information will not be available to the management accountant and his function will lose its significance.

THE MANAGEMENT ACCOUNTANT

The management accountant plays a significant role in the decision-making process of the organization. He is variously known as the controller of finance, financial controller, financial adviser, chief accounts officer, etc. He is responsible for the installation, development and efficient functioning of the management accounting systems.

He plays an important role in gathering, compiling, reporting and interpreting the internal accounting information. He designs the framework of the financial and cost control reports in order to satisfy the information needs of the different levels of the management. He computes variations by comparing the actual performance with standards or budget estimates and interprets the result of operations to all levels of management and the owners of the business.

The management accountant occupies a pivotal position in the organization. He performs a staff function and has also line authority over the accountants and other employees in his office.

He educates executives on the need for control information and on the ways of using it. He shifts relevant information from the non-relevant information and reports the same in an intelligent form to the management and sometimes to interested external parties.

However, his job is limited to the provision of required information in a comprehensive and as well as in a reliable form to the management for decision-making. But the actual decision-making responsibility lies with the management. In other words, neither the management accountant nor the internal accounting reports can make decisions of the management. But without that information decisions of the management may not be as good as they are with such information.

Functions of the Management Accountant

In the USA, the management accountant is called controller or comptroller. He is considered to be the part of the management team because he has the responsibility for collecting vital information both from within and outside the company.

He has to design a framework for the management accounting system. Thus, he safeguards the accuracy of information and develops devices required for their meaningful organization and interpretation. Functions of the controller have been laid down by the Controller's Institute of America. They are typical of the function of any management accountant by whatever name he is called. They are:

1. To establish, coordinate and administer as an integral part of the management. An adequate plan for the control of operations would provide to the extent required in the business for profit planning program for capital investments and for financing sales forecasts, expenses on budget and cost standards and together with the necessary procedures to execute the plan.
2. To compare the performance with operating plans and standards, to report and to interpret results of operation to all levels of the management and to the owners of the business. This function includes the formulation, administration of accounting policies and compiling statistical records and special reports as required.
3. To consult with all the segments of management responsible for policy or action concerning any phase of operations of the business as it relates to the attainment of objectives and the effectiveness of policies, organizational structure and procedures.
4. To administer tax policies and procedures.
5. To supervise and coordinate preparation of reports to government agencies.
6. To assure fiscal protection for assets of the business through adequate internal control and proper insurance coverage.
7. To continuously appraise economic and social forces and government influences and interpret their effects upon the business.

It may be noted that these seven functions of a controller are broad enough to include all phases of policy and organization within the controller's jurisdictions. This has elevated the position of a controller to the top management cadre to the level of Vice President or Director for finance.

REVIEW QUESTIONS

1. Define management accounting.
2. Management accounting is concerned with accounting information, which is useful to management. Comment.
3. State the main objectives of management accounting.
4. List out the main tools of management accounting.
5. Cost accounting is complementary to management accounting. How?
6. State the objectives and functions of financial accounting.
7. State the limitation of financial accounting.
8. Who are the users of the accounting information?
9. What are the objectives of cost accounting?
10. Enumerate the functions of cost accounting.
11. Explain in details the accounting concepts and conventions.
12. State the limitations of cost accounting.
13. Distinguish between financial accounting and management accounting.
14. Differentiate cost accounting from management accounting.
15. Discuss the need for management accounting.
16. Explain the advantage of management accounting.
17. Enumerate the limitation of management accounting.
18. Explain how management accounting helps to eliminate limitations of financial accounting.
19. What are the functions of a management accountant?
20. What are the qualities of a management accountant?
21. Discuss the utility of management accounting.
22. Define management accounting. Discuss the scope and functions of management accounting.
23. Explain the term management accounting and mention the objectives and practical uses.
24. Explain the importance of management accounting as a tool of management decision-making.
25. How does management accounting help planning and control functions in an organization?
26. Explain the limitation of financial accounting and point out how management accounting helps in removing them.
27. Explain the scope of management accounting in providing information to the management for the evaluation and control of business operations.
28. Explain the duties and functions of the controller.

■■■

2

Preparation of Financial Accounts

Double Entry Book Keeping System, Journal, Ledger, Trial Balance

DOUBLE ENTRY BOOK KEEPING

ACCOUNTING AS THE LANGUAGE OF BUSINESS

Arnold W Johnson in his book *'Elementary Accounting'* says that "Modern Accounting has often been called *'The Language of Business'*. Its responsibility is applying thorough knowledge of the theory of accounting i.e., generally accepted principles of accounting to the practical field of business in order that income and financial position may be stated fairly".

The basic function of language is to serve as a means of communication. Accounting serves the purpose of communicating the results of business operations to all the interested parties such as proprietors, managers, creditors and investors.

DEFINITION OF ACCOUNTING

According to the American Institute of Certified Public Accountants (AICPA) *"Accounting is the art of recording, classifying and summarizing in a significant manner and in terms of money transactions and events which are of a financial character and interpreting the results thereof"*.

OBJECTIVES OF ACCOUNTING

Objectives of accounting may differ from business to business depending upon their specific requirements. However, the following are the general objectives of accounting:

1. **Maintenance of Accounting Records:** Accounting records are the basis for the accounting work. The records have to be maintained systematically. While maintaining the accounting records, the generally accepted accounting conventions and concepts have to be followed.

   In recent years, maintenance of books and records is relegated to the lower level employees. Still, required guidance has to be provided to them as and when necessary.

2. **Ascertainment of profit or loss:** Accounting is expected to ascertain and reveal the net results of the operations of a business. Various interested parties like owners, management, investors and creditors should be supplied with the results of the operations as per their specific requirements. While finalizing the accounts, objective approach is essential, combined with consistency and conservatism.

3. **Depiction of financial position:** A true and fair view of the financial position should be presented. The properties and assets possessed by the business should be shown at appropriate values as per the prevailing practices. The stake of creditors and owners in the business should be clearly presented. All the material information must be clearly disclosed.

4. **Providing information:** In recent years, providing information has become the most important objective of accounting.

   The American Accounting Association (AAA) has listed out the following purposes for which accounting should provide information.

   (*a*) Making decisions concerning the use of limited resources including identifications of crucial decision areas and determination of objectives and goals.

   (*b*) Effectively directing the controlling of all organisation's human and material resources.

   (*c*) Maintaining and reporting on the custodianship of resources.

   (*d*) Facilitating social functions and control.

DEVELOPMENT OF ACCOUNTING CONCEPTS AND CONVENTIONS

The generally accepted principles were evolved from common experience of accountants, historical precedents, regulations of Government agencies and statements from professional bodies. Professional bodies like The Institute of Chartered Accountants of England and Wales, The American Accounting Association, The American Institute of Certified Public Accountants, The Institute of Chartered Accountants of India have evolved, modified and codified the different principles, concepts and conventions of Accounting.

These principles, concepts and conventions provide uniformity in preparation of accounts. They are the general guidelines to sound accounting practices. They facilitate the understanding the financial statements by the end users. The principles are acceptable because they satisfy three basic criteria namely:-

1. **Utility or relevance:** The principles are invaluable in providing more useful, necessary and relevant data to the interested parties.

2. **Objectivity:** The principles are supported and supplemented by facts and documents. They are not based on subjective views of individual accountants.

3. **Feasibility:** The principles are practicable since they can be applied without excessive cost and effort.

CHARACTERISTICS OF ACCOUNTING CONCEPTS AND CONVENTIONS

1. The accounting principles are developed for practical purposes. They cannot be validated or proved like the principles of Mathematics, Physics and Chemistry. They are the best possible suggestions based on practical experience, reasoning and observation of the professional accountants.
2. The principles are for common usage to ensure uniformity and understanding. They are not rigid. They can be adapted to the changing needs and circumstances of business units. They enhance the usefulness of the data relating to the activities of a firm.
3. They are not specifically made or legislated by any Government or legal authority. They are not legally enforceable.
4. They are in the process of evolution and are likely to change as per the dictates of changing circumstances and technology.

Accounting Concepts

1. **Business entity concept:** A business entity is an organisation of persons to accomplish an economic goal. According to the entity concept, the entity that represents the association of persons is considered distinct and separate from the owners, managers and employees of the enterprise. The accounting entity may be the business unit itself (sole proprietorship, partnership firm, joint stock company, cooperative societies or a Government Enterprise) or a defined part of business (i.e., a department) or an amalgamation of related businesses (i.e., a holding company) depending on the user's needs. It can be a non-business group like a club, religious body which engages in economic activities.
2. **Going concern concept:** According to International Accounting Standard–1 (AS–1), "The enterprise is normally viewed as a going concern, that is, as continuing in operation for the foreseeable future. It is assumed that the enterprise has neither the intention nor the necessity of liquidation".

   This concept assumes that a business entity has continuity of life. It will continue for an indefinite period of time. It has no need or intention to close down.
3. **Money measurement concept:** All business transactions are measured, expressed and recorded in terms of money. 'Money' provides a common denominator or unit of measurement by means of which heterogeneous facts about a business can be expressed in terms of quantities which can be added or subtracted and summarized. Money, as a common denominator of profit or loss and financial position. The 'Rupee' is the common unit of measurement for economic events and transactions in India since it is the legal tender used as the medium of exchange.
4. **Dual aspect concept:** Every business transaction recorded in the books of accounts of a business has two aspects – receiving of benefit and giving of benefit. Both the aspects of each transaction must be recorded in appropriate accounts of the business.

For example, when a building is acquired by a firm (receiving of benefit), it has to pay cash (giving of benefit) or create an obligation for payment in future (benefit to be given). Recording of the transaction takes place through debiting the building account and crediting cash account or the personal account of the seller, thus showing both the benefit receiving and giving aspects.

5. **Accounting period concept or periodicity concept:** A business unit may continue for an indefinite period. It is possible to ascertain overall profit or loss of the business when it is liquidated. But practically it is not possible to wait for an indefinite period. The interested parties like owners or shareholders, creditors, tax authorities need periodical reports about the business performance. So it is necessary to sub-divide the indefinite life span of a firm into smaller time units for measurement of performance and understanding the financial position. Such smaller and usable time frame is called an accounting period.
6. **Cost concept:** Accounting is a historical record of the transactions of a business entity. According to cost concept, assets are recorded at the price said to acquire them. This cost is the basis for all subsequent accounting for the assets. The assets are gradually depreciated on the basis of cost and the effective life of the asset. The market value of assets are not considered either for valuation or depreciation of such assets.
7. **Realisation concept or revenue recognition concept:** "Revenue is the gross inflow of cash, receivables or other consideration arising in the course of an enterprise from the sale of goods, services and from holding of assets". According to the realisation concept, revenue is considered as earned on the date when it is realised. The term 'Realisation' implies the legal liability to pay by the buyer or user or customer. The revenue should be recognised only when it is legally due and realisable.
8. **Matching concept:** Primary objective of commercial enterprises is profit making. The accountants are responsible to match the revenues earned during an accounting period with the cost associated with the period to ascertain the profit earned. Matching of revenues and costs relevant to a specific period is called the matching concept. It is the basis for finding reliable profit for a period which can be safely distributed to the owners.
9. **Accrual concept:** This concept makes a distinction between receipt of cash and the right to receive cash and payment of cash and the legal obligation to pay cash in relation to revenues and expenses respectively. Revenues and costs are accrued i.e., recognised as they are earned or incurred and not as money is received or paid. The accrual concept is the basis for mercantile system of accounting.
10. **Objectives of evidence concept:** All accounting entries must be based on objective evidence. 'Objective' refers to verifiability, reliability and absence of bias. No transaction must be recorded in the books of accounts without verifiable documentary evidence. Examples are Cash receipts for payment made, bank paying-in counterfoils or bank statements for deposits in bank, invoice copies for purchases etc. The confidence of users of financial statements can be achieved through systematic adherence to this concept.

Accounting Conventions

1. **Convention of full disclosure:** According to this convention, all accounting statements should be prepared honestly. This should be evident through the transparency of the statements. The statement should disclose fully all the significant information. Facts, figures and the details which are of material interest to the owners, investors, creditors etc., must be clearly presented in the financial statements. This type of disclosure needs proper classification, summarisation, aggregation and explanation of the numerous business transactions.
2. **Convention of consistency:** The basic aim of the doctrine of consistency is to preserve the comparability and reliability of financial statements. According to this convention, the rules, practices and concepts used in accounting should be continuously observed and applied year after year. Comparisons of results among different accounting periods can be significant and meaningful only when consistent practices were followed in ascertaining them.
3. **Convention of materiality:** Materiality means 'relative importance'. All important items and facts should be disclosed in accounting statements, Unimportant and immaterial details need not be separately given. Otherwise, the accountant becomes over burdened with unnecessary details. For example, a plastic container for drinking water can be clubbed with general expenses instead of separately being disclosed as an Asset.
4. **Convention of conservatism:** Conservatism is a policy of caution or 'playing safe'. It demands taking a 'gloomy' view of a situation. Conservatism is the defensive accounting mechanism against 'uncertainty'. According to Kohler, "Conservatism is a guideline which chooses between acceptable accounting alternatives for recording events and transactions so that the least favourable immediate effect on assets, income and owner's equity is reported".

LIMITATIONS OF ACCOUNTING

In spite of its indispensable position in modern business establishments, accounting has its own limitations.

It cannot record all the events and transactions taking place in an enterprise. It ignores transactions which cannot be expressed in terms of money. It cannot measure the qualitative aspects of the products, policies, management and the workers. It cannot quantify the morale of employees in the Organisation.

Accounting relies on estimates, and forecasts in several important matters like useful life of machinery, market value of investments. Similarly, subjective opinions of the accountant can influence valuation of stocks, provision on debtors for doubtful debts and discounts etc. Accounting results may not be accurate and reliable due to such estimates and subjective influence of individual accountants.

Accountants rely on historical cost for recording the fixed assets. Depreciation is also provided on the recorded cost of the assets. When the time for replacement comes, replacement cost is usually far more than the accumulated funds through depreciation. Accounting also ignores the price level changes which drastically alter the values of assets and liabilities. Inflation which is an universal phenomenon makes the profit ascertained and financial position shown by accounting unrealistic and unreliable.

Everyone of these limitations has been engaging the attention of the professional bodies. Recent developments like Human Resource accounting, Inflation Accounting, International Accounting Standards etc., have been aimed at improving the usefulness of Accounting by overcoming the limitations.

Groups Interested in Accounting Information

Accounting information is used by different groups of people, both inside and outside the organisation. According to Slawin and Reynolds "Conceptually, accounting is the discipline that provides information on which external and internal users of the information may base decisions that result in the allocation of economic resources in society".

1. Internal Users of Accounting Information

The internal users comprise of owners, management and employees.

(i) Owners: The sole trader or partners or shareholders who have provided the capital of a business unit are interested in its performance and progress. They are primarily interested in the revenues and expenses, profit or loss, net worth and external liabilities. They expect reasonable return on their investment in the form of profits. They are also concerned about the risk and uncertainty attached to their investment. They require detailed data about comparative earnings of the business, future prospects and divisible profits.

(ii) Management: Sole traders and partners usually manage their own business. But companies are managed by paid professionals. Management of a business involves making day to day decisions on routine matters and also policy decisions, whenever needed. Accounting data is the basis for most of the decisions made by management. The trends in sales and purchases, relationship of expenses to the turnover, productivity of workers, comparative profitability of different products and divisions etc., are some of the vital data required by management for planning and controlling the business operations.

(iii) Employees: The work force is interested in the profitability of the business which affects their bonus, incentives and working conditions. The success or failure of the business is linked to their livelihood. Labour unions use the accounting data in their bargaining strategies with the management.

2. External Users of Accounting Information

Various outside groups and individuals make use of accounting information for their own purposes:

(i) Creditors and financiers: Suppliers of goods and services, commercial banks, public deposit holders, debenture holders etc., are included in this category. They are interested in the liquidity position and repaying capacity of the business.

(ii) Potential investors: Those who are interested in investing their surplus funds should know about the financial condition of a business unit while making their investment decisions. They are more interested in future earnings and risk.

(iii) Consumers: Those who use the products and services of a firm are interested in knowing the justification for the prices charged to them. They examine the expenses, sales and profits to see if they are paying fair prices for the products and services.

(iv) Tax authorities: Accounting information helps them in computing Sales tax, Income tax etc., to be collected from business units. They scrutinise the revenues and expenses of business firms to determine their accuracy.

(v) Government: The scarce financial resources of the country are used by business enterprises. Performance of business units in different industries helps the Government in policy formulation for development of trade and industry. Government also administers prices of certain trades. In such cases, Government agencies have to ensure that the guidelines for pricing are followed.

(vi) Research scholars: The published financial statements are especially used by researchers to evaluate the performance of individual firms, industries and trade. They make use of the data relating to sales, profits, dividends, interest, taxes etc., in their analysis and evaluation.

DIFFERENT SYSTEMS OF ACCOUNTING FOR RECORDING BUSINESS TRANSACTION

There are two different systems of accounting for recording business transactions. They are cash system of accounting and mercantile system of accounting.

1. **Cash System of Accounting:** Under this system, only actual cash received and paid is recorded. No entry is made for a receipt that is merely due; any payment outstanding is accounted for. Government accounting is based on the cash system only. Professional people like lawyers, chartered accountants, etc., maintain accounts under this system only.
2. **Mercantile System or Accrual System of Accounting:** Under this system of accounting, entries are made not only for actual receipt or payment of cash but also for amounts having become due for payment or receipt. In other words, both cash transactions and credit transactions are recorded in the books of accounts. All commercial establishments and even non-trading concerns follow this system only.

   Further, accounting records can be prepared under any one of the following systems:

   1. **Single-entry system:** Under this system only, the personal and cash aspects of transactions are recorded in books. Normally, the impersonal aspects are ignored. It is not based on 'dual aspect concept'. Hence, it is incomplete, inaccurate, and unscientific.
   2. **Double-entry system:** It is the most common system of book keeping whereby the two aspects of every transaction, i.e., the receiving aspect [debit] and the giving

aspect [credit] are recorded in books of accounts. It is based on the 'dual aspect concept'. This method of writing every transaction in two accounts is known as the double entry system of book keeping. This is the most accurate, complete and scientific system of accounting.

ADVANTAGES AND LIMITATIONS OF DOUBLE ENTRY SYSTEM

The important advantages of double entry system are as follows:

1. It keeps a complete record of business transactions.
2. It provides complete information concerning the business.
3. It provides a check on the arithmetical accuracy of books of accounts.
4. It discloses the operating results, i.e., profit or loss of the business for a given period.
5. It makes possible a meaningful comparison of operating and financial performance over a period of time and enables the businessman to evaluate the progress of his business.
6. It also enables a businessman to plan and control his operations.
7. It reduces the chances of committing fraud.
8. Past details with regard to any account are easily and accurately obtainable in this system.
9. This system is highly flexible and can be adjusted to any specific needs of a business unit.

Limitations of Double Entry System

Though the system is very methodical, scientific, and accurate, it has a few shortcomings. The biggest limitation is that this method fails to detect errors of the following types:

1. It is not possible to discover a transaction, which is not recorded at all in books of original entry.
2. If the amount of a transaction is recorded wrongly, there is no way of detecting the error.
3. A compensatory error is also not detected by this system.
4. It involves more clerical labour.

SOME COMMON TERMS USED IN ACCOUNTANCY

Transactions: Transactions are those activities of businessmen, which involve transfer of money or goods or services between two persons or two accounts. These activities may be in the nature of purchase of goods, sale of goods, and borrowing from a bank or lending money to some persons, payment or receipt of certain income, like dividend or commission, etc. They may be in the nature of cash transaction or credit transaction. When cash payment or receipt takes place immediately in a transaction, it is called cash transaction. When cash is paid or received at a later date, it is called credit transaction.

Entry: An entry is a record of a transaction in account books.

Debtor: A person, who received a benefit without giving money or money's worth, is a debtor, abbreviated as 'Dr'.

Creditor: A person, who gives a benefit without receiving money or money's worth, is a creditor, abbreviated as 'Cr'.

Goods: Goods are the articles purchased for the purpose of resale. For example, for a furniture mart selling chairs and tables, furniture is considered as goods. Other articles, such as computer, a wall clock, or cycle purchased for office use, are not goods, because they are not for sale. They will be called assets of the business.

Purchases: These are goods bought for resale to customers.

Purchases returns: These are goods returned by the trader to the supplier because of poor quality or defects in the goods supplied. They may also be termed as 'returns outwards' or 'returns to suppliers'.

Sales: These are goods sold to customers. If it is for cash, it will be termed as cash sales or till takings. If cash for sales is received at a later date, it will be termed as credit sales.

Sales returns: When the trader receives back goods from any customer for poor quality or defects in the goods sold out, it is called 'Sales returns', or 'Returns outwards' or 'Returns from customers'.

MEANING OF ACCOUNT

It is statement of various dealings that occur between a customer and the firm. It can also be expressed as a clear and concise record of transactions relating to a person, or a firm, or a property, or a liability, or an income or expenditure. The short abbreviation for account is A/c.

CLASSIFICATION OF ACCOUNTS

In order to understand rules of double entry system, it is essential to know which classes of accounts are affected by a particular transaction. For this purpose, all accounts are broadly classified into two classes: **1.** Personal accounts and **2.** Impersonal accounts. Impersonal accounts are further subdivided into (*a*) Real account, and (*b*) Nominal account. Thus, all accounts can be classified into 'personal', 'real' and 'nominal' accounts.

VARIOUS TYPES OF ACCOUNTS

Personal accounts: Such accounts relate to persons. A separate account is prepared for each person. Such accounts can take the following forms:

(*i*) Natural person's accounts, e.g., Krishna's accounts, Priya's account

(*ii*) Artificial person or body of persons e.g., Bank account, any firm's account, any company's account.

(*iii*) Representative personal accounts, e.g., prepaid expenses accounts, outstanding wages account.

Real accounts or property accounts: These accounts relate to a property, an asset, or a possession, e.g., Plant account, Cash Account, Goodwill account, etc. A separate account is prepared for each class of property or asset.

Nominal accounts: These accounts relate to business expenses or losses and income or gains, e.g., Wages' account, Interest account, Discount received account, Dividends account.

RULES OF DOUBLE ENTRY

When closely analyzed, each transaction has two aspects. One aspect is either 'Receiving Aspect' or 'Incoming Aspect' or 'Expenditure Aspect'. This is termed as 'Debit Aspect'. Another aspect is 'Giving Aspect' 'Outgoing Aspect' or 'Income Aspect'. This is termed as 'Credit Aspect'. Together, they form the basis of double entry.

The rules of double entry are as follows:

1. Personal Accounts — (*a*) Debit the Receiver
(*b*) Credit the Giver

2. Real or Property Accounts — (*a*) Debit what comes
(*b*) Credit what goes out

3. Nominal Accounts — (*a*) Debit all expenses and losses
(*b*) Credit all incomes and gains

Stages of double entry system

The following are the three distinct stages of a complete system of double entry:

(*i*) Recording the transaction in the journal.

(*ii*) Classifying transactions in the journal by posting them to the appropriate ledger accounts and then preparing a trial balance.

(*iii*) Closing books and preparing the final accounts.

DISTINGUISH BETWEEN DOUBLE ENTRY SYSTEM AND SINGLE ENTRY SYSTEM

	Double Entry	*Single Entry*
1.	The double aspects of a transaction are recorded.	Only one aspect is recorded.
2.	For every debit, there is a credit of equal amount.	There may a debit without a corresponding credit and vice versa.
3.	There are personal accounts, real accounts, and nominal accounts.	There are personal accounts and cash accounts only.
4.	A trial balance can be prepared to test the arithmetical accuracy of accounts.	It cannot be prepared as the ledger does not contain all accounts.
5.	Trading and Profit and Loss Account and Balance Sheet can be prepared directly.	They cannot be prepared directly.
6.	Actual net profit can be calculated directly.	Approximate net profit can be indirectly calculated.
7.	It involves more clerical labour.	It involves less clerical labour.
8.	It is a perfect scientific system.	It is an imperfect way of book keeping.
9.	Tax authorities accept this system.	They do not accept it as such.

ACCOUNTING *vs.* BOOK KEEPING

Book keeping refers to the maintaining of the various sets of account books and deals with recording routine and repetitive business transactions in a significant and orderly manner. Assistants usually do it. On the other hand, accounting is more analytical and deals with the designing of accounting system, forecasting, preparation of financial statements and audits, cost analysis, income tax and interpretation of financial statements and reports for decision-making, etc. Senior accountants normally do them. Where book keeping ends, accounting starts. Book keeping provides necessary data for accounting in the case of big concerns. But in small concerns the same person does both.

REVIEW QUESTIONS

1. Define accounting and state the attributes of accounting.
2. List out the group of people who would like to make use of the accounting information.
3. State the basic features of accounting principles.
4. Describe the meaning and significance of any four accounting concepts.
5. What is the significance of the following accounting concepts:
   (*a*) Going Concern Concept; (*b*) Dual Aspect Concept; (*c*) Money Measurement Concept.
6. State deficiencies of financial accounting.
7. What are the different systems of accounting for recording transactions?
8. What is meant by double entry system of book keeping?
9. State advantages and disadvantages of double entry system.
10. Explain the following terms:
    (*a*) Transactions, (*b*) Account, (*c*) Goods.
11. What are the rules of double entry system of book keeping?
12. How does double entry system differ from single entry system?
13. Differentiate book keeping from accounting.

JOURNAL

MEANING OF JOURNAL

A journal may be defined as the book of original or prime entry containing a chronological record of transactions from which posting is done to the ledger. Transactions are recorded first in the journal in the order in which they occur. The process of recording transactions in a journal is called journalizing. The prescribed format of a journal is shown below.

Journal

Date *[1]*	*Particulars* *[2]*	*L.F.* *[3]*	*Debit [4]* *Amount*	*Credit [5]* *Amount*
Year Month Date	Name of the A/C to be debited Name of the A/C to be credited [Narration]			

Explanation

1. **Date.** The date on which the transaction takes place is entered here.
2. **Particulars.** The name of the account to be debited is written in the first line and the abbreviation 'Dr' is written against it. In the second line, the account to be credited is written preceded by the word 'To'. An explanation of the entry, known as 'narration' is also given within bracket explaining briefly about the transaction.
3. **L.F.** L.F. stands for Ledger Folio, which means the page number in the ledger in which the entry is posted.
4. **Debit.** In this column the amount to be debited against the 'Dr' account is entered.
5. **Credit.** In this column, the amount to be credited against the 'Cr' account is entered.

The Procedure for Journalizing

From the given business transaction, the receiving aspect and the giving aspect should be identified. Depending upon the nature of account that is affected by the transaction, the rule for journalizing should be selected as follows:

Name of Account	Rules for debiting an account	Rules for crediting an account
Personal Account	Debit the Receiver a/c	Credit the Giver a/c
Real Account	Debit what comes in	Credit what goes out
Nominal Account	Debit all expenses and losses	Credit all incomes and gains

These rules may be used either jointly or separately for journalizing each and every transaction. Examples given below would explain the same.

Transaction 1

On 1.1.2018 Vignesh started business with ₹60,000.

Journal: In this transaction, the receiving aspect is that 'cash' is received by the business, which is distinct from Vignesh's private or personal property and the giving aspect is that Vignesh is the giver. Proprietor's personal account is represented by Capital a/c.

The journal entry in the business books is as follows:

Date	*Particulars*		*L.F.*	*Amount Dr.* (₹)	*Amount Cr.* (₹)
1.1.2018	Cash a/c	Dr.		60,000	
	To Vignesh's Capital a/c				60,000
	[Being capital brought in]				

Debit what comes in, here cash comes in, hence cash a/c is debited, proprietor is the giver; hence capital a/c is credited. A short explanation to explain the entry is given within brackets by way of narration. Note that separate rules are used for debiting and crediting accounts. Real account rule is used for making the debit entry and personal rule for making credit entry.

Transaction 2

Furniture was purchased for ₹20,000

Journal: In this transaction, furniture is received and cash is paid. The receiving and giving aspects form the real a/c, i.e., furniture and cash. Hence, the real account rule, i.e., debit what comes in and credit what goes out is to be applied. Furniture comes in and cash goes out. Hence, the entry is as follows:

Date	*Particulars*		*L.F.*	*Amount Dr.* (₹)	*Amount Cr.* (₹)
2.1.2018	Furniture a/c	Dr.		20,000	
	To Cash a/c				20,000
	[Being furniture purchased for cash]				

Transaction 3

Bought goods from Raj for ₹30,000

In this transaction goods are received and Raj is the giver of goods on credit. Hence, the journal entry is as follows:

Date	*Particulars*		*L.F.*	*Amount Dr.* (₹)	*Amount Cr.* (₹)
3.1.2018	Purchase [of goods] a/c	Dr.		30,000	
	To Raj a/c				30,000
	[Being goods purchased on credit]				

Transaction 4

Sold goods for cash ₹25,000

In this transaction, cash comes in and goods go out. Hence, the entry is as follows:

Particulars		*L.F.*	*Amount Dr.* (₹)	*Amount Cr.* (₹)
Cash a/c	Dr.		25,000	
To Sales a/c				25,000
[Being cash sales]				

Transaction 5

On 15.1.2018 paid wages ₹6,000

In this transaction, wages being an expense it is debited as per the third rule, i.e., debit all expenses and losses and cash is paid for wages. Hence, it is credited. The journal entry is as follows:

Date	*Particulars*		*L.F.*	*Amount Dr.* (₹)	*Amount Cr.* (₹)
15.1.2018	Wages a/c	Dr.		6,000	
	To Cash a/c				6,000
	[Being wages paid]				

Transaction 6

16.1.2018 Interest received ₹1,500

In this transaction, interest being an income, it is credited as per the third rule, i.e., credit all incomes and gains. Interest is received in the form of cash; hence it is debited. The journal entry is as follows:

Date	*Particulars*		*L.F.*	*Amount Dr.* (₹)	*Amount Cr.* (₹)
16.1.2018	Cash a/c	Dr.		1,500	
	To Interest a/c				1,500
	[Being interest received]				

State the accounts involved in the following transactions and which account is to be debited and which account is to be credited.

1. Karthik commenced business with ₹1,00,000
2. Purchased furniture for ₹5,000
3. Sold goods for cash ₹5,000
4. Sold goods to Raj for ₹20,000
5. Paid salaries ₹10,000
6. Purchased goods from Ram for cash ₹9,000
7. Commission received ₹800
8. Paid outstanding expenses ₹900

Answer

Books of Karthik

Sl.No	Accounts involved	Account to be debited	Account to be credited
1.	Cash a/c and Capital a/c	Cash a/c [Real a/c]	Capital a/c [personal a/c]
2.	Furniture a/c and Cash a/c	Furniture a/c [asset comes in] Real a/c	Cash a/c [asset goes out] Real a/c
3.	Cash a/c and Sales a/c	Cash a/c [Asset comes in] Real a/c	Sales a/c [income] Nominal a/c
4.	Raj a/c and Sales a/c	Raj [receiver] Personal a/c	Sales a/c [Nominal a/c]
5.	Salaries a/c and Cash a/c	Salaries [expense] Nominal a/c	Cash a/c
6.	Purchases a/c and Cash a/c	Purchases a/c [expense] Nominal a/c	Cash a/c
7.	Cash a/c and Commission a/c	Cash a/c [comes in] Real a/c	Commission a/c [income] Nominal a/c
8.	Outstanding expenses a/c and Cash a/c	Outstanding expenses a/c [creditors receive] Personal a/c	Cash a/c [goes out] Real a/c

Illustration 1

Enter the following transactions in the journal of Mr. Ram Kumar.

2018 Jan.	*Particular*	*Amount (₹)*
1	Started business by investing cash	70,000
2	Purchased land for	20,000
2	Purchased goods for cash	30,000
3	Purchased goods from Ajit on credit	10,000
4	Sold goods for cash	20,000
5	Sold goods to Arun on credit	6,000
6	Paid freight	300
8	Donated to Charities	1,000
11	Paid salaries to Ramesh	1,200
12	Deposited cash into bank	16,000
13	Withdrawn from bank for office use	4,000
14	Withdrawn from bank for private use	6,000
15	Charged Interest on capital	1,000
15	Rent received	2,000
16	Loan from bank	20,000

Solution

Date	*Particulars*		*L.F.*	*Amount [Dr.] ₹*	*Amount [Cr.] ₹*
2018 January 1	Cash a/c To Capital a/c [Being cash brought in as capital]	Dr.		70,000	70,000
2	Land a/c To Cash a/c [Being land bought for cash]	Dr.		20,000	20,000
2	Purchases a/c To Cash a/c [Being cash purchases]	Dr.		30,000	30,000
3	Purchases a/c To Ajit a/c [Being credit purchases]	Dr.		10,000	10,000
4	Cash a/c To Sales a/c [Being cash sales]	Dr.		20,000	20,000
5	Arun a/c To Sales [Being credit sales]	Dr.		6,000	6,000
6	Freight a/c To Cash a/c [Being freight paid]	Dr.		300	300
8	Donation a/c To Cash a/c [Being donation paid]	Dr.		1,000	1,000
11	Salary a/c To Cash a/c [Being salaries paid]	Dr.		1,200	1,200
12	Bank a/c To Cash a/c [Being cash deposited into bank]	Dr.		16,000	16,000
13	Cash a/c To Bank a/c [Being withdrawal from bank for office use]	Dr.		4,000	4,000

(Contd...)

14	Drawings a/c Dr. To Bank a/c [Being withdrawal from bank for private use]		6,000	6,000
15	Interest a/c Dr. To Capital a/c [Being interest charged on capital]		1,000	1,000
15	Cash a/c Dr. To Rent a/c [Being rent received]		2,000	2,000
16	Cash a/c Dr. To Bank loan a/c [Being loan taken from bank]		20,000	20,000

Compound Journal Entry

If two or more transactions of the same nature occur on the same day, and either debit account and/or credit account are common in them, instead of passing a separate entry for each such transaction, one combined entry may be passed. Such type of entry is known as compound journal entry.

For example, if a trader pays postage, stationery, and cartage on the same day, then instead of passing a separate entry for each of these three expenses, the following compound entry may be passed:

Postage a/c	Dr.
Stationery a/c	Dr.
Cartage a/c	Dr.
To Cash a/c	

Discount Transactions

Discount is an allowance in the form of reduction in the value of an item. There are two kinds of discounts, viz., trade discount and cash discount.

Trade discount: is allowed at the time of purchase or sale of goods by one trader to another in order to promote sales. For example, a manufacturer may allow discount on sale of goods to wholesaler or a wholesaler may allow discount to a retailer. It is always allowed as certain percentage on sale price, i.e., invoice price. The trade discount is not normally recorded in books of account. In other words, only the net amount of purchase or sale i.e., invoice price minus trade discount is recorded in the journal.

Example: Mr. X sells goods for ₹5,000 to Mr. Y at a trade discount of 20%. For recording this transaction the net amount of ₹4,000 [i.e., ₹5,000 – 1,000 {20% of 5,000}] will be considered by both X and Y.

Entries

Books of Mr. X

Mr. Y a/c	Dr.	₹4,000
To Sales a/c		4,000
[Being goods sold at discount]		

Books of Mr. Y

Purchase a/c	Dr.	₹4,000
To Mr. X a/c		4,000
[Being goods bought at a discount]		

Cash discount is a discount allowed at the time of making payments or receipt of cash. It is allowed as certain percentage on the amounts due. It is allowed to a debtor by a creditor in order to induce him to pay on time. As the cash discount is calculated on the amounts already recorded in books, it is shown in books. Cash discount allowed to a debtor is a loss and it should be debited to discount a/c cash discount received from a creditor is a gain and it should be credited to discount a/c.

Examples 1

1. Mr. A owed ₹5,000 to the firm. He settled his account in full at a discount of 2%
   The journal entry in firm's books is as follows:

Cash a/c	Dr.	₹ 4,900
Discount allowed a/c	Dr.	₹ 100
To Mr. A a/c		₹ 5,000
[Being A settled his a/c at 2% discount]		

2. Suppose the firm owes ₹ 10,000 to Mr. X who allows a discount of 5% on full settlement of his account.
   The journal entry in the firm's books is as follows:

Mr. X a/c	Dr. ₹10,000	
To Cash a/c		₹ 9,500
To Discount received a/c		₹ 500
[Being X's a/c settled in full at 5% discount]		

Distinguish between Trade Discount and Cash Discount

	Trade discount	*Cash discount*
1.	It is allowed at the time of making purchases or sales.	It is allowed at the time of making payments or receipts of cash.
2.	It is calculated as certain percentage on the invoice price of goods purchased or sold.	It is calculated as certain percentage on the amounts due to creditors or amounts due from debtors.
3.	It is not shown in the books of accounts. Only the net amount of purchase or sale is recorded in the books.	It is shown in the books: discount allowed as debit entry and discount received as a credit entry.
4.	It is allowed in order to promote more sales or purchases.	It is allowed in order to encourage parties to make payments on time.

Illustration 2

Journalize the following transactions in the books of a trader:

2018 Jan. 1 Commenced business with ₹50,000.

3 Purchased goods for cash ₹10,000 at 5% trade discount

4 Paid carriage ₹100.

7 Purchased Machinery for ₹30,000.

8 Sold goods to Mani on account of for ₹15,000.

Solution

Date	Particulars	L.F.	Amount Dr. (₹)	Amount Cr. (₹)
2018 Jan. 1	Cash a/c Dr. To Capital a/c [Being business started with cash]		50,000	50,000
3	Purchases a/c Dr. To Cash a/c [Being goods bought for cash at 5% trade discount]		9,500	9,500
4	Carriage a/c Dr. To Cash a/c [Being carriage paid]		100	100
7	Machinery a/c Dr. To Cash a/c [Being machinery purchased for cash]		30,000	30,000
8	Mani's a/c Dr. To Cash a/c [Being credit sales]		15,000	15,000

Illustration 3

Journalize the following transactions:

Durga of Chennai started business on 1.1.2018 by investing cash of ₹50,000. She brought goods ₹20,000 and furniture of ₹25,000. She borrowed from her friend Priya ₹25,000 the same day. Her transactions for the month are as follows:

January 1	Purchased goods worth ₹25,000 less 20% trade discount and 5% cash discount.
2	Opened a current a/c in State Bank of India with ₹ 15,000.
3	Sold goods worth ₹15,000 to Vicky and allowed 10% discount.
4	Received ₹13,250 from Vicky in full settlement of his account.
5	Sold goods to Ravi for cash ₹3,500.
6	Sold goods to Krishna ₹5,000.

10	Received ₹ 4,925 from Krishna in full settlement.
15	Paid by cheque: Salaries ₹ 2,500, Postage ₹ 50 and Stationery ₹ 175
16	Repair of furniture ₹ 100.
18	Withdraw for personal use ₹ 3,500.
19	Goods to Ram at the invoice price of ₹ 10,000 on the terms of trade discount at 20% and cash discount at 10%. He paid half in cash.

Solution

Journal in the Books of Durga

Date	*Particulars*		*L.F.*	*Amount Dr.* (₹)	*Amount Cr.* (₹)
2018	Cash a/c	Dr.		50,000	
Jan. 1	Goods [stock] a/c	Dr.		20,000	
	Furniture a/c	Dr.		25,000	
	To Capital a/c				95,000
	[Being cash, goods and furniture brought in to start business]				
1	Cash a/c	Dr.		25,000	
	To Priya's Loan a/c				25,000
	[Being loan taken from Priya]				
1	Purchase a/c	Dr.		20,000	
	To Cash a/c				20,000
	To Discount a/c				
	[Being goods worth ₹ 25,000 bought for cash less 20% trade discount and 5% cash discount]				
2	Bank a/c	Dr.		15,000	
	To Cash a/c				15,000
	[Being cash paid into bank]				
3	Vicky a/c	Dr.		13,500	
	To Sales a/c				13,500
	[Being goods worth ₹ 15,000 sold at 10% discount]				
4	Cash a/c	Dr.		13,250	
	Discount a/c			250	
	To Vicky's a/c				13,500
	[Being cash received less discount]				
5	Cash a/c	Dr.		3,500	
	To Sales a/c				3,500
	[Being cash sales]				

Contd...

Date	Particulars		L.F.	Amount Dr. (₹)	Amount Cr. (₹)
6	Krishna's a/c	Dr.		5,000	
	To Sales a/c				5,000
	[Being credit sales]				
10	Cash a/c	Dr.		4,925	
	Discount a/c	Dr.		75	
	To Krishna's a/c				5,000
	[Being cash received in full settlement]				
	Salaries a/c	Dr.			
15	Postage a/c	Dr.		2,500	
	Stationery a/c	Dr.		50	
	To Bank a/c			175	
	[Being expenses paid by cheque]				2,725
	Repairs a/c	Dr.			
16	To Cash a/c			100	
	[Being repairs paid into cash]				100
18	Drawings a/c	Dr.		3,500	
	To Cash a/c				3,500
	[Being drawn for personal use]				
20	Donations a/c	Dr.		3,500	
	To Goods [Purchase] a/c				3,500
	[Being goods sold at 20% trade discount]				
31	Ram's a/c	Dr.		8,000	
	To S ales a/c				8,000
	[Being goods sold at 20% trade discount]				
31	Cash a/c	Dr.		3,600	
	Discount a/c	Dr.		400	
	To Ram's a/c				4,000
	[Being half amount received at 10% cash discount]				

Illustration 4

An accountant made the following entries in his account books. Are these entries correct? If not, give correct entries.

Date	Particulars		Amount Dr. [₹]	Amount Cr. [₹]
1	Cash a/c Dr. To Raman a/c [Sold goods to Raman for cash]		3,500	3,500
2	Goods a/c Dr. To Lakshman a/c [Purchased goods for cash from Lakshman]		6,000	6,000
3	Ravi a/c Dr. To Cash a/c [Paid salary to Ravi]		2,000	2,000
4	Purchase a/c Dr. To Cash a/c [Furniture purchased for cash]		1,000	1,000
5	Freight a/c Dr. To Cash a/c [Freight paid on behalf of the purchaser Raman]		350	350
6	Charity a/c Dr. To Sales a/c [Goods given for charity]		500	500
7	Sathya a/c Dr. To Cash a/c [Paid rent to Sathya]		1,250	1,250

Solution

All entries are wrong. The correct entries are as follows:

Date	*Particulars*		*L.F.*	*Amount Dr.* [₹]	*Amount Cr.* [₹]
1	Cash a/c To Sales a/c [Being cash sales]	Dr.		3,500	3,500
2	Purchase a/c To Cash a/c [Being cash purchases]	Dr.		6,000	6,000
3	Salary a/c To Cash a/c [Being payment of salary]	Dr.		2,000	2,000
4	Furniture a/c To Cash a/c [Being furniture purchased for cash]	Dr.		1,000	1,000
5	Raman a/c To Cash a/c [Being freight paid on behalf of Raman]	Dr.		250	250
6	Charity a/c To Sales a/c [Goods given for charity]	Dr.		500	500
7	Rent a/c To Cash a/c [Being rent paid]	Dr.		1,250	1,250

Opening Entry

In a going concern, previous year balances are brought forward at the beginning of new accounting year by means of a composite or compound journal entry. Such an entry is known as opening entry. In journalizing, all assets accounts are debited and liabilities accounts are credited. The excess of assets over liabilities is credited to *Capital account.*

Example 2

Pass the opening entry, journal entry and find out the balance in the capital a/c.

The balances as on 31st December, 2018 were as follows:

Debit balances: Cash in hand ₹ 60,000; Cash at bank ₹ 25,000; Stock ₹ 90,000; Furniture ₹ 35,000; Buildings ₹ 1,25,000; Debtors ₹ 75,000.

Credit balances: Outstanding rent ₹ 2,500; Sundry creditors ₹ 30,000.

Solution

Opening Journal Entry

Date	*Particulars*		*L.F.*	*Amount Dr.* [₹]	*Amount Cr.* [₹]
2018 Jan. 1	Cash a/c	Dr.		60,000	
	Bank a/c	Dr.		25,000	
	Stock a/c	Dr.		90,000	
	Furniture a/c	Dr.		35,000	
	Buildings a/c	Dr.		1,25,000	
	Debtors a/c	Dr.		75,000	
	To Outstanding Rent a/c				2,500
	To Sundry Creditors a/c				30,000
	To Capital a/c				3,77,500
	[Balances brought in from last year]				

Review Problems

1. Journalize the following transactions extracted from books of a bookseller in May 2018:

1 Started business with a capital of ₹ 1,50,000.

2 Borrowed from Bank ₹ 40,000.

3 Furniture purchased ₹ 10,000.

4 Purchased books ₹ 50,000 and paper ₹ 25,000.

7 Sold books and paper for cash ₹ 35,000.

8 Purchased books from Madras Book House for ₹ 50,000.

10 Sold books worth ₹ 25,000 to Madras University Library

17 Paid postage ₹ 250.

19 Paid ₹ 49,500 to Madras Book house in full settlement.

25 Received rent ₹ 750 from Rajesh who is using a portion of the shop for his business.

27 Sold books on credit to Prasad ₹ 15,000.

30 Paid rent ₹ 2,250 and salary ₹ 2,500.

2. Pass opening entry and find out the capital from the following balances:

1. Cash in hand ₹ 15,000; 2. Stock ₹ 17,500; 3. Debtors – 4. Raj ₹ 9,500, 5. Anu ₹ 8,000; 6. Creditors – Geetha ₹ 25,000; 7. Prepaid insurance ₹ 5,000; 8. Outstanding salaries ₹ 6,000.

3. Journalize the following transactions:

January 2018

1 Rajini started business with a capital of ₹ 60,000.

2 She purchased furniture for ₹ 8,000.

3 Bought goods on credit from Vicky for ₹ 12,000.

12 Sold goods to Umesh for ₹ 15,000.

13 Received cash from Umesh ₹ 9,000.

14 Purchased goods for cash ₹ 12,000.

19 Sold goods for cash ₹ 13,000.

20 Purchased stationery for ₹ 500.

28 Paid rent ₹ 1,200.

31 Paid Vicky ₹ 8,000 on account.

4. Give narration for the following entries:

Date	*Particulars*		*Amount* [₹]	*Amount* [₹]
[A]	Cash a/c	Dr.	15,000	
	Goods a/c	Dr.	10,000	
	To Capital a/c			25,000
[B]	Luna a/c	Dr.	10,000	
	To Sales a/c			10,000
[C]	Purchase a/c	Dr.	15,000	
	To Subbu a/c			15,000
[D]	Cash a/c	Dr.	9,800	
	Discount a/c	Dr.	200	
	To Luna a/c			10,000
[E]	Subbu a/c	Dr.	15,000	
	To Cash a/c			14,625
	To Discount a/c			375
[F]	Bank a/c	Dr.	4,000	
	Drawings a/c		1,000	
	To Cash a/c			5,000
[G]	Charity a/c	Dr.	1,000	
	Drawings a/c		2,000	
	To goods a/c			3,000

5. Not all of the following entries are correct. Pass correct entries wherever necessary:

Date	*Particulars*		*Amount* [₹]	*Amount* [₹]
[a]	Purchase a/c	Dr.	4,000	
	To Ajit traders a/c			4,000
	[Being furniture purchased from Ajit traders]			
[b]	Arun a/c	Dr.	1,000	
	To Bank a/c			1,000
[c]	Sundaram's a/c	Dr.	6,000	6,000
	To Sales a/c			
	[Being goods sold to Sundaram for cash]			
[d]	Ramesh a/c	Dr.	3,000	
	To Furniture a/c			3,000
	[Being old furniture sold to Ramesh on credit]			
[e]	Cash a/c	Dr.	9,000	
	To Sales a/c			9,000
	[Being cash sales for the day]			
[f]	Durga a/c	Dr.	7,500	
	To Purchase a/c			7,500
	[Being goods purchased on credit from Durga]			
[g]	Cash a/c	Dr.	9,800	
	Trade discount a/c	Dr.	200	
	Cash discount a/c	Dr.	100	
	To Sales a/c			10,100
	[Being goods sold for ₹ 10,100 and allowed trade discount ₹ 200 and cash discount ₹ 100]			
[h]	Furniture a/c	Dr.	3,000	
	To cash a/c			3,000
	[Being furniture purchased for domestic use]			

[**Note:** Entries **[d]** and **[e]** are correct entries. Others are wrong. Correct entries should be passed].

6. From the following transactions find out the nature of account and also state which account should be debited and which account should be credited: [a] Salaries paid; [b] Dividend received; [c] Land purchased for cash; [d] Furniture sold; [e] Outstanding rent; [f] Received cash from Karthik; and [g] Proprietor introduced capital.

LEDGER

MEANING OF LEDGER

A ledger is a book of main entry and it contains various accounts, such as personal accounts, real accounts, and nominal accounts. It is the principle book of accounts where identical transactions related to specific person or thing are entered. A ledger account is nothing but a summary statement of all transactions relating to persons, assets or liabilities, and expenses or incomes, which have taken place during a period of time showing their net effect. Journal records all business transactions separately and as per the order of the date of the transaction. The transaction pertaining to a particular person, asset or expenses are recorded at different places in the journal as they occur on different dates. Hence, journal fails to bring the similar transactions together and it is not useful for any reference. In order to have a consolidated view of the similar transactions, the entries in the journal are transferred to the ledger accounts. The following process from journal to ledger is known as *posting.*

SPECIMEN LEDGER ACCOUNT

Specimen Ledger Account
Name of Account

Dr. Cr.

Date	*Particulars*	*J.F.*	*Amount* [₹]	*Date*	*Particulars*	*J.F.*	*Amount* [₹]
Year month date	To [Name of credit element]			Year month date	By [N ame of the debit element]		

This is a standard form of ledger account, which is in "T" form. It is widely used. Each account in the ledger is divided into two equal parts. The left hand side is the debit side [Dr.] and the right hand side is the credit side [Cr.]. Each of the two sides are further divided into four columns for recording the date of transactions, the name of the account to be debited or credited, folio, and the amount of transaction. J.F. stands for journal folio, i.e., the page number in the journal or subsidiary book from where the posting to the account is made.

Running Balance Form of Ledger Account. This form has six columns, viz., 1. Date; 2. Particulars; 3. J.F.; 4. Dr. Amount [₹]; 5. Cr. Amount [₹]; and 6. Balance. Commercial banks and some business houses use this type of ledger.

ADVANTAGES OF A LEDGER

The main advantages of a ledger are:

1. The journal gives information regarding various transactions chronologically. But the ledger gives information regarding all transactions of a particular account in a summary form.
2. In the journal, one account is debited and another account is credited at different dates. The final effect of a series of transactions of a certain customer or certain property or

a certain expense is not disclosed by the journal. It is not designed in that way. But the final effect is known at a glance.

3. Similarly, the journal could not provide immediately the totality of certain dealings.

LOOSE-LEAF LEDGER

The ledger that is normally used in majority of business concerns is a bound book, so that it can be preserved for a long time. But in bigger concerns bound books may not be used. Appropriately ruled sheets in thick paper are introduced and fixed up with the help of a binder. The sheets can be removed whenever necessary. Therefore, this type of ledger is known as "loose-leaf ledger". There is, of course, a danger that an unscrupulous employee may remove a sheet. To prevent such removal, this type of ledger is locked and will be with a responsible official.

HOW CAN A LEDGER BE SUB-DIVIDED?

In small concerns all accounts relating to persons, assets, expenses and income, etc., can be maintained in one ledger and in one cashbook. In a broad sense, Cashbook is also a part of the ledger. But in bigger concerns, as accounts are too many, the ledger is further sub-divided. They maintain the following three types of ledger.

1. **Creditors Ledger:** All accounts of creditors are found in this ledger. It can also be called as 'Bought Ledger' or 'Supplier's Ledger.' Entries in this ledger are usually made from Purchases Daybook, Purchases Returns Book and Cashbook.
2. **Debtors Ledger:** It contains accounts of those customers to whom goods are sold on credit. It is also known as Customers' Ledger or Sales Ledger. Entries in this ledger are usually made from Sales Daybook, Sales Returns Book and Cashbook.
3. **General Ledger/Nominal Ledger:** It contains all accounts other than debtors and creditors. Accounts of properties, expenses, incomes, capital, drawings, etc., will be found in this ledger. It may also be called as 'Impersonal Ledger.'

Subdivision of Ledger

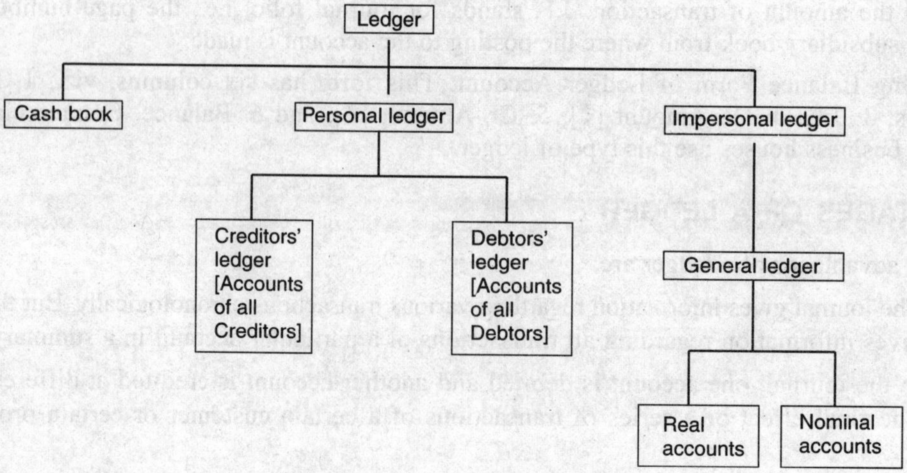

Procedure Regarding Posting of Journal Entries into Ledger Accounts

Posting means transferring debits and credits from the journal to ledger accounts. Each amount recorded in the debit column of the journal is posted to the debit side of an account in the ledger. And each amount recorded in the credit column of the journal is posted to the credit side of an account in the ledger.

Separate accounts should be opened in the ledger for posting transactions relating to separate persons, assets, expenses or incomes, as shown in the journal.

The concerned account that has been debited in the journal should also be debited in the ledger. While debiting the concerned account, the name of the other account, which has been credited in the journal, is entered in the debit side of this account with a prefix "To".

Similarly, the concerned account that has been credited in the journal should also be credited in the ledger. While crediting the concerned account, the name of the other account that has been debited in the journal, is entered in the credit side of this account with a prefix "By".

The date of the transaction in the date column, the pages number of the journal from which the entry is posted in the J.F. column, and the amount of the transaction in the amount columns should be entered in the concerned account.

Finally, the concerned account should be balanced in order to find out the net balance in the account.

What does 'Balancing of an Account' Mean?

The various transactions entered in the journal in the chronological order are posted to the concerned account in the ledger, as explained above. At the end of the period, say a month, a quarter, or a year, the account is closed in order to find out the net position shown by it. Totaling debits and credits of the account separately and finding the difference do this. The difference is entered on the side that is similar and this difference is the 'closing balance' shown by the account and this will be carried forward to the next period as the 'opening balance' in the account. This process is known as 'balancing the account'. If the debit side is similar than the credit side, the difference is entered on the debit side to close the account for the period and the balance is known as the ***credit*** balance. If total of the credit side is similar, the difference will be known as the ***debit*** balance.

Example 3

On 31st January 2018 Commission paid ₹ 5,000.

Journal entry

31.1.2018	Commission a/c	Dr.	₹ 5,000	
	To Cash a/c			₹ 5,000
	[Being commission paid]			

The concerned accounts to be opened in the ledger are Commission A/c and Cash A/c. In the ledger, the Commission A/c should be debited and the Cash A/c should be credited.

Dr. **Commission a/c** Cr.

Date	Particulars	J.F.	Amount [₹]	Date	Particulars	J.F.	Amount [₹]
2018				2018			
Jan. 31	To Cash a/c		5,000	Jan. 31	By balance c/d		5,000
Feb. 1	To balance b/d		5,000				

Dr. **Cash a/c** Cr.

Date	Particulars	J.F.	Amount [₹]	Date	Particulars	J.F.	Amount [₹]
2018				2018			
Jan. 31	To balance c/d		5,000	Jan. 31	By commission a/c		5,000
				Feb. 1	By balance b/d		5,000

Note. C/d is the abbreviation for carried/down. It means that the closing balance in the concerned account is taken [carried] down to the next period as the opening balance.

B/d is the abbreviation for brought/down. It indicates that the closing balance of the previous period has been brought down as the opening balance.

Example 4

On 31.1.2016, Purchased furniture for ₹ 5,000 and cash box ₹ 3,000 on credit from Exe Ltd.

The concerned accounts are Furniture A/c, Cash Box A/c and Exe Ltd. A/c. Furniture A/c and Cash box A/c should be debited and Exe Ltd. A/c should be credited.

Dr. **Furniture a/c** Cr.

Date	Particulars	J.F.	Amount [₹]	Date	Particulars	J.F.	Amount [₹]
2018				2018			
Jan. 31	To Exe Ltd. a/c		5,000 5,000	Jan. 31	By balance c/d		5,000 5,000
				Feb. 1	By balance b/d		5,000

Dr. **Cash box a/c** Cr.

Date	Particulars	J.F.	Amount [₹]	Date	Particulars	J.F.	Amount [₹]
2018				2018			
Jan. 31	To Exe Ltd. a/c		3,000	Jan. 31	By balance c/d		3,000
			3,000				3,000
				Feb. 1.	By balance b/d		3,000

Dr. **Exe Ltd a/c** Cr.

Date	Particulars	J.F.	Amount [₹]	Date	Particulars	J.F.	Amount [₹]
2018				2018			
Jan. 31	To balance c/d		8,000	Jan. 31	By Furniture a/c		5,000
				Feb. 1	By Cash box a/c		3,000
			8 ,000				8,000
				2018			
				Feb. 1	By Balance b/d		8,000

Illustration 5

Journalize the following transactions, post them in the ledger and balance the accounts as on 31st December 2018:

December 1 Rashmi started business with a capital of ₹ 50,000

1 She purchased furniture for ₹ 5,000

2 Bought goods on credit from Vinod for ₹ 8,000

14 Sold food items to Suresh for ₹ 5,000

15 Received cash from Suresh ₹ 3,000

18 Purchased goods for cash ₹ 8,000

28 Paid rent ₹ 1,200

31 Paid Vinod ₹ 3,000 on account

Solution

Journal of Rashmi

Date	Particulars		J.F.	Dr. [₹]	Cr. [₹]
2018 Dec. 1	Cash a/c	Dr.		50,000	
	To Rashmi capital a/c				50,000
	[Being capital introduced]				
2	Furniture a/c	Dr.		5,000	
	To cash a/c				5,000
	[Being furniture purchased]				
3	Purchases a/c	Dr.		3,000	
	To Vinod a/c				3,000
	[Being credit purchases]				
14	Suresh a/c	Dr.		5,000	
	To Sales a/c				5,000
	[Being credit sales]				
15	Cash a/c	Dr.		3,000	
	To Suresh a/c				3,000
	[Being cash received]				
18	Purchases a/c	Dr.		12,000	
	To Cash a/c				12,000
	[Being cash purchases]				
27	Cash a/c	Dr.		8,000	
	To Sales a/c				8,000
	[Being cash sales]				
28	Rent a/c	Dr.		1,200	
	To Cash a/c				1,200
	[Being rent paid]				
31	Vinod a/c	Dr.		3,000	
	To Cash a/c				3,000
	[Being cash paid]				

Ledger of Rashmi Cash a/c

Dr. Cr.

Date	Particulars	J.F.	Amount [₹]	Date	Particulars	J.F.	Amount [₹]
2018				2018			
Dec. 1	To Capital a/c		50,000	Dec. 2	By Furniture a/c		5,000
15	To Suresh a/c		3,000	18	By Purchase a/c		12,000
27	To Sales a/c		8,000	28	By Rent a/c		1,200
				31	By Vinod a/c		3,000
				31	By balance c/d		39,800
			61,000				61,000
1.1.2019	To balance b/d		39,800				

Rashmi's Capital a/c

Dr. Cr.

Date	Particulars	J.F.	Amount [₹]	Date	Particulars	J.F.	Amount [₹]
2018				2018			
Dec.1	To balance c/d		50,000	Dec. 1	By Cash a/c		50,000
			50,000				50,000
				1.1.2019	By balance b/d		50,000

Furniture a/c

Dr. Cr.

Date	Particulars	J.F.	Amount [₹]	Date	Particulars	J.F.	Amount [₹]
2018				2018			
Dec. 2	To cash a/c		5,000	Dec. 31	By balance c/d		5,000
			5,000				5,000
1.1.2019	To balance b/d		50,000				

Dr. **Purchases a/c** Cr.

Date	Particulars	J.F.	Amount [₹]	Date	Particulars	J.F.	Amount [₹]
2018				2018			
Dec. 3	To Vinod a/c		8,000	Dec. 31	By balance c/d		20,000
Dec. 18	To Cash a/c		12,000				
			20,000				20,000
1.1.2019	To balance b/d		20,000				

Dr. **Sales a/c** Cr.

Date	Particulars	J.F.	Amount [₹]	Date	Particulars	J.F.	Amount [₹]
2018				Dec.14	By Suresh a/c		5,000
Dec. 31	To balance c/d		13,000	Dec.27	By Cash a/c		8,000
			13,000				13,000
				1.1.2019	By balance b/d		13,000

Dr. **Vinod a/c** Cr.

Date	Particulars	J.F.	Amount [₹]	Date	Particulars	J.F.	Amount [₹]
2018				2018			
Dec. 31	To Cash a/c		3,000	Dec. 3	By Purchases a/c		8,000
	To balance c/d		5,000				
			8,000				8,000
				1.1.2019	By balance b/d		8,000

Dr. **Suresh a/c** Cr.

Date	Particulars	J.F.	Amount [₹]	Date	Particulars	J.F.	Amount [₹]
2018				2018			
Dec. 14	To Sales a/c		5,000	Dec. 15	By Cash a/c		3,000
				Dec. 31	By balance c/d		2,000
			5,000				5,000
1.1.2019	To balance b/d		2,000				

Dr. **Rent a/c** Cr.

Date	Particulars	J.F.	Amount [₹]	Date	Particulars	J.F.	Amount [₹]
2018				2018			
Dec. 28	To Cash a/c		1,200	Dec. 31	By balance c/d		1,200
			1,200				1,200
1.1.2019	To balance b/d		2,000				

What is Meant by 'Trial Balance?'

When transactions are recorded under *double entry system*, there is a credit for every debit. When one account is debited, another account is credited with equal amount. Therefore, it is quite evident that the total of debit balances of the ledger accounts of given transactions are equal to the total of the credit balances. If a statement is prepared with debit balances in one side/column and credit balances in other side/column, the totals of the two sides/columns are equal. Such a statement is called as 'Trial Balance'. Or simply a trial balance may be defined as "a list of balances standing on the ledger accounts and cash book of a concern".

Features: The following are its main features:

1. It is a tabular statement having separate sides/columns for debit balances and credit balances.
2. Closing balances of the various ledger accounts are brought to this statement.
3. It can be prepared on any date on which accounts are closed and balanced. But, it is usually prepared at the end of the accounting year.
4. Trial Balance is not an account. It is only a statement.

Advantages *[or Functions]* of a Trial Balance

Important advantages of a Trial Balance are:

1. It presents to the businessman a consolidated list of all ledger balances.
2. It is the shortest method of verifying the arithmetical accuracy of entries made in the ledger.
3. If the total of debit side/column is equal to the total of credit side/column, the Trial Balance is said to agree. Otherwise, it is implied that some errors have been committed in the preparation of accounts.
4. It helps in the preparation of the final accounts, i.e., Trading A/c. Profit and loss A/c and Balance sheet.

The Method of Preparing a Trial Balance

There are two methods of preparing a Trial Balance. They are: (1) Total Method and (2) Balance Method.

Total Method. In this method, ledger accounts are not balanced. They are totaled. These are entered in the debit and credit columns. The grand total of debit column will be equal to the total of the credit column. The format of a Trial Balance under this method is as follows:

Trial Balance as on .... *[closing date]*

Particulars *[Name of the Accounts]*	*L.F.*	*Dr. Total of A/c* *Amount [₹]*	*Cr. Total of A/c* *Amount [₹]*

Balance Method. Under this method, the closing balances of ledger accounts are tabulated in a separate statement. The brought down balances are brought to this statement. All debit balances are shown in the debit column and all credit balances in the credit column. This method is more commonly used one. The format of Trial Balance under this method is as follows:

Trial Balance as on .... *[closing date]*

Particulars *[Name of Accounts]*	*L.F.*	*Debit Balance* *Amount [₹]*	*Credit Balance* *Amount [₹]*

Important Note. All debtors' accounts, Assets or Properties accounts, all expenses or losses accounts will always show debit balances. They will be shown in the debit side/column of the Trial Balance.

All creditors accounts, Liabilities' accounts, Income or gains accounts will always show credit balances. They will be shown in the credit side/column of the Trial Balance.

Illustration 6

Prepare a Trial Balance using the closing balances of ledger accounts prepared for illustration 1.

Solution

The closing balances are as follows: Cash A/c ₹ 39,800; Capital A/c ₹ 50,000; Furniture A/c ₹ 5,000; Purchases A/c ₹ 20,000; Sales A/c ₹ 13,000; Vinod A/c [Cr.] ₹ 5,000; Suresh A/c [Dr.] ₹ 2,000;

Particulars	L.F.	Debit balance [₹]	Credit balance [₹]
Cash a/c		39,800	
Capital a/c			50,000
Furniture a/c		5,000	
Purchases a/c		20,000	
Sales a/c			13,000
Vinod a/c			5,000
Suresh a/c		2,000	
Rent a/c		1,200	
Total		68,000	68,000

Illustration 7

Journalize the following transactions and prepare necessary ledger accounts and verify the arithmetical accuracy of the ledger accounts:

Date		Particulars	Amount [₹]
2018			
January	1	Vicky started business with a capital of	1,00,000
	3	Purchased goods from Ajit for cash	30,000
	6	Cash sales	2,000
	8	Goods sold to Shankar on credit	6,000
	10	Purchased goods from Anil on credit	10,000
	15	Received from Shankar in full settlement	5,900
	20	Paid to Anil	5,000
	24	Purchased furniture for office use	4,000
	31	Paid shop rent ₹ 2,000 and salaries	3,000

Solution

Journal of Vicky

Date	Particulars	J.F.	Amount [₹]	Amount [₹]
2015				
Jan. 1	Cash a/c Dr.		1,00,000	
	To Capital a/c			1,00,000
	[Being capital introduced]			
3	Purchases a/c Dr.		30,000	
	To Cash a/c			30,000
	[Being cash purchases]			

Date	Particulars		J.F.	Amount [₹]	Amount [₹]
6	Cash a/c To Sales a/c [Being cash sales]	Dr.		2,000	2,000
8	Shankar's a/c To Sales a/c [Being credit sales]	Dr.		6,000	6,000
10	Purchases a/c To Anil's a/c [Being credit purchases]	Dr.		10,000	10,000
15	Cash a/c Discount a/c To Shankar's a/c [Being cash received in full settlement]	Dr. Dr.		5,900 100	6,000
20	Anil's a/c To Cash [Being cash paid]	Dr.		5,000	5,000
24	Furniture a/c To Cash a/c [Being furniture purchased]	Dr.		4,000	4,000
31	Rent a/c Salaries a/c To Cash a/c [Being rent and salaries paid]	Dr. Dr.		2,000 3,000	5,000

Dr. **Vicky's Ledger Cash a/c** **Cr.**

Date	Particulars	J.F.	Amount [₹]	Date	Particulars	J.F.	Amount [₹]
2018				2018			
Jan. 1	To Capital a/c		1,00,000	Jan. 3	By purchase a/c		30,000
6	To Sales a/c		2,000	20	By Anil's a/c		5,000
15	To Shankar a/c		5,900	24	By Furniture a/c		4,000
				31	By Rent a/c		2,000
				31	By Salaries a/c		3,000
					By Balance c/d		63,900
			1,07,900				1,07,900
1.1.2019	To balance b/d		63,900				

Dr. **Vicky's Ledger Cash a/c** Cr.

Date	*Particulars*	*J.F.*	*Amount* [₹]	*Date*	*Particulars*	*J.F.*	*Amount* [₹]
2018			1,00,000	2018			
Jan.31	To balanced c/d			Jan. 1	By Cash a/c		1,00,000
			1,00,000				1,00,000
1.1.2019	To balance b/d		63,900				

Dr. **Purchases a/c** Cr.

Date	*Particulars*	*J.F.*	*Amount* [₹]	*Date*	*Particulars*	*J.F.*	*Amount* [₹]
2018				2018			
Jan. 3	To Cash a/c		30,000	Jan. 31	By balance c/d		40,000
10	To Anil's a/c		10,000				
			40,000				40,000
1.1.2019	To balance b/d		40,000				

Dr. **Sales a/c** Cr.

Date	*Particulars*	*J.F.*	*Amount* [₹]	*Date*	*Particulars*	*J.F.*	*Amount* [₹]
2018				2018			
Jan. 31	To Balance c/d		8,000	Jan. 6	By Cash a/c		2,000
			8,000				8,000
				1.1.2019	By Balance b/d		8,000

Dr. **Shankar's a/c** Cr.

Date	*Particulars*	*J.F.*	*Amount* [₹]	*Date*	*Particulars*	*J.F.*	*Amount* [₹]
2018				2018			
Jan. 8	To Sales a/c		6,000	Jan. 15	By Cash a/c		5,900
					By Discount a/c		100
			6,000				6,000

Dr. **Anil's a/c** Cr.

Date	*Particulars*	*J.F.*	*Amount* [₹]	*Date*	*Particulars*	*J.F.*	*Amount* [₹]
2018				2018			
Jan. 20	To Cash a/c		5,000	Jan. 10	By Purchase a/c		10,000
31	To Balance c/d		5,000				
			10,000				10,000
				1.1.2019	By balance a/c		5,000

Dr. **Discount a/c** Cr.

Date	*Particulars*	*J.F.*	*Amount* [₹]	*Date*	*Particulars*	*J.F.*	*Amount* [₹]
2018				2018			
Jan. 15	To Shankar a/c		100	Jan. 31	By Balance c/d		100
			100				100
1.1.2019	To Balance b/d		100				

Dr. **Furniture a/c** Cr.

Date	*Particulars*	*J.F.*	*Amount* [₹]	*Date*	*Particulars*	*J.F.*	*Amount* [₹]
2018				2018			
Jan. 24	To Cash a/c		4,000	Jan. 31	By Balance c/d		4,000
			4,000				4,000
1.1.2019	To Balance b/d		4,000				

Dr. **Rent a/c** Cr.

Date	*Particulars*	*J.F.*	*Amount* [₹]	*Date*	*Particulars*	*J.F.*	*Amount* [₹]
2018				2018			
Jan. 31	To Cash a/c		2,000	Jan. 31	By Balance c/d		2,000
			2,000				2,000
1.1.2019	To Balance b/d		2,000				

Dr. **Salaries a/c** Cr.

Date	*Particulars*	*J.F.*	*Amount* [₹]	*Date*	*Particulars*	*J.F.*	*Amount* [₹]
2018				2018			
Jan. 31	To Cash a/c		3,000	Jan. 31	By Balance c/d		3,000
			3,000				3,000
1.1.2019	To Balance b/d		3,000				

To verify the arithmetical accuracy of ledger accounts, the Trial Balance should be prepared.

Trial Balance as on January 31, 2015

Particulars	*Amount* Dr. [₹]	*Amount* Cr. [₹]
Cash a/c	63,900	
Capital a/c		1,00,000
Furniture a/c	4,000	
Purchase a/c	40,000	
Sales a/c		8,000
Anil's a/c		5,000
Rent a/c	2,000	
Discount a/c	100	
Salaries a/c	3,000	
Total	1,13,000	1,13,000

Illustration 8

Arun commenced business with ₹ 30,000 cash and ₹ 10,000 furniture Sales amounted to ₹ 1,32,000 including ₹ 32,000 cash sales and ₹ 20,000 sales were outstanding at the end of the year. Purchases amount to ₹ 70,000, including ₹ 16,000 cash purchases and ₹ 40,000, has been paid to creditors. Salaries paid amounted to ₹ 8,000. Drawings were ₹ 12,000. Machinery was purchased for ₹ 24,000, out of which ₹ 8,000 has been paid. Prepare Trial Balance.

Solution

Trial Balance

Particulars [name of the accounts]	*Amount Dr.* [₹]	*Amount Cr.* [₹]
Capital		40,000
Furniture	10,000	
Sales		1,32,000
Purchases	70,000	
Debtors	20,000	
Creditors		14,000
Salaries	8,000	
Drawings	12,000	
Machinery	24,000	
Creditor for Machinery		16,000
Cash a/c	58,000	
Total	2,02,000	2,02,000

Workings

Cash a/c

Receipts	*Amount* [₹]	*Payments*	*Amount* [₹]
To Capital	30,000	By Cash purchases	16,000
To Cash sales	32,000	By Creditors	40,000
To Collections from debtors	80,000	By Salaries	8,000
		By Drawings	12,000
		By Machinery	8,000
		By Balance c/d	58,000
	1,42,000		1,42,000
To balance b/d	1,42,000		

Total value of machinery ₹ 24,000 less cash paid ₹ 8,000 will be Creditors for machinery i.e., ₹ 16,000.

Total sales	₹ 1,32,000
Less cash sales	32,000
Balance credit sales	1,00,000
Less debtors at the end	20,000
Collections from debtors	80,000

Illustration 9

From the following ledger balances, prepare Trial balance:

Opening Stock ₹ 30,000; Purchases ₹ 3,00,000; Closing Stock ₹ 14,000; Debtors ₹ 1,20,000; Cash ₹ 3,000; Discount allowed ₹ 3,400; Bank ₹ 5,600; Creditors ₹ 90,000; Sales ₹ 4,20,000; Salaries ₹ 42,000; Rent ₹ 9,000; Postage ₹ 4,500; Taxes ₹ 1,500; Machinery ₹ 1,20,000; Drawings ₹ 20,000; Capital ₹ 1,52,000; Purchase Returns ₹ 6,000; Sales Returns ₹ 9,000.

Solution

Trial Balance as on........

Debit balances	*Amount* [₹]	*Credit Balances*	*Amount* [₹]
Opening Stock	30,000	Purchases Returns	6,000
Purchases	3,00,000	Sales	4,20,000
Sales Returns	9,000	Creditors	90,000
Salaries	42,000	Capital	1,52,000
Rent	9,000		
Postage	4,500		
Taxes	1,500		
Debtors	1,20,000		
Discount allowed	3,400		
Drawings	20,000		
Cash	3,000		
Bank	5,600		
Machinery	1,20,000		
Total	6,68,000	Total	6,68,000

Note: Closing Stock is not included in the above Trial Balance, because it is an item of adjustment and its value is ascertained only after closing the ledger accounts.

Illustration 10

The following Trial Balance contains certain obvious errors. Point out errors and prepare a correct Trial Balance:

Name of the accounts	*Debit* [₹]	*Credit* [₹]
Purchases	70,000	
Sales		1,00,000
Purchase Returns	4,000	
Sales Returns		8,000
Opening stock	60,000	
Closing stock		56,000
Trade expenses	8,000	
Outstanding expenses	4,000	
Cash in hand	10,000	
Bank overdraft	50,000	
Debtors		56,000
Creditors		12,000
Carriage inwards	4,000	
Carriage outwards		6,000
Discount received	10,000	
Loan from Chaco	30,000	
Capital		1,12,000
Buildings	1,00,000	
Total	3,50,000	3,50,000

Solution

Obvious Errors: The following credit balances have been shown in the debit column: Purchases Returns, Outstanding Expenses, Bank Overdraft, Discount Received, and Loan from Chaco. These items should be shown in the credit column.

The following debit balances are shown in the credit column: Sales Returns, Carriage Outwards. They should be shown in the debit column.

Closing Stock, being an adjustment item, should not be shown in the Trial Balance.

Correct Trial Balance as on ....

Name of the accounts	*Amount Dr.* [₹]	*Amount Cr.* [₹]
Purchases	70,000	
Sales		1,00,000
Purchase Returns		4,000
Sales Returns	8,000	
Opening stock	60,000	
Trade expenses	8,000	
Outstanding expenses		4,000
Cash in hand	10,000	
Bank overdraft		50,000
Debtors	56,000	
Creditors		12,000
Buildings	1,00,000	
Carriage inwards	4,000	
Carriage outwards	6,000	
Discount received		10,000
Loan from Chaco		30,000
Capital		1,12,000
Total	3,22,000	3,22,000

REVIEW QUESTIONS

1. Journalize the following transactions and post them to various ledger accounts. Also prepare a Trial Balance as on 31st December 2017:

December

1 Raj started business with a capital of ₹ 50,000

2 He purchased computer for office use for ₹ 24,000

3 Bought goods on credit from Vignesh for ₹ 18,000

15 Sold goods to Subbu on credit ₹ 15,000

18 Purchased goods for cash ₹ 12,000

19 Sold goods for cash ₹ 9,000

27 Received cash from Subbu ₹ 3,000

28 Paid rent ₹ 1,500

31 Paid Vignesh ₹ 9,000 on account.

2. Mr. Nirmal commenced business on January 1, 2017 with ₹ 50,000 borrowed from his friend Ramesh. His transactions for the month of January were as follows:

January

1 Deposited in Bank ₹ 20,000.

3 Purchased goods worth ₹ 25,000 from Meeran for cash who allowed 20% trade discount and 10% cash discount.

4 Sold goods for cash ₹ 20,000.

7 Purchased goods from Raju ₹ 20,000.

10 Returned goods to Raju worth ₹ 2,000.

11 Paid ₹ 17,500 to Raju in full settlement.

20 Purchased furniture from Raghav ₹ 5,000. He paid freight ₹ 200 on our behalf.

21 Paid rent ₹ 2,500.

27 Received commission ₹ 800.

31 Paid salaries ₹ 3,000.

3. From the following information, prepare the Trial Balance of Mr. Karthik for the year ended on 31st March, 2018:

Name of the Accounts	*Amount* [₹]	*Name of the Accounts*	*Amount* [₹]
Capital Account	25,000	Sales Account	30,900
Furniture and Fittings	1,280	Bank [cr. balance]	5,700
Motor Car	12,500	Purchase Returns	250
Buildings	15,000	Commission [cr.]	750
Debtors	7,600	Sales Returns	400
Creditors	5,000	Advertisement	500
Bad Debts	250	Interest Account [Dr.]	236
Opening Stock	6,920	Cash Balance	1,300
Purchases	10,950	Insurance and Tax	2,500
		Salaries	8,164

[**Ans.** Total of Trial balance ₹ 67,600]

4. **The following Trial Balance has certain errors. Point out errors and prepare the correct Trial Balance:**

Particulars	*Amount Dr.* [₹]	*Amount Cr.* [₹]
Capital Account	1,00,000	
Furniture		10,000
Deposit with Bank		75,000
Interest Received		10,000
Miscellaneous Receipts		7,625
Sundry Creditors	12,500	
Sundry Debtors	35,000	
Cash in Hand		3,375
House Rent	2,500	
Of?ce Expenses		4,250
Total	1,50,000	1,10,250

[Ans. Total of Trial Balance ₹ 1,30,125]

3

Preparation of Financial Statements

P&L A/C, Balance Sheet, Corporate Financial Statements

PREPARATION OF FINANCIAL STATEMENTS

Final accounts refers to the final statement of accounts prepared in order to ascertain and report the result of the financial activities of a business. Having prepared the Trial Balance, which establishes the accuracy of books of accounts, the next step is to ascertain the operating results and financial position of the business. For this purpose, the final accounts are prepared, which include mainly the Trading and Profit and loss accounts, also called as Income Statement and Balance sheet. The preparation of trading account reveals the gross profit earned or gross loss incurred. The profit and loss account indicates the net profit or loss earned. The balance sheet shows the financial position of the business. Many parties, such as the owners, creditors, investors, employees, and regulatory authorities, etc., are interested in the financial information provided by the final accounts.

VARIOUS TYPES OF CONCERNS FROM ACCOUNTING POINT OF VIEW

Broadly, the concerns may be classified into two categories: business and non-business concerns. Business concerns mainly function with the profit motive and the non-business concerns, though they make some profits while performing their activities, but they do not have profit making as their main motive. Hence, these concerns may also be classified as profit making concerns and non-profit making concerns.

Business concerns may further be classified as trading concerns, manufacturing concerns, and service organizations, super markets, mega stores, etc. Manufacturing concerns are mainly engaged in manufacturing activities. They buy raw materials, convert them into finished products and sell them to customers directly or indirectly. Example: Industrial concerns manufacturing various products. Service organizations mainly provide services to customers. They do not normally engage in any of the trading or manufacturing activities. Examples: banking companies, Insurance companies, etc. These concerns may further be classified, depending on their size and area of operation, as small, medium, and large-scale organizations. Depending upon the forms of organizations, they may be classified as sole trading concerns, partnership organizations, company type and co-operative organizations.

Whatever may be the type, all concerns maintain books of accounts adopting double entry system of book keeping. All of them prepare final accounts at the end of the accounting or financial year in order to find out results of their operating performance and financial position. However, depending upon the nature of business, the items of income and expenditure will vary. For example, trading concern will prepare trading and profit and loss account to find out the profit or loss earned during the accounting year. A manufacturing concern will prepare a manufacturing account in order to find the cost of production and then trading and profit and loss account to ascertain the gross profit and net profit. A service organization, say a banking company, prepares only the profit and loss account to find out the net profit. A non-profit making institution prepares an Income and Expenditure Account in place of Profit and Loss account. However, in all cases, the income statement is followed by a Balance Sheet. But the composition of assets and liabilities vary from business to business. Further, there are no statutory form for final accounts in the case of sole trading and partnership organizations. But, there are statutory forms in the case of company type of organizations.

PREPARATION OF TRADING ACCOUNT

An income statement of a trading concern has two parts, viz., Trading Account and Profit and Loss Account. Trading Account is an account prepared to ascertain the trading results of a business, i.e., the gross profit earned or gross loss incurred from buying and selling of goods during a particular period. The excess of net sales [total sales less returns] over cost of goods sold is termed as gross profit. Adding together the opening stock, purchases and direct expenses on purchase of goods or manufacturing the foods less closing stock computes the cost of goods sold. When the cost of goods sold is more than the net sales, the difference is termed as gross loss. The gross profit or loss is transferred to Profit and Loss Accounts. The specimen of a Trading Account is given below:

Trading Account

for the year ended 31st December 2XXX

Dr. Cr.

Particulars		*Amount* [₹]	*Particulars*		*Amount* [₹]
To Opening Stock			By Sales	xxxxxx	
To Purchases	xxxxxx		Less Returns	xxxxx	
Less Return	xxxx		By closing Stock		
To Direct Expenses					
To Gross Profit transferred To P & L A/c					

Explanation of the debit side items of the Trading A/c

Opening stock: This is the stock of goods in hand at the beginning of the accounting period. Generally, this item appears in the Trial Balance. Sometimes, it may consist of stock of raw materials, work in process, and finished goods.

Purchases: This item includes total purchases less trade discount and returns. Goods taken out by the proprietor for personal use are also deducted from purchases and debited to drawings account. Purchase of assets is not included in this item.

Direct expenses: All expenses incurred in connection with purchases to make them ready for sale are termed as direct expenses. A few items of direct expenses are: carriage inwards, import duties, customs duties, wages, power manufacturing expenses, consumable stores and royalties, etc.

Explanation of Credit Side Items of Trading A/c

Sales: This item includes the total sales less returns. Items of assets sold are not included in sales.

Closing stock: It is the amount of goods, which remain unsold at the end of the accounting period. Generally, it is shown outside the Trial Balance. This item is entered in two places in final accounts, i.e., credit side of Trading Account and asset side of the Balance Sheet.

Closing entries for Trading Account

Closing entries are the journal entries necessary to close the various ledger accounts by transferring them to final accounts. Transferring them to the Trading a/c closes the balances in the opening and closing stocks, purchases and sales and direct expenses. The following closing entries are passed for the same:

For transfer of opening stock, net purchases, and direct expenses to Trading A/c

Trading a/c Dr.
To Opening stock a/c
To purchases a/c
To Direct Expenses a/c

For transfer of net sales and closing stock to Trading a/c

Sales a/c Dr.
Closing Stock a/c Dr.
To Trading a/c

For transfer of gross profit

Trading a/c Dr.
To Profit and Loss a/c

For transfer of gross loss,

Profit and loss a/c Dr.
To Trading a/c

Example 1

From the following ledger balance taken out at the close of a trading year ended on 31st December 2018 prepare Trading Account and pass necessary closing entries:

Particulars	*Amount* [₹]	*Particulars*	*Amount* [₹]
Opening stock	16,000	Carriage Inwards	2,400
Purchases	40,000	Wages	6,600
Sales	1,60,000	Freight and Dock charges	4,800
Returns Inwards	3,000	Stock on 31-12-2018	14,000
Return Outwards	800	Salaries	30,000

Solution

Trading Account

for the year ended on 31st December, 2018

Particulars		*Amount* [₹]	*Particulars*		*Amount* [₹]
To Opening Stock		1,6000	By Sales	1,60,000	
To Purchases	40,000		Less Return	3,000	1,57,000
Less Returns	800	3,9200	By Closing Stock		14,000
To Carriage Inwards		2,400			
To Wages		6,600			
To Freight and dock Charges		4,800			
To Gross Profit tfd. to P & L a/c		1,02,000			
		1,71,000			1,71,000

Note: Salaries, being an office expense, is not included in the Trading a/c.

Closing Entries

For transfer of debit side items to trading a/c

		Dr.	Cr.
Trading a/c	Dr.	69,000	
To Opening Stock			16,000
To Purchases			39,200
To Carriage Inwards			2,400
To Wages			6,600
To Freight and dock charges			4,800

For transfer of credit side items to Trading a/c

		Dr.	Cr.
Sales a/c	Dr.	1,57,000	
Closing Stock a/c	Dr.	14,000	
To Trading a/c			1,71,000

For transfer of gross profit to Profit and Loss a/c

Trading a/c	Dr.	1,02,000	
To Profit and Loss a/c			1,02,000

Preparation of Profit and Loss Account

Profit and Loss a/c is an account, which is prepared to calculate the final profit or loss of the business. All operating expenses and other non-operating income and expenditures and losses are charged to P & L a/c to find out the net profit. Operating expenses, such as office and administration expenses, selling and distribution expenses and financial charges are indirect in nature and incurred to carry on business profitably. Non-operating income, such as dividends received; interest received etc., and non-operating expenses and losses, such as donations paid, fire losses etc., are also charged to P&L a/c in order to arrive at the final net profit or loss earned by the business. This account is a nominal account and its balance–net profit or loss is transferred to Capital account. The specimen P&L a/c is given below:

Profit and Loss Account

for the year ended on 31st December 2XXX

Particulars	*Amount* [₹]	*Particular*	*Amount* [₹]
To Gross Loss [Transferred from Trading a/c]		By Gross Profit [Transferred from Trading a/c]	
To Salaries		By Dividend received	
To Rent		By Interest received	
To Commission		By Discounts received	
To Advertisement		By Commission earned	
To Discount allowed		By Net Loss transferred to Capital a/c	
To Interest paid			
To Postage			
To Printing and stationary			
To Depreciation			
To Net profit transferred to Capital a/c			

Explanation of debit side items of P&L a/c

Office and administration expenses: Salaries paid to office staff and warehouse staff, office rent, municipal rates and taxes other office expenses, like postage, stationery etc.

Selling and distribution expenses: Salesmen's salaries, selling commission, advertisement, carriage outwards/ bad debts, discount allowed, etc.

Financial charges: Interest on loans, overdrafts and bills overdue etc. Depreciation and other non-operation expenses, and abnormal losses.

Explanation of credit side items of P&L a/c

Non-operating income: Interest of investments, discount on rent received, commission earned and other abnormal gains. In short, except sales income, all other items of income are credited to P&L a/c.

Items not to be shown in P&L a/c

Domestic and household expenses: All personal expenses of the proprietor are treated as drawings and are not shown in P&L a/c. Income tax and life insurance premium paid are the personal expenses of the proprietor and are added to drawings.

Closing Entries

(*a*) For transfer of various items of expenses to P&L a/c

Profit and Loss a/c Dr.

To Carriage Expenses a/c

(*b*) For transfer of various items of income and gains to P&L a/c

Various income and gains a/c Dr.

To Profit and Loss a/c

(*c*) To transfer Net Loss

Profit and Loss a/c Dr.

To Capital a/c

To transfer Net Loss

Capital a/c Dr.

To Profit and Loss a/c

Example 2

From the following balance, taken out at the close of a year ended on 31st December 2018, prepare a Profit and Loss Account:

Particulars	*Amount* [₹]	*Particulars*	*Amount* [₹]
Gross Profit	1,02,000	Discount (Dr.)	1,000
Carriage Outwards	5,000	Apprentice Premium (Cr.)	3,000
Salaries	11,000	Printing and Stationery	500
Rent	2,200	Rates and Taxes	700
Insurances Premium	1,800	Travelling Expenses	400
Bad Debts	4,200	Depreciation	12,000
Sundry Trade Expenses	600	Repairs and Maintenance	5,600

Solution

Profit and Loss Account

for the year ended on 31st December, 2018

Particulars	*Amount* [₹]	*Particulars*	*Amount* [₹]
To Carriage outwards	5,000	By Gross Profit b/d	1,02,000
To Salaries	11,000	By Apprentice Premium	3,000
To Rent	2,200		
To Insurance Premium	1,800		
To Bad Debts	4,200		
To Sundry Trade Expenses	600		
To Discount	1,000		
To Printing and Stationery	500		
To Traveling Expenses	400		
To Rates and Taxes	700		
To Depreciation	12,000		
To Repairs and Maintenance	5,600		
To Net Profit transferred to Capita l a/c	60,000		
	1,05,000		1,05,000

PREPARATION OF MANUFACTURING ACCOUNT

Industrial concerns, in order to find out the cost of production, prepare a separate account called manufacturing account. This account includes all expenses relating to manufacturing operating such as raw materials consumed, semi-manufactured goods, productive wages, power and other manufacturing expenses. The cost of goods produced is transferred to Trading A/c. Trading A/c deals with the sale of goods and debited with the cost of production instead of purchase of goods as in the case of trading concerns. Some concerns combine trading A/c with Manufacturing A/c and calculate the Gross Profit or Gross Loss of the manufacturing operations. The specimen form of Manufacturing Account is given below:

Manufacturing Account

for the year ended on 31st December, 2018

Particulars	*Amount* [₹]	*Particulars*	*Amount* [₹]
To Opening Stock:		By Closing Stock	
Raw Materials		Raw Materials	
Goods in Process		Goods in Process	
To Purchase of Materials		By Cost of Production	
To Manufacturing Wages		Transferred to Trading A /c	
To All Factory Expenses		(Balancing Figure)	
To Repairs to Plant & Factory Building			
To Depreciation of Plant & Factory Buildings			

Distinguish between Manufacturing Account and Trading Account

Particulars	*Amount*[₹]	*Particulars*	*Amount*[₹]
Opening Stock:			
Raw Materials	20,000	Gas and Water	6,000
Semi-finished Goods	10,000	Return of Materials	2,600
Deducted from the Purchases	52,000	Coal and Fuel	6,600
		Factory Power	25,000
Purchases:		Fire Insurance	2,600
Raw Materials	1,60,000	Sales Returns	24,000
Finished Goods	34,000	Depreciation on Factory Buildings	2,400
Carriage Inwards:			
Raw Materials	6,000	Closing Stock:	
Finished Goods	700	Raw Materials	
Manufacturing		Semi-finished	16,000
Wages	20,000	Goods	26,000
Factory Rent	14,000	Finished Goods	44,000
Salary of Supervisor	7,200	Sales	4,40,000

Example 3

From the following balance extracted from the books of Arun for the year ended on 31st December, 2018, prepare Manufacturing Account:

Particular s	*Amount*[₹]	Particulars	*Amount*[₹]
Opening Stock:			
Raw Materials	20,000	Gas and Water	6,000
Semi-finished Goods	10,000	Return of Materials	2,600
Deducted from the Purchases	52,000	Coal and Fuel	6,600
		Factory Power	25,000
Purchases:		Fire Insurance	2,600
Raw Materials	1,60,000	Sales Returns	24,000
Finished Goods	34,000	Depreciation on Factory Buildings	2,400
Carriage Inwards:			
Raw Materials	6,000	Closing Stock:	
Finished Goods	700	Raw Materials	
Manufacturing Wages	20,000	Semi-finished	16,000
		Goods	26,000
Factory Rent	14,000	Finished Goods	44,000
Salary of Supervisor	7,200	Sales	4,40,000

Solution

Manufacturing Account

for the year ended on 31st December, 2018

Particulars		*Amount* [₹]	*Particulars*		*Amount* [₹]
To Opening Stock:			By Closing stock		
Raw Materials	20,000		Raw material	16,000	
Semi-finished Goods	10,000	30,000	Semi-finished goods	26,000	42,000
To Purchase of					
Raw Material	1,60,000		By Cost of Production		
Less Return	2,600	1,57,400	(Transferred to Trading a/c)		2,35,200
To Carriage Inwards		6,000			
To Manufacturing Wages		20,000			
To Factory Expenses:					
Salary of Supervisor	7,200				
Factory Rent	14,000				
Gas and Water	6,000				
Coal and Fuel	6,600				
Factory Power	25,000				
Fire Insurance	2,600				
Depreciation	2,400	63,800			
		2,77,200			2,77,200

Note: Items relating to finished goods i.e., sales, sales returns, openings stock, closing stock are not entered in the Manufacturing a/c since they are items to be entered in the Trading a/c.

Example 4

From the following relating to the year 2018, prepare Manufacturing a/c, Trading a/c, and Profit and Loss a/c:

Particulars	*Amount* [₹]	*Particulars*	*Amount* [₹]
Stock on 1.1.2018		Depreciations: Machinery	50,000
Finished Goods	66,000	Office Equipment	16,200
Raw Materials	32,000	Sundry Expenses: Factory	10,600
Work in Progress	22,000	Office	35,600
Purchase of Materials	3,01,800	Sales	7,20,000
Carriage on Purchases	8,200	Stock on 31.12.2018	
Wages	1,30,000	Finished goods	55,000
Factory Salaries	52,000	Raw Materials	36,000
Office Salaries	36,000	Work in progress	18,600
Repairs: Machinery	16,600		
Office Equipment	3,400		

Solution

Manufacturing Account
for the year ended on 31st December, 2018

Particulars		Amount [₹]	Particulars	Amount [₹]
To Opening Work in Progress		22,000		
To Materials consumed			By Cost of production	
Opening Stock	32,000		(Transferred to Trading a/c)	5,68,000
Add: Purchases	3,01,800			
	3,33,800			
Less: Closing Stock	36,600	2,97,200		
To Carriage on Purchases		8,200		
To Wages		1,30,000		
To Factory Expenses	10,600			
Salaries	52,000			
Machinery Repairs	16,600			
Depreciation of Machinery	50,000	1,29,200		
		5,86,600		
Less: Closing work in Progress		18,600		
		5,68,000		5,68,000

Trading Account
for the year ended on 31st December, 2018

Particulars	Amount [₹]	Particulars	Amount [₹]
To Opening Stock of Finished goods	66,000	By sales	7,20,000
To Cost of Production Transferred From Manufacturing A/c	5,68,000	By Closing stock in finished goods	55,000
To Gross Profit transferred to Profit and loss A/c	1,41,000		
	7,75,000		7,75,000

Profit and Loss Account

for the year ended on 31st December, 2018

Particulars	*Amount* [₹]	*Particulars*	*Amount* [₹]
To Office Salaries	36,000	By Gross profit transferred from Trading a/c	1,41,000
To Repairs of Equipment	3,400		
To Depreciation of Equipment	16,200		
To Sundry Office Expenses	35,600		
To Net Profit Transferred to Capital a/c	49,800		
	1,41,000		1,41,000

PREPARATION OF BALANCE SHEET

A Balance Sheet [B/S] may be defined as "a statement drawn upon a given date, generally at the end of each accounting year, to measure the exact financial position of a business, setting forth the various assets and liabilities of the concern at this date". From this definition, it may be understood that the B/S is a statement of assets and liabilities as on a particular date. Its assets of a given date and its liabilities indicate the financial position of a concern on that date. Excess of assets over liabilities represents the capital and is indicative of the financial soundness of a company. A B/S is also described as a 'statement showing the sources and application of capital.' It is a statement and not an account. It is prepared from real and personal accounts.

On the left hand side of the B/S, the liabilities and capital are shown. On the right hand side, all the assets are shown. Therefore, the two sides of the balance sheet must always be equal. Otherwise, there is an error somewhere in books of accounts. A properly drawn up balance sheet gives information relating to (*a*) the nature and value of asset; (*b*) the nature and extent of liabilities; (*c*) whether the firm is solvent; and (*d*) whether the firm is over trading. In short, it explains the financial condition of the concern.

(*a*) The B/S is prepared as on a particular date. The information furnished by the B/S is true only on that date and not before or later. The capital position of a concern keeps on changing from time to time. Hence, it is never prepared to cover a period.

(*b*) A B/S is not an account. It is a statement showing assets, liabilities and capital of a particular concern.

(*c*) A B/S is intended to reveal the financial position of a concern. It shows the nature and value of assets, the nature and value of liabilities and the amount of capital.

(*d*) A specimen format of a Balance Sheet is given below:

Balance Sheet of (firm's name) as on (closing date)

Liabilities	*Amount* [₹]	*Assets*	*Amount* [₹]
<u>Current Liabilities:</u>		<u>Current Assets:</u>	
Bills Payables		Cash in Hand	
Sundry Creditors		Cash at Bank	
Bank Overdraft		Sundry Debtors	
Outstanding Expenses		Bills Receivables	
Income Received in Advance		Prepaid Expenses	
<u>Long-term Liabilities:</u>		Accrued Income	
Mortgage Loans		Closing Stock	
Debentures		<u>Investments:</u>	
Owner's Equity		Government Securities	
Reserves and Surplus		Other investment	
Capital		<u>Fixed Assets:</u>	
Add: Net Profit		Furniture	
Interest on Capital		Plant and Machinery	
Less: Drawings		Land and Buildings	
Income Tax		Patents	
		Goodwill	
		Miscellaneous Expenses	

Note for any contingent liability, if any.

Form of Balance Sheet

There is no prescribed form of B/S for a sole trader and partnership concern. However, assets and liabilities may be shown either in the liquidity order or permanency order. Under liquidity order, assets, which can be converted into cash, are shown first and those which cannot be concerted into cash come next and so on. Similarly, those liabilities, which are to be paid immediately, are shown first and others payable later come next and so on. Under permanency, order of the arrangement of assets and liabilities will be reversed. Assets, which are used permanently in the business, are shown first and the most liquid assets shown at the bottom. The arrangement of assets and liabilities in any one of these methods is called as "Marshalling of the Balance Sheet". In the case of Joint Stock Companies, the B/S is prepared as per the prescribed form given in the Companies Act.

Classification of Assets

Assets represent every thing, which a business owns and has money value. In other words, assets represent the possession and properties of the business. They are valuable resources owned by a business entity that benefit future period. Land and buildings, plant and machinery, stock, cash, debtors, etc., are some examples of assets. Depending upon the nature of assets, they are classified as follows:

Fixed assets: Assets, which are acquired and held permanently and are used for the purpose of earning profits, are called fixed assets. Land and buildings, plant and machinery and furniture, etc., are some examples of these assets.

Currents assets: Assets such as cash, debtors, stock, etc., can be converted into cash, or consumed in production of goods and services; they are called current assets. They are normally owned by a business in not more than one accounting year. As their values are constantly floating from one form to another [for example, cash into stock, stock into debtors and so on], they are also called floating assets.

Liquid assets: These assets, which are in the form of cash or are readily converted into cash, are liquid assets. Examples are: cash, bank, bills receivables, marketable securities, etc.

Tangible assets: These are definite assets that can be seen, touched and have volume, such as cash, stock, machinery, etc. On the other hand, intangible assets cannot be seen and touched or felt, e.g., goodwill, copyrights, etc.

Fictitious assets: These assets have no real value and are losses not written off, e.g., P&L a/c debit balance, preliminary expenses, discount on the issue of securities, etc.

Wasting assets: Assets, such as mines, quarries, etc., that become exhausted or reduce in value by their working, are called wasting assets.

Contingent assets: Contingent asset is an asset, the existence, value and ownership of which is dependent of the occurrence or non-occurrence of a specified act or an uncertain future event. Suppose a firm has filed a suit for some specified property now in possession of someone else. If the suit is decided in firm's favour, the firm will get the property. At the moment, the specified property is a contingent asset. Contingent liability in respect of a contract for capital expenditure already entered into will give rise to an asset on payment, at present; it is only a contingent asset. Similar would be the position of a patent applied for and arising out of a firm's research efforts.

Classification of Liabilities

All claims that the business owes are liabilities. They include the credit balances of personal and real accounts together with the proprietor's capital. A liability is a claim by an outsider on the assets of the business and an amount that a business is legally bound to pay. Liabilities may be classified into four categories.

Fixed liabilities: Those liabilities that are payable only on the termination of a business are called fixed liabilities. It mainly includes the proprietor's equity, such as paid up capital, reserves and surplus.

Long-term liabilities: Liabilities, which are payable over a long period of time, say five to ten years, are called long-term liabilities. Debentures, mortgage loans, term loans, etc., are a few examples of long-term liabilities.

Current liabilities: Liabilities that are payable out of current assets within the next accounting period, usually a year or already due, are called current liabilities. Sundry creditors, bills payables, short-term bank overdraft and outstanding expense, etc., are some examples of such liabilities.

Contingent liabilities: A contingent liability is one, which is not an actual liability but will become an actual one on the occurrence of some future uncertain event. It has two characteristics (*a*) uncertainty as to whether the amount will the payable or not; and (*b*) uncertainty about the amount involved. Some examples are law suits against the company for environment pollution, patent infringement, trademark violation, etc., arrears of fixed cumulative dividend, uncalled liability partly paid up shares, and bills of exchange, and guarantees given against particular firm person.

Difference Between a Trial Balance and Balance Sheet

	Trial Balance	*Balance Sheet*
1.	It is a list of balances of all ledger accounts; no account with balance can be left out.	It is a statement of assets and liabilities; only personal and real accounts appear here.
2.	Its object is to check the arithmetical accuracy of the ledger balances.	Its object is to reveal at a glance the financial position of the business concerns.
3.	It includes the opening stock.	It includes the closing stock.
4.	It is prepared whenever desired or at the end of every month or quarterly, half yearly, or annually.	It is usually prepared at the end of a trading period or accounting year.
5.	It does not give information about the net profit or net loss.	It gives information about the profits and the capital balance includes the profit.
6.	It is not absolutely necessary to prepare the Trial Balance. It can be dispensed with.	Preparation of balance sheet is absolutely necessary to complete the accounting process.
7.	It is generally prepared without giving effect to any adjustment.	It cannot be prepared without making adjustments for outstanding and prepayments.
8.	It contains headings like 'debit' and 'credit'.	It contains the headings 'liabilities' and 'assets'.

Example 5

From the following particulars, prepare a Balance Sheet as on 31st December 2018:

Particulars	*Amount* [₹]	*Particulars*	*Amount* [₹]
Capital	1,00,000	Loan to Sumathi	10,000
Business premises	1,10,000	Investments	6,000
Furniture and Fixtures	5,000	Cash in Hand	400
Bills Receivable	7,000	Cash in Bank	7,000
Bills Payable	5,000	Proprietor's Withdrawals	6,000
Sundry Debtors	40,000	Net Pro?t	77,800
Sundry Creditors	31,600	Closing Stock	14,000
Packing Machinery	9,000		

Solution

Balance Sheet

as on 31st December, 2018

Liabilities		*Amount* [₹]	*Assets*	*Amount* [₹]
Sundry Creditors		31,600	Cash in Hand	400
Bills Payable		5,000	Cash at Bank	7,000
Capital	1,00,000		Investment	6,000
Add: Net Pro?t	77,800		Sundry Debtors	40,000
	1,77,800		Bills Receivable	7,000
Less: Drawings	6,000	1,71,800	Closing Stock	14,000
			Loan to Sumathi	10,000
			Packing Machinery	9,000
			Furniture and Fixtures	5,000
			Business Premises	1,10,000
		2,08,400		2,08,400

Example 6

The following balances are extracted from the books of Durga and Co. on 31st December, 2018. You are required to prepare the Trading and Profit and Loss Account and a Balance Sheet as on that date:

Particulars	*Amount* [₹]	*Particulars*	*Amount* [₹]
Stock on Jan. 1 2018	1,000	Discounts (Cr.)	400
B/R	4,500	Returns outwards	500
Purchases	39,000	Trade Expenses	200
Wages	2,800	Office Fixtures	1,000
Insurance	1,100	Cash in hand	500
Sundry Debtors	30,000	Cash at Bank	4,750
Carriage Inward	800	Rent and Taxes	1,100
Commission (Dr)	800	Carriage outward	1,450
Interest on Capital	700	Sales	50,000
Stationery	450	Bills Payable	3,000
Return Inwards	1,300	Creditors	19,650
		Capital	17,900

The Closing Stock valued at ₹ 25,000.

Solution

Trading and Profit and Loss a/c of Durga and Co.

for the year ended on 31st December, 2018

Particulars		*Amount* [₹]	*Particulars*		*Amount* [₹]
To Opening stock		1,000	By Sales	50,000	
To Purchase	39,000		Less Sales Return	1,300	
Less: Returns outwards	500	38,500			48,700
To Wages		2,800	By Closing Stock		25,000
To Carriage Inwards		800			
To Gross Profit c/d		30,600			
		73,700			73,700
To Insurance		1,100	By Gross Profit b/d		30,600
To Commission		800	By Discounts		400
To Interest on Capital		700			
To Stationery		450			
To Trade Expenses		200			
To Rent and Taxes		1,100			
To Carriage Outward		1,450			
To Net Profit Transferred to Capital a/c		25,200			
		31,000			31,000

Balance Sheet of Durga & Co.

as on December 31, 2018

Liabilities		*Amount* [₹]	*Assets*	*Amount* [₹]
Creditors		19,650	Cash in Hand	500
Bills payable		3,000	Cash at Bank	4,750
Capital	17,900		Bill Receivable	4,500
Add: Net Profit	25,200	43,100	Stock	25,000
			Sundry Debtors	30,000
			Office Fixtures	1,000
		65,750		65,750

Adjustments

The object of preparing the Final Account is to find out the true profit or loss for the year under consideration. This requires that all items, which are relevant for the current year, be brought into account. For example, in the case of expenses, all expenses incurred for the current year, whether paid or unpaid must be debited to the P&L a/c. The unpaid amount of a particular expense has to be brought into account. This is known as adjustment. The following are the common adjustment:

Closing stock: As the value of closing inventories is ascertained at the end of the accounting year, it appears as adjustments. It should be credited to Trading a/c and shown in the asset side of the B/S.

The adjusting entry is:

Closing stock A/c Dr.
To Trading A/c

Trading Account

Particulars	*Amount* [₹]	*Particulars*	*Amount* [₹]
		By Sales By Closing Stock	

Balance Sheet

Liabilities	*Amount* [₹]	*Assets*	*Amount* [₹]
		Closing Stock	

Outstanding expenses: These are the expenses incurred within the accounting year but the payment has not been made. Outstanding or unpaid expenses should be added to the concerned expenses a/c in P&L a/c and will be shown as a current liability in the B/S. For example, of ₹ 1,000 Rent for the month of December 2018 remains unpaid. The calendar year is the accounting year.

Adjusting Entry:

Rent account		Dr.	1,000
	To outstanding Rent A/c		1,000

Dr. **Profit and Loss Account** Cr.

Particulars	*Amount* [₹]	*Particulars*	*Amount* [₹]
To Rent Account [11 month rent] 11,000 *Add:* Outstanding [December] 1,000	12,000		

Balance Sheet as on 31st December, 2018

Liabilities	*Amount* [₹]	*Assets*	*Amount* [₹]
Outstanding Expenses Rent	1,000		

Prepaid expenses: These are the expenses, which have been paid, but part of the amount paid extends to the next year. It is also called 'un-expired expenses'. Advance amount paid should be deducted from the concerned expenses and be shown as a current asset in the B/S. For example, the insurance premium of ₹ 2,400 a year was paid on 1st July, 2018. The calendar year is the accounting year.

Since premium for one year has been paid on 1st July, the premium for 6 months, i.e., **half the** amount relates to the current year and the other half related to the next year. Hence, **₹1,200 must** be treated as prepaid and deducted from the premium paid and be shown as an asset in the B/S.

Adjusting Entry

Prepaid Insurance a/c	Dr.	1,200	
To Insurance Premium a/c			1,200

Dr. **Profit and Loss a/c** Cr.

Particulars		*Amount* [₹]	*Particulars*	*Amount* [₹]
To Insurance Premium a/c	2,400			
Less: Prepaid Insurance	1,200	1,200		

Balance Sheet

Liabilities	*Amount* [₹]	*Assets*	*Amount* [₹]
		Prepaid Insurance	1,200

Accrued income: It is the income that has already been earned; the service has already been rendered but the money has not been received. For example, interest on investments accrued 1,200. The interest for the current year is due at the close of the year. The amount may be actually received in the next year. At present, it represents an income, which has become receivable or accrued. Hence, it is credited to P&L a/c and being accounts receivable, shown as an asset in the B/S.

Adjusting Entry

Accrued Interest a/c	Dr.	1,200	
To Interest a/c			1,200

Profit and Loss a/c

Particulars	*Amount* [₹]	*Particulars*	*Amount* [₹]
By interest on investments *Add*: Interest accrued	 1,200		

Balance Sheet

Liabilities	*Amount* [₹]	*Assets*	*Amount* [₹]
			1,200

Income received in advance: It indicates incomes received during the current year, but part of the amount received relates to the next year. Such amount must be deducted from the total amount received in P&L a/c and shown on the liabilities side of the B/S as it represents an amount which the business is obliged to return. For example, a business concern has received apprentice premium for three years amounting to ₹ 6,000. In this amount ₹ 2,000 one-third of ₹ 6,000 is for the current year and should be credited to P&L a/c as income. And the balance ₹ 4,000 represents a liability, as the business is obliged to return.

Adjusting Entry

Apprentice Premium a/c	Dr.	4,000	
To Apprentice Premium received in advance a/c			4,000

Dr. **Profit and Loss Account** Cr.

Particulars	*Amount* [₹]	*Particulars*		*Amount* [₹]
		By Apprentice premium	6,000	
		Less: Received in advance	4,000	2,000

Balance Sheet

Liabilities	*Amount*[₹]	*Assets*	*Amount*[₹]
Apprentice Premium Received in Advance	4,000		

Depreciation on assets: Depreciation means diminution or fall in value of an asset due to its constant use. It may also arise on account of wear and tear, lapse of time and obsolescence. It is a loss to the business. It is usually calculated at a certain percentage on the value of asset and the amount so obtained is first shown on the debit side of the P&L a/c and then deducted from the original value of asset in the B/S. For example, a business has furniture of the value of ₹ 50,000 at the end of the year, which is depreciated at 5%.

Adjusting Entry

Depreciation a/c	Dr.	2,500	
To Furniture a/c			2,500

[5% on ₹ 50,000 = 2500]

Profit and Loss a/c

Particulars	*Amount* [₹]	*Particulars*	*Amount* [₹]
To Depreciation a/c Furniture	2,500		

Balance Sheet

Liabilities	*Amount* [₹]	*Assets*		*Amount* [₹]
		Furniture	50,000	
		Less: Depreciation	2,500	47,500

Bad debts: Debts represent money due from debtors. When debts become irrecoverable, they become bad debts and are treated a losses. The amount of bad debts is debited to P&L a/c and is deducted from Sundry Debtors in the B/S. For example, the ledger balance in respect of Sundry Debtors of a trader shows ₹ 20,000 and of this ₹ 1,000 is estimated to be irrecoverable.

Adjusting Entry:

Bad Debts a/c	Dr.	1,000	
To Sundry Debtors a/c			1,000

Provision for bad and doubtful debts: Every business has a lot of dealings by way of credit transactions. This gives rise to a sizable amount of book debts or debtors. But it is seldom that 100 per cent down the debtors balance to it shows true position. The usual practice is to calculate such doubtful debts at a certain percentage, based on past experience on debtors. It is called provision or Reserve for Doubtful Debts. However, the provision for bad and doubtful debts is calculated on good debts after deducting bad debts not adjusted earlier.

Example 7: The sundry debtors of a trader at the close of the year stood at ₹ 21,000. It is estimated that ₹ 1,000 is written off as bad debts and 5% provision is created for doubtful debts.

Adjusting Entries

Bad Debts a/c	Dr.	1,000	
To Sundry Debtors a/c			1,000
Profit and Loss a/c	Dr.	2,000	
To Bad debt a/c			1,000
To Provision for Doubtful Debt			1,000

Profit and Loss a/c

Particulars	*Amount* [₹]	*Particulars*	*Amount* [₹]
To Bad Debts	1,000		
To Reserve for Doubtful Debts	1,000		

If there is an old provision for doubtful debts, it should be adjusted against the new provision.

Balance Sheet

Liabilities	*Amount* [₹]	*Assets*		*Amount* [₹]
		Sundry Debtors	21,000	
		Less: Bad Debts	1,000	
			20,000	
		Less: Provision for Doubtful debts	1,000	
				19,000

Provision for discount on debtors: Cash discounts are allowed to debtors in order to encourage them to make prompt payments. After providing for bad and doubtful debts, the balance of debtors represents debts due from sound parties. They may try to pay their dues on time and avail themselves of the cash discounts, should which be anticipated and provided for. The usual practice in business is to provide for discount on debtors at certain percentage on good debts.

Example 8: Suppose a trader has sundry debtors amounting to ₹ 20,000 and he estimates that after a provision of 5% for doubtful debts, a provision for discount at 2% is desirable. Then, on the sound debts, ₹ 19,000 a provision of 2% is made as Reserve for Discount on Debtors.

Adjusting Entry:

Profit and loss a/c	Dr.	380	
To Reserve for Discount a/c on Debtors a/c			380

Profit and Loss a/c

Particulars	*Amount* [₹]	*Particulars*	*Amount* [₹]
To Bad Debts	?		
To Reserve for Doubtful Debts	1,000		
To Reserve for Discount on Debtors	380		

Balance Sheet

Liabilities	*Amount* [₹]	*Assets*		*Amount* [₹]
		Sundry Debtors	20,000	
		Less: Provision for Doubtful Debt	1,000	
			19,000	
		Less: Provision for Discounts on Debtors	380	18,620

Provision for discount on creditors: Creditors represent the amount owed by the business to suppliers of goods on credit. Sound business concerns make it a practice to settle accounts with creditors in time to earn goodwill of the creditors and also the discount allowed by them. Liability in respect of sundry creditors can be reduced to the extent of discount anticipated. Based on the past practice, a certain percentage on creditors, balance is calculated as provision for discount and deducted from the creditors balance in the B/S and the same amount is credited as gain in the P&L a/c.

Example 9: A trader had sundry creditors at ₹ 10,000 on 31st December 2018. It is desired to make a provision of 3% on this amount for discounts.

Adjusting Entry

Reserve for Discounts on Creditors a/c	Dr.	300	
To Profit and Loss a/c			300

Profit and Loss a/c

Particulars	*Amount* [₹]	*Particulars*	*Amount* [₹]
		By Reserve for Discount on Creditors	300

Balance Sheet

Liabilities		*Amount* [₹]	*Assets*	*Amount* [₹]
Sundry Creditors	10,000			
Less: Reserve for Discounts	300	9,700		

Interest of capital: Often, interest at a normal rate is allowed on the capital of the Proprietor employed in the business. This is necessary in order to assess the efficiency of the business. Otherwise, the profit would include the interest and appear at a higher rate. The interest so charged is a loss to the business and gain to the proprietor. So, it is debited to the profit and loss a/c and added to the capital in the Balance sheet.

Adjusting Entries

Interest on Capital a/c	Dr.
To Capital a/c	
Profit and Loss a/c	Dr.
To Interest on capital a/c	

Interest on drawings: Drawings are money withdrawn by the proprietor from his capital. Just as the business allows interest on capital, it charges interest on drawings. It is a gain to the business and a loss to the proprietor. So, it is credited to the Profit and Loss a/c and deducted from the capital in the Balance sheet.

Profit and Loss a/c

Particulars	*Amount* [₹]	*Particulars*	*Amount* [₹]
To Interest on Capital		By Interest on Drawings	

Balance Sheet

Liabilities	*Amount* [₹]	*Assets*	*Amount* [₹]
Capital *Add:* Interest of Capital *Less:* Drawings Interest on Drawing			

Guidelines for the Preparation of Final Accounts

When a Trial Balance and adjustments are given for the preparation of Final Accounts, following points should be kept in mind:

1. Trial Balance items should be entered into Final Accounts in only one place. Debit balances should be debited to Trading a/c or Profit and Loss a/c or Balance Sheet asset side. For example, wages given in Trial Balance should be debited to Trading a/c and salaries at Profit and Loss a/c and Furniture in the asset side of the Balance Sheet.

   Similarly, credit balances should be credited to Trading a/c or Profit and Loss a/c or shown in the liability side of the Balance Sheet. Examples: Sales given in the Trial Balance should be credited to Trading a/c: Interest received to profit and Loss a/c and Capital a/c shown in the liability side of the Balance Sheet.
2. Adjustments items should be entered in two places in the Final Accounts in order to complete the double entry principle. They are entered into books of accounts for the first time.
3. Guidelines for making adjustments in the Final Accounts.

Adjustment	*Profit and Loss A/c*	*Balance Sheet*
Outstanding Expenses	Add to the concerned item of expense in debit side	Show all Outstanding expenses in the Liability side.
Prepaid or Unexpired expenses	Deduct from the concerned item of expense in the debit side.	Show all prepaid expenses in the asset side.
Accrued or Outstanding income	Add to the concerned item of income in the credit side.	Show the accrued income in the Asset side.
Income received in advance	Deduct from the concerned item of income in the credit side.	Show the income received in advance in the liabilities side.
Closing Stock	Credit Trading a/c with the value of closing stock.	Show the closing stock in the Asset side.
Stock destroyed by fire [Abnormal loss]	Credit Trading a/c with full value of stock destroyed. Debit P&L a/c with the actual loss. [total stock destroyed less insurance claim].	Add the claim received in cash with Cash a/c or show the Insurance Company a/c in the Asset side.
Depreciation [Operating loss]	Debit with the amount of depreciation of individual asset.	Deduct the amount of depreciation from the concerned item of asset Or add the amount with the Depreciation Reserve in the liability side.
Bad Debts [Operating loss]		
Provision for Bad and Doubtful Debt [Reserve]	Debit the amount of bad debt.	Deduct the amount of bad debts from sundry Debtors.
	Debit the amount of bad debts.	Deduct the amount of bad debts from Sundry Debtors.

Adjustment	*Profit and Loss A/c*	*Balance Sheet*
Discount allowed and provision for discount	Debit both the items.	Deduct from debtors discounts allowed first and then deduct the provision.
Discounts received and provision for discounts received	Credit both the items.	Deduct from creditors discounts received first and then deduct provision.
Interest on Capital	Debit the amount of interest on capital.	Add the interest to the Capital a/c.
Interest on Drawings	Credit the amount of interest on drawings.	Deduct the interest from Capital a/c.

Illustration 1

From the following Trial Balance of Ever Green and Company, prepare Trading and Profit and Loss a/c and Balance Sheet:

Trading Balance

as on 31st December 2018

Particulars	*Amount Dr.* [₹]	*Amount Cr.* [₹]
Cash in hand	2,400	
Purchases	2,40,000	
Stock on 1st January 2018	70,000	
Debtors	1,00,000	
Plant and Machinery	1,20,000	
Furniture	30,000	
Bills Receivable	40,000	
Rent and Taxes	20,000	
Wages	32,000	
Salaries	37,600	
Capital		2,00,000
Bills Payable		44,000
Creditors		48,000
Sales		4,00,000
	6,92,000	6,92,000

Additional Information:

(*a*) Closing inventory as on 31st December 2018 ₹ 50,000.

(*b*) Outstanding wages ₹ 5,000.

(*c*) Depreciation on Plant and Machinery at 10% and Furniture at 5%.

Solution

BOOKS OF EVERGREEN AND COMPANY

Trading Account

for the year ended on 31st December 2018

Particulars		*Amount* [₹]	*Particulars*	*Amount* [₹]
To Opening Stock		70,000	By Sales	4,00,000
To Purchases		2,40,000	By Closing Stock	50,000
To Wages	32,000			
Add: Outstanding	5,000	37,000		
To Gross Pro?t c/d		1,03,000		
		4,50,000		4,50,000

Profit and Loss a/c

for the year ended on 31st December 2018

Particulars	*Amount*[₹]	*Particulars*	*Amount*[₹]
To Salaries	37,600	By Gross Profit b/d	1,03,000
To Rent and Taxes	20,000		
To Depreciation:			
Plant and Machinery	12,000		
Furniture	1,500		
To Net Profit Carried to Capital a/c	31,900		
	1,03,000		1,03,000

Balance Sheet

as on 31st December 2018

Liabilities		*Amount*[₹]	*Assets*		*Amount*[₹]
Creditors		48,000	Cash in Hand		2,400
Bills Payable		44,000	Debtors		1,00,000
Outstanding Wages		5,000	Bill Receivable		40,000
Capital	2,00,000		Stock		50,000
Add: Net Profit	31,900	2,31,900	Furniture	30,000	
			Less: Depreciation	1,500	28,500
			Plant and Machinery	1,20,000	
			Less: Depreciation	12,000	
					1,08,000
		3,28,900			3,28,900

Illustration 2

The following is the trial balance of Raja Jewellers as on 31st December 2018:

Debit Balance	*Amount* [₹]	*Credit Balance*	*Amount* [₹]
Opening Inventory	72,000	Capital	5,00,000
Purchases	2,25,000	Sales	3,50,000
Furniture	15,000	Purchase Return	1,800
Motor Car	30,000	Ram	32,000
Buildings	4,25,800	Shyam	24,000
Sanjay	12,000	Commission	7,500
Kishore	20,000		
Raghav	18,000		
Advertisement	22,000		
Repairs and maintenance	13,000		
General expenses	16,000		
Insurance	7,000		
Cash in Hand	3,500		
Cash at Bank	6,000		
Salaries	30,000		
	9,15,300		9,15,300

You are required to draft Profit and Loss a/c and Balance Sheet as on 31st December 2018 after taking into account the following.

Adjustment:

(*a*) Closing Inventory as at 31.12.2018 ₹ 80000.

(*b*) Interest on Capital at 6%.

(*c*) Prepaid Advertisement ₹ 2000.

(*d*) Goods used for domestic purpose ₹ 1800.

(*e*) Outstanding on buildings at 5% on furniture at 5% and motorcar at 10%.

Solution

BOOKS OF RAJA JEWELLERS

Trading and Profit and Loss a/c

for the year ended on 31.12.2018

Particulars			*Amount* [₹]	*Particulars*	*Amount* [₹]
To Opening Stock			72,000	By Sales	3,50,000
To Purchases	2,25,000			By Closing Inventory	80,000
Less: Return	1,800				
	2,23,200				
Less: Drawings	1,800		2,21,400		
To Gross Profit c/d			1,36,600		
			4,30,000		4,30,000
To Salaries	30,000			By Gross profit b/d	1,36,600
Add: Outstanding	3,000		33,000	By Commission	7,500
To Advertisement		22,000			
Less: Prepaid		2,000	20,000		
To Repairs and Maintenance			13,000		
To General Expenses			16,000		
To Insurance			7,000		
To Depreciation					
Furniture			750		
Motor car			3,000		
Building			21,290		
To Interest on Capital			30,000		
To Net Profit to Capital a/c			60		
			1,44,100		1,44,100

Balance Sheet

as on 31.12.2018

Liabilities		*Amount*[₹]	*Assets*		*Amount*[₹]
Capital	5,00,000		Building	4,25,800	
Add: Interest on			*Less:* Depreciation	21,290	4,04,510
Capital	30,000				
Net Profit	60		Furniture	15,000	
	5,30,060		*Less:* Depreciation	750	14,250
Less: Drawings	1,800	5,28,260	Motor Car	30,000	
Sundry Creditors			*Less:* Depreciation	3,000	27,000
Ram	32,000		Closing Inventory		80,000
Shyam	24,000	56,000	Sundry Debtors:		
Outstanding Salary		3,000	Sanjay	12,000	
			Kishore	20,000	
			Raghav	18,000	50,000
			Prepaid Advertisement		2,000
			Cash at Bank		6,000
			Cash in Hand		3,500
		5,87,260			5,87,260

Note: Goods used for domestic purpose should be treated as drawings.

Illustration 3

From the following particulars, prepare Final Accounts for the year ending on 31st December 2018:

Particulars	*Amount Dr.* [₹]	*Amount Cr.* [₹]
Opening Stock	10,000	
Cash and Bank	4,000	25,000
Purchases and Sales	70,000	90,000
Returns	3,000	4,000
Debtors and Creditors	30,000	21,000
Buildings	30,000	
Capital		30,000
Furniture	7,000	
Bad Debts Reserve		2,000
Petty Cash	200	
Carriage Inwards	800	
Salaries	11,000	
Interest	500	
Sundry Expenses	6,000	
Insurance	1,000	
Premium paid upto 30.6.2019		
Telephone Charges	500	
Commission		2,000

Additional information:

(*a*) Closing Stock ₹ 15,000.

(*b*) Buildings and furniture depreciated at 10% and 20% respectively.

(*c*) Bad Debts ₹ 1,000 are to be written off and a reserve for doubtful debts 5% is to be kept on remaining debtors.

(*d*) Commission received in advance ₹ 1,000.

Solution

Trading Account

for the year ended on 13 31.12.2018

Particulars		*Amount* [₹]	*Particulars*		*Amount* [₹]
To Opening stock		10,000	By Sales	90,000	
To Purchases	70,000		*Less:* Return	3,000	87,000
Less: Return	4,000	66,000	By Closing Stock		15,000
To Carriage Inwards		800			
To Gross Profit c/d		25,200			
		1,02,000			1,02,000

Profit and Loss a/c

for the year ended on 31.12.2018

Particulars		*Amount* [₹]	*Particulars*		*Amount* [₹]
To Salaries		11,000	By Gross profit b/d		25,200
To Petty cash expenses		200	By Commission	2,000	
To Interest on Overdraft		500	*Less:* Received in advance	1,000	1,000
To Insurance Premium	1,000				
Less: Prepaid	500	500			
To Telephonic charges		500			
To Sundary Trade expenses		6,000			
To Bad debts	1,000				
Add: New Bad debts	1,450				
	2,450				
Less: Old Reserve	2,000	450			
To Depreciation					
Furniture		1,400			
Buildings		3,000			
To Net Profit to Capital a/c		2,650			
		26,200			26,200

Balance Sheet

as on 31.12.2018

Liabilities		*Amount* [₹]	*Assets*		*Amount* [₹]
Creditors		21,000	Cash		4,000
Bank Overdraft		25,000	Debtors	30,000	
Commission received in advance		1,000	*Less:* Bad debt	1,000	
Capital	30,000			29,000	
Add: Net Pro?t	2,650		*Less:* New Bad debts		
		32,650	Reserve	1,450	27,550
			Closing Stock		15,000
			Prepaid Insurance		500
			Furniture & Fittings	7,000	
			Less: Depreciation @ 20%	1,400	5,600
			Buildings	30,000	
			Less: Depreciation	3,000	27,000
		79,650			79,650

Illustration 4

From the particulars extracted from the books of Gaiter Traders, prepare final accounts for the year ended 31.3.2018.

Particulars	*Amount* [₹]	*Particulars*	*Amount* [₹]
Capital	2,00,000	Land	54,000
Cash at Bank	8,000	Sales	5,00,000
Cash in Hand	2,000	Carriage inwards	3,200
Buildings	1,20,000	Gas	8,800
Wages	60,000	Sundry Creditors	48,800
Salaries	40,000	Sundry Debtors	60,000
Rent and Taxes	7,200	Purchases Returns	8,000
Printing and stationery	4,800	Sales Returns	6,000
Stock on 1.4.2017	32,000	Bills Receivable	16,000
Purchases	2,80,000	Discount Received	1,600
Insurance	3,200	Discount Allowed	2,000
Machinery	48,000	Furniture	12,000
Drawings	24,000	Travelling Expenses	7,200
		Loans	40,000

Provide the following:

(*a*) Prepaid insurance ₹ 800.

(*b*) Depreciation: 1. Machinery at 10% and 2. Furniture at 5%.

(*c*) Interest on capital at 3%.
(*d*) Outstanding Wages ₹ 3,200 Outstanding Salary ₹ 2,400.
(*e*) Write off Bad Debts ₹ 4,000 and create a Reserve for Bad Debts at 5% on Debtors. Also, create reserve for discounts on Debtors and Creditors at 1%.
(*f*) Value of closing stock ₹ 40,000.

Solution

BOOKS OF GAITER TRADERS

Trading Account

for the year ended on 31.3.2018

Particulars		*Amount*[₹]	*Particulars*		*Amount*[₹]
To Opening stock		32,000	By Sales	5,00,000	
To Purchases	2,80,000		*Less:* Return	6,000	4,94,000
Less: Return	8,000	2,72,000	By Closing Stock		40,000
To Wages	60,000				
Add : Outstanding	3,200	63,200			
To Carriage inwards		3,200			
To Gas		8,800			
To Gross Profit c/d		1,54,800			
		5,34,000			5,34,000

Profit and Loss a/c

for the year ended on 31.3.2018

Particulars		*Amount*[₹]	*Particulars*	*Amount*[₹]
To Salaries	40,000		By Gross Profit	1,54,800
Add: Outstanding	2,400	42,400	By Discounts Received	1,600
To Rent and Rates		7,200	By Reserve for discounts on	488
To Printing and Stationery		4,800	creditors	
To Insurance	3,200			
Less: Prepaid	800	2,400		
To discounts allowed		2,000		
To Reserve for discounts on Debtors		532		
To Traveling Expenses				
To Depreciation		7,200		
Machinery				
Furniture		4,800		
To Bad Debts		600		
To Reserve for Bad Debts		4,000		
To Interest on Capital		2,800		
To Net Profit to Capital A/c		6,000		
		72,156		
		1,56,888		1,56,888

Balance Sheet as on 31.3.2018

Liabilities		*Amount*[₹]	*Assets*		*Amount*[₹]
Sundry Creditors	48,800		Cash in Hand		2,000
Less: Return	488	48,312	Cash at Bank		8,000
For discounts?			Bills Receivable		16,000
Loans		40,000	Sundry Debtors	60,000	
Outstanding Expenses:-			*Less*: Bad debts	4,000	
Wages		3,200		56,000	
Salaries		2,400	*Less:* Reserve for	2,800	
Capital	2,00,000		Bad Debts		
Add: Interest on	6,000			53,200	
Capital			*Less*: Reserve for	532	52,668
Net Profit	72,156		Discounts		
	2,78,156		Prepaid Insurance		800
Less: Drawing	24,000	2,54,156	Stock		40,000
			Furniture	12,000	
			Less: Depreciation	600	11,400
			Machinery	48,000	
			Less: Depreciation	4,800	43,200
			Building		1,20,000
			Land		54,000
		3,48,068			3,48,068

REVIEW QUESTIONS

1. From the following data, prepare trading a/c of a trader for the year ending on 31st March 2018:

Particulars	*Amount* [₹]
Stock on 1.4.2017	24,000
Purchases	6,08,000
Sales	9,50,000
Purchase returns	8,000
Sales returns	10,000
Freight	10,000
Carriage	2,000
Import Duty	8,000
Clearing Duty	12,000
Cost of free sample goods distributed	5,000
Goods taken for personal use	2,000
Stock destroyed by fire	13,000
Cost of material unsold on 31.3.2016 was ₹ 1,20,000, but the market value was ₹ 1,50,000.	

(**Ans.** Gross profit ₹ 2,08,000)

2. From the following particulars prepare trading & profit & loss a/c for the year ended on 31st Dec. 2018:

Particulars	*Amount* [₹]
Stock on 1.1.2018	4,00,000
Purchases	5,10,000
Wages	2,00,000
Carriage	10,000
Purchase Returns	26,500
Export Duty	18,000
Sales	11,50,000
Coal and Coke	50,000
Sales Returns	20,000
Printing and Technology	4,500
Salaries	60,000
Rent and Rates	24,000
Depreciation	6,040
Repairs	12,000
Discount Allowed	25,010
Bad Debts	18,000
Advertisement	5,000
Gas and Water	3,000
Factory Lighting	5,000
General Expenses	800

Value of closing stock ₹ 6,00,000.

[**Ans.** Gross profit ₹ 5,78,500; Net profit ₹ 39,77,950]

3. From the following particulars, prepare Final Accounts of Mr. John for the year ended on 31.3.2018:

Debit Balances	*Amount* [₹]	*Credit Balances*	*Amount* [₹]
Cash in Hand	1,200	Capital	1,00,000
Purchases	1,20,000	B/P	22,000
Stock {1.4.2017}	35,000	Creditors	24,000
Debtors	50,000	Sales	2,00,200
Plant and Machinery	60,000	Reserve for Bad Debts	1,000
Furniture	15,000		
B/R	20,000		
Rent & Rates	10,000		
Wages	16,000		
Salaries	20,000		
	3,47,200		3,47,200

Additional information: [*a*] Closing stock ₹ 40,000, [*b*] O/S rent ₹ 2,000 and O/S salaries ₹ 4,000, [*c*] provide depreciation on plant at 5% and furniture at 10% and [*d*] increases reserve for Bad Debts on Debtors to 2.5%. From above particulars prepare Final Accounts.

[**Ans.** Gross profit ₹ 66,200; Net profit ₹ 25,450; Balance sheet Total ₹ 1,80,450]

4. From the following particulars prepare final accounts for the year ended on 30th June 2018:

Particulars	*Amount*[₹]
Capital	60,000
Sundry Expense	5,400
Manufacturing Expenses	1,500
Reserve for Bad & Doubtful Debts	1,000
Productive Wages	21,500
Office Rent	2,000
Plant and Machinery	28,000
Furniture	10,000
Insurance	1,200
B/R	3,300
B/P	4,200
Factory Rent	4,000
Salaries	16,000
Carriage in	1,500
Carriage out	1,700
Cash in Hand	4,700
Sundry Debtors	23,500
Sundry Creditors	14,300
Purchases	68,000
Sales	1,40,500
Opening Stock	20,500
Drawings	7,200

Take into account the following adjustments:

(*a*) Closing stock amounted to ₹ 27000.

(*b*) Write off ₹ 500 as bad debts and maintain the reserve for bad debts at ₹ 1150.

(*c*) Unexpired insurance amounted to ₹ 300.

(*d*) Sales include ₹ 500 worth of goods taken out by the proprietor for personal use.

(*e*) Depreciate Machinery by 10% and Furniture at 5%.

[**Ans.** Gross Profit ₹ 26,200; Net Loss ₹ 3,750; Balance Sheet total ₹ 67,550.]

[Hints: For adjustment (*d*): deduct goods used for Personal use from sales as purchases in trading account]

5. From the following particulars, prepare final accounts for the year ended on 31st March 2018:

Particulars	*Amount Dr.* [₹]	*Amount Cr.* [₹]
Drawings	10,000	
Stock [1.4.2017]	46,000	
Purchases and Returns	1,50,250	600
Cash in Hand	3,400	
Cash at Bank	22,660	
Freehold Premises	38,600	
Trade Expenses	840	
Printing and Advertisement	1,640	
Professional Charges	280	
Commission		3,300
Investment [1.4.2017, @ 10%]	4,000	
Interest on Deposit		200
Debtors and Creditors	36,000	29,000
Wages	25,000	
Salaries	14,000	
Capital		1,14,000
Income Tax	1,600	
Discounts	6,300	4,600
Sales Returns and Sales	500	2,08,950
Bill Receivables / Bill payables	3,200	10,000
Office furniture	3,050	
Rent and rates	4,000	
Bad Debts Provision		670
	3,71,320	3,71,320

Adjustments:

(*a*) Provide for Wages ₹ 5000.

(*b*) Write off 5% depreciation on free hold premises and 10% on furniture.

(*c*) Insurance paid in advance ₹ 52,000.

(*d*) Stock on 31.3.2017 is ₹ 52,000.

(*e*) Charge interest on capital at 5% and interest on drawings ₹ 300.

(*f*) Further bad debts are ₹ 1000.

(*g*) Provide for bad and doubtful debts at 5% on debtors.

(*h*) Make provision for discount on debtors and reserve for discount on creditors at 2%.

[**Ans.** Gross Profit ₹ 34,800; Net Profit ₹ 6,440; Balance sheet Total ₹ 1,57,600]

■■■

4

Valuation of Fixed Assets: Depreciation Accounting

INTRODUCTION

On the basis of fundamental accounting assumption of going concern, assets are classified as Fixed Assets and Current Assets. Fixed Assets are used in any business to derive benefit for more than one accounting period. Periodic profit is measured by charging cost against periodic revenue. Since fixed assets are used to generate periodic revenue, an appropriate proportion of cost of fixed assets, which is believed to be used or expired for generation of periodic revenue, needs to be charged as cost. Such an appropriate proportion of the cost of fixed assets is termed as Depreciation.

Generally, the term 'Depreciation' is used to denote decrease in value, but in accounting, this term is used to denote decrease in the book value of a fixed asset. Depreciation is the permanent and continuous decrease in the book value of a fixed asset, due to use, effluxion of time, obsolescence, expiration of legal rights or any other cause. According to the Institute of Chartered Accountants in England and Wales, "Depreciation represents that part of the cost of a fixed asset to its owner which is not recoverable when the asset is finally out of use by him. Provision against this loss of capital is an integral cost of conducting the business during the effective commercial life of the asset and is not dependent on the amount of profit earned."

Comprehensively, the term 'Depreciation' covers depletion, amortization and obsolescence. The term **'depletion'** refers to the physical deterioration by the exhaustion of natural resources (ore-deposits in mines, oil wells, quarries, timber stands, etc.). The term **'amortization'** refers to the economic deterioration by the expiration of intangible assets (patents, copyrights, goodwill etc.). The term **'obsolescence'** refers to the economic deterioration by (*a*) invention of improved technique or equipment (*b*) market decline due to change in taste and fashion, etc. (*c*) inadequacy of existing plant to meet the increased business.

DEPRECIATION ACCOUNTING

According to the American Institute of Certified Public Accountants (AICPA), "Depreciation Accounting is a system of accounting which aims to distribute cost or the basic value of tangible capital assets, less salvage (if any), over the estimated useful life of the unit (which may be a group of assets) in a systematic and rational manner. It is a process of allocation and not a valuation."

FACTORS DETERMINING THE AMOUNT OF DEPRECIATION

The amount of depreciation is usually based on the following three factors:

(a) **Historical cost** of a depreciation asset implies the cost incurred on its acquisition, installation, commissioning and for additions to or improvements thereof, which are capital in nature.

(b) **Expected useful life** of a depreciable asset implies either the period over which a depreciable asset is expected to be used by the enterprise or the number of production or similar units expected to be obtained from the use of the asset by the enterprise.

(c) **Estimated residual value** of a depreciable asset implies the value expected to be realized on its sale or exchange on the expiry of its useful life.

Methods of Allocating Depreciation Amount

There are several methods of allocating depreciation amount over the useful life of the assets. Those most commonly employed in industrial and commercial enterprise are the straightline method and the reducing balance method. The management of a business selects the most appropriate method(s) based on various important factors e.g., (*i*) type of asset, (*ii*) the nature of the use of such asset, and (*iii*) circumstances prevailing in the business. A combination of more than one method is sometimes used. In respect of depreciable assets which do not have material value, depreciation includes the following:

Straight Line Method (or Fixed Instalment Method)	Sum of Years' Digits Method (or SYD Method)
Written Down Value Method (or Reducing Instalment Method)	Machine Hour Method
Sinking Fund Method (or depreciation Fund Method)	Production Unit Method (or Depletion Method for Wasting Assets)
Insurance Policy Method	Repairs Provision Method
Annuity Method	Revaluation Method
Double Declining Method	Group Depreciation Method (or Block of Asset Method)

Straight Line Method

Under Straight Line Method, a fixed and equal amount in the form of depreciation, according to a fixed percentage on the original cost, is written off during each accounting period over the expected useful life of the asset. The amount and rate of depreciation is calculated as under:

(*a*) Amount of depreciation $= \dfrac{\text{Original Cost} - \text{Residual Value}}{\text{Expected Useful Life of the Asset}}$

(*b*) Rate of Depreciation $= \dfrac{\text{Amount of Depreciation}}{\text{Original Cost}} \times 100$

Written Down Value Method

Under Written Down Value Method, depreciation, according to a fixed percentage calculated upon the original cost (in the first year) and written down value (in subsequent year) of the asset, is written off during each accounting period over the expected useful life of the asset. Under this method, the rate of depreciation remains constant year after year whereas the amount of depreciation goes on decreasing. The rate of depreciation is calculated as under:

$$\text{Rate of Depreciation} = 1 - n\sqrt{\frac{S}{C}}$$

where, n = Useful Life of the Asset (in years),

S = Scrap Value at the end of useful life,

C = Cost of the Asset.

Sinking Fund Method (Or Depreciation Fund Method)

Under Sinking Fund Method, a fund is created to provide a definite amount at a certain further date for the specific purpose of replacement of the asset at the end of its useful life. The amount of depreciation may be calculated as under:

Amount of Depreciation

= Original cost **less** scrap Value × [Present value of ₹ 1 for a given rate of interest]

or $= \dfrac{\text{Original cost \textbf{less} Scrap value}}{\text{Present Value of an Annuity of ₹ 1 for a given period rate of interest}}$

or = [Original Cost **less** Scrap Value] × $\dfrac{r}{(1+r)^n - 1}$

where, r = Rate of Interest and n = Period for which accumulation is desired.

Insurance Policy Method

Insurance Policy Method is also a Sinking Fund Method under which instead of investing the money in securities, the amount is used in paying premium on an Insurance Policy.

Annuity Method

Under Annuity Method, such an amount is charged by way of depreciation which takes into account not only the cost of the asset but also interest thereon at a given rate. A fixed amount of depreciation is computed with the help of an Annuity Table which provides the amount to write off ₹ 1 over a given period and at a given rate of interest.

Amount of Depreciation = [(Original Cost less Scrap Value) × (Value of Annuity for a given Period at a given rate of interest)] +

Interest on scrap value (if any) for a year at a given rate of interest.

Double Declining Method

Double Declining Method is one of the accelerating methods of depreciation which depreciates the asset at higher rate in the earlier years and at lower rate in the later years. Under this method, a fixed double declining percentage calculated upon the diminishing value of the asset is written off in each accounting period during the expected useful life of the asset. The double declining rate is calculated ignoring the scarp value as under:

Rate of depreciation (in percentage) = $2/n$* 100, where 'n' = Useful Life Asset (in years).

Note: *In the last year of the Useful Life of the Asset, the depreciation amount should be charged in such a manner that the book value of the asset after charging depreciation is at least equal to the estimated scrap value of the asset.*

Sum of the Year's Digits Method (Or SYD Method)

Sum of Year's Digits Method is one of the accelerating methods of depreciation which depreciates the asset at higher rate in the earlier years and at lower rate in the later years. Steps involved in the working of this method are given below in Exhibit 4.1.

Exhibit 4.1 *Steps involved in the calculation of Amount of Depreciation according to SYD Method*

Step 1: *Calculate the 'Sum of years' Digits as under:*

$$\text{Sum of years' Digits} = \frac{n\,(n+1)}{2}$$

where 'n' refers to useful life of the asset (in asset).

Step 2: *Calculate the Fraction for various years up to the useful life as under:*

$$\text{Fraction for 1st year} = \frac{n^{\text{th}} \text{ year}}{\text{Sum of years' Digits}}$$

$$\text{Fraction for 2nd year} = \frac{(n-1)^{\text{th}} \text{ year}}{\text{Sum of years' Digits}}$$

$$\text{Fraction for 3rd year} = \frac{(n-2)^{\text{th}} \text{ year}}{\text{Sum of years' Digits}}$$

$$\text{Fraction for 9th year} = \frac{1}{\text{Sum of years' Digits}}$$

Step 3: *Calculate the amount of Depreciation as under:*

Amount of Depreciation = (Original Cost **less** Estimated Scrap Value) × Respective Fraction for the given year.

Machine Hour Method

Under Machine Hour Method, depreciation is provided by means of a fixed rate hour calculated by dividing the value of the asset by the estimate number of effective working hours during the useful life of the asset. In this case, the life of the asset is estimated in terms of hours for which it is expected to be used. This method is considered to be appropriate for plant and machinery, air-craft, etc. The working of this method involves steps given below in Exhibit 4.2.

Exhibit 4.2 *Steps involved in the calculation of amount of Depreciation, according to Machine Hour Method*

Step 1: *Calculate the rate of Depreciation per hour as under:*

$$\text{Rate per hour} = \frac{\text{Original Cost } \textbf{less} \text{ Residual Value}}{\text{Useful Life in Terms of Effective Hours}}$$

Step 2: *Calculate the amount of Depreciation as under:*

Amount of Depreciation = Actual Hours × Rate of Depreciation per hour (as per Step 1)

Production Unit Method (Or Depletion Method for Wasting Assets)

Under Production Unit Method, depreciation is provided by means of a fixed rate per unit of production, calculated by dividing the value of the asset by the estimated number of units to be produced during its life. In this case, the life of the asset is estimated in terms of output, which it is expected to produce. This method is considered to be appropriate for mine, quarries, etc. The working method involves steps given below in Exhibit 4.3.

Exhibit 4.3 *Steps involved in the calculation of amount of Depreciation according to Production Unit Method*

Step 1: *Calculate the rate of Depreciation per unit as under:*

$$\text{Rate per unit} = \frac{\text{Original Cost } \textbf{less} \text{ Residual Value}}{\text{Useful Life in Terms of Output}}$$

Step 2: *Calculate the amount of Depreciation as under:*

Amount of Depreciation = Actual Output (in units) × Rate of Depreciation per unit (as per Step 1)

***Note:** This method when applied to wasting assets like mines, quarries etc. is known as Depletion Method because wasting assets cannot be depreciation but can be gradually depleted.*

Repairs Provision Method

Repairs Provision Method takes into consideration not only the cost of the asset but also the estimate cost of repairs to be effected during the useful life of the asset. The salient features of this method are as under:

(*a*) The total cost of repairs to be effected during the life of the asset is estimated.

(*b*) The amount of Depreciation is calculated as under:

$$\text{Amount of depreciation} = \frac{(\text{Original Cost} - \text{Residual Value}) + \text{Estimate Total Cost of Repairs}}{\text{Useful Life}}$$

(*c*) The amount of depreciation is debited to Profit and Loss Account and credited to Provision for Depreciation and Repairs Account.

(*d*) The actual amount incurred on repairs and renewals is debited to Provision for Depreciation and Repairs Account.

(*e*) At the end of useful life of the asset, the Provision for Depreciation and Repairs Account is closed by transferring it to the Asset Account.

(*f*) The main merit of this method lies in the fact that it equalizes the Burdon on the Profit and Loss Account in respect of depreciation and repairs.

(*g*) This method is considered to be appropriate where the service rendered by the asset is uniformed over the useful life of the asset.

Revaluation Method

Under this method, at the end of each accounting period, the asset concerned is valued at its current market value, and, if the current value is less than the book value, the difference is written off as depreciation. This method is considered to be appropriate for assets like loose tools, live stock, etc. The method of calculating depreciation is given below in Exhibit 4.4.

Exhibit 4.4 *Statement Showing the Calculation of Depreciation under Revaluation Method*

	₹
A. Book Value of the Asset in the Beginning	xxxxx
B. *Add:* Purchases	xxxxx
C. *Less*: (*a*) Sale Proceeds of the Asset sold during the accounting period	xxxxx
(*b*) *Revalued figure of the Asset at the end	xxxxx
D. Depreciation to be charged (A + B – C)	xxxxxx

***Note:** *If the revalued figure of the asset at the end exceeds the book value of the asset at the end, and such appreciation should be ignored and the book value instead of revalued figure should be deducted, as aforesaid.*

Group Depreciation Method (Or Block of Assets Method)

The salient features of this method are as under:

(*a*) All similar or interchangeable assets having usually the similar useful lives are grouped together in a single Asset Account.

(*b*) Original cost of all the assets in the group is debited to this account.

(*c*) Depreciation is charged for the group in total and not item by item.

Under the Income Tax Act 1961, with effect from the assessment year 1988-89, depreciation is admissible for block of assets on the basis of written down value method. To understand the method of computation of depreciation, one must know the meaning of Block of Assets, actual cost, Written Down Value.

Block of Assets [Sec. 2 (11)]: It means a group of assets falling within a class of assets, being building, machinery, plant or furniture, in respect of which the same percentage of depreciation is prescribed.

Actual Cost [Sec. 43(1)]: It means the actual cost to the assessee, as reduced by the proportion of the cost thereof, if any, as has been met, directly or indirectly, by any other person or authority.

Written Down Value [Sec. 43 (6)]: The procedure for computing the Written Down Value and the amount of depreciation has been given below in Exhibit 4.5.

Exhibit 4.5 *Procedure for computing the Written Down Value and the amount of Depreciation*

Statement Showing the Computation of the Written Down Value and the amount of Depreciation

	₹
A. Written Down Value in the beginning	**xxxx**
B. *Add:* Actual Cost of asset (falling in the block) acquired	**xxxx**
C. *Less:* Money payable (together with scrap value) in respect of that asset (falling within that block) which is sold, discarded, demolished or destroyed.	**xxxx**

(*Note*: *The amount of such reduction cannot, however, exceed the value of block of assets, i.e.* A + B)	
D. Written Down Value (subject to depreciation) at the end (A + B – C)	**xxxx**
E. *Less:* Depreciation	**xxxx**
F. Written Down Value (after depreciation) at the (D – E)	**xxxx**

Depreciation where an asset is put to use for less than 180 days under the Income Tax Act, 1961: Where any asset falling within a block of asset is acquired by the assessee during the previous year and is 'put to use' for the purposes of business or profession for a period of less than 180 days in that previous year, the depreciation in respect of such asset shall be restricted to 50 per cent of the amount calculated at the percentage prescribed in the case of block of asset comprising such an asset. (*Note*: *The term 'use' includes ready for use.*)

Tutorial Note: *The aforesaid provision of the Income Tax Act, 1961 has been given just for information and not for the purpose of applying the same while solving problems of this chapter.*

Change in the Method of Depreciation

According to the revised Accounting Standard, issued by ICAI, the depreciation method selected should be applied consistently, to provide comparability of the results of operations of the enterprise from period to period. A change from one method of providing depreciation to another should be made only if the adoption of the new method is required by statue or for compliance with an Accounting Standard or if it is considered that the change would result in a more appropriate preparation or presentation of the financial statements of the enterprise. When such a change in the method of depreciation is made, depreciation should be recalculated in accordance with the new method from the date of the asset coming into use. The deficiency or surplus arising from retrospective recomputation of depreciation in accordance with the new method should be adjusted in accounts in the year in which the method of depreciation is changed. In case the change in the method results in deficiency in depreciation in respect of past years, the deficiency should be charged in the statement of profit and loss. In case the change in the method results in surplus, the surplus should be credited to the statement of profit and loss. Such a change should be treated as a change in the accounting policy and its effect should be quantified and disclosed. The procedure for recording a change in the method of depreciation with retrospective effect has been given below in Exhibit 4.6.

Exhibit 4.6 *Procedure for recording a change in the Method of Depreciation with retrospective effect*

Step 1: *Calculate the aggregate depreciation already provided on existing assets, i.e. assets other than sold/discarded/destroyed/exchanged, under the existing method up to the end of previous accounting year.*

Step 2: *Calculate the aggregate depreciation on existing assets retrospectively from the date of asset coming into use by adopting the new method up to the end of previous accounting year.*

Step 3: *Calculate the difference between the aggregate depreciation under existing method, as per Step 1 and that under new method as per Step 2.*

Step 4: *Adjust the short depreciation (excess of Step 2 over Step 1) by debiting Profit & Loss Account and crediting the Asset Account/Provision for Depreciation Account OR Adjust the excess depreciation (excess of Step 1 over Step 2) by debiting Asset Account/Provision for Depreciation Account and crediting Profit & Loss Account.*

Step 5: *Charge depreciation from the current accounting year and onwards by adopting new method.*

EFFECT OF A REVISION OF ESTIMATED USEFUL LIFE OF AN ASSET

According to the revised Accounting Standard 6, issued by ICAI, where there is a revision of the estimated useful life of an asset, the unauthorized depreciable amount should be charged over the revised remaining useful life.

EFFECT OF ANY ADDITION OR EXTENSION

According to the revised Accounting Standard 6, issued by ICAI, the depreciation on any addition or extension to an existing asset, which is of capital nature, should be provided as under:

(*a*) Where an addition or extension retains a separate identity and is capable of being used after the existing asset is disposed of	(*i*) Depreciation should be provided independently on the basis of an estimate of its own useful life
(*b*) In other cases	(*ii*) Depreciation should be provided on the basis of the remaining useful life of that existing asset of which an addition or extension becomes an integral part

EFFECT OF CHANGE IN LONG-TERM LIABILITY

According to the revised Accounting Standard 6, issued by ICAI, where the historical cost of a depreciable asset has undergone a change due to increase or decrease in the long-term liability on account of exchange fluctuations, price adjustments, changes in duties or similar factors, the depreciation on the revised unamortized depreciable amount should be provided prospectively over the residual useful life of the asset.

EFFECT OF REVALUATION OF ASSET

According to the revised Accounting Standard 6, issued by ICAI, where the depreciable assets are revalued, the provision for depreciation should be based on the revalued amount and on the estimate useful lives of such assets. In case, the revaluation has a material effect on the amount of depreciation, the same should be disclosed separately in the year in which revaluation is carried out.

METHODS OF RECORDING DEPRECIATION

In order to record depreciation, a provision for depreciation may or may not be maintained. In case, a 'Provision for Depreciation Account' is maintained, the asset concerned appears at its original cost since the depreciation is credited to 'Provision for Depreciation Account' instead of the 'Concerned Asset Account'. In case a 'Provision for Depreciation Account' is not maintained, the asset concerned appears at a written down values since the depreciation is credited to the 'Concerned Asset Account'. The accounting entries under both these cases are summarized as under:

Case	*When a Provision for Depreciation Account is maintained*	*When a Provision for Depreciation Account is not maintained*
(*a*) For providing depreciation	Depreciation A/c Dr. To Provision for Depreciation A/c	Depreciation A/c Dr. To Asset A/c
(*b*) For closure of Depreciation	Profit & Loss A/c Dr. To Depreciation A/c	Profit & Loss A/c Dr. To Depreciation A/c
(*c*) On disposal of an Asset	(*i*) For transfer of original cost Of asset disposal off. Asset Disposal A/c Dr. To Asset A/c (*ii*) For transfer of accumulated Depreciation on asset disposal off Provision for Depreciation A/c Dr. To Asset Disposal A/c (*iii*) For recording sale proceeds Cash A/c / Bank A/c Dr. To Asset Disposal A/c (*iv*) For transfer of the balance in Asset Disposal Account (*a*) In case of profit Asset Disposal A/c Dr. To profit & Loss A/c (*b*) In case of loss, reverse of the Above entry will be passed.	(*i*) For recording sale proceeds Cash A/c /Bank A/c Dr. To Asset A/c (*ii*) For transfer of profit & loss disposal off. (*a*) In case of profit Asset A/c Dr. To Profit & Loss A/c (*b*) In case of loss, reverse of the above entry will be passed.

Working Notes:

(*i*) Book value, as on date of sale = Original Cost – Total Depreciation till date of sale.

(*ii*) Profit = Sale Proceeds – Book Value as on date of sale.

(*iii*) Loss = Book Value as on date of sale – Sale Proceeds.

(*iv*) In case of an exchange of an asset, sale proceeds imply the 'Trade in allowance' (i.e. the amount at which the vendor agrees to acquire the old asset).

(*v*) In case of destruction/damage of an insured asset by fire or accident, sale proceeds imply claim admitted by Insurance Company together with salvage value, if any.

DEPRECIATION ON ADDITIONS TO FIXED ASSETS

Strictly for examination purpose, the following approach is suggested:

	Ans.
(*a*) When the rate of depreciation with the words, 'per annum' is given (*e.g.* 20% p.a.).	
(*i*) If the date of acquisition is given.	(*a*) (*i*) Charge depreciation only for the remaining accounting period.
(*ii*) If the date of acquisition is not given.	(*ii*) Either charge depreciation for the full accounting period or half accounting period or charge no depreciation with specific note to that effect.
(*b*) When the rate of depreciation without the accounting 'per annum' is given (*e.g.* 20%) of acquisition.	(*b*) With the words' 'per annum', charge depreciation for the full period, irrespective of the date.

SOLVED PROBLEMS

STRAIGHT LINE METHOD (SLM)

Illustration 1

On 1st April 2014, X Ltd. purchased machinery for ₹ 1,00,000 and incurred ₹ 7,000 towards freight and insurance, ₹ 1,000 towards carriage inwards and ₹ 2,000 towards installation charges. It was established that the machinery will have a scrap value of ₹ 10,000 at the end of its useful life, which is 4 years. On 1st April, 2017, ₹ 2,000 were incurred on repairs and renewals of machine.

Requirement: Determine (*a*) Amount of Depreciation, (*b*) Rate of Depreciation, (*c*) Show the Machinery Account for the first four financial years ending 31st March, each year, according to the Straight Line Method.

(*i*) If no Provision for Depreciation Account is maintained.

(*ii*) If Provision for Depreciation Account is maintained.

Solution

(*a*) Amount of Depreciation $= \dfrac{\text{Original Cost} - \text{Scrap Value}}{\text{Estimated useful life}}$

$= \dfrac{₹\,1,10,000 - ₹\,10,000}{4}$

$= ₹\,25,000$

(*b*) Rate of Depreciation $= \dfrac{\text{Amount of depreciation}}{\text{Original Cost}} \times 100$

$= \dfrac{₹\,25,000}{₹\,1,10,000}$

$= 22.73\%$

(*c*) Dr. (*i*) **Machinery Account** Cr.

Date	*Particulars*	*Amount* [₹]	*Date*	*Particulars*	*Amount* [₹]
01.04.14	To Bank A/c	1,00,000	31.03.17	By Depreciation A/c	25,000
	To Bank A/c (Freight)	7,000	31.03.17	By Balance c/d	85,000
	To Bank A/c (Carriage inwards)	1,000			
	To Bank A/c (Installation Charges)	2,000			
		1,10,000			1,10,000
01.04.15	By Balance b/d	85,000	31.03.18	By Depreciation A/c	25,000
			31.03.18	By Balance c/d	60,000
		85,000			85,000
01.04.16	By Balance b/d	60,000	31.03.19	By Depreciation A/c	25,000
			31.03.19	By Balance c/d	35,000
		60,000			60,000
01.04.17	By Balance b/d	35,000	31.03.20	By Depreciation A/c	25,000
			31.03.20	By Balance c/d	10,000
		35,000			35,000

(*c*) Dr. (*ii*) **Machinery Account** Cr.

Date	*Particulars*	*Amount* [₹]	*Date*	*Particulars*	*Amount* [₹]
01.04.14	To Bank A/c	1,00,000	31.03.12	By Balance c/d	1,10,000
	To Bank A/c (Freight)	7,000			
	To Bank A/c (Carriage inwards)	1,000			
	To Bank A/c(Installation charges)	2,000			
		1,10,000			1,10,000
01.04.15	To Balance b/d	1,10,000	31.04.13	By Balance c/d	1,10,000
01.04.16	To Balance b/d	1,10,000	31.04.14	By Balance c/d	1,10,000
01.04.17	To Balance b/d	1,10,000	31.04.15	By Balance c/d	1,10,000

Dr. **Provision for Depreciation Account** Cr.

Date	*Particulars*	*Amount* [₹]	*Date*	*Particulars*	*Amount* [₹]
31.03.15	To Balance c/d	25,000	31.03.15	By Depreciation A/c	25,000
31.03.16	To Balance c/d	50,000	01.04.16	By Balance b/d	25,000
			31.03.17	By Depreciation A/c	25,000
		50,000			50,000
31.03.17	To Balance c/d	75,000	01.04.16	By Balance b/d	50,000
			31.03.17	By Depreciation A/c	25,000
		75,000			75,000
31.03.18	To Balance c/d	1,00,000	01.04.17	By Balance b/d	75,000
			31.03.18	By Depreciation A/c	25,000
		1,00,000			1,00,000

Note: The amount spent on repairs and renewals of machinery ₹ 2,000 on 1.4.17, is of revenue nature and not of capital nature and hence not debited to **Machinery Account.**

WRITTEN DOWN VALUE METHOD

Illustration 2

Taking the same information as given in **Illustration 1** determines the rate of Depreciation and show the Machinery Account for the first four financial year ending on 31st March, each year according to the Written Down Value Method.

Solution

$$\text{Rate of Depreciation} = 1 - n\sqrt{\frac{S}{C}} \qquad = 1 - 4\sqrt{\frac{10,000}{1,10,000}} = 0.45 = 45\%$$

where, *n* refers to useful life, *S* refers to scrap value at the end of useful life, *C* refers to cost of asset.

Dr. **Machinery Account** Cr.

Date	*Particulars*	*Amount* [₹]	*Date*	*Particulars*	*Amount* [₹]
01.04.14	To Bank A/c	1,00,000	31.03.15	By Depreciation A/c	49,500
01.04.14	To Bank A/c(Freight)	7,000	31.03.15	By Balance c/d	60,500
01.04.14	To Bank A/c (Carriage inwards)	1,000			
01.04.14	To Bank A/c (Installation Charges)	2,000			
		1,10,000			1,10,000
01.04.15	To Balance b/d	60,500	31.03.16	By Depreciation A/c	27,225
			31.03.16	By Balance c/d	33,275
		60,500			60,500
01.04.16	To Balance b/d	33,275	31.03.17	By Depreciation A/c	14,974
			31.03.17	By Balance c/d	18,301
		33,275			33,275
01.04.17	To Balance b/d	18,301	31.03.18	By Depreciation A/c	8,235
			31.03.18	By Balance c/d	10,066
		18,301			18,301

LOSS ON SALE, LOSS ON EXCHANGE, LOSS BY FIRE

Illustration 3

X Ltd. purchased a machine for ₹ 60,000 on 1.1.15. Depreciation is provided @ 10% p.a. on diminishing balance method. Prepare the Machinery Account for the year 2015 in each of the following alternative cases:

(*a*) If this machine is sold on 1.7.17 for ₹ 28,600.

(*b*) If a new machine costing ₹ 60,000 is purchased on 1.7.17 after surrendering the old one and paying cash ₹ 35,000.

(*c*) If this machine was destroyed by fire on 1.7.17 and its scrap was sold for ₹ 600 and the insurance company paid ₹ 28,000 only.

Solution

Case (*a*) If this machine is sold on 1.7.17 for ₹ 28,600.

Dr. **Machine Account** Cr.

Date	*Particulars*	*Amount* [₹]	*Date*	*Particulars*	*Amount* [₹]
01.01.17	To Balance b/d	48,600	01.07.17	By Depreciation A/c	2,430
			01.07.17	By Bank A/c	28,600
			01.07.17	By P&L A/c (Loss)	17,570
		48,600			48,600

Case (*b*) If this Machine is exchanged

Dr. **Machine Account** Cr.

Date	*Particulars*	*Amount* [₹]	*Date*	*Particulars*	*Amount* [₹]
01.01.17	To Balance b/d	48,600	01.07.17	By Depreciation A/c	2,430
01.07.17	To Vendors A/c	60,000	01.07.17	By Vendors A/c	25,000
			01.07.17	By P&L A/c (Loss)	21,170
			31.12.17	By Depreciation A/c	3,000
			31.12.17	By Balance c/d	57,000
		1,08,600			1,08,600

Case (*c*) If this Machine was destroyed by fire.

Dr. **Machine Account** Cr.

Date	*Particulars*	*Amount* [₹]	*Date*	*Particulars*	*Amount* [₹]
01.01.17	To Balance b/d	48,600	01.07.17	By Depreciation a/c	2,430
				By Bank a/c (Scrap)	600
				By Bank a/c (Claim)	28,000
				By P&L a/c (Loss)	17,570
		48,600			48,600

Working Notes:

(*i*) Calculation of Book Value as on 01.01.17 and on 01.07.17

A	Original Cost as on 01.01.15	60,000
B	*Less*: Depreciation for 2015	6,000
C	Book Value as on 01.01.16	54,000
D	*Less*: Depreciation for 2016	5,400
E	Book Value as on 01.01.17	48,600
F	*Less*: Depreciation up to 01.07.017	2,430
G	Book Value as on 01.07.17	46,170

(*ii*) Loss on Sale = Book Value as on date of sale – Sale Proceeds

= ₹ 46,170 – ₹ 28,600 = ₹ 17,570

(*iii*) Loss on Exchange = Book Value as on date of **Exchange** – **Trade-in-allowance**

= ₹ 46,170 – **(₹ 60,000 – ₹ 35,000)**

= ₹ 46,170 – ₹ 25,000 = ₹ 21,170

(*iv*) Loss by Fire = Book Value as on **date of fire** – **(Scrap Proceeds + Claim received)**

= ₹ 46,170 – (₹ 600 + ₹ 28,000) = ₹ 17,570

Illustration 4

A company purchases a 3 years lease on January 1, 2015 for ₹ 25,000. It decided to provide for the replacement of the lease at the end of 3 years by setting up a Depreciation Fund. It is expected that investment will fetch interest at 5%. Sinking Fund tables show that to provide the requisite sum at 5% at the end of 3 years, an investment of ₹ 7,932.22 is required every year. Investments are made to the nearest rupee. On 31st December, 2017, investments are sold for ₹ 30,000. Prepare Lease Account, Depreciation Fund Account, Depreciation Fund Investment Account, Depreciation Account and the New Lease Account.

Solution

Dr. **Lease Account** Cr.

Date	Particulars	Amount [₹]	Date	Particulars	Amount [₹]
01.01.15	To Bank a/c	25,000	31.12.15	By Balance c/d	25,000
01.01.16	To Balance b/d	25,000	31.12.16	By Balance c/d	25,000
01.01.17	To Balance b/d	25,000	31.12.17	By Depreciation Fund a/c	25,000
		75,000			75,000

Dr. **Depreciation Fund Account** Cr.

Date	Particulars	Amount [₹]	Date	Particulars	Amount [₹]
31.12.15	To Balance c/d	7,932.22	31.12.15	By Depreciation a/c	7,932.22
31.12.16	To Balance c/d	16,261.04	01.01.16	By Balance b/d	7,932.22
			31.12.16	By Bank a/c(interest)	396.60
			31.12.16	By Depreciation a/c	7,932.22
		16,261.04			16,261.04
31.12.17	To Depreciation Fund Investment a/c	1,011.00	01.01.17	By Balance b/d	16,261.04
	To Lease a/c	25,000.00	31.12.17	By Bank a/c (interest)	813.05
				By Depreciation a/c	7,932.22
				By Profit and Loss a/c	1,004.69
		26,011.00			26,011.00

Dr. **Depreciation Fund Investment Account** Cr.

Date	Particulars	Amount [₹]	Date	Particulars	Amount [₹]
31.12.17	To Bank a/c	7,932.00	31.12.15	By Balance c/d	7,932.00
01.01.16	To Balance b/d	7,932.00	31.12.16	By Balance c/d	16,261.00
31.12.16	To Bank a/c	8,329.00			
		16,261.00			16,261.00
01.01.16	To Balance b/d	16,261.00	31.12.17	By Bank a/c (Sales)	15,250.00
				By Depreciation Fund a/c (loss on sale)	1,011.00
		16,261.00			16,261.00

Dr. **Depreciation Account** Cr.

Date	Particulars	Amount [₹]	Date	Particulars	Amount [₹]
31.12.15	To Depreciation Fund A/c	7,932.22	31.12.15	By Profit and Loss A/c	7,932.22
31.12.16	To Depreciation Fund A/c	7,932.22	31.12.16	By Profit and Loss A/c	7,932.22
31.12.17	To Depreciation Fund A/c	7,932.22	31.12.17	By Profit and Loss A/c	7,932.22

Dr. **New Release Account** Cr.

Date	Particulars	Amount [₹]	Date	Particulars	Amount [₹]
01.01.18		30,000			

INSURANCE POLICY METHOD

Illustration 5

A Ltd. purchased a machinery for ₹ 50,000 on 1.01.14 and incurred ₹ 10,000 towards freight insurance, carriage inwards and installation charges. It was estimated that the machinery will have a scrap value of ₹ 5000 at the end of its useful life, which is 4 years. It was decided to take out an insurance policy to provide necessary funds for the replacement of asset at the end of its useful life. The annual premium for the policy payable on 1st April every year was ₹ 13,000. The scrap value at the end of fourth year realized ₹ 5,200. Prepare Depreciation Fund Account, Depreciation Fund Policy Account and the Machinery Account.

Solution

Dr. **Depreciation Fund Policy Account** Cr.

Date	Particulars	Amount [₹]	Date	Particulars	Amount [₹]
01.01.14	To Bank A/c	13,000	31.12.14	By Balance c/d	13,000
01.01.15	To Balance b/d	13,000	31.12.15	By Balance c/d	26,000
	To Bank A/c	13,000			
		26,000			26,000
01.01.16	To Balance b/d	26,000	31.12.16	By Balance c/d	39,000
	To Bank A/c	13,000			
		39,000			39,000
01.01.17	To Balance b/d	39,000	31.12.17	By Bank A/c	55,000
01.01.17	To Bank A/c	13,000			
01.01.17	To Depreciation Fund A/c (profit)	3,000			
		55,000			55,000

Dr. **Depreciation Fund Account** Cr.

Date	Particulars	Amount [₹]	Date	Particulars	Amount [₹]
31.12.14	To Balance c/d	13,000	31.12.15	By Balance A/c	13,000
31.12.15	To Balance c/d	26,000	01.01.15	By Balance b/d	13,000
			31.12.15	By Depreciation A/c	13,000
		26,000			26,000
31.12.16	To Balance c/d	39,000	01.01.16	By Balance b/d	26,000
			31.12.16	By Depreciation A/c	13,000
		39,000			39,000
31.12.17	To Balance c/d	55,000	01.01.17	By Balance b/d	39,000
			31.12.17	By Profit & Loss A/c	13,000
				By Depreciation Fund Policy A/c (Profit)	3,000
		55,000			55,000

Dr. **Machinery Account** Cr.

Date	Particulars	Amount [₹]	Date	Particulars	Amount [₹]
01.01.14	To Bank A/c	50,000	31.12.14	By Balance c/d	60,000
	To Bank A/c	10,000			
		60,000			60,000
01.01.15	To Balance b/d	60,000	31.12.15	By Balance c/d	60,000
01.01.16	To Balance b/d	60,000	31.12.16	By Balance c/d	60,000
01.01.17	To Balance b/d	60,000	31.12.17	By Depreciation Fund A/c	55,000
	To Profit & Loss A/c	200		By Bank A/c	5,200
		60,200			60,200

Working Note: Amount of Insurance Policy required = ₹ 50,000 + ₹ 10,000 – ₹ 5,000
= ₹ 55,000.

ANNUITY METHOD

Illustration 6

A lease is purchased on 1st January, 2012 for 4 years at a cost of ₹ 20,000. It is proposed to depreciate the lease by the annuity method charging interest at 5 % p.a. A reference to the annuity table shows that to depreciate ₹ 1 by annuity method over 4 years charging interest at 5 % p.a. one must write off a sum of ₹ 0.2820. Show the Lease Account for four years and also the relevant entries in the Profit and Loss Account.

Solution

Lease Account

Dr. Cr.

Date	*Particulars*	*Amount* [₹]	*Date*	*Particulars*	*Amount* [₹]
01.01.14	To bank a/c	20,000	31.12.14	By Depreciation a/c (20,000*0.2820)	5,640
31.12.14	To Interest a/c (5% on ₹ 20,000)	1,000		By Balance c/d	15,360
		21,000			21,000
01.01.15	To balance b/d	15,360	31.12.15	By Depreciation a/c	5,640
31.12.15	To Interest a/c (5% on ₹ 15,360)	768		By Balance b/d	10,488
		16,128			16,128
01.01.16	To Balance b/d	10,488	31.12.16	By Depreciation a/c	5,640
31.12.16	To Interest a/c (5% on ₹ 5,372)	524		To Balance c/d	5,372
		11,012			11,012
01.01.17	To Balance b/d	5,372	31.12.17	By Depreciation a/c	5,640
31.12.17	To Interest a/c (5% on ₹ 5,372)	268			
		5,640			5,640

An Extract of Profit and Loss Account

Dr. Cr.

Date	*Particulars*	*Amount* [₹]	*Date*	*Particulars*	*Amount* [₹]
31.12.14	To Depreciation a/c	5,640	31.12.14	By Interest a/c	1,000
31.12.15	To Depreciation a/c	5,640	31.12.15	By Interest a/c	768
31.12.16	To Depreciation a/c	5,640	31.12.16	By Interest a/c	524
31.12.17	To Depreciation a/c	5,640	31.12.17	By Interest a/c	268

REVIEW QUESTIONS AND PROBLEMS

1. What is depreciation? What are its causes?
2. What are the various methods of providing depreciation?
3. On 1st April 2014 X Ltd. purchased a machine for ₹ 2,00,000 and incurred ₹ 14,000 towards freight and insurance, ₹ 2,000 towards carriage inwards and ₹ 4,000 towards installation charges. It was estimated that the machinery will have a scrap value of ₹ 20,000 at the end of its useful life (which is 4 years). On 1st April 2018, ₹ 2,000 were incurred on repairs and renewals of machine.

(*a*) Prepare the Machinery Account according to Straight Line Method if no Provision for Depreciation Account is maintained.

(*b*) Prepare the Machinery Account and the Provision for Depreciation Account according to Straight Line Method.

(*c*) Prepare a Machinery Account according to Written Down Value Method.

(*d*) Prepare the Machinery Account, Depreciation Fund Account and Depreciation Fund Investment Account according to Depreciation Fund Method if the Sinking Fund Table shows that ₹ 1 p.a at 12% compound interest amounts to ₹ 4.779 in 4 years, investments are to be made in multiplies of ₹ 20 only. On 31st March, 2015 investments realized ₹ 16,000 only.

(*e*) Prepare the Machinery Account, Depreciation Fund Account and Account and Depreciation Fund Policy Account according to the Insurance Policy Method, if the annual premium for the policy payable on 1st April, every year, was ₹ 52,000 and the scrap value of machinery realized ₹ 20,800 only.

(*f*) Prepare the Machinery Account and Profit and Loss Account according to Annuity Method if the Annuity Table shows that to depreciate ₹ 1 by annuity method over 4 years charging at 5% p.a., one must write off a sum of ₹ 0.2820.

(*g*) Prepare the Machinery Account according to Double Declining Method.

(*h*) Prepare the Machinery Account according to Sum of Year' Digits Method.

4. On 1st Jan. 2012, X Ltd. purchased a machine for ₹ 1,16,000 and spent ₹ 4,000 on its erection. On 1st July, 2014 an additional machinery costing ₹ 40,000, was purchased on 1st July 2012 the machine purchased on 1.1.14 was sold for ₹ 57,200 and on the same date, a new machine was purchased at a cost of ₹ 80,000. Prepare the Machinery Account for the first four calendar years under each of the following alternative cases:

(*a*) If the depreciation has been provided at 10% p.a. according to written Down Value Method and at the end of Method @ 5% p.a. prospectively in accordance with Accounting Standard 6;

(*b*) If the depreciation has been provided at 10% p.a. according to Written Down Value Method, and at the end of 2018, the firm decided to change the method of depreciation from Written Down value Method to Straight Line Method @ 5% p.a. retrospectively in accordance with Revised Accounting Standard 6.

5. A transport company purchases 5 trucks at ₹ 2,00,000 each on April 1, 2016. The company writes off depreciation @ 20% per annum on original cost and observes calendar year as its accounting year. On October 1, 2018, one of the trucks is involved in an accident and is completely destroyed. Insurance company pays ₹ 90,000 in full settlement of the claim. On the same day, the company purchases a used truck for ₹ 1,00,000 and spends ₹ 2,000 on its overhauling. Prepare Truck Account for the three years ending on 31st December, 2018.

■■■

5

Valuation of Inventories

INTRODUCTION

Every enterprise needs inventory for smooth running of its activities. It serves as a link between production and distribution processes. There is, generally, a time lag between the recognition of a need and its fulfillment. The greater the time-lag, the higher is the requirement for inventory. It also provides a cushion for future price fluctuations.

Investments in inventories constitute the most significant part of current assets/working capital in most of the undertakings. Thus, it its very essential to have proper control and management of inventories. The purpose of inventory management is to ensure availability of materials in sufficient quantity as and when required and also to minimise investment in inventories.

MEANING AND NATURE OF INVENTORY

The dictionary meaning of inventory is 'stock of goods, or a list of goods'. The word 'Inventory' is understood differently by various authors. In accounting language it may mean stock of finished goods only. In a manufacturing concern, it may include raw materials, work in process and stores, etc. to understand the exact meaning of the word 'inventory' we may study it from the usage side or from the 'side of point of entry' in operations. Inventory includes the following things:

1. **Raw material:** Raw material forms a major input into the organization. They are required to carry out production activities uninterruptedly. The quantity of raw materials required is determined by the rate for replenishing supplies. Factors like the availability of raw materials and government regulations, etc. too affect the stock of raw materials.
2. **Work-in-progress:** The work-in-progress is that stage of stocks which are in-between raw material and finished goods. The raw materials enter the process of manufacture but they are yet to attain a final shape of finished goods. The quantum of work-in-progress depends

upon the time taken in the manufacturing process. The greater the time taken in manufacturing, the more will be the amount of work in progress.

3. **Consumables:** Then refer to materials which need to smoothen the process of production. These materials do not directly enter production, they act as catalysts. Consumables stores do not create any supply problem and form a small part of production cost. There can be instances where these materials may account for much value than the raw materials. The fuel oil may form a substantial part of the cost.

4. **Finished goods:** There are goods which are ready for the consumers. The stock of finished goods provides a buffer between production and market. The purpose of maintaining inventory is to ensure proper supply of goods to customers. In some concerns the production is undertaken on order basis. In these concerns, there will not be a need for finished goods. The need for finished goods inventory is more when production is undertaken in general without waiting for specific orders.

5. **Spares:** Spares also form a part of inventory. The consumption pattern of raw material, consumables, finished goods are different from that of spares. The stocking policies of spares are different from industry. Some industries, like transport, require more spares than the other concerns. The costly spare parts like engines, maintenance spares, etc. are not discarded after use, rather they are kept in ready position for further use. All decisions about spares are based on the financial cost of inventory on such spares and costs that may arise due to their non-availability.

OBJECTIVES OF HOLDING INVENTORIES

Although holding inventories involves blocking of a firm's funds and the cost of storage and handling, every business enterprise has to maintain a certain level of inventories to facilitate uninterrupted production and smooth running of business. In the absence of inventories, a firm will have to make purchases as soon as it receives orders. It will mean loss of time and delays in the executing of orders which sometimes may cause loss of customers and business. A firm also needs to maintain inventories to reduce ordering costs and avail quantity discounts, etc. Generally speaking, there are three main objectives of holding inventories:

(*i*) The Transaction Motive, which facilitates continuous production and timely execution of sales orders.

(*ii*) The Precautionary Motive, which necessitates the holding of inventories for meeting the unpredictable changes in demand and supplies of materials.

(*iii*) The speculative motive which induces to keep inventories for taking advantage of price fluctuations, saving in re-ordering cost and quantity discounts, etc.

RISK AND COSTS OF HOLDING INVENTORIES

The holding of inventories involves blocking of firm's funds and incurrence of capital and other cost. It expose the firm to certain risks. The various costs and risks involved are given below:

1. **Capital cost:** Maintaining of inventories results in blocking of the firm's fund and incurrence of capital and other cost. Funds may be arranged from proprietor's own resources or from outsiders. But, in both the cases, the firm incurs cost. In the former case, there is an opportunity cost of investment while in the later case, the firm has to pay interest to outsiders.
2. **Storage and Handling costs:** Holding of inventories also involves costs on storage as well as handling of materials. The storage costs include the rental of godown, insurance charges, etc.
3. **Risk of price decline:** There is always a risk of reduction in the prices of inventories by suppliers in holding inventories. This may be due to increased market supplies, competition or general depression in the market.
4. **Risk of obsolescence:** Inventories may become obsolete due to improved technology, changes in requirements, change in customer's tastes, etc.
5. **Risk deterioration in quality:** The quality of materials may also deteriorate while inventories are kept in stores.

INVENTORY MANAGEMENT

The investment in inventory is very high in most of the undertakings engaged in manufacturing, whole-sale and retail trade. The amount of investment sometimes more in inventory than in other assets. In India, a study of 29 major industries has revealed that the average cost of materials is 64 paise and the cost of labour and overheads is 36 paise in a rupee. In industries, like sugar, the raw materials cost is as high as 68.75 per cent of the total cost. About 90 per cent part of working capital is invested in inventories. It is necessary for every management to give proper attention to inventory management. A proper planning of purchasing, handling, storing and accounting should form a part of inventory management. An efficient system of inventory management will determine (*a*) what to purchase (*b*) how much to purchase (*c*) from where to purchase and (*d*) where to store, etc.

There are conflicting interests of different departmental heads over the issue of inventory. The finance manager will try to invest less in inventory because for him it is an idle investment, whereas the emphasis of production manager is to acquire more and more inventory as he does not want any interruption in production due to shortage of inventory. The purpose of inventory management is to keep stocks in such a way that neither there is over-stocking nor under-stocking. The over-stocking means a reduction of liquidity and starving of other production processes; under-stocking, on the other hand, results in stoppage of work. The investments in inventory should be kept in reasonable limits.

Objectives

The main objectives of inventory management are operational and financial. The operational objectives mean that materials and spares should be available in sufficient quantity so that work is not disrupted for want of inventory. The financial objective means that investments in inventories should not remain idle and minimum working capital should be locked in it. The following are the objectives of inventory management:

1. To ensure continuous supply of materials, spares and finished goods so that production should not suffer at any time and demand of customers should also be met.
2. To avoid both over-stocking and under-stocking of inventory.
3. To maintain investments in inventories at the optimum level, as required by the operational and sales activities.
4. To keep material cost under control so that they contribute in reducing cost of production and overall costs.
5. To eliminate duplication in ordering or replenishing stocks. This is possible with the help of centralizing purchases.
6. To minimize losses through deterioration, pilferage, wastages and damages.
7. To design proper organization for inventory management. A clear-cut accountability should be fixed at various levels of the organization.
8. To ensure perpetual inventory control so that materials shown in stock ledgers should be actually lying in stores.
9. To ensure right quality goods at reasonable prices. Suitable quality standards ensure proper quality of stocks. The price-analysis, the cost-analysis and value-analysis ensure payment of proper prices.
10. To facilitate furnishing of data for short-term and long-term planning and control of inventory.

Tools and Techniques

Effective inventory management requires an effective control system for inventories. A proper inventory control not only help in solving the acute problem of liquidity but also increases profits and causes substantial reduction in the working capital of the concern. The following are the important tools and techniques of inventory management and control:

1. Determination of stock levels.
2. Determination of safety stocks.
3. Selecting a proper system of ordering for inventory.
4. Determination of Economic Order Quantity.
5. A.B.C. Analysis.
6. V.E.D. Analysis.
7. Inventory turnover ratios.
8. Aging schedule of inventories.

9. Classification and codification of inventories.

10. Preparation of customers inventory reports.

1. *Determination of Stock Levels*

Carrying of too much and too little of inventories is detrimental to the firm. If the inventory level is too little, the firm faces frequent stock-outs involving heavy ordering cost and if the inventory level is too high it will be unnecessary tie-up of capital. Therefore, an efficient inventory management requires that a firm should maintain an optimum level of inventory where inventory costs are the minimum and at the same time, there is no stock-out which may result in loss of sale or stoppage of production. As such various stock levels are discussed below:

(a) Minimum level

This represents the quantity which must be maintained in hand at all times. If stocks are less, than the minimum level, the work stops due to shortage of materials. Following factors are taken into account while fixing minimum stock level:

Lead time: A purchasing firm requires some time to process the order and time is also required by the supplying firm to execute the order. The time taken in processing the order and executing it is known as lead time. It is essential to maintain some inventory during this period.

Rate of consumption: It is the average consumption of materials in the factory. The rate of consumption is decided on the basis of past experience and production plans.

Nature of material: The nature of material also affects the minimum level. If material is required only against special orders of customer, minimum stock will not be required for such materials. Minimum stock level can be calculated with the help of the following formula:

Minimum stock level = Reordering level – (Normal consumption × Normal Reorder period)

(b) Reordering level

When the quantity of materials reaches at a certain level, fresh order is sent to get materials again. The order is sent before the materials reach minimum stock level. Reordering level or ordering level is fixed between minimum level and maximum level. The rate of consumption, number of days required to replenish stocks, and maximum quantity of materials required on any day are taken into account while fixing reordering level. Reordering level is fixed with the following formula:

Reordering Level = Maximum Consumption × Maximum Reorder period.

(c) Maximum level

It is the quantity of material beyond which a firm should not exceed its stocks. If the quantity exceeds the maximum level limit, it will be overstocking. A firm should avoid overstocking because it will result in high material costs. Overstocking means blocking of more working capital, more space for storing the material, more wastage of material and more chances of losses from obsolescence. Maximum stock level depends on the following factors:

1. The availability of capital for the purchase of materials.
2. The maximum requirements of materials at any point of time.
3. The availability of space for storing the material.
4. The rate of consumption of material during lead time.
5. The cost of maintaining stores.
6. The possibility of fluctuations in prices.
7. The nature of material: If the material is perishable in nature, it cannot be stored for a long time.
8. Availability of material: If the material is available only during seasons, it will have to be stored for rest of the period.
9. Restrictions imposed by the Government: Sometimes, government fixes the maximum quantity of material which a concern can store. The limit fixed by the government will become the limiting factor and maximum level cannot be fixed more than this limit.
10. The possibility of change in fashions will also affect the maximum level.

The following formula may be used for calculating maximum stock level:

Maximum Stock Level = Reordering Level + Reordering Quantity – (Minimum Consumption × Minimum Reordering period)

(d) Danger level

It is level beyond which material should not fall in any case. If danger level arises, immediate steps should be taken to replenish the stock even if more cost is incurred in arranging the materials. If material are not arranged immediately, there is a possibility of stoppage of work. Danger level is determined with the following formula:

Danger Level = Average Consumption × Maximum reorder period for emergency purchases

(e) Average stock level

The average stock level is calculated as such:

Average stock level = Minimum stock level + ½ of Reorder quantity

2. Determination of Safety Stocks

Safety stock is a buffer to meet some unanticipated increase in usage. The usage of inventory cannot be perfectly forecasted. It fluctuates over a period of time. The demand for materials may fluctuate and delivery of inventory may also be delayed, and in such a situation the firm can face a problem of stock-out. The stock-out can prove costly by affecting the smooth working of the concern. In order to protect against the stockout arising out of usage fluctuations, firms usually maintain some margin of safety or safety stocks. The basic problem is to determine the level of quantity of safety stocks. Two costs are involved in the determination of this stock, i.e. Opportunity;

cost of stock-outs and the carrying costs. The stock-outs of raw materials cause disruption in production, resulting in higher cost of production. Similarly, the stock-outs of finished goods results into the failure of the firm in competition as the firm cannot provide proper customer service. If a firm maintains low level of safety, frequent stock-outs occur resulting into the larger opportunity costs. On the other hand, the larger quantity of safety involves higher carrying costs.

3. Ordering Systems of Inventory

The basic problem of inventory is to decide the re-order point. This point indicates when an order should be placed. The re-order point is determined with the help of (*a*) average consumption rate (*b*) duration of lead time, (*c*) economic order quantity. When inventory is depleted to lead time consumption, the order should be placed. There are three prevalent systems of ordering and a concern can choose any one of these:

(*a*) Fixed order quantity system, generally known as economic order quantity (EOQ) system.

(*b*) Fixed period order system or periodic re-ordering system or periodic review system.

(*c*) Single order and scheduled part delivery system.

4. Economic Order Quantity (EOQ)

A decision about how much to order has great significance in inventory management. The quantity to be purchased should neither be small nor big, because costs of buying and carrying materials are very high. Economic order quantity is the size of the lot to be purchased which is economically viable. This is the quantity of material which can be purchased at minimum costs. Generally, economic order quantity is the point at which inventory carrying costs are equal to order costs. In determining economic order quantity it is assumed that cost of managing inventory is made up solely of two parts.

Ordering costs: There are costs which are associated with the purchasing or ordering of materials. These costs include:

1. Costs of staff posted for ordering of goods. A purchase order is processed and placed with suppliers. The labour spent on this process is included in ordering costs.
2. Cost of storage, which could have been used for other purpose.
3. The loss of materials due to deterioration and obsolescence. The material may deteriorate with passage of time. The loss of obsolescence arises when the materials in stock are not usable because of change in process or product.
4. Insurance cost.
5. Cost of spoilage in handling of materials.

The Planning Commission of India had estimated these costs between 15 per cent to 20 per cent of total costs. The longer the material is kept in stock, the costlier it becomes by 20 per cent every year. The ordering and carrying costs have a reverse relationship. The ordering cost goes up with the increase in number of orders placed. On the other hand, carrying costs go down per unit with the increase in number of units, purchased and stored. It can be shown in the diagram given on the next page:

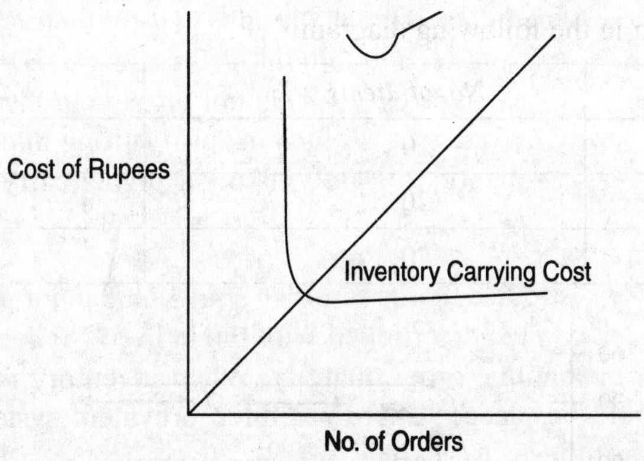

The ordering and carrying costs of materials being high, and effort should be made to minimise these costs. The quantity to be ordered should be large and smooth economy, when one can earn in transport costs and discounts. On the other hand, in storing facilities, a capital is locked up; insurance costs should also be taken into account.

Assumptions of EOQ: While calculating EOQ the following assumptions are made:

1. The supply of goods is satisfactory. Goods can be purchased whenever they are needed.
2. The quantity to be purchased by the concern is certain.
3. Prices of goods are stable. It results to stabilize carrying costs.

When above-mentioned conditions are satisfied, economic order quantity can be calculated with the help of the following formula:

$$\text{EOQ} = \sqrt{2AS/I}$$

where A = Annual consumption in rupees

S = Cost of placing an order

I = Inventory carrying costs of one unit

5. A.B.C Analysis

Materials are divided into a number of categories for adopting a selective approach for material control. It is generally seen that in manufacturing concern, a small percentage of items contribute a large percentage of value of consumption and a large percentage of items of materials contribute to a small percentage of value. In between these two limits, there are some items, which have almost equal percentage of value of materials. Under A.B.C. 'A' analysis, materials are divided into three categories, *viz.*, A, B and C. Past experience has shown that almost 10 per cent of items contribute to 70 per cent of value of consumption and this category is called 'A' Category. About 20 per cent of those items contribute about 20 per cent of value of consumption and this is known as category 'B' materials. Category 'C' covers about 70 per cent of items of materials which contribute only 10 per cent of the value of consumption. There may be some variation in different organization and an adjustment can be made in these percentages.

The information is shown in the following diagram:

Class	*No. of Items %*	*Value of Items %*
A	10	70
B	20	20
C	70	10

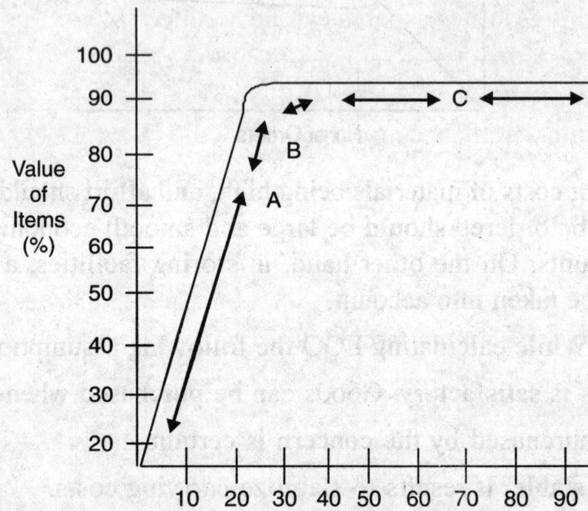

The following example explains advances of A-B-C analysis:

Suppose three items (P, Q, R) have been used and their consumption is ₹ 240000, ₹ 24000, and ₹ 2400 respectively. Let us presume that A-B-C classification is not done and annual orders are 12 in number. Each item will be ordered 4 times and average inventory will be:

Item	*Annual Consumption*	*No. of Orders*	*Average Working Inventory (₹)*
P	2,40,000	4	60,000
Q	24,000	4	6,000
R	2,400	4	600
	2,66,400	12	66,600

Suppose A.B.C. analysis is followed and the number of orders are according to the importance of the items. If the number of orders are 8, 3 and 1, for items P, Q and R respectively, the average inventory will be as follows:

Item	*Annual Consumption*	*No. of Orders*	*Average Working Inventory (₹)*
P	2,40,000	8	30,000
Q	24,000	3	8,000
R	2,400	1	2,400
Total	2,66,400	12	40,000

When A.B.C. analysis was not followed the average inventory was ₹ 66600. Urgency of spare parts is different from that of materials. A-B-C analysis may not be properly used for spare parts. The demand for spares depends upon the performance of the plant and machinery. Spare parts are classified as Vital (V), Essential (E) and Desirable (D). The vital spares are a must for running the concern smoothly and these must be stored adequately. The non-availability of vital spares will cause havoc in the concern. The E type of spares are also necessary but their stocks may be kept at low figures. The stocking of D type of spares may be avoided at times. If the lead time of these spares is less, stocking of these spares can be avoided.

The classification of spares under three categories is an important decision. A wrong classification of any spare creates difficulties for production department. The classification of spares should be left to the technical staff because they know the need, urgency and use of these spares.

6. Inventory Turnover Ratios

Inventory turnover ratios are calculated to indicate whether inventories have been used efficiently or not. The purpose is to ensure the blocking of only required minimum funds in inventory. Turnover Ratio also known as stock velocity, is normally calculated as sales/average inventory or cost of goods sold/average inventory cost. Inventory conversion period may also be calculated to find the average time taken for clearing stocks.

Symbolically,

$$\text{Inventory Turnover Ratio} = \frac{\text{Cost of Goods Sold}}{\text{Average Inventory at Cost}}$$

$$\text{or} = \frac{\text{Net Sales}}{\text{(Average) Inventory}}$$

and,

$$\text{Inventory Conversion Period} = \frac{\text{Days in a Year}}{\text{Inventory Turnover Ratio}}$$

7. *Aging Schedule of Inventories*

Classification of inventories, according to the period (age) of their holding, also helps in identifying slow moving inventories thereby helping in effective control and management of inventories. The following table shows inventories of a firm.

Aging Schedule of Inventories

Item Name/Code	*Age Classification*	*Date of Acquisition*	*Amount ₹*	*% age to Total*
001	0–15 days	June 25, 2018	30,000	15
002	16–30 days	June 10, 2018	60,000	30
003	31–45 days	May 20, 2018	50,000	25
004	46–60 days	May 5, 2018	40,000	20
005	61 and above	April 12, 2018	20,000	10
			2,00,000	100

8. Classification and Codification of Inventories

The inventories of a manufacturing concern may consist of raw materials, work in process, finished goods, spares, consumable stocks, etc. All these categories may have their sub-divisions. The raw materials used may be of 3-4 types, finished goods may also be of more than one type, spares may be of a number of types and so on. For proper recording and control of inventory, a proper classification of various types of items is essential. Inventories should first be assigned for their identification. The identification of short names are useful for inventory management not only for large concerns but also for small concerns, Lack of proper classification may also lead to reduction in production.

Inventories may be classified either according to their nature or according to use. Generally, materials are classified according to their nature such as construction, Materials are given code numbers. The coding may be done alphabetically or numerically. The third distinction needed for the quality of goods and decimals is the noting of this factor. For example, a concern has two categories of items divided into 15 groups. Two numbers will be used for main category and two in the sub-groups and then decimals will be used to the quality, etc. If mobile oil is to be coded, two digits are used in the category, lubricant oils, say 12, two digits are used for mobile oil, say 56 and one digit may be used for the quality of say mobile oil. The code of mobile oil can be 1256.1.

The classification and coding of inventories enable the introduction of mechanized accounting. It also helps in maintaining a secrecy of description and prompt issue of stores.

9. Inventory Reports

From effective inventory control, the management should be kept informed with the latest stock position of different items. This is usually done by preparing periodical inventory reports. These reports should contain necessary information for managerial action. On the basis of these reports, management takes corrective action wherever necessary. The more frequently these reports are prepared lesser are the chances of lapse in the administration of inventories.

Illustration 1

From the following information, calculate minimum stock level, maximum stock level and re-ordering level:

(*i*) Maximum consumption = **200 units per day**

(*ii*) Minimum consumption = **150 unit per day**

(*iii*) Normal consumption = **160 unit per day**

(*iv*) Reordering period = 10–15 days

(*v*) Reordering quantity = 1600 units

(*vi*) Normal reordering period = 12 days.

Solution

Reordering level = Maximum consumption × Maximum Reordering period

= 200 units × 15 = 3000 units

Minimum stock level = Reordering level – Ordering level – (Normal Consumption × Normal Reordering period)

= 3000 + 1600 – (150 × 12)

= 3000 – 1920 = 1080 units

Maximum stock level = Reordering level + Reorder quantity – (Minimum consumption × Reorder period)

= 3000 + 1600 – (150 × 10)

= 3000 + 1600 – 1500

= 3100 units

Illustration 2

Following information is given about materials:

Annual usage = ₹ 2,00,000

Cost of placing and receiving one order = ₹ 80

Annual carrying cost: 10% of inventory value

Find out the economic order quantity.

Solution

$$EOQ = \sqrt{2AS/I}$$

A = Annual usage is ₹ 2,00,000

S = Cost of placing an order is ₹ 80

I = Annual carrying cost is 10% of material value

$$EOQ = \frac{\sqrt{2 \times 2,00,000 \times 80}}{10\%}$$

$$= \frac{\sqrt{2 \times 2,00,000 \times 80 \times 100}}{10}$$

$$= \sqrt{320000000}$$

= 14833 units

VALUATION OF INVENTORIES

The value of material has a direct bearing on the income of a concern. So, it is necessary that a method of pricing material should be such that it gives a realistic value of the stock. The traditional method of valuing material 'cost price or market price whichever is less' is no longer the only method. Different methods of pricing the material give different value of closing materials and it leaves a scope for window dressing. If management is interested to show more profit, it can choose a method which will show more stock or vice-versa. To safeguard public interest the Government of India has instituted statutory controls to prevent frequent change of material valuation methods. A concern will have to use a particular valuation method for at least three years and any change therefrom must be approved by the Board.

The following methods for pricing material issues are generally used:

1. First-in First-out method
2. Last-in First-out method
3. Average price method
   (*a*) Simple average price method.
   (*b*) Weighted average price method.
4. Base stock method.
5. Standard price method.
6. Market price method.

1. **First-in first-out method:** This method, the materials received first are issued first. The materials are issued in chronological order. The recently received materials remain in stock. Whenever a requisition for material issue is presented to the store-keeper, he will use the price of the first lot and then of the second and third lot, etc. after the quantity of the first, second lot is exhausted. When prices are fluctuating, the cost of different batches of production will be different because issue prices of various lots are different. This method is suitable when prices fall because material issues will be prices at earlier figures while costs of replacements will be low. On the other hand, when price rises materials are issued at lower prices and replacement costs are higher. This method is useful for materials which are subject to obsolescence or deterioration. The following example, will explain this method.

Illustration 3

The following are the figures of receipts and issues of materials:

2018		
Jan. 1	Opening balance	500 units @ ₹ 5.00 per unit
Jan. 6	Purchase of material	400 units @ ₹ 5.25 Per unit
Jan. 8	Issue of material	600 unit
Jan. 10	Purchase of material	550 units @ ₹ 5.45 per unit
Jan. 15	Purchase of material	350 units @ ₹ 5.60 Per unit
Jan. 16	Issue of material	450 units
Jan. 22	Purchase of material	480 units @ ₹ 5.75 Per unit
Jan. 28	Issue of material	600 units
Jan. 30	Issue of material	300 units

Solution

FIFO Method (Stores Ledger Account)

Date 2018	*Particulars*	*Receipts*			*Issues*			*Balance*	
		Quantity (unit)	*Total cost [₹]*	*Cost per unit [₹]*	*Quantity (units)*	*Total cost [₹]*	*Cost per unit [₹]*	*Quantity (unit)*	*Amount [₹]*
Jan. 1	Balance b/d							500	2,500.00
Jan. 6	Purchase:								
	Order No.	400	2,100.00	5.25				900	4,600.00
Jan. 8	Issue.					3,025.00			
	Requisition					500 @ 5.00	5.00		
	Slip No.				600	100 @ 5.25	5.25	300	1,575.00
Jan. 10	Purchase:								
	Order No.	550	2,997.50	5.45				850	4,572.50
Jan. 15	Purchase								
	Order No.	350	1,960.00	5.60				1200	6,532.50
Jan. 16	Issue:					2392.50			
	Requisition					300 @ 5.25	5.25	750	4,140.00
	Slip No.				450	150 @ 5.45	5.45		
Jan. 22	Purchase:								
	Order No	480	2,760.00	5.75				1230	6,900.00
Jan. 28	Issue:					3300.00			
	Requisition					400 @ 5.45	5.45		
	Slip No.				600	200 @ 5.60	5.60	630	3,600.00
Jan. 30	Issue:					1,702.50			
	Requisition					150 @ 5.60	5.60		
	Slip no.				300	150 @ 5.75	5.75	330	1,897.50

2. **Last-in first-out method:** In this method, the last received materials are issued first and the ending inventory consists of earlier acquired materials. This method is also known as replacement cost method, because the latest purchased goods will correspond to the current market prices except that goods were not purchased much earlier. The inventories are valued at lots on hand and these values would be quite different from current invoice prices.

Last-in first-out method is suitable during rising prices because goods are issued from the latest received lots at prices which are closely related to current market to show lower profits because of increased charge to production and closing stock figures are also low, as they are valued at earlier prices. The taxable liability is also low, thus enabling the concern to retain more money in the business.

A comparison between the two jobs will not be possible if these jobs were started at the same time bit materials to the second job were issued from a different lost, the earlier lot having been exhausted. The materials may be priced at two or more prices even in the same invoice.

Illustration 4

The following figures are taken from the record materials of a concern:

2018	*Material Received (unit)*	*Price per Unit* [₹]	*Material Issue (units)*
Jan. 1	400	2.00	
Jan. 4	300	2.25	
Jan. 10			250
Jan. 18	500	2.50	
Jan. 22			450
Jan. 25	600	3.00	
Jan. 30			500

Record these transaction in the material ledger by pricing issues at weighted average price method.

3. **Average cost method:** The principle on which the average cost method is based that all of the materials in store are so mixed up that an issue cannot be made from any particular lot of purchases and, therefore, it is proper if the materials are issued at the average cost of materials in store. Average may be of two types:

   (*i*) Simple arithmetic average.

   (*ii*) Weighted arithmetic average.

   Simple average price: "A price which is calculated by dividing the total of the prices of the materials in the stock from which the material to be priced could be drawn by the number of the prices used in that total."

   Simple average price is calculated by dividing the total of unit purchase prices of different lots in stock on the date of issue by the number of prices used in the calculation and quantity of different lots is ignored. This method may lead to over-recovery or under-recovery of cost of materials from production because quantity purchased in each lot is ignored.

   Weighted average price: "A price which is calculated by dividing the total cost of materials in the stock from which the materials to be priced could be drawn by the total quantity of materials in that stock."

   The weighted average price takes into account the price and quantity of the materials in store. In the above example, the weighted average price is ₹ 11.33 per unit calculated as follows:

$$\frac{1{,}000 \times 2{,}000 \times 11 + 3{,}000 \times 12}{1{,}000 + 2{,}000 + 3{,}000} = ₹\,11.33$$

Advantages of average cost method

(1) This method is rational, systematic and not subject to manipulation. It is representative of the prices that prevailed during the entire period rather than of the price at the beginning, end, or at one point of issue during the period because it is based on the average of the material costs of the various lots available in the store.

(2) Average price method is considered to be the best method when prices fluctuate considerably because this method tends to smooth out fluctuations in prices.

(3) Issue prices are not to be calculated each time issues are made. Issue prices are charged only when new lot of materials is received.

(4) This method recovers the cost of materials from production.

(5) This method maintains the issue prices as near to the market price as possible.

(6) This method eliminates the necessity for adjustments in stock valuation.

Disadvantages of average cost method

(1) The greatest disadvantage of this method is that a fresh rate calculation will have to be made as soon as a new lot of materials are purchased which may involve tedious calculations. Thus, there are chances of clerical errors.

(2) Issue price of materials does not represent actual cost price of materials issued but it represents average cost of materials in stores. At the time of rising prices, it over-states profit but not as much as FIFO because average price is lower than the most recent price.

(3) Closing stock is not valued at current cost.

Illustration 5

The following transactions took place in respect of an item of material:

Year	*Receipts quantity*	*Rate* [₹]	*Issue quantity*
2-9-2018	200	2.00	
10-9-2018	300	2.40	
15-9-2018			250
18-9-2018	250	2.60	
20-9-2018			200

Record the above transactions in the Stores Ledger, pricing the issues at:

(*a*) Simple average rate

(*b*) Weighted average rate

Solution

(a) Simple Average Rate

STORES LEDGER ACCOUNT

Date	*Reference*	*Receipts*			*Issues*			*Balance*	
		Quantity	*Total cost* [₹]	*Cost per unit* [₹]	*Quantity*	*Total cost* [₹]	*Cost per unit* [₹]	*Quantity*	*Amount* [₹]
2-9-2018	Goods Received Note No. …	200	400	2.00	-	-	-	200	400
10-9-2018	Goods Received Note No. …	300	720	2.40	-	-	-	500	1,120
15-9-2018	Requisition Slip No. …	-	-	-	250	550	2.20*	250	550
18-9-2018	Goods Received Note No. …	250	650	2.60	-	-	-	500	1,200
20-9-2018	Requisition Slip No. …	-	-	-	250	500	2.50**	300	750

$$*\left(\frac{2+2.40}{2}\right)**\left(\frac{2.40+2.60}{2}\right)$$

(b) Weighted Average Rate

STORES LEDGER ACCOUNT

Date	*Reference*	*Receipts*			*Issues*			*Balances*	
		Quantity	*Total cost* [₹]	*Cost per unit* [₹]	*Quantity*	*Total cost* [₹]	*Cost per unit* [₹]	*Quantity*	*Amount* [₹]
2-9-2018	Goods Received Note No. …	200	400	2.00	-	-	-	200	400
10-9-2018	Goods Received Note No. …	300	720	2.40	-	-	-	500	1,120
15-9-2018	Requisition Slip No. …	-	-	-	250	560	2.20*	250	550
18-9-2018	Goods Received Note No. …	250	650	2.60	-	-	-	500	1,200
20-9-2018	Requisition Slip No. …	-	-	-	200	480	2.40**	300	720

$$*\left(\frac{400+720}{200+300}\right)**\left(\frac{560+650}{250+250}\right)$$

4. **Base stock method:** In this method, some quantity of materials is assumed to be necessary for keeping the concern going. No quantity is issued unless there is an emergency. The earlier material which is not issued as is kept in stock, is known as a base stock. The earlier material received is kept as a base and is valued at the price on which it is acquired.

   This method is not an independent method. It is used along with some the methods, such as FIFO, LIFO, Average Price Method, etc. After maintaining the base quantity in stock, the issues are priced at one of the methods mentioned above. The purpose of this method is to issue materials at current prices. This aim is achieved only when LIFO method of pricing the material is used.

5. **Standard price method:** The issue price of materials is predetermined or estimated in this method. The standard price is based on market conditions, usages rate, handling facilities, storage facilities, etc. Materials are priced at ₹ 5 per unit. Two lots of materials of 10000 units and 12000 units were purchased at ₹ 4.90 and ₹ 5.25 per unit. Every issue of materials will be priced at ₹ 5 per unit without taking into consideration the prices at which these were purchased. There will be a difference between the cost of materials and price charged to production. The difference between these the cost of materials and price charged to production. The difference between these two prices is transferred to 'Purchase Price Variance Account'. The profit or loss incurred firm then issue of materials will depend upon whether actual price paid is less or more than the standard price charged.

6. **Market price method:** In this method the prices charged to production are not costs incurred on materials, but, they are the latest market prices. The market prices may either be replacement prices or realizable prices. The replacement prices are used for the materials which are kept in stock for use in production and realizable prices are used for the goods kept for resale. The prices of issue for materials are always the replacement prices. The actual prices paid for acquiring materials are not considered at the time of issue of materials. Every issue is made at the replacement price of that day. It reflects the latest prices charged to production. This method is a check on the efficiency of the purchasing department. If prices paid are more than the market prices, it shows inefficiency and if actual prices paid are lower than the market prices, it will show efficiency.

Market price method is not generally used because of a number of difficulties. It becomes difficult to select the market price because different prices prevail in different markets. This method brings in human bias in the selection of market price. The charging of more or less prices than the price actually paid brings in the elements of profit or loss which is unnecessary.

STORES LEDGER ACCOUNT (Weighted Average Price Method)

Date 2018	Particulars	*Receipts*			*Issues*			*Balance*		
		Quantity (unit)	*Total cost [₹]*	*Cost per unit [₹]*	*Quantity (unit)*	*Total cost [₹]*	*Cost per unit [₹]*	*Quantity (unit)*	*Amount [₹]*	*Price per unit [₹]*
Jan. 1	Purchase Order No.	400	800	2.00				400	800.00	2.00
Jan. 4	Purchase Order No.	300	675	2.25				700	1,475.00	2.107
Jan. 10	Issue Requisition Slip No.				250	526.75	2,107	450	948.25	
Jan. 18	Purchase: Order No.	500	1250	2.50				950	2,198.00	2.314
Jan. 22	Issue: Requisition Slip No.				450	1,041.30	2,314	500	1,156.70	
Jan. 25	Purchase Order No.	600	1800	3.00				1100	2,986.70	2.688
Jan. 30	Issue: Requisition Slip No.				500	1,344.00	2,688	600	1,612.70	

REVIEW QUESTIONS AND PROBLEMS

1. What do you mean by inventory?
2. What is the nature of inventories?
3. Give three objectives of holding inventories.
4. What are the risks and costs of holding inventories?
5. Name various tools of inventory management.
6. Explain danger level of inventories.
7. What is VED analysis?
8. Write a note on aging of inventories.
9. What is inventory turnover ratio?
10. Write a short note on codification of inventories.
11. What is meant by Inventory Management? Why is it essential to a business concern?
12. Discuss in detail the objectives of Inventory Management.
13. Define the term 'Inventory Control'. What is Inventory Control system?
14. Explain various tools and techniques used for inventory management.
15. What is A.B.C. analysis? How is it useful as a tool of inventory management?

16. What is meant by 'Economic order Quantity'? What are the various costs which affect economic order quantity?

17. "The management of inventory must meet two opposing needs." What are these? How is a balance brought in these opposing needs?

18. What is a selective control of inventory? Why is it needed?

19. Define safety stocks. How do they affect he computation of reorder levels?

20. Find out the Economics Order Quantity and Order Schedule for raw materials and packing materials with the following data given to you:

(*a*)	Cost of ordering	Raw materials	:	₹ 1,000 per order
		Packaging materials	:	₹ 5,000 per order
(*b*)	Cost of holding inventory:	Raw materials	:	1 P. per unit p.m
		Packaging materials	:	5 P. per unit p.m
(*c*)	Production rate		:	200000 units per month

[**Ans.** 2,00,000 units ; 2,00,000 units]

21. What do you understand by maximum level, minimum level, reordering level? Calculate the above from the following data:

Reorder quantity	1500 units
Reorder period	4 to 6 weeks
Maximum consumption	400 units per week
Normal consumption	300 units per week
Minimum consumption	250 units per week

[**Ans.** Re-order quantity 2400 units; Maximum level 2900 units; minimum level 900 units]

22. Two materials, *X* and *Y* are used as follows:

Minimum usage – 50 units per week each;

Maximum usage – 150 units per week each;

Normal usage – 100 units per week each;

Ordering quantity: *X* – 600 units and *Y* – 1000 units;

Delivery period: *X* – 4 to 6 weeks; *Y* – 2 to 4 weeks.

Calculate for each material:

(*a*) Minimum Level, (*b*) Maximum Level, (*c*) Ordering Level.

[**Ans.** (*a*) *X* = 400 units, *Y* = 300 units,

(*b*) *X* = 1300 units, *Y* = 1500 units;

(*c*) *X* = 900 units, *Y* = 600 units]

23. The following information is available in respect of component 020:

Maximum stock level	:	8400 units
Budgeted consumption	:	Maximum 1500 units per month
		Minimum 800 units per month
Estimated delivery period	:	Maximum 4 months
		Minimum 2 months
You are required to calculate	:	

(*a*) Reorder level.

(*b*) Reorder quantity.

[**Ans.** (*i*) 6000 units (*ii*) 4000 units]

24. Easy Limited specialized in the manufacture of a computer component. The component is currently sold for ₹ 1,000 and its variable cost is ₹ 800. For the year ended 31.12.15, the company sold on an average 400 components per month.

At present the company grants one month credit to its customers. The company is thinking of extending the same to two months on accounts of which the following is expected:

Increase in Sales	25%
Increase in Stock	₹ 2,00,000
Increase in Creditors	₹ 1,00,000

You are required:

To advise the company on whether or not to extend the credit terms if:

(*a*) All customers avail the extended credit period of two months, and

(*b*) Exiting customers do not avail the credit terms but only the new customers avail the same. Assume in this case the entire increase in sales is attributable to the new customers.

The company expects a minimum returns of 40% on the investment.

[**Ans.** Extend the credit in both (*a*), and (*b*), Additional profit in (*a*) ₹ 8,000 and (*b*) ₹ 1,36,000]

25. Following information is available for purchase and issue of materials:

2017		
Jan. 4	Purchased	5000 units @ ₹ 4.00 per unit
Jan. 15	Purchased	1000 units @ ₹ 4.80 per unit
Jan. 20	Issued	3000 units
Feb. 10	Purchased	2000 units @ ₹ 5 per unit
Feb. 13	Issued	2500 units
Feb. 28	Purchased	6000 units @ ₹ 5.20 per unit
Mar. 10	Purchased	1500 units @ ₹ 5.50 per unit
Mar. 15	Issued	4000 units
Mar. 20	Issued	3000 units
Mar. 28	Purchased	2400 units @ ₹ 5.70 per unit

From the information given above, prepare the Stores Ledger by (*i*) FIFO and (*ii*) LIFO methods of charging issue of materials.

[**Ans.** Balance (*i*) ₹ 29730; (*ii*) ₹ 26280]

26. The following transactions took place in respect of material B. 25:

Date	*Units*	*Rate (₹ P. 0)*	*Issues (unit)*
1.3.2018	500	1.00	
15.3.2018	700	1.10	
17.3.2018			600
19.3.2018	400	1.20	
21.3.2018			300
27.3.2018	300	1.25	
31.3.2018			800

Prepare a stores ledger using:

(*a*) Simple average method, and

(*b*) Weighted average method

[**Ans.** Balance amount (*a*) ₹ 233.60; (*b*) ₹ 230.90]

27. Following transaction occur in the purchase and issue of a materials in January 2017:

Date	*Particulars*	*Units*	*Price ₹*
Jan. 1	Balance b/f	300	2.00
Jan.2	Purchase	100	1.50
Jan. 5	Issue	100	
Jan. 9	Purchase	240	2.10
Jan. 12	Issue	200	
Jan. 20	Purchase	300	2.20
Jan. 24	Issue	260	
Jan. 28	Purchase	150	2.30

Prepare stores Ledger Account by using:

(*a*) Simple average method

(*b*) Weighted average method

[**Ans.** Balance Amount (*i*) ₹ 924.80; (*ii*) ₹ 1183.36]

28. The stock of material A as on 1st July 2015 is 500 units at ₹ 1 per unit. Following purchases and issues of this item were made subsequently:

Date	*Purchase quantity (in units)*	*Rate (₹ P.)*	*Issues quantity (in units)*
July 5			100
July 12	500	1.20	
July 15	300	1.20	
July 20			400
July 22			200
July 25	600	1.40	
July 31			300

Prepare a store ledger account showing how the value of the above issues be arrived under the Base stock methods when it operates with (*i*) FIFO and (*ii*) LIFO Method. Base stock is 300 units.
[**Ans.** Balance Amount (*i*) 1140; (*ii*) 1060]

29. The standard price of the material is fixed at ₹ 5 per unit. Prepare Stores Ledger Account by using the following information:

Date 2018	*Receipts quantity (in units)*	*Rate ₹*	*Issues quantity (in units)*
Jan. 1	4000	5.25	
Jan. 5	2000	5.30	
Jan. 10			3000
Jan. 12	8000	5.00	
Jan. 15			7000
Jan. 25			2000
Jan. 29	5000	4.80	
Jan. 30	2000	5.50	
Jan. 31			2500

30. At the beginning of October, 2018, Quality Brush Company had in stock 10000 brushes valued at ₹ 10 each. Further purchases were made during the month as follows:

7th October 4000 Brushes @ ₹ 12.50
14th October 6000 Brushes @ ₹ 15.00
24th October 8000 Brushes @ ₹ 16.50
Issue to shop floor were as follows:
16th October 16000 Brushes
28th October 10000 Brushes

(*a*) Prepare a Stores Ledger Card for the month of October on the assumption that materials were issued on First-in-first-out principle, and

(*b*) State the value of closing stock at the end of October, if issues are priced at the weighted average method.

[**Ans.** Balance Amount (*a*) ₹ 33,000 (*b*) ₹ 30,000].

■■■

6

Analysis of Financial Statements

THE BASIC FINANCIAL STATEMENT

Of the various reports issued to their shareholders by companies, the annual report is by far the most important. Two types of information are given in this report. First, there is a text that describes the firm's operating results during the past year and discusses new developments that will affect the future operations. Second, there are four basic financial statements – the income statement, the balance sheet, the statement of retained earnings, sources and uses of fund statement.

Financial statements, taken together, give an accounting picture of the firm's operations and financial position. The package of financial statements subsumes such schedules as those relating to fixed assets, long term investments, inventories, long term debts, accrued liabilities, cost of goods manufactured, selling expenses, administration and general expenses. These schedules mainly supplement the data contained in the financial statements and are considered essential for the purpose of analysis. In addition, explanatory footnotes are also given in the financial statements and schedules when the information given in notes regarding methods of inventory valuation and of depreciation, description of contingent liabilities, etc. are given as footnotes.

NATURE OF FINANCIAL STATEMENTS

According to the American Institute of Certified Public Accountants, financial statements reflect a combination of recorded facts, accounting conventions, personal judgments and judgements as well as conventions applied affect them materially. This statement makes it clear that the accounting information, as depicted by the financial statements, are influenced by three factors, viz., recorded facts, accounting conventions and personal judgments.

Recorded facts: This refers to data recorded in company's accounts books. In other words, information, which finds no place in the account books, is not usually depicted in the financial statements even if, consists of highly material facts. For example, the cost of fixed assets on the date of their acquisition is shown rather than their market or replacement price, as such price is not recorded in the account book.

Accounting conventions: Accounting conventions are certain fundamental accounting principles and include those customs and traditions which guide the accountant while preparing the financial statements. For example, the convention of conservatism makes the accountant feel the need for making a provision for expected loss but, at the same time, to ignore expected profits.

Personal judgement: Besides the recorded facts and accounting conventions, personal judgments or opinions have also an important bearing on the accounting statements. For example, the choice of a particular method for determining depreciation and depletion charges for a particular year, the mode of writing off of intangible assets, the method to evaluate inventory, etc. depends mostly on the personal judgment of the accountant.

OBJECTIVES OF FINANCIAL STATEMENTS

Over a period of time the number and types of people interested in financial statements have changed radically. They need varied information and, fortunately, such an information may be classified as relating to profitability, liquidity and solvency. The main objective should be that these broad needs of information should be satisfied by a single set of financial statements. The Accounting Principles Board of America states the objectives as follows:

1. To provide reliable financial information about the economic resources and obligations of a business and other needed information about changes in such resources or obligations.
2. To provide reliable information about changes in the net resources (resources less obligations) arising out of the business activities and financial information that assists in estimating the earning potentials of the business.
3. To disclose, to the extent possible other information related to the financial statements that is relevant to the needs of users of these statements.

USES AND USERS OF FINANCIAL STATEMENTS

Different classes of people are interested in the financial statement analysis with a view to assess the economic and financial position of any business or industrial concern in terms of profitability, liquidity or solvency. Such persons and bodies include:

1. Shareholders: Divorce between ownership, management and broad based ownership of capital due to dispersal of shareholdings have made shareholders take more interest in the financial statements with a view to ascertain the profitability and financial strength of the company.

2. Debenture holders: Interested in the short term as well as the long term solvency position of the company.

3. Creditors: Potential suppliers or others doing business with the company are interested in the liquidity position of the company.

4. Financial institution and commercial banks: Interested in the solvency, short term, long term and profitability position of the company.

5. Prospective investors: Interested in the future prospects and financial strength.

6. Employees and trade unions: Profitability.

7. Important customers who want to make a long standing contract with the company: Interest in its financial strength.

8. Tax authorities: Profitability.

9. Government department dealing with the industry in which the company is engaged: Profitability.

10. The Company Law Board.

11. Economists and investment analysts.

12. Members of Parliament, the Public Accounts Committee and the Estimates Committee in respect of government companies.

13. Stock exchange: Interested in the prospect and the performance of listed companies with a view to protect the interest of investors.

14. Managers: Interested in knowing through the financial statements, the present position and the future prospects of the company. This is mainly to review the company's progress and position, and take decisions for the future.

ESSENTIALS OF FINANCIAL STATEMENTS

1. The financial statements should be relevant for the purpose for which they are prepared. Unnecessary and confusing disclosures should be avoided and all those which are relevant and material should be reported to the public.
2. They should convey the total and accurate information about the position, progress and prospects of an enterprise. It is also important that those who prepare and present financial statements should not allow their personal prejudices to colour the facts.
3. They should be easily comparable with previous statements or with those of similar concerns or industry. Comparability increases the utility of the financial statement.
4. They should be prepared in a classified form for a better and meaningful analysis.
5. The financial statements should be prepared and presented at the right time. Undue delay in their preparation would reduce the significance and utility of these statements.
6. The financial statements must have general acceptability and understanding. This can be achieved only by applying certain generally accepted accounting principles in their preparation.

7. The financial statements should not be affected by inconsistencies arising out of personal judgment and procedural choices exercised by the accountant.
8. Financial statements should comply with the legal requirements, if any, as regards form, contents, disclosures and the methods. In India, companies are required to present their financial statements according to the provisions of the Companies Act, 1956.

IMPORTANCE OF FINANCIAL STATEMENTS

The importance of financial statements lies in their utilities to satisfy the varied interests of different categories of parties, such as management, creditors, public, etc.

Importance of management: Increase in size and complexities of factors affecting the business operations necessitate a scientific and analytical approach in the management of modern business enterprises. The management team requires an up-to-date, accurate and systematic financial information for the purpose.

Financial statements help the management to understand the position, progress and prospects of business vis-a-vis the industry. By providing the management with the causes of business results, they enable them to formulate appropriate policies and courses of action for the future. The management communicates only through these financial statements, their performance to various parties and justify their activities and thereby their existence.

A comparative analysis of financial statements reveals the trend in the progress and position of the enterprise and enables management to make suitable changes in policies, to avert unfavorable situations.

Importance to the shareholders: There is divorce between management and ownership in the case of companies. Shareholders cannot directly take part in the day-to-day activities of the business. However, results of these activities should be reported to shareholders at the annual general meeting in the form of financial statements. These statements enable shareholders to know about the efficiency and effectiveness of the management and also the earning capacity and financial strength of the company.

By analyzing the financial statements, the prospective shareholders could ascertain the profit earning capacity, present position and future prospects of the company and decide to make investments in this company. Published financial statements are the main source of information for the prospective investors.

Importance to lenders/creditors: The financial statements serve as a useful guide for the present suppliers and for probable lenders in the future of a company. It is through a critical examination of the financial statements that these groups can acquaint themselves about the liquidity, profitability and long term solvency position of the company. This helps them to decide about their future course of action.

Importance to labour: Workers are entitled to bonus depending on the size of profit as disclosed by audited profit and loss account. Thus, P & L A/c is of great importance to employees. In wages, negotiations are based on the size of profits and profitability achieved.

Importance to public: Business is a social entity. Various groups of the society, though not directly connected with the business are interested in knowing the position, progress and prospects of a business enterprise. They are financial analysts, lawyers, trade associations, trade unions, financial press, research scholars, teachers, etc. It is only through these published financial statements that these people can analyse, judge and comment upon the business enterprise.

Importance to national economy: The rise and growth of the corporate sector, to a great extent, influence the economic progress of a country. Unscrupulous and fraudulent corporate managements shatter the confidence of the general public in joint stock companies which is essential for the economic progress and retard economic growth of the country. Financial statements come to the rescue of the general public by providing information by which they can examine and assess the real worth of the company and avoid being cheated by unscrupulous persons.

The emphasis of law raise the level of business morality by compelling companies to prepare financial statements in a clear and systematic form and disclose material information. This has increased the confidence of the public in companies.

Financial statements are also essential for the various regulatory bodies, such as tax authorities, Registrars of Companies Act, etc. They can judge whether regulations are being strictly followed and also whether regulations are producing the desired effects or not, by evaluating the financial statements.

LIMITATIONS OF FINANCIAL STATEMENTS

Most of the limitations are mainly due to the cumulative effect of recorded facts, accounting conventions and personal judgments on the financial statements. Unless they are specifically prepared, they fail to reflect the current economic picture of the business. As such, financial statements have a number of limitations; a few important ones are described as under:

1. Information is incomplete and inaccurate. Financial statements are essentially an interim report usually prepared for an accounting period. Hence, the financial information, as revealed by them, is neither complete nor accurate. The true financial position or the ultimate gain or loss can be known only when the business is closed down.
2. Qualitative information is ignored. Financial statements depict only those items of quantitative information which are expressed in monetary terms. But a number of qualitative factors, such as the reputation and prestige of the management with the public, cordial industrial relations and efficiency of workers, customer satisfaction, competitive strength, etc. which cannot be expressed in monetary terms, are not depicted by the financial statements.

   However, these factors are essential for understanding the real financial condition and the operating results of the business.
3. Financial statements mainly show historical information. As the financial statements are compiled on the basis of the historical costs, they fail to take into account such factors as

the decrease in money value or changes in the level of prices. Since these statements deal with past data and not considering the future, they are of little value in decision making.

4. Financial statements are based on accounting concepts and conventions. Accounting concept and conventions used for the preparation of financial statements make them unrealistic. For example, the value of fixed assets in the balance sheet is shown on the basis of going concept. This means that the value put on asset rarely represents the amount of cash which would be realized on liquidation.

   Similarly, the income statement, which is prepared on the basis of the convention of conservatism, fails to disclose the true income for it includes the probable losses but ignores the probable income.

5. Personal judgements influence financial statements. Many items in the financial statements are left to the personal judgment of the accountant. For example, the method of inventory valuation, the method of depreciation, treatment deferred revenue expenditure, etc., depend on the personal judgment of the accountant.

The true value of such items, lies on the soundness of such judgment which, in turn, depends on the experience, skills, integrity and competence of the accountant. The person preparing the financial statement may make improper assumptions either by mistake or to distort the real picture. However, such indiscreet personal judgments are controlled to a certain extent by the convention of conservatism.

PRESENTATION OF FINANCIAL STATEMENTS

Presentation of financial statements assumes greater importance, as it makes the preparation of the financial statements more meaningful as well as purposeful. Even those who do not have a good knowledge of accounting may like to read and understand these statements. Hence, the language and presentation of the text should be simple and easy to understand by ordinary people.

The conventional method used for presentation is the account "T" form. The Companies Act, 1956 has also given a prescribed form for the Profit and Loss Account and Balance Sheet in Part I, Schedule IV, only in the horizontal form (T form). However, in recent times they are presented in vertical form in a single column form. A great advantage of this form is that layman's language can be used and another is that the figures can flow logically from one to another. For example, the Balance Sheet may be presented as follows (in summary form):

What the company owns:			Amount [₹]
Fixed Assets			
Cost			5,00,000
Less: Amount written off as depreciation			2,00,000
Net fixed assets			3,00,000
Investments in outside securities (at cost)			50,000
Current assets:	Inventory	60,000	
	Debtors	65,000	
	Cash and bank	15,000	
		1,40,000	
Less: Current liabilities		80,000	60,000
			4,10,000
What the company owes			
6% debentures		1,00,000	
Borrowings from financial institutions		1,00,000	2,00,000
Shareholders funds or net worth			2,10,000
Represented by 10% preference of ₹ 100 each			50,000
By equity share capital (₹ 10 each)			1,00,000
Reserves and surplus			60,000
			2,10,000

Figures presented above are too brief. Part I of Schedule IV requires much more information. Since the vertical summary form enables one to grasp the essential message very quickly, the modern practice is to draw up financial statements more or less in vertical summary form and to give the details as required by law in separate schedules. Each schedule is being distinctly numbered giving reference to the schedule in the main financial statements. The government, by a special notification, have permitted companies to prepare the balance sheet either in the horizontal form, or in the vertical form. The vertical form as per the notification, is given below.

Schedule VI – Part I B

Name of the Company:

Balance Sheet as at:

	Schedule No	*Figures as at the end of the Current Year*	*Figures as at the end of the Previous Year*
I. *Source of funds*			
1. Shareholders fund			
(*a*) Capital	....	....	....
(*b*) Reserves and surplus	....	....	....
2. Loan funds			
(*a*) Secured loans	....	....	....
(*b*) Unsecured loans	....	....	....
Total			
II. *Application of funds*			
1. Fixed assets			
(*a*) Gross block			....
(*b*) *Less*: Depreciation	....	....	....
(*c*) Net block	....	....	....
(*d*) Capital work in progress	....		
2. Investments			
3. Current assets, loan and advanced			
(*a*) Inventories			....
(*b*) Sundry Debtors	....		....
(*c*) Cash and bank balance	....	....	....
(*d*) Other current assets	....	....	....
(*e*) Loans and advances			
Less: Current Liabilities and Provisions			
(*a*) Current Liabilities	....	....	....
(*b*) Provisions	....	....	....
(*c*) 1. Miscellaneous expenditures to the extent not written off or not adjusted	....	....	....
2. Profit and loss A/c	....	....	....
Total			

Notes:

1. Details under each of the above items shall be given in separate schedules. The schedules shall incorporate all the information required to be given under Part IA of Schedule VI and with notes containing general instructions for preparation of Balance Sheet.
2. The schedules, referred to above, accounting policies and explanatory notes that may be attached form an integral part of the Balance Sheet.
3. Figures in the Balance Sheet may be rounded to the nearest "000" or "00", as may be convenient or may be expressed in terms of decimals of thousands.
4. A footnote to the Balance Sheet may be added to show separately contingent liabilities.

Part II of Schedule VI states such particulars and information which are to be given in the Profit and Loss Account.

ANALYSIS AND INTERPRETATION

Analysis and interpretation of financial statements refers to the process of determining the significant operating and financial characteristics from the accounting data with a view of getting an insight into the activities of an enterprise. According to Myers, financial statement analysis is largely a study of relationship among the various financial factors in a business, as disclosed by a single statement and a study on the trend of these factors as shown in a series of statements.

By establishing a strategic relationship among items of a Balance Sheet, income statement and other operative data, the financial analysis (as it is simply called) unveils the meaning and significance of such items.

COMPARATIVE FINANCIAL STATEMENTS

These statements mainly include two types of analytical statements, viz. comparative balance sheets and comparative income statements. They facilitate comparison among two or more similar firms, preferably in the same industry. Comparison may be regarding profitability and financial position.

Comparative statements mainly show the following information for analytical purpose:

1. Actual data in absolute money values, as given in the financial statements for the periods under consideration.
2. Increases or decreases on various items in money values.
3. Increases or decreases on various items in percentages.

Comparative financial statements facilitate each comparison by presenting relevant figures for two or more periods or each firm side by side. The following example would illustrate the method of preparation of a comparative Balance Sheet and a comparative income statement clearly.

Comparative Balance Sheet
(as on June 2018 and 2019)

₹ in lakhs

Assets	June 30 2018 [₹]	June 30 2018 [₹]	Amount of increase or decease in 2018	Percentage of increase or decrease in 2018
Fixed assets				
Premises (less depreciation)	600	570	–30	–5
Plant and Machinery (less depreciation)	400	500	+100	+25
Furniture and fittings (less depreciation)	100	85	–15	–15
Total fixed assets	1100	1155	+55	+5
Investments	200	150	–50	–25
Current assets:				
Stock	300	300	–	–
Debtors	200	150	–50	–25
Bank	50	60	+10	+20
Cash	20	18	–2	–10
Total current assets	570	528	–42	–7.4
Total assets	1870	1833	–37	–2

Liabilities	June 30 2019 [₹]	June 30 2019 [₹]	Amount of increase or decease in 2019	Percentage of increase or decrease in 2019
Capital and Liabilities				
8% Preference capital	200	300	+100	+50.00
Equity capital	500	500	–	–
Reserves	200	250	+50	+25.00
Total Proprietors funds	900	1050	+150	+16.67
Secured loans	350	200	–150	+43.00
Current Liabilities:				
Sundry creditors	300	350	+50	+16.67
Bills payable	200	175	–25	–12.50
Taxes payable	120	58	–62	–50.00
Total Current liabilities	620	583	–37	–5.97
Total Liabilities	970	783	–187	–19.28
Total Capital and liabilities	1870	1833	–37	–2.00

From the above comparative Balance Sheet some of the following tentative conclusions may be drawn.

1. Total fixed assets have been added during 2017 by ₹ 55 lakhs compared to 2018, for which long term investments worth ₹ 50 lakhs has been realized.
2. The level of total current assets worth ₹ 42 lakhs has been reduced. This implies that addition to fixed assets have been financed partly by the sale or reduction of other assets. Increase in fixed assets and decrease in current assets reflect a poor financial policy.
3. The relationship between total current assets and total current liabilities is not satisfactory.
4. Increase in the preference share capital of ₹ 100 lakhs might have been due to the fresh issue of shares for the redemption of debentures. Also, the increase in reserves may represent redemption of debentures out of profits.

Similar to the comparative Balance Sheet, the comparative income statement contains same columns and leads to infer the same type of information. The comparative income statement explains clearly the relationship between sales and costs of goods sold and its effect on gross profits. Increase in selling expenses and office administration expenses relating to the increase in sales should be proportional. This indicates clearly the efficiency of operations by showing changes in absolute figures and also in terms of percentages of the operating profits from one period to another.

Comparative financial statements can be prepared for more than two periods or two firms in an industry. But the analysis should be very cumbersome. The Companies Act of India insists that companies should give figures for different items for the previous year together with the current year's figures in their Profit and Loss Accounts and Balance Sheets.

Comparative Profit and Loss Account

(for the years ended 30th June, 2018 and 2019)

₹ in lakhs

	June 30		*Amount of increase or decrease in 2019*	*Percentage of increase or decrease in 2019*
	2019 ₹	*2020* ₹		
Net Sales	600	800	+200	+33.33
Cost of Goods Sold	400	500	+100	+25.00
Gross Profit	200	300	+100	+50.00
Operating Expenses				
Office Expenses	20	20	–	–
Selling Expenses	20	30	+10	+50.00
Total Operating Expenses	40	50	+10	+25.00
Operating Profits	160	250	+90	+56.25

COMMON SIZE FINANCIAL STATEMENT

The main limitation of the comparative financial statements is that they fail to show changes that have taken place from year to year in relation to the total assets, total liabilities and capital of total net sales. This limitation is eliminated by common size analysis.

Common size financial statements are those statements in which items reported in the financial statements are converted into percentages taking some common base. In the common size income statement, the net sale is assumed to be 100% and the other items are expressed as percentage of sales. Similarly in the common size Balance Sheet the total assets or total liabilities is assumed to be 100% and all other items are expressed as the percentage of this total.

Common size statements are also called 100 per cent statement, because each statement is reduced to the total of 100 and each individual item is expressed as a percentage of this total.

The preparation of the common size statement based on the figures in the example of the comparative financial statements.

Common Size Balance Sheet

(as on June 2018 and 2019)

₹ in lakhs

Assets	*2018 Amount*	%	*2019 Amount*	%
Fixed Assets				
Premises (*less* depreciation)	600	32.09	570	31.09
Plant & Machinery (*less* depreciation)	400	21.39	500	27.27
Furniture & Fittings (*less* depreciation)	100	5.35	85	4.64
Total Fixed Assets	1100	58.82	1155	63.00
Investments	200	10.70	150	8.19
Current Assets:				
Stock	300	16.05	300	16.37
Debtors	200	10.70	150	8.18
Bank	50	2.61	60	3.27
Cash	20	1.06	18	28.81
Total Current Assets	570	30.48	528	100.00
Total Assets	1870	100.00	1833	

Liabilities

Capital Liabilities	*2018 Amount*	*%*	*2019 Amount*	*%*
Capital and Liabilities				
8% Preference Capital	200	10.70	300	16.37
Equity Capital	500	26.74	500	27.27
Reserves	200	10.69	250	13.64
Total Proprietor's Funds	900	48.13	1050	57.28
Secured Loans	350	18.71	200	10.91
Current Liabilities:				
Sundry Creditors	300	16.05	350	9.09
Bills Payable	200	10.70	175	9.55
Taxes Payable	120	6.41	58	3.17
Total Current Liabilities	620	33.16	583	31.81
Total Liabilities	970	51.87	783	2.72
Total Capital and Liabilities	1870	100.00	1833	100.00

Interpretation

The percentage of fixed assets to total assets was 58.83% in 2018 and it increased to 63% in 2019. At the same time, the percentage of current assets decreased from 30.47% to 28.31%. This indicates that the policy relating to current assets is wrong. The value of investments has also decreased from 10.7% to 8.19%. This may be in order to finance the increase in fixed assets. The preference share capital has increased from 10.7% to 16.37% and reserves from 10.69% to 13.64%. But, at the same time the long term as well as current liabilities to total liabilities have come down from 51.87% to 42.72%. Compared to the total current liabilities the total current assets are inadequate. Here, the working capital position is not satisfactory. In general, the financial policy of the concern is highly unsatisfactory.

Common Size Income Statement
(for the years ended 2018 and 2019)

Particulars	*2018 Amount*	*%*	*2019 Amount*	*%*
Net Sales	600	100	800	100.00
Cost of Goods Sold	400	66.67	500	62.50
Gross Profit	200	33.33	300	37.50
Operating Expenses:				
Office Expenses	20	3.33	20	2.50
Selling Expenses	20	3.33	30	3.75
Total Operating Expenses	40	6.66	50	6.25
Operating Profits	160	26.367	250	31.25

Interpretation

The gross profit percentage has increased from 33.33% to 37.50%. This increase is more proportionate compared to sales. This is because the increase in cost of goods sold is less proportionate. Similarly, the net profit percentage has also increased from 26.67% to 31.25%. In general, the overall operating efficiency of the business is highly satisfactory.

Trend Percentage or Ratios

Comparing the past data over a period of time with a base year is called Trend Analysis. Under this method, percentage relationships that statement each items bears to the same item in the base year are calculated. Any year, either the earliest or the latest year, involved in comparison or any intervening year may be taken as the base year.

The trend percentages are calculated only for some important items which can be logically connected with each other as the purpose is to highlight important changes. The concerned item in the base year is taken to be equal to 100 and then based on this trend, percentages of corresponding terms in other years are calculated. This method is a horizontal type of analysis of financial statements. Trend Ratios are shown in competitive financial analysis statements.

Trend analysis is a useful tool for the management since it reduces the large amount of absolute data into a simple and easily reasonable form. By looking at the trend in a particular ratio one can see whether the ration is increasing, decreasing or remaining constant. From this, a problem is unearthed and good management is observed.

Precautions to be Taken in Preparing the Trend Analysis

1. The base year selected should be normal and be truly representative of all years involved in the analysis.
2. The financial statement used for the analysis must have been prepared applying consistent accounting principles and practices.
3. Figures of the various accounting statements considered for the analysis should be adjusted for any price level changes as compared to the base year, before calculating trend ratio.
4. Trend percentages should be studied along with the absolute figures on which they are based. This enables us to know whether change is significant or not. For example one item may increase from ₹100 to ₹200 (i.e. 100% increase) and the other item may change from ₹15000 to ₹21000 (40% increase). Of these two, the change in the first item is not significant compared to the second item.

The Trend Ratio for the assets of a Balance Sheet is illustrated below:

Comparative Balance Sheet
(as on June 30, 2019)

Assets	*Amount in lakhs*				*Trend Percentages and Base Year in 2005*			
	2016	*2017*	*2018*	*2019*	*2016*	*2017*	*2018*	*2019*
Fixed assets								
Land	80	100	110	120	100	125	137.5	150
Plant	160	200	240	240	100	125	150	150
Furniture	20	25	25	25	100	125	125	125
Total fixed assets	260	325	375	385	100	125	144.2	148.1
Current asset								
Cash	20	25	20	30	100	125	100	150
Book debts	40	50	60	80	100	125	150	200
Stock	60	80	70	100	100	133.3	119.7	166.7
Total current assets	120	155	150	210	100	129.2	125	177.7

Working Notes:

A separate column for the base year (2016) need not be provided in the Comparative Balance Sheet. From the above statement, it is clear that both the fixed assets and current assets have registered an increasing trend. This is an indication of the company's growth over the period. Similar to this analysis, trend percentages can be computed for the important items of liabilities side of the Balance Sheet and of the income statement. The other major tools of the financial analysis, viz., ratio analysis, fund flow analysis and cash flow analysis will be discussed in the next three chapters.

PRACTICAL PROBLEMS

Illustration 1

The comparative Balance Sheet of ABC Ltd. is shown below. Comment upon the significant changes which have taken place during the year 2018.

Balance Sheet
as on 31st December, 2017 and 2018

Liabilities	Amount in lakh ₹		Assets	Amount in lakh ₹	
	2017	2018		2017	2018
Equity share capital	800	1200	Current Assets		
Capital reserves	130	220	Debtors	418	380
General reserves	444	418	Cash	236	20
Sinking fund	80	100	Stock	320	260
Fixed liabilities			Others	64	26
Debentures	400	650	Investments	540	340
Current liabilities			Fixed Assets		
Sundry creditors	510	234	Furniture *less* depreciation	18	36
Others	14	20	Building *less* depreciation	620	1,572
			Land	40	60
			Other Assets	112	148
Total liabilities	2368	2842		2,368	2,842

Solution

ABC Ltd.
Comparative Balance Sheet
as on 31st December 2017 and 2018

Assets	Amount in lakh ₹		Increase or Decrease	
	2017	2018	Absolute amount	%
Current assets				
Debtors	418	380	–38	– 9
Cash	236	20	–216	–92
Stock	320	260	– 60	– 19
Others	64	26	– 38	– 60
Total current assets	1,038	686	– 352	– 34
Investments	540	340	– 200	– 37
Fixed assets				
Furniture *less* depreciation	18	36	+18	+100
Building *less* depreciation	620	1,572	+ 952	+154
Land	40	60	+20	+50
Total fixed assets	678	1,668	+990	+146
Other assets	112	148	+36	+32

Contd...

Total assets	2368	2842	+474	+20
Liabilities and capital				
Current liabilities				
Sundry creditors	510	234	–276	–54
Others	14	20	+6	+49
Total current liabilities	524	254	–270	–52
Fixed liabilities				
Debentures	400	650	+250	+63
Total liabilities	924	904	–20	–2
Equity share capital	800	1,200	+400	+50
Retain earning or surplus				
Capital reserves	130	220	+100	+83
General reserves	444	418	–26	–6
Sinking fund	80	100	+20	+25
Total surplus	644	738	+94	+15
Total capital	1,444	1,938	+494	+34
Total liabilities and capital	2,368	2,842	+474	+20

Comments

Current assets both individual and as well as total have decreased in 2018 by 34% when compared to 2017. Investments also have decreased by 37%. Amounts realized from the assets have been mainly used to repay current liabilities (decrease by 52%) and the balance used for the purchase of fixed assets. Fixed assets, particularly buildings significantly have increased by 146% and other assets by 32%. It is heartening to note that these assets have been funded through the issue of debentures by 63% and equity and retain earnings by 65%. Generally, there is overall increase in total assets in 2018 over 2017 only by 20%.

Illustration 2

From the following income statement of ABC Ltd., prepare a comparative income statement:

Particulars	*Amount in lakh rupees for the year ending December*			
	2017		*2018*	
Net sales		6850		7210
Cost of goods sold		4190		4630
Gross profit		2,660		2,580
Operating expenses				
Selling expenses	940		910	
General administrative expenses	470	1410	460	1,370

Contd...

Operating profit	1250	1210
Add: Other income—dividend	220	250
Total	1470	1460
Less: Other deductions	220	220
Net profit before tax	1250	1240
Less: Income Tax	620	620
Net Profit after tax	630	620

Solution

ABC Ltd.

Comparative Income Statement

for the years ended on December 2017 and 2018

Assets	*Amount in lakh ₹*		*Increase or decrease*	
	2017	*2018*	*Absolute amount*	*%*
Net sales	6850	7210	+ 360	+ 5.3
Less: Cost of goods sold	4190	4630	+ 440	+10.5
Gross profit	2660	2580	– 80	– 3.0
Operating expenses				
Selling expenses	940	910	– 30	– 3.2
General administrative expenses	470	460	– 10	– 2.1
Total operating expenses	1410	1370	– 40	– 2.8
Operating profit	1250	1210	– 41	– 3.2
Add: Other income – Dividend	220	250	+ 30	+1.4
Total	1470	1460	– 10	– .07
Less : Other deductions	220	220	–	–
Net profit before tax	1250	1240	– 10	– .08
Less : Income Tax	620	620	–	–
Net Profit after tax	630	620	– 10	– 1.6

Illustration 3

Convert the following income statement into common size statement and interpret the changes in the year 2018 in the light of the conditions in 2017.

Income Statement

Particulars	*2017*	*2018*
Gross sales	30600	367230
Less: Sales return	600	700
Net sales	30000	36020
Less: Cost of goods sold	18200	20250
Gross Profit	11800	15770
Less: Operating expenses		
Administrative expanses	3000	3400
Sales expenses	6000	6600
Total operating expenses	9000	1000
Income from operation	2800	5770
Add: Non-operating income	300	400
Total income	3100	6170
Less: Non-operating expenses	400	600
Net profit	2700	2270

Solution

Common Size Income Statements

Particulars	*2017*		*2018*	
	Absolute amount	*%*	*Absolute amount*	*%*
Gross sales	30600	102.0	367230	101.9
Less: Sales return	600	2.0	700	1.9
Net sales	30000	100.0	36020	100.0
Less: Cost of goods sold	18200	60.7	20250	56.2
Gross profit	11800	39.3	15770	43.8
Less: Operating expenses				
Administrative expenses	3000	10.0	3400	18.3
Sales expenses	6000	20.0	6600	9.4
Total operating expenses	9000	30.0	1000	27.7
Income from operation	2800	9.3	5770	16.1
Add: Non-operating income	300	1.0	400	1.1
Total income	3100	10.3	6170	17.2
Less: Non-operating expenses	400	1.3	600	1.7
Net profit	2700	9.0	2270	15.5

Interpretation

The analysis of the above income statement enables us to draw the following conclusions.

1. During 2018, the cost of goods sold has declined by 4.5% (from 60.5 to 56.5). This decline may be due to a decrease in the cost of raw material. Owing to this decline, the gross profit ratio has increased from 39.3% to 43.8%.
2. The operating expenses have declined by 2.3%, which indicates high operating efficiency and economy in expenditure. Both administrative and selling expenses have declined despite the increase in the absolute values of these items.
3. The combined effect of decrease in cost of goods sold and operating expenses has caused an increase in net operating income by 6.8% in 2018 (from 9.3% to 16.1 in 2017).
4. The increase in non-operating income is a welcoming feature while the corresponding increase in non-operating expenses proportionately is not desired.
5. Finally, it is said that the company has been operating more efficiently in 2018 than in 2017.

Illustration 4

From the following information, interpret the result of operations of a manufacturing concern, using the trend ratios:

Comparative Statements
for the years 2017 to 2018

Particulars	*Absolute amount*			
	2015	*2016*	*2017*	*2018*
Gross sales	100.0	95.0	120.0	130.0
Less: Cost of goods sold	60.0	58.9	69.6	72.8
Gross profit	40.0	36.1	50.4	57.2
Less: Operating expenses	10.0	9.7	11.0	12.0
Net operating profit	30.0	26.4	39.4	45.2

Solution

Trend Ratio (base year 2015 is 100)

Particulars	*Absolute amount*			
	2015	*2016*	*2017*	*2018*
Gross sales	100	95	120	130
Less: Cost of goods sold	100	98	116	121
Gross profit	100	90	126	143
Less: Operating expenses	100	97	110	120
Net operating profit	100	88	131	151

Interpretations

1. From the above statement, it is seen that the cost of goods sold and operating expenses have all declined in 2018 as compared with 2015.
2. The decline in sales is comparatively more than the cost and operating expenses.
3. On the other hand, the sales cost and operating expenses have all increased in 2017 and 2018 than in 2015.
4. The increase in cost and operating expenses is less than the increase in sales.
5. Hence, we also conclude that from the trend ratios a large portion of cost of goods and operating expenses is fixed and they are not affected by change in sales volume. Because of this, we find that the net operating profit is more in 2017 and 2018, compared to 2015.

REVIEW QUESTIONS

1. Explain the meaning and nature of financial statements.
2. What are the objectives of financial statements?
3. Explain the essential attributes of financial statements.
4. Discuss the importance of financial statements.
5. Who are the users of financial statements?
6. What are the main limitations of the financial statements?
7. Financial statements reflect a combination of recorded facts, accounting conventions and personal judgments. Discuss.
8. Explain the meaning, objectives and importance of analysis and interpretation of financial statements.
9. Explain the various ways of presentation of financial statements.
10. Explain the vertical way of presenting the financial statements.
11. Describe briefly the major tools used in the financial statements analysis.
12. What are comparative financial statements? How are they prepared?
13. What are common sized Balance Sheet and Income Statements? Explain the technique of preparing a common size Balance Sheet.
14. What are trend ratios? How are they computed? What is their significance?
15. State the different types of financial analysis.
16. Write short notes on (*a*) common size statements (*b*) trend analysis and (*c*) comparative financial statements.
17. From the following information, prepare a proforma income statement for the months of January, February and March 2018 for a company:

    (*a*) The company has ₹ 6000 of 8% loan, interest payable monthly.

    (*b*) Sales are projected at ₹ 45000, ₹ 48000 and ₹ 43000 for January, February and March 2018 respectively.

(*c*) Cost of goods sold is ₹ 10000 plus 30% for selling price per month.

(*d*) Selling expenses are 3% of sales.

(*e*) Rent is ₹ 1500 per month, administrative expenses for January are expected to be ₹ 1200, but are also expected to rise by 1% per month over the previous month's expenses.

(*f*) Corporate tax rate is 505.

Ans.

Particulars	*January*	*February*	*March*
Gross profit	21,500	23,600	20,100
Operating expenses	14,850	15,060	15,031
Profit after tax	3,125	4,070	2,334

18. The comparative Balance Sheet for Enpees Ltd., as on December 31, 2017 and 2018, are given below. Comment upon the significant changes that have taken place during the year 2020.

Assets	*2015*	*2016*
Gross fixed assets	2,600	3,100
Less: Depreciation & Reserves	800	1,100
Profit after tax	1,800	2,000
Current assets		
Stock in trade	1,200	1,600
Debtors	200	800
Cash	300	100
Total current assets	1,700	2,500
Total assets	3,500	4,500
Liabilities		
Equity share capital	1,000	1,000
Reserves	800	1,200
6 % Debentures	200	200
Current liabilities		
Sundry creditors	400	500
Bills payable	900	1,300
Bank overdraft	200	300
	3,500	4,500

19. From the following Balance Sheet of Ram Ltd., you are required to compute the following trend percentages using 31st December, 2016 as the base year.

A. Accounts receivables, B. Current assets, C. Fixed assets,
D. Current liabilities and E. Share capital,

Liabilities	*Amount in 000s*			*Assets*	*Amount in 000s*		
	2014	*2017*	*2018*		*2016*	*2017*	*2018*
Share capital	25	20	25	Fixed assets less depreciation	20	15	16
Retained earnings	5	3	2	Investments	4	2	4
Accounts payable	8	9	7	Stock	5	3	4
Accrued expenses	3	2	1	Account receivables	12	13	11
Taxes payable	3	2	3	Cash	3	3	3
Total	44	36	38	Total	44	36	38

Also prepare a Common Size Balance Sheet for the last two years nearest to the first decimal place.

20. From the information prepare a Common Size Balance Statement and make brief comments.

Particulars	*Amount in the years*		
	2016	*2017*	*2018*
Net sales	6,20,000	4,40,000	2,80,000
Cost of goods sold	4,30,000	3,02,000	2,04,000
Gross profit	1,90,000	1,38,000	76,000
Operating profit	1,26,000	69,000	44,000
Net operating profit	64,000	69,000	32,000
Interest expenses	6,000	3,500	2,500
Profit before tax	58,000	65,500	29,500
Provisions for taxes	25,000	35,000	14,000
Total	33,000	30,500	15,500

21. Acon Ltd. and Harish Ltd. produce and sell the same type of goods. The budgeted percentage for the year ended 30th June, 2018 are

Cost (percentage of sales)	*Acon Ltd.*	*Harish Ltd.*
Fixed	50	40
Variable	40	50
Net profit	10	10
Total	100	100

Evaluate and compare the operating performance of the two companies.

22. The following Trend Ratio (base year is 2013) are taken from the financial statements of a retailer of consumer goods.

Particulars	*Percentages for the years*				
	2014	*2015*	*2016*	*2017*	*2018*
Net sales	102	118	134	152	161
Cost of goods sold	102	113	131	146	154
Gross profit on sales	103	129	138	166	178
Selling expenses	100	107	116	128	130
General and administrative expenses	105	121	132	137	153
Net profit	108	175	183	258	283
Net income after tax	110	169	186	238	266

Find the major changes in the trading position.

23. From the following accounting statements of Mona Ltd., for the year ended 31st December 2015, prepare a Common Size Analysis of the company.

Balance Sheet

as on 31st December 2018

Liabilities	*Amount in* ₹	*Assets*	*Amount in* ₹
Share capital	13,10,000	Cash	50,000
Fixed liabilities	4,50,000	Debtors	4,40,000
Sundry creditors	84,000	Stock	2,00,000
Other liabilities	1,56,000	Prepaid expenses	20,000
		Bills receivables	20,000
		Net fixed assets	12,70,000
Total	20,00,000	Total	20,00,000

Income Statement

for the year ending on 31st December 2018

Particulars	*Amount in ₹*	*Amount in ₹*
Net sales		25,38,000
Cost of good sold		14,22,000
Gross profit		1,16,000
Selling expenses	7,20,000	
Administrative expense	1,84,000	9,04,000
Operating profit		2,12,000
Other incomes		26,000
Total profit		2,38,000
Other expenses		40,000
Income before tax		1,98,000
Income tax		68,000
Income after tax		1,30,000
Loss on sale of securities		90,000
Net income transferred to surplus		40,000

■■■

7

Financial Ratio Analysis

RATIO ANALYSIS

The term "ratio" simply means one number expressed in terms of another. It describes in mathematical terms the quantitative relationship that exists between the two numbers. The term "accounting ratio", as pointed out by J. Batty, is used to describe significant relationship between figures shown on a balance sheet, in a profit and loss account and in a budgetary control system or in any part of the accounting organization.

Ratio Analysis, when simply defined, refers to the analysis and interpretation of financial statements through ratios. Now-a-days, it is used by all business and industrial concerns in their financial analysis. Ratios are considered to be the best guides for the efficient execution of basic managerial functions like planning, forecasting, controlling, etc.

Ratios are designed to show how one number is related to another. It is worked by dividing one number by another. Ratios are customarily presented either in the form of a coefficient or a percentage or as a proportion.

For example, the current assets and current liabilities of a business on a particular date are ₹ 2.5 lakhs and ₹ 1.25 lakhs respectively. The resulting ratio of current assets and current liabilities could be expressed as 2 (i.e. ₹ 2,50,000/₹ 1,25,000) or as 200%. Alternatively, in the form of a proportion the same ratio is expressed as 2 : 1, i.e. the current asset is two times that of current liabilities.

Ratios are invaluable aids to management and others who are interested in the analysis and interpretation of financial statements. Absolute figures may be misleading unless compared with one another. Ratio provides means of showing the relationship, which exists between figures. Though there is no special magic in Ratio Analysis, many prefer judgments more on ratios as they find them highly useful for making judgments more easily.

However, the numerical relationship of the kind expressed by ratios are not an end but are means for understanding the financial position of the business. Generally simple ratios or ratios compiled from a single year's financial statements of a business may not serve the real purpose. Hence, ratios are to be worked out from the financial statements of a number of years.

Ratios by themselves are meaningless. They derive status partly from the ingenuity and experience of the analysts who use the available data in a systematic manner. Besides, in order to reach valid conclusions, ratios have to be compared with some standards that are established with a view to represent the financial position of the business under review.

However, it should be borne in mind that after computing ratios, one cannot categorically say whether a particular ratio is good or bad as the conclusion may vary from business to business. A single ideal ratio cannot be applied for all types of business. Speedy compiling of ratios and their presentation in the appropriate manner is essential.

A complete record of ratios employed is advisable and explanation of each ratio, year by year, should be included. This record may be treated as a part of an accounts manual or a special ratio register may be maintained.

INTERPRETATION OF RATIO

Generally, there are four different approaches available for interpreting ratios.

1. **Interpretation of an individual ratio:** An individual ratio by itself may have a significance of its own. For example, a persistent fall in the net profit to sales may indicate inefficiency or waste in the organization. Normally, they are to be studied with a reference to some standards. However, these standards are mostly approximations. The conclusion derived from any deviation of actual ratios from them may be misleading. Hence, this approach is to be combined with others.
2. **Interpretation by referring to a group of ratios:** Sometimes, when studied individually it may be difficult to comprehend the significance of certain ratios fully. In such case, the analysis could be made more meaningful by computing/some of the additional related ratios. A change in one ratio may be of significance only when viewed with relation to other ratios. For example, the significance of profit ratio could be by calculating other ratios like return on capital employed, interest coverage, etc.
3. **Interpretation of ratios by trend:** Under this method, an individual ratio or a group of ratios are computed and compared over time. The significant trend, increasing or decreasing or being constant are considered for reaching conclusions. Some times the average of ratios calculated for a number of years are used for carrying out the analysis.
4. **Interpretations by inter-firm comparisons:** In this approach, the ratios of one firm are compared with ratios of other firms in the same industry. Such inter-firm comparisons may be significant as some of the other firms considered for comparison may be experiencing the same or similar financial problems. Generally, selected significant ratios are calculated and published by trade associations or credit rating or financial institutions

as the form of tables. Such tables may be used by individual firms for carrying out the analysis.

A full fledged investigation of the financial and economic position of any business however needs the application of all the four approaches. This is essential for generating useful information which will make the intrinsic meaning of any ratio clear.

RATIOS IN PUBLISHED ACCOUNTS

It has now become a common feature for many progressive companies to show the most significant ratios in their annual reports. These ratios are used to illustrate the most important facts and trends to show shareholders and other interested parties how the company is progressing.

For example, some significant ratios relating to the working and performance of central or state government undertakings computed from their annual financial statements are published every year. The Reserve Bank of India also publishes periodically a few significant ratios for all vital industries in India. These ratios may be used for comparative analysis of individual firms. Or, each firm may compute some important ratios for a period of five years for assessing the trend from the past to the present and for estimating the future.

ANALYSIS OF FINANCIAL ACCOUNTS

When analyzing the financial health, ascertaining the trend by studying the results of a number of years is extremely important. For this purpose, a period of five years is generally regarded as satisfactory. If only a few years' figures are available, the best use has to be made of them.

A clear understanding of the purpose or the main reason for undertaking the financial analysis is imperative before any attempt is made to carry out the work. The purpose of the analysis would tend to differ according to the analyst concerned, whether a creditor, a would-be lender, a prospective shareholder or a potential take-over bidder.

For example, if a bank or other institutions are to lend money, they will first wish to know whether the borrower is in a position to pay back and possibly whether there is adequate collateral security. In addition, the reliability of the information received for analysis should be ascertained.

For too many ratios, it is always better to use selected ratios with care instead of enlightening, which may confuse the analyst. Some of the important ratios which can be used with advantages are discussed below. A number of steps that can be followed are also outlined here.

1. Is profit adequate? This can be seen by considering the profit earned in relation to assets employed. The risk involved in the particular business should also be considered as it indicates, what is a reasonable return on the capital employed.
2. Is profit increasing or decreasing and at what rate? This can be seen by comparing the accrued profits for a number of consecutive years. Suppose, there has been a change for the worse, in that cases the investigation into volume of turnover, prices, costs, etc. may be necessary.

3. What is the position regarding solvency? Here, it is necessary to study the liquid, current ratios and debt-to equity ratios. In particular, the possibility of over trading or under trading should be looked in. Analysis of the current ratios into its main parts, related to one top over another may be useful for assessing the short-term financial positions. Debt to equity ratios is useful for measuring the long term solvency position of the business.
4. The sales turnover ratios should be computed. The purpose here is to indicate whether the volume of sales is adequate in relation to other key factors. The ratio of sales to total assets employed may be an important criterion, especially when the trend of four to five years is observed.
5. It should be ascertained as to whether the capital structure is appropriate for the business concerned.

The profit being earned should be adequate to cover the payment of interest and dividends to all the classes of creditors and shareholders. This matter depends very much upon capital gearing or usage of debt by the business.

USES OF RATIO ANALYSIS

Ratios enable the mass of accounting data to be summarized and simplified. Besides, they provide means of showing the inter relationship which exists between the various segments of business as revealed through accounting statements and thereby prevent any distortion that may result from the study of absolute figures.

Ratio analysis is an invaluable aid to management in the discharge of its basic functions such as planning, forecasting, controlling, etc. the trend ratios may be useful for predicting likely events in the future. The plans made can be signposted by accounting ratios and thereby become an integral part of the standard costing and budgetary control systems.

Ideal ratios can be established and the relationship between primary ratios may be used to establish the desirable coordination. Ratios may also be used for controlling the performance and as well as control of costs. Ratios are an effective means of communication and play a vital role in informing the position of the business and also the progress by the business concern to the owners and other parties.

Ratio analysis is an effective instrument which, when properly used, is used to assess important characteristics of business like liquidity, solvency, profitability, etc. A study on these aspects may enable conclusions to be drawn relating to financial requirements and capabilities of the business. The ratio may be used as measures of efficiency. It is the main tool of analysis for intra firm comparisons.

LIMITATIONS OF RATIO ANALYSIS

Ratios are mainly calculated from the information recorded in the financial statements. As indicated in the previous chapter, the financial statements suffer from a number of limitations and may therefore affect the quality of the ratio analysis.

Ratios gains significance only when compared with other ratios or standards. It is very difficult to lay down fixed standards for ideal ratios. Also, ratios share with each other statistical concepts with all the limitations of the latter.

Ratios are tools of quantitative analysis only and normally qualitative factors, which may generally influence the conclusions derived and are ignored while computing ratios. For example, a high current ratio may not necessarily mean sound liquidity position when current assets include a large inventory consisting mostly of obsolete items. Hence, it is very difficult to generalize whether a particular ratio is good or bad.

Lack of standard formulae for working out ratios makes it difficult to compare them. They are worked out on the basis of different items in different industries. In addition, the number of ratios is so large that the task of selecting appropriate ratios for different units becomes very difficult. Ratios also fail to indicate clearly the point where the error lies.

Ratio Analysis is only a beginning and just gives a fraction of information needed for decision making. It is just an aid and cannot replace the thinking judgment employed in the decision making process.

Ratios computed from historical data are used for predicting and projecting the likely events in the future. Such ratios may provide a glimpse of a firm's past performance but the forecast for the future may not be correct because several other factors like management policies, economic and market conditions, etc. may influence future operations.

CLASSIFICATION OF RATIOS

Ratios may be classified in a number of ways to suit any particular purpose. Different kinds of ratios are selected for different types of situations. Mostly, the purpose for which ratios are used and the kind of data available determine the nature of analysis. In general, the following bases of classifications are in practice,

A. Classifications According to Accounting Statements

This classification is based on the nature of the accounting statement on which the items are used for compiling ratios appear. Accordingly, the different sub-divisions are:

1. Balance sheet ratios: These ratios are also called financial ratios. The components for computing these ratios are drawn from the Balance Sheet. For example, current ratio, debt-equity ratio, etc.

2. Profit and account ratio: These ratios are also called operating ratios. The items used for calculating ratios are drawn from the Profit and Loss Account Statements. For examples, gross profit ratio, operating ratio, etc.

3. Inter-statement ratios or combined ratios: The information required for the compilation is normally drawn from both the Balance Sheet and Profit and Loss Account. For example, debtors' turnover ratios, stock turnover ratios, net profit to fixed assets ratios, etc.

B. Classification According to Time

The classification is based on the point of time in relation to which the ratios are compiled. Accordingly, they may be classified as follows:

1. Structural ratios: The data used for the computation of these ratios normally relate to the same point of time, for example ratio of a particular month, quarter or a year. In this sense, the Balance Sheet ratios and the Profit and Loss Account ratios of a particular year may be termed as structural ratios.

2. Trend ratios: These are ratios computed between items over a period of time and are analyzed. For example, the current ratios for a period of 3 to 6 years may be calculated and the trend observed from these ratios may be used for the analysis.

C. Classification According to Importance

Some ratios, when related to the main objective of the business for the purpose for analysis, may be more important than others. This basis of classification has been recommended by the British Institute of Management (BIM) for inter-firm computations and the BIM has suggested the following types:

1. Primary ratios: The prime motive of any commercial undertaking is profit and, therefore, ratios like profit to sales, return on capital employed may be termed as primary ratios.

2. Secondary ratios: These ratios are mainly used to explain the primary ratios. They are also known as subsidiary or supporting ratios. Taking the ratio of return on capital employed as the primary ratio, the following ratios may be grouped as secondary ratios, like profit and earning ratios, cost or expenses ratios, turnover ratios, capital and related ratios, etc.

D. Classification According to Functions or Tests Satisfied

Robert N Antony suggested that ratios may be grouped on the basis of certain tests, which satisfies the needs of parties having the financial interests in the business firm. The tests usually are:

1. Liquidity tests,
2. Profitability tests,
3. Market tests.

E. Classifications According to Nature

Under this classification ratios are grouped as

1. Liquid ratios: These ratios are used to measure the ability of the firm to meet its maturing obligations, or current liabilities, for example, current ratio or acid test ratio.

2. Leverage ratios: These ratios help to measure the financial contribution of owners, compared with that of creditors, as also the risk of debt financing. They are also known as capital structure ratios, for example, debt to equity ratio, fixed assets to net worth, interest coverage ratio, etc.

3. Turnover ratio or Activity ratio: These ratios enable measurement of the effectiveness of usage of the resources at the command of the concern, for example, fixed assets turnover ratio indicates the profitability position of the business.

4. Profitability ratios: These ratios are intended to measure the end result of the business operations, for example, gross profit ratios, return on capital employed ratios, operating ratios, etc.

It may be observed from the above discussion that one basis of classification bends into the other. Whatever classification is followed, ratios should be computed carefully and presented to the management and other interested parties at regular intervals.

For further explanation, ratios are classified into three major groups, such as liquidity ratios, solvency ratios and profitability ratios.

ANALYSIS OF LIQUIDITY OR LIQUID RATIOS

Liquidity ratios play a key role in the analysis of the short term financial position of the business. Commercial banks and other short term creditors are generally interested in such an analysis. However, managements can employ these ratios to ascertain how efficiently they utilize their working capital in the business.

Shareholders, debenture holders and other long term creditors can use these ratios to assess the prospects of dividend and interest payments. This type of ratio indicates the ability of the business to meet the maturing or current debts, the efficiency of the management in utilizing the working capital and the progress attuned in the current financial position.

DESCRIPTION OF PRINCIPLE RATIOS: CURRENT RATIO

Current ratio may be defined as the ratio of the current assets to current liabilities. It is also known as the working capital ratio. Current ratio shows the relationship between total current assets and total current liabilities. As a formula, the current ratio is:

Current ratio = Current assets/current liabilities

Components of Current Ratio

Current assets mean cash or those assets convertible or expected to be converted into cash within a year and current liabilities are those liabilities to be paid off within the same time.

Current assets normally include the following items:

1. Cash in Hand and at Bank,
2. Marketable Securities or Readily Realizable Investments,
3. Bills Receivables,
4. Book Debits (excluding Bad Debts and Provisions),
5. Inventories and Prepaid Expense.

Current liabilities normally include the following items:

1. Outstanding or Accrued Expenses,
2. Sundry Creditors,
3. Bills Payable,
4. Bank Overdraft,
5. Provisions for Taxations, etc.

However, a controversy sometime arises whether overdraft should be regarded as Current Liability or not. Often an arrangement with the bank is regarded as permanent and therefore, it may be treated as a long term liability. At the same time, the fact remains that overdraft facility may be cancelled at any time. Hence, because of this reason and the need for conservatism in interpreting a situation it seems advisable to include overdraft in Current Liabilities.

GENERAL GUIDELINES

All current assets and current liabilities should be properly valued. Therefore, all reserves and provisions created should be deducted for such current assets. Book Debts outstanding for more than 6 months and loose tools should be excluded. Investments, which are easily marketable and are meant to be sold for cash should be treated as current assets. Fictitious assets, such as preliminary expenses and discounts on issue of shares, advances made for the purpose of fixed assets, etc. are to be excluded.

Every long term liabilities, if they are payable within one year, should be treated as Current Liability. Bank Overdraft, unless specifically stated as permanent arrangement, should be treated as a current liability. As regards Bills Receivable, all bills (whether discounted or not) should be treated as current assets and, at the same time, Discounted Bills Receivables should be treated as Current Liabilities.

For example, in computing the Current Ratio from the Balance Sheet

Liabilities	*Amount* [₹]	*Assets*		*Amount* [₹]
Sundry creditors	15,000	Cash		10,000
Outstanding expenses	2,000	Short term investments		20,000
Bills payable	8,000	Bills receivables		6,000
Income tax payable	15,000	Book debts	42,500	
Bank overdraft	35,000	Reserves	2,500	40,000
		Inventories		44,000
		Prepaid expense		5,000
		Loose tools		5,000
Total	75,000			75,000

Current ratio = 1,25,000/75,000

= 1.67 or 5:3

From the above ratio, it is clear that for every rupee worth of current liability there are current assets worth ₹ 1.67. In other words it connotes that the firm can meet all its current obligations even by just realizing 60% of its current assets. Though 2:1 is often refered to as a banker's rule of thumb standard of liquidity of business, it is suggested that an ideal current ratio could be 1:5 to 2:1.

PROBLEMS OF WINDOW DRESSING

Window dressing, as used here, refers to the practice of manipulating the Current Assets and Current Liabilities in a manner as to present a more favourable ratio than the actual one. Such manipulations can be carried out in the value of inventories and by recording in advance cash sales or outstanding liabilities for credit purchase of goods taken into closing stock. Also, they may be done by treating short term obligations as a long term debts. In such cases, the Current Ratio will not be representative of the actual position of the business during the year.

SIGNIFICANCE

Current ratio is an index of the firm's financial stability, i.e. an index of technical solvency and an index of the strength of the working capital which means excess of current assets over current liabilities. The logic behind current ratio is that cash need not be immediately available to meet all Current Liabilities on a particular date but there should be good prospects for an adequate inflow of cash indicated by the amounts of the individual components of current assets.

It is closely connected with the concept of working capital. A high current ratio is an assurance that the firm will have adequate funds to pay Current Liabilities and Current Payments.

The main limitation of current ratio is that it fails to indicate the liquidity of individual components of current assets. For example, a high current ratio due to large inventories may not be regarded as an index of liquidity as one which is due to huge cash and bank balance.

Even if the ratio is favourable, the firm may be in financial trouble because more stock and work in progress which are not easily convertible into cash and therefore may have less cash to pay off current liabilities. Hence, it is suggested that the current ratio should not be used as the sole index of short term solvency.

LIQUID RATIO

Liquid Ratio is the ratio of liquid assets to liquid liabilities or current liabilities. It is concerned with the relationship between liquid assets and liquid or current liabilities. For the purpose of computation, the Current Assets and Current Liabilities could be classified as follows:

Current Assets — Liquid Assets and Deferred Assets

Current Liabilities — Liquid Liabilities and Deferred Liabilities

This classification could be made by establishing a simple rule that all assets and liabilities are liquid if they are expected to be realized or paid within a month and, if beyond, belong to the deferred category. However, the criterion for such classifications depends upon the purpose for which the current ratio is used.

Components

Liquid assets normally include cash, bank sundry debtors, bills receivables and marketable securities. In other words, they are current assets minus inventories and prepaid expenses. In the same manner, Liquid Liabilities are Current Liabilities minus Bank Overdraft. The formula is as follows:

Liquid Ratio = Liquid Assets/Liquid Liabilities

Some authorities recommended that Liquid Ratio may be computed comparing Current Liabilities with liquid assets.

General Guidelines

All guidelines which are applicable to the computation of ratio, are equally applicable to the computation of Liquid Ratio. That is Current Assets and Current Liabilities should be valued properly and the nature of the assets should be kept in view.

From the example considered for computing the current ratio the Liquid Ratio may be calculated as,

Liquid Ratio = ₹ 76,000/₹ 40,000

= 1.9 or 1.9:1

The ratio indicates that by realizing the debtors, short term investments and bills receivables at their face value, the firm could pay off all the Liquid Liabilities. In other words, the firm could meet its Liquid Liabilities without resorting to the sale of inventories. Comparing with the rule of thumb, which is 1:1 for the Liquid Ratio, the actual ratio is exceptionally good.

Significance

Liquid Ratio is a more rigorous test of liquidity than current ratio, since it eliminates inventories and prepaid expenses as a part of Current Assets. A comparison of the Current Ratio to Liquid Ratio would indicate the degree of inventory held up. A high Liquid Ratio, when compared to current ratio, may indicate under stocking while a low Liquid Ratio may indicate over stocking.

When used in conjunction with current ratio, the Liquid Ratio gives a better picture of the firm's capacity to meet its short term obligations out of the short term assets.

However, it is difficult to establish a standard for this ratio and also dangerous in relying too much on a 1:1 standard, as suggested without further investigations. A reasonable standard for Liquid Ratio may vary from season to season and also from business to business. For example, a manufacturing company may have a weak Liquid Ratio in the time of prosperity due to increased activity where there are huge stocks and less cash. Hence, it should be remembered while arriving at conclusions, though technically inventories are not immediately available to meet current liabilities, they, to a measurable extent, generate cash during the normal course of business.

Inventories are converted into cash, debtors and bills receivables when they are sold in ordinary course of business. Though this ratio is definitely an improvement over current ratio, the interpretation of this ratio also suffers from the same limitation of current ratio.

ABSOLUTE LIQUID RATIO

Absolute Liquidity is represented by cash and near cash items. Hence, in the computation of this ratio, only the Absolute Liquid assets are compared with Liquid Liabilities. The Absolute Liquid assets are cash, bank and marketable securities. It is also observed that receivables are eliminated from the list of Liquid Assets in order to obtain Absolute Liquid assets, since there are some doubters relating to their liquidity.

Formula

Absolute Liquid Ratio = (Cash + Bank + Marketable Securities)/Liquid Liabilities

This ratio gains much significance only when it is used in conjunction with the first two ratios. A standard 0.5:1 absolute liquid ratio is considered an acceptable norm. That is from the point of view of absolute liquidity, fifty paise worth of absolute liquid assets are considered sufficient for one rupee worth of liabilities. However this ratio is not in much use.

The Current Ratio, Liquid Ratio and Absolute Liquid Ratio generally indicate the adequacy of the current assets for meeting the Current Liabilities. This is one dimension of liquidity analysis. The other dimension of liquidity is the determination of the rate at which various short term assets are converted into cash.

Important ratios under the secondary category are as follows:

WORKING CAPITAL TURNOVER RATIO

This ratio indicates whether or not working capital, which relates to current assets and current liabilities, has been effectively used in making sales. It is calculated as follows:

Working Capital Turnover Ratio = Net Sales/Net Working Capital

For the sake of convenience, the figure of net working capital (Current Assets—Current Liabilities) at the end of the year, should be considered. This ratio makes it clear that the business is being carried on with the small or large amount of working capital in relation to sales.

A low working capital turnover ratio may reflect an inadequacy of net working capital as a result of low turnovers of inventories or receivables. In other words, a high ratio may be due to huge turnovers of inventory or receivables. Considerable caution should be exercised while interpreting this ratio. Working capital turnover ratio takes a number of forms in the analysis. Some of them are discussed here.

RECEIVABLES TURNOVER RATIO

Receivables or debtors normally include both debtors and bills receivable representing the uncollected portion of credit sales. Receivables institute an important component of current assets and therefore the quality receivables to a greater extent determines the liquidity of a firm. This ratio can be calculated in two ways as follows:

Receivables turnover ratio = Credit Sales/Average accounts receivable (Receivables velocity)

or

= Average accounts receivables/credit sales per day

(where credit sales per day = Total credit sales / 360 or 365 days)

Components

Book debts and bills receivables, which arise out of credit sales, should be considered. Average debtors can be arrived at by adding the opening and closing balances of the book debts and bills receivables and by dividing the result by two.

It should be noted that provisions for bad and doubtful debts should not be deducted since this may give an impression that some amount of receivables has been collected. When the credit sales are not given, the total sales may be considered for the computation. The receivable turnover ratio, when calculated in terms of days, is known as average collection period or debts collection period ratio.

For example, from the information given below:

Sundry debtors as 1-1-2018	30,000
Sundry debtors as on 31-12-2018	45,000
Bills receivables as 1-1-2018	10,000
Bills receivables as 31-12-2018	15,000
Total sales for the year 2018	3,50,000
Cash sales for the year 2018	50,000
Provisions for doubtful debts as on 31-12-2018	2,000

Debtors turnover ratio = Credit sales/average account receivables

= 30,000/50,000 = 6 times

Alternatively,

Debtors turnover ratio = Average account receivables/Credit sale per day

= 50,000 × 3/2,500 = 60 days

where credit sales per day = 3,00,000/360 = 2,500/3

In fact, these two ratios are inter-related. Debtors turnover ratio could be obtained by dividing the number of days in a year by the average collection period (i.e. 360/60 = 6).

Significance

Average collection period indicates the quality of debtors by measuring the rapidity or slowness in the collection process. A shorter collection period implies prompt payment by debtors, while a longer period implies a too liberal and inefficient credit collection performance.

In order to measure the efficiency of the credit collection department, it should be compared with the average of the industry. It should be neither too liberal nor too restrictive. When a liberal credit policy may result in more Bad Debts and over investments in receivables, a restrictive policy may result in lower sales and therefore lower profits.

It is very difficult to establish a standard collection period, since it depends on a number of factors such as the seasonal character of the business, nature of industry, credit policy of the firm, etc. Hence, it is a very good supplementary check to be used for judging the adequacy of current ratio.

CREDITORS TURNOVER RATIO

This ratio is similar to receivables turnover ratio. It compares the accounts payable with the total credit purchase. It signifies the credit period enjoyed by the firm in paying to creditors. Accounts payable include both sundry creditors and bills payable. It is calculated as follows:

Creditors turnover ratio = Credit purchase/Average account payable

or

= Average accounts payable/Average monthly (daily) credit purchase

Example 1:

Compute the creditors turnover ratio from the following particulars:

	₹
Credit purchase during 2018	2,40,000
Creditors as on 31-12-2018	40,000
Creditors as on 1-1-2018	60,000
Bills payable as on 1-1-2018	7,500
Bills payable as on 31-12-2018	12,500

Creditors turnover ratio = ₹ 2,40,000/₹ 60,000 = 4 times

Creditors payment period = ₹ 60,000/₹ 20,000 = 3 months

When average monthly credit purchase = ₹ 2,40,000/12 = ₹ 20,000

Significance

A high creditor turnover ratio signifies that creditors are being paid properly, promptly and thus boosting up the credit worthiness of the firm. Also, a very low ratio may signify that the firm is not taking full advantage of credit facilities allowed by creditors.

INVENTORY TURNOVER RATIO

Meaning

Inventory Turnover Ratio is also known as Stock Turnover Ratio, which normally establishes relationship between cost of sales and average inventory. This ratio indicates whether investments in inventory are within proper limit or not.

Besides being an index of liquidity of a firm showing the rate at which inventories are converted into sales and then into cash, this ratio helps the financial manager to evaluate inventory policy.

Components

Average inventory and cost of goods sold are constituents of the ratio. Average inventory is calculated by taking inventory level at the opening date plus the end of every month, adding them up and dividing them by two. If the monthly figures are not available, the average inventory could be derived by adding stock levels at the opening and closing dates and dividing them by two.

As regards sales, the ratio is best expressed when an average inventory is compared with the cost of goods sold. However, the ratio of net sales (sales less returns) to inventory may be used. Some firms like departmental stores, which value inventory at selling price under retail method, may compute this ratio comparing net sale to average inventory at selling price.

Formulae

Stock turnover ratio can be calculated by employing any one of the following formulae:

Stock Turnover Ratio = Cost of goods sold/average inventory at cost

= Net sales/average inventory at cost

= Cost of goods sold/average inventory at cost

= No. of units sold/average no. of units in stock

To be more realistic, the ratio should be calculated using the same units, both as numerator and denominator. Accordingly, the first and third formulae are considered to be more reasonable. However, the second may be used where the cost of goods sold is not known. The fourth formula is useful mainly to eliminate the effect of changing prices.

When the inventory consists of more kinds of items, such as raw materials, work in progress and finished goods, it is useful to break up the inventory turnover into its main constituent parts to bring out the efficiency or inefficiency at various points. In such cases, the inventory turnover ratio and its constituent parts can be calculated as follows:

Inventory Turnover Ratio (main ratio) = Cost of goods sold/average inventory

Notes:

Average Inventory is calculated by taking stock levels of finished goods, raw materials and work in progress at the opening date and at the end of each month, adding them up and then dividing by thirteen.

Raw Material Turnover Ratio = Materials consumed/average stock of raw materials and chief stores

Work in Process Turnover Ratio = Cost of completed work/average work in progress

Finished Goods Turnover Ratio = Cost of goods sold/average stock of finished products

For example, computing the stock turnover ratio from the given details below we see:

Opening stock at cost for every month	Amount [₹]
At the beginning of January 2018	12,000
At the end of January 2018	12,500
At the end of February 2018	14,000
At the end of March 2018	13,500
At the end of April 2018	13,000
At the end of May 2018	12,500
At the end of June 2018	13,500
At the end of July 2018	14,000
At the end of August 2018	14,600
At the end of September 2018	14,000
At the end of October 2018	13,800
At the end of November 2018	13,000
At the end of December 2018	12,500

Total sales for the year is ₹ 66,000 at 20% profit on cost, then

Stock Turnover Ratio = Cost of goods sold/average stock at cost

= 55,000/13,000 = 4.14 (approximately)

Calculation of cost of goods sold

= Total sales – Profit

= 66,000 – 11,000 = 55,000

(20% on cost or 16 2/3 % on sales)

Calculation of average inventory

= Opening stock + Stock at the end of 12 months)/13

= 1,72,900/13 = 13,000

Significance

Inventory Turnover Ratio is an effective tool to measure the liquidity of inventory and thereby to avoid any danger of overstocking as a prelude to the efficient utilization of a firm's resources.

While a high inventory turnover ratio indicates brisk sales, a low turnover ratio may reflect dull business, over investments in inventory, accumulation of stocks, etc. However, it should be remembered that these ratios, standing by themselves, mean absolutely nothing. Hence, for a meaningful analysis, they should be compared with similar ratios in the previous period, or with the ratios of similar firms.

It is very difficult to establish standards for inventory turnover ratios, because it differs from industry to industry. The inventory turnover ratio is also an index of profitability, where a high ratio signifies more profit and a low ratio signifies low profit.

Sometimes a high inventory ratio may not be accompanied by relatively high profits or profits may be sacrificed to push up volume of sales by reducing price. Similarly, a high turnover ratio may be due to under investments in inventories.

Precautions

The interpretation of inventory turnover ratio should always be done keeping in view the complex circumstances which have a bearing upon the formulation of inventory policies.

When ratios fall out of standards, the reasons for such results should be ascertained and conclusions can be arrived at. The following factors may be given due considerations while using the Inventory Turnover Ratio:

Price trends: Increasing or decreasing prices have their influence on inventories.

Volume of business: An increasing trend in the volume of business may necessitate larger inventories and vice versa.

Supply of conditions: Scarcity conditions may compel firms to pile up stocks for future requirements.

Seasonable conditions: The amount of inventory may differ between seasons. Hence, the nature of season (slack or busy season) to which the inventory value belongs should be duly considered.

CASH TURNOVER RATIO

This ratios relates to the average cash and bank balance to the total cash and cheque payments. It indicates whether the cash or bank balances are in tune with the actual payments to be made.

Formula

Cash Turnover Ratio = Total cash and cheque payments/average cash and bank balances

Significance

This ratio measures the efficiency of cash management. A high ratio may indicate that the cash and bank balances are kept unduly low while a low ratio may indicate that the balances are unduly high, which signifies inefficiency of cash management.

Establishing a standard is very difficult, as it is a matter for the management to decide upon proper cash and bank balance, considering possible future requirements which may vary from time to time.

ANALYSIS FOR PROFITABILITY RATIOS

Profitability is a measure of efficiency and control. It indicates the efficiency or effectiveness with which the operations of the business are carried out. Poor operational performance may result in poor sales and therefore low profits. Low profitability may be due to lack of control over expenses resulting in low profits.

Profitability ratios are employed by management in order to assess how efficiently they carry on the business operations. Profitability is the main base for liquidity as well as solvency. Creditors, banks and financial institutions are interested in profitability ratios since they indicate liquidity or capacity of the business to meet interties obligations and regular improved profits enhance the long term solvency position of the business. Owners are interested in the profitability because they indicate the growth of the business and also the rate of return on their investments.

The amount and the rate of profits earned depend on the quantum of investments committed. Hence, generally the profitability ratios are calculated relating the profits either to sales or to investments.

GROSS PROFIT (GP) RATIO

Gross profit ratio is the ratio of gross profit to net sales expressed as a percentage. It expresses the relationship between gross profit margin and sales. The basic components for the computation of this ratio are gross profit and net sales. Net sales means total sales less if there are sales returns. Gross profit would be the difference between net sales and costs of goods sold.

Costs of goods sold in case of a trading concern would be equal to the opening stock plus purchases, less closing stock and all direct expenses related to purchases, i.e. all expenses charged to trading account. In the case of manufacturing concern, it is equal to the sum of the cost of raw materials, wages, direct expenses and all manufacturing expenses.

In other words, generally, expenses as charged to Profit and Loss Account or operating expenses, excluded from the cost of goods sold, is referred to as the gross profit.

Formula

Gross profit ratio = (Gross profit/Net sales) × 100

For example, computing the ratio from the given information we find,

Opening stock	25,000
Purchases	80,000
Closing stock	35,000
Purchase returns	2,000
Sales	1,05,000
Sales returns	5,000

Gross profit ratio = (32,000 × 100)/1,00,000 = 32%

Workings Notes

Cost of goods sold = Opening stock + Net purchases (Purchase – Purchase returns) – Closing stock

= 25,000 (80,000 – 2,000) – 35,000 = 68,000

Net sales = Total sales – Sales returns

= 1,05,000 – 5,000 = 1,00,000

Gross profit = Net sales – Cost of goods sold

= 1,00,000 – 68,000 = 32,000

Significance

Gross profit ratio may indicate to what extent the selling price of goods per unit may be reduced without incurring loses on operations. It is useful to ascertain whether the average of the mark up on goods sold is maintained.

There is no standard gross profit ratio for evaluation. Trend observed may be used for the analysis. However, the gross profits earned should be sufficient to recover all operating expenses and to build up reserves after paying all fixed interest charges and dividends.

It should be observed that an increase in the gross profit ratio may be due to the following factors.

1. Increase in the selling price of goods sold without any corresponding increase in the cost of good sold.
2. Decrease in the cost of goods sold without corresponding decrease in selling price.
3. Omission of purchase invoices from accounts.
4. Under valuation of opening stock or over valuation of closing stock.

On the other hand, the decrease in the gross profit ratio may be due to the following factors:

1. Decrease in the selling price of goods sold without any corresponding decrease in the cost of good sold.
2. Increase in the cost of goods sold without corresponding increase in selling price.
3. Unfavourable purchasing or mark up policies.
4. Over valuation of opening stock or under valuation of closing stock.

Hence, an analysis of gross profit margin should be carried out in the light of the information relating to purchasing, mark-ups and mark-downs, credit, collections as well as merchandising policies. However, these items of information may not be easily available to the external analyst.

NET PROFIT (NP) RATIO

This is the ratio of net income or profit after tax to net sales. Net profit, as used here, is the balance of Profit and Loss Account which is arrived at after considering all non-operating income, such as interest on investments, dividend received, etc. and non-operating expenses like loss on sale of investments, provisions for contingent liabilities, etc.

Formula

Net profit ratio = (Net profit/Net sales) × 100

This is used as the measure of overall profitability and is useful to the owner. It is both an index of efficiency as well as profitability when used along with gross profit ratio and operating ratio.

OPERATING RATIO

This is the ratio of cost of goods sold plus operating expenses to net sales. This is closely related to the ratio of operating profit to net sales. For example, if the operating ratio is 80%, the operating profit ratio would be 20%.

Components

The main items are operating cost (cost of goods sold plus operating expenses) and net sales. Operating expenses normally include the following:

1. Office and administrative expense, and
2. Selling and distribution expense

Financial charges, such as interest, provision for taxation, etc. are generally excluded from operating expenses.

Formula

Operating Ratio = (Operating cost/Net sales) × 100

An alternate form of this may be expressed as follows:

Operating Profit Ratio = {(Net sales – Operating cost)/net sales} × 100

Computation of any one of these two would be adequate since the other one can be found out by deducting the first one from 100.

For example, if sales less returns and gross profit amounts to ₹ 2,50,000 and ₹ 75,000 respectively, the sum of selling and distribution expenses and administrative expenses amounts to ₹ 25,000, the operating ratio would be,

= {[(2,50,000 – 75,000) + 25,000]/2,00,000 } × 100

= 80%

Hence, operating profit ratio is 20% (100 – 80).

Significance

This ratio indicates the operational efficiency with which the business is being carried on. It shows the percentage of net sales that is absorbed by the cost of goods sold and operating expenses. Hence, lower the operating ratio the higher will be the operating profit.

While the ratio serves as an index of overall efficiency, its usefulness is limited by a number of financial and extraordinary factors. While interpreting the ratio it is important to note that the changing management decisions may create possible variations in expenses from one year to another or one company to another.

An operating ratio, ranging between 75% to 85%, is generally considered as standard from manufacturing organizations.

It is not necessary that the management should be concerned only when the operating ratio rises. If the operating ratio falls while the selling price per unit remains the same, it may be because of the summation of efficiency in some departments and inefficiency in others.

A dynamic management should be interested in making a full analysis. It is, therefore necessary to examine each of the individual components of the operating ratio into various expenses ratios.

EXPENSES RATIO

These expenses ratio supplement the information given by the operating ratio. Some of the important ratios are given below:

Factory expenses ratio = (Factory expense/Net sales)×100

Administrative expense ratio = (Administrative expense/Net sales) × 100

Selling expenses ratio = (Selling expenses/Net sales) × 100

RETURN ON CAPITAL EMPLOYED

Meaning

The prime objective of making investment in business is to obtain satisfactory return on the capital invested. Hence, the return on capital employed is used as a measure of success of a business in realizing his objectives. Otherwise known as return on investments this is the overall profitability ratio. It indicates the percentage of return on the capital employed in the business and it can be used to show the efficiency of the business as a whole.

Formula

Return on capital employed = (Operating profit/Capital employed) × 100

Components

Capital employed and operating profits are the main items. Capital employed may be defined in a number of ways. However, two widely accepted definitions are gross capital employed and net capital employed. Gross capital employed usually minus the total assets used in the business, while the net capital employed refers to the total assets minus Current Liabilities.

On the other hand net capital refers to total capital, capital reserves, revenue reserves (including balance of Profit and Loss Account balance), debenture and long term loans.

Computation of Capital Employed

It is computed from the assets side and comprises of

(*a*) Fixed assets
- Land and building
- Plant and machinery
- Furniture and fittings
- Motor vehicles, etc.

(*b*) Investments made in the Bank

(*c*) Current assets
- Inventories
- Book Debts less provisions

- Bank
- Cash

Less: Current liabilities

- Sundry creditors
- Bills payable
- Bank overdraft

Gross capital employed = Fixed assets + Investments + Current assets

Net capital employed = Fixed assets + Investments + Working capital

Alternatively, if it is calculated from the liabilities side, it will include the following items:

(*a*) Share capital

- Issued share capital (equity and preference)

(*b*) Reserves and Surplus

- Capital reserves
- Profit and loss account balance

(*c*) Debentures

(*d*) Other long term loans

While capital employed is calculated for the assets side, the following precautions should be taken:

(*a*) Regarding the valuation of fixed assets, it is considered necessary to value assets at their replacement cost. This is with a view to provide room for the continuing problem of inflation during recent years.

Under replacement cost method, the fixed assets are to be valued on the basis of their current market prices either by reference to reliable published index numbers or on valuation of experts.

When replacement cost method is used, provisions for depreciation should be recalculated since depreciation charges might have been calculated on original cost of assets.

(*b*) All idle assets should be excluded from the computation. However, standby plant and equipment required for normal working of the machinery may be included.

(*c*) All intangible assets like goodwill, patents, trademarks, unless they have the potential sales value and all fictious assets, like preliminary expenses, discounts on issues of share, etc. should be excluded.

(*d*) All investments made outside the business should be excluded.

(*e*) All current assets should be properly valued. Any excess bank balance, which is more than the normal requirement, should be considered.

Some people suggested that the average capital employed should be used in order to give effect to the capital investment made throughout the year. It is argued that profits earned remain in the business throughout the year and are distributed by way of dividends only at the end of the year.

Average capital employed may be calculated in two ways. In the first method, the simple arithmetic mean of the total capital employed at the end of the year is found out. But in the second method, it is calculated by adding half of the profit after tax and interest to the opening capital employed.

When the net capital employed has been calculated either from assets side or from the liabilities side, half of the profit earned during the year may be deducted from the figure so computed in order to arrive at average capital employed.

Operating profits used for the computation of return on capital employed should be the profits earned by such capital. Hence, the net profit should be adjusted if necessary for obtaining the true operating profit with the following items:

(*a*) Any abnormal and non-recurring losses or gains.

(*b*) Income from investments made outside the business.

(*c*) Depreciation based on the replacement cost of assets.

(*d*) Interest on long term loans and debentures should be added back.

(*e*) Profits before the payment of income tax.

Example 2

From the following information, calculate the return on capital employed:

SUBBU TRADING CORPORATION LTD

Profit and Loss Account

for the year ended on 31-12-2018

To Cost of good sold	1,50,000	By Sales	2,50,000
To Interest on debentures	5,000	By Income for investment	5,000
To Provisions for taxation	50,000		
To Net profit	50,000		
	2,55,000		2,55,000

Balance Sheet as on 31-12-2018

Liabilities	*Amount* [₹]	*Assets*	*Amount* [₹]
Share capital – Preference	50000	Fixed assets	2,25,000
– Equity	1,00,000	Investment in government bonds	50,000
Reserves	50,000	Current assets	75,000
10% debentures	50,000		
P and L balance	50,000		
Provision for taxation	50,000		
	3,50,000		3,50,000

Solution

Return on capital = (Operating profit/Average capital employed) × 100

Operating profit = Net profit before interest – Income from investments

= (50,000 + 5,000 + 50,000) – 5,000

= 1,00,000

Capital employed = Fixed assets + Current assets – Provisions for tax

= 2,25,000 + 75,000 – 50,000

= 2,50,000

Or by Share capital + Reserves + Debentures + P and L balance – Investments

= 1,50,000 + 50,000 + 50,000 + 50,000 – 50,000

= 2,50,000

Average capital employed = Capital employed – ½ (Profits earned during the year)

= 2,50,000 – 25,000

= 2,25,000

Return on average capital employed = (1,00,000/2,25,000) × 100

= 44.4 %

Or

Return on closing capital employed = (1,00,000/2,50,000) × 100

= 40%

Significance

Return on capital employed is considered to be the best measure of profitability in order to assess the overall performance of the business satisfactorily. It is commonly used as a basis for various managerial decisions because it relates to benefits obtained in the form of income with the sacrifice made in the form of capital invested.

A starting point in budgeting and management planning is the determination of a minimum rate of return on capital invested. All business decisions should result in a reasonable (minimum) return. Investments, which generate rates lower than the minimum rate of return on capital employed, is rejected.

However, it is very difficult to set a standard rate of return on capital employed because a number of factors, such as business risk, the type of the industry, inflation, changes in economic conditions, etc. may influence such a rate. Different views prevail with regard to the standard rate of return. Bank rate, discounted rate on gilt edged securities or some opportunity rate are some of the rates suggested as the norm for this ratio.

Anyhow, it left to the discretion of the management to set some rate against which they are going to compare the actual result with a view to measure their efficiency or the overall performance of the business. This ratio could be supplemented with a number of ratios depending upon the purpose for which it is computed. Some such ratios are dealt in the next few pages.

Advantages of the Concept of Return on Capital Employed

1. It is the only measure which can be said to show satisfactorily the benefits being obtained for the sacrifice involved for the capital invested.
2. It allows external comparisons to be made. The progress of one company or companies may be compared with that of other companies.
3. It is an effective tool for making an internal comparison in respect of different divisions or departments of a company. It may be used as an instrument of control by comparing the relative profitability of different profits.
4. It enables the management to make efficient capital budgeting decisions. The relative profitability of future course of actions, such as expansion of plant, introduction of new product, etc. may be obtained. The return on capital employed can become an integral part of the budgetary control system.
5. It gives ideas for analysis and decisions to bring out effective changes in the financial policies. For example, there should be borrowing when the rate of interest is higher than the rate of return.
6. If the management ensures that an adequate return on capital is earned, many direct benefits may accrue to the business concerned and they are:
   (*a*) Regular and satisfactory dividends to shareholders.
   (*b*) The business should be able to ward off any unexpected competition or other adversities without great difficulties.

RETURN ON SHAREHOLDERS' INVESTMENTS

It is the ratio of net profit to shareholders' investments. It is also called return on proprietors' funds or capital employed. This ratio establishes the profitability from the shareholders' point of view.

Formula

Return on share holders' fund = Net profit after tax and interest/Shareholders' funds × 100

Components

The term 'net profit' as used here, means net income after payment of interest and tax including the non-operating expenses, i.e. non-operating income minus non operation expenses. It is the final income that is available for distribution as dividend to shareholders. Shareholders' funds include both preference and equity shares capital and all reserves and surplus belonging to shareholders.

Example 3

Taking figures from the example given for the computation of return on capital employed, the return on shareholders' funds shall be calculated as follows:

Return on shareholders' fund = (₹ 50,000/ ₹ 2,50,000) × 100
= 20%

This means that the return on proprietors fund is 20 paise per rupee.

Significance

This ratio is another effective measure of the probability of a business. It is one of the most important relationships in financial statement analysis. It is an index to know whether the main objective of the business, i.e. realization of satisfactory net income, has been achieved. It is useful for inter-industry comparison. But, if comparisons are made between two companies belonging to different industries, the value of this ratio would be very much limited since margins and operating costs among industries may vary widely.

RETURN ON EQUITY CAPITAL

This ratio relates to net profits finally available to equity shareholders to the amount of capital invested by them. Alternatively, this ratio could be derived dividing profits available to equity shareholders by shares held by them.

Formula

Return on equity capital = (Net profit – Tax and preference dividend/Equity share capital) × 100

Or

Earning per equity share = (Net profit – Tax and preference dividend/No. of Equity share) × 100

Components

As profits used for calculations are the final profits available to equity shareholders as dividends, the preference dividend and taxes are deducted in order to arrive at such profits. Equity share capital would be the total called-up value of the equity shares.

Example 4

Calculate the earning's per share or return on equity share capital from the following information:

Equity Share Capital (₹ 100 per share)	₹ 10,00,000
9% Preference Share Capital (₹ 100 each)	₹ 5,00,000
Taxation Rate 50% of the net profit	
Net Profit before Tax	₹ 4,00,000

Solution

Return on Equity Share Capital = (Net profit – Tax and preference dividend/
Equity share capital) × 100

= [₹ 4,00,000 – (₹ 2,00,000 + ₹ 45,000)/₹ 1,00,000] × 100

= 15.5%

Earning Per Equity Share = (Net profit – Tax and preference dividend/No. of Equity share) × 100

= (1,55,000/10,000) × 100

= ₹ 15.50 per share.

Significance

This ratio indicates what percentage of profits earned are enjoyed by the equity shareholders. Return on equity share capital or earnings per share helps to determine the market price of the equity share of the company while comparing with the ratios of other companies. It will also indicate whether the capital is effectively used or not.

RETURN ON TOTAL RESOURCES OR TOTAL ASSETS

This ratio is compared to find out the productivity of the total assets. This ratio compares the total profits with the total assets of the business.

Formula

Return on total assets = Net profit after tax and interest/(Total assets – Fictitious assets).

DU POINT CONTROL CHART

The Du Point Control Chart is called as such, because it was first used by the Du Point Company of the USA. The various factors affecting the Return on Investment (ROI) are illustrated through this chart. Return on investment represents the earning power of the business. It depends on two ratios: net profit ratio and capital turnover ratio. A change in any of the two ratios changes the business earning power and it is affected by many factors. The chart exhibits that ROI is affected by a number of factors.

Any change in these factors will affect the return on capital employed. For example, if the cost of goods sold decreases without any corresponding decrease in selling price, the net profit increases and therefore ROI also increases. Similarity, if there is any decrease in the working capital, the total capital employed decreases and therefore in the absence of any decrease in the net profit ROI increases.

The Du Point chart helps the management to identify the areas of problems which affects the profits. In other words, the management can easily visualize different forces affecting the profits and profits which could be improved either by putting capital into effective use which, in turn, results in higher turnover ratio or by better sales efforts which results in higher profit ratio. The same rate of return could be obtained either by a higher net profit ratio but low turnover ratio or by a higher turnover ratio but a low net profit ratio.

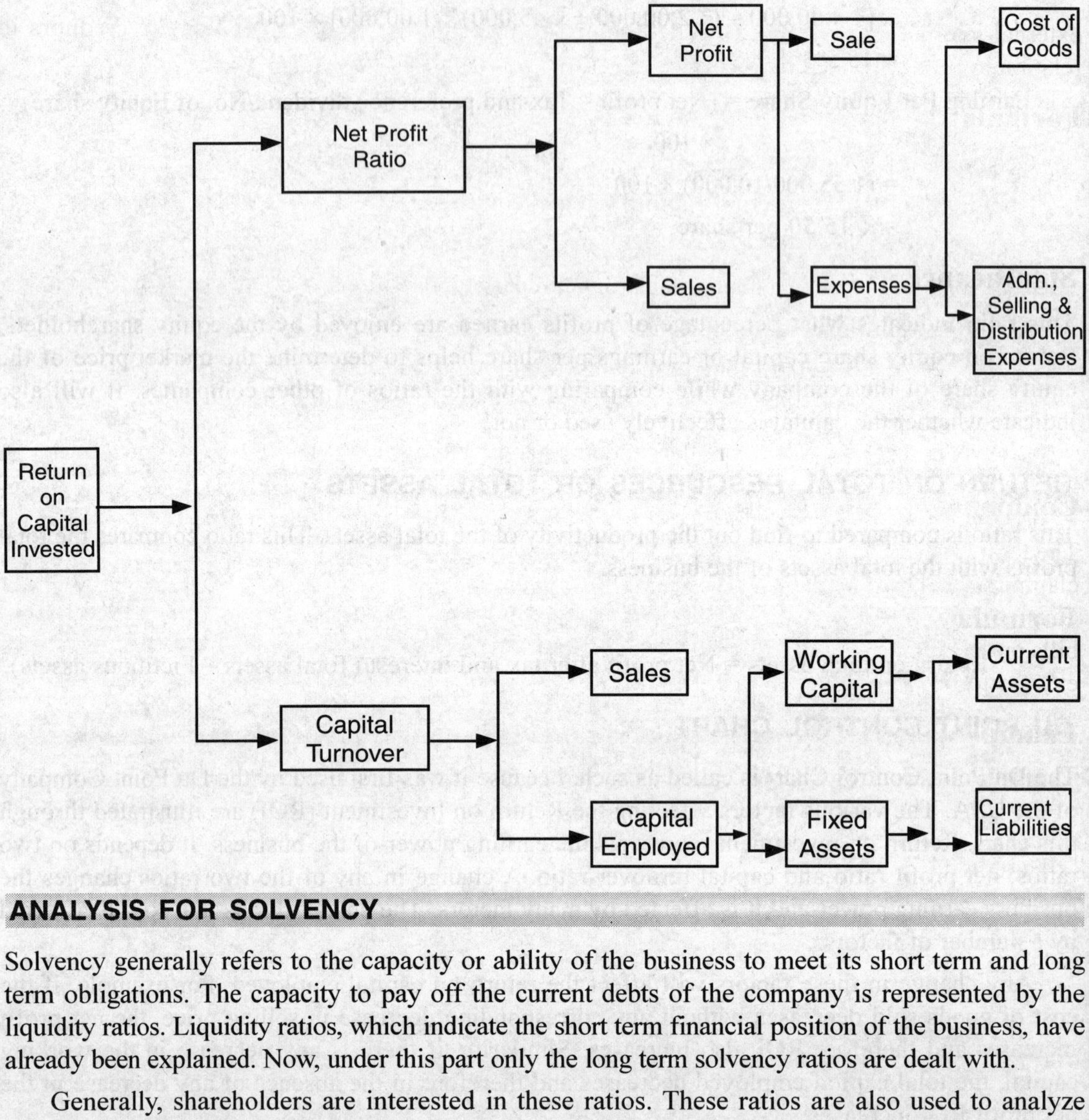

ANALYSIS FOR SOLVENCY

Solvency generally refers to the capacity or ability of the business to meet its short term and long term obligations. The capacity to pay off the current debts of the company is represented by the liquidity ratios. Liquidity ratios, which indicate the short term financial position of the business, have already been explained. Now, under this part only the long term solvency ratios are dealt with.

Generally, shareholders are interested in these ratios. These ratios are also used to analyze the capital structure of the company. They indicate the pattern of financing whether long term requirements have been met out of the long term funds or not. Some selected solvency ratios are discussed below.

DEBT EQUITY RATIO

Meaning

Debt Equity Ratio relates to all external liabilities to owners' recorded claims. It is also known as external-internal equity ratio. It is determined to measure the firm's obligations to creditors in relation to funds invested by owners.

Formula

Generally, it is calculated as

Debt Equity Ratio = External equities/Internal equities

Or

= Outsiders funds/Shareholders funds

As a long term financial ratio, it may be calculated as

= Total long term debts/Total long term funds

Or

= Total long term debts/Shareholders funds

Components

The term External Equities refers to total outside liabilities and internal equities which includes all claims of preference and equity shareholders, such as share capital and reserves and surplus. Outside liabilities include all debts whether long term or short term or in the form of mortgages, bills or debentures. But, when used as a long term financial ratio, only terms debts like debentures, etc. are to be considered.

Example 5

From the following figures, compute the Debt Equity Ratio.

1. Preference Share Capital	₹ 3,00,000
2. Equity Share Capital	₹ 11,00,000
3. Capital Reserves	₹ 5,00,000
4. Profit and Loss Account Balance	₹ 2,00,000
5. 6% Debentures	₹ 5,00,000
6. Sundry Creditors	₹ 2,40,000
7. Bills Payable	₹ 1,20,000
8. Provision for Taxation	₹ 1,80,000
9. Outstanding Creditors	₹ 1,60,000

Solution

Debt Equity Ratio = External equities/Internal equities

= 12,00,000/21,00,000 = 0.57 or 4:7

This means that the External Debts are equal to about 57% of shareholders funds. This indicates that even if the value of assets decreases by 435, creditors' position will not be affected.

Normally, this ratio is expressed as a proportion. It means that for every four rupees worth of creditors' investments the shareholders have invested seven rupees.

Significance

This ratio enables one to ascertain the proportion of shareholders' stake in the business. Excess assibilates tend to cause insolvency. The ratio indicates the extent of assets, cushion available to creditors on liquidation. However, the interpretation of the ratio depends upon the financial and business policy of the company.

While owners try to gain benefits of maintaining control with limited investments, creditors would insist that owners invest more in the business. Hence, an acceptable norm for this ratio is considered and it is 1:1 (both possessing equal interest in the business). Theoretically, if the owner's interest is greater than that of creditors, the financial position is considered to sound. In other words, the business position is highly solvent.

In the analysis of the long term financial position of the business, it enjoys the same importance as the current ratio in the analysis of the short term financial position.

PROPRIETARY RATIO

This is a variant of the Debt Equity Ratio. This ratio relates shareholders' funds to total assets. It is calculated by dividing shareholders' funds by the total tangible assets. This ratio indicates the long term or future solvency position of the company.

Formula

Proprietary Ratio = Shareholders' funds/Total assets or total resources.

Components

Shareholders' funds include preference and equity share capital plus all reserves and surplus items. Total assets include all assets including goodwill. Some authors exclude goodwill from the total assets. In that case, the total shareholders' funds are to be divided by total tangible assets. As total assets are always equal to total liabilities, the latter are also used as denominators in the above formula.

Example 6

Continuing the example used to illustrate the computation of the Debt Equity Ratio, wherein shareholders funds are ₹ 21,00,000 and total assets which are equal to total liabilities are ₹ 33,00,000, the ratio would be

Proprietary Ratio = Shareholders funds/Total liabilities

= (21,00,000/33,00,000) × 100 = 64%

Interpretation

This means that out of every ₹ 1 employed in the business shareholders contribution is about 64%. The difference between this ratio and 100% represents the ratio of other liabilities to total assets. Accordingly, contribution of the creditors would be the remaining 36 paise.

Significance

This ratio throws light on the general financial strength of the company. It has come to be regarded as a test of the soundness of the capital structure. It is of greater importance to creditors, because it enables them to find out the proportion of shareholders' fund in the total assets used in the business.

A high proprietary ratio indicates a relatively secured position to the creditors in the event of liquidation and a low proprietary ratio will include greater risk on the part of creditors. A ratio above 50% is generally considered safe for the creditors.

The Debt Equity Ratio, or proprietary ratio, may be further analyzed into the following:

1. Ratio of fixed assets to shareholders' funds
2. Ratio of current assets to shareholders' funds.

FIXED ASSETS TO PROPRIETORS' FUNDS RATIO

This ratio establishes the relationship between the fixed assets and shareholders' funds. The purpose of this ratio is to indicate the percentage of owners' investment in fixed assets.

Formula

Fixed assets to proprietors fund = (Fixed assets/Proprietors' funds) × 100.

The total fixed assets are considered at their depreciative book value and proprietors funds consist of the same items as internal equities in the case of Debt Equity Ratio. Suppose the depreciated book value of the fixed assets is ₹ 36,000 and the proprietors' funds are ₹ 48,000, the relevant ratio would be:

Fixed assets to proprietors fund = (₹ 36,000/₹ 48,000) × 100

= 75% or 0.75 : 1

From the above computation, it can be ascertained that 75% of shareholders' funds are sunk into fixed assets and 25% supplied by them is invested in working capital. The yardstick for this measure which, may differ from business to business is 65% for industrial undertakings. If the computed ratio is greater than 1, it means that creditors' obligation has been used to acquire a part of the fixed assets.

CURRENT ASSET TO PROPRIETORS' FUNDS RATIO

This ratio establishes the relationship between the current assets and the proprietor's funds. The purpose of this ratio is to indicate the percentage or owner's fund being invested in current assets.

Formula

Current assets to proprietors' fund ratio = (Current assets/Proprietors' fund) × 100

This may be expressed either as a percentage or as a proportion. To illustrate, if the value of the current assets is ₹ 36,000 and the proprietors' funds is ₹ 1,80,000, the relevant ratio is

= (₹ 36,000/1,80,000) × 100

= 20% or 0.2 : 1

This means that 20% of the proprietors' fund has been invested in current assets. Different industries have different norms and therefore this ratio should be studied carefully taking the history of individual concern before relying too much on this ratio. For meaningful, this ratio should be read along with the result given by the fixed assets to proprietors' fund ratio.

DEBT SERVICE RATIO

This ratio relates to fixed interest charges to the income earned by the business. It is also known as interested coverage ratio. It indicates whether the business has earned sufficient profits to pay periodically the interest charges. It is calculated as

Interest coverage ratio = Net profit before interest and tax/Fixed interest charges.

Example 7

The operating profit of Excel Ltd. after charging interest on debentures and tax is a sum of ₹ 1,24,000. The interest charged is ₹ 25,000 and provisions for taxes have been ₹ 1,24,000, being 50% of the actual profits. Calculating the interest on coverage ratio, we find

= (1,24,000 +1,24,000 + 25,000)/25,000

= 2,73,000/25,000 = 11 times approximately

Sometimes, there may be a need to calculate fixed charges ratio. In that case, the ratio is calculated as follows:

Fixed Charges Ratio = (Net profit before interest and tax/Interest and preference dividend)

In case it is desired to calculate the fixed dividend cover, it may be calculated as

Fixed dividend charges ratio = Net profit before interest and tax/preference dividend.

Significance

The interest coverage ratio is very important for the lenders' point of view. It gives an idea on the number of times that fixed interest charges are covered by earnings. It is an index of the financial strength of an enterprise and indicates the margin of safety for the long term creditors. The standard for this ratio for a manufacturing company is that interest charges should be covered six to seven times. A high ratio assures the lender a regular and periodical interest income. But a weak ratio may create some problems to the financial manager in raising funds from the debt sources.

CAPITAL GEARING RATIO

Closely related to solvency ratios is the capital gearing ratio which is mainly used to analyze the capital structure of the company. The term capital gearing or leverage normally refers to the proportion between fixed interest or dividend bearing funds and non-fixed interest or dividend bearing funds. While the former includes funds supplied by debenture holders and preference shareholders, the latter includes equity shareholders' funds.

This ratio relates the equity share capital to debentures and preference share capital.

Formula

Capital gearing ratio = Equity share capital/Fixed interest bearing funds.

Equity share capital for the purpose of calculation of this ratio includes equity share capital and all reserves and surplus items that belong to equity shareholders. Fixed interest bearing funds includes debentures, preference share capital and other long term loans.

It may be noted that the gearing is in inverse ratio to the equity share capital. Highly geared represents low equity share capital and low geared refers to high equity share capital.

Significance

Capital gearing reveals the stability or otherwise of the company's capitalization. It is important not only to the company but also to the prospective investors. It must be carefully planned because it affects the company's capacity to maintain an even distribution policy during difficult trading periods.

Furthermore, its immediate effect may be to enable a company to pay a higher equity dividend when there is only a narrow margin of profit, but its long term effect on the efficiency of the company are far reaching. Distribution policies and the building up of the reserves as well the dividend policy are affected by the company's gearing ratio.

In addition to the capital gearing ratio, the following ratios must also be used to analyze fully the capital structure of the company. These ratios would also throw light, to a certain extent, on the financial strength of the company.

1. Total Investment to long term liabilities ratio compare the share capital to loan capital. Generally a high proportion of long term liabilities are risky to any company which this ratio enables us to find.
2. Current Liabilities to Proprietors' Fund is an index for measuring amounts of funds supplied by short term creditors in the financing of the company.
3. Reserve to Equity Capital Ratio compares reserves to equity which reveals the company's policy with regard to the growth and distribution of dividends. It also indicates the effect of reinvesting profits on share value.

ANALYSIS OF RISK

Risks refer to the variability of the firm's expected or actual returns. The total risk of the business firm could be classified into business risk and financial risks. Business is related to the investment decisions or assets mix of the firm. It can be defined as the variability in return on assets.

The financial risk on the other hand is associated with the financing decisions on the capital mix of the firm. The Equity Shareholders Risk is resuls from the use of debt. Debt causes financial risk by increasing the variability of shareholders' return and threatens the solvency of the firm.

To measure the risk that the company may face in its day-to-day life, attention is paid to what will happen if sales decline. The extent to which shareholders suffer as a result of a fall in sales is the measure of risk. This consists of two parts and they are the effect on earnings before interest and taxes and the effect on earnings after taxes.

The first, the earnings before interest and taxes is measured by what is called the operating leverage and the second the earnings after interest and taxes is measured by financial leverage.

The third measure called the combined leverage is the combination of the first two measures.

OPERATING LEVERAGE

Operating leverage is the relationship between the contribution and earning before interest and taxes and is measure as

Operating Leverage = Contribution (Sales – Variable costs)/Earnings before interest and taxes

It signifies the change that results in earnings before interest and taxes for any change in sales. If operating leverage is 3, it means that for every 1% change in sales, the change in earnings before interest and taxes will be 3% (i.e. three times). A high ratio would indicate a high business risk and a low ratio the low business risk.

Example 8

Sales	₹ 50,000
Less: Variables cost	₹ 30,000
Contribution	₹ 20,000
Less: Fixed cost	₹ 10,000
Earnings before interest and taxes	₹ 10,000

Operating Leverage = Contribution/Earnings before interest and taxes

= 20,000/10,000 = 2 times

This implies that if sales drop to ₹ 40,000 the earnings will drop by 40% (2 times the change in sales – 2 × 20%).

Verification

Sales	₹ 40,000
Less: Variables cost	₹ 24,000
Contribution	₹ 16,000
Less: Fixed cost	₹ 10,000
Earnings before interest and taxes	₹ 6,000

Change in sales = [(₹ 50,000 – ₹ 40,000)/50,000] × 100 = 20%

Change in earnings before interest and taxes

= [(10,000 – 6,000)/10,000] × 100

= 40%.

Financial Leverage

This shows the relationship between earning before interest and taxes, and earning after interest and taxes. It is measured as

= Earning before interest and taxes/Earning after interest and taxes.

Suppose, in the above example, the interest is ₹ 6,000 paid, the earnings after interest is ₹ 4,000. The financial leverage now is 10,000/4,000 = 2.5 times.

It means that for 1% change in earnings before interest and taxes, the earnings after interest will change by 2.5 times. It means that for 1% change in earnings before interest and taxes, the earnings after interest will change by 2.5 times, i.e. 2.5%. In the above example, when sales drop by 20%, earnings before interest and taxes decline by 40%. When earnings before interest and taxes decline by 40%, earnings after interest decreases by 100% (2.5 × 40%).

A high financial leverage indicates a high financial risk and a low financials risk indicates a low risk.

Combined Leverage

Combined leverage is the combination of operating leverage and financial leverage.

Combined leverage = Operation leverage + Financial leverage.

From the above example, the Combined Leverage is 5 (2 × 2.5). This means that for every 1% change in sales, earnings after interest will change by 5%. From the above example, when sales drop by 20%, earnings after interest will decline by 100% (5 × 20%). A high combined leverage indicates a high total risk and a low value indicates a low total risk.

Example 9

From the following selected operating data, determine the degree of operating leverage. Which company has the greater amount of business risk?

Particulars	*Company A*	*Company B*
Sales	5,00,000	6,00,000
Fixed costs	1,50,000	3,00,000
Variable costs	2,50,000	1,50,000

Solution

Particulars	*Company A*	*Company B*
Sales	5,00,000	6,00,000
Less: Variable costs	2,50,000	1,50,000
Contribution	2,50,000	4,50,000
Less: Fixed costs	1,50,000	3,00,000
Operating profit before interest and tax	1,00,000	1,50,000
DOL = (EBIT)	2.50	3.00

Company B has a high business risk as its degree of operating leverage value is greater than the company A.

Example 10

Calculating operating, financial and combined leverage values from the following information we find:

Particulars	*Amount*
Sales	60,000
Variable costs	36,000
Fixed costs	10,000
Interest	4,000

Solution

Particulars	*Amount*
Sales	60,000
Less: Variable costs	36,000
Contribution	24,000
Less: Fixed costs	10,000
Operating profit before interest and tax	14,000
Less: Interest	4,000
Earnings after interest	10,000

DOL = C/EBIT = 24,000/14,000 = 1.71

DFL = EBIT/EAIT = 14,000/10,000 = 1.40

DCL = C/EAI

or = DOL × DFL

= 24,000/10,000 = 2.4

or 1.7 × 1.4 = 2.4

ANALYSIS OF SICKNESS OF FIRMS

Altman has stated that the following ratios in their totality will throw light on whether or not the firm concerned is becoming sick.

(*a*) Working capital/total assets (weight 0.012)

(*b*) Retained earnings/total assets (weight 0.014)

(*c*) EBIT/Total assets (weight 0.033)

(*d*) Market Value of equity/book value of total debt (weight 0.016)

(*e*) Sales/Total Assets (weight 0.999)

The combined value of these ratios is called Z by Altman. According to him, if the value of Z is 1.81, there is a high danger of sickness and it is 2.99, then there is no such danger. In these two values there is a possibility of sickness.

From the ratios suggested by Altman, one can see that the emphasis is mainly on liquidity (first ratio) and profitability (third and fourth). Hence, his analysis of sickness through ratios may be valid.

In India, the situation is different. The Reserve Bank of India applies a rough and ready rule that if a firm suffers a cash loss in the previous year as well in the current year, it is likely to incur cash in the next year and could be declared sick. Because cash is essential for survival, cash losses are surely a point towards sickness. If it is not rectified quickly, it leads to insolvency.

Another measure called 'No Credit Interval' has been developed which indicates how long the concerned firm can continue its operations without having to raise fresh funds. No credit interval is measured as

= [(Cash that can be immediately raised less immediate payment)/
Monthly cash operating costs]

Suppose a firm can raise ₹ 1,00,000 immediately but it will have to pay taxes soon ₹ 80,000, the balance cash will only be ₹ 20,000. If the monthly cash operating costs come to ₹ 40,000, the firm can operate only for 15 days without making further additional borrowing.

The no credit interval should be compared with the operating cycle. If it is longer than the operating cycle, there is not much danger, but if the operating cycle is much longer, the danger of solvency is very much there.

INTER-FIRM COMPARISON

Meaning

Inter firm comparison means comparison of the performance of one company with that of the other in the same industry or trade.

It provides information showing how its operating performances and financial results stand in comparison with those of other firms. It is thus concerned with the individual firm, its success and the role of the management in achieving it. Results of the inter-firm comparison provide the management an instant and vivid picture of how its profitability, its costs, its inventory turnover and other key figures indicate the success or weakness of a business when compared with those of the other firms in the same industry.

MEANING OF INTRA-FIRM COMPARISON

It means comparison of two or more departments of the same firm with a view to make a meaningful analysis for the purpose of improving the efficiency of departments involved.

Both inter and intra-firm comparisons have the same objectives of highlighting the strength and weakness of the system involved by comparative analysis. However, while the first one compares the performances of the firm with other firms the second compares the performance of one department with the other departments of the same firm.

ESSENTIAL CONDITIONS FOR THE INTER-FIRM COMPARISON

It will have to be on the basis of certain tangible figures. Usually, figures relate to costs accounting and profitability. The basis of comparison should be the same in all cases. Hence, the requisites for a meaningful comparison may be listed as follows:

Similarity of Firms

Firms to be compared should be similar in all respects of age, size, character of production, market, etc. For example, the comparison of an old firm with a new firm or a textile firm manufacturing for export market with textile firm mainly manufacturing for domestic market may not yield very significant results.

Similarity in Accounting Practices

Firms to be compared should have uniform accounting practices regarding method of depreciation, valuation of inventories, provisions for gratuity, etc.

RATIOS FOR COMPARISON

The most important ratios used for comparison are as follows:

1. Return on investments (ROI): This ratio can be broken into its two main components namely, profit margin on sales and turnover to capital. Each component may further be analyzed through a number of ratios.

2. Debt equity ratio: This is the ratio of long term debt to the total long term funds. A change in the ratio would indicate a change in the financial policy of the company.

3. Current ratio: This indicates the ability of the company to meet its short term obligations.

4. Turnover ratios: They indicate stock turnover, debtors turnover, fixed assets turnover ratio, etc.

5. Input and output ratio: This ratio is particularly used in the case of manufacturing industries.

Besides the above accounting ratios, certain other figures can also be used for throwing light on the performance of the firm, for example, product wise figure growth in sales, value of company's shares on the stock market, money spent on R & D, etc.

Merits of Comparing the Ratios

1. Ratios indicate trends of the industry or trade. Comparison, therefore, helps developing an insight to understanding business problems in their proper perspective.
2. Weak spots are identified and this leads to remedial actions.
3. Comparison leads to betterment of results.
4. This leads to the avoidance of unfair competition, rather guides in the direction of efforts in a more positive way towards improvement in performance.
5. It develops cost consciousness among the member firms.
6. Members exchange information willingly knowing that confidentiality is not lost. There is mutual trust and confidence and this leads to wider outlook. The attitude to help others finally helps the individual firms.

Demerits

1. Usually, the information for the number of firms is collected by their associations and is kept highly confidential. Even then a few firms hesitate to part with the information of a confidential nature. This would create problems for top management, some extent, for making meaningful decisions.
2. Financial statements used and ratios computed from these statements have certain limitations. Hence, these limitations are transported into the analysis. It is, therefore, necessary to keep these in view while making any comparison.
3. Financial statements ratios fail to take into account the effect of inflation. The ratios calculated may therefore, be distorted by inflationary conditions. Hence, it is necessary to adjust for effects of inflation before making any comparison.

COMPUTATION OF RATIOS

Illustration 1

From the following particulars extracted from the financial statements of ABC & Co., compute the current turnover ratio, liquid ratio, inventory ratio, debtors turnover ratio and creditors turnover ratio.

Particulars	*Amount* [₹]	*Particulars*	*Amount* [₹]
Opening stock	47,000	Sundry debtors	42,000
Closing stock	10,000	Cash	53,000
Sales less returns	2,52,000	Bank	8,000
Provisions for bad debts	2,000	Bills receivables	15,000
Sundry creditors	32,000	Provisions for taxation	15,000
Loose tools	4,000	Bills payable	29,000
Purchases	1,80,000	Marketable securities	8,000

Solution

A. Current Ratio= Current Assets/Current Liabilities

= 1,34,000/76,000 = 1.76

Current assets	*Amount* [₹]	*Amount* [₹]	*Current liabilities*	*Amount* [₹]
Sundry debtors	42,000		Sundry Creditors	32,000
Less: Provisions for bad debts	2,000	40,000	Provisions for taxation	15,000
Cash		1,000	B/P	29,000
B/R		15,000		
Securities		15,000		
Stock		53,000		
		1,34,000		76,000

B. Liquid ratio = Liquid assets/Liquid liabilities

= (1,34,000 – 53,000)/76,000

= 1.07 (approximately)

C. Inventory turnover ratio = Net sales/Average inventory

= 2,52,000/50,000 = 5.04 times

Average inventory = (Opening stock + Closing stock)/2

= (47,000 + 53,000)/2 = 50000

D. Debtors turnover ratio = Total receivables/Credit sales per day

Credit sale per day = Total sales/360 = 2,52,000/360 = 700 per day

Debtors turnover ratio = (Sundry debtors + Bills receivable)/Credit sale per day

= (42,000 + 15,000)/700

= 57,000/700 = 82 days

Alternatively

Debtors turnover ratio = Total sales/average receivable

= 2,52,000/57,000 = 4.42 times

Average collection period = 360/4.42 = 82

E. Credit turnover ratio = Total accounts payable/Credit purchase per day

Credit purchase per day = Total purchase/360

= 1,80,000/360 = 500

Creditors turnover ratio = (32,000 + 29,000) / 500

= 61,000/500 = 122 days

Interpretation

Current Ratio and Liquid Ratio are both satisfactory compared to rule of thumb used for the two ratios. Stock turnover ratio is about 5 times. As cost of goods is not known, the total sales figure has been used. Hence, it could be taken only as a rough indicator of stock velocity. For a meaningful analysis, it should be compared with ratios of the previous years.

Though the average collection period is 82 days, it seems to be very liberal but it is reasonable when compared to the credit period, i.e. 122 days enjoyed by the firm. However, all these ratios should be compared for a series of years and the trend so obtained could be used for the analysis.

Illustration 2

ABC Ltd. sells goods on cash as well as credit, though not installments deferred terms. The following particulars from their books of accounts for the calendar year 2018 is taken. Compute the average collections period.

Particulars	*Amount* [₹]
Total gross sales	2,00,000
Cash sales (included as above)	44,000
Sales returns	12,000
Book debt, as 31-12-2018	20,000
Bills receivables as on 31-12-2018	4,000
Provisions for doubtful debts as 31-12-2018	1,500
Sundry creditors, as on 31-12-2018	12,000

Compute the average collections period.

Solution

Average collection period = Credit sales/360

Credit sales = Total sales – Sales returns – Cash sales

Total gross sales	2,00,000	
Less: Sales returns	12,000	1,88,000
Less: Cash sales		44,000

Total credit sales		1,44,000
Credit sales per day	= 1,44,000/360 = 400	
Average collection period	= Total receivables/Credit sales per day	
	= (20,000 + 4,000)/400	
	= 24,000/400 = 60 days	

Note: It is assumed that the number of working days in a year is 360 and the information regarding provision for Doubtful Debts and Sundry Creditors is not relevant for computation.

Illustration 3

With the following information, calculate the Sundry Debtors, Sundry Creditors and Closing Stock:

Debtors velocity	3 months
Creditors velocity	2 months
Stock velocity	8 times
Bills payable	₹ 10,000
Bills receivables	₹ 4,000
Total sales	₹ 24,000

The Closing Stock is ₹ 2,000 more than the opening stock. Gross profit on the above sales is ₹ 40,000. There are no cash sales and cash purchases. The accounting year consists of 360 working days.

Solution

A. Sundry debtors = Total Debtors – Bills Receivables

Debtors Velocity = (Total debtors/Total credit sales) × 360

Let total debtors = a

90 = (a × 360)/2,40,000

a = (90 × 2,40,000)/360 = 60,000

Sundry debtors = 60,000 – 10,000 = 50,000

B. Sundry creditors

Creditors velocity = (Total creditors/Credit purchase) × 360

Cost of good sold = Opening stock + Purchase – Closing stock

2,00,000 = 24,000 + Purchases – 26,000

Purchase = 2,00,000 + 2,000

= 2,02,000

Let y be the total creditors

Creditors velocity – 60 = $(y \times 360)/2,02,000$

$y = (60 \times 2,02,000)/360$

$= 33,667$ (approximately)

Sundry creditors = Total creditors – Bills payable

= 33,667 – 4,000 = 29,667 (approximately)

C. Closing Stock

Stock velocity = Cost of good sold/Average stock

Cost of goods sold = Sales – Gross profit

2,00,000 = 2,40,000 – 40,000

Stock velocity × 8 = 2,00,000/Average stock

Average stock = 2,00,000/8 = 25000

Average stock = (Opening stock + Closing stock)/2

Closing stock = (2 × Average stock) – Opening stock

= 2 × 25,000 – Opening stock

Closing stock = 2,000 + Opening stock

Adding these two equations

2 closing stock = 52,000/2

Hence, closing stock = 26,000.

Illustration 4

The Balance Sheet of Sen & Co, as on 31-12-2018 is as follows:

Liabilities	*Amount* [₹]	*Assets*		*Amount* [₹]
Share capital		Fixed assets		
10% Preference share 10000 at ₹ 10 each	1,00,000	Land and building		2,00,000
Ordinary shares 20000 at ₹ 10 each	2,00,000	Plant and machinery	3,60,000	
Share premium	50,000	*Less:* Depreciation	1,20,000	2,40,000
Reserves	1,70,000			
Dividend equalization fund	25,000	Motor vehicles	50,000	
10% debentures	25,000	*Less:* Depreciation	30,000	20,000
Creditors	50,000			
Bank overdraft	20,000	Investments		50,000
Provisions for taxation	30,000	Current assets		
		Stock		70000

Contd...

		Debtors	80,000	
		Less: Provisions	2,000	78,000
		Cash		2,000
		Deferred advertisement expenditures		10,000
Total	6,70,000			6,70,000

Calculate the value of the capital employed considering the following factors with the above given data:

1. Freehold land and building are valued at ₹ 2,60,000.
2. Plant and Machinery has a replacement cost of ₹ 4,50,000 and depreciation on replacement cost amount to ₹ 1,50,000.
3. Motor Vehicles would cost ₹ 60,000 to replace and depreciation on replacement cost would be ₹ 36,000.
4. Investments have been analyzed to show that ₹ 40,000 is invested outside the business and ₹ 10,000 inside the business.
5. Included in the stock valuation are items considered obsolete, which amounts to ₹ 2,000.

Solution

Value of capital employed as an 31-12-2018.

Particulars		*Amount* [₹]
Fixed assets:		
Land and building		2,60,000
Plant and machinery	4,50,000	
Less: Depreciation	1,50,000	3,00,000
Motor Vehicles	60,000	
Less: Depreciation	36,000	24,000
Investments made in the business		10,000
Current assets:		
Stock	68,000	
Debtors	78,000	
Less: Provisions	2,000	
		1,48,000
Less: Current liabilities		
Creditors	50,000	
Bank overdraft	20,000	
Provisions for taxation	30,000	1,00,000
		48,000
		6,42,000

Alternate method:

Particulars			*Amount* [₹]
Issued capital:			
Preference capital		1,00,000	
Equity share capital		2,00,000	
			3,00,000
Share premium			50,000
Reserves			1,70,000
Dividend equalization fund			25,000
10% debentures			25,000
Add: Land and Buildings		60,000	
Plant and machinery		60,000	
Motor vehicles		4,000	
Total		1,24,000	
Less: Stock	2,000		
Assets not included in capital employed:			
Investment outside the business	40,000		
Deferred advertisement expenses	10,000		
		52,000	72,000
			6,42,000

Illustration 5

Redraft the following financial statements for the purpose of analysis and then compute the following ratios.

1. Gross profit ratio
2. Return on capital ratio
3. Operating profit ratio
4. Net profit ratio
5. Current ratio
6. Liquid ratio
7. Stock turnover ratio

Profit and Loss Account

Particulars	*Amount Dr.* [₹]	*Particulars*	*Amount Cr.* [₹]
To Opening stock		By sales	2,00,000
Raw materials	10,000	By Closing stock:	
Finished goods	20,000	Raw materials	30,000
To Purchase of raw material	60,000	Finished goods	20,000
To Wages	40,000	By Profit on sale of shares	10,000
To Factory expense	20,000		
To Administration expense	10,000		
To Selling & Distribution expense	10,000		
To Interest on debentures	2,000		
To Loss on sale point	13,000		
To Net profit	75,000		
Total	2,60,000		2,60,000

Balance Sheet

Liabilities	*Amount* [₹]	*Assets*	*Amount* [₹]
Share capital		Fixed assets	50,000
Equity @ ₹ 10	20,000	Stock of raw materials	30,000
Preference @ ₹ 10	20,000	Stock of finished goods	20,000
Reserves	20,000	Books debt	20,000
5% Debentures	40,000	Cash	15,000
Creditors	20,000		
Bills payable	10,000		
Bank overdraft	5,000		
Total	1,35,000		1,35,000

Solution

Income Statement **Amount [₹]**

Sales		2,00,000	
Less: Cost of goods sold			
Raw material consumption – opening stock	10,000		
Add: Purchase	60,000		
	70,000		
Less: Closing stock	30,000	40,000	
Wages		40,000	
Factory expenses		20,000	
Cost of production		1,00,000	
Add: Opening stock of finished goods		20,000	
		1,20,000	
Less: Closing stock of finished goods		20,000	1,00,000
Gross profit			1,00,000
Less: Operating expense			
Administrative expense	10,000		
Selling and distribution expense	10,000		20,000
			80,000
Add: Net operating profit			
Non-trading income profit on sale of shares			10,000
			90,000
Less: Plant trading expenses of losses - loss on point of sale			13,000
Net profit before interest and taxes			77,000
Less: Interest on debentures			2,000
Net Profit before taxes			75,000

Balance Sheet			Amount [₹]
Cash balance			15,000
Book debts			20,000
			35,000
Liquid assets			
Raw material stock	30,000		
Finished goods	20,000		50,000
Current assets			85,000
Less: Current liabilities			
Sundry creditors	20,000		
B/P	10,000	30,000	
Liquid liabilities; Bank overdraft		5,000	35,000
Working capital			50,000
Add: Fixed assets			50,000
Capital employed			1,00,000
Less: 5% Debentures		40,000	
Shareholders fund		20,000	60,000
Equity Shareholders' net worth			40,000
Represented by Equity share capital		20,000	
Reserves		20,000	

Calculation of Ratios

1. **Gross Profit Ratio** = (Gross profit/Sales) × 100
   = (1,00,000/2,00,000) × 100 = 50%
2. **Net Profit Ratio** = (Net profit/Sales) × 100
   = (75,000/2,00,000) × 100 = 37.5%
3. **Operating Ratio** = (Operating costs/Sales) × 100
   = (1,20,000/2,00,000) × 100 = 60%

   Alternatively

   = (Operating profit /Sales) × 100
   = (8,0000/2,00,000) × 100 = 40%
4. **Return on Capital Employed**
   = (Operating profit/Capital employed) × 100
   = (80,000/1,00,000) × 100 = 80%

5. **Current Ratio** = (Current assets/Current liabilities)
= 85,000/35,000 = 2.43 times
6. **Liquid Ratio** = (Liquid assets/Liquid liabilities)
= 35,000/30,000 = 1.17 times
7. **Stock Turnover Ratio**= Cost of goods sold/Average stock*
(*Average stock of raw materials and finished goods)
= 1,00,000/40,000 = 2.5 times
8. **Raw Material Turnover Ratio** = Materials Consumed/Average raw materials inventory
= 40,000/20,000 = 2 times
9. **Finished Goods Turnover Ratio** = Cost of goods sold/Average finished goods stock
= 1,00,000/20,000 = 5 times

Illustration 6

From the following information, find out the sales, closing stock, sundry debtors and sundry creditors:

Gross profit ratio	25%
Debtors turnover ratio	4 months
Stock turnover ratio	4 times
Creditors turnover ratio	6 months

Closing stock is ₹ 10,000 more than the opening stock. Bills Receivables amount to ₹ 65,000 and Bills Payable to ₹ 80,000. Cost of goods sold for the year is ₹ 9,00,000.

Solution

Calculation of Sales:

Gross profit ratio = 25%
Cost of good sold to sales = 75%
Sales = Cost of goods sold × (100/75)
= 9,00,000 × (100/75) = 12,00,000

Calculation of Closing Stock:

Stock turnover ratio = Cost of goods sold/average stock = 4
Average stock = 9,00,000/4
= 2,25,000
Closing stock = Average stock + ½ (Difference between opening stock and closing stock)
= 2,25,000 + {1/2 × 10,000}
= 2,30,000

Calculation of Sundry Debtors:

Accounts receivables = Sales × Debtors turnover ratio

= 12,00,000 × 4/12 = 4,00,000

Less: Bills receivables = 65,000

Sundry debtors = 3,35,000

Calculation of Sundry Creditors:

Purchases = Cost of goods sold = Closing stock – Opening stock

= 9,00,000 + 2,30,000 – 2,20,000

= 9,10,000

Accounts payable = Purchase × Creditors turnover ratio

= 9,10,000 × 6/12 = 4,55,000

Less: Bills payable = 80,000

Sundry Creditors = 3,75,000

Illustration 7

The following are the summarized profit and loss account of Sham Ltd. for the year ended on 31-12-2018 and the balance sheet as on that date:

To Opening stock	99,500	By Sales	8,50,000
To Purchases	5,45,250	By Closing stock	1,49,000
To Incidental expenses	14,250		
To Gross profit	3,40,000		
	9,99,000		9,99,000
To Operating expenses:			
Selling & distribution expenses	30,000	By Gross profit	3,40,000
Administrative expenses	1,50,000		3,000
Finance charges	15,000	By Profit on sale of shares	6,000
To Non-operating expenses			
Loss on sale of assets	4,000		
To Net profit	1,50,000		
	3,49,000		3,49,000

Balance Sheet as on 31-12-2018

Liabilities	*Amount* [₹]	*Assets*	*Amount* [₹]
Issued Capital:		Land and Building	1,50,000
2000 Equity shares of ₹ 100 each	2,00,000	Plant & Machinery	80,000
Reserves	90,000	Stock	1,49,000
Current liabilities	1,30,000	Sundry Debtors	71,000
P & L a/c	60,000	Cash and Bank	30,000
	4,80,000		4,80,000

From the above statement, you are required to calculate the following ratios and state the purpose they serve:

1. Current ratio
2. Liquid ratio
3. Operating ratio
4. Stock turnover ratio
5. Return on total resources
6. Turnover of fixed assets.

Solution

1. Current Ratio = Current assets/Current liabilities
   = (1,49,000 + 71,000 + 30,000)/1,30,000
   = 2,50,000/1,30,000 = 1.923 times (approximately)
   = or 1.923 : 1
2. Liquid Ratio = Liquid assets/Liquid liabilities
   = (71,000 + 30,000)/1,30,000
   = 1,01,000/1,30,000 = 0.78 (approximately)
   = or 0.78 : 1

Compared to the standard of 2 : 1 expected for the Current Ratio, the actual ratio of 1.923 is very near. But the liquid ratio which is 0.78 : 1 against the standard for 1 : 1, reveals that a large part of the current assets consists of stock. Hence, it may be inferred that the liquid position is not satisfactory because the stock is not easily convertible into cash.

3. Operating Ratio = (Operating cost/Net sales) × 100
   = {(5,10,000 + 1,95,000)/8,50,000} × 100
   = (7,05,000/8,50,000) × 100 = 83% (approximately)

Cost of goods sold = (Opening stock + Purchase + Incidentals expenses – Closing stock)

= 99,500 + 5,45,250 + 14,250 – 14,90,000

= 5,10,000

For every rupee worth of sales, the ratio indicates that 83 paise constitute cost of goods sold and operating expense.

4. Stock turnover ratio = Cost of goods sold/Average inventory at cost

Average inventory = (99,500 + 1,49,000)/2 = 1,24,250

Stock turnover ratio = 5,10,000/1,24,250 = 4.1 times

During 2018, the stock turned over slightly more than 4 times. However, it should be compared with the previous year's ratios for arriving at any conclusions.

5. Return on total resources = Net profit/Total assets

= 1,50,000/4,80,000 = 0.31

= or 0.31 : 1

The business has earned a return of 31 paise for everyone rupee on total resources employed. This ratio shows a favourable position.

6. Turnover of fixed assets = Net sales/Fixed sales

= 8,50,000/2,30,000 = 3.71

= or 3.71 : 1

This shows that every rupee worth of fixed assets has been used to generate net sales of ₹ 3.70. This ratio may also be calculated using the cost of goods sold instead of net sales as follows

Turnover of fixed assets = Cost of goods sold/Fixed assets

= 51,00,000/2,30,000 = 2.22

= or 2.22 : 1

This means that every rupee invested in fixed assets results in the sale of goods costing ₹ 2.22.

Illustration 8

A & C Co. has been operating for two years. The most important facts from its published accounts are given below:

Balance Sheet

Liabilities	*2018 Amount* [₹]	*2019 Amount* [₹]	*Assets*	*2018 Amount* [₹]	*2019 Amount* [₹]
Equity share capital @ ₹ 10 each	10,000	10,000	Fixed assets depreciation	20,000	22,000
Reserves	2,000	3,000	Stocks	3,000	6,000
P & L a/c	3,000	2,000	Debtors	3,000	6,000
Mortgage	8,000	8,000	Cash and bank	4,000	2,000
Bank overdraft	-	2,000			
Creditors	5,000	7,000			
Proposed dividends	1,000	2,000			
Provisions for taxes	1,000	2,000			
	30,000	36,000		30,000	36,000

Profit and Loss Account

Particulars	2018 *Amount* [₹]	2019 *Amount* [₹]	*Particulars*	2018 *Amount* [₹]	2019 *Amount* [₹]
To interest on mortgage	480	480	By balance c /d	—	3,000
To directors' remuneration	1,000	3,000	By profit for the year after normal running cost & depreciation	9,000	8,000
To provision of taxes	1,000	2,000			
To dividends	1,000	2,000			
To transfer to reserves	2,000	1,000			
To balance c/d	3,520	2,520			
	9,000	11,000		9,000	11,000

You are told that total sales amount to ₹ 60,000 in 2018 and ₹ 50,000 in 2019. Examine details from the point of view of

(*a*) profitability (*b*) solvency position

(*c*) sales (*d*) capital structure

Solution

(*a*) Profitability

(*i*) Return on capital employed = (Profit before tax and interest/ average capital employed) × 100

For 2018 = (8,000/19,740) × 100 = 40.5%
For 2019 = (5,000/21,740) × 100 = 23.0%
Profits for the year = Profits – Directors remuneration
Profits for 2018 = 9,000 – 1,000 = 8,000
Profits for 2019 = 8,000 – 3,000 = 5,000
Average capital employed

	2018 Amount [₹]	2019 Amount [₹]
Share capital	10,000	10,000
Reserves	2,000	3,000
P&L a/c	3,000	2,000
Loan on mortgage	8,000	8,000
Capital employed at the end	23,000	23,000

Or

	2018	2019
Fixed assets	20,000	22,000
Adding: Working capital	3,000	1,000
	23,000	23,000

Average Capital Employed = Capital employed at the end – ½ (Profits after tax and interest)
For the year 2018 = {23,000 – ½ (9,000 – 2,480)}
= 19740
For the year 2019 = {23,000 – ½ (8,000 – 5,480)}
= 21,740

(*ii*) Return on total resources = (Profit before tax and interest/Total assets) × 100
For the year 2018 = (8,000/30,000) × 100 = 27% (approximately)

(*iii*) Return on shareholders' fund (Net profit after tax and interest/Shareholders' fund) × 100
For the year 2018 = {(9,000 – 2,480)/15,000} × 100
= (6,520/15,000) × 100 = 43% (approximately). For the year 2019
= {(8,000 – 5,480)/15,000} × 100
= (2,520/15,000) × 100 = 17% (approximately)

(*iv*) Return on equity capital = Profit after tax and interest/Equity capital
For the year 2018 = (6,250/10,000) × 100
= 65.2% (approximately)
For the year 2019 = (2,520/10,000) × 100
= 25.2% (approximately)

(*v*) Net profit ratio = (Net profit/Sales) × 100

For the year 2018 = (6,520/60,000) × 100

= 10.8% (approximately)

For the year 2019 = (2,520/50,000) × 100

= 5.0% (approximately)

(*b*) Solvency position – Short-term solvency

(*i*) Current ratio = Current assets/Current liabilities

For the year 2018 = 10,000/7,000

= 1.4 : 1 (approximately)

For the year 2019 = 14,000/13,000

= 1.1 : 1 (approximately)

(*ii*) Liquid Ratio = Liquid assets/ Liquid liabilities

For the year 2018 = 7,000/7,000

= 1 : 1

For the year 2019 = 8,000/11,000

= 0.73: 1 (approximately)

Long term solvency

(*i*) Debt equity ratio = External equities/Internal equities

For the year 2018 = 15,000/15,000

= 1 : 1

For the year 2019 = 21,000/15,000

= 1.4: 1 (approximately)

(*ii*) Proprietary ratio = Shareholders' fund/Total assets

For the year 2018 = 15,000/30,000

= 0.5 : 1

For the year 2019 = 15,000/36,000

= 0.42: 1 (approximately)

(*iii*) Fixed assets to shareholder's fund ratio = Fixed assets/Shareholder's fund

For the year 2018 = 20,000/15,000

= 1.33 : 1 (approximately)

For the year 2019 = 22,000/15,000

= 1.46: 1 (approximately)

(*iv*) Interest coverage ratio = Profit before tax and interest/Fixed interest charges

For the year 2018 = 8,000/480

= 16.67 times (approximately)

For the year 2019 = 5,000/480

= 10.5 times (approximately)

(*c*) Sales

(*i*) Debt turnover ratio = Debtors/Sales per day

For the year 2018

Sales per day = 60,000/360 = 1,000/6

Debt turnover ratio = 3,000/(1,000/6)

= (3,000 × 6)/1,000 = 18 days

For the year 2018

Sales per day = 50,000/360 = 5,000/36

Debt turnover ratio = 6,000/(5,000/36)

= (6,000 × 36)/5,000 = 43.2 days

(*ii*) Stock turnover ratio = Sales/Average stock

For the year 2018 = 60,000/3,000

= 20 times

For the year 2019 = 50,000/4500

= 11 times (approximately)

(*iii*) Total assets turnover ratio = Sales/Total assets

For the year 2018 = 60,000/30,000

= 2 : 1

For the year 2019 = 50,000/36,000

= 1.4 : 1 (approximately)

(*d*) Capital structure

(*i*) Capital gearing ratio = Equity capital/Fixed interest bearing securities

For the year 2018 = 15,000/8,000

= 1.9 : 1

For the year 2019 = 15,000/8,000

= 1.9 : 1 (approximately)

Internal Analysis

1. Operating expenses (director's remuneration) have increased despite reduction in both sales and operating profits in 2019 compared to 2018.
2. All profitability ratios have greatly declined in 2019 compared to 2018.
3. The short term solvency or liquidity position, as revealed by current ratio and quick ratio are also highly unfavourable in the year 2019 compared to 2018. They are far below the standards expected for these ratios.
4. However, the long-term solvency ratios are not bad, though all the ratios are not found satisfactory in 2019 compared with 2018.
5. The capital structure remains the same for both the years. But the sales and profits have declined. At the same time, dividend in 2019 is 100% more than in 2018.
6. As regards Turnover Ratios, it may be said that all the ratios are highly unsatisfactory for 2019 considering the ratios in 2018. However, in the absence of further details it is very difficult to make comments about these ratios.

It may therefore be concluded that operating as well as financial performance, of the business are not satisfactory during the year 2019 as compared with 2018. Necessary steps should be taken to tone up the efficiency of financial management.

Illustration 9

From the following particulars, draw up the balance sheet of the company:

Current ratio	2.5
Quick ratio	1.5
Net working capital	₹ 30,000
Stock turnover ratio	6 times
Cost of sales/Closing stock	20%
Gross profit ratios	
Fixed asset turnover ratio (on cost of sales)	2 times
Debtors turnover ratio	2 months
Fixed assets to shareholders net worth	0.80
Reserves and surplus capital	0.50

Solution

Current ratio = 2.5 : 1

Current assets – Current liabilities = Working capital

$$2.5 - 1 = 30,000$$

$$1.5 = 30,000$$

$$1 = 20,000$$

Thus, Current liabilities is ₹ 20,000

Current assets = Current liabilities × 2.5

= 20,000 × 2.5 = 50,000

Liquid ratio = 1.5 : 1

Liquid liabilities are equal to current liabilities.

Therefore, Liquid assets = 20,000 × 1.5 = ₹ 30,000

Stock = Current assets – Liquid assets

Stock = 50,000 – 30,000 = 20,000

Stock turnover ratio = Cost of sales/Stock

6 = Cost of sales/20,000

Cost of sales = 20,000 × 6 = 1,20,000

Gross profit ratio = 20%

Therefore, cost of sales to sales ratio = 80%

Sales = (Cost of sales/Cost of sales to sales ratio) × 100

= (1,20,000/80) × 100 = 1,50,000

Fixed assets turnover ratio (Cost of sales/fixed assets) = 2

Fixed assets = Cost of sales/2

= 1,20,000/2 = 60,000

Debtors turnover ratio = (Receivables/Sales) × 360

60 days = (Debtors/1,50,000) × 360

Debtors = (1,50,000/360) × 60 = 25,000

Bank = Liquid assets – Debtors

= 30,000 – 25,000 = 5,000

Fixed assets to shareholders' net worth

0.80 = Fixed assets/Shareholders' net worth

0.80 × Shareholders' net worth = Fixed assets

Shareholders' net worth = 60,000/0.80

= 75,000

Reserves and surplus to capital = 1.5 : 1

Shareholders' net worth = Capital and reserves and surplus

According to the above ratio, it is 1.5 when reserves and surplus is 0.5 and capital is 1.

But the actual shareholders' net worth is ₹ 75,000, which is equal to 1.5.

Therefore, reserves and surplus = (75,000 × 0.5)/1.5

= 25,000

Capital = (75,000 × 1)/1.5

= 50,000

Balance Sheet

Liabilities	*Amount* [₹]	*Assets*	*Amount* [₹]
Share capital:	50,000	Fixed assets:	60,000
Reserves	25,000	Stock	20,000
Long term loans (balancing figure)	15,000	Debtors	25,000
Current liabilities	20,000	Bank	5,000
	1,10,000		1,10,000

Illustration 10

Balance Sheet of ENPEE Ltd.

as on 31-12-2018

Liabilities	*Amount* [₹]	*Assets*	*Amount* [₹]
Share capital:		Fixed assets:	
30000 share of ₹ 10 each	3,00,000	Freehold property (WDV)	1,80,000
6000 preference shares of 10 each	60,000	Plant and machinery (WDV)	2,00,000
Reserves and surplus:		Furniture (WDV)	60,000
General reserves	48,000	Vehicles (WDV)	40,000
P & L A/C	48,000	Investments in subsidiary company (market value is ₹ 75000)	60,000
Secured loans:		Current assets:	
8% debentures	2,40,000	Stock at cost	90,000
(1/10 of the debentures are to be redeemed in 2018)		Debtors (outstanding for more than 6 months) ₹ 15000	60,000
Current liabilities	60,000	Cash	30,000
		Bills receivables	30,000
		Miscellaneous expenditure:	
		Preliminary expenses	6,000
	7,56,000		7,56,000

Comment on solvency position of the company.

Solution

In order to assess the long-term financial or solvency position of the business, the following ratios may be worked out:

1. Debt equity ratio
2. Proprietary ratio – Overall, fixed assets and current assets
3. Capital gearing ratio

Debt – Equity ratio = External equities/Internal equities

External equities = Debentures + Creditors

Internal equities = Equity capital + Preference capital + Reserves and Surplus – Preliminary expenses

External equities = 2,40,000 + 60,000 = 3,00,000

Internal equities = 3,00,000 + 60,000 + 48,000 + 48,000 – 60,000
= 4,50,000

Debt – Equity ratio = 3,00,000/4,50,000
= 0.67 : 1

This ratio may be compared considering only long-term debts. In that case, the ratio is as follows:

Debt equity ratio = Long-term debt/shareholder's funds

Long-term debt = Debentures – Debentures due for redemption in 2018
= 2,40,000 – 24,000 = 2,16,000

Debt equity ratio = 2,16,000/4,50,000
= 12 : 25

In both cases, the debt equity ratio is favourable and therefore the solvency position is very sound.

Proprietary ratio = Shareholders'/(Total assets – Fictitious assets)
= 4,50,000/(7,56,000 – 6,000)

Complemented by

Fixed assets to shareholders' fund = Fixed assets/Shareholders' fund
= 4,80,000/4,50,000
= 16 : 15

Current assets to shareholders' fund = Current assets/Shareholders' fund
= 240000/450000
= 7 : 15

A variant to the first one may be computed as follows:

Fixed assets to total-term funds = Fixed assets/Total long-term funds

= 5,40,000/6,66,000

= 90 : 111

Proprietary ratio and the complementary ratios also indicate sound financial position.

Capital gearing ratio = Equity capital/Fixed interest or dividend bearing Funds

= (4,00,000 + 48,000 + 48,000 – 60,000)/(2,16,000 + 60,000)

= 3,90,000/2,76,000 = 1.41 : 1

As the equity capital is more than the amount of fixed interest or dividend bearing funds, the capital structure is low geared. Hence, the financial position is highly stable.

In an absolute sense and in the absence of comparable ratios no objection can be raised to any of the ratios and therefore the financial position of the company may be considered as highly sound.

PRACTICAL PROBLEMS

Problem 1

Calculate the operating ratio

Item	*₹ in lakhs*
Sales	17,874
Sales returns	4
Other income	53
Cost of sales	15,440
Administrative and selling expenses	1,843
Depreciation	63
Interest expense (non-operating)	456

Solution

Operating ratio = (Operating cost/Net sales) × 100

Operating cost = Cost of goods sold + Operating expenses

Net sales = Total sales – Sales returns

Operating ratio = {(15,440 + 1,843 + 63)/(17,874 – 4)} × 100

= (17,346/17,870) × 100 = 97.07%

Operating ratio is very high and therefore it is highly unsatisfactory. A high operation ratic generally indicates inefficiency.

Problem 2

The following details are taken from the books of Arun stores:

Item	*₹ in lakhs*
Sales	33,984
Sales returns and allowances	380
Stock at the beginning of the year at cost price	1,378
Stock at the close of the year at cost price	1,814
Gross profit for the year	8,068

You are required to calculate the purchases and the rate of stock turnover.

Solution

(a) Purchase

Sales	33,984
Sales returns and allowances	380
Net sales	33,604
Less: Gross profit	8,068
Cost of goods sold	25,536
Add: Closing stock	1,814
	27,350
Less: Opening stock	1,378
Purchases	25,972

(b) Stock turnover ratio

Average stock = (Opening stock + Closing stock)/2

= (1,378 + 1,814)/2 = 1,596

Stock turnover ratio = Cost of goods sold/Average stock

= 25,536/1,596 = 16.

Problem 3

(*a*) A trade carries an average stock valued at cost price of ₹ 40,000 and turnover five times per year. If he marks his stock by 20% on selling price, what is his gross profit for the year?

(*b*) Current liabilities of a company are ₹ 3,00,000. Its current ratio is 3 : 1 and quick ratio is 1 : 1. Calculate the value of the stock in trade.

Solution

(*a*) Average stock at cost = ₹ 40,000

Stock turnover ratio = 5 = Cost of goods sold/Average stock

Cost of goods sold/40,000 = 5

= 5 × 40,000

= 2,00,000

Gross profit = 20% on sales

If sales = 100, Gross profit = 20 and cost = 80

If cost = 80 then gross profit = 20

Cost = 2,00,000 then gross profit = (2,00,000 × 20)/80 = 50,000

(*b*) Current ratio = 3 : 1

Current liabilities = ₹ 3,00,000

Current asset = 3,00,000 × (3/1) = 9,00,000

Quick ratio = 1 : 1

Assuming that there is no bank overdraft, current liabilities are equal to liquid assets, i.e. ₹ 3,00,000.

Stock = Current assets – Liquid assets

= 9,00,000 – 3,00,000 = 6,00,000

Problem 4

Following is the profit and loss account of Excel Ltd:

To Opening stock	50,000	By Sales	2,60,000
To Purchases	1,25,000	*Less:* Sales returns	10,000
To Manufacturing expenses	12,500		2,50,000
To Office & administrative expenses	12,500	By Closing stock	25,000
To Selling & distribution expenses	12,000		
To Preliminary expenses written off	5500		
To Net profit	57,500		
	2,75,000		2,75,000

Calculate

(*a*) Gross profit ratio (*b*) Net profit ratio

(*c*) Operating ratio (*d*) Stock turnover ratio

(*e*) Expenses ratio.

Solution

(*a*) Gross profit ratio = (Gross profit/Net sales) × 100
= (8,75,00/2,50,000) × 100 = 35%

(*b*) Net profit ratio = (Net profit/Net sales) × 100
= (57,500/2,50,000) × 100 = 23%

(*c*) Operating ratio = {(Cost of good sold + Operating expenses gross)/ Net sales} × 100
= (1,89,500/2,50,000) × 100 = 75.8%

(*d*) Stock turnover ratio = Cost of goods sold/Net sales
Cost of goods sold = (Net sales – Gross profit)
= 2,50,000 – 87,500 = 1,62,500
= 1,62,500/2,50,000 = 4.33 times

(*e*) Expenses ratio
Manufacturing expenses ratio = (Manufacturing expenses/Net sales) × 100
= (12,500/2,50,000) × 100 = 5%

Office and administration expenses ratio
= (Office and administration expenses/Net sales) × 100
= (15,500/2,50,000) × 100 = 6%

Selling and distribution expenses ratio
= (Selling and distribution expenses/Net sales) × 100
= (12,000/2,50,000) × 100 = 4.8%

Problem 5

Presented below is the financial information or two companies X and Y belonging to the same industry

	X Ltd.	Y Ltd.
Current ratio	3.0 : 1	2.0 : 1
Acid test ratio	1.8 : 1	1.1 : 1
Debt equity ratio	30%	40%
Number of time interest earned (interest coverage ratio)	6	5

Assume that you are a loan officer of a bank and both the companies have requested a loan of equal amount to be repaid over the next two years.

(*i*) If you could grant a loan to only one company which would it be?

(*ii*) If you could grant a loan to both the companies, would you be willing to do so? Explain.

Solution

1. Loan would be granted to company X Ltd. for the following reasons:
   (*a*) Its debt equity ratio is lower than that of the company Y Ltd.
   (*b*) Its interest coverage ratio is higher than that of the company Y Ltd.
   (*c*) Because the period involved is only two years, the bank would not overlook the liquidity ratio, which too is higher than those of the company Y Ltd.
2. Yes, the loans can be granted to both the companies. Y's debt equity ratios of 40% and interest coverage of 5 times are fairly satisfactory solvency ratios. Furthermore, its liquidity ratio also meets, the desired standards.

Problem 6

From the following information of a chemical company, prepare the proforma balance sheet its sales are ₹ 32,00,000:

Sales to net worth	2.3 times
Current debt to net worth	42%
Total debt to net worth	75%
Current ratio	2.9 times
Net sales to inventory	4.7 times
Average collection period (assume 360 days)	64 days
Fixed assets to net worth	53.2 %

Solution

Liabilities	*Amount* [₹]	*Assets*	*Amount* [₹]
Net worth	13,91,304	Fixed assets	7,40,173
Long- term debt	4,59,130	Cash	4,44,869
Current debt	5,84,348	Stock	6,80,851
		Debtors	5,68,889
	24,34,782		24,34,782

Working Notes:

1. Net worth = 32,00,000/2.3 = ₹ 13,91,304
2. Current ratio = (13,91,304 × 42)/100 = ₹ 5,84,348
3. Total debt = (13,91,304 × 75)/100 = ₹ 10,43,478
4. Long-term debt = 10,43,478 – 5,84,348 = ₹ 10,43,478

5. Fixed assets = (13,91,304 × 532)/1,000 = ₹ 7,40,173
6. Current assets = 5,84,348 × 2.9 = ₹ 16,94,609
7. Inventory = 32,00,000/4.7 = ₹ 6,80,851
8. Debtors = (32,00,000 × 64)/360 = ₹ 5,68,889
9. Cash = 16,94,609 – (6,80,851 + 5,68,889) = ₹ 4,44,869

Problem 7

Using the information, complete the balance sheet given below:

Gross profit (20% of sales)	₹ 60,000
Shareholder's equity	₹ 50,000
Credit sales to total assets	80%
Total assets turnover	3 times
Inventory turnover (to cost of sales)	8 times
Average collection period (360 days year)	18 days
Current ratio	1.6
Long-term debt equity	40%

Solution

Balance Sheet

Liabilities	*Amount* [₹]	*Assets*	*Amount* [₹]
Creditors	30,000	Cash	6,000
Long term debts	20,000	Debtors	12,000
Shareholders equity	50,000	Inventory	30,000
		Fixed assets	52,000
	1,00,000		1,00,000

Working Notes:

1. Gross profit ratio = (Gross profit/Sales) × 100
   Sales = ₹ 60,000/20% = ₹ 3,00,000
   Credit sales = 80% of 300000 = ₹ 2,40,000
   Cost of sales = 300000 – 2,40,000 = ₹ 60,000
2. Inventory turnover ratio = Cost of goods sold/Inventory = 8
   Inventory = 2,40,000/8 = 30,000
3. Debtors turnover ratio = Credit sales/Debtors
   = 360 days/average collection period
   = 360/18 = 20 times

4. Total assets turnover ratio	= Sales/Total sales = 3
Total liabilities	= 3,00,000/3 = ₹ 1,00,000
5. Debt equity ratio	= 40%
Long term debt	= 40% of 50,000 = ₹ 20,000
6. Creditors	= Total liabilities – Equity – Long-term debt
	= 1,00,000 – 50,000 – 20,000 = ₹ 30,000
7. Current ratio	= Current assets/Current liabilities
1.6	= Current assets/30,000
Current assets	= 30,000 × 1.6 = ₹ 4,80,000
8. Fixed assets	= 1,00,000 – 48,000 = ₹ 52,000
9. Cash	= 48,000 – 30,000 – 12,000 = ₹ 6,000

Problem 8

From the projected financial plan of Navjeevan Trading Company Ltd., find the use of the accounting ratios:

Estimated annual sales	₹ 2,00,000
Sales to net worth	2.5 times
Current debt to net worth	25%
Total debt to net worth	60%
Current ratio	3.6 times
Net sales to inventory	4 times
Average collection period (taken as 360 days in a year)	36 days
Fixed assets to net worth	70%

On the basis of the above information, prepare a proforma balance sheet of the company.

Solution

Sales to net worth	= Net sales/Net worth
Estimated annual sales	= ₹ 2,00,000
Net worth = 2,00,000/2.5	= ₹ 80,000
Current debt to net worth	= 25%
Current debt = (80,000 × 25)/100	= ₹ 20,000
Total debt to net worth	= 60%
Total debt = (80,000 × 60)/100	= ₹ 48,000
Long-term debt	= Total debt – Current debt
	= 48,000 – 20,000 = 28,000

Current ratio	= 3.6 times
Current liabilities	= ₹ 20,000
Current assets	= 20,000 × 3.6 = ₹ 72,000
Net sales to inventory	= 4 times
Inventory	= 2,00,000/4 = ₹ 50,000
Average collection period	= 36 days
Debtors	= (Total sales × 36)/360
	= (2,00,000 × 36)/360 = ₹ 20,000
Fixed assets to net worth	= Fixed assets/Net worth = 70%
Fixed assets	= (80,000 × 70)/100
	= ₹ 56,000

Balance Sheet

as on 31-12-2018

Liabilities	*Amount* [₹]	*Assets*	*Amount* [₹]
Share capital (net worth)	80,000	Fixed assets	56,000
Long- term debts	28,000	Stocks	50,000
Current debt	20,000	Debtors	20,000
		Cash	2,000
	1,28,000		1,28,000

Problem 9

From the following data, calculate:

(*a*) Gross profit ratio

(*b*) Net profit ratio

(*c*) Operating ratio

(*d*) Inventory turnover ratio

Also rearrange the same in the form suitable for analysis.

To Opening stock	15,250	By sales	1,04,000
To Purchase less returns	64,450	*Less:* Sales return	4,000
To Gross profit c/d	40,000		1,00,000
		By closing stock	19,700
	1,19,700		1,19,700

Contd...

To Office salaries	4,800	By Gross profit b/d	40,000
To Rent and rates	4,040	By Interest on investments	1,800
To Printing & Stationeries	500	By Profit on sales of investments	600
To Postage	400		
To Depreciation	1,860		
To Selling expenses	4,000		
To Distribution expenses	400		
To Loss on sale of assets	800		
To Provisions of taxes	8,000		
To Net profit	17,600		
	42,400		42,400

Solution

Income Statement

for the year ended on 31-12-2018

Sales	1,04,000	
Less: Sales returns	4,000	
		1,00,000
Less: Cost of goods sold	15,250	
Opening stock	–	
Add: Purchases	64,450	
	79,700	
Less: Closing stock	19,700	
		60,000
Gross profit		40,000
Less: Operating expenses:		
Administrative expenses		
Office salaries	4,800	
Rent, etc.	4,040	
Printing & stationery	500	
Postage	400	
Depreciation	1,860	
Provisions for taxes	8,000	
	19,600	
Less: Selling & distribution expenses:	4,000	
Selling expenses	400	
Distribution expenses	24,000	24,000
		16,000
Add: Net non-operating income:		
Non-operating income	2400	
Less: Non-operating expenses	800	
	1600	1600
Net profit		17,600

Computation of ratios:

Gross profit ratio = (40,000/1,00,000) × 100 = 40%

Net profit ratio = (17,600/1,00,000) × 100 = 17.6%

Operating ratio = {(Cost of goods sold + Operating profit)/Net sales} × 100

= {(60,000 + 24,000)/1,00,000} × 100

= 84%

Inventory turnover ratio = (Cost of goods sold/Average stock) × 100

Average stock = (Opening stock + Closing stock)/2

= (15,250 + 19,700)/2 = 17475

= (60,000/17,475) × 100

= 3.43 times

Problem 10

The following is the Balance Sheet of Anees Ltd. as on 30-06-2018:

Liabilities	*Amount* [₹]	*Assets*	*Amount* [₹]
Share capital (20,000 shares of ₹ 10 each and ₹ 5 paid up	1,00,000	Land & building	1,25,000
Reserves & surplus	65,000	Plant & furniture	75,000
6% Debentures	1,00,000	Stock	50,000
Creditors	18,000	Debtors	10,000
Bills payable	7,000	Bills receivables	5,000
		Cash & bank	20,000
		Preliminary expenses	5,000
	2,90,000		2,90,000

Rearrange the above balance sheet in a form suitable for analysis and calculate the following ratios:

(*a*) Debt-equity ratio

(*b*) Proprietary ratio

(*c*) Current ratio

(*d*) Acid test ratio

Solution

Balance Sheet

as on 30-06-2018

Fixed assets:		
Land and building	1,25,000	
Plant and furniture	75,000	
		2,00,000
Current assets:		
Stock	50,000	
Debtors	10,000	
Bills receivables	5,000	
Cash and bank	20,000	
	85,000	
Less: Current liabilities:		
Creditors	18,000	
Bills payable	7,000	
	25,000	
Working capital:		
Current assets	85,000	
Less: Current liabilities	25,000	
		60,000
Capital employed		2,60,000
Less: 6 % debentures		1,00,000
Shareholders' net worth		1,60,000
Represented by Share capital	1,00,000	
Reserves and Surplus	65,000	
Less: Preliminary expenses	5,000	
	1,60,000	

Computation of ratios

(*a*) Debt – Equity ratio = External equities or liabilities/Internal equities or Shareholders fund

= (1,00,000 + 18,000 + 7,000)/(1,00,000 + 65,000 + 5,000)

= 1,25,000/1,60,000 = 25 : 32

Alternatively this ratio can be calculated

= Long-term debts/Long-term funds

= (1,00,000)/(1,00,000 + 60,000)

= 1,00,000/2,60,000 = 5: 13 or 0.38

(*b*) Proprietary ratio = Shareholders' fund/Total assets

= 1,60,000/2,85,000 = 32 : 57 or 0.56

This ratio could be supplemented with the following ratio:

Fixed assets to shareholders' fund ratio = Fixed assets/Shareholders' fund

= 2,00,000/1,60,000 = 1.25 or 5 : 4

Current assets to shareholders' funds ratio = Current assets/Shareholders' fund

= 85,000/1,60,000 = 0.53 or 17 : 32

(*c*) Current ratio = Current assets/Shareholders' fund

= 3.4 or 3.4 : 1

(*d*) Acid test ratio = Liquid assets/Current or Liquid liabilities

= 35,000/25,000 = 1.4 or 1.4 : 1

Problem 11

From the following figures and ratios, draw out the Balance Sheet, Trading and Profit and Loss Account:

Share capital	₹ 1,80,000
Working capital	₹ 63,000
Bank overdraft	₹ 10,000
Current ratio	2.5
Proprietary ratio	0.7 (Fixed assets/Shareholder's fund)
Stock velocity	4
Net profit ratio (to net capital employed)	10%
Quick ratio	1.5
Gross profit ratio (to sales)	20%
Debtors velocity	36.5 days

There is no fictitious asset. In current assets, there is no asset other than stock, debtors and cash. Closing stock is 20% higher than the opening stock.

Solution

Current ratio = 2.5

If Current asset = 2.5, then Current liabilities = 1

Working capital = Current asset – Current liabilities = 2.5 – 1 = 1.5

If Working capital = 1.5 = 63,000, then Current assets = (63,000/1.5) × 2.5

= 1,05,000

and Current liabilities = (63,000/1.5) × 1

= 42,000

Quick ratio = 1.5

If Quick assets = 1.5 then Quick liabilities = 1

Quick liabilities = 42,000 – 10,000 = 32,000

Current assets – Quick assets = Closing stock

Closing stock = 1,05,000 – 48,000 = 57,000

Closing stock is 20% higher than the opening stock. If opening stock is 100, then closing stock is 120

Closing stock = 57,000, then

Opening stock = (57,000/ 120) × 100 = 47,500

Average stock = Opening stock + Closing stock/2

= (57,000 + 47,500)/2 = 52,250

Stock velocity = Cost of goods sold/Average stock = 4

Cost of goods sold = Average stock × 4 = 52,450 × 4 = 2,09,000

Gross profit ratio to sales = 20%

Cost of goods sold to sales = 80%

If Cost of goods sold = 80 then Sales = 100

If Cost of goods sold is ₹ 2,09,000 then Sales = (2,09,000/80) × 100

= 2,61,250

Gross profit = ₹ 2,61,250 – 2,09,000 = ₹ 52,250

Debtors velocity (average collection period) = 36.5 days

Debtors = (Total credit sales/365) × Average collection period

= (2,61,250/365) × 36.5 = ₹ 26,125

Proprietary ratio = Fixed assets/Shareholders' fund = 0.7

If Fixed assets = 0.7 then Shareholders' fund = 1

Shareholders' fund – Fixed assets = 1 – 0.7 = 0.3

Shareholders' fund + Current liabilities = Fixed assets + Current assets

Shareholders' fund – Fixed assets = Current assets – Current liabilities

= 63,000

Hence, 0.3 = 63,000

Shareholders fund	= 1 = 63,000/0.3 = 2,10,000
Fixed assets	= 0.7 = (63,000/0.3) × 0.7 = 1,47,000
Reserves and Surplus	= 2,10,000 – 1,80,000 = 30,000
Net profit employed	= 10% of capital employed
Capital employed	= Fixed assets + (Current assets – Current liabilities)
	= 1,47,000 + 63,000 – 2,10,000
Net profit	= 10% of 2,10,000 = 21,000
Purchase	= Cost of goods sold – Opening stock + Closing stock
	= 2,09,000 – 47,500 + 57,000 = 2,18,500

Trading and Profit Account

To Opening stock	47,500	By Sales	2,61,250
To Purchases	2,18,500	By Closing stock	57,000
To Gross profit	52,250		
	3,18,250		3,18,250
To Sundry expenses	31,250	By Gross profit b/d	52,250
To Net profit	21,000		
	52,520		52,250

Balance Sheet

Liabilities	*Amount* [₹]	*Assets*	*Amount* [₹]
Share capital	1,80,000	Fixed assets	1,47,000
Reserves and Surplus	30,000	Current assets: Stock	57,000
Current liabilities: Sundry creditors	32,000	Debtors	26,125
Over draft	10,000	Cash (1,05,000 – 57,000 – 26,125)	21,875
	2,52,000		2,52,000

Problem 12

From the following information relating to PSV Ltd. in respect of the year ended 30th June 2018, prepare a trading and a profit and loss account:

Gross profit ratio	25%
Net profit ratio	20%
Stock turnover ratio	10
Net profit/capital	1/5
Fixed assets/Capital	5/4
Fixed assets	₹ 10,00,000
Closing stock	₹ 80,000

Solution

Calculation of Capital

Fixed assets/Capital = 5/4

1,00,000/Capital = 5/4

Capital = (10,00,000 × 4)/5

= 8,00,000

Calculation of Net Profit

Net profit/Capital = 1/5

Net profit/8,00,000 = 1/5

= 8,00,000/5 = 1,60,000

Calculation of Sales

Net profit ratio = Net profit/Sales = 20% = 1/5

1,60,000/Sales = 1/5

Sales = 5 × 1,60,000

= 8,00,000

Calculation of Gross Profit and Cost of Sales

Gross profit ratio = 25%

= 800000 × 25% = 200000

Cost of goods sold = Sales – Gross profit

= 8,00,000 – 2,00,000

= 6,00,000

Calculation of Opening Stock

Stock turnover ratio = Cost of sales/Average stock

10 = 6,00,000/Average stock

Average stock = 6,000 Net profit/8,00,000 = 1/5

= 60,000

= (Opening stock + Closing stock)/2

60,000 = (Opening stock + 80,000)/2

Opening stock = (2 × 60,000) – 80,000

= 40,000

Calculation of Purchases

Purchases = Cost of Sales + Closing stock – Opening stock

= 6,00,000 + 80,000 – 40,000

= 6,40,000

Trading and Profit and Loss Account
for the half year ended 30-06-2018

To Opening stock	40,000	By sales	8,00,000
To Purchases	6,40,000	By closing stock	80,000
To Gross profit c/d	2,00,000		
	8,80,000		8,80,000
To Administrative, selling & distribution expenses	40,000	By gross profit b/d	2,00,000
To Net profit	1,60,000		
	2,00,000		2,00,000

Problem 13

Excel Ltd., a large manufacturer of consumer durables is seeking a medium term loan of ₹ 500 lakhs essentially to finance a part of its working capital requirements and following its decision to significantly improve its credit terms to its customers, with a view to substantially increase the demand for its products. Following are the company's summarized financial data compiled from published accounts:

Particulars	*2018 ₹ in lakhs*	*2017 ₹ in lakhs*
Gross fixed assets at cost	220	200
Accumulated depreciation	160	150
Trade investments	10	10
Inventories	48	39
Receivables	59	40
Trade creditors	17	9
Tax & other provisions	40	40
Net assets employed	120	90
Financed by:		
Equity capital	30	30
Reserves	25	20
Long-term loans	40	20
Over draft and short-term facilities	25	20
	120	90
Sales income	180	160
Profit before interest and tax	28	28
Interest	10	6
Tax	10	12
Dividends	3	3
Retentions	5	7

The Company's fully paid up equity shares of ₹ 10 each are quoted as ₹ 15 in the stock market. It is known that the plant utilization of the Company's facilities is around 60% of its capacity and there are adequate technical and marketing skills in the company to handle a much higher volume of business.

Making such other assumptions as you consider necessary prepare a brief note on key indicators bearing on the Company's financial position and its credit and liquidity status from the prospective lenders view point for use at an exploratory meeting scheduled with the company.

Solution

Key financial ratios (from the point of view of perspective lender)

Particulars	*2018*	*2017*
Debt equity ratio = (Long term debts/Shareholders)	440 /35 = 0.73	30/50 = 0.4
Current ratio = Current assets/Current liabilities	107 / 82 = 1.3	79 / 69 = 1.14
Acid test ratio = Quick assets/Quick liabilities	590 / 570 = 1.04	400/490 = 0.82
Inverses coverage ratio	2.8	4.7
Inventory turnover ratio	108 / 48 = 3.75	160 / 39 = 4.1
Average collection period = Receivables'/Average monthly sales	590 / 150 = 3.93 months	400 / 133 = 3 months
Return on investments	(28/95) ×100 = 29.5%	(28/70) × 100 = 40%
Margin on sales = (Profit before interest & taxes/Sales) × 100	(28/180) ×100 = 13.6%	(28/160) × 100 = 17.5%
Capital turnover ratio = Sales/capital employed	180 /95 = 1.89 times	160 /70 = 2.29 times
Return on shareholders investments = Profit after tax/shareholders' fund	14.55%	20%
Earning per share = Earning after tax/No. of shares	₹ 2.67	₹ 3.33

Comment on the Company's Financial Position:

1. The Company has adopted very conservative policy regarding long term borrowings. The debt equity ratio is very low. The standard for the ratio is 2. Thus, the company can still make more long-term borrowings.
2. The current ratio is not at all satisfactory when compared to commercial banks standard ratio of 2. However, it has improved in 2018 as compared to 2017.
3. The acid test ratio has also improved in 2018 as regards to 2017. However, it is just satisfactory.
4. The inventory ratio has also deteriorated in 2018 as compared to 2017. This may cause considerable hold up of inventories.

5. The rise in credit period from 3 months to 3.93 months indicates that the credit policy has become very lenient and more funds have been locked up in receivables.
6. The interest coverage ratio has also deteriorated very much from 4.7 in 2018 to 2.8 in 2018. This is a matter of serious concern to the present as well as the prospective lenders. The profitability position should be improved very much.
7. The return on investments has declined very much in 2018 to 29.5% from 40% in 2017. Return on shareholders' fund and earnings per share have also declined. The causes for these declines have to be investigated thoroughly.

Suggestions for Improvements

The above analysis reflecting the sorry states of affairs in the liquidity position are due to locking up of funds in inventories, receivables and very much declining in its profitability and deteriorating the working capital position.

It is suggested that the company may be given a further loan of ₹ 50 lakhs. However, the lender must make sure that such lending will enhance the profitability position of the company and the company provides adequate securities for the loan. As things stand, lending to the company is not an attractive proposition from the lender's point of view.

Workings:

Particulars	*2018*		*2017*	
Gross fixed assets		220		200
Less: Depreciation		160		150
		60		50
Trade investments		10		10
Working capital	107		79	
Less: Current assets	82		69	
		25		10
Current liabilities				
Capital employed		95		70

Problem 14

Following is the profit and loss account of Laxmi Enterprises Ltd. for the year ended on 31st December, 2018 and balance sheet as on that date:

Profit and loss account for the year ended on 31st December, 2018.

Particulars	*Amount* [₹]	*Particulars*		*Amount* [₹]
To Opening stock	25,000	By Sales	3,06,800	
To Purchases	2,68,000	*Less*: Returns	6,800	3,00,000
To Gross profit	42,000			
		By Closing stock		35,000
	3,35,000			3,35000
To Office expenses	4,000	By Gross profit b/d		42,000
To Rent	2,800	By Interest on investments		1,500
To Depreciation	10,000			
To Selling expenses	2,200			
To Interest on debentures	4,200			
To Interest on overdraft	300			
To Tax	10,000			
To Net profit	10,000			
	43,500			43,500

Balance Sheet
as on 31-12-2018

Liabilities	*Amount* [₹]	*Assets*	*Amount* [₹]	*Amount* [₹]
Equity share capital	50,000	Fixed assets	1,80,000	
7% preference share capital	10,000	*Less*: Depreciation	50,000	
Reserves & surplus	40,000			1,30,000
6 % Debentures	70,000	Stock		35,000
Creditors	17,000	Debtors		20,000
Provisions for taxes	13,000	Marketable securities		10,000
		Cash		5,000
	2,00,000			2,00,000

Calculate all significant ratios and give a broad interpretation of every one of them and also give a comprehensive evaluation of Laxmi Enterprises Ltd. in the light of ratios calculated.

Solution

Analysis of Liquidity Position

Current ratio = Current assets/Current liabilities = 70,000/30,000 = 2.3 :1

Compared to the standard for the ratio 2:1, the position is highly satisfactory. The company could pay all its current liabilities just by realizing 43.5% of the current assets.

Acid test ratio = Liquid assets/Liquid liabilities = 35,000/30,000 = 1.17 :1

Compared to the standard for the ratio 1:1, the position is highly satisfactory. However the real effects depend upon the collection from the debtors and sales proceeds of marketable securities.

Stock turnover ratio = Cost of goods sold/Average stock

= 2,58,000/30,000 = 8.6 times

The interpretation of this ratio largely depends upon the nature of business and therefore there is no standard ratio. However the ratio of 8.6 times may be taken as satisfactory for this type of business.

Debtors turnover ratio = Total credit sales/Average debtors

= 3,00,000/20,000 = 15 times

Average collection period = 360/15 = 24 days

Conclusions could be drawn only by comparing the average collection period with the credit period allowed by creditors. Suppose the credit period is more than 24 days, the ratio is satisfactory. Assumptions that the number of working days in a year is 360 and all sales are credit sales.

Analysis of Solvency Position

Debt equity ratio = Outsiders fund/Shareholders fund

= 1,00,000/1,00,000 = 1:1

This ratio is highly satisfactory when compared to standard of 2:1 for this ratio. The company can still increase its external long term liability in order to take advantage of debt capital.

Interest coverage ratio = Net profit before tax and fixed interest charges/Fixed interest

= 24,500/4,500 = 5.5 times

In the case of industrial company, it is expected that this ratio should be 7 to 8 times. This company has a low ratio which indicates a low margin of safety and therefore not satisfactory.

Note: Though there is no bank overdraft in balance sheet, it is possible that the company might have paid the same during the year. Interest on overdraft has been treated as fixed interest charges.

Proprietary ratio = Shareholders funds/Total assets

= 1,00,000/2,00,000 = 0.5 : 1

Shareholders have provided funds up to 50% of the total assets. Hence, the ratio is satisfactory. In other words, the company can meet all external claims just by realizing 50% of the total assets.

Analysis of the Probability

General profitability

Gross profit ratio = (Gross profit/Net sales) × 100

= (42,000/3,00,000) × 100 = 14%

Net profit ratio = (Net profit/Net sales) × 100

= (10,000/3,00,000) × 100 = 3.33%

Operating turnover ratio = (Operating Cost/Net Sales) × 100

= (2,58,000 + 4,000 + 2,800 + 10,000 + 20,000/3,00,000) × 100

= (2,77,000/3,00,000) × 100 = 92.33%

There are no norms to judge these ratios and therefore they can be compared over a period of time for the same concern or at one time for different concerns in the same industry.

Overall profitability,

Return on shareholders investments = (Net profit after tax and interest/ Shareholders' fund) × 100

= (10,000/1,00,000) × 100

= 10%

This ratio is very low and not satisfactory when it is compared with the average return of the above 15% for the industrial concerns.

Return on capital employed = (Net profit before tax and interest/ Average capital employed fund) × 100

= (23,000/1,50,000) × 100

= 15.33%

Compared with the interest on debentures 6%, this ratio is satisfactory. It clearly indicates that the company has derived the benefit of trading on equity. However, for better comparison inter-form and inter-industry comparisons have to be made.

Workings:

Computation of capital, employed

Balances (Closing date):	Equity share capital	50,000
	Preference share capital	10,000
	Reserves and surplus	40,000
	6% debentures	70,000
		1,70,000
Less: Investments made in outside securities		15,000
Closing capital employed		1,55,000
Less: Half of the net profit		5000
Average capital employed		1,50,000

Return on equity capital = (Net Profit after preference dividend/Equity capital) × 100

= {(10,000 – 700)/50,000} × 100

= 18.6%

This ratio is highly satisfactory. However, this ratio may be compared with those or previous year for better evaluation.

Fixed Assets Turnover Ratio = Cost of goods sold/Fixed assets

= 2,58,000/1,30,000 = 2 times.

The turnover of fixed assets is very low and therefore not satisfactory. The standard is about 5 times for individual concerns.

Analysis of Capital Structure

Capital gearing ratio = Equity shareholders fund/Fixed income bearing securities

= 90,000/80,000 = 1.125 : 1

The company follows more or less the traditional method of capitalization. This ratio is satisfactory.

Ratio of reserves to equity capital = Reserves/Equity capital

= 40,000/50,000

= 0.8 : 1

This ratio is highly satisfactory. The high ratio indicates that the management has followed a conservative dividend policy.

Evaluation of Laxmi Enterprises Ltd.

Though it is necessary that qualitative consideration should be taken in account for a full fledged evaluation, some broad conclusions may be drawn from the ratios calculated.

1. Generally, the liquidity and solvency ratios reveal a satisfactory position. They indicate that the company is following a very conservative policy. However the profitability ratios, particularly the general profitability ratios, do not show a satisfactory performance. It is ascertained from the fixed assets turnover ratio that the company has failed to make use of fixed assets because the ratio is very poor.
2. Apparently, the company has built for the future. It will have to increase sales in order to benefit from the fixed assets which it has acquired.

Problem 15

The following table gives the comparative figures of ratios of the actual conditions for a given period and the standard selected. Give *in a few words your general*; conclusions on an examination of the several ratios:

Particulars	*Actual condition*	*Standard selected*
Current Assets/Current Liabilities	650	250
Cash/Current Liabilities	60	20
Fixed Assets/Net worth	40	50
Trade Debtors/Sales	8	10
Stock/Sales	60	40
Sales/Net worth	13	20
Liabilities/Net worth	7	10
Sales/Fixed assets	3	4
Net Profits/Net worth	3	7

Solution

1. The ratio of Current assets to current Liabilities is far higher than the standard. It is very comfortable for the creditors but for the company it indicates idle funds and a certain lack of enthusiasm for the work.
2. The above is also true of the second ratio–cash to current liabilities.
3. This ratio of fixed assets to net worth show that the company is not as mechanized as other companies or it may be because of idle funds.
4. The ratio of trade debtors to sales is lower than the standard. It is comforting to note that the debts are collected more promptly but in view of comments in (1) above, the ratio may be favourable because of low activity rather than prompt collections. Further, the company may be insisting more on cash and thus missing sales opportunities.
5. The ratio of stocks to sales clearly shows that the company is not rapidly turning over the stocks. Sales are low ratio numbers 6, 8 and 9, confirm this. The facilities of the company are not being fully utilized.
6. Liabilities to net worth ratio is more favourable ratio than the standard but in view of the extremely high current ratio, this ratio is rather high. It indicates that long term liabilities preponderate and perhaps working capital needs have also been raised by issue of long term loans.

On the whole, it is clear that company seems to be missing its opportunity and is not as active as it ought to be. It must use all the facilities fully.

Problem 16

Make an assessment of the comparative position of the following three companies engaged in the same line of business based on the following information:

2018	*X Ltd.*	*Y Ltd.*	*Z Ltd.*
Sales	2,64,000	3,33,000	3,60,000
Cost of goods sold	2,40,000	3,00,000	3,20,000
Inventory as on 31-12-18	40,000	60,000	80,000
Office administration expenses	20,000	30,000	40,000
Accounts receivables (360 days)	52,800	99,900	1,42,000

Solution

Particulars	*X Ltd.*	*Y Ltd.*	*Z Ltd.*
Gross profit ratio	9.1 %	9.9 %	11.1 %
Inventory turnover ratio	6 times	5 times	4 times
Average collection period	72 days	108 days	142 days
Percentages of office expenses to sales	7.6 %	9 %	11.1 %

Comments

A comparative study of the performance of three companies based on the above ratios reveals that the affairs of X Ltd. has been managed, efficiently compared to the other two companies. However, its Gross profit ratio is lower than those of other companies which may be due to reduced sale volume.

Its inventory turnover ratio is high and its average collection period is also very low. Expenses ratio is also very low. All these factors indicate the efficient utilization of resources of X Ltd. and a sound credit policy of the company.

Problem 17

A trader purchases goods on cash and credit terms. The following particulars are obtained from this record:

Total purchases	60,000
Cash purchases	6,000
Purchase returns	5,600
Creditors at the end	14,000
Bills payable at the end	8,000
Reserves for discount on creditors	500

Calculate average payment periods.

Solution

Total purchases	60,000
Less: Cash purchases	6,000
Credit purchases	54,000
Less: Purchase returns	5,600
	48,400
Net: Creditors purchase	48,400

Net purchases per day = 48,400/360 days

Average payment period = (Creditors + Bills payable)/Credit purchases per day.

= {(14,000 + (8,000 × 360)}/48,400

= 164 days (approximately)

Problem 18

Excel Ltd. intends to supply goods on credit to Ram Ltd. and Raj Ltd. The relevant information relating to the companies for the year ended on 30th June 2018 is as follows:

Terms of payment – 3 months	*Ram Ltd.*	*Raj Ltd.*
Stock	1,60,000	20,000
Debtors	34,000	28,000
Cash	6,000	12,000
Creditors	60,000	32,000
Bank overdraft	8,000	6,000
Expenses outstanding	12,000	2,000
Total purchases	1,86,000	1,32,000
Cash purchases	6,000	4,000

As per the management accountant advise, give reasons as to which of the companies should be preferred for dealings.

Solution

Computation of Short-term Solvency Ratios

Current ratio = Current assets/Current liabilities

Ram Ltd. = 20,000/80,000 = 2.5

Raj Ltd. = 60,000/40,000 = 1.5

Liquid Ratio = Quick assets/Quick liabilities

Ram Ltd. = 40,000/72,000 = 0.56

Raj Ltd. = 40,000/34,000 = 1.18

Average payment period = (Trade creditors/Credit purchases) × 360

Ram Ltd. = (60,000/1,80,000) × 360 = 120 days

Raj Ltd. = (32,000/1,28,000) × 360 = 90 days

Comments:

1. Current ratio of Ram Ltd. is better than that of Raj Ltd. But, when we compare the liquid ratios of two companies Raj Ltd. turns out to be a better choice.
2. This is owing to excessive holding of stock. Such high stock of Ram Ltd. may be due to unsaleable or obsolete items included in stocks. This factor makes the current ratio highly unreliable.
3. Comparisons of creditors' velocity also prove that Raj Ltd. is better than Ram Ltd. While Raj Ltd. is availing of 90 days' credit, Ram Ltd is taking 120 days to pay their creditors.

Considering all the factors and ratios that indicate the short term solvency position of the companies, Raj Ltd. is highly preferable.

REVIEW QUESTIONS

1. What is meant by ratio analysis?
2. Explain the following concept: Liquidity, solvency and profitability.
3. Explain the importance of ratio analysis.
4. Discuss the uses of ratio analysis.
5. What do you mean by inter-firm comparison?
6. Describe the following ratios:
   (*a*) Acid test ratio (*b*) Debt equity ratio
   (*c*) Return on capital employed, and (*d*) Capital gearing ratio.
7. How can ratios be classified?
8. Why is ratio analysis considered better than more comparison of figures?
9. What procedure would you adopt to study the liquidity of a business firm?
10. State the purpose of computing inventory ratio, operating ratio and debtor's turnover ratio.
11. What is the relationship of the assets turnover ratios to the rate of return on total assets?
12. Ratio analysis is a widely used tool of financial analysis, yet it suffers from various limitations. Explain.
13. How can the solvency of a firm be measured?
14. Critically examine the various methods of measuring return on capital investments.
15. Find out the long term solvency ratio and comment on the solvency based on the information from the balance sheet.

Liabilities		*Amount* [₹]	*Assets*	*Amount* [₹]
Equity share capital		2,000	Goodwill	1,200
Capital reserves		400	Fixed assets	2,800
Loans (mortgage)		1,600	Stocks	600
Creditors		800	Debtors	600
Bank overdraft		200	Investments	200
Taxation Current	200		Cash in hand	600
Future	200	400		
Profit after tax and fixed deposit	1,200			
Less: Transfer to reserve	400			
Less: Dividends	200	600		
		6,000		6,000

16. Balance sheet of X Ltd. as on 31st December 2015 is given and you are required to calculate the following ratios testing liquidity, testing profitability and testing capital gearing:

Liabilities		*Amount* [₹]	*Assets*	*Amount* [₹]
Equity share capital		20,000	Goodwill	12,000
Capital reserves		4,000	Fixed assets	28,000
8% Loans (mortgage)		16,000	Stocks	6,000
Trade creditors		8,000	Debtors	6,000
Bank overdraft		2,000	Investments	2,000
Taxation Current	2,000		Cash in hand	6,000
Future	2,000	4,000		
Profit after tax and fixed deposit	12,000			
Less: Transfer to reserve	4,000			
Less: Dividends	2,000	6,000		
		60,000		60,000

17. A company has an inventory of ₹ 7,20,000, debtors for ₹ 4,30,000 and an inventory Turnover Ratio of 1:2. The gross profit margin is 10% and its credit sales are 20% of the total sales. Calculate the average collection period. **[Ans.** 81 days**]**

18. Srinivasa Cotton Company's stock turnover is 5 times, stock at the end of year is for ₹ 2,000, more than that of the beginning. Sales (all credit) are for ₹ 8,00,000, rate of gross profit on cost is one fourth. Current Liabilities ₹ 1,20,000, Quick Ratio is 0.75. Calculate the current assets. **[Ans.** 1,64,000**]**

19. From the following information, calculate the current Ratio and acid test ratio:

Current assets loans and advances	*Amount* [₹]	*Current liabilities*	*Amount* [₹]
Stock in trade	77,000	Sundry creditors	23,300
Sundry debtors	47,300	Acceptance	9,460
Cash in hand	6,700	Dividend warrants issued but not cashed	190
Loans and advances	13,300	Provisions for taxation	10,150
Prepaid taxes	700		

[**Ans.** Current ratio = 3.37 and acid test ratio = 1.56]

20. Velan & Co. sell their goods on cash as well as credit. The following particulars are taken out from their records for the year 2018. Calcualte the average collection period:

Particulars	*Amount* [₹]
Total gross sales (including cash sales of ₹ 3,0000	1,60,000
Sales returns	10,000
Total debtors for sales upto 31-12-2018	15,000
Bills receivables as on 31-12-2018	3,000
Provisions for Doubtful debts, as on 31-12-2018	2,000
Sundry creditors	18,000
Prepaid Expenses	600

[**Ans.** 54 days, working days are assumed to be 360 days]

21. Calculate the following ratios from the balance sheet: debt equity ratio, liquidity ratio, fixed assets to Current Ratio and fixed assets Turnover ratio. The sales for the year were ₹ 5,60,000.

Liabilities	*Amount* [₹]	*Assets*	*Amount* [₹]
Equity share @ of ₹ 10	1,00,000	Goodwill	60,000
Reserves	2,000	Fixed assets (cost)	1,40,000
Profit and loss account	30,000	Stock	30,000
Secured loans	98,000	Sundry debtors	30,000
Sundry creditors	50,000	Advances	10,000
Provisions for tax	20,000	Cash balances	30,000
	3,00,000		3,00,000

[**Ans.** 1:1, 1:1, 1.4:1 and 4]

22. From the data find the Working Capital, Net Capital employed, current ratio and debt equity ratio.

Liabilities	*Amount* [₹]	*Assets*	*Amount* [₹]
Equity share capital	25,000	Fixed assets	30,000
Preference share capital	5,000	Stores	4,000
Reserves & surplus	4,000	Stock in Trade	4,000
Debentures	8,000	Sundry debtors	3,000
Bank loans	4,000	Cash in Hand	500
Sundry creditors	1,000	Balance with bank	2,500
Proposed dividends	1,000	Preliminary expenses	8,000
Provisions for taxes	2,000		
Contingent liabilities	2,000		
Total	52,000		52,000

[**Ans.** 8000, 38000, 3 and 0.53]

23. The standard ratios for the industry and the ratios of the company X & Co. is given. Determine the efficiency of the working capital of the X & Co.

Particulars	*Industry standard*	*Company X & Co.*
Current ratio	2.50	1.90
Gross pro?t	0.30	0.35
Fixed expenses ratio to sales	0.15	0.20
Variable expenses ratio to sales	0.10	0.08
Sales to capital	3.00	4.00
Fixed assets to long term funds	1.00	0.90
Rate of return on capital	15%	20%

24. The following details are worked out from the financial statements of a business concern for the year ended on 31-03-2018. You are required to reconstruct the balance sheet of the concern as on 31-03-18:

Particulars	*Amount* [₹]
Fixed assets (after writing off 30% depreciation)	10,50,000
Fixed assets turnover ratio	2.00
Finished goods turnover ratio	6.00
Gross profit to sales (%)	25.00
Net profit before interests to sales	8.00
Interest covers (debenture interest at 7%)	8.00
Debt collection period in months	1.5
Materials consumed to sales (%)	30.00
Stock of raw materials (in months of consumption)	3.00
Current ratio	2.40
Quick ratio	1.00
Reserves to capital	0.21

[**Ans.** B/S total is ₹ 20,00,000; CA ₹ 9,60,000, CL ₹ 4,00,000, debentures ₹ 4,00,000, capital ₹ 10,00,000 and reserves ₹ 2,10,000]

25. From the following information, you are required to prepare a balance sheet:

Particulars	
Current ratio	1.75
Liquid ratio	1.25
Stock turnover ratio (cost of sales / closing stock)	9
Gross profit ratio	25
Debt collection period	1 month
Reserves & surplus to capital	0.2
Turnover to fixed assets	1.2
Capital gearing ratio	0.6
Fixed assets to net worth	1.25
Sales for the year	12,00,000

[**Ans.** B/S ₹ 11,00,000, share capital ₹ 5,00,000, reserves and surplus ₹ 1,00,000, Long term debt ₹ 3,00,000, current liabilities ₹ 2,00,000, fixed assets ₹ 7,50,000, stock ₹ 1,00,000, debtors ₹ 1,50,000 and cash and bank balance ₹ 1,00,000].

26. The following are the financial statements of a leasing company. Find the

(*a*) current ratio

(*b*) acid test ratio

(*c*) debtors' turnover ratio

(*d*) earnings per share (equity share) and

(*e*) total debt to shareholders equity

Liabilities	*Amount*[₹]	*Assets*	*Amount*[₹]	*Amount*[₹]
Equity share capital	50,000	Plant and machinery	2,00,000	
6% Preference share capital	20,000	Less: Depreciation	1,60,000	40,000
Profit & loss	44,000	Inventory		1,00,000
5.25% mortgage	80,000	Debtors – previous year 40000		60,000
Loans payable	30,000	Investments		24,000
Taxes payable	20,000	Cash		20,000
Total	2,44,000			2,44,000

Profit and loss account for the year ended on 31st December 2018.

Particulars	*Amount* [₹]	*Particulars*	*Amount* [₹]
To Stock in the beginning	80,000	By Sales	2,40,000
To Purchase	1,20,000	By Stock at the end	1,00,000
To Gross profit	1,40,000		
	3,40,000		3,40,000
To Operating expense		By Gross profit	1,40,000
Selling expense	30,000		
General & admin.	40,000		
Net operating income	70,000		
	1,40,000		1,40,000
To Interest expenses	4,200	By Net operating income	70,000
To Income before tax	65,800		
	70,000		70,000
To Income tax	29,800		
To Net income after tax	36,000	By Income before tax	65,800
	65,800		65,800

[**Ans.** 4.08, 2.08, 4.80, ₹ 6.96 and 1.14]

27. Find the following from the given information:

1. Sales
2. Sundry Debtors
3. Sundry Creditors
4. Closing Stock
5. Fixed Assets
6. Proprietor Fund
7. Make out the balance sheet

Debtors Velocity : 3 months
Creditors Velocity : 2 months
Stock Velocity : 8 times
Capital turnover ratio : 2.5 times
Fixed asset turnover ratio : 8 times
Gross profit turnover ratio : 25%

Gross profit amounted in a year is ₹ 80,000. There is no long term loan or overdraft. Reserves and surplus amount to ₹ 28,000. Liquid assets are ₹ 97,333, closing stock is ₹ 2,000 more than the opening stock. Bills receivable amount to ₹ 5,000 and bills payable's is ₹ 5,000.

[**Ans.** A share capital is ₹ 4,00,000, creditors ₹ 60,000, Fixed assets ₹ 3,60,000, stock ₹ 1,10,000, other assets ₹ 90,000 and total is ₹ 5,60,000]

28. From the following information, prepare a summarized balance sheet as on 31st March 2018.

Working capital	₹ 1,20,000
Reserves & surplus	₹ 80,000
Bank overdraft	₹ 20,000
Fixed assets to proprietor fund	0.75
Current ratio	2.50
Liquid ratio	1.50

Assuming the current ratio is 2, state in each of the following cases whether the ratio will improve or decline or will not have any change:

1. Payment of current liabilities
2. Purchase of fixed assets
3. Cash collected from debtors
4. Bills receivables dishonoured
5. Issue of new shares

29. In projecting the financial plan of Navjeevan Trading Company Limited, the use of the following ratios is made:

Estimated annual sales	₹ 2,00,000
Sales to net worth	2.5 times
Current debt to net worth	25%
Total debt to net worth	60%
Current ratio	3.60 times
Net sales to inventory	4 times
Average collection (360 working days)	36 days
Fixed assets to net worth	70%

On the basis of the above information, prepare a program balance sheet of the company.

30. With the following ratios and further information given below, prepare a trading account, profit and loss account and the Balance Sheet:

Gross profit ratio	25%
Net profit to sales	20%
Stock turnover ratio	10
Net profit to capital	1/5
Capital to total liabilities	1.20
Fixed assets to capital	5/4
Fixed assets to total current assets	5/7
Fixed assets	₹ 2,00,000
Closing stock	₹ 20,000

[**Ans.** Purchase ₹ 1,36,000, other current assets ₹ 2,60,000 – both are balancing figures]

31. From the following details prepare the statement of propertied funds with as many details as possible:

Stock velocity	6
Capital turnover ratio	2
Fixed assets turnover ratio	4
Gross profit turnover ratio	20%
Debtors' velocity	2 months
Creditors' velocity	73 days

The Gross Profit was ₹ 60,000, reserves and surplus amounted to ₹ 20,000 and Closing Stock was ₹ 5,000 in excess of the Opening Stock.

[**Ans.** Proprietor fund is ₹ 1,20,000]

32. From the following ratios worked out from the financial statements of a company and standard ratios, make comments:

	Actual	*Standard*
Current ratio	5	2
Liquid ratio	2	1
Fixed assets to Proprietor fund ratio	4	6.7
Debtors' velocity	40 days	60 days
Stock velocity	7	12
Net profit to net worth	5	12
Fixed assets to turnover	4	6
Net worth turnover ratio	10	15
Creditors velocity	30 days	40 days
GP ratic	25%	25%
Net profit to sales	8%	12%

[**Comment:** The Company has a lot of funds and therefore has a low profit].

■ ■ ■

8

Funds Flow Analysis

FUNDS FLOW ANALYSIS

The 'traditional package' of final accounts and statements, though very significant statements, have as such, a limited role to play in financial analysis. The balance sheet is a statement of assets and liabilities on a particular date and portrays the financial position as on that particular date. Similarly, the income statement shows in greater detail only the profit or loss i.e., change in owners' equity arising during an accounting period as a result of the productive and commercial activities in that period. However, they fail to throw light on those major financial transactions which are behind the balance sheet changes. The main criticism against the balance sheet is that it is merely a static statement. In order to ascertain such major financial transactions or movement of financial resources of funds, the balance sheet of two periods should be compared, and changes in assets and liabilities should be shown in a separate statement. This statement is variously known as "funds flow statement", "statement of sources and application of funds", "where got and where gone statement" or "simply funds statement".

Funds Flow Analysis is an invaluable analytical tool for a financial manager or a creditor for evaluating the employment of funds by a firm, and in determining the sources for such funds. In addition to study past flows, the analyst can evaluate future flows by means of funds–statement based upon forecasts. Such a statement provides an efficient method for the financial manager to assess the growth of the firm and its resulting financial needs, and to determine the best way to finance those needs. In particular, funds flow analysis is very useful in planning intermediate and long-term financing.

CONCEPT OF FUNDS

Some define the term 'funds' as cash and they concern themselves only with the movements in the cash account. The statement showing changes in cash balances is termed as 'Cash flow statement'. This is a very narrow definition. Though a record of cash inflows and outflows is valuable in its own way, it however, fails to throw light on many important changes involving the disposition of resources.

At the other end, there are those who view funds in a broader sense as all assets to which the firms resources stand committed and all liabilities from these resources are obtained. This is known as the financial resources' concept of funds. In between these two concepts is the third and the most acceptable one which views 'funds' as net working capital. Net working capital denotes excess of current assets over current liabilities. The term 'Working Capital' is considered the most appropriate expression since the wealth of the enterprise continuously revolving through the various current assets is supplemented by current liabilities.

The broad categories of current assets include such items as cash (including fixed deposits with banks), sundry debtors, bills receivable, marketable securities, inventories, advances recoverable and prepaid expenses. Generally, the term 'current assets' may be used here to designate any asset which is reasonably expected to be realised in cash, or consumed during the normal operating cycle of the business. Similarly, the term 'current liabilities' may be used to denote such liabilities or obligations which should be repaid within the accounting year out of current assets, or by creating current liabilities. The broad categories of current liabilities include such items as sundry creditors, bills payables, outstanding expenses, bank overdraft and other short-term loans and income received in advance.

Long-term liabilities may be treated as current liabilities if their maturity date falls within the accounting year and they are payable out of current assets, or by current liabilities. But, if they are to be paid by raising long-term funds (for example, by issuing shares or debentures), such liabilities should not be treated as current liabilities.

To conclude, funds may be defined in different ways, depending upon the purpose of the analysis. Other definitions are possible, although the three described above are the most common by far, viz.,

(*a*) Funds mean cash;

(*b*) Funds mean net working capital; and

(*c*) Funds mean all financial resources.

In this chapter, the term 'funds' has been used to mean 'net working capital'.

CONCEPT OF FLOW

The term 'flow' refers to change or transfer, and therefore, 'the flow of funds' means transfer of economic values from one asset to another, from one, liability to another, from one asset to a liability or vice-versa, or a combination of these. But, as per the working capital concept of funds, it means 'changes in working capital' i.e., any increase or decrease in working capital the change in funds (i.e. current assets and current liabilities) occurs when changes occurring in non-current assets (all assets other than current assets) and in non-current liabilities (all liabilities other than current liabilities) are offset by corresponding changes in current assets and current liabilities. If any transaction results in increase of funds, it will be considered as a "source of funds". For example, issue of shares for cash is taken as a "source of funds", as it increases the cash (working capital item). Similarly, a transaction, if it results in decrease of funds is treated as an application of funds. For example, purchase of fixed assets for cash is taken to be "application of funds" as it reduces the cash (i.e. working capital). The Transactions which do not affect the working capital items would be treated as non-fund transactions and are excluded from funds flow analysis. For example, purchase of machinery by issuing shares is a non-fund transaction.

Principal Sources of Funds

1. Issue of shares and debentures,
2. Long and medium-term borrowings,
3. Sale of fixed assets, and long term investments,
4. Funds from operations or trading income,
5. Non-trading income, such as income from investments, gifts, damages awarded in legal action, etc.

Possible Uses of Funds

Though there are numerous applications of funds, the main categories are as follows:

1. Redemption of shares and debentures,
2. Repayment of long and medium-term loans,
3. Purchase of fixed assets and long-term investments,
4. Funds lost in operations, or trading losses,
5. Non-trading losses, such as loss of cash by embezzlement, fines, etc.

Concept of Funds Flow Statements

Funds Flow Statement is a statement in summary form that indicates changes in items of financial position between two different balance sheet dates showing clearly the different sources and applications of funds. The major purpose of funds statement is to provide a detailed presentation of results of financial management, as distinguished from operating management. It summarises the financing and investing activities of enterprises. The statement shows directly information that readers of financial reports could otherwise obtain only by making an analysis and interpretation of published balance sheets and statements of income and retained earnings.

Balance Sheet is a statement of financial position, whereas funds statement is a obviously statement of 'changes' in financial position. Balance sheet shows the status on a, day. In contrast, funds statement, income statement and statement of retained earnings cover periods of time; they provide the explanation of why the balance sheet items have changed. The conventional financial statements show mostly the position of accounting, rather than the financial condition of the business in terms of flow of funds. However, since all financial events are reflected in the conventional statements, it becomes easy to unearth unusual trends and proportions by the use of analytical methods like the funds flow statement. Thus, the funds flow statement is intended to supplement, and not to supplant the conventional financial statements.

Uses of Funds Flow Statements

By highlighting changes in the distribution of resources of an undertaking, the funds flow statement enables the financial manager to have a clear perspective of the organisation's financial strengths and weaknesses. It provides answers to a number of difficult questions. The use of funds flow statement may be listed as follows:

Firstly, it explains the financial consequences of business operations. For example, a business may be earning huge profits but its liquidity position can be highly unsatisfactory. The Funds flow statement explains the causes of such a seemingly irreconcilable situation by showing what has become of the profits earned. Further, the Statement would point out the direction of flow of funds into activities considered more beneficial for the efficient working of the enterprise and which is very essential for effective managerial control. When a Balance Sheet presents a distorted picture of an undertaking because of a number of non-fund transactions, funds statement would be an illuminating document.

Secondly, debt capital is very essential for increased profitability of any enterprise. But, creditors or lenders ask the financial manager a number of questions in order to ascertain the creditworthiness and funds generating capacity of the organisation. Also, they would like to know in what way the management has utilised funds in the past and how they would be utilised in future. By providing the required information or clues, funds flow statement enables the financial manager to answer such questions in a befitting manner.

Thirdly, it acts as an instrument for allocation of the company's scarce resources. A proposed funds flow statement helps to find out how the management is going to allocate resources for meeting the future productive programmes of the business. When a Projected Funds Statement is tied to the capital budget, it helps the management to maintain the financial health of the organisation. Further, problems faced by a firm do not arise all of a sudden. They take time to reach a critical stage and are affected by a number of factors. A projected funds flow statement, by providing a perspective for considering the financial implications of evolving issues, would help management to reverse an unfavourable trend.

Lastly, it is a test for evaluating the effective use of working capital by the management. Information on the adequacy or inadequacy of working capital enables the management to decide what possible steps it should take for effective use of surplus Working Capital, or in case of inadequate working capital to make suitable arrangements make up the deficiency.

Limitations of Funds Flow Statements

Despite its multiple managerial uses, the Funds flow statements suffer from certain limitations.

1. As this statement ignores non-fund items, it becomes a crude device compared to the Income Statement and Balance Sheet.
2. The statement does not reveal shifts among the items making up the current assets and current liabilities. It does not show whether any loss of working capital has unduly weakened the financial position. Only an examination of the Balance Sheet at the end of the period will show the end-effects of these changes. Therefore, Funds Flow statement cannot supplant but only supplement the conventional financial statements, either in whole or in part.
3. The information used for the preparation of Funds flow statement is essentially historical in nature, though attempts are made to project funds statement for future.

Despite these limitations, the information supplied by funds flow statement is really an invaluable aid to management in planning capital expenditure, devising dividend and other financial policies, etc. Taken in conjunction with Ratio Analysis, and other financial statements, Funds Flow Analysis provides a rich source of information regarding possible managerial uses.

Preparation of Funds Flow Statements

Mainly two comparative balance sheets at the beginning and end of a period are used for preparing Funds flow statement. In addition, a summarised income statement and retained earnings statement or, at least material information from these statements are required in order to obtain information relating to funds from operations and ownership transactions. These are the basic minimum and not maximum. Additional information, if available, sharpens the firm's financial profile, as revealed by the funds statement.

The funds flow Analysis involves the preparation of two statements, viz.

(*a*) Statement or schedule of changes in working capital; and

(*b*) Sources and uses of funds statement.

Since a funds flow statement depicts changes in the working capital, it is better to prepare first the schedule of changes in the working capital before preparing a Funds Flow Statement. The statement of changes in working capital or simply called "Working capital statement" is prepared with the help of current assets and current liabilities. The purpose of this statement is to find out the net change in working capital. The format of this statement is as follows:

Statement of Changes in Working Capital

Particulars	*Previous year*	*Current year*	*Effect of change in working capital*	
			Decrease	*Increase*
Current Assets:				
Cash	XXX	XXX	–	XXX
Bank	XXX	XXX	–	XXX
Bills receivable	XXX	XXX	XXX	–
Debtors	XXX	XXX	XXX	–
Stock	XXX	XXX	–	XXX
Prepaid expenses	XXX	XXX	XXX	–
Total (*a*)	XXX	XXX	XXX	XXX
Current Liabilities:				
Outstanding expenses	XXX	XXX	–	XXX
Bills payable	XXX	XXX	–	XXX
Creditors	XXX	XXX	XXX	–
Total (*b*)	XXX	XXX	XXX	XXX
Working capital (*a* – *b*)			XXX	–
Net increase/decrease in working capital				

The total difference between the total sources and application are shown as either increase or decrease in working capital or funds and this could be verified with the net increase/decrease in working capital as derived from the above statement. The change in working capital may also be verified by calculating working capital separately.

Example 1

From the following two balance sheets on December 31, 2017 and December 31, 2018, prepare a Schedule of Changes in the working capital.

Liabilities	*2017 Amount* [₹]	*2018 Amount* [₹]	*Assets*	*2017 Amount* [₹]	*2018 Amount* [₹]
Share capital	3,25,000	3,00,000	Land and buildings	5,00,000	4,00,000
Profit and Loss A/c	1,20,000	1,00,000	Machinery	1,00,000	1,60,000
9% Debentures	2,00,000	2,00,000	Stock-in trade	1,10,000	80,000
Trade creditors	98,000	75,000	Debtors	30,000	36,000
Outstanding creditors	2,000	5,0000	Cash	5,000	4,000
	7,45,000	6,80,000		7,45,000	6,80,000

Solution

Schedule of Changes in Working Capital

Particulars	2017 Amount [₹]	2018 Amount [₹]	Effect on working capital	
			Increase (+) Amount [₹]	Decrease (–) Amount [₹]
Current Assets:				
Stock-in-trade	80,000	1,10,000	30,000	
Debtors	36,000	30,000		6,000
Cash	4,000	5,000	1,000	
Total of current assets (*a*)	1,20,000	1,45,000		
Current liabilities:				
Trade creditors	75,000	98,000	–	23,000
Outstanding creditors	5,000	2,000	3,000	–
Total current liabilities (*b*)	80,000	1,00,000		
Working capital (*a* – *b*)	40,000	45,000		
Net increase in working capital	5,000	–		5,000
	45,000	45,000	34,000	34,000

Proforma of Funds Flow Statement
Statement of Sources and Applications of Funds

Sources	*Amount* [₹]
1. Issue of shares at par/discount/premium	XXX
2. Issue of debentures at par/discount/premium	XXX
3. Long- and medium-term borrowings	XXX
4. Sales of investments	XXX
5. Sales of ? xed assets	XXX
6. Funds from operation	XXX
7. Non-trading income	XXX
Total	
Applications	
1. Redemption of shares/at par/discount/premium	XXX
2. Redemption of debentures at par/discount/premium	XXX
3. Repayment of loans	XXX
4. Purchase of investments	XXX
5. Purchase of ? xed assets	XXX
6. Funds lost from operations	XXX
7. Non-trading payments — dividends paid.	XXX
Total	XXX

Increase/decrease in working capital as per statement of changes in working capital.

Alternatively, it may be prepared as follows:

Statement of Sources and Applications of Funds

Sources	*Amount* [₹]	*Applications*	*Amount* [₹]
Issue of shares	XXX	Redemption of shares	XXX
Issue of debentures	XXX	Redemption of debentures	XXX
Long-term and medium-term loans taken	XXX	Repayment of loans	XXX
		Purchase of investments	XXX
Sale of investments	XXX	Purchase of fixed assets	XXX
Sale of fixed assets	XXX	Payment of dividends (last year and interim)	XXX
Trading profits	XXX		
Non-trading income	XXX	Funds lost from operations	XXX
Net decrease in working capital, as per schedule of changes in working capital	XXX	Non-trading payments	
		Net increase in working capital as capital per schedule of changes in working	XXX
Total	XXX	Total	XXX

The given balance sheet items should be classified into current accounts (i.e., current assets and current liabilities) and non-current accounts (i.e. non-current assets and non-current liabilities). The following extract from the balance sheet of a company will explain the above method of classification:

Non-current liabilities share capital	*Amount* [₹]	*Non-current assets fixed assets*	*Amount* [₹]
Equity share capital	50,000	Goodwill	15,000
Preference share capital	40,000	Premises	60,000
		Plant	50,000
Reserves and surplus:			
Share premium	2,000	Furniture	10,000
Reserve fund	10,000	*Investments:*	
Sinking fund	15,000	6% Government *bonds*	20,000
Compensation fund	5,000	Miscellaneous expenditure	
P & L A/c	10,000	Preliminary Expenses	2,000
Secured loans:			
12% Debentures	25,000	Discount on issue of debentures	3,000
Mortgage loans	20,000		
Unsecured loans			
Deposits	8,000	Total non-current Assets	
Total non-current liabilities	1,85,000		1,60,000

Contd...

Sundry creditors	12,000		Inventories	25,000	
Bills payable	8,000		Debtors	21,000	
Bank overdraft	15,000		Bills receivable	9,000	
Outstanding expenses	5,000		Prepaid expenses	2,000	
			Outstanding income	3,000	
Total current liabilities,		40,000	Cash	5,000	
			Total assets		65,000
Total liabilities		2,25,000			2,25,000

The following points should be noted while preparing the working capital statement:

1. An increase in current assets and decrease in current liabilities will increase the working capital.
2. A decrease in current assets and increase in current liabilities will decrease the working capital.

It should be noted that the schedule of changes in the Working capital is prepared only from the current accounts appearing in the Balance Sheet. There is no effect of additional information given separately, and such an information will affect only the funds flow statement.

While preparing the statement of changes in the working capital, the current assets may be shown either at their gross values, showing provisions as current liabilities, or at their net values after deducting such provisions. The usual items are: provision for doubtful debts, provision for loss of stock, provision for discount on debtors, etc.

Calculation of Funds from Operations or Trading Profits

The current operating profit is the main source of funds. The operating profit is the excess of operating or sales revenue over operating cost which includes cost of goods sold and operating expenses. While sales result in inflow of funds in the form of cash, bills receivable and sundry debtors, the operating cost results in outflow of funds in the form of reduction in cash and bank balances and *increase in* sundry and expense creditors and acceptances. Thus, the net inflow would amount to *sources of funds,* and the net outflow would be *applications of funds.*

While calculating funds from operations, only those transactions which affect the movement of funds should be considered. In other words, all non-fund transactions, such as depreciation, write-off and write-up of fixed assets or fictitious assets, appropriation etc. should be readjusted to current net profit if they have already been charged to such profits. Similarly, if the profit and loss account has been credited with certain non-operating income, viz. dividends received, transfer back of excess provision for taxation, interest on investment, refund for tax, profit on sales of fixed assets, etc., such items should be readjusted to the current profits and be shown separately as a source in the funds flow statement. For making such readjustments, an adjusted profit and loss statement should be prepared in a statement form or account form, as shown below:

Proforma of Adjusted Profit and Loss A/c

Debit	*Amount* [₹]	*Credit*	*Amount* [₹]
To Depreciation written off	XXX	By Opening balance	XXX
To Provision for tax	XXX	By Dividends already credited to P & L a/c	XXX
To Proposed dividend	XXX		
To Preliminary expenses written off	XXX	By Over-provision for taxation written back	XXX
To Goodwill written-off	XXX		
To Discount on issue of shares and debentures	XXX	By Gain on sale of fixed assets	XXX
To Deferred revenue expenses already charged	XXX	By Funds from trading operations (Balancing figure)	XXX
To Transfer to general reserve	XXX		
To Transfer to sinking fund, etc.	XXX		
To Loss on sale of fixed assets written-off	XXX		
To Closing balance	XXXX		
	XXXX		XXX

In the case of accumulated losses, the opening balance should be shown in the debit side of the Adjusted Profit and Loss A/c, and the closing balance should be shown on *the credit* side.

Alternatively

Calculation of Funds from Operations

Particulars	*Amount* [₹]
Net profit for the current year	XXX
Add: Non-fund/Non-operating items charged to Profit and Loss account, Depreciation on fixed assets, Goodwill written-off, Preliminary expenses written-off, Loss on sale of non-current assets etc.	XXX
	XXX
Less: Non-fund/non-operating credits appearing in the Profit and Loss account, Dividends received, Interest on investments received, Profit on sales of non-current assets etc.	XXX
Funds from Operations	XXX

Determination of Net Funds in Cash of Net Loss

If the Profit and Loss A/c for the year shows net loss, it does not necessarily mean that the funds have been lost in operations. If the total of items to be added back (expenses and losses written-off and transfers to reserve, etc.) exceeds the total of net loss plus items to be deducted (dividend, etc.) the difference would represent funds provided by operations.

On the other hand, if the total of items to be added back is less than the total of the net loss, plus items to be deducted, the difference would reflect funds lost in operations. Funds so lost may be shown under the heading "Application of Funds" in the Statement of Sources & Application of Funds.

Example 2

From the following Profit and Loss Account, calculate the funds from operations;

Profit and Loss Account

Particulars	*Amount* [₹]	*Particulars*	*Amount* [₹]
To Salaries	28,000	By Gross profit	1,50,000
To Rent	12,000	By Profit on sale of furniture	12,000
To Printing and Stationery	6,000	By Interest on investment	8,000
To Depreciation on plant	25,000		
To Goodwill written-off, Loss	10,000		
on sale of plant	5,000		
To Provision for taxation	15,000		
To Proposed dividend	14,000		
To Net profit taken to Balance sheet	55,000		
	1,70,000		1,70,000

Solution

Calculation of Funds from Operation

Net profit as per P & L (appropriation) A/c ₹55,000

Add: Non-fund/Non-operating items appearing in P & L a/c

	Amount [₹]	*Amount* [₹]
Depreciation on plant	25,000	
Goodwill written-off	10,000	
Loss on sale of plant	5,000	
Provision for taxation	15,000	
Proposed dividends	14,000	69,000
Less: Non-fund/non-operating credits appearing in the P&L a/c		1,24,000
Profit on sale of furniture	12,000	
Interest on investments	8,000	20,000
Funds from operations		1,04,000

TREATMENT OF PROVISION FOR TAXATION AND PROPOSED DIVIDENDS

Provision for Taxation

There are two ways of treating this item in the Funds Flow Statement.

(*a*) Provision for Taxation made during the year may be treated as current liability. If this is the treatment, provision for taxation made during the year is not used for adjusting the net profit made during the year for calculating funds from operations. As such, tax paid during the year is not treated as 'Application of Fund'.

(*b*) Provision for taxation may be treated as internal appropriation and thus a non-current liability. Then, it will be used for adjusting the net profit made during the year, and tax paid during the year is treated as an 'Application of Funds.'

Proposed Dividends

This item is also treated in two ways in the Funds Flow Statement:

(*a*) Proposed dividend may be treated as current liability. Then it will not be used for adjusting the net profit made during the year for calculating funds from operations.

(*b*) The proposed dividend may be treated as non-current liability i.e., an appropriation of profits. In that case, dividends paid during the year are shown as application of funds. It may be noted that it is the payment of dividend (and not the declaration of dividend) which reduces the working capital. The declaration of dividend does not affect the working capital because, it is a mere appropriation of funds. In order to find out funds from operations, such proposed dividends should be added back to the current year's net profit.

Hidden Transactions

Sometimes, the information required for the funds flow statement may have to be found out difference in the values of fixed assets and investments in the comparative balance sheet would generally represent either sources, or application by way of sale or purchase thereof, subject to an amount written-off as depreciation. A separate fixed assets account may be prepared to find out the inflow and/or outflow of funds from fixed assets. In the same way, the inflow and/or outflow of funds from long-term liabilities could be found but by taking into consideration the difference in the values of such liabilities. A separate ledger account may be prepared to locate such differences. For example, if the balance sheets on two different dates show Machinery Account at ₹ 50,000 and ₹ 60,000 respectively, and it is given that depreciation on Machinery has been provided to the extent of ₹ 10,000, the hidden information can be ascertained by preparing a Machinery Account as under:

Dr. **Machinery Account** cr.

Particulars	Amount [₹]	Particulars	Amount [₹]
To Opening balance	50,000	By Depreciation	10,000
To Cash (purchase of machinery during year)	20,000	By Closing balance	60,000
(Balancing figure-application of funds)	70,000		70,000

Suppose the opening balance of the machinery in the above-example is ₹ 80,000, the Machinery Account would appear as follows:

Dr. cr.

Particulars	Amount [₹]	Particulars	Amount [₹]
To Opening balance	80,000	By Depreciation	10,000
		By cash (sale of Machinery) balancing figure source of funds)	10,000
		By closing balance	60,000
	80,000		80,000

It may be noted that while preparing the fixed assets account as shown above, the opening and closing balances of such assets should be shown at cost. If the balance of fixed assets and provision for depreciations are given separately in the balance sheets, the fixed assets' accounts are prepared at original cost and a separate provision for Depreciation Account is prepared to find out depreciation, provided during the year. But, if assets are shown at their written down values in the balance sheets, and the provision for depreciation in the adjustments, such provisions should be added back to the concerned balances of fixed assets and be shown as balances in their respective account. These points are illustrated as follows:

Example 3

Opening and closing balances of the Machinery Account (at W.D.V.) appearing in the comparative balance sheet are ₹ 1,50,000 and ₹ 2,50,000 respectively. The opening and closing balances of Accumulated Depreciation Account were ₹ 25,000 and ₹ 40,000 respectively. Further, it is given that during the year (*a*) a machine costing ₹ 50,000 was purchased in exchange for fully paid up shares, and (*b*) an old machine costing ₹ 10,000 (accumulated depreciation ₹ 4,000) was sold for ₹ 4,500. Show the ledger accounts,

Solution

Machinery Account (at Original Cost)

Dr. cr.

Particulars	Amount [₹]	Particulars	Amount [₹]
To Opening balance (₹ 1,50,000 + ₹ 25,000)	1,75,000	By Cash (sale of old machine)	4,500
Share capital (1) (issued for thepurchase machinery	50,000	Accumulated depreciation A/c	4,000
Cash (purchase of new machinery-balancing figures)	75,000	Loss on sale (2) (P & L A/c)	1,500
		Closing balance (₹ 2,50,000 + ₹ 40,000)	2,90,000
	3,00,000		3,00,000

Accumulated Depreciation Account

Debit	*Amount* [₹]	*Credit*	*Amount* [₹]
To Machinery A/c (Depreciation on machine sold)	4,000	By Opening balance	25,000
To Closing balance	40,000	By P&L A/c (balancing figure – depreciation provided during the year)	19,000
	44,000		44,000

Notes: 1. Purchase of machinery by exchanging fully paid-up shares is non-fund item which will not affect working capital and therefore will not be shown in the funds flow statement.

2. Original cost Accumulated Depreciation amount sold (i.e. ₹ 10,000 – ₹ 4,000 – ₹ 4,500)

Effect of Depreciation on Funds Flow (or is Depreciation a Source of Funds?)

Depreciation refers to the decrease in the value of assets, particularly fixed assets. Fixed assets may lose their values due to wear and tear, obsolescence, passage of time, exhaustion and accident. As this loss in value, i.e. depreciation arises out of operations of fixed assets, in the business, it is treated as an operating expense to profit and loss account. The usual treatment of depreciation in final account is to debit the same to profit and loss account and credit the concerned fixed asset account (i.e. deducted from fixed asset in balance sheet). Since, in Profit and Loss account fixed assets are non-current accounts, depreciation is treated as a non-fund item while preparing the fund flow statement. In other words, depreciation is added back to operating profit to find out funds from operations since it does not affect the flow of funds. Hence, it is neither a source nor an application of funds. If depreciation is really a source of funds by itself then any business could improve its funds position by providing periodical depreciation charge.

However, depreciation may be considered as a source in a limited sense due to reasons given below:

(*a*) Depreciation reduces taxable income and therefore tax liability. For example, a company is in 40% tax bracket and the amount of depreciation charged to its Profit and Loss account is, say, ₹40,000. The company reduces the taxable income by ₹ 40,000 and the tax liability by ₹16,000 (i.e., 40% on ₹40,000). The opportunity saving of cash outflow may be taken as a source of funds.

(*b*) Depreciation may not generate funds but it definitely saves funds. For example, if a company has taken an asset on lease, it must pay lease rentals which are cash outflows. But it may avoid this situation by owning the same assets.

(*c*) Depreciation forms part of current asset when it is charged as overheads. For example, the value of closing stock may include depreciation as an element of cost and in that case, it becomes a fund item.

Illustration 1

A company's reported current profit is ₹ 70,000 after incorporating the following:

Particulars	*Amount* [₹]	*Particulars*	*Amount* [₹]
Loss on sale of equipment	10,000	Gain from sale of non- current assets	40,000
Premium on redemption of debentures	1,500	Excess provision of taxation	22,000
Discount on issue of debentures	2,000	Dividend income in investments	4,000
Depreciation on machinery and building	20,000	Transfer to general reserve	5,000
Depletion of natural resources	10,000	Preliminary expenses	1,000
Amortization of goodwill	30,000	Profit on revaluation of investments	2,500
Interim dividend	25,000		
Derive the net inflow of funds-from the operation.			

Solution

Particulars	*Amount* [₹]	*Amount* [₹]
Reported Current Profit		70,000
Add: Items not affecting the funds:		
Loss on sale of equipment	10,000	
Discount on issue of debentures	2,000	
Depreciation on machinery and building	20,000	
Depletion of natural resources	10,000	
Amortization of goodwill	30,000	
Excess provision for taxation	22,000	
Transfer to general reserve	5,000	
Preliminary expenses	1,000	
		1,00,000
Items affecting the funds but separately shown		
Premium on redemption of debentures	1,500	
Interim dividend	25,000	
		26,500
		1,96,500
Deduct: Items not improving the funds		
Profit on revaluation	2,500	
Items improving the funds but separately dealt with:		
Gain from sale of non-current assets	40,000	
Dividend income on investments	4,000	
		46,500
Net inflow of funds from operation		1,50,000

Alternatively, this figure of ₹ 1,50,000 may be derived by preparing an adjusted profit and loss account as below:

Adjusted Profit and Loss A/c

Debit	*Amount* [₹]	*Credit*	*Amount* [₹]
To Loss on sale of equipment	10,000	By Profit on revaluation of investment	2,500
To Discount on issue of Debentures	2,000	By Gain from sale of non-current assets	40,000
To Depreciation on machinery and building	20,000	By Dividend income on investments	4,000
To Depletion of natural Resources	10,000	By Net inflow of fund from operation from operation (balancing figures)	1,50,000
To Amortization of goodwill	30,000		
To Excess provision for taxation	22,000		
To Transfer to general reserve	5,000		
To Preliminary expenses	1,000		
To Premium on redemption of debentures	1,500		
To Interim dividend	25,000		
To Closing balance	70,000		
	1,96,500		1,96,500

Illustration 2

From the following information, work out figures of (*a*) fixed assets purchased, and (*b*) items to be shown in the Funds Flow Statements:

	₹
Fixed Assets WDV on 1-1-2009	7,60,000
Fixed Assets WDV on 31-12-2009	7,20,000
Depreciation charged during the year	1,40.000
WDV of Asset sold during the year	20,000
Sale proceeds of scrapped assets	15,000

Solution

Fixed Assets Account

Date	*Particulars*	*Amount* [₹]	*Date*	*Particulars*	*Amount* [₹]
1-1-2017	To Balance	7,60,000	*31-12-17*	By Depreciation[2]	1,40,000
	To cash (Fixed Assets Purchased)[1]	1,20,000		By Cash (Sale of the Assets)[3]	15,000
				By Loss on Sale of Assets[4]	5,000
				By Balance c/d	
		8,80,000			8,80,000

1. Fixed assets purchased to be shown as application of funds ₹ 1,20,000
2. Depreciation to be adjusted to operating profit ₹ 1,40,000
3. Sale of asset to be shown as a source of funds ₹ 15,000
4. Loss on sale to be adjusted to operating profit ₹ 5,000

Illustration 3

The following transactions in fixed assets section of the balance sheet of a company took place in 2018.

The fixed assets at cost amounted to ₹ 1,92,680 on 1-1-2018 and ₹ 2,02,240 on 31-12-2018. The accumulated depreciation account increased from ₹ 85,600 in 2017 to ₹ 88,500 in 2018. A piece of asset sold in 2017 for ₹ 5,000 was originally purchased at ₹ 20,000. Accumulated depreciation on the asset sold was ₹ 12,000. The loss was charged against profit of the year.

Find out the amount of fixed assets acquired during the year. What other items shown above should appear in the funds flows statement?

Solution

Fixed Assets Account

Date	*Particulars*	*Amount* [₹]	*Date*	*Particulars*	*Amount* [₹]
1.1.2018	To Balance b/d	1,97,680	*31.12.2018*	By Asset Sold (Cost)	20,000
	To Cash (assets purchased) (balancing figure)[1]	29,560		By balance c/d	2,02,240
		2,22,240			2,22,240

Accumulated Depreciation A/c

Date	*Particulars*	*Amount* [₹]	*Date*	*Particulars*	*Amount* [₹]
31.12.2014	To Asset sold (dep)	12,000	1.1.2018	By balance b/d	85,600
	To Balance c/d	88,500		By Depreciation[2] (balancing figures)	14,900
		1,00,500			1,00,500

Asset Sold Account

Particulars	*Amount* [₹]	*Particulars*	*Amount* [₹]
To Fixed Asset (Cost)	20,000	By Accumulated Dep.	12,000
		By Cash (sale proceeds)	5,000
		By Adjusted P&L a/c (*Loss*—balancing figure)	3,000
	20,000		20,000

1. Fixed assets acquired ₹ 29,560 should be shown "as an application of funds".
2. Depreciation of ₹ 14,900 will be added back to operating profits in order to find out funds from operations.

3. Sale proceeds of assets scrapped ₹ 5,000 will be shown as a source of funds.

4. Loss on sale of assets ₹ 3,000 will be added back to operating profits.

Illustration 4

From the following particulars, prepare a Funds Flow Statement for the year ended on 31st December, 2018.

	Particulars	*Amount* [₹]
(*a*)	Net profit before writing off goodwill	21,500
(*b*)	Depreciation written off on fixed assets	3,500
(*c*)	Goodwill to be written off from profit	5,000
(*d*)	Dividends paid	7,000
(*e*)	Shares issued for cash	10,000
(*f*)	Purchase of machinery	20,000
(*g*)	Ease in working capital	8,000

Solution

Particulars	*Amount* [₹]
Working Notes:	
Funds from operations	21,500
Net profit before writing off goodwill	3,500
Add: Depreciation	
	25,000

Funds Flow Statement

Sources	*Amount* [₹]	*Applications*		*Amount* [₹]
Issue of shares	10,000	Machinery purchased	20,000	
Funds from operations	25,000	Dividend paid	7,000	27,000
		Increase in working capital		8,000
	35,000			35,000

Illustration 5

From the following information relating to X and Company, prepare a Funds Flow statement:

Particulars	*2017* [₹]	*2018* [₹]	*(In Thousands of Rupees)*	*2017* [₹]	*2018* [₹]
Share capital	300	400	Cash	30	90
Reserve	100	50	Accounts receivables	105	150
Retained earnings	30	60	Inventories	150	195
Accounts payable	45	135	Fixed assets	190	210
	475	645		475	645

The company issued bonus shares for ₹ 50,000 and shares for cash ₹ 50,000. Depreciation written off during the year ₹ 15,000.

Solution

Schedule of Changes in Working Capital

Particulars		2017	2018	Effect on working capital	
				Increase (+)	*Decrease (–)*
		Amount [₹]	*Amount* [₹]	*Amount* [₹]	*Amount* [₹]
Current Assets:					
Cash		30,000	90,000	60,000	–
Assets receivable (Dr.)		1,05,000	1,50,000	45,000	–
Inventory (stock)		1,50,000	1,95,000	45,000	–
Total of current assets	(*a*)	285,000	4,35,000		
Current liabilities					
Assets payable (Cr.)	(*b*)	45,000	1,35,000	–	90,000
Total current liabilities		2,40,000	1,35,000	–	90,000
w.c.	(*a* – *b*)	60,000			60,000
Net Increase in working capital		3,00,000	3,00,000	1,50,000	1,50,000

Adjusted P&L A/c (Retained Earnings)

Particulars	*Amount*[₹]	*Particulars*	*Amount*[₹]
To Opening balance	1,90,000	By Depreciation	15,000
To Cash	35,000	By Closing balance	2,10,000
	2,25,000		2,25,000

Fixed Assests A/c

Particulars	*Amount*[₹]	*Particulars*	*Amount*[₹]
To Opening balance	1,90,000	By Depreciation	15,000
To Cash	35,000	By Closing balance	2,10,000
	2,25,000		2,25,000

Total Shares issued	1,00,000
Less: Bonus shares issued (Out of general reserve)	50,000
Issued for cash	50,000

Funds Flow Statement

Sources	*Amount* [₹]	*Applications*	*Amount* [₹]
Issue of shares	50,000	Purchase of fixed assets	35,000
Funds from operation	45,000	Net increase in working capital	60,000
	95,000		95,000

Illustration 6

From the following comparative Balance Sheet of Shri Ram Ltd. as on June 30, 2017 and June, 30, 2018 you are required to prepare

1. A Statement of Changes in the Working Capital
2. Funds Flow Statement

Liabilities	*2017 Amount [₹]*	*2018 Amount [₹]*	*Assets*	*2017 Amount [₹]*	*2018 Amount [₹]*
Share capital	1,80,000	2,00,000	Goodwill	24,000	20,000
Reserve fund	28,000	36,000	Buildings	80,000	72,000
P&L A/c	39,000	24,000	Machinery	74,000	72,000
Trade creditors	16,000	10,800	Investments	20,000	22,000
Bank overdraft	12,400	2,600	Inventories	60,000	50,800
Provision for taxation	32,000	34,000	Debtors	40,000	44,400
Provision for doubtful debts	3,800	4,200	Cash	13,200	30,400
	3,11,200	3,11,600		3,11,200	3,11,600

Additional information:

(*a*) Depreciation charged on machinery was ₹ 8,000, and on building ₹ 8,000.
(*b*) Interim dividend paid on January, 2018 was ₹ 15,000.
(*c*) Provision of ₹ 10,000 was made for taxation during the year ending 30th June, 2018.

Solution

Schedule of Changes in Working Capital

Particulars		*2017 Amount [₹]*	*2018 Amount [₹]*	*Effect on working capital*	
				Increase Amount [₹]	*Decrease Amount [₹]*
Current assets:					
Inventories		60,000	50,800	–	9,200
Debtors, less provision for doubtful debts		36,200	40,200	4,000	–
Cash		13,200	30,400	17,200	–
	Total (*a*)	1,09,400	1,21,400		
Current liabilities:					
Trade creditors		16,000	10,800	5,200	–
Bank overdraft		12,400	2,600	9,800	–
Provision for tax		32,000	34,000	–	2,000
	Total (*b*)	60,400	47,400		
Working capital	(*a – b*)	49,000	74,000		
Net increase in working capital		25,000	–	–	25,000
		74,000	74,000	36,200	36,200

Funds Flow Statement

Sources	*Amount* [₹]	*Applications*		*Amount* [₹]
Issue of shares	20,000	Purchase of investments	2,000	
Funds from operations	28,000	Purchase of machinery	6,000	
		Interim dividend paid	15,000	
				23,000
		Net increase in working capital		25,000
	48,000			48,000

Adjusted P&L A/c

Particulars	*Amount* [₹]	*Particulars*	*Amount* [₹]
To Goodwill written o ff	4,000	By Opening balance	39,000
To Depreciation on m achinery	8,000	By Funds from operations/Balancing fig	28,000
To Building	8,000		
To Interim dividend paid	15,000		
To Reserve fund	8,000		
To Closing balance	24,000		
	67,000		67,000

Building A/c

Particulars	*Amount* [₹]	*Particulars*	*Amount* [₹]
To Opening balance	80,000	By Depreciation	8,000
		By Closing balance	72,000
	80,000		80,000

Machinery A/c

Particulars	*Amount* [₹]	*Particulars*	*Amount* [₹]
To Opening balance	74,000	By Depreciation	8,000
To Cash (Purchase of machinery balancing figure)	6,000	By Closing balance	72,000
	80,000		80,000

Note: Since the provision for Taxation has been treated as a non-current liability, the adjustment item relating to this provision is omitted.

Alternatively, if the provision for taxation is treated as a non-current liability, it will appear as follows:

Provision for Taxation A/c

Particulars	*Amount* [₹]	*Particulars*	*Amount* [₹]
To Cash (taxes paid balance figure)	8,000	By Opening balance	32,000
To Closing balance	34,000	By (Adjusted) P&L A/c (taxation provided during the year)	10,000
	42,000		42,000

The net effect would be that (*i*) the net increase in working capital will increase by ₹ 2,000, (*ii*) Funds from operations will increase by ₹ 10,000, and (*iii*) ₹ 8,000 will be shown as application of funds in the Funds Statement.

Illustration 7

From the following data, prepare "Statement of Sources" and "Uses of Funds":

1. Income Statement

For the year ending on 31st December, 2018 (₹/in 000's)

Particulars		*Amount* [₹]	*Amount* [₹]
Sales		600	
Less: Cost of goods sold		337	
Gross margin on sales		263	
Less: Operating expenses			
Depreciation on machinery	50		
Depreciation on building	80		
Other expenses	100	230	
Net margin on sales			33
Add: Gain on sales of long term investments			12
		Total	45
Less: Loss on sale of machinery (Proceeds from sale of machinery ₹15)			5
Net Income			40

Balance Sheet (₹ in 000's)

As on 31st December 2017 and 31st December, 2018

Liabilities	*2017 Amount [₹]*	*2018 Amount [₹]*	*Assets*	*2017 Amount [₹]*	*2018 Amount [₹]*
Accumulated depreciation	227	150	Cash	315	285
Creditors	100	75	Marketable securities	106	50
Bills payable	50	25	Debtors	150	125
Debentures	500	250	Long-term investments	70	110
Equity share capital	550	400	Inventories	95	70
Premium on shares	60	-	Machinery	500	350
Retained earnings	336	325	Building	600	200
			Land	35	35
	1,871	1,225		1,871	1,225

Solution

Particulars	*Amount (₹ in 000)*	*Amount [₹]*
Income from operation		
Net margin from operations	33	
Add : Depreciation —on machinery	50	
—on building	80	
(or Sales *minus* cost of goods sold, *minus* other expenses ₹ 600 – 337 – 100 = 163)		163

2. Accumulated Depreciation A/c

Particulars	*Amount [₹]*	*Particulars*	*Amount [₹]*
To Closing balance	275	By Opening Balance	150
To Machinery A/c (Depr t. on machinery sold out—balancing figure)	5	By P&L A/c (Dept. on machinery)	50
		By On building	80
	280		280

3. Sales of Machinery ₹ 15 – Source Machinery A/c

Particulars	*Amount* [₹]	*Particulars*	*Amount* [₹]
To Opening balance	350	By Depreciation	5
To Purchase of machinery (balancing figures)	175	Loss on sales (P&L A/c)	5
		Cash (sale of machinery	15
		Closing balance	500
	525		525

4. Purchase of Machinery, ₹ 175 – Application

Statement of Changes in Working Capital (₹ in 000's)

Particulars	*2017 Amount* [₹]	*2018 Amount* [₹]	*Decrease Amount* [₹]	*Increase Amount* [₹]
Current assets:				
Cash:	285	315	–	30
Marketable securities	50	106	–	56
Debtors	125	150	–	25
Inventories	70	95	–	25
	530	666		
Current liabilities:				
Creditors	100	75	25	–
B/P	50	25	25	–
	150	100		
Net increase in working capital			86	–
			136	136

5. It is better to prepare long-term investments A/c

Particulars	*Amount* [₹]	*Particulars*	*Amount* [₹]
To Opening Balance	110	By Closing balance	70
To Gain on sale (P&L A/c)	12	By Cash (Sale of Investments) Balancing figure	52 (Source)
	122		122

6. Sale of Long-term Investments … ₹ 52

Particulars	*Amount* [₹]
Retained earnings: Opening balance …	325
Add: Net income as per income statement	40
	365
Less: Retained earnings at end	336
Balance represents dividend or tax paid	29

Statement of Sources and Uses of Funds

for the Year ended on 31st December, 2018

Sources	*Amount* [₹]
Funds from:	(in 000's)
Trading operations	163
Sale of machinery	15
Sale of investment	52
Issue of equity shares	150
Share premium	60
Issue of debentures	250
	690

Uses		
Funds used for:		
Purchase of machinery	175	
Purchase of building	400	
Payment of dividend/tax	29	604
Net increase in working capital		86

Illustration 8

From the following Balance Sheet of M/s Gamma Ltd. make out:

1. Schedule of changes in the working capital and
2. Statement of sources and application of funds.

Balance Sheet of M/s Gamma Ltd.

₹ in (000)

Liabilities	*2017 Amount* [₹]	*2018 Amount* [₹]	*Assets*	*2017 Amount* [₹]	*2018 Amount* [₹]
Equity Share Capital	300	400	Goodwill	100	80
8% Redeemable preference shares	150	100	Land	200	170
Capital reserve	...	20	Plant	80	200
General reserve	40	50	Investment	20	30
Profit and Loss a/c	30	48	Sundry debtors	140	170
Proposed dividends	42	50	Stock-in-trade	77	109
Sundry creditors	25	47	Bills receivable	20	30
Bills payable	20	16	Cash in hand	15	10
Liabilities for expenses	30	36	Cash at bank	10	8
Provision for taxation	40	50	Preliminary expenses	15	10
	677	817		677	817

Notes: 1. A machine has been sold for ₹ 10,000. The written down value of the machine was ₹ 12,000. Depreciation of ₹ 10,000 is charged on Plant in 2018.

2. A piece of land had been sold out in 2016 and/the profit on sale has been credited to capital reserve.
3. Investments are trade investments. ₹ 3,000 is received by way of dividends including ₹ 1,000 from pre-acquisition which has been credited to Investment Account.
4. An interim dividend of ₹ 20,000 has been paid in 2018.

Solution

Gamma Ltd.
Schedule of Changes in Working Capital

(₹ in .000)

Particulars		2017 Amount [₹]	2018 Amount [₹]	Effect on working capital: Increase Amount [₹]	Decrease Amount [₹]
Current assets:					
Sundry debtors		140	170	30	–
Stock		77	109	32	–
Bill receivable		20	30	10	–
Cash in hand		15	10	–	5
Cash at bank		10	8	–	2
Total of current assets	(*a*)	262	327		
Current liabilities:					
Sundry creditors		25	47	–	22
Bills payable		20	16	4	–
Liability for expenses		30	36	–	6
Total of current liabilities	(*b*)	75	99		
Working capital	(*a* – *b*)	187	228		
Net increase in working capital		41	–	–	41
		228	228	76	76

Gamma Ltd.
Statement of Sources and Application of Funds

Sources	Amount [₹](in 000's)	Applications	Amount [₹](in 000's)
Funds from:		*Funds used for:*	
Trading operations	143	Redemption of preference shares	50
Issue of equity capital	100	Purchase of plant	142
Sale of land	50	Purchase of investments	11
Sale of machine	10	Payment of proposed dividend for 2019	42
Dividends received	3	Payment of interim dividend	20
			265
		Net increase in working capital as per schedule of changes in working capital	41
	306		306

Working Notes ('000 omitted)

Plant A/c

Particulars	*Amount* [₹]	*Particulars*	*Amount* [₹]
To Opening balance	80	By Cash (Sale proceeds)	10
To Cash (purchase of plant) (Balancing ? gure)	142	By P&L A/c (Loss on sale)	2
		By Depreciation	10
		By Closing balance	200
	222		222

Land A/c

Particulars	*Amount* [₹]	*Particulars*	*Amount* [₹]
To Opening balance	200	By Cash (Sale) (Balancing figure)	50
To Capital Reserve (Profit on sale)	20	By Closing balance	170
	220		220

It has been assumed that depreciation has been written off in respect of Land A/c during the year 2017, and land costing ₹ 30,000 (2,00,000 minutes 1,70,000) was sold for ₹ 50,000.

Investment A/c

Particulars	*Amount* [₹]	*Particulars*	*Amount* [₹]
To Opening balance	20	By Dividends Received (Preacquisition)	1
To Cash (purchase) (Balancing ? gure)	11	By Closing balance	30
	31		31

Goodwill A/c

Particulars	*Amount* [₹]	*Particulars*	*Amount* [₹]
To Opening balance	100	By P&L A/c written-off (BalancingFig.)	20
		By Closing balance	80
	100		100

Preliminary Expenses A/c

Particulars	*Amount* [₹]	*Particulars*	*Amount* [₹]
To Opening balance	15	By P&L A/c written-off (BalancingFig.)	5
		By Closing balance	10
	15		15

Proposed Dividend A/c

Particulars	*Amount* [₹]	*Particulars*	*Amount* [₹]
To Cash (paid)	42	By Opening balance	42
To Closing balance	50	By P&L A/c	50
	92		92

It has been assumed that proposed dividend for 2017 was paid during the year 2018.

General Reserve A/c

Particulars	*Amount* [₹]	*Particulars*	*Amount* [₹]
To Opening balance	50	By Opening balance	40
		P&L A/c – Transfer (Balancing figure)	10
	50		50

Provision for Taxation A/c

Particulars	*Amount* [₹]	*Particulars*	*Amount* [₹]
To Opening balance	50	By Opening balance	40
		P&L A/c (Balancing figure)	10
	50		50

Adjusted Profit & Loss A/c

Particulars	*Amount* [₹]	*Particulars*	*Amount* [₹]
To Plant A/c (Dep)	10	By Opening balance	30
To Plant A/c (Loss)	2	By Dividends received	2
To Proposed dividend	50	By Funds fromoperation (Balancing fig)	143
To Goodwill A/c (W/off)	20		
To General reserve A/c (Transfer)	10		
To Provision for taxation	10		
To Preliminary exp. A/c (W/off)	5		
To Interim dividend	20		
To Closing balance	48		
	175		175

Illustration 9

The Comparative Balance Sheet of Subbulakshmi Ltd. as on 31st March 2017 and 31st March 2018 are:

Liabilities	2017 Amount [₹]	2018 Amount [₹]	Assets	2017 Amount [₹]	2018 Amount [₹]
Sundry creditors	39,500	41,135	Cash at Bank	2,500	2,700
Bills payable	33,780	11,525	Sundry debtors	85,175	72,625
Bank overdraft	59,510		Sundry advances	2,315	735
Provision for taxation	40,000	–	Stock	1,11,040	97,370
Reserve	50,000	–	Land & building	1,48,500	1,44,250
Profit and Loss A/c	39,690	–	Plant & machinery	1,12,950	1,16,200
Share capital	2,00,000	–	Goodwill	–	20,000
	4,62,480	4,53,880		4,62,480	4,53,880

The following information is obtained from the General Ledger:

(*a*) During the year ended 31st March, 2018, an interim dividend of ₹ 20,000 was paid.

(*b*) The assets of another company were purchased for ₹ 60,000 payable in fully paid shares of the company.

The assets consisted of:	₹
Stock	21,640
Machinery	18,360
Goodwill	20,000

(*c*) Income-Tax paid during the year amounted to ₹ 25,000.

(*d*) The net profit for the year, before tax, was ₹ 62,530.

You are required to prepare a statement showing the sources and application of funds for the year ended on 31st March, 2018 and the schedule setting out changes in working capital.

Solution

Subbulakhsmi Ltd.
Schedule of Changes in Working Capital

Particulars		*2017 Amount* [₹]	*2018 Amount* [₹]	*Effect on working capital*	
				Increase Amount [₹]	*Decrease Amount* [₹]
Current assets:					
Cash at bank		2,500	2,700	200	
Sundry debtors		85,175	72,625	–	12,550
Sundry advances		2,315	735	–	1,580
Stock		1,11,040	97,370	–	13,670
	Total (*a*)	2,01,030	1,73,430		
Current liabilities:					
Sundry creditors		39,500	41,135	–	1,635
Bills payable		33,780	11,525	22,255	–
Bank overdraft		59,510	–	58,510	–
	Total (*b*)	1,32,790	52,660		
Working capital	(*a* – *b*)	68,240	1,20,770		
Net increase in working capital		52,530	–	–	52,530
		1,20,770	1,20,770	81,965	81,965

Workings Provision for Taxation A/c

Particulars	*Amount* [₹]	*Particulars*	*Amount* [₹]
To Cash income-tax paid	25,000	By Opening balance	40,000
To Closing balance	50,000	By Adjusted P&L A/c	
		(Balancing figure)	35,000
	75,000		75,000

Share Capital A/c

Particulars	*Amount* [₹]	*Particulars*		*Amount* [₹]
To Closing balance	2,60,000	By Opening balance		2,00,000
		By Stock	21,640	
		By Goodwill	20,000	
		By Machinery	18,360	60,000
	2,60,000			2,60,000

Land and Buildings A/c

Particulars	*Amount* [₹]	*Particulars*	*Amount* [₹]
To Opening balance	1,48,500	By Closing balance	1,44,250
		By Adjusted P&L A/c (Depreciation) (Balancing ?gure)	4,250
	1,48,500		1,48,500

Plant and Machinery A/c

Particulars	*Amount* [₹]	*Particulars*	*Amount* [₹]
To Opening balance	1,12,950	By Closing balance	1,16,200
To Share capital A/c	18,350	By (Adjusted P&L A/c)	
To Cash (sundry purchase)	5,650	By (Depreciation)	
		By (Balancing figure)	20,760
	1,36,960		1,36,960

Adjusted Profit Loss A/c

Particulars	*Amount* [₹]	*Particulars*	*Amount* [₹]
To Provision for taxation	35,000	By Opening balance	39,690
To Depreciation on Land	4,250	By (Income from operations) (Balancing figure)	81,540
To Depreciation on plant	20,760		
To Dividend paid	20,000		
To Closing balance	41,220		
	1,21,230		1,21,230

Funds Flow Statement

Sources	*Amount* [₹]	*Application*		*Amount* [₹]
Issue of shares (stock)	21,640	Purchase of plant	5,650	
Funds from operation	81,540	Taxes paid	25,000	
		Dividend paid	20,000	
				50,650
		Net increase in working capital		52,530
	1,03,180			1,03,180

Illustration 10

The comparative balance sheets of M/s. Venkat and Subbu as on 31.12.2017 and 31.12.2018 were as follow:

Liabilities	2017 Amount [₹]	2018 Amount [₹]	Assets	2017 Amount [₹]	2018 Amount [₹]
Sundry creditors	80,000	85,000	Cash	20,000	15,000
Loan from Prasanna	40,000	35,000	Receivables	50,000	90,000
Bank loan	80,000	90,000	Inventories	70,000	60,000
Combined capital	1,25,000	1,50,000	Plant and machinery	80,000	55,000
			Land and buildings	1,05,000	1,40,000
	3,25,000	3,60,000		3,25,000	3,60,000

During the year, a machine costing ₹ 10,000 (accumulated depreciation ₹ 4,000) was sold fo ₹ 7,000. The provision for depreciation against plant and machinery, as on 31.12.2017, wa ₹ 25,000, and on 31.12.2018, ₹ 40,000, net profit for the year 2018 amounted to ₹ 46,000.

Prepare (1) Schedule of changes in working capital, and

(2) Statement of sources and applications of funds.

Solution

(1) Schedule of changes in working capital

Particulars		2017 Amount [₹]	2018 Amount [₹]	Effect on working capital: Increase Amount [₹]	Effect on working capital: Decrease Amount [₹]
Current assets:					
Cash		20,000	15,000	–	5,000
Receivables		50,000	90,000	40,000	–
Inventories		70,000	60,000	–	10000
	Total (*a*)	1,40,000	1,65,000		
Current liabilities:					
Sundry creditors		80,000	85,000		5,000
	Total (*b*)	80,000	85,000		
Working capital	(*a–b*)	60,000	80,000		
Net increase in working capital		20,000	–	–	20,000
		80,000	80,000	40,000	40,000

Workings:

Plant and Machinery A/c

Particulars	Amount [₹]	Particulars	Amount [₹]
To Opening balance (₹ 80,000 + ₹ 25,000)	1,05,000	By Provision for depreciation a/c (Depreciation on machine sold)	4,000
To Adjusted P&L A/c (Profit on sale)	1,000	By Cash (machine sold)	7,000
		By Closing balance (₹ 55000 + 40000)	95,000
	1,06,000		1,06,000

Provision for Depreciation A/c

Particulars	Amount [₹]	Particulars	Amount [₹]
To Plant and machinery A/c (P&L A/c)	4,000	By Opening balance	25,000
To Closing balance	40,000		
		By (Balancing figure – depreciation charged)	19,000
	44,000		44,000

Combined Capital A/c

Particulars	Amount [₹]	Particulars	Amount [₹]
To Combined drawings (balancing Fig.)	21,000	By Opening balance	1,25,000
To Closing balance	1,50,000	By Net profit	46,000
	1,71,000		1,71,000

To Calculation of funds from operation:	
To Net profit for the year	46,000
Add: Depreciation charged	19,000
	65,000
Less: Profit on sale of machinery	1,000
To Opening profits	64,000

Sources and Applications of Fund Statement

Sources	Amount [₹]	Applications		Amount [₹]
Funds from operations	64,000	Purchase of land & buildings	35,000	
Sale of machinery	7,000	Loan paid	5,000	
Bank loan	10,000	Drawings	21,000	
				61,000
		Net increase in working capital		20,000
	81,000			81,000

Illustration 11

The Comparative Balance Sheets of M/s. Alpha and Beta on 31.12.2017 and 31.12.2018 are shown on the next page.

The provision for depreciation against machinery as on 1.1.2017 was ₹ 42,000, and on 31.12.2018. ₹ 54,000. During the year, the partners withdrew ₹ 45,000 for personal expenses. The delivery van was purchased on 31.12.2018 on hire purchase basis; a payment of ₹ 75,00 was made immediately, and the balance is to be paid in 20 monthly instalments of ₹ 1,500 each, together with interest at 12% p.a.

Prepare the funds flow statement, with the supporting schedule of changes in Working Capital.

Liabilities	*2017 Amount* [₹]	*2018 Amount* [₹]	*Assets*	*2017 Amount* [₹]	*2017 Amount* [₹]
Capital	2,20,000	2,30,000	Land	30,000	45,000
Hire purchase Vendor	–	30,000	Buildings	75,000	82,500
Loan from Bank	47,000	38,500	Machinery	1,20,000	1,29,000
Mrs. Alpha's loan	–	30,000	Delivery van	–	37,500
Creditors	30,000	45,000	Stock	37,500	33,000
Bills payable	20,000	14,000	Debtors	30,000	45,000
Expenses creditors	4,000	2,500	Bills receivables	20,500	12,000
			Cash	8,000	6,000
	3,21,000	3,90,000		3,21,000	3,90,000

Solution

Working Notes:

Capital Account

Particulars	*Amount* [₹]	*Particulars*	*Amount* [₹]
To Cash (drawings)	45,000	By Opening balance	2,20,000
To Closing balance	2,30,000	By Net profits (balancing figure)	55,000
	2,75,000		2,75,000

Machinery Account (at Cost)

Particulars	*Amount* [₹]	*Particulars*	*Amount* [₹]
To Opening balance (₹ 1,20,000 + ₹ 42,000)	1,62,000	By Closing balance (₹ 1,29,000 + ₹ 54,000)	1,83,000
To Cash (Purchase of machinery (Balancing figure)	21,000		
	1,83,000		1,83,000

Provision for Depreciation A/c

Particulars	*Amount* [₹]	*Particulars*	*Amount* [₹]
To Closing balance	54,000	By Opening balance	42,000
		P&L A/c (depreciation – balancing Fig.)	12,000
	54,000		54,000

To Funds from operations:

Net profit during 2018	55,000
Add: Depreciation	12,000
Operating profit	67,000

Schedule of Changes in Working Capital

Particulars		*2017 Amount* [₹]	*2018 Amount* [₹]	*Effect on Working capital*	
				Increase Amount [₹]	*Decrease Amount* [₹]
Current assets:					
Stock		37,500	33,000	–	4,500
Debtors		30,000	45,000	15,000	–
Bills receivable		20,500	12,000	–	8,500
Cash		8,000	6,000	–	2,000
	Total (A)	96,000	96,000		
Current liabilities:					
Creditors		30,000	45,000	–	15,000
Bills payable		20,000	14,000	6,000	–
Expenses creditors		4,000	2,500	1,500	–
Hire purchase vendor		–	18,000	–	18,000
	Total (B)	54,000	79,500		
Working capital	(A – B)	42,000	16,500		
Net decrease in working capital		–	25,500	25,500	–
	(A – B)	42,000	42,000	48,000	48,000

Funds Flow Statement

Sources	*Amount* [₹]	*Applications*	*Amount* [₹]
Funds from operations	67,000	Land	15,000
Mrs. Alpha's Loans	30,000	Buildings	7,500
Hire Purchase vendor	12,000	Machinery	21,000
	1,09,000	Delivery van	37,500
Net decrease in working capital	25,500	Bank loan repaid	8,500
		Partners drawings	45,000
	1,34,500		1,34,500

Of the total amount of ₹ 30,000, due to HP vendor, the instalment amount payable within the next 12 months period is treated as Current Liability and is included in the working capital statement The balance is shown as a source towards the purchase of delivery van value of ₹ 37,500 which is treated as application.

Illustration 12

The following are Balance Sheets of Shantha Ltd., for the years 2017 and 2018:

Liabilities	*2017 Amount* [₹]	*2018 Amount* [₹]	*Assets*	*2017 Amount* [₹]	*2018 Amount* [₹]
Share Capital	600	700	Fixed assets	1000	1200
Reserve fund	200	250	*Less:* Accumulated depreciation	200	250
Capital reserve (Profit on sales of investments)	-	10		800	950
Profit and Loss A/c	100	200	Investments (at cost)	180	180
6% Debentures	300	200	Stock	200	270
Sundry creditors	170	260	Debtors less provision	225	245
Proposed dividends	30	35	Bills receivable	40	65
Provision for taxation	70	75	Preliminary expenses	15	10
			Prepaid expenses	10	10
	1,470	1,730		1,470	1,730

Additional Information

1. During the year 2018, Bad debts written off were ₹ 15,000 against the provision account and fixed asset (WDV) ₹ 20,000 (accumulated depreciation ₹ 30,000) was sold for ₹ 15,000.

2. During the year 2018, investments costing ₹ 60,000 were sold and, later in the year, investments of the cost were purchased.
3. Debentures were redeemed at a premium of 5% in 2018.
4. Tax Liability for the 2017 amounted to ₹ 65,000.

Prepare a funds flow statement.

Solution

Workings Fixed Assets A/c

Particulars	*Amount* [₹]	*Particulars*	*Amount* [₹]
To Balance b/d	10,00,000	By Cash (sales)	15,000
To Cash (Balancing figure – purchase of assets)	2,50,000	By Adjusted P&L A/c (Loss on sale)	5,000
		By Accumulated depreciation	30,000
		By Balance c/d	12,00,000
	12,50,000		12,50,000

Accumulated Depreciation A/c

Particulars	*Amount* [₹]	*Particulars*	*Amount* [₹]
To Fixed assets a/c	30,000	By Balance b/d	2,00,000
To Balance c/d	2,50,000	By Adjusted P&L A/c (Balancing Fig.)	80,000
	2,80,000		2,80,000

Investments A/c

Particulars	*Amount* [₹]	*Particulars*	*Amount* [₹]
To Balance b/d	1,80,000	By Cash (sales)	70,000
To Cash (purchase)	60,000	By Balance c/d	1,80,000
To Capital reserve	10,000		
	2,50,000		2,50,000

Adjusted P&L Account

Particulars	*Amount* [₹]	*Particulars*	*Amount* [₹]
To Depreciation	80,000	By Opening balance	1,00,000
To Loss on sale of fixed assets	5,000	By Funds from operations	3,50,000
To Reserve fund	50,000	(Balancing figure)	
To Proposed dividends	35,000		
To Provision for taxation	70,000		
To Preliminary expenses written off	10,000		
To Closing balance	2,00,000		
	4,50,000		4,50,000

Provision for Taxation A/c

Particulars	*Amount* [₹]	*Particulars*	*Amount* [₹]
To Cash (Taxes paid)	65,000	By Balance b/d	70,000
To Balance c/d	75,000	By Adjusted P&L A/c (Provided during the year balancing figure)	70,000
	1,40,000		1,40,000

Schedule of Changes in Working Capital (₹ in 000's)

Particulars		*2017 Amount* [₹]	*2018 Amount* [₹]	*Effect on w orking capital*	
				Increase Amount [₹]	*Decrease Amount* [₹]
Current assets					
Stock		200	270	70	–
Debtors, less provision		225	245	20	–
Bills receivable		40	65	25	–
Prepaid expenses		10	10	–	–
	Total (A)	475	590		
Current liabilities:					
Sundry creditors		170	260	–	90
	Total (B)	170	260		
Working capital	(A – B)	305	330		
Net increase in working capital		25	–	–	25
		330	330	115	115

Funds Flow Statement

Sources	*Amount* [₹]	*Applications*	*Amount* [₹]
Sales of fixed asset	15,000	Purchase of investme nts	60,000
Sales of investments	70,000	Purchase of fixed assets	2,50,000
Issue of shares	1,00,000	Redemption of debentures	1,05,000
Funds from operations	3,50,000	Dividends paid	30,000
		Taxes paid	65,000
			5,10,000
		Net increase in working capita l statement	25,000
	5,35,000		5,35,000

Illustration 13

From the following comparative summary and information, prepare a statement of sources and application of funds:

Supplementary Information (for 2017–2018)

1. Accumulated depreciation on property, plant and equipment amounts to ₹ 4,24,000 on December 31, 2017 and to ₹ 4,11,000 on December 31, 2018.
2. In addition to a machine being scrapped to the end of its effective life, another machine was sold for ₹ 20,000. The original cost of the machine sold was ₹ 70,000, and its net book value on the date of sale was ₹ 30,000.
3. Fixed assets acquired during the period amounted to ₹ 2,13,000.
4. An agency business run by a partnership firm in which one of the directors was a partner was acquired—the purchase consideration of ₹ 1,00,000 was paid in the form of fully paid shares, the consideration was arrived at as follows: Book debts—₹ 30,000, Inventories—₹ 20,000, and ₹ 50,000 towards goodwill.
5. Investments, the book cost of which was ₹ 80,000, were sold for ₹ 1,00,000.
6. During the year 2018 debentures of the face value of ₹ 25,000 were redeemed at a premium of 5 per cent.
7. The net loss for the year after providing for all written-off was ₹ 66,465.
8. A dividend of ₹ 50,000 was declared for the year.

PRODUCTS LIMITED
Balance Sheet
as on December 31

Liabilities	Amount [₹] 2017	Amount [₹] 2018	Assets	Amount [₹] 2017	Amount [₹] 2018
Equity share capital	7,25,000	6,25,000	Investments	25,000	1,05,000
Reserves	2,52,000	2,52,000	Debenture discount	5,000	6,875
Surplus	59,070	1,75,535	Patents	24,000	30,000
6% Debentures	1,00,000	1,25,000	Inventories	3,37,670	2,85,800
Accrued interest on debentures	3,000	3,750	Goodwill	55,000	85,000
Sundry creditors	1,33,000	1,02,000	Property, plant and equipment	5,13,000	4,26,000
Dividends payable	25,000	–	Cash at bank	2,37,800	2,20,650
Provision for taxation	48,000	8,000	Book debts	1,43,000	1,28,760
			Prepaid expenses	4,600	3,200
	13,45,070	12,91,285		13,45,070	12,91,285

Workings:

Funds Flow Statement
for the year ended 31.12.2018

Sources	Amount [₹]	Applications	Amount [₹]
Issue of shares (for purchase consideration towards debtors and inventories)	50,000	Purchase fixed assets	2,13,000
Sale of investments	1,00,000	Redemption of debentures (at a premium)	26,250
Funds from operations	1,56,660	Taxes paid	8,000
Sale of assets	20,000	Dividends paid	25,000
			2,72,250
		Net increase in working capital	54,410
	3,26,660		3,26,660

Workings:

Calculation of Funds from Operations

Particulars	Amount [₹]	Amount [₹]
Net loss for the year	–	(–) 66,465
Add: Depreciation written-off	96,000	
Loss on sale of assets	10,000	
Goodwill written-off	80,000	
Debenture discount written-off	1,875	
Patents written-off	6,000	
Premium on redemption of debentures	1,250	
Provision for tax	48,000	2,43,125
		1,76,660
Less: Profit on sale of investments		20,000
Funds from Operation		1,56,660

Fixed Assets Account

Particulars	*Amount* [₹]	*Particulars*	*Amount* [₹]
To Opening balance	8,50,000	By Cash (Sales)	20,000
To Cash (Purchase)	2,13,000	By Accumulated depreciation	40,000
		By Adjusted P&L A/c (Loss)	10,000
		By Accumulated depreciation (Balancing figure asset scrapped)	69,000
		By Closing balance	9,24,000
	10,63,000		10,63,000

Accumulated Depreciation A/c

Particulars	*Amount* [₹]	*Particulars*	*Amount* [₹]
To Fixed assets A/c (Depreciation of assets sold)	40,000	By Opening balance	4,24,000
		By adjusted P&L A/c (Depreciation written - off) (Balancing figure)	96,000
By Fixed assets A/c (assets scrapped)	69,000		
By Closing balance	4,11,000		
	5,20,000		5,20,000

Changes in Working Capital

Particulars		*2017 Amount* [₹]		*2018 Amount* [₹]
Current assets:				
Cash at bank		2,37,800		2,20,650
Book debts		1,43,000		1,28,760
Inventories		3,37,670		2,85,800
Prepaid expenses		4,600		3,200
Total		7,23,070		6,38,410
Less: Current Liabilities				
Sundry creditors	1,33,000		1,02,000	
Accrued interest on debentures	3,000	1,36,000	3,750	1,05,750
Working Capital		5,87,070		5,32,660

Increase in Working Capital ₹ 54,410 (₹ 5,87,070 – ₹ 5,32,660).

FUNDS OR WORKING CAPITAL FORECAST

Working capital means net current assets, i.e., excess of current assets over current liabilities or cash costs incurred on Current Assets less current liabilities. Hence, the following items are usually taken into account while estimating the working capital requirement of a business.

(*a*) Costs to be incurred on materials, wages and overheads.

(*b*) Length of time during which raw materials are to remain in stock before they are issued to production departments.

(*c*) Length of time during which the work in progress is to remain for completion.

(*d*) Length of time during which the finished goods remain in stock for sales.

(*e*) Period of credit allowed to debtors and period of credit availed of from creditors.

(*f*) Time-lag involved in the payment of wages and overheads expenses.

After estimating the amount of working capital, required by taking the above factors into account, a percentage would be added to the amount for contingencies.

From the following information, calculate the average amount of working capital required, allowing 10% for contingencies.

Example 4:

From the following information, calculate the average amount of working capital required, allowing 10% for contingencies.

	Per annum [₹]
(i) Average amount locked up in stocks:	
Stock of finished goods	10,000
Work in progress	5,000
Stock of stores and raw materials	10,000
(ii) Average credit given:	
Within the state—2 weeks credit	78,000
Outside the state—4 weeks credit	3,12,000
(iii) Time lag in payments:	
For purchases—4 weeks	96,265
For wages—4 weeks	2,60,000

Solution

Working Capital Forecast

Current Assets	*Amount* [₹]	*Amount* [₹]
Stock of finished goods	10,000	
Work in progress	5,000	
Stock of stores and raw material	10,000	25,000
Debtors within the state		
78,000 × 2/52	3,000	
Outside the state 3,12,000 × 4/52		
Total current a sset	24,000	27,000
Less: Current Liabilities		52,000
Creditors 96, 265 × 4/52	7,405	
Outstanding wages 2,60,000 × 2/52		
	10,000	
		17,405
		34,595
Add: 10% for contingencies		3,460
working capital required		38,055

STATEMENT OF CHANGES IN FINANCIAL POSITION (SCFP)

Preparation of funds statements on the aforesaid pattern, however, excludes all those transactions which do not affect working capital. Consequently, many important activities, where fund flows take place between non-current assets to one another, or from one non-current liabilities to another, or from non-current assets to non-current liabilities and vice versa, remain altogether unreported. But, these transactions influence significantly the financial position of the business enterprise, and also the flow of funds. To incorporate all these interfirm non-current exchange transactions, on all financial resources flow statement, termed the Statement of Changes in Financial Position (SCFP) is constructed.

Like the funds statement, it is also prepared from financial data generally identifiable in the income statement, balance sheet and related notes. There is no standard format for this statement However, the International Accounting Standard (IAS-71) states that the presentation of the SCFP should be informative. It also requires that SCFP should be (*i*) presented for each period for which the income statement is prepared, (*ii*) included as an integral part of the financial statements (*iii*) the funds gained or lost in operations should be presented in SCFP separately from other sources or uses of funds. Unusual items, which are not part of the ordinary activities of the enterprise, should be separately disclosed in the statement.

SCFP is thus designed to report causes of changes in financial position (all financial resources, i.e., all assets and liabilities, including owner's equities) of a business during the period that result from its financing and investment activities with others. It thus improves our understanding of operations and activities of an enterprise for the relative period.

Illustration 14

From the figures given below, prepare a statement showing application and sources of funds during the year 2019.

Particulars	*Dec. 31, 2018 Amount [₹]*	*Dec. 31, 2019 Amount [₹]*
Assets:		
Fixed assets (Net) cross	5,10,000	6,20,000
Investment	30,000	80,000
Current assets	2,40,000	3,75,000
Discount on debenture	10,000	5,000
	7,90,000	10,80,000
Liabilities and Capital:		
Share capital (Equity)	3,00,000	3,50,000
Share capital (9% preference)	2,00,000	1,00,000
8% Debentures	1,00,000	2,00,000
Reserves	1,10,000	2,70,000
Provision for doubtful debts	10,000	15,000
Current liabilities	70,000	1,45,000
	7,90,000	10,80,000

The provision for depreciation stood at ₹ 1,50,000 on 31st December, 2018 and at ₹ 1,90,000 on 31.12.2019. During the year:

(*i*) A machine costing ₹ 70,000 (book value ₹ 40,000) was disposed of for ₹ 25,000;

(*ii*) Preference share redemption was carried out at a premium of 5% on 1.1.2019.

(*iii*) Dividend @ 15% was paid on equity shares for the year 2019.

Solution

Statement of Sources and Application of Funds of Exe. Ltd.

for the year ended on December 31, 2019

1. Profit Earning During the year	2,34,000	Purchase of Fixed Assets		2,20,000
Add: Non-cash charges		Purchase of Investment		50,000
Depreciation	70,000	Redemption of preference shares		1,05,000
Discount on Debenture written off	5,000	Payment of Dividend:		
		Preference	9,000	
	3,09,000	Equity	45,000	
Issue of shares	50,000			54,000
Issue of debentures	1,00,000	Increase in working capital		55,000
Sale of machine	25,000			
	4,84,000			4,84,000
Working notes:	*31-12-2012*			*31-12-2012*
Current assets	2,40,000			3,75,000
Less: Provision for doubtful debts	10,000			15,000
	2,30,000			3,60,000
Current liabilities	70,000			1,45,000
Working capital	1,60,000			2,15,000
Increase	55,000			
	2,15,000			2,15,000
2. Depreciation provided during the year: Provision as on 31.12.2018				1,50,000
Less: Provision relating to the machine sold, during the year (Cost₹ 70,000 book value₹40,000)				30,000
Provision as on 31.12.2019				1,20,000
Fresh provision made during the year				1,90,000
3. Profit earned during the year				70,000

Adjusted Profit and Loss A/c

Particulars	Amount [₹]	Particulars	Amount [₹]
To Loss on sale of machine	15,000	By Balance b/d	1,10,000
To Premium Redemption of preference shares	5,000	By profit earned during the year	2,34,000
To Pref. dividend	9,000		
To Equity dividend	45,000		
To Balance c/d	2,70,000		
	3,44,000		3,44,000
Fixed assets acquired:			
Book value of fixed assets on 31.12.2017			5,10,000
Add: Provision for depreciation on 31.12.2017			1,50,000
Cost of fixed Assets as on 31.12.2017			6,60,000
Less: Cost of machine disposed of			70,000
New assets acquired during 2018 (balancing figure) Cost of fixed assets as on 31.12.2018 (₹ 6,20,000 + 1,90,000)			8,10,000

Illustration 15

The summarized balance sheets of Exe. Ltd., as on 31st December 2017 and 2018 are as follows:

Particulars	*December 31, 2015*	*December 31, 2016*
Fixed assets: Cost	8,00,000	9,50,000
Less: Depreciation	2,30,000	2,90,000
	5,70,000	6,60,000
Trade investment	1,00,000	80,000
Current assets	2,80,000	3,30,000
Preliminary expenses	20,000	10,000
	9,70,000	10,80,000
Share capital	3,00,000	4,00,000
Capital reserve	–	10,000
General reserve	1,70,000	2,00,000
Profit and loss account	60,000	75,000
Debentures	2,00,000	1,40,000
Liabilities for goods and services	1,20,000	1,30,000
Provision for income-tax	90,000	85,000
Unpaid dividend	–	4,000
Proposed dividend	30,000	36,000
	9,70,000	10,80,000

During 2018, the company:

1. Sold one machine for ₹ 25,000; the cost of the machine was ₹ 50,000 and the depreciation provided on it amounted to ₹ 21,000;
2. Provided ₹ 95,000 as depreciation;
3. Redeemed 30% of debentures @ 103;
4. Sold some trade investments at a profit credited to capital reserve; and
5. Decided to value the stock at cost whereas previously the practice was to value stock at cost less 10%. The stock according to books on 31.12.2017 was ₹ 54,000; the stock on 31.12.2018 of ₹ 75,000 was correctly valued at cost.

You are required to prepare the statement of sources and application of funds during 2018.

Solution

Statement of Sources and Application of Funds

for the year ended on December 31, 2018

Sources	Amount [₹]	Amount [₹]	Application	Amount [₹]
Profit earned	80,800		Purchase of fixed assets	2,14,000
Add: Non-cash charges			Redemption of debentures	61,800
Depreciation	95,000		Increase in working capital	35,000
Preliminary expenses	10,000	1,85,800	Capital reserve	
Issue of shares		1,00,000		
Sale of trade investments		30,000		
Sale of machine		25,000		
		3,40,800		3,40,800

Working Notes:

1. Profit earned during the year

Adjustment Profit and Loss Account for 2018

	Amount [₹]		Amount [₹]
To Loss on redemption of debentures (3% on ₹ 60,000)	1,800	By Balance b/d	60,000
To Loss on sale of machine	4,000	By Opening stock (54,000 × 10/90)	6,000
To Transfer to general reserve	30,000	By Net profit earned (Balancing figure)	80,800
To Proposed dividend	36,000		
To Balance c/d	75,000		
	1,46,800		1,46,800

2.	**(I) Working capital 31.12.2017**		
	Current assets on 31.12.2017 as given	2,80,000	
	Add: writeup for opening stock	6,000	
			2,86,000
	Less: Current liabilities:		
	Liabilities for goods and services	1,20,000	
	Provision for income-tax	90,000	2,10,000
			76,000
	(ii) Working capital on 31.12.2018		
	Current assets on 31.12.2018		3,30,000
	Less: Liabilities for goods & services	1,30,000	
	Provision for income-tax	85,000	
	Unpaid dividend	4,000	2,19,000
			1,11,000
	(iii) Increase **(ii–i)**		35,000
3.	**Depreciation provision**		
	Balance on 31.12.2017	2,30,000	
	Less: Machine that was sold	21,000	
			2,09,000
	Add: Amount provided in 2017		95,000
	Total that should be on 31.12.2017		3,04,000
	Less: Amount shown in the balance sheet		2,90,000
	Difference, presumably the provision in respect of a discarded machine		14,000
4.	**Fixed assets acquired during 2018 cost as on 31.12.2017**		8,00,000
	Less: Cost of machine		
	Sold	50,000	
	Discarded (see (3) above)	14,000	
			64,000
			7,36,000
	Cost as per Balance Sheet as on 31.12.2018		9,50,000
	Addition : (9,50,000 – 7,36,000)		2,14,000

7. Trade investments have declined by ₹ 20,000 (book value) in addition, there is profit of ₹ 10,000 credited to capital Reserve. Hence, total amount realised is ₹ 30,000.

Illustration 16

A statement of retained earnings of A Ltd. is given below:

Particulars		*Amount* [₹]
Balance of retained earnings 1st July, 2018		2,08,640
Add: Net income after taxes		4,16,330
Tax refund		14,215
		6,39,185
Less: Dividends	2,92,605	
Cost of investment written off	61,150	
Loss on sale of plant	6,670	3,60,425
Balance of retained earnings 30th June 2019		2,78,760

Depreciation of ₹ 39,760 was deducted in arriving at net income for the accounting year.

Plant having a net book value of ₹ 21,605 was sold in August' 2019.

Plant and equipment were purchased during the accounting year at a cost of ₹ 1,60,000 and this purchase was financed by the issue of debentures.

Preference shares were reduced for ₹ 38,700.

Preference a statement of the sources and uses of net working capital for the year ending 30th June, 2019.

Solution

Funds Flow Statement

Sources	*Amount* [₹]	*Uses*	*Amount* [₹]
Sale of plant	14,935	Dividends paid	2,92,605
Tax refund	14,215	Preference shares reduced	38,200
Funds from operations	4,56,050	Net increase in	3,30,805
		Working capital	1,54,395
		(Balance figure)	
	4,85,200		4,85,200

Workings:	*Amount* [₹]
Calculations of funds from operations	4,16,330
Net income after taxes	39,760
Add: Depreciation	4,56,090

Illustration 17

AM and BN are carrying-on business in partnership since January 1st, 2017, sharing profit and losses in the ratio of 3 : 2. Not all the necessary books and records have been maintained. However, the following figures have been ascertained from the available records:

Particulars	*Dec. 31, 2017 Amount [₹]*	*Dec. 31, 2018 Amount [₹]*
Drawings for the year:		
AM	5,000	15,000
BN	10,000	10,000
Sundry creditors	24,000	27,000
Stock	30,000	50,000
Sundry debtors	28,000	48,000
Profit for the year	15,000	28,425
Purchase of machineries	25,000	15,000
Purchase of furniture	10,000	–
Bills payable	12,000	7,000
Bills receivable	8,000	6,000
Sale of furniture	–	2,000
Bank loan obtained	–	50,000
Bank loan discharged	–	10,000
Salaries outstanding	–	2,000
Prepaid insurance	–	500

Cash in hand and at bank amounts to ₹ 7,000 on 31st December, 2018. Partners have been regularly charging depreciation on machineries @ 10% and on furnitures @ 5% excluding sold items.

In 2017, AM and BN introduced further capital of ₹ 10,000 and ₹ 15,000 respectively (other than initial capital).

On 31st December, 2017, the assets of business included cash and bank balances. The book value of furniture sold was ₹ 3,000.

Prepare a statement showing sources and application of funds for the year ended on 31st December, 2018. Show your workings properly.

Solution

M/S AM and BN
Statement of Sources and Application of Funds
for the Year ending on 31st December, 2018

Particulars	*Amount* [₹]	*Amount* [₹]
Sources of funds		
Funds from business operations		33,500
Sale of non-current assets:		2,000
Furniture		
Increase in long-term liabilities:		
Bank loan (long-term)		50,000
Total sources of funds		85,500
Application of funds		
Purchase of non-current assets:		
Machineries		15,000
Payment of long-term liabilities:		
Bank loan		10,000
Recurring withdrawals by partners;		
AM	15,000	
BN	10,000	25,000
Total application of funds		50,000
Increase in working capital (₹ 85,500 – ₹ 50,000)		35,000
Working Notes:		
Profit for the year		
Add: expenses not involving the use of funds:		
Depreciation on machineries		28,425
10% on ₹ 22,500 (2017)	2,250	
10% on ₹ 15,000 (2018)	1,500	3,750
Depreciation on furniture		
5% on (₹ 9,500 (2017) – ₹ 3,000)		325
Loss on sale of furniture (₹ 3,000 – ₹ 2,000)		1,000
		33,500

Machineries A/c

Date	*Particulars*	*Amount* [₹]	*Date*	*Particulars*	*Amount* [₹]
2017	To Bank	25,000	2017	By Depreciation	2,500
			2017	By Balance c/d	22,500
		25,000			25,000
2018	To Balance c/d	22,500	2018	By Depreciation	3,750
2018	To Bank	15,000	2018	Balance c/d	33,750
		37,500			37,500

Furniture A/c

Date	*Particulars*	*Amount* [₹]	*Date*	*Particulars*	*Amount* [₹]
2017	To Bank	10,000	2017	By Depreciation	500
			2017	By Balance c/d	9,500
		10,000			10,000
2018	To Balance c/d	9,500	2018	By Cash	2,000
				By P&L A/c (loss on sale of furniture)	1,000
				By Depreciation	325
				By Balance c/d	6,175
		9,500			9,500

Illustration 18

The following is the balance sheet of a concern as on 30th June, 2017.

Liabilities	*Amount* [₹]	*Assets*	*Amount* [₹]
Capital	12,00,000	Fixed assets (at cost less depreciation)	5,00,000
Trade creditors	2,50,000	Stock	4,50,000
Profit and Loss A/c	80,000	Debtors	2,50,000
		Cash and bank balance	3,30,000
	15,30,000		15,30,000

The management makes the following estimates for the year ending 30th June, 2018

Particulars	*Upto to 31st May, 2018*	*June, 2018*
Purchases	₹ 15,20,000	₹ 1,05,000
Sales	₹ 22,40,000	₹ 2,50,000

Additional Information:

(*a*) It has been decided to invest ₹ 1,50,000 in purchase of fixed assets which are depreciated @ 10%.

(*b*) The time-lag for payment of creditors and receipts from debtors is one month.

(*c*) The business earns a gross profit of $33\frac{1}{3}\%$ on turnover.

(*d*) Sundry expenses against gross profit will amount to 12% of the turnover (excluding depreciation on fixed assets).

You are required to prepare a projected funds flow statements for the year ending 30th June, 2018 (workings to be shown along with the answer).

Solution

Working Notes:

Let us first prepare Projected Income Statement for the year ending 2017 and Balance Sheet as on that date.

Particulars	*Amount* [₹]
Gross profit (1/3) of sales, i.e. ₹ 24,90,000 × 1/3)	8,30,000
Less: Sundry expenses (12% of ₹ 24,90,000)	–2,98,800
Less: Depreciation 10% (₹ 5,00,000 + ₹ 1,50,000)	–65,000
Net income	4,66,200
Add: Profit and loss A/c (Opening balance)	80,000
Profit and loss account (Closing balance)	5,46,200

Projected Balance Sheet for 2018

Liabilities	*Amount* [₹]	*Assets*	*Amount* [₹]
Capital	12,00,000	Fixed assets (at cost less depreciation)	5,85,000
Creditors (June purchases)	1,05,000	Stock	4,15,000
Profit and Loss A/c	5,46,200	Debtors (June sales)	2,50,000
		Cash & Bank balance	6,01,200
	18,51,200		18,51,200

Trading Account

Particulars	*Amount* [₹]	*Particulars*	*Amount* [₹]
To Opening stock	4,50,000	By Sales	24,90,000
To Purchases	16,25,000	By Closing stock	4,15,000
To Gross profit	8,30,000	(Balancing figure)	
	29,05,000		29,05,000

Cash and Bank Account

Particulars	Amount [₹]	Particulars	Amount [₹]
To Balance b/d	3,30,000	By Cash payment to creditors:	
To Cash receipts from debtors:		Creditors opening	2,50,000
		Purchases	15,20,000
To Debtors opening	2,50,000	By Cash expenses	2,98,800
To Sales	22,40,000	(12% of Rs.24,90,000)	
		By Fixed assets	1,50,000
		By Balance c/d	6,01,200
	28,20,000		28,20,000

Projected Fund Flow Statement

for the year ending on 30th June, 2017

	Amount [₹]	Amount [₹]
Sources of funds:		
Funds from business operations:		
Net income	4,66,200	
Add: Depreciation	65,000	5,31,200
Uses of funds:		
Purchase of fixed assets		1,50,000
Net increase in working capital (sources – uses)		3,81,200

Verification:

Working Capital Calculations

			CA		CL	WC
	2018		₹ 12,66,200	-	₹ 1,05,000	₹ 11,61,200
	2017		₹ 10,30,000	-	₹ 2,50,000	₹ 7,80,000
						₹ 3,81,200

Illustration 19

The following are the summarised Trial Balances of H Co. Ltd., as at 31st December, 2017 and 31st December, 2018:

Particulars	*31st December, 2017*		*31st December, 2018*	
	Dr.	Cr.	Dr.	Cr.
Issued share capital	–	80,000		80,000
Capital reserve				20,000
8% Debentures				25,000
Discount on issue of Debentures			500	
Land and building	50,000		40,000	
Plant and machinery	1,00,000		1,25,000	
Provision for depreciation on fixed assets		40,000		50,000
Profit and Loss Account				
Salaries on 1st Jan.		30,000		45,000
Net Profit for the year		23,000		30,000
Dividend for the previous year	8,000		8,000	
Provision for doubtful debts		2,000		3,500
Trade investments (at cost)	10,000		30,000	
Current assets	70,000		85,000	
Current liabilities		35,000		25,000
Bank overdraft		28,000		10,000
	2,38,000	2,38,000	2,88,500	2,88,500

The following additional information is available:

1. During the year, Land and Building, having an original cost of ₹ 10,000 and a written down value of ₹ 7,500, have been sold for ₹ 30,000. The capital profit has been transferred to Capital Reserve and the profit equivalent to the depreciation written off in the past has been included in the profit for the year.
2. On 1st January, 2018, the company issued debentures of a face value of ₹ 25,000 at a discount of 5 per cent. Part of the discount has been written off out of profits.

   Prepare a Statement of Sources and Application of Funds during the year.

Solution

Workings:

Adjusted Profit and Loss A/c

Particulars	*Amount* [₹]	*Particulars*	*Amount* [₹]
To Discount on debentures written off	750	By Profit on sale of Buildings	2,500
To Depreciation written off	12,500	Funds from operations	40,750
Net profit for the Current Year	30,000		
	43,250		43,250

Provision for Depreciation A/c

Particulars	*Amount* [₹]	*Particulars*	*Amount* [₹]
To Land and building A/c	2,500	By Balance c/d	40,000
To Balance c/d	50,000	Adjusted P & L A/c (dep. W/off)	12,500
	52,500		52,500

Land and Buildings A/c

Particulars	*Amount* [₹]	*Particulars*	*Amount* [₹]
To Balance b/d	50,000	By Cash (Sale)	30,000
Capital reserve	20,000	Depreciation	2,500
P&L A/c	2,500	Balance c/d	40,000
	72,500		72,500

Schedule of Changes in Working Capital Effect on W/C

Particulars	*2017* *Amount* [₹]	*2018* *Amount* [₹]	*Increase* *Amount* [₹]	*Decrease* *Amount* [₹]
Current assets:	70,000	85,000		
Less: Provision for doubtful debts	2,000	3,500		
	68,000	81,500	13,500	–
Current liabilities:	35,000	25,000	10,000	–
Bank overdraft	28,000	10,000	18,000	–
	63,000	35,000		
Net increase in working capital			–	41,500
			41,500	41,500

Funds Flow Statement

Sources	Amount [₹]	Application	Amount [₹]
Sale of land and Buildings	30,000	Plant and Machinery	25,000
8% Debentures	23,750	Purchased	
Funds from operations	40,750	Investments purchased	20,000
		Dividends Paid	8,000
			53,000
		Increase in working capital	41,500
	94,500		94,500

Illustration 20

A Ltd. gives you the following statement regarding Assets and Liabilities on 30th June, 2017 and 30th June, 2018:

Particulars	Amount [₹] As at 30th June 2017	Amount [₹] As at 30th June 2018
Fixed assets	2,50,000	3,50,000
Current assets	1,45,000	1,30,000
(Provision for bad debts, ₹ 10,000 and ₹ 9,000 respectively)		
Underwriting commission	10,000	7,000
Profit and Loss account	40,000	68,000
	4,45,000	5,55,000

Liabilities	Amount [₹]	Amount [₹]
Equity share capital	1,50,000	1,50,000
Loan	30,000	60,000
Sundry creditors	1,00,000	1,50,000
Bank overdraft	90,000	1,30,000
Provision for depreciation	75,000	65,000
	4,45,000	5,55,000

During the year, an old asset costing ₹ 10,000 (Depreciation provided for ₹ 6,000) was disposed of for ₹ 3,000. In the previous years, depreciation had been provided for in excess of needs and hence the Provision for Depreciation was brought down to its proper figure on 30th June, 2018. Further, stock, which was previously valued at 10% below cost was valued at its proper figure on 30th June, 2018 after the preparation of the Profit and Loss account. Stock now appears in the Balance Sheet at ₹ 30,000.

Prepare a statement showing sources and application of funds during 2017-18 and comment upon the financial policies of the company.

Solution

Statement of Sources and Application of Funds of A Ltd.

for the Year ended on 30th June 2018

Sources	*Amount* [₹]	*Application*	*Amount* [₹]
Loan	30,000	Cash outflow on account of operations-loss	31,000
Sale of machine	3,000		
Decrease in Working Capital	1,08,000	Fixed assets (purchase)	1,10,000
	1,41,000		1,41,000

Comment

The company's financial position, judged from the current ratio is precarious. It should have not acquired fixed assets at the present juncture. If these are necessary, long-term loans should be raised to the full extent.

Working Notes:

Adjusted Profit and Loss A/c

Particulars	*Amount* [₹]	*Particulars*	*Amount* [₹]
To Balance b/d	40,000	By Provision for depreciation	4,000
To Loss on sale of machine	1,000	By Balance c/d	68,000
To Loss during the year	31,000		
	72,000		72,000

Provision for Depreciation A/c

Particulars	*Amount* [₹]	*Particulars*	*Amount* [₹]
To Machine disposal A/c	6,000	By Balance b/d	75,000
To P&L A/c (Balancing figure)	4,000		
To Balance c/d	65,000		
	75,000		75,000

For ascertaining change in the working capital, current assets should be taken to be ₹ 1,27,000 – excluding the ₹ 3,000 to stock added by revaluation.

Changes in working capital	*30.6.2017 Amount [₹]*	*30.6.2018 Amount [₹]*
Current assets	1,45,000	1,27,000
Current liabilities, Sundry creditors and bank overdraft	1,90,000	2,80,000
Working capital	– 45,000	–1,53,000
Decrease in working capital		1,08,000

Illustration 21

The following Balance Sheets have been prepared from the books of Raj Limited as appearing on 31.12.2017 and 31.12.2018.

Balance Sheet

Liabilities	*2017 Amount [₹]*	*2018 Amount [₹]*	*Assets*	*2017 Amount [₹]*	*2017 Amount [₹]*
Equity capital	4,00,000	6,00,000	Buildings	5,70,000	5,00,000
Share premium	1,00,000	1,10,000	Plant and machinery	3,60,000	3,51,000
General reserve	2,00,000	2,20,000	Furniture	90,000	81,000
Debenture redemption			Cash in hand	5,000	8,000
reserve	1,00,000	1,10,000	Stock	1,55,000	1,45,000
Debenture	3,00,000	2,90,000	Debtors	1,80,000	1,60,000
Taxation provision	40,000	35,000	Bills receivable	4,000	40,000
Secured loan	2,00,000	1,00,000	Investments	–	2,10,000
Current liabilities	24,000	30,000			
	13,64,000	14,95,000		13,64,000	14,95,000

(*a*) During 2018, the company paid 12% dividend on its equity share capital of ₹ 4,00,000.

(*b*) The shares are of ₹ 100 each fully paid.

(*c*) Taxation provision of 2017 was utilised to the extent of ₹ 30,000, for income tax paid in 2018.

(*d*) Depreciation was charged on buildings at 5% on plant and machinery at 10% and on furniture at 10% for a full one year.

(*e*) A building worth ₹ 70,000 was sold on 1.1.2018 at ₹ 60,000 and new building was constructed at a value of ₹ 25,000 on 31.12.2018.

(*f*) A machine was purchased at a cost of ₹ 40,000 on 1.1.2018 while a machine having a book value of ₹ 10,000 was sold on 1.7.2018 at ₹ 20,000.

Prepare a statement showing movement in working capital, profit and loss appropriation account and a statement showing sources and application of funds.

Solution

Profit and Loss Appropriation Account

Particulars	*Amount* [₹]	*Particulars*	*Amount* [₹]
To Dividend paid 12% on ₹ 4,00,000	48,000	By Balance b/d	78,000
To Debenture redemption reserve	10,000	(Balancing figure)	
To General reserve	20,000		
	78,000		78,000

Statement Showing Movement in Working Capital

Particulars	*2017*	*2018*	*Change in working capital*	
			Increase	*Decrease*
Current Assets				
Cash in hand	5,000	8,000	3,000	–
Investments		2,10,000	2,10,000	–
Stock	1,55,000	1,45,000	–	10,000
Debtors	1,80,000	1,60,000	–	20,000
Bills receivable	4,000	40,000	36,000	
Total current assets 'A'	3,44,000	5,63,000		
Current Liabilities				
Taxation provision secured loans	40,000	35,000	5,000	
Current liabilities	2,00,000	1,00,000	1,00,000	
	24,000	30,000		6,000
Total current liabilities 'B'	2,64,000	1,65,000		
Working capital A -B	80,000	3,98,000		36,000
Increase in Working capital	3,18,000	–		3,18,000
	3,98,000	3,98,000	3,54,000	3,54,000

Notes:

1. Investment is treated as a current asset.
2. Taxation provision has been treated as a current liability.
3. Secured loan has been treated as a bank loan secured by the hypothcation of stock, etc.

Statement Showing the Source and Application of Funds

Sources		*Amount* [₹]
Funds from operations (see working note 1)		1,51,000
Issue of equity shares		2,00,000
Share premium		10,000
Sale of buildings		60,000
Sale of machinery		20,000
Total (A)		4,41,000
Application		
Purchase of buildings		25,000
Purchase of plant and machinery		40,000
Redemption of debentures		10,000
Dividend paid		48,000
Total (B)		1,23,000
Increase in working capital (A – B)		3,18,000

Working Notes:

1.	Funds from operations have been computed as follows:		
	Net profit as per Profit & Loss Appropriation A /c		78,000
	Add: Depreciation (see working note 2)		73,500
	Add: Loss on sale of buildings		10,000
			1,61,500
Less:	Gain on sale of machinery (see working note 3)		10,500
	Funds from operations		1,51,000
2.	Computation of depreciation:		
	(*i*) Depreciation on buildings:		
	On ₹ 5,00,000 @ 5% for full one year		25,000
	(*ii*) Depreciation on plant & machinery:		
	On ₹ 3,00,000 (3,60,000 + 40,000 – 10,000)		
	@10% for full one year	39,000	
	On ₹ 10,000 @ 10 for 6 months	500	39,500

Contd...

(*iii*) Depreciation on furniture: On ₹ 90,000 @ 10% for full year	9,000
	73,500
3. Gain on sale of machine is determined as follows:	
Sales proceeds	20,000
Less: Net depreciation value of the machine (10,000 – 500)	9,500
	10,500

Illustration 22

Prepare a working capital forecast from the following information:

	₹
Issued share capital	2,00,000
8% Debentures	75,000

The fixed assets are valued at ₹ 2 lakhs. Production during the previous year is 50,000 units. The same level of activity is intended to be maintained during the current year. The expected ratio of cost to selling price are:

Raw materials	50%
Wages	10%
Overheads	25%

The raw materials normally remain in stores for two months before production. Every unit of production remains in process for one month. Finished goods remain in the warehouse for four months. Credit allowed by creditors is three month and credit allowed to debtors is three months. Selling price is ₹ 6 per unit. Both production and sales are in a regular cycle. Add 10% for contingencies.

Solution

Workings:

Total Sales = 50,000 × 6 = 3,00,000

Cost of Sales: Raw materials (50%)	= ₹ 1,50,000
Wages (10%)	= ₹ 30,000
Overheads (25%)	= ₹ 75,000
Stock of raw materials = 1,50,000 × 2/12 (two months)	= ₹ 25,000

Work in process (one month)

Raw materials 1,50,000 × 1/12	= ₹ 12,500
Wages 30,000 × 1/12	= ₹ 2,500
Overheads 75,000 × 1/12	= ₹ 6,250
	= ₹ 21,250

Stock of finished Goods (4 months) 2,55,000 × 4/12 = ₹ 85,000

Debtors: 2,55,000 × 3/12 = ₹ 63,750

Creditors: 1,50,000 × 3/12 = ₹ 37,500

Working Capital Forecast

Current Assets:	
Stock of raw materials	25,000
Work in process	21,250
Stock of finished goods	85,000
Debtors	63,750
	1,95,000
Less: Creditors	37,500
	1,57,500
Add: Contingencies (10%)	15,750
Working capital required	1,73,250

Illustration 23

A Ltd. commenced production on 1-1-2018. The material cost is ₹ 16 per unit and wages ₹ 24 per unit. In addition, variable expenses are expected to be ₹ 8 per unit and fixed expenses ₹ 30,000 per month. Payment for materials is to be made in the month following the purchase. One-third of sale units to be for cash and the rest on credit for settlement in the following month. Expenses are payable in the month in which they are incurred. The selling price is fixed at ₹ 80 per unit. The number of units manufactured and sold are expected to be as under:

January—900; February—1,200; March—1,800; April—2,100; May—2.100; June—2,400. Draw a statement showing requirement of working capital from month to month, ignore the question of stocks.

Solution

Statement Showing Requirement of Working Capital

Particulars	Jan Amount [₹]	Feb Amount [₹]	Mar. Amount [₹]	Apr. Amount [₹]	May Amount [₹]	June Amount [₹]
Receipts:						
Sales: Cash	24,000	32,000	48,000	56,000	56,000	64,000
Credit	–	48,000	64,000	96,000	1,12,000	1,12,000
Total (A)	24,000	80,000	1,12,000	1,52,000	168,000	17,600
Requirements:						
Materials	–	14,400	19,200	28,800	33,600	33,600
Wages	21,600	28,800	43,200	50,400	50,400	57,600
Variable expenses	7,200	9,600	14,400	16,800	16,800	19,200
Fixed expenses	30,000	30,000	30,000	30,000	30,000	30,000
Total (B)	58,800	82,800	1,06,800	1,26,000	1,30,800	1,40,400
Cash Surplus (Deficits) (A-B)	(34,800)	(2,800)	(5,200)	26,000	37,200	35,600
Cumulative surplus/ Deficit	(34,800)	(37,600)	(32,400)	(6,400)	30,800	66,400

Illustration 24

From the following data, construct a funds flow statement and the SCFP (Statement of Changes in financial position) for the year ended on 31st December, 2018)

Particulars	Jan. 1, 2017 [₹]	Dec. 31, 2018 [₹]	Particulars	Jan. 1, 2017 [₹]	Dec. 31, 2018 [₹]
Goodwill	6,000	5,000	Share capital	30,000	36,000
Land	19,800	19,800	Share premium		300
Furniture	2,000	1,000	Reserves	8,000	9,200
Machinery	26,400	23,400	P&L A/c	5,260	5,500
Investments	4,000	6,000	Debentures	5,000	5,000
Inventory	12,080	8,680	Trade creditors	11,740	9,100
Book debts	8,000	8,320	B/P	8,540	400
Bank	1,080	1,100	Outstanding expenses	160	60
Prepaid expenses	220	280	Unclaimed dividend	—	100
			Accumulated depreciation	8,300	5,140
			Provision for bad debt	380	480
			Provision for taxation	2,200	2,300
	79,580	73,580		79,580	73,580

Additional information: During the year 2018 (*a*) in addition to goodwill, machinery worth ₹ 3,400 and inventory worth ₹ 1,900 were acquired by issue of fully paid shares; (*b*) 2,000 debentures were redeemed for ₹ 1,950; (*c*) Furniture acquired for ₹ 1,000 (with an accumulated depreciation of ₹ 500) was sold for ₹ 150; (*d*) Machinery costing ₹ 8,000 (with an accumulated depreciation of ₹ 4,500) realised ₹ 3,800; and (*e*) Interim as also final dividends declared were ₹ 720 and ₹ 1,200 respectively.

Solution

Funds Flow Statement

for the Year ended on 31st December 2018

Sources	*Amount* [₹]	*Uses*	*Amount* [₹]
Sale of furniture	150	Debenture redemption	1,950
Sale of Machinery	3,800	Investment acquisition	2,000
Share issue (inventory acquisition)	1,900	Dividend appropriations (720 + 1,200)	1,920
Debenture issue	2,000	Machinery acquisition	1,600
Funds from operations	7,200	Increase in funds, viz., net working capital (balancing figure)	7,580
	15,050		15,050

Statement of Changes in Financial Position

Working Notes:

Machinery Account

Particulars	*Amount* [₹]	*Particulars*		*Amount* [₹]
Opening balance	26,400	Sundries		
Share capital A/c (Purchase of machine)	3,400	Cash (Sale proceeds of machine)	3,800	
Profit and Loss A/c (Transfer of gain on sale)	300	Accumulated depreciation for sold machine	4,500	8,300
Cash (Acquisition of machine balancing figure)	1,600	Closing balance		23,400
	31,700			31,700
		Adjusted Profit and Loss Account		
Write off goodwill (6,000 + 1,000 – 5,000)	2,000	Opening balance Non-operating gains	300	5,260
Transfer to reserve (9,200 – 8,000)	1,200	Debenture redemption	50	350
Non-opening loss:		Funds from operations (Balancing figure)		7,200
Furniture sold (1,000 – 500 – 150)	350			
Current years depreciation (See Accum. Dept. A/c)	1,840			
Closing balance	5,500			
	12,810			12,810

Sources		*Amount* [₹]	*Uses*		*Amount* [₹]
Items raising funds			Items using funds		
Sale of furniture	150		Debenture redemption	1,950	
Sale of machinery	3,800		Investment acquisition	2,000	
Share issue	1,900		Dividend appropriations	1,920	
Debenture issue	2,000		Machinery acquisition	1,600	7,470
Funds from operation	7,200	15,050	Items not using funds (confined) to external exchanges of one type of non-current item with that of another		
Items not raising funds (Attributable to inter firm conversion of one – type of non – current item with that of another): share issue (including share premium Rs. 300)		4,400	Machinery acquisition	3,400	
			goodwill	1,000	4,400
			Increase in funds (balancing figure)		7,580
		19,450			19,450

Accumulated Depreciation Account

Particulars	*Amount* [₹]	*Particulars*	*Amount* [₹]
Machinery (Transfer in respect of sold machine)	4,500	Opening balance	8,300
Furniture (Transfer for disposed furniture)	500	Profit & loss A/c (Current year depreciation) (balancing figure)	1,840
Closing balance	5,140		
	10,140		10,140

REVIEW QUESTIONS

1. Define the term 'funds of funds' and funds statement.
2. What is Working Capital? Give some examples of expenses and losses which do not affect the Working Capital.
3. Examine the major sources and applications of Working Capital.
4. Explain the managerial uses of funds flow statement.
5. Give your comments on the following statements.

   (*a*) "Net losses mean drains on working capital",

   (*b*) "Depreciation is usually a big source of working capital".
6. Explain the following (*a*) Funds from operations, (*b*) non current accounts (*c*) non fund items.
7. What is the purpose of the statement of change in financial position.
8. Explain the procedure for the construction of funds flow statement.
9. Explain the various techniques of fund reporting
10. From the following Balance sheet as on 31st Dec. 2017 and 2018, prepare a Schedule of Changes in Working Capital for 2020:

Particulars	*2017 Amount* [₹]	*2018 Amount* [₹]
Assets		
Cash	30,000	47,000
Debtors	1,20,000	1,15,000
Stock in-trade	80,000	90,000
Land	50,000	66,000
Capital and Liabilities	2,80,000	3,18,000
Share capital	2,00,000	2,50,000
Trade creditors	70,000	45,000
Retained earnings	10,000	23,000
	2,80,000	3,18,000

[**Ans.** Increase in Working Capital ₹ 47,000]

11. "An analysis of the flow of funds through an organisation can be very useful to the management." Elucidate this statement.
12. From the following summarised Balance Sheet of YZ Ltd 'for two years as on 31st March, 2017 and, 31st March, 2018:

   (*i*) Explain how the increase assets was financed.

   (*ii*) Find out the working capital for each of the two years, and comment on the significance of changes.

Particulars	*31.3.2017 Amount* [₹]	*31.3.2018 Amount* [₹]
Share capital	10,00,000	15,00,000
Share premium	1,00,000	1,50,000
Profit and Loss account	4,00,000	7,00,000
Trade creditors	2,50,000	3,00,000
Bank overdraft	–	1,00,000
Proposed dividend	50,000	50,000
	18,00,000	28,00,000
Land and Buildings	5,00,000	5,00,000
Plant and Machinery	7,00,000	16,00,000
Stock	1,75,000	3,00,000
Debtors	2,25,000	3,50,000
Cash	2,00,000	50,000
	18,00,000	28,00,000

(B. Com, Madras, Nov. 1979)

[Ans. (*i*) Increase in Fixed Assets has been financed by issue of shares of ₹ 5,50,000 funds from operations ₹ 3,00,000 and ₹ 50,000 from working capital.

(*ii*) Working capital in 2008 — ₹ 3,00,000

Working capital in 2009 — ₹ 2,50,000

[**Hint.** proposed dividend has been taken as a current liability]

13. Prepare a Funds Flow Statement from the following data:

Particulars	*31.3.2017 Amount* [₹]	*31.3.2018 Amount* [₹]
Cash	2,000	2,500
Accounts receivable	2,400	2,700
Inventories	300	3,200
Other assets	800	700
Fixed assets	5,000	5,800
Accumulated depreciation	2,100	2,500
Accounts payable	2,000	2,100
Long term debt	1,400	1,300
Equity capital	5,000	5,300
Retained earnings	2,800	3,700

Notes:

(*a*) Fixed assets costing ₹ 1,200 were purchased for cash.

(*b*) Fixed assets (original cost ₹ 400, accumulated depreciation ₹ 150) were sold for ₹ 200.

(*c*) Depreciation for the year 2018 amounted to ₹ 550 and duly debited to Profit and Loss Account. Dividends paid amounted to ₹ 300 in 2018.

(*d*) Reported income for 2016 was ₹ 1,200.

[**Ans.** Increase in the working capital ₹ 700 sources ₹ 2,300, Application ₹ 1,600]

14. The comparative Balance sheets of Bharat Trading Corporation Limited are indicated in condensed form as under:

Particulars	*Amount* [₹]	*Amount* [₹]	*Amount* [₹]	*Amount* [₹]
Fixed assets	5,20,000		4,80,000	
Less: Depreciation to date	1,40,000	3,80,000	1,08,000	3,72,000
Investment at cost		50,000		1,00,000
Stocks	95,500			55,600
Sundry debtors	1,62,800			1,18,300
Cash and bank balance	47,500			7,200
	7,35,800			7,02,900
Share capital ordinary shares of ₹ 100 each issued for cash	4,00,000			3,60,000
General reserve	60,000			1,10,000
Surplus in profit and loss a/c	33,450			20,450
Sundry creditors	1,95,350			1,33,650
Proposed dividend	15,000			28,800
Provision for taxation	32,000			50,000
	7,35,800			7,02,900

Additional Information:

The net profit for the year (after providing for depreciation ₹ 40,000, writing off preliminary expenses ₹ 7,200 and making provision for taxation ₹ 32,000) amounted to ₹ 38,000.

The company sold during the year old machinery costing ₹ 9,000 for ₹ 3,000. The accumulated depreciation on the said machinery was ₹ 8000.

A portion of the company's investment became worthless and was written off to general reserve. The cost of such investment was ₹ 50,000.

During the year, the company paid an Interim dividend to ₹ 10,000 and final dividend of ₹ 15,000 recommended for 2018.

Prepare a Funds Flow Statement.

Answers: Increase in the working capital ₹ 52,000

Funds from operations ₹ 83,200

Total Sources ₹ 1,26,200

Applications ₹ 74,000

15. From the following Balance Sheet on 1-1-2018 and the budgeted Balance Sheet as on 31.12.2018 prepare a Funds Flow Statement, as estimated:

Particulars	*1.1.2018*		*31.12.2018*	
	Amount [₹]	*Amount* [₹]	*Amount* [₹]	*Amount* [₹]
Equity share capital		20,00,000		25,00,000
Share premium account		–		1,00,000
Profit on sale of leasehold property		–		25,000
Profit on redemption of debentures		–		4,000
Profit and Loss A/c (Balance b/f)		4,50,000		4,50,000
Profit for the year, before taxation		–		4,85,000
4% Debentures		5,00,000		4,50,000
Creditors		6,40,000		4,00,000
Reserve for income-tax		3,10,000		5,90,000
Proposed dividend (Net)		1,00,000		31,200
		40,00,000		45,85,200
Freehold property at cost		14,50,000		18,50,000
Leasehold property at cost		50,000		5,00,000
Plant and machinery at cost	18,00,000		21,00,000	
Less: Depreciation to date	7,20,000	10,80,000	9,30,000	11,70,000
Investments		1,60,000		2,24,000
Work-in-progress		1,70,000		1,50,000
Stock in trade		2,70,000		3,60,000
Debtors		6,20,000		1,47,200
Bank balance		2,00,000		1,84,000
		40,00,000		45,85,200

During 2018, it was anticipated that plant, costing ₹ 1,30,000 (Depreciation ₹ 90,000) would be sold for ₹ 30,000. The transaction had been allowed for in preparing the estimated Balance Sheet as on 31-12-2018, the loss on sale having been charged against profit for the year.

16. Given below are the Balance Sheets on December 31, 2017 and December 31, 2018 and a statement of income and reconciliation of earnings for 2018 of Electronics Ltd. The only item in the Building and Equipment Account sold during the year was a specialised machine that originally cost ₹ 15,000. The accumulated depreciation on this machine at the time of sale was ₹ 8,000. The machine was sold for 6,000 and full payment was received in cash.

Particulars	*Dec. 31, 2017 Amount* [₹]	*Dec. 31, 2018 Amount* [₹]
Cash	74,000	37,000
Account receivable	54,000	47,000
Inventories	3,12,000	2,77,000
Prepaid expenses	6,000	4,000
Land	60,000	60,000
Patents	55,000	65,000
Buildings and Equipment	4,20,000	4,80,000
Less: Accumulated depreciation	(1,05,000)	(1,20,000)
Total assets	8,76,000	8,50,000
Account payable	58,000	94,000
Notes payable	28,000	8,000
Estimated income-tax	86,000	12,000
Social security taxes accrued	3,000	5,000
Debentures	2,20,000	60,000
Capital	2,50,000	4,60,000
Retained earnings	2,31,000	2,11,000
	8,76,000	8,50,000

Electronics Limited

Statement of Income and Reconciliation of Earning for 2018

Net sale		19,70,000
Less: Cost of goods sold		14,80,000
		4,90,000
Less: Operating expenses (including depreciation on building and equipment of ₹ 23,000, patent amortization of ₹ 6,000)		50,00,000
Net loss from operation		10,000
Less: Other revenue		7,000
Net loss		3,000
Add: Retained earnings, December, 31, 2018		2,31,000
		2,28,000
Less: Dividend paid	16,000	
Loss on sale of assets	1,000	
		17,000
Retained earnings, December 31, 2018 Prepare a funds flow statement		2,11,000

[**Ans.** Increase in W.C. ₹ 99,000; Funds from operations ₹ 16,000; Total application ₹ 4,40,000]

17. From the following Balance Sheet of Y Ltd. on 31st December, 2017 and 2018 you are required to prepare

(*a*) A schedule of changes in the working capital

(*b*) A funds flow statements.

Liabilities	*2017 Amount* [₹]	*2018 Amount* [₹]	*Assets*	*2017 Amount* [₹]	*2018 Amount* [₹]
Share capital	1,00,000	1,00,000	Goodwill	12,000	12,000
General reserve	14,000	18,000	Building	40,000	36,000
Profit and loss A/c.	16,000	13,000	Plant	37,000	36,000
Sundry creditors	8,000	5,400	Investments	10, 000	11,000
Bills payable	1,200	800	Stock	30,000	23,400
Provision for taxation	16,000	18,000	Bills receivable	2,000	3,200
Provision for doubtful debts	400	600	Debtors	18,000	19,000
			Cash at Bank	6,600	15,200
	1,55,600	1,55,800		1,55,600	1,55,800

The following additional information has also been given:

(*i*) Depreciation charged on plant was ₹ 4,000 and on building ₹ 4000

(*ii*) Provision for taxation of ₹ 19,000 was made during the year 2018

(*iii*) Interim dividend of ₹ 8,000 was paid during the year 2018

[**Ans.** Increase in working capital ₹ 5,000 Funds from operation 17,000. Total sources ₹ 17,000). (*Note:* Total Provision for taxation as current liability]

18. For each of the following transactions state whether items involved would appear on funds statements for the period. For these items appearing on the funds statement, state whether each item would be a source of net working capital or a use of net working Capital, and where appropriate state the amount of the source or use.

(*a*) Sold 1500 Equity shares of ₹ 100 each at a premium of 10 per cent.

(*b*) Retired fully depreciated equipment which had an original cost of ₹ 15,000.

(*c*) Sold fixed assets for ₹ 20,000 that had an original cost of ₹ 50,000 and accumulated depreciation of ₹ 30,000.

(*d*) Declared and paid a cash dividend of ₹ 50,000 and issued a stock dividend for ₹ 50,000.

(*e*) Amortised goodwill on the income statement ₹ 20,000.

(*f*) Purchased ₹ 35,000 inventory on account.

(*g*) Purchased an equipment for ₹ 5,000 on a 2 month 6% note.

19. A statement of retained earnings of back Ltd. is shown as follows:

		Amount [₹]
Balance of retained earnings (1.1.2018)		2,08,640
Add: Net profit after taxes		4,16,330
Tax refund		14,215
		6,39,185
Less : Dividends	2,92,605	
Goods written off	61,150	
Loss on sale of plant	6,670	3,60,425
Balance of retained earnings (31.12.2018)		2,78,760

Depreciation of ₹ 39,760 was in arriving at net profit for the accounting year.

Plant having a net book value of ₹ 21,605 was sold in August 2018. A new plant costing ₹ 27,500 was purchased and the purchase was financed by the issue of preference shares of ₹ 10 each at a premium of 10 per cent.

300, 8% Debentures of ₹ 100 each were redeemed at a premium of 20 per cent during the accounting year.

Prepare a statement of the Sources and Uses of Net Working Capital for the year ending 31-12-2015. (Answer: Net increase in Working Capital ₹ 1,56,635).

20. Balance Sheets of M/s Bee and Kee as on 1.1.2018 and 31.12.2018 were as follows:

Liabilities	*1 Jan. 2018*	*31 Dec. 2018*	*Assets*	*1 Jan.. 2018*	*31 Dec. 2018*
Creditors	40,000	44,000	Cash	10,000	7,000
Mr. Kee's loan	25,000	–	Debtors	30,000	50,000
Loan from			Stock	35,000	25,000
P.N. Bank			Machinery	35,000	55,000
Capital	40,000	50,000	Land	40,000	50,000
	1,25,000	1,53,000	Building	35,000	60,000
	2,30,000	2,47,000		2,30,000	2,47,000

During the year, machine costing ₹ 10,000 (accumulated depreciation ₹ 3,000) was sold for ₹ 5,000. The provision for depreciation against machinery as on 1.1.2018 and on 31.12,2018; ₹ Net Profit for the year 2018 amounted to ₹ 45,000. You are required to prepare Funds (working capital) Flow Statement.

[**Ans.** Increase in working capital ₹ 3,000; Funds from operations ₹ 65,000; Total sources ₹ 80,000.

21. The Balance Sheets of A Co., Ltd., as at the end 2017 and 2018 are given below:

Liabilities	*2017*	*2018*	*Assets*	*2017*	*2018*
Share capital	20,000	30,000	Freehold land	20,000	20,000
Share premium	—	1,000	Plant at cost	20,800	20,000
General reserve	10,000	12,000	Furniture at cost	1,400	1,800
Profit and loss account	2,000	3,400	Investment at cost	12,000	16,000
6% Debenture	14,000	10,000	Debtors	6,000	14,000
Provision for	10,000	11,200	Stock	12,000	13,000
Depreciation on plant			Cash	6,000	9,000
Provision for depreciation on furniture	1,000	1,200			
Provision for taxation	4,000	6,000			
Sundry creditors	17,200	19,000			
	78,200	93,800		78,200	93,800

A plant purchased for ₹ 800 (Depreciation ₹ 400) was sold for cash for ₹ 160 on September 30, 2018. On June 30, 2018, an item of furniture was purchased for ₹ 400. These were the only transactions concerning fixed assets during 2018. A dividend of 22.½% on original shares was paid.

You are required to prepare a Funds Flow Statement and verify the results by preparing a schedule of changes in the working capital.

Note: Treat provision for taxation as non-current liability. Answer: (Increase in working capital ₹ 10,200; Funds from operations ₹ 15,940; Total sources ₹ 27,100.

22. The following schedule shows the Balance Sheets in condensed form of B Co. Ltd., at the beginning and end of the year 2018.

Asset	*1 Jan. 2018 Amount*[₹]	*31 Dec. 2018 Amount*[₹]
Cash and Bank balances	10,000	8,000
Sundry debtors	15,400	14,600
Temporary investments	22,000	16,800
Prepaid expenses	200	400
Stock in trade	18,400	21,200
Land and buildings	20,000	20,000
Machinery	14,400	16,000
Total	1,00,400	97,000
Liabilities and Capital:		
Sundry creditors	20,600	19,200
Outstanding expenses	2,600	4,400
5% Debentures	18,000	14,000
Depreciation fund	8,000	8,800
Reserve for contingencies	12,000	10,000
Profit and Loss account	3,200	4,600
Capital	36,000	36,000
Total	1,00,400	97,000

The following information concerning transactions is available:

(*i*) 10% dividend was paid in cash.

(*ii*) New Machinery for ₹ 4,000 was purchased but old machinery costing ₹ 2,400 was sold for ₹ 800, accumulated depreciation was ₹ 1,200.

(*iii*) ₹ 4,000, 5% Debentures were redeemed by purchsase from open market @ ₹ 96.

(*iv*) ₹ 2,000 was debited to Contingency Reserve for settlement of previous tax liability.

(*v*) ₹ 5,200 investments' were sold at book value.

You are required to prepare a schedule of change in working capital and a statement showing the sources and application of funds.

[**Ans.** Decrease in working capital. ₹ 5,400; Funds from operations ₹ 7,240; Total applications ₹ 13,440].

■ ■ ■

9

Cash Flow Analysis

CONCEPT OF FUNDS

As discussed in the previous chapter, the term "funds" has different connotations ranging from the narrow one of "cash" to that of "all financial resources". But the most common connotation is "working capital". While the broader concept of "all financial resources" takes into account all significant transactions relating to current as well *as* non-current accounts, the intermediate connotation, i.e. "working capital", considers only such information which relate to significant fluctuations in working capital. When it is used as equivalent to cash, the funds flow analysis would be called cash flow analysis. Under cash flow analysis, all movements of cash, rather than the inflow and outflow of working capital would be considered. Such movements are depicted in a statement called Cash Flow Statement.

TYPES OF CASH FLOW

While preparing a cash flow statement, two types of cash flows, viz. actual cash flows and notional cash flows, are identified. Actual cash flows refer to the actual movements of cash into or out of business. Purchase of fixed assets, borrowings from bank or financial institutions, trading profits and redemption of debentures are all examples of actual cash flows. But notional cash flows result only in the case of increase or decrease in current assets. Notional cash flows result in indirect cash movements into or out of business. For example, increase in balance of debtors does not result in any actual cash outflow since it is part of credit sales. But, at the same time, cash flows out of the business in the form of material cost, labour cost, overheads, etc. are locked up in goods sold on credit.

The sources of cash (funds) include:

1. Issue of shares and debentures for cash,
2. Disposal of fixed assets and investments for cash,

3. Borrowings from banks and other financial institutions,
4. Cash from operations or trading profit,
5. Decrease in current assets. For example, credit sale of goods involves creation of assets in the form of debtors and bills receivable. When payment is received (cash inflow) from the customer.

There will be a reduction of current assets (debtors and bills). Thus, decrease in current assets involves cash inflows.

6. Increase in current liabilities. For example, purchase of goods on credit results in creation of current liabilities in the form of creditors and bills payable. Here, it is assumed that creditors have given a loan of cash (notional cash inflow) which has been used to acquire goods.

Application of cash include:

1. Redemption of shares and debentures by cash,
2. Purchase of fixed assets and investments by cash,
3. Repayment of loans,
4. Cash lost in operations or trading losses,
5. Increase in current assets,
6. Decrease in current liabilities

PREPARATION OF CASH FLOW STATEMENT

Format of a Cash Flow Statement

Cash Flow Statement

(for the year ending)

	Amount [₹]		Amount [₹]
Balances as on 1.1.20 x x		Cash outflows:	
Cash in hand		Redemption of shares and debentures	
Cash at bank		Purchase of fixed assets and investments	
Add: Cash inflows		Repayment of loans	
Issue of shares		Increase in current assets	
Issue of debentures		Decrease in current liabilities	
Sales of fixed assets		Payment of taxes and dividends	
Sale of investments		Outstanding expenses of previous year paid	
Borrowings (Long, medium and short term)		Expenses paid in advance	
Cash from operations:		Balances as on 31.12.20xx	
Decrease in current assets		Cash in hand	
Increase in current liabilities		Cash in bank	
Outstanding income of previous year collected			
Income received in advance			
Total		Total	

Alternatively, it may be shown in the form of a statement as follows:

Cash Flow Statement

(for the year ended on.................)

		Amount [₹]
Balances as on 1.1.20 xx		
Cash in hand		x x x
Cash in bank		x x x
Add: Cash inflows	x x x	
	x x x	
(Refer the first alternative for details)		x x x
Total cash available (a)		
Less: Cash outflows		x x x
(Refer the first alternative for details)		x x x
Total applications (b)		x x x x
Balance as on 31.12.20 xx		
Cash in hand		x x x
Cash in bank		x x x

Note: The total closing balance should tally with the balance as shown by (a) – (b)

Calculation of Cash Flow from Operations

The ultimate result of all business operations would be either net profit or net loss. When net profit results in the cash inflow, the net loss would result in cash outflow. Further, when all transactions are cash transactions, the net profit or loss, as shown by the income statement, may be taken as the amount of cash from operations. However, in actual practice it does not happen. A number of credit transactions take place, such as credit purchases, credit sales, outstanding expenses, etc. In such cases, the profit or loss, as shown by the Income Statement, may be more or less than actual cash flows. There are possibilities for a business with net loss to have positive cash flow from operations. Such a situation may arise owing to charging of non-cash or non-fund items to profit and loss account.

The cash from operations can be calculated by preparing one Adjusted Profit and Loss Account, as in the case of Funds Flow Analysis. That is, all non-fund items, such as depreciation, goodwill written-off etc., should be readjusted. In addition to non-fund items all non-cash transactions, such as outstanding expenses, outstanding income, etc., should be readjusted. The proforma of the Adjusted Profit and Loss Account would be as follows:

Adjusted P&L A/c

To	Depreciation	By	Opening balance
"	Goodwill written-off	"	Dividends received
"	General reserve	"	Interest on investments
"	Loss on sale of fixed assets and investments	"	Profit on sale of assets
"	Current year's outstanding expenses	"	Current year's outstanding income
"	Expenses paid in advance during last year	"	Income received in advance during last year
"	Closing balance	"	Cash profits from operations (Balancing figure)

It may be noted that adjustments relating to stock, debtors, creditors, bills receivable and bills Payable in the form of increase/decrease are shown in the cash flow statement. Alternatively, increase or decrease in the above mentioned items may be adjusted to cash profit from operations, as follows:

Adjusted P&L A/c

To All debit items as shown in the proforma given previously		By All credit items as shown in the proforma given previously	
" Decrease in current assets		" Increase in current assets	
" Increase in current liabilities		" Decrease in current liabilities	
" Closing balance		" Cash from operations (balancing figure)	

Illustration 1

From the following balances, you are required to calculate cash from operations:

Particulars	December, 31 2017 Amount [₹]	December, 31 2018 Amount [₹]
Profit and Loss Account balance	25,000	1,55,000
Debtors	45,000	42,000
Creditors	20,000	26,000
Bills receivable	12,000	15,000
Prepaid expenses	1,600	1,400
Bill Payable	18,000	16,000
Outstanding expenses	1,200	1,600
Outstanding income	800	900
Income received in advance	250	300

Solution

Calculation of Cash from Operations

Adjusted Profit and Loss Account

Particulars	*Amount* [₹]	*Particulars*	*Amount* [₹]
To Decrease in debtors	3,000	By Opening balance	25,000
" Increase in creditors	6,000	" Increase in B/R	3,000
" Decrease in prepaid expenses	200	" Decrease in B/P	2,000
" Increases in outstanding expenses	400	" Increase in outstandi ng income	100
" Increase in income received in advance	50	" Cash from operations	1,34,550
" Closing balance	1,55,000		
	1,64,650		1,64,650

Illustration 2

The Profit and Loss Account of an enterprise for the year ended on 31st December, 2018 was as follows:

Particulars		*Amount* [₹]	*Particulars*		*Amount* [₹]
To Opening stock		10,000	By Sales		1,40,000
To Purchases		98,000	" Closing stock		12,000
To Wages 15,000					
Add: Outstanding 3,000		18,000			
To G.P. c/d		26,000			
		1,52,000			1,52,000
			By G.P. b/d		26,000
To Salaries paid	10,000		" Interest received	2,000	
Add: Outstanding	2,000	12,000	" *Add*: accrued	500	2,500
" Insurance	1,200				
Less: Prepaid	200	1,000	" Net Loss		8,500
" Selling expenses		8,000			
" Depre ciation		10,000			
" Goodwill written off		5,000			
" Preliminary expenses written off		1,000			
		37,000			37,000

From the above Profit and Loss Account, cash from operations may be calculated as follows:

Adjusted Profit and Loss Account

To Outstanding wages	3,000	By Interest accrued	500
" Outstanding salaries	2,000	" Cash from operations	12,000
" Depreciation	10,000	" Closing balance (Net loss)	8,500
" Goodwill written off	5,000		
" Preliminary expenses written off	1,000		
	21,000		21,000

Note: Prepaid expenses (insurance) of ₹ 200 will be shown as application in the cash flow statement.

Preparation of Non-current Accounts

Preparation of non-current accounts in order to ascertain the sale or purchase of such assets is similar to that of the Funds Flow Statement. Provision for tax is treated as a non-current liability and a separate Provision for Taxation account may be prepared to ascertain either the amount of taxes paid, or the amount of provision created during the year. Taxes paid are shown as cash outflow and the tax provision is readjusted to Adjusted Profit and Loss account to find out cash from operation.

DISTINCTIONS BETWEEN CASH FLOW ANALYSIS AND FUNDS FLOW ANALYSIS

1. The concept of fund refers to actual cash under cash flow analysis. Under "funds flow analysis" it means either all financial resources or net working capital.
2. Cash flow analysis deals with the cash transactions only. They may be either actual or notional cash flows. But funds flow is concerned with all items constituting funds i.e., net working capital. Cash is one of the components of working capital.
3. Cash flow statement shows causes for the change in cash, i.e., cash receipts and disbursement of cash only. Funds flow statement shows causes for the change in net working capital. It is a flexible device designed to disclose and emphasise all significant changes in the current assets and current liabilities of the firm during the period under study.
4. Cash flow analysis is a tool of short-term financial analysis while funds flow analysis is a comparatively long-term one.
5. Fund flow statement is consonant with the actual basis of accounting, while in cash flow statement, data obtained on accrued basis are converted into the cash basis.
6. Funds flow statement tallies the funds generated from various sources with various uses to which they are put. Cash flow statement starts with the opening balance of cash and reaches to the closing balance of cash by proceeding through sources and uses.
7. In cash flow analysis cash from operations are calculated after adjusting the increase and decrease in current assets and current liabilities. In fund flow analysis, such changes in current account items are adjusted in the schedule of charges in working capital.

USES OR ADVANTAGES OF CASH FLOW ANALYSIS

1. It is very helpful in understanding the cash position of a firm. Since cash is the basis for carrying on business operations, the cash flow statement is very useful in evaluating the current cash position.
2. It helps the management to understand the past behaviour of the cash cycle, and to control uses of cash in future.
3. The repayment of loans, replacement of assets and other such programmes can be planned on its basis.
4. It throws light on factors contributing to the reduction of cash balance, in spite of increase in income or vice versa.
5. A comparison of the cash flow statement with the cash budget for the same period helps in comparing and controlling cash expenditure.

6. The cash flow statement is helpful in making short-term financial decisions relating to liquidity, and the ways and means position of the firm.

Illustration 3

Following are the condensed balance sheets of Subha Ltd.:

Particulars	*2017* *Amount* [₹]	*2018* *Amount* [₹]
Equity share capital	4,00,000	4,00,000
Reserves and surplus	2,82,000	3,46,000
Depreciation reserve	20,000	28,000
Secured loans	40,000	60,000
Creditors for goods	1,29,000	1,06,000
Outstanding expenses	17,000	3,000
	8,88,000	9,43,000
Plant and equipment (cost)	5,70,000	6,00,000
Inventories	1,96,000	2,26,000
Debtors	79,000	57,000
Cash at bank	43,000	60,000
	8,88,000	9,43,000

You are required to work out figures of funds from operations and cash from operations.

Solution

Particulars		*Amount* [₹]
Computation of funds from Operations, Reserves and Surplus in 2018		3,46,000
Less: Balance in 2017		2,82,000
Profit added during the year		64,000
Add: Depreciation		8,000
		72,000
		₹
Computation of cash from operations, Profit earned		64,000
Add: Depreciation	8,000	
Decrease in Dr.	22,000	30,000
		94,000
Less: Decrease in Cr.	23,000	
Decrease in outstanding expenses	14,000	
Increase in inventories	30,000	67,000
Cash from operations		27,000

Illustration 4

Statements of the financial position of Mr. Ram are given below:

Liabilities	1.1.2018	31.12.2018	*Assets*	1.1.2018	31.12.2018
Accounts Payable	2,900	2,500	Cash	4,000	3,000
Capital	73,900	61,500	Debtors	2,000	1,700
			Stock	800	1,300
			Building	10,000	8,000
			Other fixed assets	60,000	50,000
	76,800	64,000		76,800	64,000

Additional information:

(*a*) There were no drawings

(*b*) There were no purchases or sales of either building or other fixed assets.

Prepare a statement of cash flow.

Solution

Statement of Cash Flow for the Year Ended 31.12.2018

Cash balance on 1.1.2018	4,000	Cash outflows	
Add: Cash inflows		1. Addition to stock	500
1. Decrease in debtors	300	2. Decrease in accounts payable	400
		3. Funds lost in trading operations	400
			1,300
		Cash Balance on 31.12.2018	3,000
	4,300		4,300

Workings:

	Particulars	*Amount* [₹]
(1)	Net Loss for the year 2018	61,500
	Capital at end	73,900
	Capital at beginning	12,400
(2)	Funds (cash) lost in operation/trading Net loss for 2018	12,400
	Less: non-cash charges	
	Depreciation on building (10,000 – 8,000) = 2,000	
	Depreciation on other fixed Assets (₹ 60,000 – 50,000) 10,000	12,000
		400

Illustration 5

Following are the Comparative Balance Sheets of Brown Company Ltd.

Liabilities			*Assets*		
	Dec. 31, 2018	*Dec. 31, 2019*		*Dec. 31, 2018*	*Dec. 31, 2019*
Share Capital	70,000	74,000	Bank balance	9,000	
Debentures	12,000	6,000	Accounts receivable	14,900	17,700
Accounts payable	10,360	11,840	Stock in trade	49,200	42,700
Provision for doubtful debts	700	800	Buildings	20,000	40,600
Profit and Loss A/c	10,040	10,560	Goodwill	10,000	5,000
Bank O/D	–	2,800			
	1,03,100	1,06,000		1,03,100	1,06,000

Additional information:

1. Buildings were acquired for ₹ 20,600.
2. Amount provided for the amortisation of goodwill, totalled ₹ 5,000.
3. Dividends paid, totalled ₹ 3,500.
4. Debenture loan repaid, was ₹ 6,000.

Explain how the overdraft of ₹ 2,800 as on 31st December, 2019 has arisen.

Solution

1. Calculation of Operating Profit made during the year (An increase in the Profit and Loss A/c may be taken as profit made (10,560 – 10,040) = 520).

		Amount [₹]
Profit		520
Add: amortisation of goodwill	5,000	
Dividend paid	3,500	
Provision for doubtful debts	100	8,600
Operating profit made during the year		9,120

Brown & Co. Ltd.
Statement of Cash Flow
for the year ended on 31st December, 2019

Particulars	*Amount* [₹]	*Particulars*	*Amount* [₹]
Bank Balance as on 1.1.2019	9,000	Cash outflows:	
Add: Cash inflows		1. Increase in accounts receivables	2,800
1. Decrease in stock in trade	6,500	2. Payment of dividend	3,500
2. Increase in accounts payable	1,480	3. Acquisition of building	20,600
3. Issue of shares	4,000	4. Repayment of debenture	6,000
4. Operating profit	9,120		
Bank overdraft as on 31.12.2019	2,800		
	32,900		32,900

Illustration 6

Balance Sheets of X and Y on 1.1.2019 and 31.12.2019 were as follows:

Balance Sheet

Liabilities	1.1.19 *Amount* [₹]	31.12.19 *Amount* [₹]	*Assets*	1.1.19 *Amount* [₹]	31.12.19 *Amount* [₹]
Creditors	40,000	44,000	Cash	10,000	7,000
Mrs. X's loan	25,000	–	Debtors	30,000	50,000
Loan from bank	40,000	50,000	Stock	35,000	25,000
Capital	1,25,000	1,53,000	Machinery	80,000	55,000
			Land	40,000	50,000
			Building	35,000	60,000
	2,30,000	2,47,000		2,30,000	2,47,000

During the year, a machine costing ₹ 10,000 (accumulated depreciation ₹ 3,000) was sold for ₹ 5,000. The provision for depreciation against machinery, as on 1.1.2019, was ₹ 25,000, and on 31.12.2019 it was ₹ 40,000. Net profit for the year 2017 amounted to ₹ 45,000. You are required to prepare a cash flow statement.

Solution

Cash Flow Statement

Particulars		Amount [₹]
Cash balance as on 1.1.2019		10,000
Add: Cash inflows:		
Cash from operation	59,000	
Loan from bank	10,000	
Sale of machinery	5,000	74,000
		84,000
Less: Cash outflows:		
Purchase of land	10,000	
Purchase of building	25,000	
Mr. X's Loan repaid	25,000	
Drawings	17,000	77,000
		7,000
Working Notes:		
Cash from operations: Profit made during the year		45,000
Add: Depreciation on machinery	18,000	
Loss on sale of machinery	2,000	
Decrease in stock	10,000	
Increase in creditors	4,000	34,000
		79,000
Less: Increase in debtors		20,000
Cash from operations		59,000

Machinery Account

Particulars	Amount [₹]	Particulars	Amount [₹]
To Balance b/d	1,05,000	By Bank	5,000
		" Loss on sale of machinery	2,000
		" Provision for depreciation	3,000
		" Balance c/d	95,000
	1,05,000		1,05,000

Provision for Depreciation

Particulars	Amount [₹]	Particulars	Amount [₹]
To Machinery A/c	3,000	By Balance b/d	25,000
" Balance c/d	40,000	" P & L A/c (depreciation charged, balancing figure)	18,000
	43,000		43,000

Note: It may be observed that the increase/decrease in current assets have been adjusted to cash from operations. Alternatively, those items may also be shown in the cash flow statement.

Additional Information:

(*a*) Depreciation of ₹ 10,000 and ₹ 20,000 have been charged on plant land and buildings respectively in 2019.

(*b*) An interim dividend of ₹ 20,000 has been paid in 2019.

(*c*) Income Tax of ₹ 35,000 was paid during the year 2019.

Illustration 7

From the following Balance Sheets of Exe. Ltd., make out the statement of sources and uses of cash:

Liabilities	*2017 Amount* [₹]	*2018 Amount* [₹]	*Assets*	*2017 Amount* [₹]	*2018 Amount* [₹]
Equity share capital	2,00,000	3,00,000	Goodwill	1,15,000	90,000
8% Redeemable Preference share capital	2,50,000	2,00,000	Land and buildings	2,00,000	1,70,000
General reserve	40,000	70,000	Plant	80,000	2,00,000
Profit and Loss account	30,000	48,000	Debtors	1,50,000	1,90,000
Proposed dividend	42,000	50,000	Stock	77,000	1,09,000
Creditors	45,000	73,000	Bills receivable	30,000	40,000
Bills payable	30,000	26,000	Cash in hand	15,000	10,000
Provision for taxation	40,000	50,000	Cash at bank	10,000	8,000
	6,77,000	8,17,000		6,77,000	8,17,000

Solution

Cash Flow Statement

for the year ending on 31st Dec., 2018

Particulars		*Amount* [₹]
Cash balance as on 1.1.2018		
Cash in hand	15,000	
Cash at bank	10,000	25,000
Add: Sources (cash inflows):		
Issue of share capital	1,00,000	
Sale of land and buildings	10,000	
Cash from operations	1,60,000	2,70,000
Total sources		2,95,000
Less: Applications (cash outflows):		
Redemption of redeemable preference shares	50,000	
Interim dividend paid	20,000	
Dividend paid	42,000	
Income-tax paid	35,000	
Plant purchased	1,30,000	2,77,000
Cash balance as on 31.12.2018		
Cash in hand	10,000	
Cash at bank	8,000	18,000

Alternatively, the cash flow statement can also be prepared as follows:

Cash Flow Statement

for the year ended on 31st December, 2018

Cash balance as on 1.1.2018	*Amount* [₹]	Outflow of cash	*Amount* [₹]
Cash in hand	15,000	Redemption of Redeemable	
Cash at bank	10,000	Preference shares	50,000
Add: Inflows of cash Issue of shares	1,00,000	Payment of interim dividend	20,000
Sale of land and buildings	10,000	Payment of dividend	42,000
Cash from operations	2,18,000	Payment of tax	35,000
Increase in creditors	28,000	Purchase of plant	1,30,000
		Decrease in bills payable	4,000
		Increase in debtors	40,000
		Increase in stock	32,000
		Increase in bills receivable	10,000
		Cash balance as on 31.12.2018	
		Cash in hand	10,000
		Cash at bank	8,000
	3,81,000		3,81,000

Working Notes:

(i) **Adjusted Profit and Loss Account**

Particulars	*Amount* [₹]	*Particulars*	*Amount* [₹]
To Depreciation on Plant	10,000	By Balance b/d	30,000
" Depreciation on building	20,000	" Cash from operations (Balancing figure)	2,18,000
" Goodwill written	25,000		
" Provision for tax-off	45,000		
" Interim dividend	20,000		
" Dividend proposed	50,000		
" Transfer to general reserve	30,000		
" Balance c/f	48,000		
	2,48,000		2,48,000

(ii) **Provision for Taxation Account**

Particulars	*Amount* [₹]	*Particulars*	*Amount* [₹]
To Bank	35,000	By Balance b/d	40,000
" Balance c/f	50,000	" P & L A/c	45,000
	85,000		85,000

(iii) **Land and Building Account**

Particulars	*Amount* [₹]	*Particulars*	*Amount* [₹]
To Balance b/d	2,00,000	By Depreciation	20,000
		" Bank (Sale)	10,000
		" Balance c/d	1,70,000
	2,00,000		2,00,000

(iv) **Plant Account**

Particulars	*Amount* [₹]	*Particulars*	*Amount* [₹]
To Balance b/d	80,000	By Depreciation	10,000
Bank (Purchases)	1,30,000	Balance c/d	2,00,000
	2,10,000		2,10,000

(v) **Cash from Operations**

Particulars	Amount [₹]	Amount [₹]
Cash from operations (See note i)		2,18,000
Add: Increase in creditors		28,000
		2,46,000
Less:		
Decrease in bills Payable	4,000	
Increase in debtors	40,000	
Increase in stock	32,000	
Increase in Bills receivable	10,000	86,000
Cash from operations		1,60,000

(vi) In the absence of information, it has been presumed that there is no profit (or loss) and no accumulated depreciation on that part of land and building which has been sold.

Illustration 8

A company finds on 1st January, 2018 that it is short of funds with which to implement its programme of expansion. On 1st January, 2017, it had a credit balance of ₹ 1,80,000. From the following information, prepare a statement for the Board of Directors to show how the overdraft of ₹ 68,750, as on 31st December, 2017, has arisen.

Figures as per Balance Sheet

as on 31st December........

Assets	*2017* ₹	*2018* ₹
Fixed assets	7,50,000	11,20,000
Stock and stores	1,90,000	3,30,000
Debtors	3,80,000	3,35,000
Bank balance	1,80,000 (Cr)	68,750 (O/D)
Share capital (in shares of Rs.10 each)	2,50,000	3,00,000
Bills receivable	87,500	95,000

(*a*) The profit for the year ended 31st December, 2018, before charging depreciation and taxation, amounted to ₹ 2,40,000.

(*b*) 5,000 shares were issued on 1st January, 2018 at a premium of ₹ 5 share. ₹ 1,37,500 were paid in March 2018 by way of Income tax. Dividend was paid as follows:

(*c*) 2017 (final) on the capital on 31.12.2017 at 10 per cent less tax at 25 per cent.

(*d*) 2018 (interim) 5 per cent free of tax.

Solution

Cash from Statement
for the year ended on 31.12.2018

Particulars	*Amount* [₹]	*Particulars*	*Amount* [₹]
Bank balance on 1.1.2018	1,80,000	Cash outflows	
Add: Sources of cash inflow		Purchase of fixed Assets	3,70,000
Issue of shares	50,000	Increase in stock stores	1,40,000
Share premium	25,000	Increase in Bills Receivable	7,500
Decrease in debtors	45,000	Income tax paid	1,37,500
Increase in creditors	80,000	Final dividend for 2017	18,750
Operating cash profit	2,40,000	Interim dividend for 2018	15,000
Balance bal. (O/D)	6,20,000		
on 31.12.18	68,750		
	6,88,750		6,88,750

Workings Notes:

1. Final dividend works out to $\frac{₹\ 2{,}50{,}000 \times 10}{100} = ₹\ 25{,}000$

   = ₹ 25,000 – 6,250 = ₹ 18,750

   Since income tax is to be deducted at source at 25% of ₹ 25,000.
2. Interim dividend has been calculated at 5% on ₹ 3,00,000.
3. Interim dividend is free of tax and hence nothing is deductible from ₹ 15,000 on account of income-tax. In addition, ₹ 5,000, i.e. $\frac{₹15{,}000 \times 25}{75}$ is payable to the government on account of income-tax.
4. It is assumed that the figure of income-tax; paid, i.e. ₹ 1,37,500 includes ₹ 11,250 (₹ 6,250 + 5,000) in respect of final and interim dividend.
5. It is assumed that fixed Assets are appearing at cost.
6. It is obvious that the profit for the year 2015, i.e. ₹ 2,40,000 is before charging the final and interim dividend.

Illustration 9

The financial position of M/s. X Y on January 1 and Dec. 31, 2018 was as follows:

Liabilities	1st Jan Amount [₹]	31st Dec. Amount [₹]	Assets	1st Jan Amount [₹]	31st Dec. Amount [₹]
Current liabilities for goods	36,000	40,000	Cash	4,000	3,000
Mrs. X's loan	–	20,000	Debtors	35,000	58,000
Loan from bank	30,000	25,000	Stock	25,000	22,000
Hire-Purchase vendor	–	20,000	Land	20,000	30,000
Capital	1,48,000	1,54,000	Buildings	50,000	35,000
			Machinery	80,000	86,000
			Delivery van	–	25,000
	2,14,000	2,59,000		2,14,000	2,59,000

The delivery van was purchased in December, 2018 on hire-purchase basis, a payment of ₹ 5,000 was made immediately and the balance of the amount was to be paid in 20 monthly instalments of ₹ 1,000 each, together with interest at 12% p.a. During the year, the partners withdrew ₹ 26,000 for domestic expenditure. The provision for depreciation against machinery on 31.12.2017 was ₹ 27,000, and on 31.12.2018 it was ₹ 36,000. You are required to prepare the Cash-Flow Statement. Also, prepare the Funds Flow Statement.

Solution

M/S X Y

for the year ending on 31st Dec., 2018

Particulars		Amount [₹]
Cash balance on 1st January, 2018		4,000
Sources:		
Cash from operations (see note 2)		45,600
Loan from Mrs. X		20,000
Total Sources		69,600
Applications:		
Payment of bank loan		5,000
Payment for delivery van		5,000
Machinery acquired		15,000
Building acquired		5,000
Land acquired		10,000
Withdrawn by partners		26,000
		66,000
Cash balance on 31st December, 2018		3,600

Funds Flow Statement

for the year ended on 31.12.2018

Particulars	*Amount* [₹]	*Particulars*	*Amount* [₹]
Funds from operations	41,000	Repayment of bank loan	5,000
Loan from Mrs. X	20,000	Payment for delivery van	5,000
Increase in working capital	17,000	Payable in a year for delivery van	12,000
		Machinery acquired	15,000
		Land acquired	10,000
		Buildings acquired	5,000
		Partner's drawings	26,000
	78,000		78,000

Working Notes:

	Particulars		*Amount* [₹]
1.	Funds from operations		
	Capital as on 31st December, 2018		1,54,000
	Add: Drawings during the year		26,000
			1,80,000
	Less: Capital as on 1st January 2018		1,48,000
			32,000
	Add: Depreciation for the year (₹ 36,000 – ₹ 27,000)		9,000
			41,000
2.	Cash from Operations		
	Funds from Operations		
	Add: Decrease in stock	3,000	
	Increase in creditors	4,600	7,600
			48,600
	Less: Increase in debtors		3,000
	Cash from operations		45,600

Machinery Account

Particulars	*Amount* [₹]	*Particulars*	*Amount* [₹]
To Balance b/d	80,000	By Depreciation for the year	9,000
To Bank (acquired during the year)	15,000	By Balance c/d	86,000
	95,000		95,000

Illustration 10

AB Ltd., had the following figures on 1st January, 2017:

Particulars	*Amount* [₹]	*Amount* [₹]
Fixed Assets – Cost	6,00,000	
Less: Depreciation	2,10,000	3,90,000
Bank balance		35,000
Current assets other than bank balance		2,50,000
Current liabilities		1,00,000
Equity capital (share of ₹ 100 each)		3,00,000

The company made the following estimates for the year 2018:

(*a*) The profit would be ₹ 58,000 after depreciation of ₹ 60,000.

(*b*) The company would acquire fixed assets costing ₹ 1,00,000 after selling one machine for ₹ 20,000 costing ₹ 50,000 on which depreciation provided amounted to ₹ 35,000.

(*c*) Current assets and current liabilities, other than bank balance at the end of 2018 are expected to be ₹ 2,95,000 and ₹ 1,30,000 respectively.

(*d*) The company will pay a free of tax dividend of 10%, the rate of tax being 25%.

Ascertain the bank balance (or overdraft) of the company at the end of 2018.

Solution

Projected Cash Flow Statement for the year ending 31.12.2018

Particulars	*Amount* [₹]	*Particulars*	*Amount* [₹]
Opening Bank balance on 1.1.2018	35,000	Cash outflows:	1,00,000
Add: Cash inflows:		Purchase of Fixed Assets	
From operations	98,000	Proposed dividends	30,000
Sale of machinery	20,000	Taxes payable on Dividends	7,500
			1,37,500
		Closing bank Balance on 31.12.2018	15,500
	1,53,000		1,53,000

Workings:

Adjusted Profit and Loss A/c

Particulars	*Amount* [₹]	*Particulars*	*Amount* [₹]
To Depreciation	60,000	By Increase in Current Assets	45,000
To Increase in Current Liabilities	30,000	By Profit on Sale of Machinery	5,000
To Current year's profit	58,000	By Cash from operation	98,000
	1,48,000		1,48,000

Illustration 11

Prepare a Cash Flow Statement of a Corporation from the following information:

Balance Sheet

as on 1st January and 31st December, 2018

Particulars	*January 1* *Amount* [₹]	*December 31* *Amount* [₹]
Current Assets	40,000	44,400
Accounts receivable	10,000	20,700
Inventories	15,000	15,000
Land	4,000	4,000
Business premises	20,000	16,000
Plant and equipment	15,000	17,000
Accumulated depreciation on Building	(5,000)	(2,800)
Patents and trade marks	1,000	900
Total Assets	1,00,000	1,15,200
Current Liabilities	30,000	32,000
Bonds payable	22,000	22,000
Bonds payable discount	(2,000)	(1,800)
Capital Stock	35,000	43,500
Retained earnings	15,000	19,500
Total Liabilities	1,00,000	1,15,200

Additional information:

(*a*) Income for the period was ₹ 10,000.

(*b*) A building that costs ₹ 4,000 and which had a book value of ₹ 1,000 was sold for ₹ 1,400.

(*c*) The depreciation charges for the period was ₹ 800.

(*d*) There was a ₹ 5,000 issue of capital stock.

(*e*) Cash dividend of ₹ 2,000 and a stock dividend for ₹ 3,500 were declared.

Solution

Cash Flow Statement

from the year ended 31.12.2018

Particulars	*Amount* [₹]	*Particulars*	*Amount* [₹]
		Cash outflows:	
Cash and Bank Balance on 1.1.18	40,000	Dividends paid	2,000
Add: Cash inflows:		Increase in debtors	10,700
(from operations)	10,700	Plant purchased	2,000
Sale of building	1,400		14,700
Issue of shares	5,000	Cash and Bank:	
Increase in Current Liabilities	2,000	Balance on 31.12.18	44,400
	59,100		59,100

Workings:

Calculation of Cash from Operations

Particulars	*Amount* [₹]	*Particulars*	*Amount* [₹]
Income for the period	10,000		
Add: Depreciation	800		
Discount W/off	200		
Patents W/off	100		
	11,100		
Less: Profit on sale of Buildings	400		
	10,700		

Illustration 12

Progressive Ltd., presents you the following Balance Sheets as on December 31st, 2017 an 2018.

Liabilities	*As at Dec. 31, 2017 Amount* [₹]	*As at Dec. 31, 2018 Amount* [₹]	*Assets*	*As at Dec. 31, 2017 Amount* [₹]	*As at Dec. 31.1, 2018 Amount* [₹]
Equity share capital	50,000	60,000	Fixed Assets	85,000	1,04,000
8% Redeemable preference share capital	20,000	–	Investments	10,000	8,000
Capital redemption reserve a/c	–	10,000	Preliminary expenses	4,000	3,000
Share premium	5,000	5,000	Stock	20,000	28,000
Profit and Loss a/c	14,000	27,000	Debtors	18,000	17,000
General Reserve	10,000	13,000	Cash	6,000	11,000
Taxation Reserve	7,000	9,000			
Proposed dividend	5,000	6,000			
Sundry Creditors	14,000	18,000			
Provision for depreciation	18,000	23,000			
	1,43,000	1,71,000		1,43,000	1,71,000

During 2018, the proposed dividend was paid in addition to the preference dividend up to 30th June, 2018 on which date the preference shares were redeemed at a premium of 5%. The premium had been provided out of share premium account. Tax liability in respect of 2017 amounted to ₹ 5,500; the balance in the Taxation reserve, as on 31st December, 2017 was transferred to General reserve. During the year, a fixed assets, costing ₹ 3,000 (depreciation provided for ₹ 1,600), was sold for ₹ 1,000. Investment costing ₹ 2,000 were realised for ₹ 1,600. These matters have been adjusted in the profit and loss account. Prepare a statement showing the source and application of cash during 2018.

Solution

Adjusted Profit & Loss A/c

Particulars	*Amount* [₹]	*Particulars*	*Amount* [₹]
To Loss on sale of fixed assets	400	By Opening balance	14,000
To Preliminary expenses W/off	1,000	By Cash from operations (balancing figure)	48,700
To Loss on sale of investments	400		
To Preference dividend	800		
To Proposed dividend	6,000		
To Capital redemption reserve	10,000		
To General reserve	1,500		
To Taxation provision	9,000		
To Depreciation	6,600		
To Closing balance	27,000		
	62,700		62,700

Fixed Assets A/c

Particulars	*Amount* [₹]	*Particulars*	*Amount* [₹]
To Opening balance	85,000	By Cash (Sales)	1,000
To Cash (Purchases)	22,000	By Provision for depreciation	1,600
		By Adjusted P&L A/c	400
		By Closing balance	1,04,000
	1,07,000		1,07,000

Provision for Depreciation A/c

Particulars	*Amount* [₹]	*Particulars*	*Amount* [₹]
To Fixed assets A/c	1,600	By Opening balance	18,000
To Closing balance	23,000	By Adjusted P&L A/c (balance)	6,600
	24,600		24,600

Illustration 13

The Balance Sheets of A Ltd., as on 31st December, 2017 and 31st December, 2018 are as follows:

Liabilities	(Amount [₹] in Lakhs) 2017	2018	Assets	(Amount [₹] in Lakhs) 2017	2018
Share capital	300.00	300.00	Freehold property (at cost)	225.00	240.00
Reserves	225.00	240.00	Plant and machinery (at cost less Dep)	135.00	165.00
6% Debentures (unsecured)	75.00	75.00	Investments: Share of companies under the same management (unquoted)	150.00	150.00
Mortgage on freehold property	27.00	14.25	In other companies	112.50	122.50
Creditors	45.00	45.00	Market value:		
Proposed dividend (subject to deduction of tax)	22.50	23.25	(2010 150 lakhs 2011 120 lakhs)		
Provision for taxation	21.00	37.50	Stock	52.50	75.00
Secured overdraft (by a floating charge on assets)	15.00	82.50	Debtors	45.00	75.00
			Bank	10.50	-
	730.50	817.50		730.50	817.50

The following additional information for the year 2018 is relevant:

	Particulars	Amount [₹](in lakhs)
(i)	Credit sales	675
(ii)	Credit purchases	520
(iii)	Overheads	83.75
(iv)	Depreciation on plant and machinery	17.50
(v)	Dividend for 2017 was paid in full	
(vi)	Amount paid towards taxation for the year 2017	21.50

In view of the credit squeeze, the company has been asked by the Bank to reduce the overdraft by 50% within six months, if possible, by 50%.

You are required to prepare a Cash Flow Statement.

Solution

Statement of Sources and Applications of Cash
(For the Year ended on 31st December, 2018)

Particulars	*Amount [₹] (in lakhs)*
Sources:	
Cash from operations	41.25
Total	41.25
Payment:	
Purchase of freehold property	15.00
Purchase of plant and machinery	47.50
Proposed dividend paid for 2019	22.50
Tax paid for 2019	21.50
Repayment of mortgage	12.75
	119.25

Calculation of Overdraft on 31st December 2018

Particulars	*Amount [₹] (in lakhs)*
Total cash payments	119.25
Less: Total cash receipts	41.25
Additional overdraft required	78.00
Add: Overdraft on 1st January, 2018	4.50
Overdraft on 31st December, 2018	82.50

Cash Flow Statement for the Year ended on 31.12.2018

Particulars	*Amount [₹]*	*Particulars*	*Amount [₹]*
Opening cash balance	6,000	Cash outflows:	
Add: Cash inflows:		Purchase of fixed assets	22,000
Issue of shares at premium	11,000	Redemption of preference shares at a premium of 5%	21,000
Sale of fixed Assets	1,000	Preference dividends paid	800
Sale of investments	1,600	Equity dividends (2017) Paid	5,000
Cash from operations	48,700	Taxes paid	5,500
Increase in creditors	4,000	Increase in stock	8,000
			62,300
Decrease in debtors	1,000	Closing balance	11,000
	73,300		73,300

Workings

Particulars		*Amount* [₹] *(in lakhs)*
(*i*) Calculation of cash from operation		240.00
Closing balance of reserves		
Add: Non-cash items written back:		
Depreciation of plant and machinery	17.50	
Provision for taxation for 2018 (37.50 + .50)	38.00	
Proposed dividend for 2018	23.25	78.75
		318.75
Less: Increase in current asset:		
Stock	22.50	
Debtors	30.00	52.50
		266.25
Less: Opening balance of reserves		225.00
Cash from operations		41.25

Particulars	*Amount* [₹] *(in lakhs)*
(*ii*) Calculation of fresh provision for tax in 2018	37.50
Closing balance on provision for taxation	
Add: Tax paid for 2017	21.50
	59.00
Less: Opening balance on provision for taxation	21.00
Fresh povision	38.00

Particulars	*Amount* [₹] *(in lakhs)*
(*iii*) Calculation of plant and machinery purchased in 2018	
Closing balance on plant and machinery A/c	165.00
Add: Depreciation provided in 2018	17.50
	182.50
Less: Opening balance on plant and machinery A/c	135.00
Fresh purchase	47.50

Particulars	*Amount* [₹] *(in lakhs)*
(*iv*) Calculation of overdraft amount of Ist January 2018	
Overdraft (secured by a floating charge on assets)	
on Ist January, 2018	15.00
Less: Bank balance on 1st January 2018	10.50
Net Amount of Overdraft	4.50

Illustration 14

A Co., Ltd., gives you its Balance Sheet as at 31st December, 2017 and its Projected Profit and Loss Account (summarised) for 2018.

Balance Sheet

Liabilities	*Amount* [₹]	*Assets*	*Amount* [₹]
Share Capital: (Fully paid shares of Rs. 100 each)	3,00,000	Plant and Equipment	10,50,000
7% Redeemable Preference Equity	5,00,000	*Less*: Depreciation	2,70,000
Share Premium	50,000		7,80,000
General Reserve	1,30,000	Goodwill	1,50,000
6% Debentures	2,50,000	Patents	50,000
Creditors for goods	1,20,000	Stock	2,70,000
Outstanding Expenses	20,000	Book Debts	2,50,000
Provisions for Taxation	1,55,000	Cash	90,000
Proposed Dividend (Equity)	80,000	Underwriting commission	15,000
	16,05,000		16,05,000

Profit and Loss Account

Particulars	*Amount* [₹]	*Particulars*	*Amount* [₹]
To Opening stock	2,70,000	By Sales: Cash	3,50,000
To Purchases	15,00,000	Credit	21,00,000
To Wages	1,70,000		24,50,000
To Manufacturing expenses	1,30,000	By Stock	2,90,000
To Depreciation	1,05,000	By Miscellaneous income	10,000
To Selling and adm.expenses	1,10,000	By Profit on sale of machinery	6,000
To Office and adm. expenses	95,000		
To Interest	15,000		
To Goodwill	20,000		
To Patents	10,000		
To Provision for taxation	1,70,000		
To Pref. dividend	21,000		
To Proposed dividend (Equity)	75,000		
To Balance of profits	65,000		
	27,56,000		27,56,000

Both the preference shares and debentures are due for redemption on 31st December, 2018. Half the debenture holders in value will accept new 9% Redeemable preference shares; also the company propose to issue equity capital with a nominal value of ₹ 2,000 at a premium of 20%.

Fixed Assets will be acquired for ₹ 1,60,000. The cost of the assets to be sold in 2018 is ₹ 60,000 with a depreciation provision of ₹ 30,000. It is expected that:

(*i*) Tax Liability upto 31.12.17 will be settled for ₹ 1,40,000.

(*ii*) Book Debts will be 10% more than that warranted by the credit period of 1½ months.

(*iii*) Creditors for goods will continue to extend one month's credit and expenses outstanding and prepaid at the end of 2018 will be ₹ 25,000 and ₹ 2,000 respectively.

You are required to:

(*i*) Prepare the statement showing sources and application of funds during 2018, and

(*ii*) Draft the company's projected balance sheet as at December 31, 2018.

Solution

Funds Flow Statement for the Year ended on 31.12.2018

Particulars	*Amount* [₹]	*Particulars*	*Amount* [₹]
Sources		Applications	
Issue of Preferences shares	1,25,000	Purchase of fixed assets	1,60,000
Issue of equity shares at a premium	2,40,000	Redemption of debentures	2,50,000
Sale of machinery	31,000	Redemption of preferences shares	3,00,000
Funds from operations (including miscellaneous income and Tax savings)	3,05,000	Equity dividend	80,000
		Preference dividend	21,000
	7,01,000		
Decrease in working capital	1,10,000		
	8,11,000		8,11,000

Projected Balance Sheet of A Ltd. as on 31.12.18

Liabilities		*Amount* [₹]	*Assets*		*Amount* [₹]
Equity share capital (₹ 100 each)		7,00,000	Goodwill		1,30,000
9% Redeemable preference shares		1,25,000	Plant and Equipment	10,50,000	
Share premium A/c		90,000	*Less*: Plant sold	60,000	
				9,90,000	
General Reserve		1,30,000	Additions	1,60,000	
P&L a/c	65,000			11,50,000	
Add: Tax savings	15,000	80,000	*Less*: Provision for depreciation	3,40,000	
Sundry creditors		1,25,000			8,10,000
Outstanding expenses		25,000	Patents		40,000
Bank overdraft		55,750	Stock		2,90,000
Provision for Taxation		1,70,000	Debtors		2,88,750
Proposed dividends		75,000	Prepaid expenses		2,000
			Underwriting commission		15,000
		15,75,750			15,75,750

Cash Flow Statement for the Year ended on 31.12.18

Particulars	*Amount* [₹]	*Particulars*	*Amount* [₹]
Opening cash balance	90,000	Cash out?ows:	
Add: Cash in?ows:		Purchase of fixed Assets	1,60,000
Sale of machinery	31,000	Increase in stock	20,000
Issue of equity shares at a premium	2,40,000	Increase in debtors	38,750
		Redemption of preference shares	3,00,000
Increase in outstanding Expenses	5,000	Redemption of debentures	1,25,000
Increase in creditors	5,000	Taxes paid	1,40,000
Cash from operating pro?ts	4,60,000	Preference dividends paid	21,000
Bank O/D (closing balance)	55,750	Equity dividends paid	80,000
		Increase in prepaid expenses	2,000
	8,86,750		8,86,750

Schedule of Changes in Working Capital

Particulars	*2017* *Amount* [₹]	*2018* *Amount* [₹]	*Increase* *Amount* [₹]	*Decrease* *Amount* [₹]
Current Assets:				
Stock	2,70,000	2,90,000	20,000	–
Debtors	2,50,000	2,88,750	38,750	–
Prepaid expenses	–	2,000	2,000	–
Cash	90,000	–	–	90,000
Total (*a*)	6,10,000	5,80,750		
Current Liabilities:				
Sundry creditors	1,20,000	1,25,000	–	5,000
Outstanding expenses	20,000	25,000	–	5,000
Bank overdraft	–	55,750	–	55,750
Provision for taxation	1,55,000	1,70,000	–	15,000
Total (*b*)	2,95,000	3,75,750		
W.C. (*a–b*)	3,15,000	2,05,000		
Net decrease in working capital		1,10,000	1,10,000	
	3,15,000	3,15,000	1,70,750	1,70,750

Debtors at the End

Total credit sales ₹	21,00,000
Amount for 1½ months	2,62,500
Add: 10%	26,250
Total	2,88,750

Provision for Depreciation A/c

Particulars	*Amount* [₹]	*Particulars*	*Amount* [₹]
To Machinery (sold) A/c	35,000	By Opening balance	2,70,000
To Closing balance	3,40,000	By Depreciation	1,05,000
	3,75,000		3,75,000

Statement Showing Cash from Operations

Particulars	*Amount* [₹]	*Amount* [₹]
Profit for the year		65,000
Add: Non-cash or non-operating items:		
Depreciation	1,05,000	
Goodwill	20,000	
Patents	10,000	
Provision for Taxation	1,70,000	
Preference dividend	21,000	
Equity dividend	75,000	4,01,000
		4,66,000
Less: Profit on sale of machinery		6,000
Cash from operation (including miscellaneous income)		4,60,000

Illustration 15

Mr. Ram owns a substantial block of shares in Jayanthi Mills Ltd. He has first received a copy of the Mills annual report in which the following comparative balance sheet data were reported for the year ending on 31st December, 2018.

Particulars	*2017* *Amount* [₹]	*2018* *Amount* [₹]
Cash	3,10,000	1,60,000
Debtors	4,20,000	5,00,000
Stock	10,00,000	8,75,000
Fixed assets	40,00,000	46,00,000
(Accumulated depreciation)	(15,00,000)	(16,50,000)
Investment	3,00,000	3,00,000
	45,30,000	47,85,000
Creditors	8,00,000	9,00,000
Tax provision	75,000	1,30,000
Mortgage loans	10,00,000	9,00,000
Equity share capital	20,00,000	20,00,000
Retained earnings	6,55,000	8,55,000
	45,30,000	47,85,000

After looking into the comparative balance sheet data, Ram commented to a friend, that there was something strange going on. These balance sheets clearly indicate that cash decreased by ₹ 1,50,000 during the year. The company paid only ₹ 50,000 in dividends; so, rather than decreasing by ₹ 1,50,000 it seems to him that it would have increased by ₹ 2,00,000. The company retired no fixed assets during the year. Prepare a cash flow statement of the company for the year 2018.

Solution

Cash Flow Statement for 2018

Particulars	*Amount* [₹]	*Particulars*	*Amount* [₹]
Cash balance (1.1.18)	3,10,000	Cash outflows	
Add: Cash inflow		Purchase of fixed assets	6,00,000
Cash from operations	6,00,000	Dividends paid	1,50,000
			7,50,000
		Cash balance (31.12.18)	1,60,000
	9,10,000		9,10,000

Working

Adjusted P&L A/c

Particulars	*Amount* [₹]	*Particulars*	*Amount* [₹]
To Depreciation	1,50,000	By Opening balance	6,55,000
Dividends	50,000	Funds from operations	4,55,000
Tax provision	55,000		
Closing balance	8,55,000		
	11,10,000		11,10,000

Funds from Operations

Particulars	*Amount* [₹]
Funds from operations	4,55,000
Add: Increase in creditors	1,00,000
Decrease in stock	1,25,000
	6,80,000
Less: Increase in debtors	80,000
Cash from operations	6,00,000

Illustration 16

From the following condensed comparative Balance Sheets of XYZ Ltd. and additional information, prepare a Cash Flow Statement.

Comparative Balance Sheet

Liabilities	*2017 Amount* [₹]	*2018 Amount* [₹]	*Assets*	*2017 Amount* [₹]	*2018 Amount* [₹]
Plant and machinery				62,000	66,000
Accumulated depreciation on plant and machinery				(37,000)	(26,200)
Buildings				95,000	1,16,000
Accumulated dep. on buildings				(43,000)	(45,000)
Land				10,000	12,000
Stock				10,220	9,620
Debtors				8,600	7,600
Prepaid expenses				720	800
Cash				6,180	9,800
				1,12,720	1,50,620

Liabilities	*2017 Amount* [₹]	*2018 Amount* [₹]	*Assets*	*2017 Amount* [₹]	*2018 Amount* [₹]
Share capital (₹ 10 each)				70,000	80,000
Share premium account				9,000	11,000
Retained earnings				23,820	30,820
7% Mortgage loan				-	20,000
Sundry creditors				6,900	6,000
Outstanding salaries				2,000	1,400
Provision for taxation				1,000	1,400
				1,12,720	1,50,620

Additional Information:

(*i*) Plant costing ₹ 16,000 (accumulated depreciation ₹ 14,800) was sold during the year for ₹ 1,200.

(*ii*) Buildings were acquired during the year at a cost of ₹ 21,000. In addition to a cash payment of ₹ 1,000, a 7% Mortgage loan was raised for the balance.

(*iii*) Dividends ₹ 8,000 were declared during the year.

(*iv*) A sum of ₹ 13,900 was transferred to provision for Taxation Account.

(*v*) Net income before tax was ₹ 28,900.

Solution

Cash Flow Statement (for the Year ended on 31.12.2018)

Particulars	*Amount* [₹]	*Particulars*	*Amount* [₹]
Cash balance (1.1.18)	6,180	*Cash Outflows:*	
Add: Cash inflows:		Dividends paid	8,000
Sale of Plant	1,200	Taxes paid	13,500
Issue of shares at a premium	12,000	Purchase of P&M	20,000
Operating profit	37,020	Purchase of building	1,000
Decrease in stock	600	Prepaid expenses (2018) paid	2,800
Decrease in debtors	1,000	Outstanding Salaries (2017) paid	2,000
		Decrease in creditors	900
			48,200
		Cash balance 31.12.18	9,800
	58,000		58,000

Workings

Adjusted P&L A/c

Particulars	*Amount* [₹]	*Particulars*	*Amount* [₹]
To Depreciation on plant and machinery	4,000	By Opening balance	23,820
To Buildings	2,000	By Operating profit (Balancing figure)	37,020
To Dividends paid	8,000		
Provision for taxation	13,900		
To Prepaid expenses (2017)	720		
To Outstanding salaries (2018)	1,400		
To Closing balance	30,820		
	60,840		60,840

Plant and Machinery A/c

Particulars	*Amount* [₹]	*Particulars*	*Amount* [₹]
To Balance b/d	62,000	By Cash (Machinery sold)	1,200
To Machinery Cash (purchased)	20,000	By Accumulated depreciation	14,800
		By Balance c/d	66,000
	82,000		82,000

Buildings A/c

Particulars	*Amount* [₹]	*Particulars*	*Amount* [₹]
To Balance b/d	95,000	By Balance c/d	1,16,000
Cash (Purchased Building)	1,000		
7% Mortgage loan Building Purchase	20,000		
	1,16,000		1,16,000

Accumulated Dep A/c (Buildings)

Particulars	*Amount* [₹]	*Particulars*	*Amount* [₹]
To Plant & machinery	14,800	By Balance b/d	37,000
To Balance c/d	26,200	By Adjusted P & L A/c	4,000
	41,000		41,000

Provision for Taxation A/c

Particulars	*Amount* [₹]	*Particulars*	*Amount* [₹]
To Cash (Taxes paid)	13,500	By Balance b/d	1,000
To Balance c/d	1,400	By Adjusted P&L A/c	13,900
	14,900		14,900

Illustration 17

Subbu Ltd. has submitted the following condensed Balance Sheet (as on 31.12.2017 and 31.12.2018) and additional information for the year ended 31.12.2018.

Balance Sheet

Liabilities	*(₹ in Lakhs)*		*Assets*	*(₹ in lakhs)*	
	2017	*2018*		*2017*	*2018*
Share capital	50,000	60,000	Fixed Assets	1,20,000	1,35,000
Reserve fund	10,000	15,000	*Less*: Accumulated		
P&L A/c	7,000	9,000	Depreciation	40,000	45,000
5% Debentures	40,000	30,000		80,000	90,000
Mortgage loan	–	5,000	Stock	25,000	35,000
Creditors	21,800	14,400	Debtors	20,000	17,000
Outstanding expenses	400	600	Cash	10,000	3,000
Provision for taxation	8,000	15,000	Prepaid expenses	200	400
			Preliminary expenses	2,000	1,500
	1,37,200	1,47,000		1,37,200	1,47,000

Additional Information:

Taxes paid during the year were ₹ 8,000. Net income after taxes ₹ 15,000. A sum of ₹ 10,000 was paid in dividends to shareholders. During the year 2018, the company purchased a building for ₹ 15,000 out of which ₹ 10,000 was paid in cash and for the rest the building was mortgaged to the vendor.

Solution

Cash Flow Statement

for the year ended on 31.12.2018

Cash Inflows:	*Amount* [₹]	*Cash Outflows:*	*Amount* [₹]
Cash balance on 1.1.2018	10,000	Reduction of Debentures	10,000
		Income tax paid	8,000
Add: Cash inflows:		Purchase of building	10,000
Issue of shares	10,000	Payment of dividends	10,000
Increase in Debtors	3,000	Increase in stock	10,000
Opening Profit	36,300	Decrease in Creditors	7,400
		Outstanding expenses as on 31.15.2017 paid	400
		Prepaid expenses for 2018	500
			56,300
		Cash balance on 31.12.18	3,000
	59,300		59,300

Workings

Adjusted P&L A/c

Particulars	*Amount* [₹]	*Particulars*	*Amount* [₹]
To Depreciation provision (45,000 – 40,000)	5000	By Opening balance	7,000
To Preliminary expenses written off (2,000 – 1,500)	500	By Operating cash profit (balancing figure)	36,300
To Outstanding expenses (2018)	600		
To General Reserve	5,000		
To Provision for taxation	15,000		
To Dividends paid	10,000		
To Prepaid expenses (2018)	200		
To Closing balance	9,000		
	43,300		43,300

Alternatively the operating cash profit may be calculated as follows:

Particulars	*Amount* [₹]
Net Income After Taxes	15,000
Add: Depreciation	5,000
Taxation Provisions	15,000
Outstanding Expenses (31.12.18)	600
Prepaid Expenses (31.12.18)	200
Preliminary Expenses written off	500
	36,300

Note: Outstanding expenses after 2020 and unexpired expenses for 2019 are non-cash items. Hence, these are readjusted to Adjusted P & L A/c.

Illustration 18

Following are the Summarised Balance Sheets of Vas Ltd. as on 31st December, 2017 and 2018.

Liabilities	*2017 Amount [₹]*	*2018 Amount [₹]*
Share Capital	3,00,000	3,75,000
Reserve Fund	75,000	90,000
Profit and Loss A/c	45,000	46,000
Mortgage Loan	1,00,000	–
Creditors	2,25,000	2,10,000
Provision for Taxation	45,000	52,500
	7,90,000	7,73,500

Assets:		
Land and Buildings	3,00,000	2,85,000
Plant & Machinery	2,25,000	2,53,500
Stock	1,50,000	1,20,000
Debtors	1,14,000	96,000
Cash	1,000	1,500
Bank	–	10,000
Goodwill	–	7,500
	7,90,000	7,73,500

Additional Information: During the year ended 31st December, 2018:

1. Dividends were paid for ₹ 32,000.
2. Assets of another company were purchased for a consideration of ₹ 75,000, payable in shares. The following assets were purchased: Stock ₹ 30,000 Machinery ₹ 37,500.
3. Machinery was further purchased for ₹ 12,000.
4. Loss on sale of machinery ₹ 300 was written off to Reserve Fund.
5. Income Tax provided during the year ₹ 50,000.

Prepare the Cash Flow Statement.

Solution

Cash Flow Statement
for the Year ending on 31st December, 2018

Particulars	*Amount* [₹]	*Particulars*		*Amount* [₹]
Cash Balance on 1.1.18	1,000	Application of Cash:		
Add: Sources of Cash		Payment of Dividend		32,000
Sale of Machinery	2,700	Purchase of Machinery		12,000
Cash from Operations	1,94,300	Tax Paid		42,500
		Mortgage Loan paid		1,00,000
				1,86,500
		Closing Balances:		
		Cash	1,500	
		Bank	10,000	11,500
	1,98,000			1,98,000

Decrease in stock

Stock on 31.12.2017	1,50,000
+ Stock purchased by shares	30,000
	1,80,000
Less: Closing balance 31.12.18	1,20,000
Increase in cash	60,000

Working Notes:

Machinery Account

Particulars	*Amount* [₹]	*Particulars*	*Amount* [₹]
To Balance b/d	2,25,000	By Depreciation	18,000
To Share Capital	37,500	By Reserve Fund	300
To Cash	12,000	By Cash (sale) (balancing figure)	19,400
		By Balance c/d	2,53,500
	2,74,500		2,74,500

Reserve Fund A/c

Particulars	*Amount* [₹]	*Particulars*	*Amount* [₹]
To Machinery A/c	300	By Balance b/d	75,000
To Balance c/d	90,000	By Profit and Loss	15,300
	90,300		90,300

Provision for Taxation A/c

Particulars	*Amount* [₹]	*Particulars*	*Amount* [₹]
To Cash (taxes paid)	42,500	By Balance b/d	45,000
To Balance c/d	52,500	By Profit and Loss	50,000
	95,000		95,000

Adjusted Profit and Loss A/c

Particulars	*Amount* [₹]	*Particulars*	*Amount* [₹]
To Dividends	32,000	By Balance b/d	45,000
To Depreciation on L & B	15,000	By Decrease in creditors	15,000
To Depreciation on Machinery	18,000	By Cash from Operations	1,94,300
To Provision for Taxation	50,000	(Balancing figures)	
To Transfer to Reserve	15,300		
To Decrease in Stock	60,000		
To Decrease in Debtors	18,000		
To Balance c/d	46,000		
	2,54,300		2,54,300

Accounting Standard [AS 3] - Revised Format

AS 3 revised in 1997, has recommended revised Cash Flow Statement [CFS] for listed companies and other industrial, commercial, and business undertakings in the private and public sector. It is, at present, recommendatory in character. According to revised AS 3, CFS should be prepared in such a way as to report the cash flows during the period separately for operating, investing, and financing activities.

1. *Cash Flows from Operating Activities*. Examples are as follows:

(*a*) Cash receipts from sale of goods and services;

(*b*) Cash receipts from royalties, fees, commission, and other revenue;

(*c*) Cash payments to suppliers of goods and services;

(*d*) Cash payments to employees;

(*e*) In the case of insurance companies, cash receipts and payments for premium received and claims and other benefits to policy holders;

(*f*) Payment and refund of income tax;

(*g*) Cash receipts and payments relating to futures and options contracts taken up for trading purposes.

2. *Cash Flows from Investing Activities*. Examples of such activities are as follows:

(*a*) Purchase of fixed assets, including intangibles and payments relating to capitalized research and development cost and self-constructed fixed assets.

(*b*) Cash receipts from sale of fixed assets including intangibles.

(c) Purchase of securities for Cash, such as shares, warrants, and debt instruments of other enterprises.

(d) Sale of securities for cash.

(e) Loans and advances given to third parties.

(f) Loans and advances collected from third parties.

(g) Cash receipts and payments relating to futures and option contracts entered into for investment purposes.

3. *Cash Flows from financing activities.* Examples of such activities are as follows:

(a) Cash receipts from the issue of shares and other similar instruments,

(b) Cash receipts from the issue of debentures, bonds, long or other short-term borrowings,

(c) Redemption of shares and repayment of amounts borrowed.

The following, illustrations would make clear the preparation of CFS under AS 3 method and Traditional methods.

Illustration 19

The same information given in Illustration 18 is used for the preparation of CFS under AS 3 [Revised] method.

Cash Flow Statement [AS-3 (Revised) Method]

I. Cash Flow from Operating Activities:	Amount [₹]	Amount [₹]
Net Profit made during the year	45 , 000	
Adjustment for Depreciation	18 , 000	
Loss on Sale o f Machinery	2 , 000	
Operating Profit before Working Capital Changes	65, 000	
Decrease in Stock	10 , 000	
Increase in Creditors	4 , 000	
Increase in Debtors	[20 , 000]	
Net Cash Flow from operating activities		59, 000
II. Cash Flows from Investing Activities:		
Sale of Machinery	5 , 000	
Purchase of Land	[10 , 000]	
Purchase of Building	[25 , 000]	
Net Cash Flow from investing activities		[30, 000]
III. Cash Flows from Financing Activities:		
Loan from Bank	10 , 000	
Mrs. X's Loan Repaid	[25 , 000]	
Drawings	[17 , 000]	
Net Cash Flow from Financing Activities		[32, 000]
Net Increase [decrease] in Cash and Cash Equivalent		[3 , 000]
Cash and Cash Equivalents Opening Balance		10, 000
Cash and Cash Equivalents Closing Balance		7, 000

Notes: 1. Cash and cash equivalents include cash and bank balances and risk less short-term investments.

2. Cash flow from operations are computed in the statement itself instead of preparing a separate statement showing cash from operations as in the case of traditional method.

3. Figures given within brackets represent cash outflows.

Illustration 20

Prepare Cash Flow Statement from the following Balance Sheets of Excel Ltd.:

Liabilities	*2017 Amount* [₹]	*2018 Amount* [₹]	*Assets*	*2017 Amount* [₹]	*2018 Amount* [₹]
Share Capital	17,00,000	18,35,000	Buildings	8,00,000	10,00,000
Reserves	40,000	83,700	Plant and Machinery	2,50,000	3,70,000
P & L App. A/c	1,00,000	1,30,000	Furniture	5,000	6,000
Provision for Dividends	70,000	50,000	Cash	2,000	2,200
Creditors	1,00,000	95,000	Debtors	1,00,000	45,000
Bank Overdraft	8,000	18,000	Bills Receivable	8,000	9,000
Bills Payable	14,000	13,000	Stock	4,00,000	3,43,700
Mortgage Loan	10,000	70,000	Prepaid Expenses	3,000	3,100
			Investments	1,64,000	1,70,000
			Goodwill	3,00,000	3,43,700
			Preliminary Expenses	10,000	2,000
	20,42,000	22, 94, 700		20,42,000	22,94,700

(*a*) Depreciation is charged on buildings at 3% of cost of ₹ 9,00,000; on Plant and Machinery at 8% of cost ₹ 4,00,000; Furniture at 5% of cost ₹ 8,000.

(*b*) Investments were purchased and interest received ₹ 3,000 was used in writing down the book value of investments.

(*c*) The declared dividends for 2017 were paid and Interim Dividend for ₹ 20,000 was paid out of P & L App. A/c.

Solution

Workings

Net Profit as per P&L A/c	Amount [₹]
Closing Balance of P&L App. A/c	1,30,000
Add: Transfer to Reserves	43,700
Provision for Dividends for 2018	50,000
Interim Dividend Paid	20,000
	2,43,700
Less : Opening Balance of P&L App A/c	1,00,000
Net Profit before Tax and Extraordinary Items	1,43,700

Investment Account

Particulars	*Amount* [₹]	*Particulars*	*Amount* [₹]
To Balance b/d	1,64,000	By Bank [interest]	3,000
To Bank [Purchase of investments]	9,000	By Balance c/d	1,70,000
	1,73,000		1,73,000

Cash Flow Statement [Revised Method]

		Amount [₹]	Amount [₹]
I.	Cash Flows from Operating Activities:		
	Net Profit before tax and extraordinary items	1,43,700	
	Adjustments for Depreciation for Furniture	400	
	Adjustments for Depreciation on Plant and machinery	32,000	
	Adjustments for Depreciation on Buildings	27,000	
	Preliminary Expenses written off	8,000	
	Operating Profit before Working Capital Changes	2,11,100	
	Decrease in Debtors	55,000	
	Decrease in Stock	56,300	
	Decrease in Creditors	[5,000]	
	Increase in Bills Receivable	[1,000]	
	Decrease in Bills Payable	[1,000]	
	Increase in Prepaid Expenses	[100]	
	Net Cash Flow from Operating Activities		3,15,300
II.	Cash Flows from Investing Activities:		
	Interest on Investments	3,000	
	Purchase of Investments	[9,000]	
	Purchase of Buildings	[2,27,000]	
	Purchase of Machinery	[1,52,000]	
	Purchase of Furniture	[1,400]	
	Purchase of Goodwill	[43,700]	
	Net Cash Flow from Investing Activities		[4,30,100]
III.	Cash Flows from Financing Activities:		
	Issue of Shares	1,35,000	
	Mortgage Loan	60,000	
	Dividend Paid for 2017	[70,000]	
	Interim Dividend Paid	[20,000]	
	Net Cash Flows from Financing Activities		1,05,000
	Net Increase [decrease] in cash and cash equivalents		[9,800]
	Cash and Cash Equivalents Opening Balance [Bank O/D – Cash]		[6,000]
	Cash and Cash Equivalents Closing Balance [Bank O/D – Cash]		[15,800]

Note: Figures given within brackets represent cash outflows.

Illustration 21

A company finds on 1st January, 2018 that it is short of funds with which to implement its expansion program. On 1st January, 2017, it had a credit balance of ₹ 1,80.000. From the following information, prepare a statement for the Board of Directors to show how the Overdraft of ₹ 68,750, as on 31st December, has arisen.

Figures as Per Balance Sheet [as on 31st December]

	2017 Amount [₹]	*2018 Amount [₹]*
Fixed Assets	7,50,000	11,20,000
Stock and Stores	1,90,000	3,30,000
Debtors	3,80,000	3,35,000
Bank Balance	1,80,000	68,750 [O/D]
Share Capital [Shares of Rs.10 each]	2,50,000	3,00,000
Bills Receivable	87,500	95,000

The profit for the year ended 31 December, 2017 before charging depreciation and taxation which amounted to ₹ 2,40,000. On 1st January 2017, 5000 shares were issued at a premium of ₹ 5 per share. ₹ 1,37,500 was paid in March 2017 by way of income tax. Dividends were paid as follows:

2016 [final] on the capital on 31st December, 2016 at 10% less tax at 25%,

2017 [interim] 5 per cent free of tax.

Solution

Preparation of Cash Flow Statement [as per Traditional Method]

Cash Flow Statement

For the Year Ended on 31st December, 2018

Sources (Cash inflows)	*Amount [₹]*	*Application (Cash outflows)*	*Amount [₹]*
Bank balance as		Cash outflows:	
on 1 – 1 - 2018	1,80,000	Purchase of Fixed Assets	3,70,000
Add: Cash Inflows:		Increase in Stock and Stores	1,40,000
Issue of shares	50,000	Increase in Bills Receivable	7,500
Share Premium	25,000	Income Tax Paid	1,37,500
Decrease in Debtors	45,000	Final Dividend for 2017	18,750
Increase in Creditors	80,000	Interim dividend for 2018	15,000
Cash from Operations	2,40,000		
Bank Balance [O/D] on 31-12-18	68,750		
	6,88,750		6,88,750

Workings

1. Final dividend works out to ₹ 2,50,000 × 10% = ₹ 25,000

   Less: Tax deducted at source at 25% on ₹ 25,000 = 6,250

   Net Dividend amount paid = 18,750
2. Interim Dividend at 5% on ₹ 3,00,000 = ₹ 15,000
3. Interim Dividend is free of tax, hence, nothing is deductible from ₹ 15,000 on account of tax. However, a sum of ₹ 5,000 i.e., ₹ 15,000 × 25/75 is payable to the Government on account of tax.
4. It is assumed that the figure of income tax paid ₹ 1,37,500 includes ₹ 11,250 [₹ 6,250 + 5,000] in respect of final and interim dividends.
5. It is assumed that fixed assets are appearing at cost.
6. It is obvious that the profit for the year 2018 ₹ 2,40,000 is before charging the final dividend and interim dividends.

The Cash Flow Statement as per revised method, is as follows:

Cash Flow Statement for the Year Ended on 31 December, 2018

	Amount [₹]	Amount [₹]
II. Cash Flows from Operating Activities:		
Net Profit Before Tax and Extraordinary Items	2 ,40,000	
Add: Decrease in Debtors	45,000	
Increase in Creditors	80,000	
Increase in Stock and Stores	[1,40, 000]	
Increase in Bills Receivables	[7, 500]	
Income tax paid	[1,37, 500]	
Net Cash Flows from Operating Activities		80, 000
III. Cash Flows from Investing Activit ies:		
Purchase o f Fixed Assets	[3,70, 000]	
Net Cash Flows from Investing Activities		[3,70,000]
IV. Cash Flows from Financing Activities:		
Issue of Shares	50,000	
Share Premium	25,000	
Final Dividend Paid	[18,750]	
Interim Dividend Paid	[15,000]	
Net cash flows fro m financing activities		41, 250
Net increase [decrease] in cash and cash equivalent		[2,48,750]
Cash and cash equivalents at the beginning of the year		1,80, 000
Cash and cash equivalents at the end of the year [O/D]		[68 750]

REVIEW QUESTIONS

1. What is a Cash Flow Statement?

2. Explain the meaning of 'Notional Cash'.

3. What do you mean by Non-Cash Items?

4. List out the various sources of cash.

5. Enumerate the applications of cash.

6. What is meant by Cash Flow?

7. State the uses of a Cash Flow Statement.

8. What are the limitations of Cash Flow Analysis?

9. Differentiate Cash Flow Analysis from Fund Flow Analysis.

10. Explain the method of calculating cash from operations for the purpose of preparing a (cash) Flow Statement

11. Explain the technique of preparing a Cash Flow Statement.

12. State the effect of each of the following transactions on cash flow:

(*a*) Purchase of goods on credit.

(*b*) Borrowing of ₹ 5,000, issuing a short-term Promissory Note.

(*c*) Purchase of building for ₹ 5,000 against a Long-Term Promissory Note.

(*d*) Purchase of office furniture on account.

(*e*) Issue of shares for cash of ₹ 10,000.

(*f*) Bonus paid in the form of Fully Paid Shares.

(*g*) Redemption of Debenture by payment in cash

13. Explain the importance of Cash Flow Analysis in a business undertaking.

14. From the following balances, you are required to calculate cash from operations:

Particulars	*Dec 31, 2017 Amount* [₹]	*Dec 31, 2018 Amount* [₹]
Debtors	1,00,000	94,000
Bills Receivable	20,000	25,000
Creditors	40,000	50,000
Bills Payable	16,000	12,000
Outstanding Expenses	2,000	2,400
Prepaid Expenses	1,600	1,400
Accrued Income	1,200	1,500
Income received in advance	600	500
Profit made during the year		2,60,000

(Ans. 2,67,200)

(Ans. 2,67,200)

15. Is it possible for a firm to have cash for paying dividend when actually there is a loss?

16. Is it possible for a firm to have profits and, at the same time, have no cash for paying, dividends?

17. From the following Balance Sheet of A Ltd., as on December, 31, 2017 and 2018, you are required to prepare a statement of Sources and Uses of Cash.

1. Depreciation of ₹ 3,000 and ₹ 6,000 have been charged on Plant Account and Land and Buildings Account respectively.
2. Dividends paid totalled ₹ 3,000.

(Ans. Operating Profits; ₹ 22,000. Sources; ₹ 34,000 Uses: ₹ 29,000)

Liabilities	*2017*	*2018*	*Assets*	*2017*	*2018*
Share Capital	80,000	85,000	Land & Building	50,000	50,000
Profit and Loss			Plant	24,000	34,000
Appropriation A/c	14,500	24,500	Stock	9,000	7,000
Creditors	9,000	5,000	Debtors	16,500	19,500
Mortgage		5,000	Cash at Bank	4,000	9,000
	1,03,500	1,19,500		1,03,500	1,19,500

18. See: Balance Sheets of ABC Limited in here.

Additional information

In 2017, Plant and Machinery costing ₹ 5 lakhs (accumulated depreciation ₹ 3 lakhs) was sold for ₹ 1 lakh. Tax paid for the last year ₹ 6 lakhs.

Prepare the cash flow statement.

(Rupees in thousands)

Liabilities	*2017*	*2018*	*Assets*	*2017*		*2018*
Equity Shares	3,000	4,000	Property		2,000	
Share Premium	–	100	Plant and Machinery	4,000		4,500
P&L A/c balance	1,000	1,000		1,400		1,500
Profit for the year	–	2,000	Depreciation		–	–
6% Debentures	1,500	1,000			2,600	3,000
Profit on redemption of debentures	–	20	Loan to Subsidiary		–	150
			Shares in Subsidiary	200		200
Sundry Creditors	1,400	1,100	Stock	1,400		1,500
Provision for Taxation	500	1,000	Debtors Bank	1,000		1,500
Proposed Dividend	150	200		350		1,570
	7,550	10,420		7,550		10,420

19. The comparative Balance Sheets of Royal Ltd., on June 30, 2018 and 2017 are given below in a condensed form.

Assets	2018 Amount [₹]	2017 Amount [₹]
Cash	20,000	28,100
Accounts Receivable	21,100	30,800
Prepaid Expenses	3,000	3,950
Merchant's Inventory	89,200	93,400
Fixed Assets	2,00,000	1,52,000
Accumulated Depreciation on Fixed Assets	(42,000)	(60,000)
	2,91,300	2,48,250

Liabilities and Shareholder's equity

Accounts Payable	48,000	28,000
Mortgage Debentures	–	50,000
Equity Capital (in shares of ₹ 10 each)	1,50,000	1,00,000
Premium on Shares	10,000	–
Retained Earnings	83,300	70,250
	2,91,300	2,48,250

Additional data obtained from the income statement and from an examination of the non-current assets, non-current liabilities, and shareholders' equity accounts in the ledger are as follows:

(*a*) Net Income for the year: ₹ 27,050

(*b*) Depreciation for the year: ₹ 10,000

(*c*) Cash Dividend declared during the year: ₹ 12,000

(*d*) An addition to the building was made during the year at a cost of ₹ 78,000 and fully depreciated equipment costing ₹ 30,000 was discarded. No salvage being realised.

Prepare:

(*a*) A Statement of Source and Application of Funds (Working Capital concept) including a schedule of changes in Working Capital.

(*b*) A statement of cash flow.

(Ans. (*a*) Increase W.C. ₹ 42,950. Funds from operation ₹ 57,050)

(*b*) Cash from operations - ₹ 41,000

(Total of sources and App. ₹ 1,43,000 and ₹ 1,34,900 respectively)

20. From the following figures compute cash from operations:

Particulars	*2017* *Amount* [₹]	*2018* *Amount* [₹]
Stock	7,500	12,000
Debtors	15,000	18,000
Bad Debts Reserve	1,500	1,800
Bills Receivable	6,000	4,500
Bills Payable	7,500	9,000
Creditors	12,000	13,500
Marketable Securities	15,000	18,000
Outstanding Salaries	1,500	2,250
Unexpired Insurance	3,000	1,500
Outstanding Income	4,500	6,000
Income received in advance	3,000	1,500

Profit earned during 2018 is ₹ 15,000 after providing for depreciation of ₹ 3,000.

(B.Com. Madras) (Ans. ₹ 11,550).

21. The following are the summarised Balance Sheets of a company as on 31st December, 2013 and 2015.

Liabilities	*2014* *Amount* [₹]	*2015* *Amount* [₹]	*Assets*	*2014* *Amount* [₹]	*2015* *Amount* [₹]
Share Capital				2,00,000	2,50,000
General Reserve				50,000	60,000
Profit & Loss				30,500	30,600
Bank Loan (Long-term)				70,000	–
Sundry Creditors				1,50,000	1,35,200
Provision for Taxation				30,000	35,000
				5,30,500	5,10,800

Liabilities	*2014* *Amount* [₹]	*2015* *Amount* [₹]	*Assets*	*2014* *Amount* [₹]	*2015* *Amount* [₹]
Land and Buildings				2,00,000	1,90,000
Machinery				1,50,000	1,69,000
Stock				1,00,000	74,000
Sundry Debtors				80,000	64,200
Cash				500	600
Bank				–	8,000
Goodwill				–	5,000
				5,30,500	5,10,800

Additional Information:

(*a*) Dividend of ₹ 23,000 was paid.

(*b*) Assets of another company were purchased for a consideration of ₹ 50,000 payable in shares.

The following assets were purchased: Stock ₹ 20,000; Machinery ₹ 25,000.

(*c*) Machinery was further purchased for ₹ 8,000

(*d*) Depreciation (written off) of machinery ₹ 12,000.

(*e*) Income-Tax provided during the year ₹ 33,000.

(*f*) Loss on sale of machinery ₹ 200 was written off to general reserve.

Prepare the Cash Flow Statement.

(**Ans.** Cash from Operations ₹ 1,35,200; Sources ₹ 1,37,100; Applications ₹ 1,29,000).

22. Prepare Cash Flow Statement, as per AS 3 Format from the following Balance Sheet of XL Engineering Ltd.

Liabilities	*(₹ in Lakhs)*		*Assets*	*(₹ in lakhs)*	
	2017	*2018*		*2017*	*2018*
Share Capital	17,00,000	18,35,000	Buildings	8,00,000	10,00,000
Reserves	40,000	83,700	Plant and Machinery	2,50,000	3,70,000
Profit and Loss Appropriation A/c	1,00,000	1,30,000	Fixtures and Fittings	5,000	6,000
			Cash	2,000	2,200
Dividends	70,000	50,000	Debtors	1,00,000	45,000
Creditors	1,00,000	95,000	Accounts Receivable	8,000	9,000
			Stock	4,00,000	3,43,700
Bank Overdraft	8,000	18,000	Prepaid Expenses	3,000	3,100
Bills Payable	14,000	13,000	Investments	1,64,000	1,70,000
Loan on Mortgage	10,000	70,000	Goodwill	3,00,000	3,43,700
			Preliminary Expenses	10,000	2,000
	20,42,000	22,94,700		20,42,000	22,94,700

(*a*) Depreciation is charged on building at 3 per cent of cost ₹ 9,00,000. On Plant and Machinery at 8 per cent cost ₹ 4,00,000. On Fixtures and Fittings at 5 per cent of cost ₹ 8,000.

(*b*) Investments were purchased and interest received ₹ 3,000 was used in writing down the book value of investments.

(*c*) The declared dividend for 2016 was paid and Interim Dividend for ₹ 20,000 paid out of the Profit and Loss Appropriation Account.

(**Ans.** Sources ₹ 5,13,300; Applications ₹ 5,23,100; Cash from operations ₹ 3,15,300).

■ ■ ■

10

Cost Accounting—Cost Analysis Concepts and Classifications

ELEMENT OF COSTS

Mere knowledge of total costs cannot satisfy the needs of the management. For proper control and managerial decisions, the management is to be provided with necessary data to analyze and classify the total costs.

For this purpose, the total costs are analyzed by elements of cost by the nature of expenses. Strictly speaking, the elements of costs are three:

(*a*) Materials

(*b*) Labour

(*c*) Other expenses.

By grouping the above elements of cost, we find the following divisions of costs are obtained:

1. Prime cost	= Direct materials + direct labour + direct expenses
2. Works or factory costs	= Prime cost + works or factory overheads
3. Cost of production	= Works cost + Administrative overheads
4. Total cost or cost of sales	= Cost of production + Selling and distribution overheads

Illustration 1

Ascertain the prime cost, work cost, cost of production, total cost and profit for the undertaking given the following information:

(*a*) Direct materials	= ₹ 5,000
(*b*) Direct labour	= ₹ 3,500
(*c*) Factory expense	= ₹ 1,500

(*d*) Administrative expenses = ₹ 800

(*e*) Selling expenses = ₹ 700

(*f*) Sales = ₹ 15000

Solution

Prime cost	= Direct materials + direct labour
	= ₹ 5,000 + ₹ 3,500 = ₹ 8,500
Works or factory costs	= Prime cost + works or factory overheads
	= ₹ 8,500 + ₹ 1,500 = ₹ 10,000
Cost of production	= Works cost + Administrative overheads
	= ₹ 10,000 + ₹ 8,00 = ₹ 10,800
Total cost or cost of sales	= Cost of prediction + Selling and distribution overheads
	= ₹ 10,800 + ₹ 700 = ₹ 11,500
Profit = Sales – Total cost	= 15,000 – 11,500 = ₹ 3,500

DIRECT MATERIAL

Direct materials are those materials which can be identified in the product and can be conveniently measured and thus directly charged to the product. Thus, they form a part of the finished product. For example, timber in furniture making, cloth in dress material making and bricks in a building are direct materials. The following are normally classified as direct materials:

(i) All **Raw Materials,** like jute in the manufacture of gunny bags, pig iron in foundry, fruits in canning industry, etc.

(ii) **Special Materials,** specifically purchase for a specific job, process or order like glue for book binding, starch powder for dressing yarn, etc.

(iii) **Parts or Components** purchased or produced like batteries for transistors/radios and tyres for cycles, etc.

(iv) **Primary Packing Materials** like cartons, wrappings, cardboard boxes, etc. used to protect the finished products from climatic conditions or for easy handling inside the factory, etc.

From the above discussion, it becomes clear that indirect materials are those which cannot be classified as direct materials. For example, cotton waste, lubricants, brooms, rags, cleaning materials, materials for repair, maintenance, diesel used in power generators, etc.

Classification of materials into direct and indirect facilitates material control. Direct materials are usually high value items as compared to indirect materials and need strict control and critical analysis for reducing their costs. On the other hand, simple control techniques are sufficient in case of indirect materials being low value items.

However, in some cases, though materials are a part of the finished products yet they are not treated as direct material. For example, sewing thread in dress making nails in furniture making, etc. This is because they are used in comparatively small quantities and it would be futile elaboration to make their analysis for the purpose of direct charges.

Such materials are treated as indirect materials. Thus, it can be concluded that the ease and flexibility with which a material can be traced into the composition of a finished product will determine what is to be treated as direct material and indirect material.

DIRECT LABOUR

Direct labour is all labour expenses in altering the construction, composition, confirmation or condition of the product. In simple words, it is that labour which can be conveniently identified or attributed wholly to a particular job, product or process or expenses in converting raw materials into finished goods. Wages of such labour are known as direct wages. Thus, it includes the following group of activities:

(*i*) Labour engaged on the actual production of the product or in carrying out an operation or in process.

(*ii*) Labour engaged in aiding the manufacture by way of supervision maintenance, setting of tools, transportation of materials, etc.

(*iii*) Inspectors, analysts, etc. specifically required for such production, etc.

The wages paid to supervisors, inspectors, etc., though not direct labour, can be treated as direct labour if they are directly engaged on specific product or process and the hours they spend on it can be directly measured without much of an effort. Similarly, where the cost is not significant, like wages of trainees or apprentices, their labour, though directly spent on a product, is not treated as direct labour.

OVERHEADS

Overheads may be defined as the aggregate of the cost of indirect materials, indirect labour and other such expenses, including services which cannot conveniently be charged direct to specific cost units. Thus, overheads are all expenses other than direct expenses.

In general terms, overheads comprise all expenses incurred for or in connection with the general organization of the whole or a part of the undertaking. It is a sort of operating supplies and services used by the undertaking, including the maintenance of capital assets. The main groups comprising overheads may be sub-divided are:

(*i*) Manufacturing overheads,

(*ii*) Administrative overheads,

(*iii*) Selling overheads,

(*iv*) Distribution overheads, and

(*v*) Research and development overheads.

Overheads can also be classified as

(*a*) Expenses on indirect materials,

(*b*) Expenses on indirect labour, and

(*c*) Expenses on other indirect actions.

These have been discussed in the subsequent topics.

EXPENSES EXCLUDED FROM COSTS

The total cost of a product should include only those items of expenses which are charged against profit. Items of expenses, which are related to capital assets, capital losses, payment by way of distribution of profits and matters of pure finance, should not form a part of the cost.

For example, such expenses like income tax, dividends, abnormal wastages of materials, abnormal idle time, interest on capital given or received, expenses of raising capital, discount on shares and debentures, profits or loss from sale of assets or investments, excessive depreciation, appropriation of profits, writing off the goodwill, preliminary expenses and underwriting commission. Cash discount, debentures interests and incomes, which are not connected with the business, like transfer fees, rent, interest or dividend received and capital expenditures form part of overheads.

COST SHEET OR STATEMENT OF COSTS

Cost sheet is a statement designed to show the output of a particular accounting period along with the break up of costs. The data incorporated in cost sheet are collected from various statements of accounts, which have been written in cost accounts, day-to-day or regular records.

There is no fixed form for preparation of a cost sheet but in order to make the cost sheet norms useful it is generally presented in columnar form. Columns are for the total costs of the current period, per unit for the current period, total cost and per unit cost for the preceding period and total per unit cost budgeted for this period and so on. The information to be incorporated in a cost sheet depends on the requirement of the management for the purpose of control.

Cost sheet is also called a memorandum statement. Therefore it does not form a part of double entry cost accounting records. In spite of this, the relationship between cost sheet and financial accounts, which are maintained as a double entry system is very important as cost sheet derives its data from the financial accounting. Where predetermined rates are not used, the entire data required for preparation of cost sheet is derived from the financial accounting. Therefore, periodically it becomes necessary to reconcile the information obtained from cost accounting and financial accounting separately.

Advantages of Cost Sheet

The advantages of cost sheet are:

1. It discloses the total costs and the cost per unit of the units produced during the period.
2. It enables a manufacturer to keep a close watch and control over the cost of production.

3. By providing a comparative study of the various elements of current cost with the past results and standard costs, it is possible to find out the causes of variation in costs and to eliminate the adverse factors and conditions which has an impact on the increase of the total costs.
4. It acts as guide to the manufacturer and helps him in formulating a definite useful production policy.
5. It helps in fixing up the selling price more accurately.
6. It helps the businessman to minimize the cost of production where there is a cut throat competition.
7. It helps the businessman to submit quotations with reasonable degree of accuracy against tenders for the supply of goods.

Specimen of Cost Sheet

Particulars	*Total cost in* [₹]	*Cost per unit in* [₹]
Direct Materials	XXX	
Direct labour	XXX	
Prime cost	XXX	
Add: Works overheads	XXX	
Works cost	XXX	
Add: Administrative overheads	XXX	
Cost of Production	XXX	
Add: Selling and distribution overheads	XXX	
Total Cost or Cost of Sales	XXX	

Illustration 2

Calculate the prime cost, factory cost, cost of production, cost of sales and profit from the following information.

Particulars	*Amount* [₹]	*Particulars*	*Amount* [₹]
Direct materials	1,00,000	Depreciation : Plant	500
Direct wages	30,000	Office premises	1,250
Wages of foremen	2,500	Stores consumables	2,500
Electric power	500	Manager's salary	5,000
Lighting factory	1,500	Director's fees	1,250
Lighting office	500	Office stationary	500
Wages of storekeepers	1,000	Telephone charges	125

(Contd...)

Particulars	Amount [₹]		Amount [₹]
Oil and water	500	Postages and telegrams	250
Rent factory	5,000	Salesman salaries	1,250
Rent office	2,500	Travelling expenses	500
Repairs and renewals: Factory plant	3,500	Advertising	1,250
Office premises	500	Warehouse charges	500
Transfer to reserves	1,000	Sales	1,89,500
Discount on shares written off	500	Carriage outward	375
Dividend	2,000	Income tax	10,000

Solution

Cost Sheet

Particulars		Amount [₹]
Direct materials		1,00,000
Direct wages		30,000
Prime cost		1,30,000
Add: Factory overheads:		
Wages of foreman	2,500	
Electric power	500	
Lighting factory	1,500	
Storekeepers wages	1,000	
Oil and water	500	
Rent factory	5,000	
Repairs and renewals: Factory plant	3,500	
Depreciation: Factory plant	500	
Stores consumables	2,500	17,500
Factory costs		1,47,500
Add: Administrative Overheads:		
Rent office	2,500	
Repairs and renewals office	500	
Lighting office	500	
Depreciation: Office premises	1,250	
Manager's salary	5,000	

(Contd...)

Particulars		*Amount* [₹]
Director's fees	1,250	
Office stationary	500	
Telephone charges	125	
Postages and telegrams	250	11,875
Cost of production		1,59,375
Add: selling and distribution overheads		
Carriage outward	375	
Salesman salaries	1,250	
Travelling expenses	500	
Advertising	1,250	
Warehouse charges	500	3,875
Cost of sales		1,63,250
Profit		26,250
Sales		1,89,500

Notes: (1) Transfer to reserves, income tax and dividends are excluded from cost accounts being the items of appropriation of profits.

(2) Discount on shares written off being an item of non-operating nature is excluded from cost accounting.

TREATMENT OF STOCK

Stock requires special treatment while preparing a cost sheet. Stock may be of raw materials, work in progress and finished goods.

Stock of Raw Materials

If opening stock of raw material, purchases of raw materials and closing stock of raw material are given then with the help of those data raw materials consumed can be calculated.

Particulars	*Amount* [₹]
Opening stock of raw materials	1,000
Add: Purchase of raw material	5,000
	6,000
Less: Closing stock	2,000
Cost of raw material consumed	4,000

Stock of Work in Progress

Work in progress means units on which some work has been done but which are not yet complete. Work in progress is valued at prime cost or work costs basis, but the latter is usually preferred.

Instructions in this respect should be carefully noted from the language of the question. If it is valued at works or factory cost, the opening and closing cost will be adjusted as follows:

	Amount [₹]
Prime cost	1,000
Add: Factory overheads incurred	5,000
Work in progress (beginning)	2,000
	8,000
Less: Work in progress closing	2,000
Factory or manufacturing or work cost	6,000

Stock of Finished Goods

If opening stock and closing stock of finished goods are also given, they must be adjusted before calculating the cost of goods sold as under:

	Amount [₹]
Cost of production	1,000
Add: Opening stock of finished goods	5,000
	6,000
Less: Closing stock of finished goods	2,000
Cost of goods sold	4,000

Illustration 3

The following information has been obtained from the records of Left Centre Inc. for the period from 1st January, 2018 to 30th June, 2018. Calculate prime cost of materials consumed, factory cost incurred, factory cost and income statement showing the gross profit and net profit.

Particulars	*January* *Amount* [₹]	*June* *Amount* [₹]
Cost of raw material stock	30,000	25,000
Cost of work in progress stock	12,000	15,000
Cost of finished goods stock	60,000	55,000
Transaction during the six months, period:		
Purchases of raw materials	4,50,000	
Wages paid	2,30,000	
Factory overheads	92,000	
Administrative overheads	30,000	
Selling and distribution overheads	20,000	
Sales	9,00,000	

Solution

Opening stock of raw material	30,000
Purchases of raw materials	4,50,000
	4,80,000
Less: Closing stock of raw materials	25,000
Cost of materials consumed	4,55,000
Add: Direct wages	2,30,000
Prime Costs	6,85,000
Add: Factory overheads	92,000
Factory cost incurred	7,77,000
Add: Work in progress	12,000
	7,89,000
Less: Opening work in progress	15,000
Factory or manufacturing cost or works cost	7,74,000

Income Statement

Particulars		*Amount* [₹]
Sales		9,00,000
Less: Cost of goods sold		
Opening stock	60,000	
Add: Factory cost of the year	7,74,000	
	8,34,000	
Less: Closing stock of finished goods	55,000	7,79,000
Gross profit		1,21,000
Less: Indirect expenses		
Administrative expenses	30,000	
Selling and distribution expenses	20,000	50,000
Net Profit		71,000

Sometimes, the entire output is not sold and in that case the cost of production of goods sold is to be calculated in order to calculate the profit or loss after adding the selling and distribution overheads.

Illustration 4

The following extract of costing information relates to commodity A for the half year ending December 2018. Calculate the cost of raw materials used, cost of output for the period, cost of sales, net profit for the period and net profit for one tonne of the commodity.

Particulars	Amount [₹]	Particulars	Amount [₹]
Purchase of raw material	1,20,000	Stock on 31st December 2015	
Works overheads	48,000	Raw material	22,240
Director wages	1,00,000	Finished goods (2000 tonnes)	32,000
Carriage on purchase	1,440	Work in progress (1st July 2018)	4,800
Stock on 1st July 2018		Work in progress (1st–31st December 2018)	16,000
Raw materials	2,000	Sales – Finished goods	3,00,000
Finished products (1000 tonnes)	16,000		

Selling and distribution overheads are Re. 1 per tone sold. 16000 tonnes of commodity were produced during the period.

Solution

Particulars	Amount [₹]	Amount [₹]
Opening stock		20,000
Purchase of raw material		1,20,000
Carriage on purchase		1,440
		1,41,440
Less: Closing stock		22,240
Value of raw material used		1,19,200
Add: Direct wage		1,00,000
Prime cost		2,19,200
Add: Work overheads	48,000	
Opening stock of work in progress	4,800	52,800
		2,72,000
Less: Closing stock of work in progress		16,000
		2,56,000
Add: Cost of output for the period		
Opening stock of finished goods		1,000
		2,57,000
Less: Closing stock of finished goods		2,000
Cost of sales		2,55,000
Net profit for the period		45,000
Sales		3,00,000

Net profit per tonne = ₹ 45,000/15,000 = ₹ 3.

Sometimes selling price is to be determined on the basis of cost of production but profit percentage is generally given on sales. For calculating of profit,

Profit = (Rate percentage on sale × total costs)/(100 – percentages on sales)

Suppose if the profit of 25 on sales is to be realized and total cost is ₹ 33000, then the profit to be added to total cost will be calculated as = (25 × ₹ 33000)/(100 – 25) = ₹ 11000.

Illustration 5

From the following information extracted from the trial balance of XYZ as on September 2016, prepare the statement of cost showing various elements and the statement of profit.

Debit balances	*Amount* [₹]	*Credit balances*	*Amount* [₹]
Opening Inventories		Sales	7,68,000
Finished stock	80,000	Purchase returns	4,800
Raw materials	1,40,000		
Work in progress	2,00,000		
Office appliances	17,400		
Plant and machinery	4,60,500		
Building	2,00,000		
Sales return and rebates	14,000		
Materials purchased	3,20,000		
Freight incurred on materials	16,000		
Direct labour	1,60,000		
Indirect labour	18,000		
Factory supervision expense	10,000		
Repairs and upkeep of the Factory	14,000		
Heat, light and power	65,000		
Rates and Taxes	6,300		
Miscellaneous factory Expenses	18,700		
Sales commissions	33,600		
Sales travelling	11,000		
Sales promotion	22,500		
Distribution department salaries	18,000		
Office salaries and expenses	8,600		
Interest on borrowed funds	2,000		

Further information are

Particulars	*Amount*[₹]
Closing inventories:	
Finished goods	1,15,000
Raw materials	1,80,000
Work in progress	1,92,000
Accrued expenses:	
Direct labour	8,000
Indirect labour	1,200
Interest on borrowed Funds	2,000
Depreciation to be provided on:	
Office appliances	5%
Plant and machinery	10%
Buildings	4%
Distribution of following costs:	
Heat, Light and power, office and distribution	8:1:1
Rates and Taxes: Two thirds to factory and one third to office	2/3 : 1/3
Depreciation on Building to Factory, Office and Plant & Machinery	8:1:1

Solution

Statement of Profit

Particulars	*Amount*[₹]	*Amount*[₹]	*Amount*[₹]
Opening raw material inventory		1,40,000	
Add: Materials purchase		3,20,000	
Freight on materials		16,000	
Total cost of raw materials		4,76,000	
Less: Purchase returns	4,800		
Closing stock of raw material	1,80,000	1,84,800	
Material consumed			2,91,200
Direct labour		1,60,000	
Add: Accrued wages		8,000	1,68,000
Prime cost			4,59,200
Add: Overheads-factory			
Indirect labour (18,000 + 1,200)		19,200	
Factory supervision		10,000	
Repairs and upkeep		14,000	
Heat, light and power (4/5 of ₹ 65,000)		52,000	
Rates and taxes (2/3 of ₹ 6,300)		4,200	
Miscellaneous factory expenses		18,700	

(Contd...)

Particulars	Amount [₹]	Amount [₹]	Amount [₹]
Depreciation on plant & Machinery (10% on ₹ 4,60,500)		46,050	
Depreciation on building (4% on 4/5 of ₹ 2,00,000)		6,400	1,70,550
Gross work costs			6,29,750
Add: Opening work in progress Stock			2,00,000
			8,29,750
Less: Closing work in progress Stock			1,92,000
Works costs			6,37,750
Add: Administrative expenses			
Office salaries		8,600	
Depreciation on office appliance		870	
Depreciation on building		800	
Heat, light and power (1/10 of ₹ 65,000)		6,500	
Rates and taxes		2,100	18,870
			6,56,620
Cost of production			
Add: Opening finished goods inventory			80,000
			7,36,620
Less: Closing finished inventory			1,15,000
Total cost of production			6,21,620
Cost of goods sold			
Add: Selling and distribution expenses			
Selling commission		33,600	
Sales travelling		11,000	
Sales promotion		22,500	
Distribution department salaries		18,000	
Heat, light and power (1/10 of ₹ 65000)		6,500	
Depreciation on building		800	92,400
Total cost of sales			7,14,020

Statement of Profit

Particulars	*Amount*[₹]	*Amount*[₹]
Sales	7,68,000	
Less: Sales returns	14,000	7,54,000
Less: Cost of sales		7,14,020
Gross operating profit		39,980
Less: Interest on borrowed Funds		4,000
Net operating profit		35,980

COST CONCEPTS

Some concepts, which are used in cost accounting, are discussed below:

COST

It is the amount of resources given up in exchange for some goods or services. The resources given up are expressed mostly in monetary terms. Cost is defined as the amount of expenditure (accrual or notional) incurred on or attributable to a given thing or to ascertain in the cost of a given thing.

The Committee on Cost Terminology of the American Accounting Association has defined cost as the foregoing in monetary terms incurred or potentially to be incurred in the realization of the objective of the management which may be manufacturing of a product or rendering a service.

Thus, cost is that which is given or is sacrificed to obtain something. The cost of an article consists of actual outgoings or ascertained charges incurred in its production and sale. Cost is a generic term and it is always advisable to qualify the word cost to show exactly what it means. For example, prime cost, factory cost, sunk cost, etc.

Cost is also defined from value as cost is measured in terms of money whereas value is measured in terms of usefulness or utility of an article.

The objective for which costs are computed is also important. For example, if the purpose is to fix the selling price, the total cost is considered, for valuation of stock cost means the cost of production only. If the objective is to measure efficiency, cost will have to be compiled differently than if the purpose is to quote or value the stock. So, the term cost has different interpretations.

A cost must always be studied with reference to its purpose and conditions. Different costs may be ascertained for different purposes and under different conditions. For the valuation of the work in progress cost is used but for the valuation of finished goods cost of production is used.

If the purpose of the study of cost is the same, different conditions may lead the variation in costs. The cost per unit of product changes with the increase or decrease in volume of output as the amount of fixed expenditure to be borne by each unit of output decreases or increases with the increase or decrease in the units of production.

It is to be noted carefully that there is no such thing as exact cost or a true cost, as no figures of the cost in all circumstances and for all purpose are the same. True costs can only be up to the stage of prime cost. But as soon as overheads are included in total cost on estimated basis the total cost becomes estimated costs, which can be used to obtain a reasonable degree of accuracy.

Expenses: Expenses are costs which have been applied against revenue of a particular accounting period in accordance with the principle of matching cost to revenue. For example, cost of goods sold, office salaries of the period in which they are incurred, etc.

Loss: It represents diminution in ownership equity, other than from the withdrawal of capital for which no compensating value has been received. For example, destruction of property by fire, etc. Thus, the central idea of the cost concept is that of giving up or parting with or sacrificing something or a value to acquire something or an equivalent value. Expense refers to this portion, that of such sacrifices which are assigned to a particular accounting period. Loss denotes sacrifice for which there is no corresponding return whereas cost implies sacrifices for the sake of or accompanied by or securing the value.

COST CENTRE

A cost centre is the smallest segment of activity or area or responsibility for which costs are accumulated. Typically, cost centres are departments but in some instances a department may contain several cost centres. These cost centres are the departments or sub-departments of an organization in reference to which cost is collected for cost ascertainment and cost control.

For example, an assembly department may be supervised by one foreman. This may contain many assembly lines. Sometimes, each assembly line is regarded as a separate cost centre with its own assistant foreman.

A cost centre can be a location, an area, such as a department, store yard, or sales area or an item or equipment, like a lathe machine, delivery vehicle, etc.

The determination of a suitable cost centre is very important for ascertainment and control of cost. The manager in charge of cost centre is held responsible for control of costs of his cost centre. It enables the accumulation of all such costs at one place for which a common base of recovery may be used.

TYPES OF COST CENTRE

1. **Personal and Impersonal:** Personal cost centre is one which consists of a person or group of persons. On the other hand, impersonal cost centre consists of a machine, a department or a plant.
2. **Operation and Process Centre:** Operation cost centre consists of those persons and / or machine carrying out the same kind of operation. On the other hand, a centre which has a continuous sequence of operations is called a process cost centre.
3. **Product and Service Cost Centre:** Product centre refers to a centre through which a product passes through and, generally, corresponds to a product department. In such centre, the raw materials are converted into finished goods. Service Centre is a department or a centre which incurs direct and indirect costs but does not work directly in products. Maintenance department and, generally, factory office are cited as examples.

   Such centres are also known as ancillary centre and they render services to the production department to enable them to carry out the work of production smoothly. The number of cost centres vary from organization to organization. In engineering industry, the cost centre may be a machine shop, welding shop, assembly shop, maintenance department, general administrative department, service centre, etc.
4. **Profit Centre:** A profit centre is that segment of activity of a business which is responsible for both revenues and expenses and also discloses the profit of a particular

segment of activity. Profit centres are created to delegate responsibilities to individuals and measure their performances. The profit centre is different from a cost centre. The main points of difference between a cost centre and a profit centre are:

- Cost is the smallest unit of activity or area of responsibility for which costs are collected whereas a profit centre is that segment of an activity of a business which is responsible for both revenue and expenses.
- Cost centres are created for accounting conveniences of costs and their control whereas a profit centre is created because of decentralization of operations like delegation of responsibilities to individuals who have greater knowledge of local conditions, etc.
- Cost centres are not autonomous whereas profit centre are autonomous.
- A cost centre does not have target costs but efforts to adopt such policies as are necessary to achieve its targets by a profit centre.
- There may be a number of cost centres in a profit centre, such as production or service cost centre, personal or impersonal cost centre, but a profit centre is a subsidiary company within a group or division of a company.

The selection of suitable cost centre or cost units for which costs are to be ascertained in an undertaking depends upon the organization of the factory, conditions of incidence of costs, requirements of costing.

Cost Driver Centre: A cost driver is that factor which can influence costs. A change in the cost drive leads to change in the total cost of a related cost object. For example, number of units produced, number of set ups, number of items distributed, number of customers served, etc. influence the total costs of the organization. It is for the management to see whether any change in the cost driver is to be made or not keeping in view the cost benefit analysis of the change.

Conversion Cost: Conversion cost is the sum of direct wages, direct expenses and overhead costs of converting raw material from one stage of production to another. In other words, conversion cost is works cost minus the cost of direct materials.

Contribution Margin: This is the excess of sales price over the variable costs. This can be expressed in total or a ratio of sales or percentage of sales.

Carrying Cost: Carrying costs are also known as holding costs. Basically they are costs incurred on the maintenance of inventory and include cost of money locked up in the inventory, inventory obsolesce, storage space rent, etc.

Out of Stock Cost: This cost takes place when shortage in a stock occurs and includes loss of sales, loss of goodwill on account of disgruntled customers and employees ill-will and cost of idle machine.

Ordering Costs: These costs are incurred each time an order for the purchase of material is placed and are expressed as rupee cost per order and also include the cost of getting an item into the firm's inventory.

Development Cost: It is the cost which begins with the implementation of the decision to produce a new or improved method and ends with the commencement of formal production of the product by the new method.

Policy Costs: This cost is in addition to normal requirement incurred in accordance with the policy of an undertaking.

Discretionary Cost: It is also known as managed costs or programmed costs which includes fixed costs that arise from periodic and appropriate decisions that is directly affected by the management policies.

Idle Facility Costs: It is the cost of abnormal idleness of fixed assets or available services.

Expired Costs: It is the cost which is related to the current period as an expense or loss.

Incremental Revenue: This incremental revenue reflects the difference in revenue between two alternatives. While making an assessment of profitability of a proposed alternative, incremental revenues are compared and thereby a decision taken.

Added Value: It is the change in the market value resulting from an alteration in the form of locations, availability of a product or service excluding costs of bought out materials or service. Unlike the conversion cost, it includes the profit.

Urgent Costs: These costs are to be incurred immediately in order to avoid the hampering of the production line. These are absolutely essential and their shifting to future period will have adverse effect on the efficiency of operation in hand.

Postponing Costs: These are activities that can be postponed or shifted to the future period and, generally, without any effect on the efficiency of operations in hand. Such costs are only determinant cost and not avoided altogether.

Pre-production Cost: These are costs incurred during the period when a new factory is in the process of being established, a new project is undertaken or a new product line or product is taken up but there is no established or formal production to which such costs may be charged. These costs are normally treated as deferred revenue expenditure (except the portion which is capitalized) and are charged to future production.

Research Costs: These are costs incurred in the discovery of new ideas or processes by experiment or otherwise and for putting the result of such experiments on a commercial basis. Research cost is also defined as the cost of searching for new or improved product, a new application of material or new improved methods, process, system or services.

Training Costs: The cost of training workers, apprentices, and staff which generally comprises their wages or salaries, pay and allowance of the training and other staff members involved, payments of fees, etc. for training or for attending courses sponsored by outside agencies, cost of materials, cost of tools and equipments used in the training modules, etc. All these costs are booked for the various functions understanding order members. Usually, there is a service cost centre, known as the training section to which all training costs are allocated. The total costs of training section are there after appropriated to production centre.

COST CLASSIFICATIONS

Cost classification is the process of grouping costs according to their common characteristics. It is the placement of like items together according to their common characteristics.

A suitable classification of costs is of vital importance to identify the cost with cost centre or cost units. Costs may be classified according to their nature, like material, labour, expenses and many other characteristics.

The same cost figures are classified according to difference in costing depending on the purpose to be achieved and requirements of a particular concern. The important ways of classifications are:

1. By nature of elements
2. By functions
3. By degree of traceability
4. By changes in activity or volume
5. By controllability
6. By normality
7. By relationship with accounting period (capital and revenue)
8. By time
9. By association with the product
10. For managerial decisions.

BY NATURE OR ELEMENTS OR ANALYTICAL CLASSIFICATION

According to this classification, the costs are divided into three categories. They are:

- Material
- Labour
- Expenses, etc.

They can be further sub-classified by each item such as material, into raw material components, spare parts consumables in stores, packing material, etc. This classification is important for it helps to find out the total costs, how the total cost is constituted and valuation of work in progress.

BY FUNCTIONS OR FUNCTIONAL CLASSIFICATION

According to this classification, costs are divided in the light of the different aspects of basic management activities involved in the operations of a business undertaking. It leads to grouping of costs according to the broader division of functions of a business undertaking such as:

- Production
- Administration
- Selling and distribution, etc.

Manufacturing and production cost represents the total cost involved in a manufacturing business, construction, fabrication of units of production, etc.

Commercial cost represents the total cost incurred in the operations of a business undertaking other than the cost of manufacturing and production. Commercial cost may further be sub-divided into:

(*a*) Administrative cost,

(*b*) Selling and distribution cost.

BY DEGREE OF TRACEABILITY TO THE PRODUCT (DIRECT AND INDIRECT)

According to this classification, the total cost is divided into the following two categories:

1. Direct cost,
2. Indirect cost.

Direct cost is incurred for and may be conveniently identified with a particular cost centre or cost unit. Materials used and labour employed are common examples of direct cost.

Indirect cost is incurred for the benefit of number of cost centre or cost units and cannot be conveniently identified with a particular cost centre. Examples of indirect cost include rent of the building, management salaries, machinery depreciation, etc.

The nature of the business and the cost unit chosen determines which costs are direct and which are indirect. For example, the hire of a mobile crane for use by the contractor at site would be regarded as direct cost because the crane is used as a part of the services of the factory, the hire charges could be considered as indirect because it benefits one of the cost centres.

The importance of the distinction of costs into direct and indirect lies in the fact that the cost of a product or activity can be accurately determined while indirect cost has to be apportioned on certain assumptions as regards their incidences.

BY CHANGES IN THE ACTIVITY OR VOLUME

According to this classification, costs are classified according to the behaviour in relation to their changes in the level of activity or volume of production. On this basis, costs are classified in the following three ways:

1. Fixed,
2. Variable,
3. Semi-variable.

Fixed costs are commonly described as those which remain fixed in total amount with the increase or decrease in the volume of output or productivity activity for a given period of time. Fixed costs per unit decreases as production increases, and increases, as production declines.

Examples of fixed costs are rent, insurance for building and machinery, factory manager's salary, etc. These fixed costs are constant in a total amount but fluctuate per unit as production charges. These charges are also known as period costs, because these departments are on time rather than on output basis. Such costs remain constant for per unit of time, such as factory rent, basis say ₹ 10,000 per month which remains the same every month irrespective of output of every month.

Fixed costs can also be classified into the following categories:

(*a*) **Committed Costs:** These costs are the result of inevitable consequences of commitment previously made or are to be incurred to maintain certain facilities and cannot be quickly eliminated. The management has little or no discretion in such types of costs, such as rent, insurance, depreciation on building and machinery, etc.

(*b*) **Policy or Management Costs:** Policy costs are incurred for implementing some management policies, such as executive development, housing, etc. and are often discretionary. Managed costs are incurred to ensure the operating existence of the company, say staff services.

(*c*) **Discretionary Costs:** These costs are related to the operation but can be controlled by the management. These costs arise due to some policy decisions, new researches, etc. Again and can be eliminated or reduced to the desired level at the discretion of the management.

(*d*) **Step Costs:** Steps costs are constant for a given level of output and then increases by a fixed amount at a higher level.

Variable costs are those which vary in total costs in direct proportion to the volume of output. These costs per unit remain relatively constant with changes in production. Thus, variable costs fluctuate in total amount but tend to remain constant per unit as production activity changes. Examples are direct and they are, say, materials costs, labour costs, power, repairs, etc. Such costs are also known as product costs because they depend on the quantum of output rather than on time.

Semi-variable costs are those which are partly fixed and partly variable. For example, the telephone expense includes a fixed portion of annual charges plus a variable according to calls and thus total telephone expenses are semi-variable. Other examples are depreciation, repairs and maintenance, etc.

BY CONTROLLABILITY

Under this, costs are classified according to their influence by an action of a given member of an undertaking. On this basis, either they influence or they do not influence the costs by actions and are classified into two following categories:

- Controllable costs
- Uncontrollable costs.

Controllable costs are those which can be influenced by the action of a specified member of an undertaking. It can also be said that these costs are at least partly within the control of the management.

An organization is divided into a number of responsibility centres and controllable costs are incurred in a particular cost centre that can be influenced by the action of the manager responsible for the centre. Generally speaking, all direct costs including direct materials, direct labour and some of the overhead expenses, are controllable by lower level of management.

Uncontrollable costs are those which cannot be influenced by actions of a specified member of an undertaking. It can also be said that they are not within the control of the management. Most of the fixed costs are uncontrollable. For example, rent of the building is not controllable and so is the management salaries. An overhead cost, which is incurred by one service section and is apportioned to another, which receives the service, is uncontrollable by the latter. The distinction between controllable and uncontrollable costs is sometimes left to individual judgments and is not sharply maintained.

In fact, no cost is controllable. It is only in relation to a particular level of management or an individual manager that we may say whether a cost is controllable or uncontrollable. A particular item of cost, which may be controllable from the point of view of one level of management, may be uncontrollable from another level of management.

Moreover there may be an item of cost which is controllable from long term point of view and uncontrollable for short term. This is so partly in the case of fixed costs.

BY NORMALITY

Under this, costs are classified according to their normality character that whether these costs which are normally incurred at a given level of output in the conditions in which that level of activity is normally attained or not. On this basis it is classified into two and they are:

- Normal costs
- Abnormal costs.

Normal cost is the cost which is normally incurred at a given level of output in the conditions in which that level of output is normally attained. It is part of cost production.

Abnormal cost is the cost which is not incurred normally at a given level of output in conditions in which that level of output is normally attained. It is not a part of the production cost and charged to costing profit and loss account.

BY RELATIONSHIP WITH ACCOUNTING PERIOD

The cost which is incurred in purchasing an asset either to earn income or increase the earning capacity of the business is called Capital cost. For example, the cost of a rolling machine in case of a steel plant enhances the capacity of earning. Such a cost is incurred at one point of time but benefits accruing from it are spread over a number of accounting years.

If any expenditure is incurred in order to maintain the earning capacity of the concern, such as cost of maintaining assets or running a business, it is called revenue expenditure. For example cost of materials used in production, labour charges paid to convert the material into production, salaries, depreciation, repairs and maintenance, selling and distribution charges, etc.

The distinction between capital and revenue items is important in costing, as all items of revenue expenditure are taken into considerations while calculating costs whereas capital items are completely ignored.

BY TIME

Costs are classified in two ways under consideration of time. They are:

- Historical costs,
- Predetermined costs.

Historical costs are costs which are ascertained after they are incurred. Such costs are available only when production of a particular thing has already been complete. They are only of historical value and will not help in cost controlling purpose. Basic characteristics of such costs are:

(*a*) They are based on recorded facts.

(*b*) They can be verified because they are always supported by the evidence of their occurrences.

(*c*) They are mostly objective, because they relate to happenings which have already taken place.

Predetermined costs are costs that are estimated or computed in advance of production, taking into account the previous costs and factors affecting such costs. Predetermined costs that are determined on scientific basis become standard costs. Such costs, when compared with actual costs, give the reasons for variance and help the management to fix the responsibility and to take remedial action to avoid its reoccurrences in the future.

Historical costs and predetermined costs are not mutually exclusive, they work together in the accounting system of an organization. In competitive age it is better to lay down standards so that after comparison with actuals, the management may be able to take stock of the situation to find out, as far the standards fixed by it have been achieved, and take suitable action in the light of such a situation.

Therefore, even in a system when historical costs are used, predetermined costs have a very important role to play because a figure of historical cost by itself has no meaning unless it is related to some other standard figure to give meaningful information to the management.

ACCORDING TO PLANNING AND CONTROL

Planning and control are two important functions of the management. Cost accounting furnishes information to the management which is helpful in the due discharge of these two functions. According to this, costs can be classified as:

- Budgeted costs,
- Standard costs.

Budgeted costs represent an estimate of the expenditure for different phases of business operations, such as manufacturing, administration, sales, research and development, etc.

These costs are coordinated in a well conceived framework for a period of time, in future, which subsequently becomes the written expression of managerial targets to be achieved. Various budgets are prepared for various phases, such as raw material, cost budget, labour cost budget, cost of production budget, manufacturing overhead budget, office and administration overhead budget, etc. With continuous comparison of actual performances to standards budgeted is made so as to report variations from the budgeted cost to the management for corrective action if required.

Standard costs are the instrument through which the budgeted costs are translated into actual operations. The Chartered Institute of Management Accountants, London, defines standard costs as the predetermined costs based on a technical estimate of materials, labour and overhead for a selected period of time and for a prescribed set of working conditions. Thus, standard cost is determined in advance of production of what should be the cost.

Similarities between the two are more or less equal to the extent that both of them represent the estimates for costs for a period of time in future. In spite of this, they differ in the following aspects:

1. Standard costs are scientifically predetermined costs of every aspect of business activity, whereas budgeted costs are mere estimates made on the basis of past actual financial accounting data, adjusted to future trends. Thus, budgeted costs are projections of financial accounts whereas standard cost are projections of cost accounts.
2. The primary emphasis of budgeted costs is on the planning function of the management whereas the main thrust of standard cost is on the control because the standard costs lay emphasis on what should be the costs.
3. Budgeted costs are extensive, whereas standard costs are intensive in their application. Budgeted costs represent a macro approach of business operation because they are estimated in respect of the operations of the department. Contrary to this, standard costs are concerned with each and minute aspects of business operations carried in a department. Thus, budgeted costs deal with aggregates whereas standard costs are concerned with individual parts which makes the aggregate.

For example, budgeted costs are calculated for different functions of the business like production, sales, purchase, etc. whereas standard costs are compiled for various elements of costs.

BY ASSOCIATION WITH THE PRODUCT

Under this classification, cost can be:

- Product costs,
- Period costs.

Product costs are those which are traceable to the product and are included in inventory valuation. Product costs are inventoriable costs and they become the basis for product pricing and cost plus contracts. They comprise direct materials, direct labour and manufacturing overheads in a manufacturing concern. They are used for valuation of inventory and are shown in the Balance Sheet till they are sold because such costs provide income or benefit only after sales. The product cost of goods sold is transferred to the cost of goods sold account.

Period costs are incurred on the basis of time, such as rent, salaries, etc. These may be related to administration, selling cost essential to keep the business running. Though these are not associated with the production and are necessary to generate revenue, they cannot be assigned to a product. These are charged to the period in which these are incurred and treated as expenses.

The net income of a concern is influenced by both product and period costs. Product costs are included in the cost of production and do not affect income till goods are sold. Period costs are not at all related to production and as such, are not inventoried but are charged to the period in which these are incurred.

FOR MANAGERIAL DECISIONS

On the basis of this, interpretation costs may be classified into the following:

- Marginal cost,
- Out of pocket costs,
- Differentials cost,
- Sunk cost,
- Imputed or notional costs,
- Opportunity cost,
- Replacement costs, and
- Avoidable and unavoidable costs.

Marginal Costs: Marginal cost is the total of variable costs. It is the prime cost plus the variable overheads. It is based on the distinction between fixed and variable costs. Fixed costs are ignored and variable costs are taken into consideration for determining the cost of products, the value of work in progress and finished goods.

Out of Pocket Costs: This is that portion of costs which involves payment to outsiders which give rise to cash expenditure as opposed to such costs as depreciation which do not involve any cash expenditure of such costs, which are relevant for price fixation during recession or when make or buy designs is to be made.

Differential Costs: The change in costs due to the change in the level of activity or pattern or method of production is known as differential costs. If the change increases costs, it will be called as incremental cost and if there is a decrease in cost resulting from a decrease in output, it is known as detrimental cost.

Sunk Costs: A sunk cost is an irrevocable cost and is caused by complete abandonment of a plant. It is the written disown value of the abandoned plant less its salvage value. Such costs are historical costs incurred in the past which are not relevant for decision making. They do not affect increase or decrease in volume. Thus, the expenditure which has taken place and is irrevocable in a situation is treated as a sunk cost. If a decision has to be made for replacing the existing plant, the book value of the plant less the salvage value, if any, will be treated as a suck cost and will be irrelevant for taking decision in replacing the existing plant.

Imputed or Notional Costs: Imputed costs or notional costs have the same meaning. The American equivalent term of the British term 'notional' is imputed. These costs are notional in nature and do not involve any cash outlay. The Chartered Institute of Management Accountants, London, defines notional costs as the value of a benefit where no actual cost is incurred.

Even though such costs do not involve cash outlay, they are taken into consideration while making managerial decisions. Examples of such costs are notional rent charged on business promises owned by the proprietor, interest on capital for which no interest has been paid, etc. When alternative capital investment projects are being evaluated, it is necessary to consider the imputed interest on capital before a decision is arrived at to which is the most profitable project.

When actual interest is not paid on capital, the basic concept is that the fund had been invested somewhere else as it would have earned interest. Therefore, imputed costs or notional costs can be known as opportunity costs. It can be hypothetical to represent the benefit enjoyed by a firm in respect of which actual expense is not made.

Opportunity Costs: It is the maximum possible alternative earning that might have been earned if the productive capacity or services had been put to some alternative use. In simple words, it is the advantage in measurable terms which has been foregone because of not using the facility in the manner originally planned. For example, when the owned building is proposed to be sued for a project, the likely rent of the building is the opportunity cost which should be taken into consideration while evaluating the profitability of the project.

Replacement Costs: It is the cost at which there could be a purchase of an asset or material identical to what is being replaced or revalued. It is cost of replacement at current market rate.

Avoidable Cost or Unavoidable Costs: Avoidable costs are those which can be eliminated if a particular product or department with which they are directly related is discontinued. For example, salary of clerks employed in a particular department can be eliminated if the department is discontinued. Unavoidable cost is that which will not be eliminated even with the discontinuation of a product or department. For example, the salary of a factory manager or even the factory rent cannot be eliminated even if a product is eliminated.

DISTINCTION BETWEEN COST CONTROL AND COST REDUCTION

Cost control involves predetermination of targeted costs measuring the actual costs, investigating into the causes of variations and instituting the corrective action, whereas cost reduction is the achievement of real and permanent reduction in unit of goods manufactured or services rendered without impairing their suitability or diminuition in the quality of product. Cost reduction in the saving of values in unit cost, such saving, is of permanent nature and the utility of the goods and services remain unaffected. Thus, cost control and cost reduction are two different tools of management but their concepts and procedures are widely different. The main points of difference between the two are:

1. Cost control aims at achieving the predetermined costs, whereas cost reduction aims at reduction of costs by finding new ways or methods.
2. Cost control is a routine exercise, which is carried out for attainment of operational efficiency whereas cost reduction aims at permanent and real savings by a continuous search for improvement.
3. The process of cost control is to lay down a target, ascertain actual performance, compare it with the target and take corrective action. On the other hand, cost reduction is not concerned with maintenance of performance according to the predetermined standards.
4. Cost control seeks adherence to standards whereas cost reduction is a challenge to the standards themselves. Cost reduction assumes that there are chances of improvements in predetermined standards.
5. The aim of cost control is to see that actual costs do not exceed the predetermined costs; so, it is a preventive function. On the other hand, cost reduction is a corrective function because it challenges the predetermined costs and seeks to improve the performance by reducing cost of increasing production. It is a continuous function of self-analysis for making more and more improvement in performance.

REVIEW QUESTIONS

1. Prepare a chart showing the different element of costs.
2. Define cost and cost centre.
3. Give five factors to be taken into consideration for selection of a suitable cost centre.
4. Define cost classification.
5. Distinguish between direct and indirect costs.
6. Define fixed cost, variable cost and semi-variable costs.
7. Define period costs.
8. Distinguish between product costs and period cost.
9. Describe the three different purposes for computing period costs.
10. Ascertain prime cost, work cost, cost of production and total cost from the following data:

Factory expenses	₹ 30,000
Administrative expenses	₹ 20,000
Labour	₹ 25,000

(**Ans.** (*a*) ₹ 60,000, (*b*) ₹ 90,000, (*c*) ₹ 1,10,000, (*d*) ₹ 1,20,000)

11. From the following data, calculate the value of the raw material consumed:

Raw material purchase	₹ 88,000
Opening stock of raw materials	₹ 1,00,000
Closing stock of raw material	₹ 1,23,500

(**Ans.** ₹ 64,500)

12. From the following data, calculate the value of the works cost:

Material	₹ 64,500
Direct wages	₹ 80,000
Factory overheads	₹ 29,500
Opening stock of work in progress	₹ 13,000
Closing stock of work in progress	₹ 34,500

(**Ans.** ₹ 1,52,500)

13. From the following data, calculate the value of the cost of goods sold:

Cost of production	₹ 1,83,500
Opening stock of finished goods	₹ 71,500
Closing stock of finished goods	₹ 42,000

(**Ans.** ₹ 2,13,000)

14. From the following data calculate the profit

Cost price	₹ 30,375
Profit	10% of sales

(**Ans.** Profit is ₹ 3,375)

15. From the following, calculate the prime cost:

Direct Material	₹ 4,98,000
Direct labour	₹ 1,71,000
Opening stock of work in progress	₹ 51,000
Closing stock of work in progress	₹ 45,000
Work in progress is valued at prime cost basis	

(**Ans.** ₹ 6,75,000)

16. Tabulate elements of cost, showing the usual terms of expenditure pertaining to cash.

17. Bring out clearly the significance of each of the cost classifications and explain the meaning of the terms, like

(*a*) Direct and indirect,

(*b*) Variable and fixed,

(*c*) Controllable and uncontrollable.

18. Describe the following:

(*a*) The classifications of costs as controllable and noncontrollable depend upon a point of reference.

(*b*) Direct costs and controllable costs are not necessarily the same.

(*c*) Product cost is a general term that denotes different costs allocated to products for different purpose.

(*d*) The composition of product cost for the purpose of external financial reporting along with its rationale.

19. Write short notes on:

(*a*) Conversion cost (*b*) Sunk cost

(*c*) Opportunity cost (*d*) Capital costs

(*e*) Revenue cost (*f*) Operating cost

(*g*) Differential cost (*h*) Decision making cost

(*i*) Relevant cost (*j*) Product costs

20. Distinguish between the following:

(*a*) Avoidable and unavoidable costs

(*b*) Cost centre and cost unit

(*c*) Product costs and period costs

(*d*) Capital costs and revenue costs

(*e*) Opportunity cost and imputed cost

(*f*) Sunk cost and incremental cost

(*g*) Differential cost and residual cost

(*h*) Absolute cost and alternative cost

(*i*) Out of pocket cost and opportunity cost

(*j*) Variable cost and variance cost

(*k*) Conversion cost and added value cost

(*l*) Estimated cost and standard cost

(*m*) Expired cost unexpired cost.

21. Notional cost and imputed costs means the same. Explain.

22. Do you agree that cost should be presented in different ways for different purpose?

23. Explain the direct and indirect expenditure.

24. Describe the three major elements of costs.

25. Describe the classification of cost in reference to time.

26. Distinguish between product cost and period cost.

27. Describe the various costs used in decision making and explain their characteristics.

28. Describe briefly the principal aims of classifying costs.

29. Cost may be classified in a variety of ways according to their nature and information needs of the management. Explain.

30. What is cost centre and how does it differ from a department of a factory?

31. Explain the meaning of formulation of product cost for the purpose of income measurement and determination of financial position.

32. From the following information, prepare the cost sheet:

Raw materials	33,000
Productive wages	38,000
Unproductive wages	1,05,000
Factory rent and taxes	7,500
Factory lighting	2,200
Factory heating	1,500
Motive power	4,400
Haulage	3,000
Director's fees – works	1,000
Director's fees – office	2,000
Factory cleaning	500
Sundry office expenses	200
Estimated works expenses	800
Factory stationary	750
Office stationary	900
Loose tool written off	600
Rent and taxes – office	500
Water supply – works	1,200
Factory insurance	1,100
Office insurance	500
Legal expenses	400
Rent on warehouse	300
Depreciation of –	
– Plant and machinery	2,000
– Office building	1,000
– Delivery van	200
Bad debts	100
Advertising	300
Sales department's salaries	1,500
Upkeep of delivery vans	700
Bank charges	50
Commission on sales	1,500

The total output for the period has been 14775 tonnes.

(**Ans.** Cost per tonne is ₹8, prime cost is ₹71,000, factory cost is ₹1,08,050, cost of production is ₹1,13,000, and total cost is ₹1,18,200)

33. From the following information, compute (*a*) materials prime cost, (*b*) factory cost, (*c*) cost of production, (*d*) total cost (*e*) net profit:

Factory office salaries:		6,500
General office salaries:		12,600
Carriage outwards		4,300
Carriage on purchases		7,150
Bad debts written off		6,500
Repairs of plant, machinery and tools		4,450
Rent, rates, taxes and insurances – Factory		8,500
– Office		2,000
Sales		4,61,100
Stock of Materials		
- 31st December 2017		62,800
- 31st December 2018		48,000
Materials purchased		1,85,000
Travelling expenses		2,100
Traveller's salaries and commissions		77,00
Productive wages		1,26,000
Depreciation		
- Plant and machinery		65,00
- Furniture		300
Director's fees		6,000
Gas and water – Factory		1,200
– Office		400
Rent		10,000
General expenses		3,400
Income tax		500
Dividend		1,000

(**Ans.** (*a*) ₹ 2,06,950, (*b*) ₹ 3,32,950, (*c*) ₹ 3,67,600, (*d*) ₹ 3,94,800, (*e*) ₹ 4,15,400 and (*f*) ₹ 45,700)

MISCELLANEOUS COST TECHNIQUES

(A) TARGET COSTING

Definition

Target costing is "a cost management tool for reducing the overall cost of a product over its entire life cycle with the help of the production, engineering, and R&D".

The target costing is the estimated cost of a product that enables a company to remain and complete in the market in the long run. Sakurai discusses the most common procedure of target costing as follows:

- To plan and design high quality products that meet customer needs.
- To set a target cost for products through the use of value engineering.
- To attain the target cost at the production stage by use of standard costs.

Meaning

The idea of target costing, originally promoted in Japan, is about going upstream to achieve cost reduction. Target costing is not really a method of costing. But it is a technique used in cost management. The intent of target costing is reduction aimed at the entire life cycle of any product. Target costing can also help in achieving broader objectives, such as, identifying and delivering various customer requirements in a product through effective management of different processes.

The target cost is maximum allowable cost at a particular point of time and is specified by reference to the successive stages in a product's life cycle. The important feature of the target costing is that it is used only after the product has reached its established production phase. However, it follows the conventional material, labour and overhead classification.

Features

The important features of target costing is its market orientation, i.e. it involves ascertaining of the product cost beforehand by working back from an expected future market price. Thus, it includes the following two fundamental steps:

- Keeping track of the external market information which would affect the organization, decision making.
- Internal cost planning process that is based on the external market information.

This technique is a powerful tool for reducing cost not only at the production stages but also at the planning and design stages of the product life cycle. Target costing is an approach that is widely used by Japanese companies, and has recently received a considerable amount of attention in the USA and European accounting literature. Target costing is driven by external market factors.

Nature

The target costing makes the system to support the cost reduction process not only in the manufacturing phase of the existing product but also the developing and designing phase of an entirely new product. It acts as a motivator of much of the creative and innovative activity in an organization. The following may be constructed as the components in the product target costing:

- Type of product,
- Technical specification,
- Customer,
- Resource consumption (acquisition price),
- Resource consumption (cost).

Another important aspect of the target costing is the concept of design to cost. This concept, which originated in 1975, find its use in the target costing by setting the largest cost at level which can be achieved with the greatest possible efforts from planners and it aims at improving the internal capabilities of an organization. The approach of design to cost coupled with the market-based target cost provides an excellent basis for cost management.

Target Costing Methodology

Target costing forces an organization to 'manage upstream' during product planning and design stage and provides a framework of strategic work of strategic guide to 'managing downstream' during production and later phases. Employs concurrent engineering analyses of market forces, customer needs, relevant technology, competitor's models, product configuration and performance features, design alternatives, process capabilities, maintenance, service requirements, etc. and life cycle costs. Such an analysis reveal innovative possibilities in several areas, especially for:

- Reducing cycle times for design, development, manufacturing and service.
- Reducing costs for design, development, manufacturing and service.
- Reducing the number of unique parts per model.
- Reducing the rate of design, rework and repair.

The end result is a product design that builds in competitive barriers and guarantees a target profit and a target cost against a planned selling price. A new product or a derivative will be approved for productions only after all concerned managers are satisfied that targets are aggressive enough and can be achieved.

A firm's business plan and product market strategies provide the framework and basic guidelines for applying the target costing methodology. Specific steps involved in target costing may be summarized as follows:

- Determine customer wants precisely,
- Translate them into the desired product performance feature,
- Estimate the proportion of value added by each feature and component,
- Choose a product design to assure a targeted profit, and cost targets for each component in total,
- Choose manufacturing designs that assure targeted costs,
- Choose suppliers that assure buying at targeted costs,
- After each cost review, conduct value engineering to reduce targeted costs, and
- Monitor initial production to ensure that all product performance, cost, profit, targets are met.

Target costing is a method used in product design that involves estimating a target cost for a new product, then designing the product to meet the cost.

Customer Requirements

The first element of target costing understands customer requirements, including the performance and cost characteristics of competitor's products. Target costing can then be applied during the product design phase to create a product that meets the customer's requirements and beat the competition.

Collecting Market Information

Collecting market information is an important step in the target costing and product development process. Various characteristics of selected product available in the market should reflect customer values and expectations about

- Price,
- Quality,
- Delivery,
- Service,
- Technology, and
- Product Performance.

Documenting Customer Requirements

A structural method for documenting customer requirements and competitor comparisons helps ensure that all relevant market factors and product characteristics are considered during product development. The framework of documentation should take into consideration the following:

- Product characteristics,
- Competitor performance comparisons,
- Target performance values, and
- Customer rating comparisons.

The above data is obtained from

- Customer surveys,
- Experience with previous products,
- Market research studies,
- Calculations and modeling, and
- Experimentation.

Comparing competitors products: When developing a competitive comparison, a manufacturer should select two sets of comparisons:

- Competitors that represent a cross section of global market,
- Upcoming competitors not having significant market share,

- The representative products of each competitor chosen should have price and performance parameters similar to those planned for the new product. The data used to make the decision are based on
    - Published performance data and specifications,
    - Customer input,
    - Comparative test data, and
    - Information from annual reports, trade shows, and other external sources of information that may provide insight into plans for new products.

Once selection process is completed, the manufacturer should obtain several samples of each chosen product for performance testing and reverse engineering.

Applying Reverse Engineering: Reverse engineering determines design characteristics and provides information about competitor's materials and processes. The purpose of this information is to help the manufacturer in ascertainment of target cost. Reverse engineering should involve a cross functional team of people from product and process engineering, manufacturing, industrial engineering, procurement and estimating.

- ❖ **Cost Structure Analysis:** The target costing makes the target cost development an aspect of ongoing design process. The manufacturer should develop estimate of competitor's cost structures by analyzing the internal costs of existing products, categorizing them by cost driver and developing comparative ratios by cost driver to translate internal costs into estimated competitor costs.
- ❖ **Best Practices Model:** The model of best practices consider the best design characteristics, best manufacturing process and best economics as factors. The product costs determined through the modeling of best levels of performances are an indication of improvement over the competitors.
- ❖ **Competitor Information:** Depending on the level of accuracy required for the target cost, competitor information is available from a variety of sources. The external data sources include:
    - Annual reports,
    - Marketing brochures,
    - Commercially available information databases,
    - Government reports, and
    - Newspapers and other industry and commercial publications.
- ❖ **Product Design:** The target costing considers the impact of various cost drivers during product design and can help a company create a different perspective. This information allows engineers to factor many cost saving design processes.
- ❖ **Value Engineering:** Once a conceptual design is complete, internal cost models can help estimate the cost of the new product. The internal cost models give value engineering team's detailed information about current production costs.
- ❖ **JIT Environment:** Target costing provides a framework for justifying changes in the production environment. It provides a means for identifying benefits that could result from the comprehensive application of JIT.

- **Coordination:** The primary element in the target costing is that of coordination. A target costing project works by bringing together all concerned (functions, units and supply-chain partners) to develop a product, with its related cost that can be achieved. The cost must be capable of bringing the product to its target, and this may mean that the group will continue to work together in an operational sense.

Methods of Establishment of Target Costs

Three basic methods are used for setting target costs:

- First is the subtraction method which is based on the price of competitor's product where the target cost is worked backwards from the market price. The result may represent a very rigorous target and it may be impossible to achieve, it.
- The second method of setting up the target cost is the addition method which is based on the existing technology and past cost data of the company. Normally, it results in the achievable targets because it is basically an extension of what has already been happening within the company. The greatest disadvantage of this method is that it is very inward looking and grossly ignores the market situation.
- The third method is the integrated method, a mixture of the subtraction and addition methods. However, in practice, this integrated method involves many difficult problems.

Illustration 6

In a period, a company has the following transactions:

Purchase of raw materials	(₹)	85,000
Conversion	(₹)	68,600
Production	(units)	4,900
Sales	(units)	4,850

There were no opening stocks of raw materials, WIP of finished goods, the standard cost per unit is ₹ 31 (₹ 17 materials + ₹ 14 conversion cost). There was no closing WIP at the end of the period.

Show journal entries for a back-flush accounting system using a raw material and in Process Account.

Journal entries under back flush accounting system

Particulars		*Debit (in ₹)*	*Credit (in ₹)*
RIP A/c To Creditors (Being purchase of raw materials on credit)	Dr.	85,000	 85,000
Finished Goods Stock A/c To RIP A/c To Conversion Cost Control A/c (Being cost of goods produced for 4,900 units)	Dr.	1,51,900	 83,300 68,600
Cost of Sales A/c To Finished Goods Stock A/c (Being the cost of goods sold for 4,850 units)	Dr.	1,50,350	 1,50,350

At the end of the period, there will be two separate stock balances:

RIP Account (85,000 – 83,300) = ₹ 1,700

Finished goods (50@ ₹ 31) = ₹ 1,550

Notes: (*a*) All entries shown above are at standard cost.

(*b*) For simplicity, figures have been chosen so that no variance arises.

REVIEW QUESTIONS

1. Define target costing.
2. Discuss the features of target costing.
3. Explain the importance of target costing.

(B) ACTIVITY BASED COSTING

Concept

ABC has been defined by CAM-1 organization of Arlinton Taxas as "the collection of financial and operation performance information to trace to the significant activities of the firm of product costs."

ABC is a recent development in Cost Accounting which attempts in absorbing overheads into product costs on a more realistic basis. Supporters of the technique argue that many costs are unnecessarily treated as common costs and are arbitrarily absorbed using a basis such as direct labour hours, machine hours, etc. Many organizations have now adopted advanced manufacturing technology (AMT) with the result that overheads are increasing and labour costs are becoming a smaller portion of total costs portion of total costs. Costing system which absorbs overheads on a direct labour basis are therefore not relevant in an AMT environment. The basic idea of ABC is that costs are grouped according to what drives them or causes them to be incurred. The cost driver is then used as an absorption base.

The CIMA official terminology defines ABC as "Cost attribution to cost units on the basis of benefit received from indirect activities, e.g., ordering, setting up, assuring quality."

Kalpan and Cooper's Approach to ABC

Kalpan and Cooper of Harvard Business School, who have developed this new approach in costing to calculate product costs, claim that costs should be classified as long-term variable costs and short-term variable costs. Traditionally, short-term variable costs are known as variable costs and long-term variable costs are known as fixed costs. Short-term variable costs are volume related and change proportionately with the volume of production. Long-term variable costs vary in long-term but not instantaneously. For example, production scheduling cost can be changed in the long-term by changing number of runs rather than changing number of units produced.

They further claim that this approach is related to overhead costs and forces behind them. Forces behind overhead costs are named 'cost drives'. Cost drivers can be defined as those activities or transactions that are significant determinants of costs. Under ABC system, product cost is determined by obtaining a greater understanding of the cost behaviour and using new measures of quantity of resources consumed by each product. A cost driver is 'an activity which generates cost'. ABC system is based on the belief that activities cause costs and that a link should, therefore, be made between activities and products by assigning costs of activities to products based on an individual product's demand for each activity.

Characteristics of ABC

The important characteristics of ABC are noted below:

Simple traditional distinction made between fixed and variable cost is not enough guide to provide quality of information to design a cost system.

- The more appropriate distinction between cost behaviour patterns are volume (scale) related, diversity (scope) related, events (decisions) related and time related.
- Cost drives need to be identified. A cost driver is a structural determinant, of cost related activity. The logic behind is that the cost behaviour pattern must be understood so that behavior pattern is dictated by cost drivers. In tracing the overhead cost product, a cost behaviour pattern must be understood so that appropriate cost driver could be identified.

How to Develop an ABC System?

The following are the three key areas of ABC:

- Product cost differentiation,
- Activities and their cost drivers, and
- Identification of non-value added cost.

In ABC system, a cost centre is established for each cost driver and identification, measurement and control of cost drivers is essential in ABC.

ABC is the planned and systematic study and determination of cost of each of the branches of business activities that add to the value of product and services. The matrix of activities, showing the short-term and long-term cost strategy, is presented as follows:

Short-term	Long-term
Product value	Value addition
Pricing	Corporate growth

Steps to develop ABC system are as under:

Identify the main activities performed in the organization, such as manufacturing, assembly, etc., as well as support activities, including purchasing, packing and dispatching.

- Identify factors which influence the cost of each activity–the cost drivers.
- Collect accurate data on direct labour, material and overhead costs.
- Establish the demand made by a particular product on activities, using the cost drivers as a measure of demand.
- Trace the cost of activities to products according to a product's demand for each activity.

The rules developed by Kalpan and Cooper for this process is:

- Focus on expensive resources, thus directing attention to resource categories where the new costing process has the potential to make big differences on product costs.
- Lay emphasis on resources whose consumption varies significantly by product and product type-look for diversity, and
- Focus whose demand patterns are un-correlated with traditional allocation measures.

How to Implement ABC System?

In ABC, the hidden weaknesses and high cost segments are identified for maximum effectiveness of cost accounting system. The process of designing and implementing an ABC system for support departments usually by a way of interviewing the concerned departmental heads to have an insight into the departmental operations and into the factors that trigger departmental activities. Subsequent analysis trace these activities to specific products. Suppose the inventory control department is responsible for raw materials and purchased components, the relevant questions that could be asked are:

- How many people work in the department?
- What do they do?
- What determines the time required to process an incoming shipment? Does it matter if the shipment is large or small?
- What other factors affect your department's work load?
- Do you usually disburse the total amount of material requirement for a production run all at once or does it go out in smaller quantities?

How ABC System Supports Corporate Strategy?

ABC supports corporate strategy in many ways, such as:

- ABC system can effectively support the management by furnishing data, at the operational level and strategic level. Accurate product costing will help the management to compare profits that various customers, product lines, brands or regions generate and to decide on pricing strategy, dropping unprofitable products, lines, etc.,
- Information generated by ABC system can also encourage management to re-design the products.
- ABC system can change the method of evaluation of new process technologies, to reduce set-up times, rationalization of plant layout in order to reduce or lower material handling cost, improve quality, etc.
- ABC system will report on the resource spending vis-à-vis resource consumption, and reduced demand in organizational resources leading to increase in profits,
- ABC analysis helps managers to focus their attention and energy on improving activities and the actions allow the insights from ABC to be translated into increased profits.
- Rates of the cost drivers established by the system can be used to measure activity performance and efficiency and provide a more suitable basis for budgeting,

- The accurate feedback can be provided to cost centre managers on their performance based on their consumption of resources during a period rather than the allocations of cost over which they have no control, and
- The provision of accurate information of product costs enables better decisions to be made on pricing, marketing design and product mix.

Illustration 7

A company manufactures two products, A and B, using the same equipment and similar processes. An extract of the production data for these products in one period is shown below:

Particulars	*A*	*B*
Quantity produced (units)	5,000	7,000
Direct labor hours per unit	1	2
Machine hours per unit	3	1
Setups in the period	10	40
Orders handled in the period	15	60
Overhead costs:		
Relating to machine activity	2,20,000	
Relating to production run set-up	20,000	
Relating handling of orders	45,000	
	2,85,000	

Required

Calculate the production overheads to be absorbed by one per unit of each of the products using the following costing methods:

(*a*) A traditional costing approach, using a direct labour hour rate to absorb overheads.

(*b*) An activity based costing approach, using suitable cost drives to trace overheads to products.

(*a*) Direct labour Hours

Product A	(5,000 units × 3 hours)	5,000
Product B	(7,000 units × 1 hour)	14,000
	Total	19,000

Therefore, overhead absorbed rate = (₹ 2,85,000)/(19,000 DLH) = ₹ 15 per hour

Product A	(1 hour × ₹15)	= ₹ 15 per unit
Product B	(2 hours × ₹15)	= ₹ 30 per unit

(*b*) Machine Hours

Product A	(5,000 units × 3 hours)	= 15,000
Product B	(7,000 units × 1 hour)	= 7,000
	Total	= 22,000

Using ABC the overhead costs are absorbed according to the cost drivers.

Machine-hour driven costs	(₹ 2,20,000/22,000 M.H)	= ₹ 10 per M.H.
Setup-driven costs	(₹ 20,000/50 setups)	= ₹ 400 per setup
Order-driven costs	(₹ 45,000/75 orders)	= ₹ 600 per order

Overhead costs:

Particulars	*Product A*	*Amount* [₹]	*Product B*	*Amount* [₹]
Machine driven costs	(15,000 hrs × ₹ 10)	1,50,000	(7,000 hrs × ₹ 10)	70,000
Setup costs	(10 × ₹ 400)	4,000	(40 × ₹ 400)	16,000
Order handelling costs	(15 × ₹ 600)	9,000	(60 × ₹ 600)	36,000
		1,63,000		1,22,000

Units produced	5,000	7,000
Overhead cost per unit	₹ 32.60	₹ 17.43

These figures suggest that product B absorbs an unrealistic amount of overhead using a direct labour hour basis. Overhead absorption should be based on activities which drive the cost, in this case machine hours, the number of production run set-ups and the number of orders handled for each product.

REVIEW QUESTIONS

1. Explain the concept of ABC.
2. Explain the key plan and cooperatives approach to ABC.
3. What are the characteristics of ABC?
4. How to develop an ABC system?
5. Explain the steps to develop an ABC system.
6. How to implement ABC system?
7. What are the benefits from adoption of ABC system?
8. When to use ABC?

(C) LIFE CYCLE COSTING

Introduction

Many products generally have characteristics of perishable distinctiveness. The distinctiveness of a product degenerates over a period into a common commodity. This process by which the distinctiveness gradually disappears as the product merges with other competitive products has been rightly termed by Joel Dean as 'the cycle of competitive degeneration'. The cycle begins with the identification of new consumer need and the invention of a new product and is often followed by patent protection and further development to make it saleable. This is usually followed by a rapid expansion in its sales as the product gains market acceptance. Then competitors enter the field with limitation and rival products and the distinctiveness of the new product starts diminishing. The speed of degeneration differs from product to product. The innovation of a new product and its degeneration into a common product is termed as the 'life-cycle of a product'.

Products and services typically pass through a series of distinct phases and is termed as the product life-cycle. Product life-cycle is the pattern of expenditure, sales level, revenue, and profit over the period from new idea generation to the deletion of a product from the product range.

Product life-cycle costing is a way to enhance the control of manufacturing costs. The thrust of product life-cycle costing is the distribution of costs among categories changes over the life of the product, as does the potential profitability of a product. Hence, it is important to track and measure costs during each stage of a product's life-cycle: research and development, design of a product, production, marketing, distribution and after sales service. It is known that the majority of products are determined at an early stage of product life-cycle. It is critical to control costs in the development stage of a product even though much of the product costs are not actually incurred until later. In the traditional cost accounting system, however, cost analysis is usually conducted at the end of the life-cycle (i.e., production stage) when not much can be done to change the cost structure.

Product life-cycle costing approach is used to provide a long term picture of product line profitability, feedback on the effectiveness of the life-cycle planning and the cost data to clarify the economic impact of alternatives chosen in the design engineering phase, etc. Depending upon scientific management needs, varying levels of detailed information may be captured by Management Accountants for selected phases of life-cycle. The major benefit of adopting product life-cycle costing is that it provides an overall framework for considering total incremental costs over the entire life span of a product, which, in turn, facilitates the analysis of parts of the whole where cost effectiveness might be improved.

Characteristics of product life-cycle

The major characteristics of product life-cycle concept are as follows:

- Products have finite lives and pass through the cycle of development, introduction, growth, maturity, decline and deletion at varying speeds.
- Product cost, revenue and profit patterns tend to follow predictable courses through the product life-cycle. Profits first appear during the growth phase and after stabilizing during the maturity phase, and decline thereafter to the point of deletion.
- Profit per unit varies as products moves through their life-cycles.
- Each phase of the product life-cycle poses different threats and opportunities that give rise to different strategic actions.
- Products require different functional emphasis in each phase, e.g. such as an R&D emphasis in the development phase and a cost control emphasis in the decline.

Activities in Product Life Cycle

Typically, the life-cycle of a manufactured product will consider the following activities:

- **Market Research:** Before any investment is made, the investor must believe that what the company proposes to make can be sold at a price which will permit a profit to be made. This usually means that market research will establish what product the customer wants, how much he is prepared to pay for it and how much he will buy.
- **Specification:** When market research has established what is to be made, it will be necessary to turn the general statement of requirements into a detailed specification which will tell the designer and the manufacturing engineer precisely what is required. The design specification will give such details as required in life, maximum permissible maintenance costs, maximum permissible manufacturing cost, the number required, the delivery rate, and the required performance of the product.
- **Design:** With a precise specification, the designers can produce drawings and process schedules which define the geometry of the product and some of the manufacturing processes.
- **Prototype Manufacture:** From the drawings it will be possible to manufacture a small number of the product. These prototypes will be used to develop the product and eventually to demonstrate that it meets the requirements of the specification.
- **Development:** When a product has been made for the first time, it is necessary to prove that it meets the requirements of the specification. In fact, when a product is first made, it rarely meets requirements of the specification and changes have to be made until it does. This period of testing and changing is 'development'. Development can be very expensive and often generates a large negative cash flow before any product has been sold and hence, before any positive cash flows have been generated.
- **Tooling:** When a product is shown to meet requirements of the specification and its calculations suggest that it will be profitable, the decision will be made to make it to sell. This is not a decision that it will be taken lightly because, in many cases, the decision to make a product for sale is a commitment to tool up for production. Tooling up for production can mean building a production line costing several lakhs of rupees, building expensive jigs, buying special purpose machine tools or, in some other way, making a very large initial investment.
- **Manufacture:** The manufacture of a product involves the purchase of raw materials, the purchase of bought out components, the use of labour to make and assemble the product, and the use of supervisory labour.
- **Selling:** When the product is fit to sell and be available, it may be necessary to spend money on campaign to sell the product.
- **Distribution:** In the process of selling the product, it must be distributed to sales outlets and to customers.

- **Product Support:** When the product has been bought, the customer will expect it to be supported. The manufacturer or supplier will have to make sure that spares and expert servicing are available for the life of the product. The manufacturer or the supplier may even have to offer free servicing and replacement of parts during the early life of the product.
- **Decommissioning or Replacement:** When a manufacturing product comes to an end, the plant used to build the product must be re-used, sold, scrapped, or decommissioned in a way that is acceptable to society.

REVIEW QUESTIONS

1. What is Target costing? What are its features?
2. What is the nature of Target costing?
3. Explain Target costing methodology.
4. What is ABC? What are its characteristics?
5. How to develop and implement ABC?
6. What is Life-cycle costing? What are its activities?
7. What are the characteristics of Life-cycle costing?

■ ■ ■

11

Marginal Costing and CVP Analysis

MARGINAL COSTING

Marginal Costing is a technique of ascertaining marginal costs or variable costs. It is not a system for cost ascertainment; it is mainly a technique to deal with the effect on profits of changes in the volume or type of output. This technique may be used in conjunction with other methods of costing. Marginal costing is also known as 'direct costing' or 'variable costing'. The latter expressions are mainly used in the United States.

CONCEPT OF MARGINAL COSTING

The concept of 'marginal cost' has been borrowed from economic theory. To the economist, marginal cost is an incremental cost; he considers it as the addition to total cost which results from the production of one more unit of output. That is, it does not arise if the additional unit is not produced.

The Institute of Cost and Management Accountants, London, defines marginal cost as "the amount at any given volume of output by which aggregate costs are changed if the volume of output is increased or decreased by one unit." As already explained, a unit may indicate a single article, a batch of articles, an order, a stage of production capacity, a process or a department, i.e., it relates to the change in output in the particular circumstances under consideration.

The Institute of Chartered Accountants of England defines marginal cost as "every expense (whether of production, selling or distribution) incurred by the taking of a particular decision." In the short-term period, marginal cost is equal to prime cost plus all overheads which vary with volume.

According to the Institute of Cost and Management Accountants, London, "Marginal costing is the ascertainment, by differentiating between fixed costs and variable costs, of marginal cost and of the effect of profit of changes in the volume or type of output." An understanding of the concept of marginal costs, however, requires a thorough understanding of the various classes of costs and their relation with the change in the level of activity. Under marginal costing, costs are mainly classified into fixed costs and variable costs. The essential feature of marginal costing is that the product or marginal cost, i.e., those costs which are dependent on the volume of activity, are separated from the period or fixed costs, i.e., costs which remain unchanged with a change in the volume of activity. Variability with the volume of output is the main criterion for the classification of costs into product and period categories. Even the semi-variable costs have to be bifurcated into their fixed and variable components based on the variability criterion. In this regard, the absorption or conventional costing system differs from marginal costing. Under absorption costing system, all manufacturing costs, whether of fixed or variable nature, are treated as product costs. All companies, which use marginal costing as an aid to managerial decision-making, mainly use the absorption costing system.

ABSORPTION COSTING vs. MARGINAL COSTING

Absorption costing, which generally refers to the practice of charging all costs, both variable and fixed, to operations, processes, or products, treats all costs, whether fixed or variable as product costs. And as such, the product is made to bear the burden of full costs even though these costs have no relevance to current operations. But under the marginal costing technique, only variable costs are regarded as product cost and the fixed costs are transferred to the Profit and Loss Account.

Absorption costing also differs from marginal costing with regard to inventory valuation. While under marginal costing, closing stocks are valued at the marginal costs, under absorption costing, they are valued at full cost. Such a method of valuation has the effect of carrying over fixed costs from one period to another. This procedure would normally affect the trading results and vitiate cost comparison as well.

In absorption costing, fixed overheads can never be absorbed exactly because of the difficulty in forecasting costs and volume of output. But the exclusion of fixed costs from product costs in the case of marginal costing does not give rise to the problem of over or under-absorption of the fixed overheads.

In the case of absorption costing, profit is the difference between sales revenue and total cost. But under the marginal costing technique, the excess of sales revenue over marginal cost of sales is known as contribution. It is the contribution that is the guiding principle for decision-making under the marginal costing technique. In order to ascertain net profits, fixed costs are absorbed in total contribution.

What is CVP Analysis?

Cost Volume Profit (CVP) Analysis is an analytical tool for studying the relationship between volume, cost, prices and profits. It is an integral part of the profit planning process of a firm. Though formal profit planning and control include the use of budgets and other forecasts, the CVP analysis provides an overview of the profit planning process. Besides, it helps to evaluate the purpose and reasonableness of such budgets and forecasts. Generally, it provides answers to such questions as follows:

(*i*) What will be the effect of changes in prices, costs, and volume on profits?

(*ii*) What minimum sales volume need be affected to avoid losses?

(*iii*) What should be the level of activity to earn a target profit?

(*iv*) What product is the most profitable one and which product or operation should be discontinued?

The managers of profit-seeking organizations usually study the relationships of revenues (sales), expenses (costs) and net income (net profit). Managers of non-profit organizations will also benefit from the study of CVP relationships, primarily because knowledge of how costs fluctuate in response to changes in volume is valuable regardless of whether profit is an objective. After all, all types of organizations have only limited resources to employ in order to achieve the objective functions.

Importance of CVP Analysis

The CVP analysis is quite useful to management as it provides an insight into effects and other relationship of factors, which has a bearing on profit of the firm. As the relationship between the cost, volume and profit makes up the profit structure. CVP relationship becomes essential for budgeting and profit planning. To start with, it helps to determine the sales volume required to avoid losses and sales volume needed to achieve the profit analysis to predict and evaluate implications of its short-run decisions about fixed costs, variable costs, sales volume and selling prices for its profit plans on a continuous basis.

BREAK-EVEN ANALYSIS

The break-even analysis is the most widely known form of CVP analysis. The study of CVP relationship is frequently referred to as break-even analysis. Break-even analysis is basically concerned with the determination of sales volume at which a company makes neither profit nor loss. As a control technique, the break-even volume, therefore, sets the floor, which a company should not allow its sales volume to drop if operations are to be profitable. Over the years, the break-even concept has found application in a wide variety of decision areas, such as profit planning, flexible budgeting, pricing, product mix, make or buy decision, etc.

Fixed Costs vs. Variable Costs

CVP analysis is based on marginal costing principles. Marginal costing may be defined as the ascertainment of marginal cost by differentiating between fixed costs and variable costs and studying the effect of profit of changes in the volume or type of output. Marginal cost is defined as every expenses (whether of production, selling or distribution) incurred in, taking a particular decision. In the short-term period, marginal is equal to prime cost plus all overheads that vary with volume. Under marginal costing, costs are mainly classified into fixed or period costs and variable or product or marginal costs. The essential feature of marginal costing is that marginal costs vary with the volume of activity and fixed costs remain unchanged with a change in the volume of activity.

Break-even analysis recognizes the fact that all cost items do not behave in the same manner as volume of activity (production or sales) changes. This recognition makes the relationship among cost, volume and profits a significant basis for the analysis. Depending from their behaviour, the costs are classified into three categories: (a) Fixed, (b) Variable, and (c) Semi-variable costs.

Fixed costs are those items of costs that remain constant or fixed irrespective of changes in the level of activity. Depreciation, rent, salaries, insurance, etc., are examples of fixed cost items for a typical manufacturing concern. Fixed costs can further be classified into committed fixed costs and discretionary fixed costs. Committed fixed costs, arise out of commitments made to keep the organization in readiness for productive operations. Thus, commitment of resources into fixed assets and personnel will give rise to fixed costs, like depreciation, insurance, rent, salaries, etc. Discretionary fixed costs arise out of decision taken towards the incurrence of expenditure on items like research and development, training programmes, sales promotion, etc. While the first exhibits greater rigidity, the discretionary costs are more flexible and allow room for reduction. Full understanding of the distinction between these two types of fixed costs is highly useful for cost control purpose.

Variable costs are costs that vary with the level of activity proportionately. Raw material cost, direct wages, salesmen's commission, etc., are a few examples. These costs can further be classified into 'engineered' costs and other variable costs. In the case of engineered costs, the relationship between production and cost is created by technical or engineering specifications in the form of input-output relations. However, other variable costs do change with the level of activity but such change is not due to technical considerations.

Semi-variable costs are costs that are partly variable and partly remain constant. Costs on repairs and maintenance, transport, telephone charges, etc., are a few examples of this category. They are decomposed into their fixed and variable components and are added to their respective elements for the purpose of break-even analysis.

Assumptions of Break-even Analysis

Break-even analysis can be carried out in two ways: (*a*) Algebraic method and (*b*) Graphical method. Both the methods are based on certain assumptions, which are rarely found in practice. Some of these assumptions are as follows:

(*i*) All costs can be classified into fixed and variable elements.

(*ii*) While variable costs vary proportionately with volume, the fixed costs remain constant.

(*iii*) Selling price remains constant despite the volume changes.

(*iv*) In the case of multiple products, sales mix also remains constant.

(*v*) Productivity per worker, and efficiency of plant, etc., remains mostly unchanged.

Any change in any one of the above factors will alter the break-even point or break-even volume and the profits will be affected by factors other than volume. Hence, results of the break-even analysis should be interpreted subject to limitations of the above assumptions.

Mathematical Representation of Break-even Analysis

Many terms and techniques have been developed, which now form part of break-even analysis. The most important term and formula for the computation of break-even point are explained. Break-even point (BEP) refers to that volume of sales where total sales is equal to total costs (fixed as well as marginal or variable costs) or total contribution (total sales minus total marginal costs) is equal to total fixed costs. It is simply a no profit or no loss sales volume or point. It is calculated as follows:

$$\text{Break-even Point (in units)} = \frac{\text{Fixed Costs}}{\text{Sales Price per unit} - \text{Variable cost per unit}}$$

Where P/V Ratio $\dfrac{\text{Contribution per unit}}{\text{Selling price per unit}} \times 100$ and where contribution = Sales – Marginal Costs

Calculation of Profit/Volume Ratio (P/V Ratio)

This ratio shows the relationship between the value of sales and contribution. A more appropriate term might be the Contribution/Sales Ratio. This ratio is often expressed as a percentage. The formula is as follows:

$$\text{P/V Ratio} = \frac{\text{Contribution}}{\text{Sales}} \times 100$$

The P/V Ratio may be calculated using either per unit contribution and sales or total contribution and total sales. When total sales and total costs (without break up for fixed and variable components) are given to periods of activity, the following formula may be used to calculate P/V Ratio.

$$\text{P/V Ratio} = \frac{\text{Contribution}}{\text{Sales}} \times 100\text{, where Sales} - \text{Costs} = \text{Profit}$$

Uses of P/V Ratio

1. It enables us to determine the marginal costs for any volume of sales by using marginal cost percentage. Deducting P/V Ratio from 100% we can arrive at marginal cost percentage. For example, if P/V Ratio is 25%, marginal cost percentage is 75% (100% – 25%).
2. Calculations of the desired volume of output, profit or other essential facts.
3. Comparisons can be made by calculating the P/V ratio for each factor to be compared, viz., (*a*) Line of product, (*b*) Sales area, (*c*) Method of sales, e.g., sales through wholesalers or retailers, (*d*) individual factories, and (*e*) separate companies.

Example 1

The fixed costs for the year are ₹ 80,000. Variable cost per unit is ₹ 12. Estimated sales for the period are valued at ₹ 3,20,000. The number units produced and sold are the same. Each unit is sold at ₹ 20. Calculate the P/V Ratio and Break-even Point.

Solution

$$\text{P/V Ratio} = \frac{\text{Contribution per unit}}{\text{Selling Price per unit}} \times 100$$

Contribution = Sales – Variable Cost = ₹ 20 – ₹ 12 = ₹ 8

$$\text{P/V Ratio} \quad \frac{8 \times 100}{20} = 40\%$$

$$\text{BEP (in units)} = \frac{80000}{20-12} \; 10{,}000 \text{ units}$$

BEP (in ₹) = 10,000 × ₹ 20 = ₹ 2,00,000

Example 2

Assuming that the cost structure and selling prices remain the same in periods I and II, find out the P/V Ratio and Break-even Point.

Periods	Sales (₹)	Total cost (₹)
I	1,20,000	1,08,000
II	1,40,000	1,24,000

Solution

Periods	Sales (₹)	minus	Cost (₹)	=	Profit (₹)
I	1,20,000	–	1,08,000		12,000
II	1,40,000	–	1,24,000		16,000

P/V Ratio = 1,08,000 × 100/1,20,000 = 90%

From the formula of P/V Ratio, Contribution and Sales values may be ascertained as follows:

P/V Ratio = (Contribution/Sales) × 100

Contribution = Sales × P/V Ratio

Sales = Contribution/P/V Ratio

By applying the above equation to period I, we can find out the contribution for period I as follows:

Contribution for Period I = Sales for Period I × P/V Ratio

= ₹ 1,20,000 × 90% = ₹ 1,08,000

Contribution – Profit = Fixed Cost

₹ 1,08,000 – ₹ 12,000 = ₹ 96,000

$$\text{Break-even Point} = \frac{\text{Fixed cost}}{\text{Sales price per unit} - \text{variable cost per unit}}$$

Note: Here the quantity is not mentioned so we assume quantity to be 1,000 units.

$$* \text{ BEP (in units) } \frac{96,000}{120-108} = 8000 \text{ units}$$

BEP (in Rupees) 8000 × 120 = 96000

Margin of Safety (MS)

The margin of safety is the difference between the total sales and break-even sales. It may be expressed in monetary terms or as a percentage, i.e., the margin of safety in relation to total sales. It is an extremely valuable guide and indicates the financial strength of the business. It is calculated as follows:

(*a*) MS = Actual Sales – Break-even Sales

(*b*) MS (in ₹) = Profit/P/V Ratio

(*c*) MS (in units) = Profit/Contribution per unit

(*d*) MS (in ₹) MS units × sp

Example 3

Current sales are 20,000 units per annum. Selling price is ₹ 12 per unit. Prime cost is ₹ 6 per unit. Variable overheads are ₹ 2 per unit. Fixed cost is ₹ 60,000. Calculate (*a*) P/V Ratio, (*b*) Break-even Point, and (*c*) Margin of safety.

Solution

Particulars		*Per unit* (₹)		*Total* (₹)
Sales (S)		12.00		2,40,000
Less: Marginal costs:				
Prime cost	₹ 6.00		₹ 1,20,000	
Variable Overheads	2.00	8.00	40,000	1,60,000
Contribution (C)		4.00		80,000
Less: Fixed costs (F)		—	—	60,000
Profit (P)				20,000

$$\text{P/V Ratio} = (C/S) \times 100 = (₹\ 80,000/2,40,000) \times 100 = 33\frac{1}{3}\%$$

$$\text{BEP in units} = \frac{60000}{12-8} = 15,000 \text{ units}$$

BEP (in ₹) 15000 units × ₹ 12 = ₹ 1,80,000

MS = Actual sales – Break-even sales = ₹ 2,40,000 – ₹ 1,80,000 = ₹ 60,000

MS (in units) = 20,000 units – 15,000 units = 5,000 units

MS (in ₹) = 5,000 units × ₹ 12 = ₹ 60,000

Break-even Chart

The break-even point can also be computed graphically. A break-even chart portrays a pictorial view of the relationship between costs, volume, and profit. The break-even point, indicated in the chart, is one of which the total cost line and total sales line intersect. It is an important aid to profit planning.

Construction of Break-even Chart

(*a*) Select a scale for sales or production in units on horizontal axis.
(*b*) Select a scale for costs and revenue on the vertical axis.
(*c*) Draw the fixed cost line parallel to the horizontal axis.
(*d*) Draw the variable cost line starting from the point on the vertical axis, and
(*e*) Draw the sales line starting from the point of origin (zero) and finishing at point of maximum scales.

Example 4

From the following data compute the break-even point by means of a break-even chart:
Volume of sales (units): 5,000, 10,000, 15,000, 20,000
Fixed cost ₹ 60,000 for all levels of sales volume
Selling price per unit is ₹ 10
Variable cost per unit is ₹ 6
Current sales: 20,000 units

Solution

Output Units	*Variable Costs* (₹)	*Fixed Costs* (₹)	*Total cost* (₹)	*Sales* (₹)
5,000	30,000	60,000	90,000	50,000
10,000	60,000	60,000	1,20,000	1,00.,000
15,000	90,000	60,000	1,50,000	1,50,000
20,000	1,20 000	60,000	1,80,000	2,00,000

At Break-even Point the total sales is equal to total cost and at 15,000 units they are equal. Hence, the BEP is 15,000 units or ₹ 1,50,000. This can be verified algebraically.

BEP = 15,000 units

Contribution per unit = Selling price per unit – Variable cost per unit = ₹ 10 – ₹ 6 = ₹ 4

The data can now be shown graphically as follows:

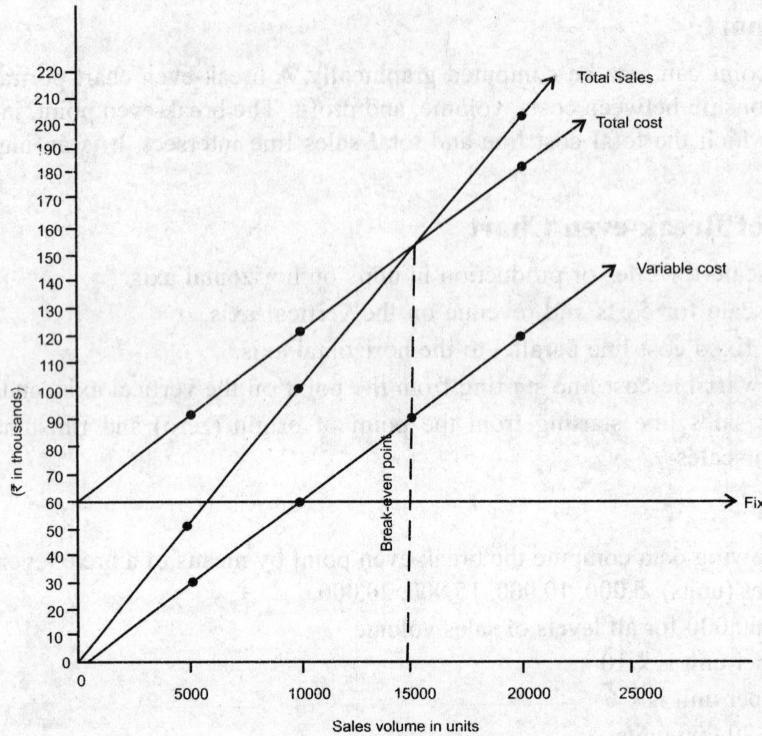

Fig. 1: Break-even Chart

Angle of Incidence

This is an angle formed between the total sales line and total cost line at the break-even point (Refer Fig. 1). A large angle of incidence indicates a high rate of profit while a narrow angle shows a relatively low rate of profit. This angle is important in boom periods when sales are expanding. Once the BEP is reached, additional sales show a good profit.

Profit Volume Graph or Chart

Profit Volume Graph is a graphical representation of the relationship between profit and volume. It is based on the same information and assumptions which are necessary for a break-even chart. It also suffers from the same limitations.

Construction of a Profit Volume Graph

(*a*) Select a scale for sales on the horizontal axis.

(*b*) Select a scale for profit and fixed costs on the vertical axis.

(*c*) Divide the graph into two areas, one representing profit and the other representing loss. The sales line that divides the graph horizontally forks these areas.

(*d*) On the vertical axis, the area below the sales line represents fixed costs and that above the sales line represents profits.

(*e*) Points are plotted for the required fixed costs and for profit, and a line is drawn to connect the two points.

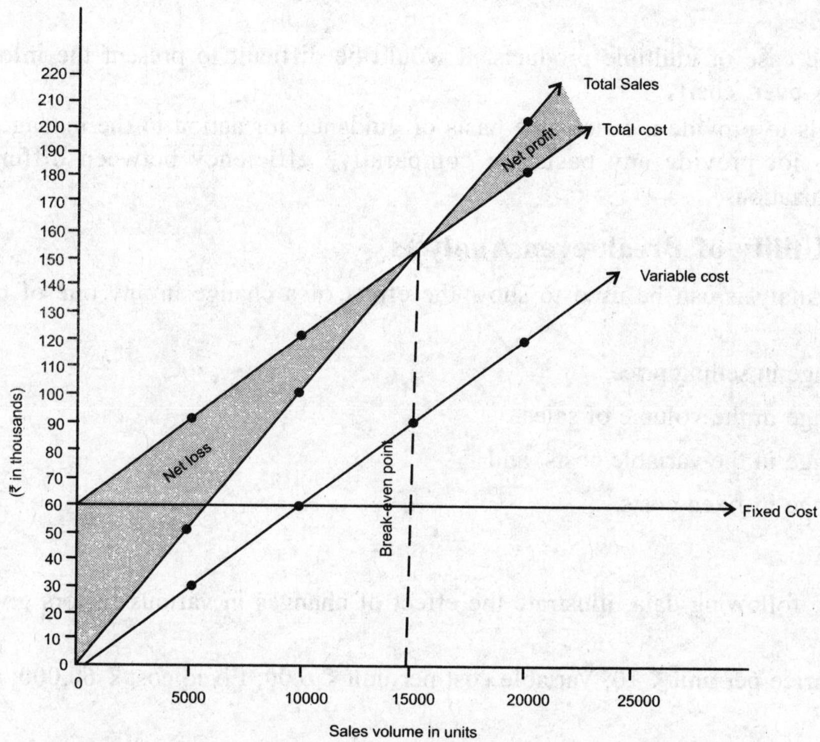

Fig. 2: Profit Volume Graph

Advantages of Break-even Charts

1. The break-even chart visualizes the information very clearly and at a glance it provides a vivid picture of the whole affair of the business in a detailed and easily understandable form.
2. It portrays clearly the effect of changes in costs and selling price.
3. Besides clearly showing the break-even point, it enables us to know the profitability of different products.
4. It is a managerial tool for control and reduction of costs, elimination of wastages and to achieve better efficiency.
5. It is very useful for forecasting, long-term planning, and growth.

Limitations

1. Break-even Chart is based on a number of assumptions, which may hold well in practice. For example, the assumption relating to selling price, variabie cost and fixed cost may not be correct in practice. It may change over a period and upset the decision taken on such an assumption.

2. Only a limited amount of information of what could be presented in a single break-even chart.
3. In the case of multiple products, it would be difficult to present the information in a break-even chart.
4. It fails to provide a conclusive basis or guidance for action to the management. It also does not provide any basis for comparative efficiency between different units or organizations.

Practical Utility of Break-even Analysis

Break-even Analysis can be used to show the effect of a change in any one of the following profit factors:

1. Change in selling price,
2. Change in the volume of sales,
3. Change in the variable costs, and
4. Change in fixed costs.

Example 5

From the following data, illustrate the effect of changes in various factors given below on profit:

Selling price per unit ₹ 10; Variable cost per unit ₹ 6.00; Fixed cost ₹ 60,000; Current sales 20,000 units.

Find out the effect of the following:

1. 20% increase in selling price,
2. 10% decrease in sales volume,
3. 20% decrease in variable costs, and
4. 10% increase in fixed costs.

Solution

Marginal Cost Statement		*Output 20, 000 units*
Sales	₹ 10	₹ 2,00,000
Less: Variable cost	6	1,20,000
Contribution	4	80,000
Less: Fixed costs		60,000
Profit		20,000

P/V Ratio = (4/10) × 100 = 40%

BEP = ₹ 60,000/4 = 15,000 units

MS = 20,000 – 15,000 = 5,000 units

MS Ratio = (15,000/20,000) × 100 = 75%

1. Effect of 20% increase in selling price

Marginal Cost Statement *Output 20,000 units*

Particulars	*Per Unit* (₹)	*Total* (₹)
Sales (₹ 10 plus 20%)	12.00	2,40,000
Less: Variable costs	6.00	1,20,000
Contribution	6.00	1,20,000
Less: Fixed cost		60,000
		60,000

P/V Ratio = (6/12) × 100 = 50 %

Break-even Point = 10,000 units

Margin of safety = 20,000 units – 10,000 units = 10,000 units

MS Ratio = (10,000/20,000) × 100 = 50%

It may be observed that due to 20% increase in selling price; the profit has increased by ₹ 40,000 (i.e., from ₹ 20,000 to ₹ 60,000). BEP has decreased to 10,000 units or ₹ 1,20,000. MS has increased by 5,000 units. The same effect may be illustrated through break-even chart.

2. Effect of 10% decrease in sales volume

Marginal Cost Statement *Output 18,000 units*

Particulars	*Per unit* (₹)	*Total* (₹)
Sales	10.00	1,80,000
Less: Variable costs	6.00	1,08,000
Contribution		72,000
Less: Fixed cost		60,000
Profit		12,000

P/V Ratio = (₹ 4/10) × 100 = 40%

BEP = ₹ 60,000/4 = 15,000 units

MS = 18,000 – 15,000 = 3,000 units

It may be observed that 10% decrease in sales volume has affected only the margin of safety. There is no change in BEP since the P/V Ratio and fixed costs are the same.

3. Effect of 20% decrease in variable costs

Marginal Cost Statement *Output 20,000 units*

	Particulars	*Per unit* (₹)	*Total* (₹)
	Sales	10.00	1,80,000
Less:	Variable costs	4.80	96,000
	Contribution	5.20	1,04,000
Less:	Fixed cost		60,000
	Profit		44,000

P/V Ratio = [₹ 5.20/₹ 10] × 100 = 52%

BEP = ₹ 60,000/5.2 = 11,539 units or ₹ 1,15,390

MS = 20,000 – 11,539 = 8,461 units [approx.]

Reduction in variable cost has improved the P/V Ratio by 12% and reduced BEP to 11,539 units. Ultimately the MS has improved.

4. Effect of 10% increase in fixed costs

Marginal Cost Statement *Output 20,000 units*

	Particulars	*Per unit* (₹)	*Total* (₹)	
	Sales		10.00	2,00,000
Less:	Variable costs	6.00	1,20,000	
	Contribution	4.00	80,000	
Less:	Fixed cost		66,000	
	Profit			14,000

P/V Ratio = (4/10) × 100 = 40%

BEP = ₹ 66,000/4 = 16,500 units or ₹ 1,65,000

MS = 20,000 – 16,500 = 3,500 units or ₹ 35,000

Increase in fixed costs has increased the BEP and reduced the MS.

Limitations of Break-even Analysis

Break-even analysis is a static concept and is useful only for short-run analysis. However, having a series of charts for different time horizons could derive its benefit. It is difficult to separate costs with fixed and variable components.

Another limitation is that the preparation of break-even charts for multi-product companies becomes cumbersome.

Break-even analysis in the conventional form assumes certainty about revenue and cost factors. But, in reality, uncertainty is the most common phenomenon. However, refinements have been made to incorporate uncertainty factors into the analysis. Despite its limitations, the break-even analysis is simple, and is very useful for decision-making, profit planning and control.

Illustration 1

The Income Statement of C Ltd., is summarized as follows:

Net Income from 1000 units sold	₹ 2,00,000
Less: Expenses (including ₹ 1,00,000 of Fixed expenses)	2,20,000
Net Loss	20,000

The sales manager believes that an increase of ₹ 50,000 in advertising outlays will increase sales substantially. The Chairman of the Board approved his plan.

Show (*a*) At what sales volume will the company achieve its break-even? (*b*) What sales will result in a net profit of ₹ 10,000?

Solution

Marginal Cost Statement

	Sales	₹ 2,00,000
Less:	Variable expenses ₹ 2,20,000 – ₹ 1,00,000	1,20,000
	Contribution	80,000
Less:	Fixed expenses	1,00,000
	Net Loss	20,000

$$\text{P/V Ratio} = \frac{80,000}{2,00,000} \times 100 = 40\%$$

When the proposed advertising expenditure is incurred and treated as Fixed Expense, the total fixed expenses would amount to ₹ 1,50,000 (i.e., ₹ 1,00,000 + 50,000).

$$\text{Break-even Point} = (\text{in units}) \frac{1,50,000}{200 - 120} = 1875 \text{ units}$$

Break-even Point (in ₹) 1875 units × ₹ 200 = 3,75,000

Required sales to earn the profit of ₹ 10,000

Required Sales = Net Loss + Profit required + B.E.P

Required sales = 20,000 + 10,000 + 3,75,000 = 4,05, 000

Illustration 2

Mr Raja has ₹ 1,50,000 investment in a business; he wants a return of 15% on his investment. From an analysis of recent cost figures, he finds that his variable cost of operation is 60% of sales; fixed costs are ₹ 75,000 per annum. Show the supporting computations for each answer of the following questions:

(*a*) What sales volume must be obtained for break-even?

(*b*) What sales volume must be obtained to get his 15% return on investment?

Solution

P/V Ratio = 1 – Variable Cost Ratio = 1 – 60% = 40%

(*a*) BEP = (in units) $\dfrac{75{,}000}{1500 - 900} = 125$ units

(*b*) Required return on his investment = 15% on ₹ 1,50,000 = ₹ 22,500

Required Sales Volume = 1,87,500 + 22,500 = BEP (in ₹) = 125 units × 1500 = 1,87,500

= × 2,10,000

= ₹ 2,43,750

Illustration 3

A factory can sell 20,000 units of its product in home market at ₹ 20 each. The marginal cost is ₹ 14 per unit and fixed overheads ₹ 50,000. It can also sell another 10,000 units in the foreign market at ₹ 16 per unit. The additional cost for export is Re. 1 per unit. The total capacity of the factory is 35,000 units. Is the foreign market worth trying?

Solution

The foreign market is worth trying. The reason is that the foreign order is within the total capacity and therefore the factory will not incur any additional fixed expense to meet the order. The foreign sale price is ₹ 16 per unit and marginal cost is ₹ 15 per unit (including extra distribution cost). Thus, it contributes ₹ 1 per unit towards profit without any increase in fixed expense. The following Profitability Statement should explain the point explicitly.

Profitability Statement

Particulars	*Domestic Market (20,000 units)* (₹)	*Foreign Market (10,000 units)* (₹)	*Total (30,000 units)* (₹)
Sales	4,00,000	1,60,000	5,60,000
Less: Marginal cost	2,80,000	1,50,000	4,30,000
Contribution	1,20,000	10,000	1, 30,000
Less: Fixed expenses	50,000		50,000
Profit	70,000	10,000	80,000

As the contribution of ₹ 10,000 increases the total profit, the foreign sale is worth trying.

Illustration 4

A company is considering a proposal to buy a certain part from outside market, which it is manufacturing at present.

The cost data of that part is as under:

Variable cost per unit:	Amount [₹]
Material	800
Wages	280
Overheads	140
Fixed cost per unit:	
Depreciation	84
Others	100
Total cost per unit	1,404

Should the company continue to make the part or buy it from outside if the purchase price is (*a*) ₹ 1,300 per unit (Brand A), and (*b*) ₹ 1,200 per unit (Brand B)?

Solution

In the case of 'make or buy' decisions, only the variable costs are relevant since the Fixed Costs remain constant.

Variable cost per unit:	Amount [₹]
Material	800
Wages	280
Overheads	140
Total	1,220

If the purchase price is ₹ 1,300 per unit (Brand A) it is better to manufacture the product (part) since the manufacturing cost is only ₹ 1,220. The company can save ₹ 80 per unit.

If the purchase price is ₹ 1,200 per unit (Brand B) the wise policy is to buy it from outside market.

However, these decisions will hold good only when the fixed costs remain constant irrespective of the decision taken.

Illustration 5

Polestar Electronics Ltd. decides to effect a 10% reduction in the price of its product because it is felt that such a step may lead to a greater volume of sales. It is anticipated that there are no prospects of any change in total fixed costs and variable cost per unit. The directors wish to maintain net profits at the present level. The following information has been obtained from its records:

Sales: 10,000 units	₹ 2,00,000
Variable cost per unit	₹ 15.00
Fixed cost	₹ 40,000

How does the management proceed to implement this decision?

Solution

Marginal Cost Statement *No. of Units: 10,000*

Particulars	*Per unit* (₹)	*Total* (₹)
Sales	20.00	2,00,000
Less: Variable cost	15.00	1,50,000
Contribution	5.00	50,000
Less: Fixed cost		40,000
Profit		10,000

$$\text{P/V Ratio} = \frac{10000}{40000} \times 100 = 25\%$$

$$\text{BEP} = \text{Fixed Cost/P/V Ratio} = ₹\ 40{,}000/25\%$$

$$= ₹\ 1{,}60{,}000$$

Effect of Change of 10% reduction in selling price

Marginal Cost Statement

	Per unit [₹]
Sales [₹ 20 less 10%]	18.00
Less: Variable cost	15.00
Contribution	3.00

$$\text{P/V Ratio} = (₹\,3/₹\,18) \times 100 = 16\frac{2}{3}\%$$

$$\text{New BEP} = ₹\,40{,}000/16.67\% = ₹\,2{,}40{,}000$$

Sales to earn present level of Profit, i.e. ₹ 10,000

$$\text{Sales} = 3000 \times 100$$

$$\text{Sales} = ₹\,3{,}00{,}000$$

Comments: The management should proceed to implement this decision if it can effect sales above new BEP, i.e., ₹ 2,40,000. If it wants to earn profit of ₹ 10,000 (present level profit), it should make sales amounting to ₹ 3,00,000.

Illustration 6

The following figures relate to a company manufacturing a varied range of products:

Period	*Total Sales (₹)*	*Total Cost (₹)*
Year ended 31-12-2017	22,23,000	19,83,600
Year ended 31-12 -2018	24,51,000	21,43,200

Assuming stability in prices, with variable costs carefully controlled to reflect predetermined relationship, and an unvarying figure for fixed costs, calculate.

(*a*) The P/V Ratio to reflect the rates of growth for profit and sales; and (*b*) any other cost figures to be deduced from the data.

Solution

Period	*Sales (₹)*	*Cost (₹)*
31st December 2016	24,51,000	21,43,200
31st December 2015	22,23 ,000	19,83,600
Difference or Change	2,28,000	1,59,600

Variable Cost Ratio = (Change in Cost/Change in Sales) × 100

= (₹ 1,59,600/ ₹ 2,28,000) × 100 = 70%

P/V Ratio = 1 – Variable Cost Ratio = 1 – 70% = 30%

Variable cost for period 2017 = 22,23,000 × 70% = ₹ 15,56,100

Variable cost for period 2018 = 24,51,000 × 70% = ₹ 17,15,700

Other Cost Figures

Fixed Cost = Total cost – Variable cost

For 2017 = ₹ 19,83,600 – 15,56,100 = ₹ 4,27,500

For 2018 = ₹ 21,43,200 – 17,15,700 = ₹ 4,27,500

BEP = (Fixed Cost/P/V Ratio) = ₹ 4,27,500/30%

= ₹ 14,25,000

MS = Actual Sales – BEP

MS for 2017 = ₹ 22,23,000 – ₹ 14,25,000 = ₹ 7,98,000

MS for 2018 = ₹ 24,51,000 – ₹ 14,25,000 = ₹ 10,26,000

Illustration 7

From the following data, calculate the break-even point:

Selling price per unit	₹ 10.00
Trade discount	5%
Direct material Cost per unit	3.00
Direct labour per unit	2.00
Fixed overheads	10,000

Variable overheads 100% on direct labour cost

If sales are 15% above the break-even volume, determine the net profits.

Solution

Marginal Cost Statement

Selling price per unit		₹ 10.00
Less: Variable Cost per unit:		
Trade discounts	₹ 0.50	
Direct material	3.00	
Direct wages	2.00	
Variable overheads (100% on wages)	2.00	7.50
Contribution per unit		2.50

Break-even Point =

= 4,000 units

BEP in ₹ = 4,000 × ₹ 10 = ₹ 40,000

Note: Trade discount has been considered as variable cost, as it is provided on the sale of every unit. If it is not considered as variable, the computation is as follows:

Selling price	₹ 10.00
Less: Trade discount	0.50
Net sales per unit	9.50
Less: Variable cost	7.00
Contribution per unit	2.50

BEP = ₹ 10,000/2.50 = 4,000 units

BEP in ₹ = 4,000 × 9.50 = ₹ 38,000

Profit when sales are 15% above BEP

Sales	= 4,000 units + 15% of 4,000 = 4,600 units	
Contribution	= 4,600 × ₹ 2.50 =	₹ 11,500
Less: Fixed costs		10,000
Profit		1,500

Illustration 8

The budgeted analysis of A Co. Ltd., include

Product	*Sales value (₹)*	*P/V Ratio*
A	50,000	50%
B	80,000	40%
C	1,20,000	30%

Fixed overhead for the period is ₹ 1,00,000. The directors are worried about the results of the company. They have requested you to prepare a statement showing the amount of the loss expected and to recommend a change in the sales of each product or in the total mix, which will eliminate the expected loss.

Solution

Statement of Loss and Additional Sales

Product	*Sales* (₹)	*P/V Ratio* %	*Contribution* (₹)	*Additional Sales* (₹)
A	50,000	50	25,000	14,000
B	80,000	40	32,000	17,500
C	1,20,000	30	36,000	23,333
Total	2,50,000	37.2	93,000	18,817
Fixed Overheads			1,00,000	
Loss			[7,000]	

Notes: 1. Contribution = Sales × P/V Ratio. The total contribution of all products comes to ₹ 93,000, which could not recover fixed overheads of ₹ 1,00,000 and therefore total loss is ₹ 7,000.

The overall P/V Ratio of budgeted sales mix = 37.2%

2. In order to recoup the loss of ₹ 7,000, it is necessary to increase the sales of any of the following products to the extent, as shown in the table.

Additional sales required for

Product A = (₹ 7,000/50) × 100 = ₹ 14,000

Product B = (₹ 7,000/40) × 100 = ₹ 17,500

Product C = (₹ 7,000/30) × 100 = ₹ 23,333

Additional sales of same mix may be increased by (₹ 7,000/37.2) × 100 = ₹ 18,817

3. Care should be taken to increase sales of more profitable products. Accordingly, the sales of Product A should be increased to the maximum and next that of Product B and last that of Product C. Thus, if the total volume of sales is constant, the mix is as follows:

Product	*Sales* (₹)	*P/V Ratio* (%)	*Contribution* (₹)
A	1,20,000	50	60,000
B	80,000	40	32,000
C	50,000	30	15,000
Fixed overheads	2,50,000	42.8	1,07,000
Profit			1,00,000
			7,000

Illustration 9

Nilgiri Tea Industries manufactures and markets quality tea in domestic market. The following data are available:

	₹ per kg.
Raw material	16
Conversion cost (variable)	12
Dealer's margin (10% of sales)	4
Selling price	40

Fixed cost: ₹ 5,00,000

Present sales: 90,000 kgs

Capacity utilization: 60%

There is acute competition. Extra efforts are necessary to sell. Suggestion has been made for increasing the sales.

(*a*) By reducing sale price by 5%

(*b*) By increasing dealer's margin by 25% of the existing rate.

Which of the above two suggestions would you make if the company desires to maintain the present profit? Show calculations indicating the quantity to be sold to earn the existing profit.

Solution

Marginal Cost Statement

Particulars		*Per unit* (₹)	*Total* (₹)
Sales		40.00	36,00,000
Less: Marginal Costs:			
Materials	16.00		
Conversion cost	12.00		
Dealer's margin	4.00	32.00	28,80,000
Contribution		8.00	7,20,000
Less: Fixed costs			5,00,000
Profit			2,20,000

Marginal Cost Statement for Future Proposals

Particulars		*Proposal I (Reduction in selling price) per unit* (₹)		*Proposal II (Increase in Dealer's margin) per unit* (₹)
Sales		38.00		40.00
Less: Marginal costs:				
Materials	16.00		16.00	
Conversion cost	12.00		12.00	
Dealer's margin	3.80	31.80	5.00	33.00
Contribution		6.20		7.00

Contribution to be earned = Fixed costs + Present profit

= ₹ 5,00,000 + ₹ 2,20,000 = ₹ 7,20,000

Number of units to be produced = Total contribution/contribution per unit

Under Proposal I: units to be produced = ₹ 7,20,000/₹ 6.20 = 1,16,129 units (approx).

Under Proposal II: units to be produced = ₹ 7,20,000/₹ 7 = 1,02,857 units (approx).

Comments: Since the contribution per unit is more under the second alternative, it is better than the first one. Further, the number of units to be produced to earn the present profit is also less.

Illustration 10

A toy manufacturer earns an average net profit of ₹ 6 per unit at a selling price of ₹ 30 by producing and selling 30,000 units at 60% of the potential capacity. The composition of his cost of sales is:

Direct material	₹ 8.00
Direct wages	₹ 2.00
Works overheads	₹ 12 (50% variable)
Sales overheads	₹ 2.00 (75% fixed)

During the current year, he intends to produce the same number but anticipates that

(*a*) His fixed charges will go up by 10%

(*b*) Rates of direct labour will increase by 20%

(*c*) Rates of material will increase by 5%

(*d*) Selling price cannot be increased.

Under these circumstances, he obtains an order for a further 20% of his capacity. What minimum price will you recommend for accepting the order to give the manufacturer an overall profit of ₹ 1,80,000?

Solution

Particulars		(₹)	*Capacity: 60%* *Per unit* (₹)	*(30, 000 units)* *Total* (₹)
Sales		—	30.00	9,00,000
Less: Marginal cost:				
Direct materials		8.40		
Direct wages		2.40		
Variable works overheads		6.00		
Variable sales overheads		0.50	17.30	5,19,000
Contribution			12.70	3,81,000
Less: Fixed overheads:				
Works overheads	1,80,000			
Add: 10% increase	18,000	1,98,000		
Sales overheads	45,000			
Add: 10% increase	4,500	49,500		2,47,500
Net profit				1,33,500

Calculation of minimum price for special order: (10,000 units at 20% capacity)

Planned profit	₹ 1,80,000
Less: Actual profit	1,33,500
Profit to be earned from the order	46,500
Minimum price	
Marginal cost to be recovered – 10,000 × ₹ 17.3	= ₹ 1,73,000
Increase in profit to be earned from the order	46,500
Minimum selling price for 10,000 units	2,19,500
Minimum selling price per unit (₹ 2,19,500/10, 000)	= ₹ 21.95

Illustration 11

If P/V Ratio is 30% and Margin of Safety is 40%, find out the current fixed cost, break-even point and net profit if actual sales is ₹ 5,00,000.

Solution

Actual sales	100	₹ 5,00,000
Margin of safety	40	2,00,000
Break-even point (AS – MS)	60	3,00,000

Fixed Cost = BEP × P/V Ratio

= ₹ 3,00,000 × 30% = ₹ 90,000

Net Profit = MS × P/V Ratio

= ₹ 2,00,000 × 30% = ₹ 60,000

Illustration 12

A firm has ₹ 5,00,000 invested in plant, and 20% as minimum required rate of return on investment. Fixed costs in the factory, presently, amount to ₹ 2,50,000 per annum, and variable costs amount to ₹ 15 per unit produced. In the past year, the firm produced and sold 30,000 units at ₹ 25 each and earned a profit of ₹ 50,000. How can management achieve its target profit goal by varying different variables like variable costs, fixed costs, quantity sold, or increasing the selling price per unit?

Solution

Investment = ₹ 5,00,000

Required rate of return = 20%

Target profit = ₹ 5,00,000 × 20% = ₹ 1,00,000

Profit Equation = Sales – Marginal cost – Fixed cost

Profit = (Qty. sold × SP per unit) – (Qty. sold × Variable cost per unit) – Fixed cost

(a) Achievement of Target Profit by Varying Variable Costs

Let variable cost be ₹ V per unit

₹ 1,00,000 = (30,000 × ₹ 25) – (30,000 × ₹ V) – ₹ 2,50,000

₹ 1,00,000 = ₹ 7,50,000 – 30,000V – ₹ 2,50,000

30,000V = ₹ 7,50,000 – 2,50,000 – 1,00,000

V = ₹ 4,00,000/30,000 = ₹ $13\frac{1}{3}$

The target profit can be achieved by reducing the variable cost by ₹ $1\frac{2}{3}$ (i.e., ₹ 15 – $13\frac{1}{3}$)

(b) Achievement of Target Profit by Varying Fixed Costs

Let fixed costs be F

₹ 1,00,000 = (30,000 × ₹ 25) – (30,000 × 15) – F

₹ 1,00,000 = ₹ 7,50,000 – ₹ 4,50,000 – F

F = ₹ 2,00,000

The target profit can be achieved by reducing the fixed costs by ₹ 50,000 (i.e., ₹ 2,50,000 – ₹ 2,00,000).

(c) Achievement of Target Profit by Varying quantity sold

Let the quantity sold be Q units.

₹ 1,00,000 = (Q × ₹ 25) – (Q × 15) – ₹ 2,50,000

₹ 1,00,000 = 25Q – 15Q – ₹ 2,50,000

10Q = ₹ 3,50,000

Q = 35,000 units.

The target profit can be achieved by increasing the sales volume by 5,000 units.

(d) Achievement of Target Profit by varying selling price

Let the selling price be S

₹ 1,00,000 = (30,000 × S) – (30,000 × ₹ 15) – ₹ 2,50,000

₹ 1,00,000 = 30,000S – ₹ 4,50,000 – ₹ 2,50,000

30,000S = 8,00,000

S = ₹ 8,00,000/30,000 = ₹ $26\frac{2}{3}$

The target profit can be achieved by increasing the selling price by ₹ $1\frac{2}{3}$.

BREAK-EVEN AND CVP ANALYSIS

PROBLEM – 1

Titan Engineering is operating at 70 per cent capacity and presents the following information:

Break-even point	₹ 200 crores
P/V ratio	40 per cent
Margin of safety	₹ 50 crores

Titan's management has decided to increase production to 95 per cent capacity level with the following modifications:

(*i*) The selling price will be reduced by 8 per cent.

(*ii*) The variable cost will be reduced by 5 per cent.

(*iii*) The fixed cost will increase by ₹ 20 crores, including depreciation on additions, but excluding interest on additional capital.

(*iv*) Additional capital of ₹ 50 crores will be needed for capital expenditure and working capital.

Required

(*a*) Indicate the sales figures, with the working, that will be needed to earn ₹ 10 crores over and above the present profit and also meet 20 per cent interest on the additional capital.

(*b*) What will be the revised?

(*i*) Break-even point

(*ii*) P/V Ratio

(*iii*) Margin of safety. **(CA Final Adopted)**

Solution

Working Notes:

Calculation of sales and profit

Total Sales	= Break-even sales + Margin of safety	
	= ₹ 200 crores + ₹ 50 crores	= ₹ 250 crores
P/V Ratio	= 40%	
Variable Cost	= 60% of sales	
	= ₹ 250 crores × 60/100	= ₹ 150 crores
Fixed Cost	= Break-even sales × P/V Ratio	
	= ₹ 200 crores × 40/100	= ₹ 80 crores
Total Cost	= ₹ 150 crores + ₹ 80 crores	= ₹ 230 crores
Profit	= Total sales – Total cost	
	= ₹ 250 crores – ₹ 230 crores	= ₹ 20 crores

Sales with desired profit (₹ in crores)

Present fixed cost			80
Add: Increase in fixed cost		20	
Interest on additional capital	(₹ 50 crores × 20%)	10	30
Total revised fixed capital			110

Present selling price		100.00
Present variable cost		92.00
Revised selling price	(8% less of present selling price)	
Revised variable cost (i.e., ₹ 92 × 55/100)	(reduced from 60% to 55% of Sale price)	50.60
Contribution per unit		41.40

New P/V ratio = (41.40/92.00) × 100 = 45%

$$\text{Required sales for desired profit} = \frac{\text{Revised fixed cost + Expected profit}}{\text{P/V ratio}}$$

$$= \frac{₹\ 110 \text{ crores} + ₹\ 30 \text{ crores}}{45\%} = ₹\ 311.11 \text{ crores}$$

Revised Break-even point = Fixed Cost/ P/V Ratio

= ₹ 110 crores/45% = ₹ 244.44 crores

Revised Margin of safety = Revised sales – Revised Break-even sales

= ₹ 311.11 crores – ₹ 244.44 crores = ₹ 66.67 crores.

PROBLEM – 2

Y Ltd., produces P, Q and R. The following are the results for the year ending 31st March, 2016:-

Product	*Sales ₹*	*Marginal Cost ₹*
P	1,00,000	30,000
Q	50,000	30,000
R	50,000	60,000
Total	2,00,000	1,20,000

Fixed overhead were ₹ 50,000 during 2015-2016.

Draw a profit graph plotting the profit for each product as well as for the company as a whole. Also ascertain the break-even point of sales from the graph.

(C.A. Final Adopted)

Solution

Profitability Statement

Product	Sales	Variable cost	Contribution	Cumulative sales	Cumulative V. cost	Cumulative contribution	Total fixed cost	Cumulative net profit
P	1,00,000	30,000	70,000	1,00,000	30,000	70,000	50,000	20,000
Q	50,000	30,000	20,000	1,50,000	60,000	90,000	50,000	40,000
R	50,000	60,000	(10,000)	2,00,000	1,20,00	80,000	50,000	30,000

PROBLEM–3

Navbharat Commerce College, Mumbai has six sections of B.Com. And two sections of M.Com. with 40 and 30 students per section respectively. The college plans one day pleasure trip around the city for students once in an academic session during winter break to visit park, Zoo, Planetarium and Aquarium.

A transporter used to provide the required number of buses at a flat rate of ₹ 700 per bus for the aforesaid purpose. In addition, a special permit fee of ₹ 50 per bus is required to be deposited with city Municipal Corporation. Each teacher is paid daily allowance of ₹ 100 for the day. No other costs in respect of teachers are relevant to the trip.

The approved caterers of the college supply breakfast, lunch and afternoon tea respectively at ₹ 7, ₹ 30 and ₹ 3 per student.

No entrance fee is charged at the park. Entrance fees come to ₹ 5 per student, both for the zoo and the aquarium.

As regards planetarium, the authority charges block entrance fees, as under, for group of students of educational institutions depending upon the number of students in a group:

Number of Students in a Group	*Block Entrance Fee Amount [₹]*
Up to 100	200
101–200	300
201 and above	450

Cost of prizes to be awarded to winners in different games being arranged in the park depends upon the strength of students in a trip. Cost of prizes to be distributed is:

Number of Students in a Trip	*Cost of Prizes Amount [₹]*
Upto 50	900
51–125	1,050
126–150	1,200
151–200	1,300
201–250	1,400
251 and above	1,500

To meet the above costs the college collects ₹ 65 from each student who wish to join the trip. The college releases subsidy of ₹ 10 per student in the trip towards it.

You are required to:

(*a*) Prepare a tabulated statement showing total costs at the levels of 60, 120, 180, 240 and 300 students indicating each item of cost.

(*b*) Compute average cost per student at each of the above levels.

(*c*) Calculate the number of students to break even for the trip as the college suffered loss during the previous year despite 72% of the students having joined the trip.

(C.A. Final Adopted)

Solution

Working Notes

1. Computation of the requirement of buses, rent payable, special permit fee and allowance paid to teachers

No. of Students		*60*	*120*	*180*	*240*	*300*
No. of Buses	(A)	2	3	4	5	6
Rent per Bus (₹)	(B)	700	700	700	700	700
Total Rent (₹)	(A×B)	1,400	2,100	2,800	3,500	4,200
Special permit fee [(A) × ₹ 50]		100	150	200	250	300
Allowance paid to teachers [(A) × ₹ 200]		400	600	800	1,000	1,200

2. Contribution Statement

Per Student (₹)

Student's collection	65
Subsidy from college	10
	75
Less: Variable cost	45
Contribution	30

(a) Statement Showing Total Costs at Different Levels of Students

No. of Students	*60*	*120*	*180*	*240*	*300*
Variable Cost:					
Breakfast	420	840	1,260	1,680	2,100
Lunch	1,800	3,600	5,400	7,200	9,000
Tea	180	360	540	720	900
Entrance fee for Zoo and Aquarium	300	600	900	1,200	1,500
Total (A)	2,700	5,400	8,100	10,800	13,500

No. of Students	*60*	*120*	*180*	*240*	*300*
Semivariable Costs:					
Rent of buses	1,400	2,100	2,800	3,500	4,200
Special permit fee	100	150	200	250	300
Allowance to teachers	400	600	800	1,000	1,200
Block entrance fee	200	300	300	450	450
Cost of prizes	1,050	1,050	1,300	1,400	1,500
Total (B)	3,150	4,200	5,400	6,600	7,650
(A) + (B)	5,850	9,600	13,500	17,400	21,150

(b) Computation of Average Cost Per Student at Each of the Above Levels

No. of Students	*60*	*120*	*180*	*240*	*300*
Total Costs (₹)	5,850	9,600	13,500	17,400	21,150
Average Cost per student (₹)	97.50	80	75	72.50	70.50

(c) Statement Computing the Number of Students of Break-even

Amount (₹)

No. of Students in Trip	*51–100*	*101–125*	*126–150*	*151–200*	*201–250*	*251–300*
No. of Buses required	*2*	*3*	*3*	*4*	*5*	*6*
Semi Variable Costs:						
Bus rent	1,400	2,100	2,100	2,800	3,500	4,200
Permit fee	100	150	150	200	250	300
Block entrance fee	200	300	300	300	450	450
Daily allowance to teachers	400	600	600	800	1,000	1,200
Cost of prizes	1,050	1,050	1,200	1,300	1,400	1,500
Total (A)	3,150	4,200	4,350	5,400	6,600	7,650
Contribution per Student (B)	30	30	30	30	30	30
Break-even No. Students (A)/(B)	105	140	145	180	220	255

Analysis

It is not viable to run each trips if students range between 51 to 100 and 101 to 125. In the other trips, the college authorities will meet the cost of trips and also some contribution will remain net of costs.

During the previous year, the college has incurred loss for the following reasons:

No. of Buses hired	5 Buses
No. of Students joining the Trip (72% of 300)	216 Students
Break-even when 5 Buses engaged	220 Students

The number of students in the trip could not even meet the break-even and hence the college had incurred loss.

PROBLEM–4

A food processing firm recently introduced a new product of processed and formed potato chips. Chips are sold in packed cases and a case is considered the basic sales unit. Although management made detailed estimates of cost and volume before it undertook this venture, new projections based on actual cost experience are now needed.

Income statements for the last two quarters are each thought to be representative of the costs and productive efficiency that can be expected in the next few quarters. There were virtually no inventories on hand at the end of either quarter. These income statements reveal the following:

First Quarter	*Amount* [₹]	*Second Quarter*	*Amount* [₹]
Sales (50,000 @ Rs. 24)	12,00,000		16,80,000
Cost of goods sold	7,00,000	(70,000 @ 24)	8,80,000
Gross margin	5,00,000		8,00,000
Selling and Administration	6,50,000		6,90,000
Net income before tax	(–) 1,50,000		1,10,000

Earnings and losses incurred by this product line are, so far, negligible in relation to the firm's overall earnings.

The firm's overall marginal and average income-tax rate is 40% and the same is to be used to estimate the tax liability arising from the potato chips operation.

Required

(*a*) Management would like to know the break-even point in terms of quarterly case sales for the chips.

(*b*) Management estimates that an investment of ₹ 30 lakhs is made in this product line. What quarterly case sales and total revenue are required each quarter to earn an after-tax return of 20% on investment?

(*c*) The firm's marketing people predict that if the selling price is reduced by ₹ 1.50 per case and ₹ 1,50,000 advertising campaign is mounted to call customers, attention to the new reduced price, sales will increase by 20% over second quarter sales, should the plan be implemented?

(I.C.W.A. Final Adopted)

Solution

1. Calculation of Variable Manufacturing Cost per Unit

$$= \frac{₹\,8{,}80{,}000 - ₹\,7{,}00{,}000}{70{,}000 - 50{,}000}$$

$$= \frac{₹\,8{,}80{,}000 - ₹\,7{,}00{,}000}{70{,}000–50{,}000} = \frac{₹\,1{,}80{,}000}{20{,}000 \text{ units}} = ₹\,9 \text{ per unit}$$

2. Calculation of Fixed Manufacturing Cost

Amount [₹]

Cost of goods sold		7,00,000
Less: Variable Mfg. Cost	(50,000 units × ₹ 9)	4,50,000
Fixed Mfg. Cost		2,50,000

3. Calculation of Variable Selling and Administration Cost per Unit

$$= \frac{₹\,6{,}90{,}000 - ₹\,6{,}50{,}000}{70{,}000 - 50{,}000} = \frac{₹\,40{,}000}{20{,}000} = ₹\,2 \text{ per unit}$$

4. Calculation of Fixed Selling and Administration Cost

Amount [₹]

Total Selling and Administration cost	6,50,000
Less: Varia ble Selling and Administration cost (50,000 units × ₹ 2)	1,00,000
Fixed Selling and Administration cost	5,50,000

Cost Structure

Particulars	*Total fixed cost per Quarter*	*Variable cost per unit*
Manufacturing cost	2,50,000	9
Selling and Administration cost	5,50,000	2
Total Cost	8,00,000	11

(*a*) The selling price per unit is ₹ 24

Sales – Variable cost – Fixed cost = Profit

At break-even sales, the profit is zero.

Let 'q' be the quantity

$$₹\,24q - ₹\,11q - ₹\,8{,}00{,}000 = 0$$

$$13q = ₹\,8{,}00{,}000$$

$$q = ₹\,8{,}00{,}000/13 = 61{,}538 \text{ units}$$

(*b*) Profit after tax = ₹ 30,00,000 × 20/100 = ₹ 6,00,000

Profit after tax per quarter = ₹ 6,00,000/4 = ₹ 1,50,000

Profit before tax for the quarter = ₹ 1,50,000 × 100/60 = ₹ 2,50,000

Desired Sales to earn profit of ₹ 2,50,000

$$24q - 11q - 8,00,000 = ₹\ 2,50,000$$
$$13q = 10,50,000$$
$$q = 10,50,000/13 = 80,769 \text{ units}$$
$$\text{Desired sales revenues} = 80,769 \text{ units} \times ₹\ 24 = ₹\ 19,38,456.$$

(c) Calculation net profit after reduction in selling price by ₹ 1.50 per case and increase in advertising cost by ₹ 1,50,000 (Fixed) to increase sales by 20%.

$$\text{Sales} - \text{Variable cost} - \text{Fixed cost} = \text{Profit}$$
$$22.50q - 11q - 9,50,000 = \text{Profit}$$
$$(22.50 \times 84,000) - (11 \times 84,000) - 9,50,000 = \text{Profit}$$
$$18,90,000 - 9,24,000 - 9,50,000 = ₹\ 16,000.$$

PROBLEM – 5

A limited company operates a lodging house with a restaurant, shops and recreational facilities attached. Its manager has entrusted you with the planning of the coming year's operations, more particularly on the level of profits the company was likely to earn.

The lodging house has 100 double-bed rooms, which are likely to be rented at ₹ 150 per day. The manager expects an occupancy ratio of 75% for a period of 250 days during the tourist season. It is also anticipated that both the beds in a room will be occupied during the period.

Each person staying in the lodging house is expected to spend, on the basis of past statistic, ₹ 30 per day in the shops attached to the lodge and ₹ 60 per day in the restaurant. The recreational facilities are not charges to the customer.

Some other relevant data available to you is as under:

(*i*) Variable cost to volume ratio:

Particulars	*Shops*	*Restaurant*
Cost of goods sold	40%	30%
Supplies	5%	15%
Others	5%	10%

(*ii*) For lodging house, the variable costs are ₹ 25 per day per occupied room for cleaning, laundry etc.

(*iii*) Annual fixed costs for the entire complex are ₹ 19,50,000.

From the above, you are required to prepare:

(*a*) An income statement for the coming year and,

(*b*) An analysis to indicate whether the manager's suggestion of reducing the room rent to ₹ 125 per day to enhance the occupancy ratio to 90% should be accepted.

Solution

Estimated Income Statement for the Coming Year

Amount [₹]

		Amount [₹]
Revenue:		
Hotel room rent	(100 rooms × 250 days × ₹ 150 × 75/100)	28,12,500
Receipts from shop	(100 rooms × 2 persons × 250 days × ₹ 30 × 75/100)	11,25,000
Receipts from restaurant	(100 rooms × 2 persons × 250 days × ₹ 60 × 75/100)	22,50,000
	Total (A)	61,87,500
Variable Cost:		
Hotel Rooms	(100 rooms × 250 days × ₹ 25 × 75/100)	4,68,750
Shops	(₹ 11,25,000 × 50/100)	5,62,500
Restaurant	(₹ 22,50,000 × 55/100)	12,37,500
		22,68,750
	Total (A–B)	
Contribution		39,18,750
Less: Fixed cost		19,50,000
Estimated Profit		19,68,750

(*a*) Revised estimated income statement for the coming year if room rent reduced to ₹ 125 per day to enhance occupancy to 90%. *Amount* [₹]

		Amount [₹]
Revenue:		
Hotel room rent	(100 rooms × 250 days × ₹ 125 × 90/100)	28,12,500
Receipts from Shop	(100 rooms × 2 persons × 250 days × ₹ 30 × 90/100)	13,50,000
Receipts from restaurant	(100 rooms × 2 persons × 250 days × ₹ 60 × 90/100)	27,00,000
	Total (A)	68,62,500
Variable Cost:		
Hotel room	(100 rooms × 250 days × ₹ 25 × 90/100)	5,62,500
Shops	(₹ 13,50,000 × 50/100)	6,75,000
Restaurant	(₹ 27,00,000 × 55/100)	14,85,000
		27,22,500
	Total (A–B)	41,40,000
Contribution		19,50,000
Less: Fixed cost		21,90,000
Estimated profit		

(*b*) **Analysis**

With the reduction in room rent from ₹ 150 per day to ₹ 125, the occupancy will increase to 90% which will result in increase of profit by ₹ 2,21,250 (i.e., ₹ 21,90,000 – ₹ 19,68,750).

PROBLEM – 6

ACE Office Supplies Corporation retails two products—a standard and a deluxe version of a designer ball point pen. The budgeted Income Statement is as under:

Sales (in units)		Standard	Deluxe	Total
		1,50,000	50,000	2,00,000
Sales:	@ ₹ 20 per unit	30,00,000	–	45,00,000
	At ₹ 30 per unit	–	15,00,000	
Variable costs:				
	At ₹ 14 per unit	21,00,000	–	
	At ₹ 18 per unit	–	9,00,000	30,00,000
Contribution		9,00,000	6,00,000	15,00,000
Less: Fixed Costs				12,00,000
Profit				3,00,000

Required

(*i*) Calculate the break-even point in units assuming that the planned sales mix is maintained.

(*ii*) Calculate the break-even point in units:

(*a*) If only standard version is sold, and

(*b*) If only deluxe version is sold.

(*c*) Suppose 2,00,000 units are sold, but only 20,000 units are deluxe quality. Calculate the profit. Calculate the break-even point if the relationship persists in the next accounting period. Compare your answer with the original plan and the answer in requirement (*a*) What is your major finding?

Solution

(i) Calculation of break-even point in units assuming that the planned sales mix is maintained.

Contribution per unit:

Standard = ₹ 20 – ₹ 14 = ₹ 6

Deluxe = ₹ 30 – ₹ 18 = ₹ 12

Let the number of budgeted units be

Deluxe = x

Standard = 3x

Break-even point:

Sales – Variable cost = Fixed cost

[(3x × ₹ 20 + x × ₹ 30) – (3x × ₹ 14 + x × ₹ 18)] = ₹ 12,00,000

30x = 12,00,000

x = 12,00,000/30 = 40,000 units

Break-even units of deluxe Ball pen = 40,000 pens

Break-even units of standard Ball pen = 1,20,000 pens

(ii) (a) Break-even point, if only standard version is sold:

= ₹ 12,00,000/₹ 6 = 2,00,000 pens

(b) Break-even point, if only deluxe version is sold:

= ₹ 12,00,000/₹ 12 = 1,00,000 pens

(c) Computation of profit if 1,80,000 units of standard quality are sold and 20,000 units of deluxe quality are sold:

= (1,80,000 × ₹ 6 + 20,000 × ₹ 12) – ₹ 12,00,000

= (₹ 10,80,000 + ₹ 2,40,000) – ₹ 12,00,000 = ₹ 1,20,000

Computation of break-even Point at 1,80,000 Standard Quality and 20,000 Deluxe Quality

Let

Break-even units of Standard quality = 9x

Break-even units of Deluxe quality = x

At break-even point

[(9x × ₹ 20 + x + ₹ 30) – (9x × ₹ 14 + x × ₹ 18)] = ₹ 12,00,000

66x = 12,00,000

x = 18,182 (Deluxe Ball Pens)

9x = 1,63,638 (Standard Ball Pens)

Major Findings on Comparing Budgeted Sales and Original Sales Plan

Sales Mix Ratio of Standard and Deluxe Model	*Units to be sold at break-even*		*Total Units Sold*	*Profit on the Sale of 2,00,000 units*
	Standard	*Deluxe*		
3:1 (as per budgeted sales plan)	1,20,000	40,000	1,60,000	3,00,000
9:1 (as per original sales plan)	1,63,638	18,182	1,81,820	1,20,000

1. The above figures clearly reflect that a change in sales mix changes break-even point and profit as well.
2. Though the total figure of budgeted and original actual sales units were identical, viz 2,00,000 units, but the proportion of the product with higher contribution declined.
3. The profit figure fall from ₹ 3,00,000 to ₹ 1,20,000 and break-even point rose from 1,60,000 units to 1,81,820 units.

PROBLEM–7

Saraju Ltd. produces electronic components with a selling price per unit of ₹ 100. Fixed cost amounts to ₹ 2,00,000. 5000 units are produced and sold each year. Annual profits amount to ₹ 50,000. The Company's equity financial assistance is ₹ 5,00,000.

The Company proposes to change its production process, adding ₹ 4,00,000 to investment and ₹ 50,000 to fixed operational costs. The consequences of such a proposal are:

(*i*) Reduction in variable cost per unit by ₹ 10.

(*ii*) Increase in output by 2000 units.

(*iii*) Reduction to selling price per unit to ₹ 95.

Assuming an average cost of capital 10%, examine the above proposal and advise whether or not the company should make the change. Also, measure the degree of operating leverage and break-even point.

Solution

Calculation of Current variable cost P.U. *Amount* [₹]

Sales	(5,000 units × ₹ 100)		5,00,000
Less: Contribution:			
Profit		50,000	
Fixed cost		2,00,000	2,50,000
Variable cost			2,50,000
Variable cost per unit	(₹ 2,50,000/5,000 units)		₹ 50

Revised profitability statement (Production and sales: 7,000 units) *Amount* [₹]

Sales	(7,000 units × ₹ 95)	6,65,000
Less: Variable cost	(7,000 units × ₹ 40)	2,80,000
Contribution		3,85,000
Less: Fixed cost	(₹ 2,00,000 + ₹ 50,000)	2,50,000
Revised Profit		1,35,000

Incremental profit = ₹ 1,35,000 – ₹ 50,000

= ₹ 85,000

New investment = ₹ 4,00,000

Incremental return on new investment

$$= \frac{₹\ 85,000}{₹\ 4,00,000} \times 100 = 21.25\%$$

Suggestion – The average cost of capital of the company is 10% and the incremental return of new investment is 21.25%. Hence, it is suggested that new investment be made.

Degree of Operating Leverage

$$= \frac{\text{Contribution}}{\text{EBIT}}$$

$$= \frac{\text{Contribution}}{\text{Contribution} - \text{Fixed Cost}}$$

$$\text{Current} = \frac{₹\,2{,}50{,}000}{₹\,2{,}50{,}000 \times ₹\,2{,}00{,}000} = 5$$

$$\text{Revised} = \frac{₹\,3{,}85{,}000}{₹\,3{,}85{,}000 \times ₹\,2{,}50{,}000} = 2.85$$

Break-even Point

$$= \frac{\text{Fixed cost}}{\text{Contribution per unit}}$$

$$\text{Current} = \frac{₹\,2{,}00{,}000}{₹\,20} = 40{,}000 \text{ units}$$

B.E.P. in ₹ = 4000 units × ₹ 100 = ₹ 4,00,000

$$\text{Revised} = \frac{₹\,2{,}50{,}000}{₹\,55} = ₹\,4545 \text{ units}$$

B.E.P. in ₹ = 4545 units × ₹ 95 = ₹ 4,31,775

PROBLEM – 8

ABC Co. fixes the inter-division transfer prices for its product on the basis of cost plus a return on investment in the division. The budget for the division A for 2013-16 is as under:

	Amount [₹]
Fixed assets	2,50,000
Current assets	1,50,000
Debtors	1,00,000
Annual fixed cost of the division	4,00,000
Variable cost per unit of the product	10

Budgeted Volume –2,00,000 Units per year

Desired ROI – 28%

Determine the transfer price for Division 'A'.

If the volume (in units) can be increased by 10%, what will be the impact on transfer price?

Solution

Calculation of desired Return of Investment *Amount* [₹]

Fixed assets	2,50,000
Current assets	1,50,000
Stock	1,00,000
Total investment in business	5,00,000
Desired return (₹ 5,00,000 × 28/100)	1,40,000

Calculation of Transfer Price *Amount* [₹]

Variable cost (2,00,000 units × ₹ 10)	20,00,000
Fixed cost of Division A p.a	4,00,000
Total cost	24,00,000
Add: Desired return	1,40,000
Total amount to be charged	25,40,000
Inter-divisional transfer price P.U. (₹ 25,40,000/2,00,000 units)	12.70

Impact on transfer price if the volume is increased by 10% *Amount* [₹]

Variable cost (2,20,000 units × ₹ 10)	22,00,000
Fixed cost	4,00,000
Total cost	26,00,000
Add: Desired return on investment	1,40,000
Total amount to be charged	27,40,000

Inter-divisional Transfer Price

= ₹ 27,40,000/2,20,000 units = ₹ 12.45 P.U.

Due to increase in sales volume, the transfer price will be reduced by ₹ 0.25 (i.e., ₹ 12.70 – ₹ 12.45) per unit.

PROBLEM–9

Satish Enterprises are the leading exporters of Kid's Toys, J. Ltd. of U.S.A. have approached Satish Enterprises for exporting a special toy named "Jumping Monkey". The order for 3,000 toys per month will be valid for next three years.

The export price of the toy will be $4.

Cost data per toy is as follows:

Amount [₹]

Materials	60
Labour	25
Variable overheads	20
Primary packing of the toy	15

The toys will be packed in lots of 50 each. For this purpose a special box, containing 50 toys, will have to be purchased, cost being ₹ 400 per box.

Satish Enterprises will also have to import a special machine for making toys. The cost of the machine is ₹ 24,00,000 and duty thereon will be 12%. The machine will have an effective life of three years and depreciation is to be charged on straight-line method. Apart from depreciation, annual fixed overheads is estimated at ₹ 4,00,000 for the first year with 6% increase in the second year. Fixed overheads are incurred uniformly over the year.

Assuming the average conversion rate to be ₹ 50 per $, you are required to

(*i*) Prepare a monthly and yearly profitability statements for the first year and second year assuming the production at 3,000 toys per month.

(*ii*) Compute monthly and yearly break-even units in respect of the first year.

(*iii*) In what contingency can there be a second break-even point for the month and for the year as a whole?

(*iv*) Do you have any comment to offer on the above?

Solution

Profit Statement of M/s. Satish Enterprises for the first and the second year on monthly and yearly basis

(*₹'in thousand)*

Particulars	*First year*		*Second year*	
	Monthly ₹	*Yearly* ₹	*Monthly* ₹	*Yearly* ₹
Sales revenue: (A)	600 (3,000 units × ₹ 200)	7,200	600	7,200
Material cost	180 (3,000 units × ₹ 60)	2,160	180	2,160
Labour cost	75 (3,000 units × ₹ 25)	900	75	900
Variable overheads	60 (3,000 units × ₹ 20)	720	60	720
Primary packing cost	45 (3,000 units × ₹ 15)	540	45	540
Boxes cost	24 $\frac{3,000 \text{ units}}{50 \text{ units}}$ × ₹ 400	288	24	288
Total fixed overhead (Refer to working note *i*)	108 $\frac{₹ 1,296}{12 \text{ months}}$	1,296	110 $\frac{₹ 1,320}{12 \text{ months}}$	1,320
Total cost: (B)	492	5,904	494	5,928
Profit: C = (A) – (B)	108	1,296	106	1,272

Working Note:

(i) Fixed Overhead:

Particulars	*First year: (₹)*	*Second year: (₹)*
Depreciation ₹ 24,00,000 + 2,88,000 duty 3 years	8,96,000	8,96,000
Other fixed overheads	4,00,000	4,24,000
Total fixed overheads	12,96,000	13,20,000

(*ii*) Statement of monthly break-even units of the first year

Levels–No. of units (Refer to working note)	*1351–1400* (₹)	*1401–1450* (₹)	*1451–1500* (₹)	*1501–1550* (₹)
Fixed costs: Total fixed overheads per month (A)	1,08,000	1,08,000	1,08,000	1,08,000
Semi-variable costs (Special boxes cost) (B)	11,200 (28 boxes × ₹ 400)	11,600 (29 boxes × ₹ 400)	12,000 (30 boxes × ₹ 400)	12,400 (31 boxes × ₹ 400)
Total fixed and semi-variable costs (A+B)	1,19,200	1,19,600	1,20,000	1,20,400
Break-even level of units	1490	1495	1500	1505
Total fixed and semi-variable costs Contribution per unit	₹ 1,19,200 ₹ 80	₹ 1,19,600 ₹ 80	₹ 1,20,000 ₹ 80	₹ 1,20,400 ₹ 80

The first and second break-even of units, viz., 1490 and 1495 units, fall outside the range of 1351–1400 and 1401–1450 units respectively. Here is a monthly break-even level of units, which lies in the range 1451–1500 units.

Statement of Yearly Break-even Points of the First year

Levels-No. of Units	*17851-17900* (₹)	*17901-17950* (₹)	*17951-18000* (₹)	*18001-18050* (₹)
Fixed costs (A)	12,96,000	12,96,000	12,96,000	12,96,000
Semi-variable costs (Cost of special boxes) (B)	1,43,200 (358 boxes × ₹ 400)	1,43,600 (359 boxes × ₹ 400)	1,44,000 (360 boxes × ₹ 400)	1,44,400 (361 boxes × ₹ 400)
Total fixed and semi-variable costs (A + B)	14,39,200	14,39,600	14,40,000	14,40,400
Break-even level units	17,990 ₹ 14,39,200 ₹ 80	17,995 ₹ 14,39,600 ₹ 80	18,000 ₹ 14,40,000 ₹ 80	18,005 ₹ 14,40,400 ₹ 80

Here a break-even level of units (on yearly basis) is 18,000 units, which lies in the range of 17,951–18,000 units as well. The other first two figures do not lie in the respective ranges, so they are rejected.

Working Note: 1

Amount [₹]

Fixed overhead in the first year	12,96,000
Fixed overhead per month	1,08,000
Contribution per unit (S.P. per unit–V.C. per unit) (₹ 200 – ₹ 120)	80

Hence, the break-even number of units will be above 1,350 units

$$= \frac{₹\,1,08,000}{₹\,80}$$

(*iii*) If the number of toys goes beyond the level of 1,500 numbers, one more box will be required to accommodate each 50 additional units of toys. In that case the additional cost of a box will be ₹ 400. This amount can be recovered by the additional contribution of five toys. Hence, the second Break-even Point in such a contingency is 1,505 toys.

If the number of toys goes beyond the level of 18,000 one more box will be required. The additional cost of this box will be ₹ 400; which can be recovered by the additional contribution of five toys. Hence, the second Break-even Point is 18,005 toys.

(*iv*) **Comments:** Yearly Break-even Point of 18,000 units of toys in the first instance is equal to 12 times the monthly Break-even Point of 1500 units, because the monthly and yearly figures of Break-even Point fell on the upper limit of the respective ranges.

In the second instance, it is not so because the monthly and yearly Break-even Point fell within the range of 50 toys.

PROBLEM – 10

Veejay Ltd., makes and sells two products, Vee and Jay. The budgeted selling price of Vee is ₹ 1,800 and that of Jay is ₹ 2,160. Variable costs associated with production and sale of Vee is ₹ 900 and that of Jay ₹ 1,800. Annual fixed production and selling cost of Veejay Ltd. are ₹ 88,000.

The company has two production/sales options. The Vee and Jay can be sold either in the ratio of two Vees to three Jays or in the ratio of one Vee to two Jays.

What will be the optimal mix and why?

(C.A. Final Adopted)

Solution

Selection of Best Optimal Mix

Amount [₹]

Particulars	*Products*	
	Vee	Jay
Budgeted Selling Price p.u.	1800	2,160
Less: Variable Cost p.u.	900	1,800
Contribution p.u	900	360

(I) Production/Sales option (2 units of Vee and 3 units of Jays) Total contribution under 1st option

= (2 units × ₹ 900 + 3 units × ₹ 360)
= ₹ 1,800 + ₹ 1,080 = ₹ 2,880

$$\text{Break-even Point} = \frac{\text{Annual Fixed Production and Selling Cost}}{\text{Total Contribution under 1st option}}$$

$$= \frac{₹\ 88{,}000}{₹\ 2{,}880} = 30.56 \text{ (sets of 5 units each)}$$

Particulars	*Products*		*Total*
	Vee	*Jay*	
Break-even point (units)	30.56 × 2 units = 61 units	30.56 × 3 units = 92 units	
Break-even sales (₹)	1,09,800 (61 units × ₹ 1,800)	1,98,720 (92 units × ₹ 2,160)	3,08,520

(II) Production/Sales Option : (1 unit of Vee and 2 units of Jays)

Total Contribution under IInd option
= (1 unit × ₹ 900 × + 2 units × ₹ 360) = ₹ 900 + ₹ 720 = ₹ 1,620

$$\text{Break-even Point} = \frac{₹\ 88{,}000}{₹\ 1{,}620} = 54.32 \text{ (sets of 3 units each)}$$

Particulars	*Products*		*Total*
	Vee	*Jay*	
Break-even Point (units)	54.32 × 1 unit = 54 units	54.32 × 2 units = 109 units	
Break-even Sales (₹)	97,200 (54 units × ₹ 1,800)	2,35,440 (109 units × ₹ 2,160)	3,32,640

Note: The given amount of annual fixed production and selling cost is such that it fails to determine the exact figure of Break-even Point under two given sales options. The approximations made in the above solution under Option I, at break-even sales level recovers ₹ 20; whereas under Option II of the solution, there is an under, recovery of fixed cost to the extent of ₹ 160.

Decision and Reasoning: Option I is preferred over Option II, as it results in a lower level of sales to reach Break-even, because of higher average contribution per unit sold. The average contribution per unit (under Option I) is ₹ 576 (₹ 2,880/5 units) and (under Option II) it is ₹ 540 (₹ 1,620/3 units). Option I contains a higher percentage (40% as against 33 1/3%) of more profitable products.

REVIEW QUESTIONS

1. What is CVP Analysis?
2. Explain the importance of CVP analysis.
3. How are costs classified in CVP analysis?
4. State the basic assumptions of Break-even Analysis.

5. What is Break-even Point? How is it ascertained?
6. Explain the meaning and uses of P/V Ratio.
7. Define the concepts: 'Margin of Safety' and 'Angle of Incidence'.
8. What is a break-even Chart? How it is constructed?
9. Illustrate a Profit Volume Graph.
10. Discuss the practical utility of Break-even Analysis.
11. Enumerate the limitations of Break-even Analysis.
12. What is Marginal Costing? What are its uses?
13. Differentiate Marginal Costing and absorption costing?

REVIEW PROBLEMS

1. From the following data, find out the Break-even Point, P/V Ratio, and Margin of Safety Ratio:

Fixed costs	₹ 60,000
Variable costs	1,20,000
Net Profit	20,000
Sales	2,00,000

[**Ans.** P/V Ratio – 40%; BEP – ₹ 1,50,000; MS Ratio – 25%]

2. Two businesses A Ltd., and B Ltd., sell the same type of product in the same market. Their budgeted Profit and Loss Account for the year ending 30th June 2018 is as follows:

		A Ltd. Amount [₹]		*B Ltd.* Amount [₹]
Sales		3,00,000		3,00,000
Less: Variable Cost	₹ 2,40,000		₹ 2,00,000	
Fixed Cost	30,000	2,70,000	70,000	2,70,000
Net Budgeted Profit		30,000		30,000

You are required to (*a*) calculate the Break-even Points of each business, and (*b*) state which business is likely to earn greater profits in conditions of (*i*) heavy demand for the product; (*ii*) low demand for the product.

[**Ans.** (*a*) A Ltd., – ₹ 1,50,000; B Ltd., – ₹ 2,10,000, (*b*) (*i*) B Ltd., (*ii*) A Ltd.]

3. The projected capacity of a plant, when sold, would return ₹ 70,000 in sales income to the company. The variable costs for this production volume were determined to be ₹ 30,000. The fixed costs are ₹ 20,000. Determine the following:

(*a*) The Break-even Point of the business,
(*b*) The profit or loss to the business on sales of ₹ 49,000 and ₹ 28,000,
(*c*) The amount of sales that will enable the business to earn a net profit of ₹ 26,000.

[**Ans.** (*a*) ₹ 35,000; (*b*) Profit ₹ 8,000, Loss ₹ 4,000; (*c*) ₹ 80,500]

4. The sales turnover and profit during the two periods were as follows:

Period	Sales (₹)	Profit (₹)
I	60,000	6,000
II	90,000	12,000

What would be the trading results with sales of ₹ 54,000? What amount of sales will yield a profit of ₹ 15,000?

[**Ans.** P/V Ratio – 20%; Profit – ₹ 4,800; Sales – ₹ 1,05,000]

5. Rajesh Ltd. decides to effect a 10% reduction in the price of its product, because it is through such a step that it would increase sales volume. It is expected that there are no prospects of a change in total fixed cost and variable cost per unit. Directors of the company would like to maintain the net profit at present level. The following information has been obtained from its books:

Sales: 20,000 units	₹ 2,00,000
Variable Costs	₹ 7.50 per unit
Fixed Costs	₹ 40,000

How would management proceed to implement this decision?

[**Ans.** Profit – ₹ 10,000; Units to be sold 33,334; If management wants to reduce the selling price by 10%, it must be able to increase the sales volume by 13,334 units.]

6. R Ltd. is a large retailer in equipment. The company's Profit and Loss Account for the year ended 31st March 2018 is as follows:

	Amount [₹]	*Amount* [₹]
Sales		24,00,000
Less: Cost of Sales		15,00,000
Gross Margin		9,00,000
Less: Operating Expenses:		
Selling Expenses	3,00,000	
Administration Expenses	1,50,000	4,50,000
Net Profit		4,50,000

The selling expenses are 90% variable and administration expenses are 80% fixed. You are required to rewrite the Profit and Loss Account in the contribution format and also calculate the Break-even Sales.

[**Ans.** P/V Ratio – 25%; BEP – ₹ 6,00,000]

7. A Ltd. sold in two successive years 21,000 units and 27,000 units and incurred a loss of ₹ 30,000 and earned a profit of ₹ 30,000 each respectively. The selling price per unit is ₹ 100. **Calculate:** (*a*) the amount of fixed cost, (*b*) the number of units to break-even, and (*c*) the number of units to earn a profit of ₹ 1,20,000.

[**Ans.** P/V Ratio – 10%; (a) ₹ 2,40,000, (b) 24,000, (c) 36,000]

8. From the following data, calculate Break-even Point:

Budgeted Output	70,000 units
Fixed Cost	₹ 4,00,000
Variable Cost per unit	₹ 12.00
Selling Price per unit	₹ 22.00

If the selling price is reduced to ₹ 20 per unit, what will be the revised Break-even Point?

[**Ans.** BEP – ₹ 8,80,000 or 40,000 units; Revised BEP – ₹ 10,00,000 or 50,000 units]

9. Any change in fixed costs, variable costs or selling price has the effect of shifting the Break-even point although the impact of each such change on the BEP and profit is different. Illustrate this with the help of the figures given below assuming a 10% increase individually in each of the three elements stated. Also, show how the profit figure is affected if all the elements increase collectively, each by 10%.

Sales		₹ 1,20,000
Variable Cost	₹ 40,000	
Fixed Cost	₹ 50,000	90,000
Profit		30,000

[**Ans.** Refer Illustration 5]

■■■

12

Standard Costing and Variance Analysis

STANDARD COSTING

The word 'standard' means a bench-mark or yardstick. Standard cost is a predetermined or expected cost which determines what each product or service should cost under given conditions. In other words, it is the expected cost of producing one unit. It is, in effect, a budget for one unit. Standard costing may be defined basically as a technique of cost accounting which compares the standard cost of each product or service with the actual cost to determine the efficiency of operation so that remedial action may be taken immediately. The Institute of Cost and Management Accountants, England, defines standard costing as "the preparation and use of standard costs, their comparison with the actual costs, and the analysis of variances to their causes and points of incidence". Variance is the difference between a budgeted or standard amount and the actual amount during a given period.

The following steps are thus involved in standard costing:

(*i*) Preparation and use of standard;

(*ii*) Comparison of actual costs with standards to determine the variances; and

(*iii*) Investigating the variance and taking appropriate action, where necessary.

BUDGETARY CONTROL vs. STANDARD COSTING

Budgetary control and standard costing are comparable systems of cost accounting in that they are both predetermined or forward-looking. The common objective is of controlling business operations by establishing predetermined targets. The *modus operandi* is also the same for Systems where the actual performance is compared with the predetermined targets (standards or budgets) in order to ascertain variances. The cause of such a variances is investigated and appropriate action taken where necessary. However, there are a few distinctions between these two systems which are given below:

BUDGETARY CONTROL SYSTEM

1. Budgetary control is related to all types of items of revenue and expenditure, whether they belong to the product or not, i.e. to all types of business activities. Hence, it is more extensive.
2. Budget is based on past experience and, in most cases, a projection of financial accounts.
3. Budgets are comparatively less rigid and 'should be' estimates. They fix limits.
4. Budgetary control can be operated without a standard costing system. It can also be adopted in part.
5. The study of variances is not the subject of special study as in the case of standard costing.

STANDARD COSTING SYSTEM

1. Standard Costing is related to production and production costs. Hence, it is more rigorous and intensive.
2. Standard is established on the basis of technical estimates. It is the 'projection' of accounts.
3. Standards are very rigid and 'ought to be' estimates. They fix targets.
4. Standard costing system cannot operate well without a budgetary control system. Also, it is not possible to operate the system in parts.
5. Variance analysis is a subject of special study of standard costing.

STANDARD COSTING vs. ESTIMATED COSTING

Standard costing differs from estimated costing in the manner of predetermining the cost of production. Standard costs are based on carefully and scientifically established cost figures of a product. But, estimated costs represent merely figures based on an average of past experience, or mere expression of opinion as to what the production cost will be. While the estimated cost can be used in any business, which is using the traditional costing system, standard cost can be applied only in a business operating under the standard costing system.

ADVANTAGE OF STANDARD COSTING

1. Weakness of the traditional costing system can be estimated by compiling standard costs more carefully.
2. Standard costs can be used as yardstick against which actual costs can be compared. It is an effective tool for planning production costs. Hence, cost control is greatly facilitated.
3. Variance analysis helps management to have regular as well as better checks over costs incurred. It marks the application of the principle of management by exception more easy. The management can concentrate its attention on variances only, leaving the other aspects of cost control to be taken care of at the later level.

4. It is a valuable guide to management and price policies in advance with the areas of profit, planning and product.
5. Standard costing makes reporting of operating data more meaningful and also fast. This makes the interpretation of management reports easy.
6. With an emphasis on standard, it makes the entire organization cost conscious. It makes, the importance of efficiency reduced to joint efforts.
7. Men, materials and machines can be effected in addition to increased use as the basis for introducing incentive schemes.

Limitations of Standard Costing

1. Setting of standards is a very tough part of studies. Small firms may find it very difficult to reach the standard costing of a product.
2. Standards are very rigid estimates for a considerable time. This makes industries which face fluctuation and changes in material and labour costs in any case the revision costs would effect the sales of a company's product.
3. The utility of variance analysis, is set. While a loosely set, standard set, very high it may create frustration, some time setting of correct standard is also very difficult.
4. It is not suitable for industries producing not-standardised products. It is of little value in job or contract system when production takes more than one accounting period.

ESTABLISHING A STANDARD COSTING SYSTEM

The procedure for establishing a standard costing system is as follows:

1. Establishment of Cost Centres

A cost centre is a location, person or item of equipment (or a group of these) for which costs may be ascertained and used for the purposes of cost control. The cost centre may be classified into a 'personal cost centre' which relates to persons, or an 'impersonal cost centre' which relates to equipment or location. Cost centres are set up for cost ascertainment and cost control. In many cases the department or functions will form the natural cost centres, but it may happen that there are a number of cost centres in a department. For example, if there are five machine groups in a production department, each group may be taken as a cost centre. Cost centres are essential for establishing standards and analysing the variances.

2. Classification of Accounts

The accounts are classified for the purpose of collection and analysis. Codes and symbols are used to facilitate this purpose. For example, the code for elements of cost may be as follows:

Direct materials	001—010
Direct labour	011—020
Indirect material	021—030
Indirect labour	031—040 and so on.

3. Determination of Type of Standard

The standard is the level of attainment accepted by the management as the basis upon which standard cost are determined. The standards are classified mainly into four types. These types are:

Ideal standard. This is one which is set up under ideal conditions. The ideal conditions may be such as maximum output and sales, best possible prices for materials and most satisfactory rates for labour and overhead costs. As these conditions do not continue to remain ideal, this standard is of little practical value. It also calls efficiency of a high order in the task of working out of the standard.

Expected standard. This is the level which is actually expected. Standards set are normally on a short-term basis and frequent revisions may be necessary. This standard is more realistic than the ideal standard.

Normal standard. This represents an average figure which it is hoped will smooth out fluctuations caused by seasonal and cyclical changes. This should be attainable and it provides a challenge to the staff.

Basic standard. This is the level fixed in relation to a base year. The principle used in setting the basic standard is similar to that used in statistics when calculating an index number. Thus, if 2015 is the base year and the standard wage rate then is ₹ 5 per hour, and in 2020 the rate is ₹ 6 per hour, the basic standard must be adjusted by 20%. This standard is set on a long-term basis and is seldom revised.

ORGANISATION FOR STANDARD COSTING

The success of the standard costing system depends upon the reliability of standards. Hence the responsibility for setting standards should be entrusted to a specific person or a committee. The persons involved in the setting of the standards in a large concern are as follows:

(*a*) *Purchase Manager.* He will give details of prices of materials and the trend of market prices.

(*b*) *Personnel Manager.* He will give details of wage rates and possible future changes in rates.

(*c*) *Production Manager.* He will give details of production requirements in terms of materials, labour and overheads.

(*d*) *Time and Study Engineer.* He will give details of standards time for the different operations in the production process.

(*e*) *Cost Accountant.* He will furnish all necessary cost data such as overheads absorption rates. He will also coordinate the activities of the committee. His duty is to present standard in the most satisfactory manner.

(*f*) *Setting of standards.* Details of the element of cost must be ascertained. In many cases costs will be established as shown below.

Direct Material

Quantity. Material specifications' quantity of each type of material required. Normal loss in process must also be estimated before the standard cost can be ascertained.

Price. A standard price will be calculated for each type of material.

Direct Labour

Time. Standard time, based on the best way of performing will be computed for each grade of labour for each operation involved.

Rate. The standard rate for the job will be determined.

Variable Overhead

This is defined by the I.C.M.A. with "the volume of output". It is constant, irrespective of the quantity produced, so it is necessary to calculate only a standard cost per unit or per hour.

Fixed Overhead

This is defined by I.C.M.A. as "a cost which tends to be unaffected by variations in volume of output".

Expenditure. The budgeted expenditure for the period will be ascertained.

Volume. The budgeted output in units or standard hours will be used to calculate the overhead recovery rate.

The Standard Hour

In a system of standard costing, the introduction of standard hours can be very valuable. The I.C.M.A. defines a standard hour as "a hypothetical hour which represents the amount of work which should be performed in one hour under standard conditions". Time and motion study engineers can calculate what the output of each process in one hour should be. For example, if 20 units of A should be produced in one hour, then an output of 100 units would represent five standard hours.

VARIANCE ANALYSIS

The main advantage of the standard costing system is variance analysis. The principle of 'management by exception' is practised easily with the help of variances. Variance may be defined as the difference between standard and actual for each element of cost and sometimes for sales. And 'variance analysis' may be defined as the process of analysing variance by subdividing the total variance in such a way that management can assign responsibility for off-standard performance. When the actual results are better than expected, a 'favourable' variance arises; where they are not up to the standard, an 'adverse variance' occurs.

Variances help to fix the responsibilities so that management can ascertain the person responsible for the poor results. For example, an adverse material usage variance would indicate that excess material cost was due to inefficient use of materials. This would enable management to fix the responsibility on the supervisor in charge of a particular operation in which the inefficiency occurred. It may be discovered that the variance was caused by (say) inefficient handling, purchase of poor quality materials or employment of trainees. The important point is that the reason for the variance must be found, explained and wherever necessary, corrective measures taken.

CLASSIFICATION OF VARIANCES

Different variances are used in different industries. However, only variances which are commonly used are listed here and explained in the following pages:

1. Direct material variances
2. Direct labour variances
3. Variable overhead variance
4. Fixed overhead variance:
   (*i*) Based on units
   (*ii*) Based on standard hours
5. Sales variance: (*i*) Based on value (*ii*) Based on profit. Basically, there are only two types of variances: (*a*) Price variance and (*b*) Volume variance. Price variance refers to prices of materials, labour rates, expenditure on overheads or selling prices of products. Volume variances refers to quantity of units in terms of raw materials consumed, number of hours worked, utilisation of plant and number of units sold. The total of price variance and volume variance for each element of cost is known as the Cost Variance, and the same for sales is known as the Value Variance. Thus, the basic variances may be listed as follows:
   1. Direct material cost variance:
      (*a*) Material price variance
      (*b*) Material usage variance
   2. Direct labour cost variance:
      (*a*) Labour rate variance
      (*b*) Labour efficiency variance
   3. Variable overhead cost variance:
      (*a*) Variable overhead expenditure variance
      (*b*) Variable overhead efficiency variance
   4. Fixed overhead cost variance:
      (*a*) Fixed overhead expenditure variance
      (*b*) Fixed overhead volume variance
   5. Sales value variance:
      (*a*) Sales price variance
      (*b*) Sales volume variance

It may be noted that in most cases the variable cost variance is represented by only one variance, viz., the Expenditure Variance. This is because the variance that may arise due to inefficiency is so small per unit of output that it may be generally ignored.

Advanced Variances

Basic variances, though useful, do not meet all the needs of the management. Further, they are useful only when one type of material is used in die manufacture of a product. When more than one type of materials are used, the simple basic variances may not serve the required purposes fully. Particularly, die volume variance is not enough to know that die volume has changed since the important point to know is the cause of change. From this point of view, the basic variances analysis may be extended further and the list of advanced variances may be shown as follows:

Basic variances	Advanced variances
1. Material cost variances:	
(*a*) Material price variance	Revised usage variance
(*b*) Material usage variance	Yield variance
	Mix variance
2. Labour cost variance:	Revised efficiency variance
(*a*) Labour rate variance	or Idle time variance
(*b*) Labour efficiency variance	Mix variance
3. Variable overhead cost variance	
Variable overhead expenditure variance	
Variable overhead efficiency variance	
4. Fixed overheads cost variance	
(*a*) Fixed overheads expenditure variance	Efficiency variance
(*b*) Fixed overheads volume variance	Capacity variance
	Calendar variance
5. Sales value variance:	
Based on value	
(*a*) Sales value price variance	Mix variance
(*b*) Sales value volume variance	Quantity variance
Based on margin	
(*a*) Sales margin price variance	Mix variance
(*b*) Sales margin volume variance	Quantity variance

An adverse variance will be denoted by the symbol 'A' and a favourable variance by 'F'.

Material Cost Variance (MCV)

Material cost variance is the difference between the standard cost of materials specified for the actual output achieved, and the actual cost of material consumed.

MCV = Standard cost – Actual cost

Standard cost = Standard price per unit × Standard quantity used for actual output achieved

Actual cost = Actual price × Actual quantity used

Material price variance (MPV) represents the difference between the actual price and standard price of materials consumed. It is calculated as follows:

MPV = AQ (SP – AP) AQ = Actual Quantity
SP = Standard Price
AP = Actual Price

The cause for MPV may be a combination of factors such as changes in prices, uneconomical size of purchase orders, poor purchasing procedures, excessive freight charges and failure to avail of discounts allowed, etc. For example, the adverse material price variance may show that unfavourable prices were paid for materials consumed during the period. The buyer would be asked to explain the position.

Material usage variance (MUV) represents the difference between the actual quantity consumed and the standard quantity which should have been consumed for actual achieved, expressed in terms of money.

MUV = Standard price (Standard quantity–Actual quantity) or SP (SQ – AQ)

This variance will be considered favourable when the standard quantity is more than actual quantity and vice versa. The supervisor would be asked to explain this variance.

Example 1

It is estimated that a product requires 100 kgs of material at the rate of ₹ 5 per kg. The actual consumption of material for manufacturing, the same product came to 120 kgs at the rate of Rs 4.75 per kg. Calculate material cost variances.

Solution

	Standard	*Actual*
Price	₹ 5/- kg	₹ 4.75/- kg
Quantity	100 kgs	120 kgs

MCV = (SQ × SP) – (AQ × AP)
= (100 × ₹ 5) – (120 × ₹ 4.75)
= ₹ 500 – ₹ 570 = ₹ 70 (A)

(Adverse variance, since the actual cost is more than the standard cost)

MPV = AQ (SP – AP)
= 120 (₹ 5 – ₹ 4.75)
= 120 (₹ 0.25) = ₹ 30 (F)

(Favourable, since the actual price is less than the standard price)

MUV = SP (SQ – AQ)

= ₹ 5 (100 – 120)

= ₹ 100 (A)

(Adverse, since the actual quantity consumed is more than the standard quantity established)

Check

MCV = MPV + MUV

₹ 70 (A) = ₹ 30 (F) + ₹ 100 (A)

Example 2

From the following particulars, calculate

(*a*) Material price variance

(*b*) Material usage variance

(*c*) Material cost variance

Materials purchased: 3,000 kgs at ₹ 3 per kg

Standard quantity of material–fixed for one unit of finished

Product: 25 kgs at ₹ 2 per kg

Opening stock of material: nil

Closing stock of material: 500 kgs

Actual output during the period: 80 units

Solution

Material cost variance = Standard cost of actual output—Actual cost

MCV = (SQ × SP) – (AQ × AP)

= (2000 × ₹ 2 – 2500 × ₹ 3)

= ₹ 4,000 – ₹ 7,500 = ₹ 3,500 (A)

SQ = Actual output in units × Standard quantity of materials per unit

= 80 × 25 = 2000 kgs

Material price variance = AQ (SP – AP)

= ₹ 2,500 (2 – 3) = ₹ 2,500 (A)

Material usage variance = SP (SQ – AQ)

= ₹ 2 (2,000 – 2,500) = ₹ 1,000 (A)

Material cost variance = ₹ 3,500 (A)

Check

MCV = MPV + MUV

Advanced Variances

When more than one type of material is used, the total usage variance will be classified into material mix variance, material revised usage variance or yield variance.

Material Mix Variance (MMV): It is that portion of total usage variance which is due to the difference between the standard mix or proportion of materials, and actual mix or proportion of materials.

Material mix variance is calculated as follows:

MMV = SP (Revised standard quantity–Actual quantity)

$$\text{RSQ} = \frac{\text{SQ for each material}}{\text{Total SQ}} \times \text{Total AQ}$$

or Total AQ × (Standard Mix Ratio)

If the AQ is more than RSQ, an Adverse variance will occur and vice versa.

Material Revised Usage Variance (MRUV):

This is that portion of total usage variance which is due to the difference between the total standard quantity for actual output and total actual quantity. Both the standard and actual quantities will be compared at standard proportion.

MRUV = SP (SQ – RSQ)

SQ refers to the total standard quantity of materials for actual output at standard proportion. If the RSQ is greater than SQ, then the variance would be termed as 'Adverse', and vice versa.

Material Yield Variance (MYV):

While the other variances are calculated on the basis of input, MYV is calculated on the basis of output. It represents that portion of total usage variance which is due to the difference between the standard output and the actual output. If the actual output is greater than the standard output, then variance would be favourable, and vice versa. The MYV may be caused by such factors as defective method of operation, sub-standard quantity of materials purchased, lack of due care in handling, and lack of proper supervision, etc.

MYV = SC per unit of output × (SY – AY)

Where several types of materials are used, MRUV and MYV imply the same thing, though they are computed using different formulae. The numerical results would work out to the same figure.

Example 3

From the following information, calculate material cost variances:

	Standard kg
Material X	100 at ₹ 3 per kg
Material Y	80 at ₹ 4 per kg
Material Z	60 at ₹ 5 per kg
	240
	Actual kg
Material X	120 at ₹ 3.25 per kg
Material Y	70 at ₹ 4.50 per kg
Material Z	50 at ₹ 6.00 per kg
	240

Solution

Material cost variance = (SQ × SP) – (AQ × AP)

Material X = (100 × 3) – (120 × 3.25)
= 300 – 390 = 90 (A)

Material Y = (80 × 4) – (70 × 4.50)
= 320 – 315 = 5(F)

Material Z = (60 × 5) – (50 × 6)
= 300 – 300

Total material cost variance = 85 (A)

Material price variance = AQ (SP – AP)

Material X = 120 (3 – 3.25) = ₹ 30 (A)

Material Y = 70 (4 – 4.50) = ₹ 35 (A)

Material Z = 50 (5 – 6) = ₹ 50 (A)

Total ₹ 115 (A)

Material usage variance = SP (SQ – AQ)

Material X = 3 (100 – 120) = 60 (A)

Material Y = 4 (80 – 70) = 40 (F)

Material Z = 5 (60 – 50) = 50 (F)

Total 30 (F)

MCV = MPV + MUV

MCV = ₹ 115 (A) + ₹ 30 (F) = 85 (A)

Material mix variance = SP (RSQ – AQ)

Material X	= 3 (100 – 120)	= 60 (A)
Material Y	= 4 (80 – 70)	= 40 (F)
Material Z	= 5 (60 – 50)	= 50 (F)
		Total 30 (F)

RSQ = Total AQ × Standard Ratio

Material	= 240 × (5 : 4 : 3)
X	= 240 × 5/12 = 100
Y	= 240 × 4/12 = 80
Z	= 240 × 3/12 = 60

Note: As the total actual quantity used is the same as the total standard quantity established, there is no material revised usage variance. Also the number of units of output is not given. Hence, there is no yield variance.

Example 4

From the following data, calculate material cost variances:

Standard Mix	Actual Mix
Material X : 60 kgs at ₹ 20	72 kgs at ₹ 20
Material Y : 40 kgs at ₹ 10	31 kgs at ₹ 11
100	103

Solution

MCV = (SQ × SP) – (AQ × AP)

Standard cost – Actual cost	
	72 × 20 = 1,440
Material X = (60 × 20) = 1,200	31 × 11 = 341
Material Y = (40 × 10) = 400	
1600	1,781

MCV = 1,600 – 1,781 = ₹ 181 (A)

MPV = AQ (SP – AQ)

Material X = 72 (20 – 20)	= ₹ 0
Material Y = 31 (10 – 11)	= ₹ 31 (A)
Total	= ₹ 31 (A)

MUV = SP (SQ – AQ)

Material X = 20 (60 – 72)	= ₹ 240 (A)
Material Y = 10 (40 – 31)	= ₹ 90 (F)
	= ₹ 150 (A)

MMV = SP (RSQ – AQ)

Material X = 20 (309/5 – 72) = ₹ 204 (A)

Material Y = 10 (206/5 – 31) = ₹ 102 (F)

Total = ₹ 102 (A)

Calculation of RSQ

Material X = 103 × 3/5 = 309/5

Material Y = 103 × 2/5 = 206/5

MRUV = SP (SQ – RSQ)

Material X = 20 (60 – 309/5) = ₹ 36 (A)

Material Y = 10 (40 – 206/5) = ₹ 12 (A)

Total = ₹ 48 (A)

MUV = MMV + MRUV

= ₹ 102 (A) + ₹ 48 (A) = ₹ 150 (A)

MCV = MPV + MMV + MRUV

= ₹ 31 (A) + ₹ 102 (A) + ₹ 48 (A)

= ₹ 181 (A)

Example 5

ABC Limited manufactures a simple product, the standard mix of which is

Material A	60% at ₹ 20
Material B	40% at ₹ 10

Normal loss in production is 20% of input. Due to shortage of Material A, the standard mix was changed. Actual results for April 2017 were:

Material A	105 kg at ₹ 20
Material B	95 kg at ₹ 9
Input	200
Loss	35 kg
Output	165 kg

Calculate material cost variances.

Solution

Material price variance = AQ (SP– AP)

Material A = 105 (20 – 20) = 0

Material B = 95 (10 – 9) = 95 (F)

Total 95 (F)

Material usage variance = SP (SQ – AQ)

Material A = ₹ 20 (495/4 – 105) = ₹ 375 (F)

Material B = ₹ 10 (165/2 – 95) = ₹ 125 (A)

Total ₹ 250 (F)

Standard quantity for actual production

$$\text{Material A} = \frac{60 \times 165}{80} = \frac{495}{4} \text{ kg}$$

$$\text{Material B} = \frac{40 \times 165}{80} = \frac{165}{2} \text{ kg}$$

MMV = SP (RSQ – AQ)

Material A = 20 (120 – 105) = ₹ 300 (F)

Material B = 10 (80 – 95) = ₹ 150 (A)

Total ₹ 150 (F)

Calculation of RSQ

Material A = 200 × 3/5 = 120 kg

Material B = 200 × 2/5 = 80 kg

MRUV = SP (SQ – RSQ)

Material A = 20 (495/4 – 120) = ₹ 75 (F)

Material B = 10 (165 – 80) = ₹ 25 (F)

Total 100 (F)

Calculation of SQ

Material A = 120/160 × 165 = 495/4

$$\text{Material B} = \frac{800}{160} \times 165 = \frac{165}{2}$$

$$\text{MYV} = \text{Standard cost per unit of output} \begin{pmatrix} \text{Standard} & - & \text{Actual} \\ \text{output} & & \text{output} \end{pmatrix}$$

= ₹ 20 (160 – 165) = ₹ 100 (F)

Calculation of Standard Cost per Unit of Output

Material A = 60 × 20		= ₹ 1,200
Material B = 40 × 10		= ₹ 400
100		1,600

20% Loss 20

Output 80

Cost per unit = ₹ 1,600 = ₹ 20

Note: MYV and MRUV have the same value. They are two sides of the same coin. While the MRUV is calculated from the input angle, the MYV is calculated from the output angle. MRUV is the difference between the standard quantity of input (at standard proportion) for the actual output. MYV is the difference between the standard output for the actual input and the actual output for the actual input.

Labour Cost Variance (LCV)

LCV is the difference between the standard direct wages specified for the activity attained, and the actual direct wages paid. As the wages of labour is determined by labour rate and labour time, the LCV consists of either or both of two variances, relating to rate and time, viz., Labour rate variance and Labour (Time) efficiency variance.

Symbolically

LCV = SC – AC

= (Standard time in hours × Standard rate) – (Actual time in hours × Actual rate)

or

(SHrs × SR) – (AHrs × AR)

If the actual cost, is less than standard cost, the variance is favourable and vice versa.

Labour Rate Variance (LRV)

This is the difference between the standard rate of payment specified and the actual rate paid.

LRV = Actual Hours (Standard rate – Actual rate) = AH (SR – AR). If the actual rate paid is less, the variance is favourable, and vice versa. The LRV may reveal one or more of the following reasons:

(*a*) Changes in the basic wage rates; this may be caused by an award of the labour tribunal in fulfilment of union demands subsequent to the setting of standard rates;

(*b*) Employment of one or more workers of different grades than the standard grade;

(*c*) Overtime work in excess of that provided in the standard rate; and

(*d*) Faculty recruitment and placement of workers.

Labour Efficiency Variances (LEV)

This is the difference between the standard labour hours specified for the activity attained (i.e. for actual output) and the actual hours paid for. It provides a key to the control of workers' efficiency and labour cost. LEV may reveal one or more of these reasons:

(*a*) Defective machinery and equipment;

(*b*) Lack of proper supervision;

(*c*) Low employee morale due to inefficient organisation and poor working conditions; and

(*d*) Inadequate training of workers, and strained industrial relations.

To check

LEV = Standard rate (Standard hours – Actual hours)

= SR (SH – AH)

If the actual hours taken is less than the standard, than the variance is favourable and vice versa.

Example 6

From the following data, calculate labour cost variances

Standard rate of wages per hour	₹ 5
Standard time set	500 hours
Actual rate of wages per hour	₹ 6
Actual time taken	490 hours

Solution

LCV = (SH × SR) – (AH × AR)

= (500 × 5) – (490 × 6)

= ₹ 2,500 – 2,940 = ₹ 440 (A)

LRV = AH (SR – AR)

= 490 (5 – 6) = ₹ 490 (A)

LEV = SR (SH – AH)

= 5 (500 – 490) = ₹ 50 (F)

LCV = ₹ 440 (A)

Advanced Variances

When more than one type or grade of labour is used for a job, standards are set for the labour mix as well as total labour hours used. In such cases, advanced variances such as labour mix variances and labour revised efficiency variance may arise.

Labour Mix Variance (LMV)

This is similar to Material Mix Variance. LMV is the difference in labour cost due to changes in the composition of the labour force (i.e., difference between standard composition of mix, and actual labour mix). In order to calculate this variance the total actual hours spent is compared with the revised standard hours. The revised standard hours are calculated as follows:

Actual hours (Total) × Standard ratio

LMV = SR (RSH – AH)

If the actual hours taken are lesser than the revised standard hours, the variance is favourable, and vice versa.

Example 7

Standard

Grade A 40 workers at ₹ 5 per hour

Grade B 60 workers at ₹ 3 per hour

100

Actual

Grade A 50 workers at ₹ 6 per hour

Grade B 40 workers at ₹ 2 per hour

90

Calculate the labour mix variance.

Solution

Calculation of RSH (Revised standard hours)

Grade A = 90 × 2/5 = 36

Grade B = 90 × 3/5 = 54

LMV = SR (RSH – AH)

Grade A = 5 (36 – 50)	= ₹ 70 (A)
Grade B = 3 (54 – 40)	= ₹ 42 (F)
Total	₹ 28 (A)

Labour Revised Efficiency Variance (LREV)

This variance arises due to the difference between the total actual hours taken, and the total standard hours specified for the actual activity achieved. They are compared at standard ratio. The formula is as follows:

LREV = SR (SH – RSH)

If the RSH is less than standard, the variance is favourable, and vice versa. From example 7, the LREV may be calculated as follows:

LREV = SR (SH – RSH)

Grade A = 5 (40 – 36) = ₹ 20 (F)

Grade B = 3 (60 – 54) = ₹ 18 (F)

Total = ₹ 38 (F)

LMV and LREV are the sub-variances of LEV. For the above example, the LEV may be calculated as follows:

LEV = SR (SH – AH)
Grade A = 5 (40 – 50) = ₹ 50 (A)
Grade B = 3 (60 – 40) = ₹ 60 (F)

To check

LEV = LMV + LREV
= ₹ 28 (A) + ₹ 38 (F) = ₹ 10 (F)

Idle Time Variance

The standard wage payable during the idle hours due to abnormal circumstances like strikes, lockout, breakdown of machinery, power-cut, etc. is termed as idle time variance. This abnormal idle time is shown separately and not normally concealed in the LEV as it is due to reasons beyond their control. This variance will always be adverse. The formula is as follows:

Idle time variance = Idle hours × Standard rate

Example 8

100 workers are employed in a factory and the average rate of wage is ₹ 1 per hour. Standard working time per week is 48 hours. During the week in May, wages paid for 50 workers were at the rate of ₹ 1.10 per hour, 20 workers at ₹ 1.00 per hour, and 30 workers at ₹ 0.90 per hour. The factory did not work for 8 hours due to power failure. Calculate suitable labour variances.

Solution

LRV = AH (SR – AR)

Category I (50 workers) = 2,400 (1 – 1.0)	= ₹ 240 (A)
Category II (20 workers) = 960 (1 – 1.0)	= 0
Category III (30 workers) = 1,440 (1 – 0.90)	= ₹ 144 (F)
Total	= ₹ 96 (A)

Workings

Actual hours paid	=	50 × 48	=	2,400
		20 × 48	=	960
		30 × 48	=	1,440
				4,800

LEV = SR (SH – AH)

Category I (50 workers)	= 1 (2,000 – 2,400)	= ₹ 400 (A)
Category II (20 workers)	= 1 (800 – 960)	= ₹ 160 (A)
Category III (30 workers)	= 1 (1,200 – 1,440)	= ₹ 240 (A)
	Total	= ₹ 800 (A)

LEV = SR (SH – AH),

= ₹ 1 (4,000 – 4,200) = ₹ 200 (F)

Idle time variance = ₹ 100 × 8 = ₹ 800 (A)

LEV = ₹ 600 (A)

Example 9

Calculate the labour variances from the following information:

Standard wages

Grade A = 90 workers at ₹ 2 per hour

Grade B = 60 workers at ₹ 3 per hour

Actual wages

Grade A = 80 workers at ₹ 2.50 per hour

Grade B = 70 workers at ₹ 2.00 per hour

Budgeted hours : 1,000; Actual hours: 900

Solution

LRV = AH (SR – AR)

Grade A = 72,000 (2 – 2.5) = ₹ 36,000 (A)

Grade B = 63,000 (3 – 2.0) = ₹ 63,000 (F)

Total = ₹ 27,000 (F)

LEVE = (SR – AH)

Grade A = ₹ 2 (90,000 – 72,000) = ₹ 36,000 (F)

Grade B = ₹ 3 (60,000 – 63,000) = ₹ 9,000 (A)

Total = ₹ 27,000 (F)

LMV = SR (RSH–AH)

Grade A = ₹ 2 (81,000 – 72,000) = ₹ 18,000 (F)

Grade B = ₹ 3 (54,000 – 63,000) = ₹ 27,000 (A)

Total = ₹ 9,000 (A)

Workings

Labour Group	*Standard hours*	*Actual hours*	*Revised Standard hours*
Grade A	90,000	72,000	1,35,000 × 9/15 = 81,000
Grade B	60,000	63,000	1,35,000 × 6/15 = 54,000
	150,000	135,000	135,000

LREV = SR (SH – RSH)

Grade A = ₹ 2 (90,000 – 81,000) = ₹ 18,000 (F)

Grade B = ₹ 3 (60,000 – 54,000) = ₹ 18,000 (F)

LEV = LMV – LREV

Overhead Cost Variances

Variable Overhead Cost Variance (VOHV)

This is the difference between standard variable-overheads for actual production and the actual variable overheads.

Symbolically

VOHV = SC – AC. It can be subdivided into VOH expenditure variance, and VOH efficiency variance.

VOH expenditure variance is the difference between the standard variable overheads for the actual hours worked, and the actual variable overheads incurred. The formula is as follows:

Workings

Standard hours per week 100 × 48	=	4,800 hours
Less idle hours 100 × 8	=	800 hours
Actual hours worked		4,000

Idle time variance= Standard rate per gang hour × Idle hours

= ₹ 100 × 8 = ₹ 800 (A)

Standard rate per gang hour = No. of workers × Rate per hour

Category I = 50 × 1	= ₹ 50
Category II = 20 × 1	= ₹ 20
Category III = 30 × 1	= ₹ 30
	₹ 100

Note: In this example, the main component of LEV is idle time variance. Suppose the actual hours worked is, say 4,200 hours, then the LEV will have Labour revised efficiency variance and Idle time variance.

VOH Exp. variance = AVOH – SVOH for actual hours worked

VOH efficiency variance arises when the actual output produced differs from the standard output for actual hours worked. It is a measure of extra overhead (for saving) incurred solely because of the efficiency shown during the actual hours worked. The formula is as follows:

VOH efficiency variance = (SVOH for actual hours worked) – (SVOH for actual output)

VOH cost variance = VOH exp. variance + VOH efficiency variance.

Example 10

From the following information calculate VOH cost variances:

Budgeted output	5000 units
Budgeted hours	10,000
Budgeted variable overheads	₹ 2,000
Actual variable overheads	₹ 3,000
Actual output	4,000 units
Actual hours	12,000

Solution

VOH cost variance	= AVOH – SVOH for actual production	
VOH expenditure variance	= AVOH – SVOH for actual hours worked	
VOH efficiency variance	= SVOH for A Hrs – SVOH for actual output	
VOH cost variance	= ₹ 3,000 – (4,000 × 0.40)	
	= ₹ 3,000 – ₹ 1,600	= ₹ 1,400 (A)
VOH expenditure variance	= 3,000 – (12,000 × 0.20)	= ₹ 600 (A)
VOH efficiency variance	= ₹ 2,400 – ₹ 1,600	= ₹ 800 (A)
		= ₹ 1,400 (A)

Workings

SVOH per hour = ₹ 2,000/10,000 = 0.20 per hour

SVOH per unit of output = ₹ 2,000/5,000 = ₹ 0.40 per unit

Fixed Overheads Cost Variance (FOHV)

This is the difference between the standard fixed overheads for actual output and actual fixed overheads. The reasons for the variance are over-absorption or under-absorption of overheads for the actual production. The budgeted production may be different from the actual production for the actual overheads incurred. The major sub-divisions of FOHV are FOH expenditure variance and FOH volume variance. The formula for FOHV is as follows:

FOH = AFOH – SFOH for actual production.

If the AFOH is less than the SFOH, the variance is favourable, and vice versa.

FOH Expenditure Variance (FOHEV)

This is the difference between AFOH and BFOH.

FOHEV = AFOH – BFOH

If the actual is greater than the budgeted, the variance is adverse, and vice versa.

FOH Volume Variance (FOHVV)

This is the difference between the budgeted fixed overheads and the standard fixed overheads absorbed on actual production. The formula is as follows:

FOHVV = BFOH – SFOH on actual production.

If the BFOH is greater than the SFOH on actual production, the variance is adverse and vice versa.

Example 11

From the following data calculate FOH cost variances: Budgeted hours: 10,000; Budgeted Output: 5,000 units; Budgeted FOH: ₹ 3,000. Actual hours: 12,000; Actual output: 4,800 units; Actual FOH: ₹ 3,600.

Solution

SFOH per hour = ₹ 3,000/10,000 = ₹ 0.30 per hour

SFOH per unit = ₹ 3,000/5,000 = ₹ 0.60 per unit

FOHV = AFOH – SFOH on actual output
= ₹ 3,600 – (0.60 × 4,800)
= ₹ 3,600 – 2,880 = ₹ 720 (A)

FOHEV = AFOH – BFOH
= ₹ 3,600 – 3,000 = ₹ 600 (A)

FOHVV = BFOH – SFOH on actual output
= ₹ 3,000 – (0.60 × 4,800)
= ₹ 3,000 – 2,880 = ₹ 120 (A)

FOHV = FOHEV + FOHVV
= ₹ 600 (A) + ₹ 120 (A) = ₹ 720 (A)

Advanced Variances

FOHV may be classified into the three sub-variances as follows: (*a*) Calendar variance, (*b*) Capacity variance, and (*c*) Efficiency variance.

Calendar variance. This is a part of capacity variance. It arises only when the actual number of working days differs from the budgeted working days. It is an indicator of variations in overhead recovery of different months due to changes in number of working days. The formula is as follows:

Calendar variance = BFOH – SFOH for revised budgeted hours.

Revised budgeted hours are equivalent to the standard hours for actual working days. If BFOH is greater than the SFOH, the variance is adverse, and vice versa.

Capacity variance. This is the difference between the SFOH for revised budgeted hours and SFOH for actual hours worked. This may arise due to strikes, lockouts, breakdown of machinery, short supply of labour, absenteeism, etc. Overtime, change in number of shifts etc., may also contribute towards this variance. It is an indicator of the degree of utilisation of available capacity. The formula is as follows:

Capacity variance = SFOH for RBH – SFOH for AH = SFOH (RBH – AH)

If the SFOH for RBH is greater than for AH, the variance is adverse, and vice versa.

Efficiency variance. This variance arises when the actual production differs from the standard output for actual hours worked. It is the difference between the SFOH recovered on actual output and SFOH for actual hours worked. The major causes for this variance are lack of proper supervision and inspection, improper handling of materials and machines, variation in production methods and changes in efficiency of machine operations, etc. The formula is as follows:

Efficiency variance = SFOH for AH worked – SFOH for actual output.

If the SFOH for actual output is greater, the variance is favourable and vice versa.

FOHEV = Calendar variance + capacity variance + efficiency variance.

Example 12

From the following data calculate FOH cost variances:

	For the Month of July 2019	
	Budget	*Actual*
Fixed overheads in ₹	30,000	31,000
Output in units	20,000	22,000
No. of working days	25	27

Budgeted fixed overhead rate is ₹ 1 per hour. In July 2019, the actual hours worked were 31,500.

Solution

SFOH per unit = ₹ 30,000/20,000 = ₹ 1.50

SFOH per unit = ₹ 1

FOHV = AFOH – SFOH on actual output

= 31,000 – (1.50 × 22,000)

= 31,000 – 33,000

= ₹ 2,000 (F)

FOHEV = FOHEV + FOHVV

₹ 2,000 (F) = ₹ 1,000 (A) + ₹ 3,000 (F)

Calendar variance = BFOH – SFOH for RBH

= 30000 – (₹ 1 × 32,400)

= ₹ 2,400 (F)

Calculation of RBH = Standard hours per day × Actual working days

$$= \frac{30,000}{25} \times 27 = 32,400 \text{ hours}$$

Since the budgeted fixed overhead rate is ₹ 1 per hour, and the total budgeted fixed overhead is ₹ 30,000, the number of budgeted hours is 30,000 (i.e. 30,000/1)

Capacity variance = SFOH for RBH – SFOH for AH
= (₹ 1 × 32,400) – (₹ 1 × 31,500)
= ₹ 32,400 – 31,500
= ₹ 900 (A)

Efficiency variance = SFOH for AH – SFOH for actual output
= (₹ 1 × 31,500) – (₹ 1.5 × 22,000)
= ₹ 31,500 – 33,000
= ₹ 1,500 (F)

FOHVV = Calendar variance + Capacity variance + Efficiency variance
= ₹ 2,400 (F) + ₹ 900 (A) + ₹ 1,500 (F)
= ₹ 3,000 (F)

FOHV = FOHEV + Calendar variance + Capacity variance + Efficiency variance
= ₹ 1,000 (A) + ₹ 2,400 (F) + ₹ 900 (A) + ₹ 1,500 (F)
= ₹ 2,000 (F)

Sales Variances

The standard costing system is complete only when sales variances are dovetailed with it as part of comprehensive information-presented to management. Sales variances are calculated by two methods, viz., sales value method, and sales margin or profit method. Basically, changes in price and changes in sales volume give rise to sales variances. A change in value may, in its own turn, result due to a change in quantity, or a change in sales mix.

Sales Value Method

The value method is used to denote variances arising due to change in sales price, quantity mix, etc., or the sales value. The sales variances may be classified as follows: (*a*) sales price variance and (*b*) sales volume variance. Sales volume variance may be further divided into sales mix variance and sales quantity or sub-volume variance.

Sales value variance (SVV) is the difference between standard sales and the actual sales.

$$SVV = (SS - AS) - (SP \times SQ) - (AP \times AQ)$$

Sales price variance (SVV) is the difference between standard price of actual quantity and actual price of the actual quantity of goods sold.

$$SPV = AQ\ (SP - AP)$$

If the actual price is greater than the standard price, the variance is favourable, and vice versa.

Sales Volume Variance (SVLV) is the difference between the actual quantity or volume and the standard quantity or volume of sales. It shows the effect of a change in volume of total sales.

$$SVLV = SP (SQ - AQ)$$

If the actual quantity sold is greater than the standard, the variance is favourable, and vice versa.

Sales Mix Variance

Where two or more items are used in the composition of sales, the difference between the standard composition of sales and the actual composition or mix is called the Sales Mix Variance. It is a part of the value variance arising due to change in the mix. It highlights the fact that the actual mix of sales has not been in the same ratio as budgeted.

$$SMV = SP (\text{Revised standard sales} - \text{Actual sales})$$

The revised standard sales is calculated by dividing the total actual sales quantity in the standard proportion. If the actual sales quantity is greater than the revised standard quantity, the variance is favourable, and vice versa.

Sales quantity variance. This is the difference between the revised standard quantity of sales and the standard quantity budgeted. This variance shows the position of actual quantity of sales, as distinct from the mix of sales, in comparison with budgeted or expected sales.

$$SQV = SP (SQ - RSQ)$$

If the RSQ is greater than the SQ, the variance is favourable, and vice versa.

$$SVLV = SMV + SQV$$

Example 13

Calculate (*i*) Sales variance, (*ii*) Sales price variance, (*iii*) Sales volume variance, (*iv*) Sales mix variance and (*v*) Sales quantity variance from the following:

Product	*Standard*		*Actual*	
	Qty (Units)	*Price (₹)*	*Qty (Units)*	*Price (₹)*
A	5,000	5.00	5,000	5.00
B	4,000	6.00	6,000	6.25
C	3,000	7.00	4,000	6.75
	12,000		15,000	

Solution

Sales Value Variance = SS – AS

= (SQ × SP) – (AQ × AP)

Product A = (5,000 × 5) – (5,000 × 5)	= 0
Product B = (4,000 × 6) – (6,000 × 6.25)	= ₹ 13,500 (F)
Product C = (3,000 × 7) – (4,000 × 6.75)	= ₹ 6,000 (F)
Total	= ₹ 19,500 (F)

Sales price variance = AQ (SP – AP)

	Amount [₹]
Product A – 5,000 (5 – 5)	= 0
Product B = 6,000 (6 – 6.25)	= 1,500 (F)
Product C = 4,000 (7 – 6.75)	= 1,000 (A)
Total	= 500 (F)

Sales voiume variance = SP (SQ – AQ)

	Amount [₹]
Product A = ₹ 5 (5,000 – 5,000)	= 0
Product B = ₹ 6 (4,000 – 6,000)	= 12,000 (F)
Product C = ₹ 7 (3,000 – 4,000)	= 7,000(F)
Total	= 19,000 (F)

Sales volume variance = Sales price variance + Sales volume variance

= 500 (F) + ₹ 19,000 (F) = 19,500 (F)

Sales mix. variance = SP (RSQ – AQ)

Product A = ₹ 5 (6,250 – 5,000)	= 6,250 (A)
Product B = ₹ 6 (5,000 – 6,000)	= 6,000 (F)
Product C = ₹ 7 (3,750 – 4,000)	= l,750 (F)
Total	= 1,500 (F)

Calculation of RSQ: Total AQ × Standard ratio

= 15,000 units × (5 : 4 : 3)

Product A = 15,000 × 5/12	= 6,250 Units
Product B = 15,000 × 4/12	= 5,000 Units
Product C = 15,000 × 3/12	= 3,750 Units
Total	= 15,000

Sales quantity variance = SP (SQ – RSQ)

	Amount [₹]
Product A = ₹ 5 (5,000 – 6,250)	= 6,250 (F)
Product B = ₹ 6 (4,000 – 5,000)	= 6,000 (F)
Product C = ₹ 7 (3,000 – 3,750)	= 5,250 (F)
Total	= 17,500

Sales volume variance = Sales mix variance + Sales quantity variance

19,000 (F) = ₹ 1,500 (F) + ₹ 17,500 (F)

Sales Margin Method or Profit Method

Sales margin variance. This is the difference between the standard margin appropriate to the quantity of sales budgeted for a period, and the margin between standard cost and the actual selling price of the sales effected. This variance arises due to the difference between Total Budgeted Profit and Total Actual Profit.

Sales Margin Variance = Budgeted Profit – Actual Profit

Sales margin variance may be classified into sales margin price variance and sales margin volume variance which is due to the difference between the standard price of the quantity of sales effected, and the actual price of the sales. It is the difference between the standard profit and actual profit. This variance is similar to the price variance calculated under value method, and the formula is as follows:

Margin price variance = AQ (Standard profit – Actual profit)

If the actual profit is greater than the standard profit, the variance is favourable, and vice versa.

Sales margin volume variance. This is that portion of total margin variance which is due to the difference between the budgeted quantity and actual quantity of sales. This is the amount by which standard profit differs from budgeted profit. The formula is as follows:

Margin volume variance = Standard profit (SQ – AQ)

If the actual quantity is greater than standard quantity the variance is favourable, and vice versa.

Sales margin mix variance. This is that portion of total margin variance which is due to the difference between the budgeted and actual quantities of each product of which the sales mixture is composed, valuing sales at the standard net selling prices and cost of sales at standard. That is, the difference between the revised standard profit is the mix variance.

Margin Mix Variance: Standard profit (RSQ – AQ)

If the actual quantity is greater than the revised standard quantity the variance is favourable, and vice versa.

Example 14

ABC Ltd., had budgeted the following sales for December 2019:

Product A	9,000 units at	₹ 5 per unit
Product B	6,500 units at	₹ 10 per unit
Product C	12,000 units at	₹ 7.5 per unit

As against this, the actual sales were:

Product A	10,000 units at	₹ 5.5 per unit
Product B	7,000 units at	₹ 9.5 per unit
Product C	11,000 units at	₹ 7.8 per unit

The cost per unit of A, B and C was ₹ 4.5, ₹ 8.5 and ₹ 6.5 respectively. Compute the different variances to explain the difference between budgeted profit and actual profit (see next page).

Solution

Sales margin variance = (SM × SQ) – (AM × AQ)

Product A = (0.5 × 9,000) – (1 × 10,000) = ₹ 5,000 (F)

Product B = (1.5 × 6,500) – (1 × 7,000) = ₹ 2,750 (A)

Product C = (1 × 12,000) – (1.3 × 11,000) = ₹ 2,300 (F)

Total = ₹ 5,050 (F)

Sales margin price variance = AQ (SM – AM)

Product A = 10,000 (0.5 – 1.0) = ₹ 5,000 (F)

Product B = 7,000 (1.5 – 1.0) = ₹ 3,500 (A)

Product C = 11,000 (1.0 – 1.3) = ₹ 3,300 (F)

Total = ₹ 4,800 (F)

Sales margin volume variance = SM (SQ – AQ)

Product A = 0.5 (9,000 – 10,000) = ₹ 500 (F)

Product B = 1.5 (6,500 – 7,000) = ₹ 750 (F)

Product C = 1.0 (12,000 – 11,000) = ₹ 1,000 (A)

Total = ₹ 250 (F)

SMV = SMPV + SMVV

₹ 5,050 (F) = ₹ 4,800 (F) + ₹ 250 (F)

Sales margin mix variance = SM (RSQ – AQ)

Product A = 0.5 (9,164 – 10,000) = ₹ 418 (F)

Product B = 1.5 (6,618 – 7,000) = ₹ 573 (F)

Product C = 1.0 (12,218 – 11,000) = ₹ 1,218 (A)

Total = ₹ 227 (A)

Budget

Product	*SQ*	*SP* ₹	*Total Sale* ₹	*Cost per unit* ₹	*Total cost* ₹	*Profit per unit* ₹	*Total Profit* ₹
A	9,000	5	45,000	4.5	40,500	0.5	4,500
B	6,500	19	65,000	8.5	55,250	1.5	9,750
C	12,000	7.5	90,000	6.5	78,000	1.0	12,000
	27,500		2,00,000		1,73,750		26,250
				Actual			
A	10,000	5.5	55,000	4.5	45,000	1.0	10,000
B	7,000	9.5	66,500	8.5	59,500	1.0	7,000
C	11,000	7.8	85,800	6.5	71,500	1.3	14,300
	28,000		2,07,300		1,76,000		31,300

Workings

RSQ = AQ × (Standard ratio)

= 28,000 × (18 : 13 : 24)

Product A = 28,000 × 18/55	9,164
Product B = 28,000 × 13/55	6,618
Product C = 28,000 × 24/55	12,218

Sales-margin quantity variance = SM (SQ – RSQ)

Product A = 0.5 (9,000 – 9,164)	= ₹ 82 (F)
Product B = 1.5 (6,600 – 6,618)	= ₹ 177 (F)
Product C = 1.0 (12,000 – 12,218)	= ₹ 218 (F)
Total	= ₹ 477 (F)
SM volume variance	= SMMV + SMQV
	= ₹ 227 (A) + ₹ 477 (F)
	= ₹ 250 (F)

Causes and Disposition of Variances

In order to make the variance analysis a control instrument, the management should investigate the causes of variances and take the necessary corrective measures. There is no uniformity of opinion regarding the disposal of variances. Where it is desired to maintain the same standard in future, the variances must be written off to P & L account. According to strict principle, the amount of variances resulting from incorrect standards or condition beyond control, like material price changes, wage rate increases due to fair legislation, etc., are allocated to inventories and cost of sales in proportion to their value of closing balances. Another method is to carry forward the variances to the next financial year by crediting the same to a reserve account to be set off in the subsequent year or years. The favourable and adverse variances may cancel each other in the course of reasonable time and thus be disposed off.

1. *Materials price variance:* (*a*) *Causes.* Change in market price, delivery costs; purchase of non-standard materials, emergency purchases, incorrect shipping instruction, loss of discounts, etc. *Disposition.* If all or a portion of the price variance is the result of inefficiencies or a saving has resulted from efficient purchasing, the amount may be adjusted to P & L account. If it is due to incorrect standards or change in market price the amount may be adjusted to inventories and cost of goods sold. It may be mentioned that under Method I, such adjustment must be made for inventories under materials control, work-in-progress, finished goods, and cost of goods sold. Under Methods II and III, such adjustments are required for inventories under work-in-progress, finished goods, and cost of goods sold.

2. *Materials usage variance: (a) Causes.* Poor quality of materials; change in material mix, product or production methods; careless handling; excessive waste or scrap; incorrect setting of standards. *(b) Disposition.* The amount of usage variance resulting in inefficiency in handling

and processing materials' is trasferred to profit and loss account. The amount of usage variance due to incorrect standards is apportioned to work in progress, finished goods, and cost of goods sold.

3. *Direct wages rate variances: (a) Causes.* General rise due to award or agreement, non-standard grade, abnormal overtime or payment above or below standard rates during seasonal or emergency operations. *(b) Disposition.* The amount of variance arising out of inefficiency can be controlled if transferred to profit and loss account. The amount of variance resulting from the use of out-of-date standards or from conditions beyond the control of management is adjusted to work-in-progress, finished goods and cost of goods sold, on the basis of wages or time.

4. *Direct labour efficiency variance:* (*a*) *Causes.* Poor working conditions, abnormal idle time i.e., power failure, breakdown, go-slow technique, quality of supervision, non-standard grade of material, or employee non-cooperation in service departments. (*b*) *Disposition.* The amount of variance attributed to various forms of inefficiency which are controllable is transferred to profit and loss account. The amount of variance resulting from improperly prepared standards and from conditions beyond the control of management may be adjusted to work-in-progress, finished goods, and cost of goods sold.

5. *Overhead expenditure variance: (a) Causes.* Under or over utilization of a service; seasonal conditions; inefficiency in the use of a service (e.g. electricity in lieu of gas). *(b) Disposition:* The amount of variance due to seasonal conditions should be treated as a deferred item. The amount arising out of inefficiency which is controllable is transferred to profit and loss account. The amount resulting from incorrectly prepared standard and from conditions beyond control is adjusted to work in progress, finished goods, and cost of goods sold.

6. *Overhead cost capacity variance: (a) Causes.* Calendar variations, abnormal idle time such as strikes, breakdowns, absenteeism, labour shortage, etc. *(b) Disposition.* The amount of seasonal variations is reasonably a deferred item. The amount arising from inefficient operations controllable by management is transferred to profit and loss account. The amount of variance arising out of abnormal idle time and beyond control of management is transferred to profit and loss account.

REPORTING OF VARIANCES

In order to make the variance analysis more effective the following conditions should be fulfilled:

(*a*) The variance arising out of each factor should be correctly separated. If it is not done properly or one merged with another, the reporting would be misleading or wrong inferences may be drawn.

(*b*) Variances, particularly the controllable variances should be reported immediately. This would enable remedial measures being taken on time.

(*c*) Analysis of uncontrollable variances should be made with the same case as for controllable variances since it may reveal far-reaching effects on the operating results of the company.

(*d*) The forms of reports for the different types of variances should be designed taking into consideration the needs of the management, size of the company.

It is better to present the profit figures by way of reconciliation of budgeted or standard and actual profits on the basis of variances:

Profit and Loss (Reconciliation) Statement for the Month

		Dr. (A)	Cr (F)
Standard Profit Variances			
Materials —	Price		
	Usage	–	–
Labour —	Rate		
	Efficiency	–	–
	Idle Time		
Variable overheads –	Expenditure		
	Efficiency	–	–
Fixed overheads –	Expenditure		
	Capacity	–	–
	Calendar		
Efficiency Sales —	Price		
	Quantity	–	–
Actual Profit			

A statement of this type may enable the management to locate points that need special attention. It is also possible to isolate the factors responsible for the profit variation and measures could be taken to control such factors to ensure planned profits in future.

Trading and Profit and Loss Account of Excel Ltd. for the Period ended 31st March 2019

Materials	68,000	Sales (14400 units)	1,44,000
Labour	44,000		
Direct expenses	7,200		
Works expenses	8,800		
Office expenses	6,400		
Net profit	9,600		
	1,44,000		1,44,000

The standard output for the period was 20,000 units and the standard cost and profit per unit is as under:

Materials (3 units at ₹ 1.50)
Labour (3 hours at ₹ 1.00)
Direct expenses
Works expenses: Fixed
Variable
Office expenses (fixed)
Profit
Selling price

Labour was paid for at ₹ 1.10 per hour and materials prices were ₹ 1.60 per unit. Actual work expenses include ₹ 5,600 fixed and the rest one variable.

Ascertain the standard profit that should have been earned and reconcile the actual profit showing the figures for various variances.

Solution

The standard profit to be earned at ₹ 1.15 per unit on 14,400 units is ₹ 16,560.

Profit and Loss Reconciliation Statement (for the period 31-3-2019)

Standard profit			16,560
Variances:	Adverse Dr. ₹	Favourable Cr. ₹	
Materials: Price	4,250	—	
Usage	—	1,050	
Labour: Rate	4,000		
Efficiency	—	3,200	
Works overheads:	—		
Variable expenditure	—	400	
Fixed expenditure	—	400	
Volume	1,680	—	
Office overheads:			
Expenditure	400	—	
Volume	1,680	—	
	12,010	5,050	(6,960)
		Actual profit	9,600

Computation of Variances

Materials: Price Variance = AQ (SP – AP)
= 42,500 (1.50 – 1.60)
= ₹ 4,250 (A)

Usage	= SP (SQ – AQ)
	= ₹ 1.5 (43,200 – 42,500) = ₹ 1,050 (F)
	AQ = (68000 + l units)
	SQ = (14400 × 3) = 43,200

Workings

Labour variances

A Hrs	= 44,000 + ₹ 1.1 = 40,000 hrs
S Hrs	= 14,400 × 3 = 43,200 hrs
Rate variance	= 40,000 (1.0 – 1.1) = ₹ 4,000 (A)
Efficiency Variance	= SR (S Hrs – A Hrs)
	= ₹ 1 (43,200 – 40,000)
	= ₹ 3,200 (F)

Work Expenses:

Variable Expenditure	= SC – AC
	= (14,400 × 0.25) – ₹ 3,200
	= ₹ 3,600 -- ₹ 3,200 = 400 (F)
Fixed Expenditure	= AC – BC
	= ₹ 5,600 – ₹ 6,000
	= ₹ 400 (F)
Volume variance	= BC – SC
	= ₹ 6,000 – ₹ 4,320
	= ₹ 1,680 (A)
Office overheads	= AC – BC
Expenditure	= ₹ 6,400 – ₹ 6,000
	= ₹ 400 (A)
Volume	= BC – SC
	= ₹ 6,000 – 4,320
	= ₹ 1,680 (A)

Direct Expenses Variance – NIL

PRACTICAL PROBLEMS

Illustration 1

From the following information calculate material cost variances:

Material	Standard Qty.	Standard Price	Actual Qty.	Actual Price
	kg	₹	kg	₹
X	10	4	12	3.75
Y	15	5	18	4.50
	25		30	

Solution

Material cost variance = (SQ × SP) – (AQ × AP)

Material X = (10 × 4) – (12 × 3.75) = ₹ 40 – ₹ 45 = ₹ 5 (A)

Material Y = (15 × 5) – (18 × 4.50) = ₹ 75 – ₹ 81 = ₹ 6 (A)

Total = ₹ 11 (A)

Material price variance = AQ (SP – AP)

Material X : 12 (4 – 3.75) = ₹ 3.00 (F)

Material Y : 18 (5 – 4.50) = ₹ 9.00 (F)

Total = ₹ 12.00 (F)

Material usage variance = SP (SQ – AQ)

Material X = ₹ 4 (10 – 12) = ₹ 8 (A)

Material Y = ₹ 5 (15 – 18) = ₹ 15 (A)

Total = ₹ 23 (A)

MCV = MPV + MUV

MCV = ₹ 12 (F) + ₹ 23 (A) = ₹ 11 (A)

Material mix variance = SP (RSQ – AQ)

Material mix variance is nil, since the actual mix is the same as the standard mix.

Material sub-usage variance = SP (SQ – RSQ)

This is the same as the material usage variance.

Illustration 2

From the following information calculate materials cost variances:

Material	*Standard*		*Actual*	
	Quantity Tons	*Price* ₹	*Quantity* Tons	*Price* ₹
Material X	20	20	10	30
Material Y	40	30	20	40
Material Z	40	50	30	45

Solution

Material cost variance = (SQ × SP) – (AQ × AP)

Material X = (20 × 20) – (10 × 30) = ₹ 100 (F)

Material Y = (40 × 30) – (20 × 40) = ₹ 400 (F)

Material Z = (40 × 50) – (30 × 45) = ₹ 650 (F)

Total = ₹ 1150(F)

Material price variance = AQ (SP – AP)

Material X = 10 (20 – 30) = ₹ 100 (A)

Material Y = 20 (30 – 40) = ₹ 200 (A)

Material Z = 30 (50 – 45) = ₹ 150 (F)

Total = ₹ 150(A)

Material usage variance SP (SQ – AQ)

Material X = 20 (20 – 10) = ₹ 200 (F)

Material Y = 30 (40 – 20) = ₹ 600 (F)

Material Z = 50 (40 – 30) = ₹ 500 (F)

Total = ₹ 1300(F)

MCV = MPV + MUV

MCV = ₹ 150 (A) + ₹ 1,300 (F) = ₹ 1,150 (F)

Material mix variance = SP (RSQ – AQ)

Calculation of RSQ = AQ × Standard Ratio = 60 × (1:2:2)

Materials X, Y, Z, 12, 24, 24 respectively

Material X = 20 (12 – 10) = ₹ 40 (F)

Material Y = 30 (24 – 20) = ₹ 120 (F)

Material Z = 50 (24 – 30) = ₹ 300 (A)

Total = ₹ 140(A)

Material revised usage variance = SP (SQ – RSQ)

Material X = 20 (20 – 12) = ₹ 160 (F)

Material Y = 30 (40 – 24) = ₹ 480 (F)

Material Z = 50 (40 – 24) = ₹ 800 (F)

Total = ₹ 1,440 (F)

MUV = MMV + MRUV

MUV = ₹ 140 (A) + ₹ 1,440 (F) = 1,300 (F)

Illustration 3

The following standard and actual data relate to a manufacturing concern:

Standard

Material X 40 kgs at ₹ 6 = 240

Material Y 60 kgs at ₹ 4 = 240

Standard output is 80% of input i.e., 700 units. Process loss is 20%.

Actual

Material X 600 kgs at ₹ 4

Material Y 400 kgs at ₹ 6

Actual output is 70% of input i.e., 700 units. Process loss is 30%.

You are required to calculate material cost variances.

Solution

Calculation of standard quantity for actual output

For 80 units SQ of materials is 100 units for 700 units

$$\text{SQ of materials is } \left(\frac{100}{80} \times 700 = 875 \text{ units}\right)$$

SQ for material X = 875 units × 4/10 = 350 units

SQ for material Y = 875 × 6/10 = 525 units

Material cost variance = SC for actual output – AC

Material X = (350 × ₹ 6) – (600 × ₹ 4)	= ₹ 360 (A)
Material Y = (525 × ₹ 4) – (400 × ₹ 6)	= ₹ 300 (A)
Total	= ₹ 600 (A)

Material price variance = AQ (SP – AP)

Material X = 600 (6 – 4)	= ₹ 1,200 (F)
Material Y = 400 (4 – 6)	= ₹ 800 (A)
Total	= ₹ 400 (F)

Material usage variance = SP (SQ – AQ)

Material X = ₹ 6 (350 – 600)	= ₹ 1500 (A)
Material Y = ₹ 4 (525 – 400)	= ₹ 500 (F)
Total	= ₹ 1,000 (A)

Verification MCV = MPV + MUV

MCV = ₹ 400 (F) + ₹ 1,000 (A) = ₹ 600 (A)

Calculation of RSQ = AQ × Standard ratio

Material X = 1000 × 4/10 = 400 units

Material Y = 1000 × 6/10 = 600 units

Material mix variance = SP (RSQ – AQ)

Material X = ₹ 6 (400 – 600)	= ₹ 1,200 (A)
Material Y = ₹ 4 (600 – 400)	= ₹ 800 (F)
Total	= ₹ 400 (A)

Material revised usage variance = SP (SQ – RSQ)

Material X = ₹ 6 (350 – 400)	= ₹ 300 (A)
Material Y = ₹ 4 (525 – 600)	= ₹ 300 (A)
Total	= ₹ 600 (A)

Material yield variance = SC per unit of output × (Standard yield – Actual yield) Calculation of SC per unit of output = Total material cost/Total standard output

= (40 × ₹ 6) + (60 × ₹ 4)/80 units = ₹ 6

Standard yield for actual input = 1,000 less 20% loss = 800 units

Material yield variance = ₹ 6 (800 – 700) = ₹ 600 (A)

MYV will always be same as MRUV.

Illustration 4

The standard mix of a product is as follows:

The standard loss in production is 100% of input. There is no scrap value. Actual production for a month was 7,240 lbs from 80 mixes. Actual consumption of material during the month were:

Material	*Quantity (lbs.)*	*Price per lb. (₹)*
A	4,160	5.50
B	1,680	3.75
C	2,560	9.50
Total	8,400	

You are required to calculate and present the following variances:

(*i*) Material cost, (*ii*) Material price, (*iii*) Material mix and (*iv*) Material yield.

Solution

(*i*) Material variance (see working note)

(Standard quantity for actual production × SP) – (AQ × AP)

Material A ([36,200/9] × 5) – (4,160 – 5.50)

= (1,81,000/9) – (22,880) = 24,920/9 = 2768.88 (A)

Material B (14,480/9 × 4) – (1,680 – 3.75)

= 57,920/9 – 6,300 = 1,220/9 = 135.55 (F)

Material C (21,728/9 × 12) – (2,560 × 9.50)

= 2,17,200/9 – 24,320 = 1,680/9 = ₹ 186.67 (A)

Total material cost variance = ₹ 2,820 (A)

(*ii*) Material price variance

(SP – AP) × AQ

Material A (5 – 5.50) × 4,160	= ₹ 2,080 (A)
Material B (4 – 3.75) × 1,680	= ₹ 420 (F)
Material C (10 – 9.50) × 2,560	= ₹ 1,280 (F)
Total material price variance	= ₹ 380 (A)

(*iii*) Material mix variance

(Revised standard mix on the basis of actual input – actual mix × SP)

Material A (4,200 – 4,160) × 5	= ₹ 200 (F)
Material B (1,680 – 1,680) × 4	= nil
Material C (2,520 – 2,560) × 10	= ₹ 400 (A)
Total material mix variance	= ₹ 200(A)

(*iv*) Material yield variance

(Standard loss on actual input – actual loss) ×

Average standard price (840 – 1,160) × 7 = (320 × 7) = ₹ 2,240 (A)

Check

Material mix variance + Material yield variance + Material price variance

= Material cost variance

₹ 200 (A) + ₹ 2,240 (A) + ₹ 380 (A) = ₹ 2,820 (A)

Working Notes

1. Calculating of standard quantity for actual production.

   For 90 units of output material input is 100 lbs.

   For 7240 units of output, the total[1] input is 100/90 × 7,240 = 72,400/9 lbs.

For material A standard quantity = (72,400/9) (5/10) = 36,200/9

For material B standard quantity = (72,400/9) (2/10) = 14,480/9

For material C standard quantity = (72,400/9) (3/10) = 21,720/9

2. Revised standard quantity-total AQ × (Standard Ratio)

   Material A = 8,400 × 5/10 = 4,200 lbs.

   Material B = 8,400 × 2/10 = 1,680 lbs.

   Material C = 8,400 × 3/10 = 2,520 lbs.

3. Standard loss for actual output at 10% = 8,400 × 10/100 = 840

   Actual loss : 8,400 – 7,240 = 1,160

4. Standard cost per unit = Total standard cost/Total standard quantity

   = (50 × ₹ 5) + (20 × ₹ 4) + (30 × ₹ 10)/90 = ₹ 7

Illustration 5

	Standard		*Actual*	
	Hours	*Rates (₹)*	*Hours*	*Rate (₹)*
Workman A	20	3	30	2.90
Workman B	25	4	15	4.50

Calculate the labour cost variance

Solution

Labour cost variance = (SH × SR) – (AH × AR)

Workman A = 20 × 3 – 30 × 2.9 = ₹ 27 (A)

Workman B = 25 × 4 – 15 × 4.5 = ₹ 32.5 (F)

Total = ₹ 5.5 (F)

Labour rate variance = AH (SR – AR)

Workman A = 30 × (3 – 2.90) = ₹ 3 (F)

Workman B = 15 × (4 – 4.5) = ₹ 7.5 (A)

Total = ₹ 4.5 (A)

Labour efficiency variance = SR (SH – AH)

Workman A = ₹ 3 (20 – 30) = ₹ 30 (A)

Workman B = ₹ 4 (25 – 15) = ₹ 40 (F)

Total = ₹ 10 (F)

Labour cost variance = Labour price variance + Labour rate variance

= ₹ 4.50 (A) + ₹ 10 (F) = ₹ 5.5 (F)

Illustration 6

The data obtained from a manufacturing concern are as follows:

	Standard	*Actual*
Number in the gang	Men 20; Women 10:	Men 16; Women 18
Wage rate per hour	₹ 0.90; ₹ 0.80	₹ 1; ₹ 0.50
Output per gang hour	50 units	Total output 2,400 units

Actual gang hour paid for 40

Actual gang hours worked 30

Abnormal idle time is one gang hour

Compute the labour variance.

Solution

Labour cost variance = SC – AC

= ₹ 1,248 – ₹ 1,000 = ₹ 248 (F)

Workings

Actual output in gang hours = 2,400/50 = 48 std. gang hours; Standard cost, per gang hour = (20 × 0.90) + (10 × 0.80) = ₹ 26. Hence, standard cost 48 × ₹ 26 = ₹ 1,248, Actual cost = (16 × 40 × 1) + (18 × 40 × 0.50) = ₹ 1,000

Labour rate variance = AH (SR – AR)

Men = (40 × 16) × (₹ 0.90 – ₹ 1)	= ₹ 64 (A)
Women = (40 × 18) × (₹ 0.80 – ₹ 0.50)	= ₹ 216 (F)
Total	= ₹ 152 (F)

Labour efficiency variance = SR (SH – AH)

Men = 0.90 (960 – 640) = ₹ 288 (F)	
Women = 0.80 (480 – 720)	= ₹ 192 (A)
Total	= ₹ 96 (F)

Workings

Standard hours for men	= 48 × 20	= 960
Standard hours for women	= 48 × 10	= 480
Total		= 1,440 hours

Now the sub-variances of total efficiency variance may be calculated thus:

Idle Time Variance

Standard rate × idle hours

Men 0.90 × 16	= ₹ 14.40 (A)
Women 0.80 × 18	= ₹ 14.40 (A)
Total	= ₹ 28.80 (A)

Mix Variance

Standard rate (revised standard hours – actual hours)

Men Re. 0.90 (884 – 624)	= ₹ 234.00 (F)
Women Re. 0.90 (442 – 702)	= ₹ 208.00 (A)
Total	= ₹ 26.00 (F)

Workings

Actual hours worked = hours paid for – idle hours

For men : 640 – 16	= 624
For women : 720 – 28	= 702
Total	= 1,326

Revised standard hours = actual hours worked expressed in standard ratio

For men = (960/1440) × 1,326	= 884
For women = (480/1,440) × 1,326	= 442
Total	= 1,326

Efficiency Variance

Standard rate (standard hours – revised standard hours)

Men : Re. 0.90 (960 – 884)	= ₹ 68.40 (F)
Women : Re. 0.80 (480 – 442)	= ₹ 30.40 (F)
Total	= ₹ 98.80 (F)

Yield Variance

Standard cost of standard gang per hour (Standard yield* – Actual yield)

₹ 26 (44.20 – 48) = 98.80 (F)

*Both have been expressed in standard gang hours.

Workings

(*a*) Standard yield expressed in standard gang hours

= Yield (in terms of standard gang hours) which should have resulted from actual hours.

= Actual hours worked/hours in one standard gang hour

= 1,326/30 = 44.20 standard gang hour

(*b*) 50 units of output = one standard gang hour

2400 units (actual output) = 2,400/50 = 48 standard gang hours

Alternatively, yield variance can be calculated thus:

Standard labour cost per unit output (SY* – AY*)

₹ 26/50 (2,210 – 2,400)

or (₹ 26/50) × 190 = ₹ 98.80 (F)

* Both expressed in units of output

Workings

Standard yield = Actual hours × Yield per standard hour

= 1,325 × (50/30) = 2210 units

Verification

Total efficiency variance = idle time variance + mix variance

= Either efficiency or yield variance

or 96 (F) = ₹ 28.80 (A) + ₹ 26 (F) + ₹ 98.80 (F) or 96 (F) = 96 (F)

Illustration 7

A company gives you the following information. Calculate the variances.

Standard data		*Actual data*	
Material [*Kg.*]	*Amount* [₹]	*Material* [*Kg.*]	*Amount* [₹]
450 Material A @ ₹ 20	9,000	450 Material A @ ₹19	8,550
360 Material B @ ₹ 10	3,600	360 Material B @ ₹11	3,960
810	12,600	810	12,510
90 Normal loss		50 Actual loss	
720		760	

Hours	*Labour*	*Labour Hours*	
2,400 skilled hours @ ₹ 2	4,800	2,400 skilled hours @	2.25
1,200 unskilled hrs. @ ₹ 1	1,200		5,400
Total cost ₹		1,200 unskilled hours @ ₹ 1.25	1,500
	18,600	Total cost	**19,410**

Solution

Material cost variance:

(SQ × SP) – (AQ × AP)

SQ of material A = 450 × (760/720) = 475 kg

SQ of material B = 360 × (760/720) = 380 kg

Material A = (475 × 20) – (450 × 19) = 9,500 – 8,550 = ₹ 950 (F)

Material B = (380 × 10) – (360 × 11) = 3,800 – 3,960 = ₹ 160 (A)

Total = ₹ 790 (F)

Material Price Variance:

(SP – AP) AQ

Material A = (20 – 19) × 450 kg = 450 (F)

Material B = (10 – 11) × 360 kg = 360 (A)

Total = 90 (F)

Material Yield Variance:

(Std. loss – Actual loss) × SC per unit of output

(₹ 12,600/720) × (90 kg – 50 kg)

= (12,600/720) × 40 = ₹ 700 (F)

(a) Labour cost variances

(SH × SR) – (AH × AR) = 600 (A)

Skilled (2,400 × 2) – (2,400 × 2.25) = 300 (A)

= 4,800 – 5,400

Unskilled (1,200 × 1) + (1,200 × 1.25) Total = 900 (A)

(b) (i) Rate variance

(SR × AR) AH	Amount [₹]
Skilled (₹ 2 – ₹ 2.25) × 2,400	= 600 (A)
Unskilled (₹ 1 × ₹ 1.25) × 1,200	= 300 (A)
Total	= ₹ 900 (A)

Illustration 8

Find out variable variances from the following:

Budgeted variable overhead for January	₹ 8,000
Budgeted production for the month	500 Units
Standard time for one unit of production	10 Units
Actual variable overhead	₹ 6,600
Actual production for the month	400 Units
Actual hours worked	3,800

Solution

Standard variable overhead rate per unit = ₹ 16

Standard variable rate per hour $\frac{8,000}{500 \times 10}$ = ₹ 1.60

Computation of variable overhead variance

	Amount [₹]
(*a*) Actual variable Overhead during the period	6,600
(*b*) Actual hours worked × Std. var. overhead rate per hour	
3,800 Hrs. × ₹ 1.60	6,080
(*c*) Actual Production × Std.variable overhead Rate per unit	
400 units × ₹ 16	6,400

Variable overhead variances:

(*i*) Expenditure variance (*a* – *b*)	₹ 520 (A)
(*ii*) Efficiency variance (*b* – *c*)	₹ 320 (F)
(*iii*) Total variable Overhead variance (*a* – *c*)	₹ 200 (A)

By application of formulae:

Variable Overhead váriance = (SVO – AVO)
= ₹ 6,400 – 6,600 = ₹ 200 (A)

(*i*) Expenditure variance = (AH – SR) – AVO
= (3,800 Hrs. × ₹ 1.60) ₹ 6,600
= ₹ 6,600 = ₹ 6,080 – ₹ 6,600 = ₹ 520 (A)

(*ii*) Efficiency variance = Std. overhead rate (Actual Hrs–Std. Hrs. for actual production)
= ₹ 1.60 (3,800 Hrs—4,000 Hrs.) = ₹ 320 (F)

Total variable overhead variance ₹ 200

Illustration 9

From the following data calculate the overhead variances which have arisen and present them in a form suitable for management appraisal:

	Budget	*Actual*
No. of working days	20	21
Man-hours in period	40,000	43,000
Output per man-hour in units	3.2	3
Total output in units	1,28,000	1,29,000
Overheads:		
Variable	₹ 1,02,400	₹ 1,14,400
Fixed	₹ 25,600	₹ 25,000

Solution

Standard hours for actual production:

For 1,28,00 units . . . 40,000 hours

For 1,29,000 units . . . 40,312.5 hours

$$\left(\frac{40{,}000\times 1{,}29{,}000}{1{,}28{,}000} \quad 40{,}312.50 \text{ hour } 1\right)$$

Standard overhead rate:

For 40,000 hours ... ₹ 25,600

For 1 hour ... Re. 0.64

For 1 unit ... Re. 0.20

$$\left(\frac{25{,}600}{40{,}000} = ₹\,\frac{16}{25} = 0.64 \text{ and } \frac{25{,}600}{1{,}28{,}000} ₹\,0.20\right)$$

(*a*) Overhead cost variance

Standard hours for Standard overhead – Actual overhead cost actual output × rate

$$\left(40{,}312.50\times\frac{16}{25}\right) - 25{,}000$$

(25,800 – 25,000) = ₹ 800 (F)

(*b*) Overhead budget variance =

Budgeted overhead cost – Actual overhead cost

(25,600 – 25,000) = ₹ 600 (F)

(*c*) Overhead volume variance

When rate per hour is given:

(Standard hours for actual production – Budgeted hours) × Standard rate per hour

(40,312.50 – 40,000) x – = ₹ 200 (F)

When rate per unit is given:

(Budgeted production – Actual production) × standard rate per unit i.e., Overhead calendar variance Standard number Actual number × Standard overhead of working days/number of days (20 – 21) × 25,600/20 = ₹ 1,280 (F)

Overhead efficiency variance

Standard production is actual hours:

For 40,000 hours ... Production 1,28,000 units

For 43,000 hours ... (1,28,000 × 43,000)/40,000 = 1,37,600 units

$$\begin{pmatrix}\text{Standard production for actual hours} - \text{Actual production}\\ (1,37,600 - 1,29,000) \times 0,20\end{pmatrix} \times \text{Standard rate per unit}$$

= 1,720 (A)

Overhead capacity variance = (SH – AH) × Standard overhead rate

(42,000 × 43,000) × 0.64 = ₹ 640 (F)

Overhead cost variance = ₹ 600 (F) + ₹ 1,280 (F) + ₹ 640 (F) + ₹ 1,720 (A) = ₹ 800

Illustration 10

From the following data calculate sales value variances:

Product	*Standard*		*Actual*	
	Qty	*Sp (₹)*	*Qty*	*Sp (₹)*
Product X	500	5	500	5
Product Y	400	6	600	6.25
Product Z	300	7	400	6.75

Solution

Sales value variance = (SQ × SP) – (AQ × AP)

Product X = (500 × 5) – (500 × 5) = nil

Product Y = (400 × 6) – (600 × 6.25) = 1,350 (F)

Product Z = (300 × 7) = 600 (F)

Total = ₹ 1,950 (F)

Sales price variance = AQ (RSQ – AQ)

Product X = 5 (625 – 500)	= ₹ 625 (A)
Product Y = 6 (600 – 600)	= ₹ 600 (F)
Product Z = 7 (375 – 400)	= ₹ 175 (F)
Total	= ₹ 150 (F)

RSQ = Total AQ × Standard ratio = 1,500 × (5:4:3)

Product X = 1,500 × 5/12	= ₹ 625 units
Product Y = 1,500 × 4/12	= ₹ 500 units
Product Z = 7,500 – 3/12	= ₹ 375 units

Sales quantity variance = SP (SQ – RSQ)

Product X = 5 (500 – 625)	= ₹ 625 (F)
Product Y = 6 (400 – 500)	= ₹ 600 (F)
Product Z = 7 (300 – 375)	= ₹ 525 (F)
Total	= ₹ 1,750 (F)

Illustration 11

From the following figures calculate the variance on sales margin basis:

Budget

Sales 2,000 units at ₹ 15 each	= ₹ 30,000
Cost of sales at ₹ 12 each	= ₹ 24,000
Profit Actual	= ₹ 6,000

Actual

Sales 4,900 units at ₹ 14 each	= ₹ 26,600
Cost of sales at ₹ 10 each	= ₹ 19,000
Profit	= ₹ 7,600

Solution

Standard margin = ₹ 15 – ₹ 12 = ₹ 3 per unit

Actual margin – ₹ 14 – ₹ 10 = ₹ 4 per unit

Sales margin quantity variance = SM (SQ – AQ)

= ₹ 3 (2,000 – 1,900) = ₹ 300 (A)

Sales margin price variance = AQ (SM – AM)

= 1,900 (3 – 4) = ₹ 1,900 (F)

Sales margin variance = ₹ 300 (A) + ₹ 1,900 (F)

= 1,600 (F)

= Total actual margin – Total budgeted margin

= ₹ 7,600 – ₹ 6,000 = ₹ 1,600

Illustration 12

From the following information calculate the variances:

Standard direct cost per unit:

Material cost: 10 kg	₹ 100
Labour cost: 40 hours	20
Total	₹ 120

For the production of 250 units materials consumption amounted to ₹ 25,625 against 2,600 kgs. Wages payment was ₹ 5,950 for 10,900 hours including 10 hours idle time due to power failure.

Solution

Material variance

MCV – SC – AC = (SQ × SP) – (AC × AP)

– (2,500 × 10) – ₹ 25,625

– ₹ 25,000 – ₹ 25,625

– ₹ 625 (A)

MPV – AQ (SP – AP) = (AQ × SP) – (AQ × AP)

– (2,600 × ₹ 10) – ₹ 25,625

– ₹ 26,000 – ₹ 25,625

– ₹ 375 (F)

MUV – SP (SQ – AQ)

– ₹ 10 (2,500 – 2,600)

– ₹ 1,000 (A)

Check

MCV – MPV + MUV

₹ 625 (A) – ₹ 375 (F) + ₹ 1,000 (A)

Labour Variance:

LCV – (SR × SH) – (AR × AH)

– (₹ 0.50 × 10,000) – ₹ 5,950

– ₹ 5,000 – ₹ 5,950 = ₹ 950 (A)

LRV – AH (SR – AR)

– (AH × SR) – (AH × AR)

– (10,900 × 0.5) – ₹ 5,950

– ₹ 5,450 – ₹ 5,950

	–	₹ 500(A)
LEV	–	SR (SH – AH)
	–	0.5 (10,000 – 10,900)
	–	₹ 450 (A)

Check

LCV	–	LRV + LEV
₹ 950 (A)	–	₹ 500 (A) + ₹ 450 (A)

Illustration 13

Using the following information calculate each of three labour variance for each department:

Particulars	*Dept. X*	*Dept. Y*
Gross wages direct (Rs.)	28,080	19,370
Standard hours produced	8,640	6,015
Standard rate per hour	3	3.40
(Rs.) Actual hours worked	8,200	6,345

Solution

(*i*) Labour cost variance

(Standard hours × Standard rate) – (Actual hours × Actual rate)

Dept. X (8,640 × 3) – 28,080

₹ 25,920 – 28,080 = ₹ 2,160 (A)

Dept. Y (6,015 × 3.40) – 19,370

₹ 20,451 – 19,370 = ₹ 1,081 (F)

(*ii*) Labour rate variance

(SR – AR) × Actual hours

Dept. X (3 × 8,200) – 28,080

₹ 24,600 – 28,080 = ₹ 3,480 (A)

Dept. Y (3.40 × 6,345) – 19,370

₹ 21,573 – 19,370 = ₹ 2,203 (F)

(*iii*) Labour efficiency variance

(SH – AH) × SR

Dept. X (8,640 – 8,200) × 3

440 × 3 = ₹ 1,320 (F)

Dept. Y (6,015 – 6,345) × 3.40

= 330 × 3.40 = ₹ 1,122 (A)

Illustration 14

The standard time and rate for unit component A are given below:

Standard hours	15
Standard rate	₹ 4 per hour
The actual data and related information are as under:	
Actual production	1,000 units
Actual hours	15,300 hrs.
Actual rate	₹ 3.90 per hour;

Calculate (*i*) Labour cost variance (*ii*) Labour efficiency variance (*iii*) Labour rate variance.

Solution

(*i*) Labour cost variance

(Standard hour for actual production × SP) – (AH × AP)

= (15,000 × 4) – (15,300 × 3.90)

₹ 60,000 – 59,670 = ₹ 330 (F)

(*ii*) Labour efficiency variance (AH – SH) × Standard rate

= (15,300 – 15,000) × ₹ 4

300 × 4 = ₹ 1,200 (A)

(*iii*) Labour rate variance

(SR – AR) × Actual hours

= (4 – 3.90) × 15,300

0.10 × 15,300 = ₹ 1,530 (F)

Check

Labour efficiency variance + Labour rate variance = Labour cost variance ₹ 1,200 (A) + ₹ 1,530 (F) = ₹ 330 (F)

Working Note

Standard hours for actual production

For 1 unit standard hours = 15

1,000 units standard hours = 15 × 1,000 = 15,000 hours.

Illustration 15

From the following data calculate (*i*) Labour cost variance (*ii*) Labour Rate variance and (*iii*) Labour Efficiency variance for each department.

Particulars	*Departments*	
	Polishing	*Painting*
Standard hours	8,640	6,015
Standard rate per hours (₹)	2	1.70
Actual hours worked	8,200	6,295
Actual wages (₹)	18,090	9,685

Solution

LCV = SC – AC = (SR × S Hrs) – (AR × A Hrs)

LRV = A Hrs (SR – AR)

LEV = SR (S Hrs – A Hrs)

Polishing Department

LCY = (8,640 × 2) – (18,090)

= ₹ 17,280 – ₹ 18,090 = ₹ 810 (A)

LRV = (8,200 × 2) – 18,090

= ₹ 16,400 – 18,090 = ₹ 1,690 (A)

LEV = 2 – (8,640 – 8,200) = ₹ 880 (F)

Painting Department

LCV = ₹ (6,015 × 1.7) – ₹ 9,685

₹ 10,225.5 – 9,685 = ₹ 540.5 (F)

LAV = (6,295 × 1.7) – 9,685

₹ 10,701.5 – 9.685 = ₹ 1,016.5 (F)

LEV = ₹ 1.70 (6,015 – 6,295) = ₹ 476 (A)

Illustration 16

The standard time and rate for product are given below:

Standard time per unit 10 hours

Standard rate ₹ 3 per hour. The actual date and related information are given below:

Actual output 1,000 units

Actual time 10,200 hours

Actual rate ₹ 2.90 per hour

Calculate (*i*) Labour cost variance (*ii*) Labour efficiency variance (*iii*) Labour rate variance.

Solution

Labour cost variance	= Standard cost – Actual cost
	= (SR × S Hrs) – (AR – A Hrs)
	= (₹ 3 × 10,000) – (₹ 2.9 – 10,200)
	= ₹ 30,000 – ₹ 29,580
	= ₹ 420 (F)
Labour rate variance	= A Hrs (SR – AR)
	= 10,200 (₹ 3 – ₹ 2.9)
	= ₹ 1,020 (F)
Labour efficiency variance	= A Hrs (SR – AR)
	= ₹ 3 (10,000 – 10,200)
	= ₹ 600 (A)

Check

LCV	= LRV + LEV
₹ 420 (F)	= ₹ 1,020 (F) + ₹ 600 (A)

Illustration 17

The following data relate to a factory:

	Men	Women
Number in Standard Group	20	10
Standard rate per hour	₹ 2.00	₹ 1.20
Number in Actual group	16	14
Actual Rate per hour	₹ 1.80	₹ 1.40

A 48 hours week was worked and the actual output was 1,200 standard hours. There was idle time of one hour due to power failure.

Compute labour cost variances (simple as well as advanced variances).

Solution

Standard cost per hour for the Standard Group

Men	20 × 2.0	= ₹ 40.00
Women	10 × 1.2	= ₹ 12.00
		₹ 52.00

Standard Group hours for the actual output

= 1200 – 30 = 40 hours

Labour cost variance	= SC – AC
	= ₹ (40 × 52) – ₹ (48 × 48.40)
	= ₹ 2,081 – ₹ 2,323.20
	= ₹ 243.20 (A)
Labour rate variance	= A Hrs (SQ – AR)
Men	= (48 × 16) × (₹ 2 – ₹ 1.80)
	= 786 × 0.20
	= ₹ 153.6 (F)
Women	= (48 × 14) × (₹ 1.20 – ₹ 1.40)
	= 672 × 0.20
	= ₹ 134.4 (A)
LRV Total	= 19.2 (F)
Labour efficiency variance	
Men	= SR (S Hrs – A Hrs)
Women	= ₹ 2 (40 × 20) – (48 × 16)
	= ₹ 2 (800 – 768)
LEV Total	= ₹ 64 (F)
	= ₹ 1.2 (40 × 10) – (4 × 14)
	= ₹ 1.2 (400 – 672)
	= ₹ 326.4 (A)
LEV total	**= ₹ 262.4 (A)**

LCV = LRV + LEV ₹ 243.20 (A) = ₹ 19.2 (F) + ₹ 262.4 (A)

Advanced Variances

Labour Mix Variance = SR (S Hrs — A Hrs)

R S Hrs = Standard Proportion of Actual Effective Hours Actual Hours

= Men 47 × 16 = 752 = Women 47 × 14 = 658

= 1,410

Standard proportion R S Hrs	= 2:1
Labour mix variance LMV	= Men – 1,410 × 2/3 = 940
Labour mix variance	= Women – 1,410 × 1/3 = 470
	= Men – ₹ 2 (940 – 752) = 376.0 (F)
Women – ₹ 1.2 (470 – 658)	= 225.6 (A)
L.M.V.	= ₹ 150.4 (F)

Labour efficiency or yield variance

= SR (S Hrs – RS Hrs)

Men = ₹ 2 (800 – 940) = ₹ 280 (A)

Women = ₹ 1.2 (400 – 470) = ₹ 84 (A)

Idle time variance = ₹ 364 (A) = SC per hour × No. of idle hours

= ₹ 48.80 × 1 = ₹ 48.80 (A)

LMV + LYV + Idle time variance

= 150.40 (F) + 364 (A) + 48.80 (A)

Illustration 18

A factory has estimated its overheads for the next year at ₹ 48,000. The factory works 300 days in a year. It works for 8 hours a day. The total-budgeted production for the year is 24,000 units.

Actual data for the month of April are given as under:

Actual overheads	₹ 4,250
Actual output	2,100 units
Idle time	4 hours

Calculate: (*i*) Overhead cost variance (*ii*) Overhead expenditure variance (*iii*) Overhead efficiency variance (*iv*) Idle time variance.

Solution

Overhead cost variance = (Standard overhead cost for actual output) – (Actual overhead cost for actual output)

Overhead expenditure variance = ₹ (2,100 × 2) (₹ 4,250) = ₹ 50 (A)

Overhead efficiency variance = Budgeted overheads – Actual overheads

Variance = ₹ 4,000 – ₹ 4,250

= ₹ 250 (A)

Overhead efficiency variance = (Standard overhead – Actual hours worked) – Standard overheads for actual production

= ₹ (20 × 196) – ₹ (2 × 2,100)

= ₹ 3,920 – ₹ 4,200 = ₹ 280 (F)

Idle time variance = ₹ 4 × ₹ 20 = ₹ 80 (A)

Check

Overhead expenditure variance = Overhead efficiency variance + Overhead Efficiency variance + Idle time variance

= ₹ 50 (A) = ₹ 250 (A) + ₹ 280 (F) + ₹ 80 (A)

Standard overhead rate per unit $= \dfrac{₹\,48{,}000}{24{,}000} = ₹\,2$

Standard overhead rate per hour $= \dfrac{₹\,48{,}000}{300 \times 8} = ₹\,20$

Illustration 19

A factory has estimated its overheads for some year at ₹ 96,000. The factory runs for 300 days in a year. It works for, 8 hours a day. The total budget production for the year is 24,000 articles.

Actual data is also given to you as under for the month of April 2019.

Actual overhead	₹ 8,500
Output	2,100 articles
Idle time	4 hours

Calculate: (1) Overhead cost variance (2) Overhead budget variance (3) Overhead efficiency variance (4) Idle time variance.

Solution

1. Overhead cost variance

   Formula = Standard overhead cost – Overhead cost of actual output

   = ₹ 8,400 – ₹ 8,500 = ₹ 100 (A)

2. Overhead budget variance or expenditure variance

   Budgeted overheads – Actual overheads

   = ₹ 8,000 – ₹ 8,500 = ₹ 500 (A)

3. Overhead efficiency variance

   (*i*) Where standard overhead rate per unit is given

   (Actual production – Standard production in actual hours) × Standard overhead rate per unit.

   (2,100 – 1,960) × ₹ 40 = 14 × ₹ 40 = ₹ 560 (F)

   (*ii*) Where standard overhead rate per hour is given

   (Actual hours – Standard hour per actual production) × Standard overhead rate per hour.

   (196 – 210) × ₹ 40 = 14 × ₹ 40 = ₹ 560 (F)

4. Idle time variance

   (*i*) Where standard overhead rate per unit is given

Formula: Production lost in idle time × Overhead standard rate per unit

40 × ₹ 4 = ₹ 160 (A)

(*ii*) Where standard overhead rate per hour is given: Idle time × overhead standard rate per hour 4 × 40 = ₹ 160 (A)

Check

Overhead efficiency variance + overhead idle time variance = overhead volume variance ₹ 560 (F) + ₹ 160 (A) = ₹ 400 (A)

Overhead volume variance + overhead budget variance = overhead cost variance ₹ 400 (F) + ₹ 500 (A) = ₹ 100 (A)

Working Notes

(*i*) Standard overhead cost of annual output. If monthly production is 2000 units, overhead cost is ₹ 8,000. If monthly production is 2,100 units, overhead cost is

$$= \frac{8{,}000 \times 2{,}100}{2{,}000}$$

Monthly production $= \dfrac{24{,}000}{12}$

Monthly overhead cost $= \dfrac{96{,}000}{12}$

(*ii*) Standard overhead rate per unit Standard units 2,000. Overhead cost ₹ 8,000. Rate per unit $\dfrac{8{,}000}{2{,}000}$ = ₹ 4 per unit

Illustration 20

Items	*Budget*	*Actual*
No. of working days	20	22
Man-hours per day	8,000	8,400
Output per man – hour in unit	1	0.9
Overhead cost (₹)	80,000	84,000

Calculate overhead variances:

Solution = Actual overheads – Standard overhead for actual production

= ₹ 84,000 – (0.50 × 1,66,320)

= ₹ 84,000 – 83,160 = ₹ 840 (A)

Overhead cost variance = Actual overheads – Budgeted overhead

Overhead expenditure variance = ₹ 84,000 – 80,000 = ₹ 4,000 (A)

Overhead volume variance = Budgeted overheads – Std. overhead for actual production
= ₹ 80,000 – ₹ 83,160 = ₹ 3,160 (F)

Overhead calendar variance = Revised Budgeted overheads – Standard overheads for actual man-hours ₹ 88,000 – (₹ 0.5 × 1,84,800) ₹ 88,000 – ₹ 92,400 = ₹ 4,400 (F) (Standard overheads for actual man-hour – Standard overheads for actual output)

Workings

Standard overhead per hour = ₹ 80,000 ₹ 0.50

Standard overhead per unit = 1,60,000

Budgeted man hours = 0.50

Budgeted output = 20 × 8,000 = 1,60,000 h

Budgeted man hours for actual working days = 1,60,000 × 1 = 1,60,000 h

Actual men hours per actual working days = 8,400 × 22 = 1,84,800 h

Actual output for actual hours = 1,84,800 × 0.9 = 1,66,320 unit

Revised budgeted overheads $= \dfrac{₹\ 80{,}000}{20} \times 22 = ₹\ 88{,}000$

= ₹ 92,400 – ₹ (0.5 × 1,66,320)

= ₹ 92,400 – ₹ 83,160 = ₹ 9,240 (A)

Volume variance = Calendar variance + capacity variance + efficiency variance

= ₹ 3,160 (A) = ₹ 8,000 (F) + ₹ 400 (F) + ₹ 9,240 (A)

Illustration 21

From the following basic data calculate (*a*) Overhead cost variance (*b*) Overhead expenditure variance (*c*) Overhead volume variance (*d*) Overhead capacity variance and (*e*) Efficiency variance

Standard output for 40 hours	1,400 units
Standard fixed overheads (₹)	1,400
Actual output	1,200 units
Actual hours worked	32
Actual fixed overheads (₹)	1,500

Solution

Overhead cost variance	= AC – SC for actual output
	= ₹ 1,500 – ₹ 1,200
	= **₹ 300 (A)**
Overhead expenditure, variance	= AFOH – HFOH
	= ₹ 1,500 – ₹ 1,400
	= **₹ 100 (A)**
Overhead expenditure	= BFOH – SFOH for actual output
	= ₹ 1400 – ₹ 1,200
	= **₹ 200 (A)**
Cost variance	= Expenditure variance + volume variance
₹ 300 (A)	= ₹ 100 (A) + ₹ 200 (A)
Capacity variance	= SFOH for HRs – SFOH for A Hrs.
	$= \frac{\textbf{₹ 1,400 (40 – 32)}}{40}$
Efficiency variance	= SFOH for A Hrs – SFOH for actual ouptut

Check

Volume variance = ₹ 200 (A)

Workings

SFOH for Actual hour = ₹ 1,400/40 × 32 = ₹ 1,120

Illustration 22

From the following data calculate (*a*) Overhead cost variance (*b*) Over-head expenditure variance (*c*) Overhead efficiency variance (*d*) Overhead capacity variance (*e*) Calendar variance (*f*) Volume variance date for the month of March, 2019.

Particulars	*Standard Budget*	*Actual*
Number of working days	24	22
Number of hours worked	2,200	1,950
Overhead cost (₹)	1,100	1,200
Production in units	1,100	1,000

Solution

(*a*) Overhead cost variance	= Actual overheads – Standard overheads for actual production
	= ₹ 1,200 – ₹ 1,000 = ₹ 200 (A)
(*b*) Overhead expenditure variance	= Budgeted overheads — Standard overheads for actual = 1,100 – 1,200 = ₹ 100 (A)
(*c*) Overhead volume variance	= Budgeted overheads – Standard over-heads for actual production – ₹ 1,100 – 1,000
	= ₹ 100 (A)
(*d*) Overheads efficiency variance	= (Standard overheads for actual hours worked) – (Standard overheads for actual production)
	= (1,950 × 0.5) – (1,000 × l)
	= ₹ 975 – 1,000 = ₹ 25 (F)
(*e*) Overhead calendar variance	= (Standard overheads for working days) (Std. overhead for actual working day) = ₹ 1,100 – ₹ 1,100 × 22/24
	= ₹ 91.67 (A)
(*f*) Overhead capacity variance	= (Standard overhead for actual working days) – (Standard overheads for actual hours worked) = ₹ 1,100 × 22 – (1950 × 0.50) 24 = ₹ 1,008.33 – ₹ 975 = ₹ 33.33 (A)

Check

Volume variance = Capacity + Calendar + Efficiency

₹ 100 (A) = ₹ 33.33 (A) + ₹ 91.67 (A) + ₹ 25 (F)

Illustration 23

A Ltd. has estimated its overheads for 2019 at ₹ 48,000. The factory run for 300 days of 8 hours per day. The total Budget production for the year is 12,000 units. Actual data for the month of May 2019 is as follows:

Actual overheads ₹ 4,250

Actual output 1,100 units and

Idle time 4 hours.

Calculate (*a*) Overhead cost variance (*b*) Overhead expenditure or budget variance (*c*) Overhead volume variance (*d*) Idle time variance and (*e*) Efficiency variance.

Solution

Overhead cost variance = Actual overheads – Standard overheads for actual production ₹ 4,250 – ₹ 4,400 = ₹ 150 (F)

= ₹ 4,250 – ₹ 4,000 = ₹ 250 (F)

= ₹ 150 (F)

Overhead expenditure variance = Actual overheads – Standard overheads

= ₹ 4,250 – ₹ 4,000 = ₹ 250 (F)

= ₹ 250 (F)

Overheads volume variance = Budget overheads – Standard overheads for actual output

= ₹ 4,000 – ₹ 4,400

= ₹ 400 (F)

Check

Overhead expenditure = Expenditure variance + Volume variance

₹ 150 (F) = ₹ 250 (A) + ₹ 400 (F)

Illustration 24

From the following data calculate sales variances:

Product	*Qty*	*Standard Price per unit*	*Qty*	*Price per unit ₹*
X	200	15	220	12.5
Y	120	20	100	22.5
Z	80	10	120	15.0
	400		440	

Solution

Sales value variance = Standard Sales – Actual Sales

(SP × SQ) (AP × AQ)

X = 3,000 – 2,750 = ₹ 250 (A)

Y = 2,400 – 2,250 = ₹ 150 (A)

Z = 800 – 1,800 = ₹ 1,000 (F)

= ₹ 600 (F)

Sales volume variance = SP (SQ – AQ)

X = ₹ 15 (200 – 220) = ₹ 300 (F)

Y = ₹ 20 (120 – 100) = ₹ 400 (A)

Z = ₹ 10 (80 – 120) = ₹ 400 (F)

Check

Sales volume variance = Price variance + Volume variance

₹ 600 (F) = ₹ 300 (F) + ₹ 300 (F)

Sales Mix variance X = ₹ 15 (220 – 220) = 0

Y = ₹ 20 (100 – 132) = ₹ 640 (A)

Z = ₹ 10 (120 – 88) = ₹ 320 (F)

= ₹ 320 (A)

Sales Quantity variance = SP (RSQ – SQ)

X = ₹ 15 (220 – 200) = ₹ 300 (F)

Y = ₹ 20 (100 – 132) = ₹ 240 (F)

Z = ₹ 10 (120 – 88) = ₹ 80 (F)

Volume variance ₹ 300 (F) = ₹ 320 (A) + ₹ 620 (F) ₹ 620 (F)

Calculation of revised standard quantity:

RSQ = Standard proportion of actual quantity

X = 440 × 5/10 = 220 units

Y = 440 × 5/10 = 132 units $= 440 \times \frac{3}{10} = 132$

Z = 440 × 5/10 = 88 units $= 440 \times \frac{2}{10} \times 88$

Illustration 25

From the following data calculate (*a*) Sales value variance (*b*) Sales price variance and (*c*) Sales volume variance.

Budget :	10,000 units at	₹	5 per unit
Actual :	5,000 units at	₹	5 per unit
	8,000 units at	₹	4.50 per unit

Solution

Sales value variance = Standard sales – Actual sales

= (10,000 × 5) – (5,000 × 5) + (8,000 × 4.5)

= 50,000 – (25,000 + 36,000)

= 50,000 – 61,000

= ₹ 11,000 (F)

Sales price variance	= AQ (SP – AP)
	= 5,000 (5 – 5) = 0
	= 8,000 (5 – 4.5) = ₹ 4,000 (A)
Sales volume variance	= SP (SQ – AQ)
	= ₹ 5(10,000 – 13,000) = ₹ 15,000 (F)

Check

Sales value variance	= Price variance + Volume variance
₹ 11,000 (F)	= ₹ 4,000 (A) + ₹ 15,000 (F)

Illustration 26

The standard labour mix for producing 100 units of a product is:

10 men of Grade I for 6 hours at ₹ 2 per hour

10 men of Grade II for 8 hours at ₹ 1 per hour

Actual production is 1,000 units. But due to shortage of Grade I labour, the standard mix had to be revised as 50 hours of Grade I and 90 hours of Grade II for producing 100 units.

Actual hours paid for were:

Grade I — 480 hours at ₹ 2.20 per hour Grade II — 940 hours at ₹ 1.10 per hour

Calculate the labour cost variances.

Solution

Labour rate variance	= A Hrs (SR–AR)
Grade I	= 480 (2 – 2.2) = ₹ 96 (A)
Grade II	= 940 (1 – 1.1) = ₹ 94 (A)
Total	= ₹ 190 (A)
Labour efficiency variance	= SR (S Hrs – A Hrs)
Grade I	= ₹ 2 (500 – 480) = ₹ 40 (F)
Grade II	= ₹ 1 (900 – 940) = ₹ 40 (A)
Total	= Nil

Labour efficiency variance may be divided into labour mix variance and labour revised efficiency variance

Labour mix variance	= SR (RSM–AM)
Grade I	= 2 (3,550 – 480) = ₹ 54.30 (F)
Grade II	= 1 (6,390 – 940) = ₹ 27.10 (A)
Total	= 27.20 (F)

Labour revised efficiency variance = SQ (SM – RSM)

Grade I $= 2\left(500 - \frac{3,550}{7}\right) = 14.20\text{ (A)}$

Grade II $= 1\left(900 - \frac{6390}{7}\right)\text{A} = 13.00\text{ (A)}$

Total = 27.20 (A)

Revised standard mix of A Hrs (RSM)

Grade I = 1,420 × 50/140 = 507 1/7

Grade II = 1 1,420 – 507 1/7 = 912 6/7

$= 1420 - 507\frac{1}{7}$

Illustration 27

From the following data, calculate:

(*a*) Expenses variance

(*b*) Efficiency variance

(*c*) Capacity variance

Budgeted direct labour hours	4,000
Standard direct labour hours for actual production	4,200
Actual direct labour hours	4,300
Actual overhead expenses incurred	
Variable	₹ 4,500
Fixed	₹ 8,500

Applied overhead rate: ₹ 3.00 per direct labour hour (of which are ₹ 2.00 per hour being fixed overheads)

Solution

(*a*) Budget of Expenses Variance:

Fixed: Actual expenses	₹ 8,500
Budgeted hours × Std. rate	
4,000 hours × ₹ 2.00/hour	₹ 8,000
	₹ 500 Adverse
Variable: Actual expenses	₹ 4,500

Actual hours × Std. rate		
4300 hours × ₹ 1.00/hour	₹ 4300	
	₹ 200 Adverse	
(*b*) Efficiency variance:		
Fixed Earned Std. hours – Actual hours		
X Std. rate (4,200 – 4,300) ₹ 2.00/hour Variable:		₹ 200 Adverse
(*c*) Same formula as above (4,200 – 4,300) ₹ 1.00/hour		₹ 100 Adverse
(*d*) Capacity variance:		
Fixed: Actual hours – Budgeted		
hours × Std. rate (4,300 – 4,000) ₹ 2.00/hour		₹ 600 Favourable

Reconciliation

Overheads recovered through production Std. hours for actual production × Std. rate	₹ 12,600
Actual overheads	₹ 13,000
	₹ 400 Adverse
(*a*) Budget or expense variance	₹ 700 Adverse
(*b*) Efficiency variance	₹ 300 Adverse
(*c*) Capacity variance	₹ 600 Favourable
Total	₹ 400 Adverse

Illustration 28

Actual overheads for the month	₹ 10,500
Budgeted overheads for the month	₹ 10,000
Budgeted labour hours	5,000
Budgeted no. of days	25
Actual hours	5,500
Actual no. of days	26
Standard hours required per unit	5
Standard overhead rate per hour	₹ 2
Actual output in units	1,000

Using the above data, calculate:

(*a*) Expenses variance
(*b*) Calendar variance
(*c*) Capacity variance
(*d*) Efficiency variance
(*e*) Volume variance
(*f*) Total variance

Solution

(*a*) *Expenses Variance:*

1. Actual overheads incurred	₹ 10,500
2. Budgeted overheads	₹ 10,000
	₹ 500 Adverse

(*b*) *Calendar Variance:*

1. Budgeted labour hours	
$\frac{5,000}{25} \times 26^* \times ₹\ 2$	₹ 10,400
25 (budgeted days)	
2. Budgeted overheads	₹ 10,000
	₹ 400 Favourable

(*d*) *Volume Variance*:

1. as per (*d*) above	₹ 10,000
2. as per (*b*) above	₹ 10,400
	₹ 400 Adverse

(It is checked Capacity + Efficiency = Volume Variances)

(*f*) *Total Variance:*

1. Overheads recovered through jobs as per (*d*) above	₹ 10,000
2. Actual overheads	₹ 10,500
	₹ 500 Adverse

Reconciliation:

Expense variance	₹ 500 Adverse
Calendar variance	₹ 400 Favourable
Volume variance	₹ 400 Adverse
(Capacity + Efficiency)	—
Total	500 Adverse

Illustration 29

The following are the standard and actual cost figures for the month of January 2019:

	Standard	*Actual*
Production (units)	*20,000*	*20,000*
	₹	₹
Material at ₹ 1 per kg.	20,000 @ ₹ 1.10	23,100
Labour @ ₹ 0.5 per hour	15,000 @ ₹ 52	15,340
Fixed expenses	30,000	33,000

Compute the variance for January 2019.

Solution

Computation of Variance for January 2019

Material variances

Price = AQ (SP – AP = 21,000 units (1.00 – 1.10)	= ₹ 2,100 (A)
Usage = SP (SQ – AQ) = ₹ 1 (20,000 – 21,000)	= ₹ 1,000 (A)
Cost = (Price + Usage)	= ₹ 3,100 (A)

Labour variances

Rate = A Hrs (SR – AR) = 29,500 (0.50 – 0.52)	= ₹ 590 (A)
Efficiency = SR (S Hrs – A Hrs) = ₹ 0.50 (30,000 – 29,500)	₹ 250 (F)
Cost = (Rate + Efficiency)	= ₹ 340 (A)

Fixed overheads variances

Expenditure = (AFOH – BFOH) = (₹ 33,000 – ₹ 30,000)	= ₹ 3,000 (A)
Volume = (BFOH – SFOH) = (₹ 30,000 – ₹ 30,000)	= Nil
Cost (AFOH – SFOH)	₹ 3,000 (A)

Workings

AQ of materials used = ₹ 23,100 + ₹ 1.10 = 21,000 units

A Hrs. of labour = 15,340 + 0.52 = 29,500 hrs

Illustration 30

The results of Progressive Co. Ltd. for the year 2018 and 2019 were as a under:

	2016	2017
	₹	₹
Direct Materials	50,000	66,000
Direct Labour	30,000	33,000
Variable overheads	6,000	7,000
Fixed overheads	10,000	12,000
Net Profit	4,000	8,500
Sales	1,00,000	1,26,500

Materials prices wage rates and selling prices had all an increase of 10% in 2019 as compared to 2018. Prepare a statement showing how each factor has contributed to the variance in Net profit.

Solution

1. *Sales*

After eliminating the effect of selling price increase of 10% from 2019 sales value. The sales at 2018 base prices were ₹ $\dfrac{1,26,500 \times 100}{110}$

= ₹ 1,15,000 and therefore

Volume increase was 15%

(*a*) Sales volume variance (₹ 1,15,000 – 1,00,000) ₹ 15,000 F

(*b*) Sales price variance (₹ 1,26,000 – 1,15,000) ₹ 11,500 F

Total sales variance ₹ 26,500 F

2. *Direct Material*

After eliminating 10% cost increase material cost at 2018 comparable price was

$$\frac{₹\,66,000 \times 100}{100} = ₹\,60,000$$

(*a*) Material price variance (₹ 60,000 – 66,000) ₹ 6,000 A

(*b*) Material usage variance (₹ 50,000 + 15% volume increase = ₹ 57,500 – 60,000) ₹ 2,500 A

Total Material Cost Variance ₹ 8,500 A

3. *Direct Labour*

Similarly, after eliminating wage rate increase, wage cost at 2019 level works out to

$$\frac{₹\,33,000 \times 100}{110} = ₹\,30,000$$

(*a*) Rate of pay variance (₹ 30,000 – 33,000) ₹ 3,000 A

(*b*) Efficiency variance (₹ 30,000 + 15% volume increase = ₹ 34,500 – 30,000) ₹ 4,500 F

Total Labour Cost Variance ₹ 1,500 F

4. *Variance Overheads*

Efficiency variance (₹ 6,000 + 15% volume increase = ₹ 6,900 – 7,000)

5. *Fixed Overheads*

(*a*) Capacity/Efficiency Variance (₹ 10,000 – 11,500) i.e. ₹ 10,000 + 15% for activity increase)

Expense variance (₹ 11,500 – 12,000) ₹ 1,500 A

(*b*) Expense variance (₹ 11,500 – 12,000) ₹ 500 A

Profit Reconciliation Statement

Particulars	*2018*	*2019*	*Variances*			
	Amount [₹]	*Amount* [₹]	*Volume Amount* [₹]	*Price Rate Amount* [₹]	*Efficiency usage Amount* [₹]	*Total Amount* [₹]
Sales	10,0001	26,500	15,000 (F)	11,500 (F)	–	26,500 (F)
Costs:						
Direct material	50,000	66,000	7,500 (A)	6,000 (A)	4,500 (F)	16,000 (A)
Direct labour	30,000	·33,000	4,500 (A)	3,000 (A)	4,500 (F)	3,000 (A)
Variable overhead	6,000	7,000	900 (A)	–	100 (A)	1,000 (A)
Fixed overheads	10,000	12,000	–	500 (A)	500 (A)	2,000(A)
Total Cost	96,0001	18,0001	29,000(A)	9,500 (A)	400 (F)	22,000 (A)
Profit	4,000	8,500	2,100 (F)	2,000(F)	400 (F)	4,500 (F)

Impact of volume variance on profit can also be checked in another practical way.

Sales volume variance ₹ 15,000 @ 14% contribution in 1979 = ₹ 2,100 (F).

Illustration 31

The standard selling price of a product produced by Champion Engineering (P) Ltd., is built up as follows:

	₹ per unit.
Materials 4 kg @ ₹ 3/-	12
Labour 2 hours @ ₹ 2/-	4
Variable overheads	1
Fixed overheads	3
	20
Profit	5
Selling price	25

During a month, actual production was 9,000 units as against the budgeted production of 10,000 units. The Profit and Loss A/c. of the Company disclosed the following information for the period under consideration. Profit and Loss Account for the month.

To Direct materials (₹ 3.06 per kg)	1,10,160	By Sales	9,000 units @ 26/- each
To Wages (18,000 hours including 500 hours lost due to power failure)	36,900		
To Variable overheads	8,500		
To Fixed overheads	27,500		
To Profit	50,940		2,34,000

There was no opening or closing work in progress or finished goods. Calculate the relevant variance and reconcile the actual profit with budgeted profit.

Solution

Variance Analysis.

Material

Price = Actual Qty × difference in price

(9,000 units × 4 kg = 36,000 kg. @ ₹ 3.00 – 3.06) = ₹ 2,160 Adverse

Labour

Rate = Actual Hours × difference in rates

(9,000 units × 2 hrs = 18,000 hrs @ ₹ 2.00 – 2.05) = ₹ 900 Adverse

Efficiency = Standard hours–Actual hours × Standard rate (18,000 hrs – 17,500 excluding abnormal hours

due to power failure × ₹ 2/--	₹ 1,000 Favourable
Idle time = Idle hours × Standard rate 500 hours	
lost due to power failure @ ₹ 2	₹ 1,000 Adverse
Lost Labour variance	₹ 900 Adverse
Overheads:	
Expenditure – Variable and Fixed	
Standard allowed expenditure (–) Actual Expenditure	
Variable:	
(9,000 units @ ₹ 1/- = ₹ 9,000 – 8,500)	₹ 500 (F)
Fixed	
(9,000 units @ ₹ 3/- = ₹ 22,000 – 27,500)	₹ 500 (A)
Total overhead variance	0
Sales	
Volume = Actual volume – Budgeted volume	
× Standard profit per unit	
(9,000 unit – 10,000 units @ ₹ 5/-)	₹ 5,000 Adverse
Price = Actual Qty × difference in selling price	
9,000 units × (₹ 26 – 25) per unit	₹ 9,000 Favourable
Total Sales Variance	₹ 4,000 Favourable

Reconciliation of Profit	Amount [₹]	Amount [₹]
Budgeted profit (10,000 Units @ 5/-)		50,000 (F)
Variance:		
Materials	2,160 (A)	
Labour	900 (A)	
Sales	4,000 (F)	
Net Variation		940 (F)
Actual Profit		50,940 (F)

Illustration 32

Reconcile the standard sales with actual sales and the standard profit with the actual on the basis of variances from the information given below:

Standard product	*Qty sold units*	*Selling price per unit* [₹]	*Cost per unit* [₹]
A	3,000	50	35
B	2,000	60	40
Actual			
A	3,250	55	36
B	2,750	58	37

Solution

Reconciliation of Standard Sales and Profit with Actual Sales and Profit

	Sales [₹]	*Profit* [₹]
Standard	2,70,000	85,000
Variances		
Price	10,750 (F)	10,750 (F)
Quantity	54,000 (F)	17,000 (F)
Mix	3,500 (F)	1,750 (F)
Cost	–	–
Actual	3,38,250	1,19,500

Workings

Sales variances		Profit variances		
Price Variance	= AQ (SP – AQ)	AQ (SM – AM)		
Product	A = 3,250 (50 – 55) = 16,250 (F)	3,250 (15 – 20)	=	16,250 (F)
	B = 2750 (60 – 68) = 5,500 (A)	2,750 (20 – 18)	=	5,500 (A)
	Total	10,750 (F)		10,750 (F)

Fixed overhead = Total semivariable – Variable overheads

= 30,000 – (10,000 × 2.5) = ₹ 5,000

Normal fixed overhead rate per hour = ₹ 5,000 + 10,000 = ₹ 0.50

Actual fixed overheads at 8,750 hours = ₹ 5,250

Actual variable overheads at 8,750 hrs = ₹ 28,750 – ₹ 5,250 = ₹ 23,500

Standard working hours = 8,750 less 5% = 8,312.5 hours

Computation of overhead variances

Variable overhead variances:

Expenditure variance = AVOH – SVOH on A Hrs worked

= ₹ 23,500 – (₹ 25 × 8,750) = ₹ 1,625 (A)

Efficiency variance = SVOH – (A Hrs worked – S Hrs)

= ₹ 2.50 (8,750 – 8,312.5) = ₹ 1,093.75 (A)

Total variance = ₹ 1,625 (A) + ₹ 1,093.75 (A) = ₹ 2,718.75 (A)

Fixed overhead variance = AFOH – BFOH

= ₹ 5,250 – ₹ 5,000 = ₹ 250 (A)

Volume variance = ₹ 5,000 – (₹ 0.50 × 8,212.5) = ₹ 84.75 (A)

Efficiency variance = SFOH (A Hrs – 8 Hrs)

Capacity variance = SFOH (B Hrs – A Hrs)

Total variance = ₹ 250 (A) + ₹ 218.75 (A) + ₹ 625 (A) = ₹ 1,093.75

REVIEW QUESTIONS

1. Define the following terms: Standard costing, Estimating costing.
2. What is Standard costing? State its main objectives.
3. Describe the various types of standards.
4. Distinguish between Standard costing and Budgetary control.
5. What is Estimating costing, and how does it differ from Standard costing?
6. What is meant by historical costing?

7. Explain the following: Material mix variance, Labour efficiency variance, Overhead expenditure variance, Sales quantity variance.
8. Distinguish between Current Standard and Basic Standard.
9. State to which type of industries Standard Costing may be applied.
10. Explain the major advantages of Standard Costing.
11. How are standards fixed? Explain.
12. Discuss the causes for material price and usage variances.
13. List out the reasons to labour efficiency variance.
14. State the preliminaries to be considered while setting production standards.
15. "Proper managerial control of manufacturing operations depends upon standard costing." Do you agree? Explain the above statement.
16. Explain the limitations of standard costing.
17. Explain the term 'variance' under standard costing, and discuss significance.
18. What do you mean by variance analysis? What are its advantages?
19. From the following particulars calculate material cost variance:
    Materials purchased: 3,000 kgs at ₹ 3 per kg.
    Standard quantity of materials required per unit of output: 30 kgs.
    Standard rate of materials: ₹ 2.50 per kg.
    Opening stock of materials: ₹ 2.50 per kg.
    Closing stock of materials: 500 kgs.
    Production during the period: 80 units.

REVIEW PROBLEMS

1. Excel Ltd. manufactures a product X. It is estimated that for each **ton of materials** consumed, 100 articles should be produced. The standard price per ton of material is **₹ 10.** During the first week in January 2019, 100 tons of material were issued to production, the **price of which** was ₹ 10.5 per ton.

   Production during the week was 10,200 articles.

   Compute the variances from above.

   [**Ans.** MPV ₹ 18.75 (A); MUV ₹ 7.5 (F); MCV ₹ 11.25 (A)]
2. The standard and actual mix of materials used in the manufacturing a product are as under:

Material	*Standard*	*Actual*
A	60 tons @ ₹ 5 per ton	80 tons @ ₹ 4 per ton
B	40 tons @ ₹ 10 per ton	70 tons @ ₹ 8 per ton

   Reconcile actual material cost with standard material cost.

   [**Ans.** RCV ₹ 1.5(A) ; LRV ₹ 4 (A); LEV ₹ 2.5 (F)]
3. It is estimated that in the manufacture of a product, for each tonne of material used, 100 pieces should be produced. The standard price per tonne of material is ₹ 10. During the second week of June 2019, 100 tonnes of material were used for the production. The issue price was ₹ 10.50 per tonne. The actual output for the period was 10,250 pieces. Calculate the material cost variances.

   [**Ans.** MCV – ₹ 25(A); MPV – ₹ 50(A); MYV – ₹ 25 (F)]

4. From the following information, calculate (*i*) MCV, (*ii*) MPV, (*iii*) MUV, (*iv*) MMV, (*v*) MYV and (*vi*) MRUV.

Material	*Qty.(kg)*	*Standard Price (₹)*	*Actual Qty. (₹)*	*Price (₹)*
X	50	6	40	6
Y	40	3.75	50	3.60
Z	30	3.00	40	2.80
Total	120		130	
Less 10% Normal loss	12	Actual loss	22	
	108		108	

[**Ans.** MCV ₹ 8 (F); MPV ₹ 15.5 (F); MUV ₹ 7.5 (A); MMV ₹ 37.5 MMV; ₹ 37.5 (F); MYU and MRUV ₹ 45 (A)]

5. The standard cost of a certain chemical mixture is as follows:

₹ 6 per unit Wages paid with bonus: ₹ 8,000

Time taken : 50 hrs Time taken: 40 hrs

[**Ans.** LCV ₹ 800 (A), LRV ₹ 3,200 (A), LEV ₹ 2,400 (F)]

6. Calculate the labour cost variances:

	Standard	Actual
Output	1,000 Units	1,200 Units
Rate of payment	₹ 6 per unit	Wages paid with bonus ₹ 8,000
Time taken :	50 hrs	Time taken: 40 hrs.

[**Ans.** LCV ₹ 1.5 (A); LRV ₹ 4 (A); LEV ₹ 2.5 (F)]

7. The production of a certain unit is assumed to require 18 hours' labour at a rate of ₹ 1.25 per hour. On completion of the production of a unit it was found that the time taken was 16 hours, the wage rate being ₹ 1.50 per hour.

Calculate the Labour variances.

[**Ans.** LCV ₹ 1.5 (A); LRV ₹ 4 (A); LEV ₹ 2.5 (F)]

8. Details regarding the composition and the weekly Wage rates of 3 labour force engaged on a job scheduled to be completed in 30 weeks are as follows:

Category of workers	*No. of labourers*	*Weekly wage rate per labourer (₹)*	*No. of labourers*	*Weekly wage rate per labourer (₹)*
Skilled	75	60	70	70
Semi-skilled	45	40	30	50
Unskilled	60	30	80	20

The work is actually completed in 32 weeks. Calculate the various labour variances.

[**Ans.** LCV = ₹ 13,000 (A), LRV = ₹ 6,400 (A); LEV = ₹ 6,600 (A)]

9. The following figures have been extracted from the cost books of a factory for the month of March 2019:

	Standard	*Actual*
Number of units produced	15,000	16,000
Capacity	100%	100%
Number of days worked	25	26
Variable overheads	₹ 30,000	₹ 31,500
Fixed overheads	₹ 45,000	₹ 46,500

Analyse the total overhead variance into:

(*a*) Expenditure

(*b*) Capacity

(*c*) Calendar

(*d*) Efficiency variance.

[**Ans.** (*a*) ₹ 300 (F) (*b*) ₹ 1,800 (F) (*c*) ₹ 1,800 (F) (*d*) ₹ 1,200 (F)]

10. The budgeted output of a product is 5,00,000 units per annum. Fixed overheads for the same period are ₹ 2,25,000. Each year the factory closes for two weeks' annual holiday.

During the First week in January, the actual output was 10,250 units while the actual expenditure was ₹ 4,750.

Standard performance is 250 units per hour on a 40-hour week basis. One hour a week was lost due to abnormal idle time.

Calculate various fixed overhead variances.

[**Ans.** FOH Exp. V. ₹ 250 (A); Vol. V. ₹ 112.5 (F); Eff.V. ₹ 225 (F); Capacity ₹ 112.5 (A)]

11. The standard overhead rate of a product is developed as follows:

Variable	₹ 4.00
Fixed (Budgeted production 10,000 units)	₹ 6.00

Standard time allowed for production of each unit of product is 5 hours. The following actual data are available for a month:

Production	₹ 9,600 units
Time taken	₹ 47,900 hours
Overheads:	
Variable	₹ 38,500
Fixed	₹ 60,500

Compute overhead variances.

[**Ans.** VOH Exp. V. ₹ 180 (A); Eff. V. ₹ 80 (F) VOH Cost V. ₹ 100 (A); FOH Exp V. ₹ 500 (A); Vol. ₹ 2,400 (A); Efficiency V. ₹ 120 (F); Capacity ₹ 2,520 (A); VOH Cost V. ₹ 2,900 (A)]

12. In a manufacture process, the following standards apply:

Standard Price	: Raw material X ₹ 1 per kg.
Standard Price	: Raw material Y ₹ 5 per kg.
Standard Mix	: 75% X; 25% Y (by weight)
Standard Yield	(weight of product as percentage of weight of raw material) : 90%

In a period, the Actual Costs, Usages and Output were as follows:

Used	: 4,400 kgs. X costing ₹ 4,620
	1,600 kgs. Y costing ₹ 7,840
Output	: 5,670 kgs. of products.

The budgeted output of the period was 7,200 kgs. Prepare a statement; showing how material cost variance is built up, and give activity and yield percentages. (Adapted I.C.W.A. London)

13. A tonne of a particular standard of material 'M' is obtained from the following mixture:

330 kg. material X at ₹ 10 per kg.

275 kg. material Y at ₹ 8 per kg.

495 kg. material Z at ₹ 5 per kg.

During a month 200 tonnes of material 'M' were produced by actually using: 70 tonnes of material X at ₹ 9 per kg. 60 tonnes of material Y at ₹ 9 per kg., 110 tonnes of material Z at ₹ 6 per kg.

Calculate: (*a*) Material price variance, (*b*) Material usage variance, (*c*) Material mix variance, (*d*) Material yield variance (Adapted from I.C.W.A X inter)

[**Ans.** (*a*) ₹ 1,00,000 (A); (*b*) ₹ 1,25,000 (A); (*c*) ₹ 10,000 (F); (*d*) ₹ 1,45,000 (A)]

14. A gang of workers normally consists of 30 men, 15 women, and 10 boys. They are paid at standard hourly rates as under:

Men – ₹ 0.80, Women – ₹ 0.60; Boys – ₹ 0.40. In a normal working week of 400 hours, the gang is expected to produce 2,000 units of output.

During the week ended 31st December 2017 the gang consisted of 40 men, 10 women and 5 boys. The actual wages paid were at ₹ 0.70, 0.65, and 0.30 respectively and 4 hours were lost due to abnormal idle time and 1,600 units were produced.

Calculate (*i*) Wage variance (*ii*) Wage rate variance (*iii*) Labour Revised efficiency variance (*iv*) Labour Composition or Mix variance and (*v*) Labour idle time variance.

(C.A. Final)

[**Ans.** (*i*) ₹ 256 (A), (*ii*) ₹ 160 (F), (*iii*) ₹ 148 (A), (*iv*) ₹ 120 (A), (*v*) ₹ 148 (A)]

15. C.M.K. Company operates a standard costing system with flexible budgets. From the following details, compute the different overhead variances separately for the fixed and variable overheads Flexible Budget.

Standard production in units	*Overhead costs*
	₹
1,000 units	5,000
800 units	4,600
700 units	4,400

Each unit of production is equivalent to 10 standard hours. The actual results of a particular month are:

Output in standard hours:	9,000
Clock hours worked:	9,500
Actual overhead incurred during the month:	
Fixed	₹ 2,900
Variable	₹ 1,950

The budget is based on 1,000 standard units of production.

	Standard data			*Actual data*		
	Qty Units	*S.P.* ₹	*Total* ₹	*Qty Units*	*S.P.* ₹	*Total* ₹
Product A	500	5.00	2,500	625	5.40	3,375
Product B	700	8.00	5,600	875	8.20	7,175
			₹ 8,100			₹ 1,550

Calculate (1) Sales value variance, (2) Sales price variance, (3) Sales volume variance.

[**Ans.** (1) ₹ 2,450 (F) (2) 425 (F) (3) 2,025 (F)

16. For unit of product A, the standard data are given below:

Material	
5 kgs @ ₹ 40 per kg.	₹ 200
Labour	
40 hrs. @ ₹ 100 per hour	₹ 40
	₹ 240

Actual data	
Actual production : 100 units	
Material 490 kg. @ ₹ 42 each	₹ 20,580
Labour 3960 hrs @ 1.10 per hour	₹ 4,356
	₹ 24,936

Calculate variances.

[**Ans.** MCV ₹ 580 (A); MPV ₹ 980 (A); MUV ₹ 400 (F); LCV ₹ 356 (A); LRV ₹ 396 (A); LEV ₹ 40 (F)]

■ ■ ■

13

Budgets and Budgetary Control

The management is efficient if it is able to accomplish the objective of the enterprise. It is effective when it accomplishes the objectives with minimum effort and cost. In order to attain long-range efficiency and effectiveness, management must chart out its course in advance. A systematic approach to facilitate effective management performance is profit-planning and control, or budgeting. Budgeting is therefore an integral part of management. In a way, a budgetary control system has been described as a historical combination of a "goal-setting machine for increasing an enterprise's profits, and a goal-achieving machine for facilitating organisational coordination and planning while achieving the budgeted targets".

DEFINITIONS

The Institute of Cost and Management Accountants, London, gives the following definitions:

A budget is "a financial and/or quantitative statement, prepared and approved prior to a defined period of time, of the policy to be pursued during that period for the purpose of attaining a given objective. It may include income, expenditure and the employment of capital."

Budgetary control. "The establishment of departmental budgets relating the responsibilities of executives to the requirements of a policy, and the continuous comparison of actual with budgeted results, either to secure by individual action the objectives of that policy, or to provide a firm basis for its revision."

Thus, a budget is a predetermined statement of management policy during a given period which provides a standard for comparison with the results actually achieved. Budgetary control is a system of controlling costs which includes the preparation of budgets, coordinating the departments and establishing responsibilities, comparing actual performance with that of budgeted and acting upon results to achieve maximum profitability. Budgeting is essentially concerned with planning, and can be broadly illustrated by comparison with the routine a ship's captain follows, on each voyage.

OPERATION OF BUDGETARY CONTROL

The steps involved in a Budgetary Control system can be outlined as follows:

1. Establish a plan or target of performance which coordinates all the activities of the business.

2. Record the actual performance.

3. Compare the actual performance with that planned.

4. Calculate the differences, or variances, and analyse the reasons for them.

5. Act immediately, if necessary, to remedy the situation.

OBJECTIVES OF BUDGETARY CONTROL

Briefly, the main objectives of budgetary control are:

1. To combine the ideas of all levels of management in the preparation of the budget.

2. To coordinate all the activities of the business.

3. To centralise control.

4. To decentralise responsibility to each manager involved.

5. To act as a guide for management decision-making when unforeseeable conditions affect the business.

6. To plan and control income and expenditure so that maximum profitability is achieved.

7. To direct capital expenditure in the most profitable direction.

8. To ensure that sufficient working capital is available for the efficient operation of the business.

9. To provide a yardstick against which actual results can be compared.

10. Show management where action is needed to remedy a situation.

BASIC CONDITIONS FOR THE SUCCESSFUL OPERATION OF BUDGETARY CONTROL

Realistic Budget: The quality of the budget is very important for the successful operation of budgetary control. 'It should be realistic and operationally feasible. Flexible budget is normally a good budget as it takes into consideration the dynamics of the business. It must be based on what is attainable, must suit the organisational facilities and complexities and must be flexible to accommodate the changing environment of the business.

Qualitative and Timely Reporting: Variances must be analysed, interpreted and reported in a manner which is easily understandable. Reporting must be on time and bring out significant areas/ points and be precise, simple and meaningful. Time is the essence of reporting and maintenance of time schedule enhances the value of reporting and leads to correction of many adverse events/ trends which otherwise would have taken a heavy toll.

Managements Attitude: The management must have a positive attitude towards budgetary control. Any scheme of control is a discipline and regulation. Management must have faith and confidence in the scheme. Management must take keen interest in the scheme of budgetary control and render whole-hearted support and cooperation in making this a success.

ADVANTAGES OF BUDGETARY CONTROL

The following are some of the most significant advantages of budgeting:

1. Budgeting compels management to plan for the future. The budgeting process forces management to look ahead and become more effective and efficient in administering business operations. It instils into managers the habit of evaluating carefully their problems and related variables before making any decisions.
2. Budgeting helps to coordinate, integrate, and balance the efforts of various departments in the light of the overall objectives of the enterprise. This results in goal congruency and harmony among the departments.
3. Budgeting facilitates control by providing definite expectations in the planning phase that can be used as a frame of reference for judging the subsequent performance. Undoubtedly, budgeted performance's a more relevant standard for comparison than past performance, since past performance is based on historical factors which are constantly changing.
4. Budgeting improves the quality of communication. The enterprise's objectives, budget goals, plans, authority and responsibility and procedures to implement plans are clearly written and communicated through budgets to all individuals in the enterprise. This results in better understanding and harmonious relations among managers and subordinates.
5. Budgeting helps to optimise the use of the firm's resources, both capital and human. It aids in directing the total efforts of the firm into the most profitable channels.
6. Budgeting increases the morale and thereby the productivity of the employees by seeking their meaningful participation in the formulation of plans and policies, bringing about a harmony between individual goals and the enterprise's objectives, and by providing incentives for better performance.
7. Budgeting develops profit-mindedness and cost consciousness.
8. Budgeting permits the management to focus attention on significant matters through budgetary reports. Thus, it facilitates management by exception and thereby saves the management's time and energy.
9. Budgeting measures efficiency and thereby enables self-evaluation by the management, it also indicates the progress made in attaining the enterprise's objectives.

PROBLEMS OF THE BUDGETING SYSTEM

The major problems in developing a budgeting system are:

1. Getting the support and involvement of all levels of management.
2. Developing meaningful forecasts and plans, especially the sales plan.
3. Inducing all individuals to get involved in the budgeting process, and gaining their full participation.
4. Establishing realistic objectives, procedures and standards of desired performance.
5. Applying the budgeting systems in a flexible manner.
6. Maintaining effective-follow-up procedures, and adapting the budgeting system to changing circumstances.

LIMITATIONS OF BUDGETARY CONTROL

Management must consider the following limitations in using the budgeting system as a device to solve managerial problems:

1. Budgeting is not an exact science; its success depends upon the precision of estimates. Estimates are based on facts and managerial judgement. Managerial judgement can suffer from subjectivity and personal biases. The efficacy of budgeting thus depends upon the quality of managerial judgement.
2. A perfect system of budgeting cannot be organised in a short period. Business conditions change rapidly. Therefore, the budgeting system should be continuously adapted to changing circumstances. Budgeting has to be a continuous exercise; it is a dynamic process. Management should not lose patience; it should go on trying various techniques and procedures in developing and using the budgeting system.
3. A skillfully prepared budget system will not by itself improve the management of an enterprise unless it is properly implemented. For the success of the budgetary system, it is essential that it is understood by all, and that the managers and subordinates put in concerted effort for accomplishing the budget goals. All persons in the enterprise must be fully involved in the preparation and execution of budgets, otherwise budgeting will not be effective.
4. Budgeting is a management tool; a way of managing, not the management itself. The presence of a budgetary system should not make management complacent. To get the best results, management should use budgeting with intelligence and foresight, along with other managerial techniques. Budgeting assists management; it cannot replace management.
5. Budgeting will be ineffective and expensive if it is unnecessarily detailed and complicated. A budget should be precise in format and simple to understand; it should be flexible in application.

6. The purpose of budgeting will be defeated if the budget goals are set carelessly. Budget goals are the definite targets to achieve the overall objectives of the enterprise. They must be in harmony with the aims of the enterprise.
7. Budgeting will hide inefficiencies instead of revealing them if there is no evaluation system. There should be continuous evaluation of the actual performance. The standards should also be re-examined regularly.

Budgeting will lower the morale and productivity of the personnel if unrealistic targets are set and if it is used as a pressure tool. To some extent budgeting may be used as a pressure device but its extent must be carefully determined.

ORGANISATION FOR BUDGETARY CONTROL

It is essential that there should be an efficient organisation if budgetary control is to be operated effectively. Budgetary control is not only an accounting exercise, but also a tool of management at all levels. In organising a system, it is essential to obtain the full cooperation of each member of the management team. A number of preliminaries will be necessary if the staff are to have confidence in the system; these include:

1. *Creation of budget centres*: Centres or departments should be established for each of which budgets can be set with the help of the head of department concerned. A budget centre is a centre or department or a segment of an organisation for which budgets are prepared. Budgets should be set with the help of the heads of these centres so that these may be implemented more effectively.
2. *Introduction of adequate accounting records*: It is imperative that the accounting system should be able to record and analyse the information required. A chart of accounts should be maintained which corresponds with the budget centres.
3. *All personnel should be trained in operating the system*: Each person must know what a budget is, what it has to accomplish and how he fits into the plan. He must feel that he is capable of handling the budget centres.
4. *Preparation of an organisation chart:* This defines the functional responsibilities of each member of the management, and ensures that he knows his position in the company and his relationship with other members.

The organisation chart will obviously depend upon the nature and size of the company, but a simplified specimen is given in Fig.13.1 to show the general principles involved. Other budgets such as the raw materials or labour budgets may be prepared by heads of departments: for example by the accountant, in conjunction with the production manager. It should be appreciated that in the preparation of each of these budgets the accountant will play a big part, especially those activities involving costs, such as the sales cost budget. Budgets will be prepared by heads of departments as shown in the following page.

5. *Establishment of a budget committee:* In small companies a budget officer or the accountant may coordinate all the work connected with budgets, but in large companies a budget committee is often established to formulate a general programme for preparing budgets and exercising overall control. The Chief Executive of the company may establish guiding principles but usually he delegates the responsibility for operating the system to the budget officer as secretary of the committee. This committee is composed of the chief executive, budget officer and heads of the main departments such as those shown in Fig. 13.1. Each member will prepare his own initial budget or budgets, which will then be considered by the committee, and all budgets will be coordinated. Usually many changes are necessary before the budgets can be finally integrated and approved. The main functions of the committee are:

(*i*) To provide historical information to help managers in forecasting.
(*ii*) To issue instructions regarding budget requirements, final dates for the receipt of budgets, etc.
(*iii*) To define the general policies of management in relation to the budget.
(*iv*) To advise in the preparation of budgets.
(*v*) To review budgets.
(*vi*) To suggest revisions and amendments to budgets.
(*vii*) To approve budgets.
(*viii*) To ensure that budgets are submitted in due time.
(*ix*) To prepare budget summaries wherever necessary.
(*x*) To prepare the master budget after functional budgets have been approved.
(*xi*) To analyse comparison of budgeted and actual results, and to recommend corrective action where necessary.
(*xii*) To coordinate the budget programme.

6. *Preparation of budget manual*. This is defined (by the I.C.M.A.) as a document which sets out the responsibilities of the persons engaged in the routine of, and the forms and records required for budgetary control. It is usually in loose-leaf form so-that alterations can easily be made as and when required; appropriate sections can be issued to executives requiring them. An index will be provided so that information can be located quickly. Such a manual will usually prove invaluable, as it will include information such as:

Description of the system and its objectives.

(*i*) Procedure to be adopted in operating the system.
(*ii*) Definition of responsibilities and duties.
(*iii*) Reports and statements required for each budget period.
(*iv*) The accounts code in use.
(*v*) Deadline by which data are to be submitted.

Type P
Chief Executive

Budget Officer

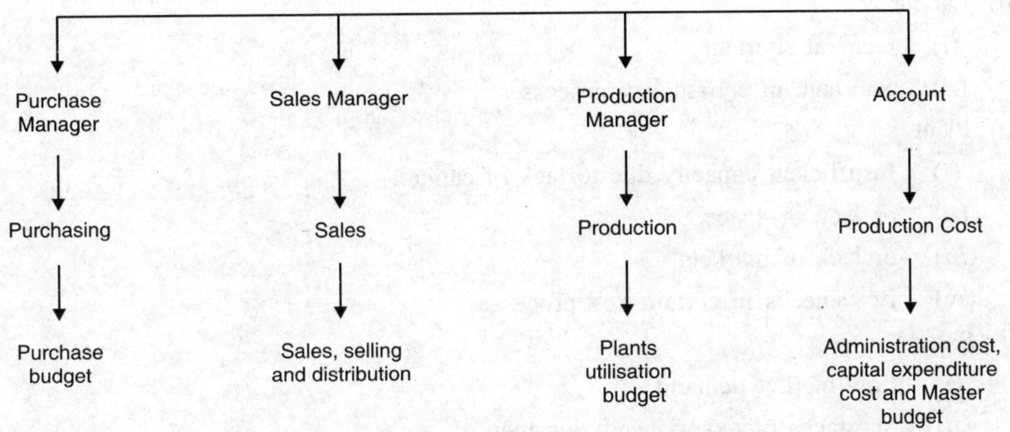

Fig 13.1. Organisation Chart for Budgetary Control

7. *Budget period*: There is no "right" period for any budget. Budget periods may be short term and long term. If a business experiences seasonal fluctuations, the budget period will probably extend over one seasonal cycle. If this cycle covers, say two or three years, the long-term budget would cover that period, while the short-term budgets would perhaps be prepared on a monthly basis for control purposes. Short-term budgeting is usually costly to prepare and operate, while long-term budgeting may be considerably affected by unforeseen conditions. Budget periods frequently used in industry vary between one month and one year, the latter probably being the most commonly used as it fits in with the normally accepted accounting period. However, forecasts of much longer periods than a year may be used in the case of capital expenditure budgets, for example, which must be planned well in advance. A common practice in industry is to have a series of budget periods. Thus, the sales budget may cover the next five years, while production and cost budgets may cover only one year. These yearly budgets will be broken down into quarterly or even monthly periods. Where long-term budgets are operated; it is usual to supplement them with short-term ones.
8. *The key factor*: This is the factor whose influence must first be assessed in order to ensure that functional budgets are reasonably capable of fulfilment. The key factor—known variously as the "limiting" or "governing" or "principle budget" factor — is of vital importance. It may not be the same for each budget period, as the circumstances may change.

It determines priorities in functional budgets. Among the many key factors which may affect budgeting are the following:

(*a*) Materials

(*i*) Availability.

(*ii*) Restrictions imposed by licences, quotas, etc.

(*b*) Labour

(*i*) General shortage.

(*ii*) Shortage in certain key processes.

(*c*) Plant

(*i*) Insufficient capacity due to lack of capital.

(*ii*) or lack of space.

(*iii*) or lack of markets.

(*iv*) Bottlenecks in certain key processes.

(*d*) Sales

(*i*) Low market demand.

(*ii*) Shortages of experienced salesmen.

(*iii*) Insufficient advertising due to lack of money.

(*e*) Management

(*i*) Lack of capital, restricting policy.

(*ii*) Lack of knowhow.

(*iii*) Inefficient executives.

(*iv*) Insufficient research into product design and methods. The factor which is most often the key factor in industry is probably the sales demand. Very often the success or otherwise of budgetary control rests on the forecast of sales during the budget period. If the sales figure proves to be inaccurate, most of the budgets will be affected.

9. *Level of activity*. It will be necessary to establish the normal level of activity, that is the level the company can reasonably be expected to achieve. This level is important in forecasting, for example, material and labour requirements, and particularly production overhead budgets which are to be recovered on machine-hour rates.

CLASSIFICATION OF BUDGETS

Though budgets can be classified according to various points of view.

The following bases of classification are generally in vogue:

(A) Classification according to time factor;

(B) Functional classification;

(C) Classification according to flexibility factor.

(A) Classification According to Time Factor

In terms of time factor, budgets are broadly of the following three types:

1. *Long-term Budgets:* They are concerned with planning the operations of a firm over a perspective of five to ten years. They are usually in the form of physical quantities.
2. *Short-term Budgets:* They are usually for a period of a year or two and are in the form of production plan in monetary terms.
3. *Current Budgets:* They cover a period of a month or so and as short-term budgets, they get adjusted to prevailing circumstances. Sometimes, within the framework of a short-term budget, there are quarterly plans which are prepared by recasting the budget for a still shorter period on the basis of the performance of the immediate past. In a way, these quarterly budgets are meant to be an elaboration of the annual budget.

(B) Functional Classification

According to this basis of classification, budgets correspond, and are co-terminous, with a particular function and are integrated with the master budget of the business. These are called functional budgets whose number depends on the size and nature of the business. The usual functional budgets of a business are:

Sales Budget: This is a forecast of total sales, classified according to groups of products, salesmen and geographical locations.

Selling and Distribution Cost Budget: This is concerned with an estimate of the cost of selling and distribution of goods.

Production Budget: This is a forecast based on sales, productive capacity and requirements of inventories, etc.

Production Cost Budget: This is related to the cost of production, including direct material cost, direct labour cost and expenses—fixed, variable and semi-variable.

Purchase Budget: Correlated with sales forecast and production planning, it deals with purchases that are required for planned production. Purchase would include both direct and indirect materials and goods.

Personnel Budget: This has reference to the utilisation of men and would include labour employed in productive activity. This would be split up between direct and indirect labour.

Research Budget: This relates to improvement in the quality of the products or research for new products.

Cash Budget: This is a sum total of the requirements of cash in respect of various functional budgets as well as anticipated cash receipts.

Plant Utilisation Budget: This is intended to cover the plant and machinery requirements to meet the budgeted production during the period. Schedules will be produced showing the available load in each department expressed in standard hours or units.

Office and Administration Budget: This budget represents cost of all administrative expenses, such as managing director's salary, staff salaries and expenses of office management like lighting and cleaning.

Capital Budget: This is a forecast of outlay on fixed assets as also of the sources of capital budget. It may differ from that of other budgets as, such expenditure is frequently planned a number of years in advance.

Master Budget: The ultimate integration of separate budgets by the accountant provides the Master Budget which includes estimated profit and loss account for the future period, and an estimated Balance Sheet at the end thereof.

(C) Classification According to Flexibility Factor

1. *Fixed Budget:* This is a budget in which targets are rigidly fixed. Such budgets are usually prepared from one to three months in advance of the fiscal year to which they are applicable. Thus, twelve months or more may elapse before figures forecast for the December budget are used to measure actual performance. Many things may happen during this intervening period and they may make the figures go widely out of line with the actual figures. Though it is true that a fixed, or static budget as it is sometimes called, can be revised whenever the necessity arises, it smacks of rigidity and artificially so far as control over costs and expenses are concerned.' Such budgets are preferred only where sales can be forecasted with the greatest of accuracy which means, in turn, that the cost and expenses in relation to sales can be quite accurately ascertained.
2. *Flexible Budget:* The figures used in this form of cost and expense budget are made adaptable to any given set of operating conditions within any month of the fiscal year. The figures range from the lowest to the highest probable percentages of operating activity in relation to the standard operating performance. From this point of view, a flexible budget prepared for an expenses group can be for the entire fiscal year, or as long as there is no need of material changes in the standards. Thus, the flexible budget proposes a distinct advantage over the static budget particularly where it is difficult to forecast sales costs and expenses with any degree of accuracy.

PREPARATION OF BUDGET

Sales Budget

This is a forecast of total sales expressed and incorporated in quantities and/or money. A sales budget may be prepared by expressing turnover under any one or combination of the following:

1. Product or product group;
2. Territories, areas and countries;
3. Types of customers, e.g., National, Government, export, home, wholesales or retails;
4. Salesmen, agents or representatives, and
5. Period, such as quarters, months, weeks, etc.

A sales budget may be prepared with the help of any one or more of the following methods:

1. Analysis of past sales with adjustment for current conditions.
2. Field estimates by own sales staff.

3. Analysis of the potential market for the firm's products.
4. Studying the impact of other sundry factors affecting the sales budget.

1. *Analysis of past sales:* Analysis of past sales for a number of years, say 5 to 10 years, viz long-term trend, seasonal trend, cyclical trend, sundry other factors. The long-term trend represents the movement of the fortunes of a business over many years. The seasonal trend may affect many types of business and hence this factor must be taken into account when studying figures for consecutive months over a number of years. The cyclical trend represents the fluctuations in the business activity due to the effect of the trade cycle. In order to study the cyclical trend it is desirable to disregard the effects of the long-term and seasonal trends. Sundry factors include, such as a strike in the industry or a serious fire or flood. From such analysis it will be possible to suggest future trends. In analysing such sales, considerable help can be obtained from statistical reports produced by the trade units and commercial intelligence units, government publications, etc.
2. *Field estimates by own sales staff:* The salesman in each area should have an intimate knowledge of the factors likely to affect his sales in the next few months or years. He can probably make a guess about the unsold stock in the shops of his customers. He is then in a position to make an estimate of future sales. When such estimates are available for a number of years, the actual sales for the year can be compared with the estimated sales and a correction factor calculated to allow for each salesman's tendency to over-estimate.
3. *Analysis of the potential market:* Market research people may report on the state of the market, population in area, fashion, trends, the type of product design required by customers, purchasing power of people, activities of competitors and the prices the consumers are likely to pay.
4. *Studying the impact of factors affecting sales:* Any change in the company policy or methods should always be considered. For example, introduction of special discounts, special salesmen, a new design of the product, new or additional advertising campaigns, improved deliveries, after-sales service should have some market effect on a sales budget. While preparing such forecasts, the sales manager must consider the opinion of divisional managers and other sales staff, the budget officer and the accountant. It will be observed that the preparation of a sales budget involves many factors and calls for a high degree of knowledge of conditions, and of ability to deduce from the known facts and various estimates the probable course of sales over the budget period. If sales be the principal budget factor, then the sales budget is prepared first. If production is the key factor, the production budget should be built up first and the sales budget must be drawn up within the limits imposed by the production budget.

Illustration I

AB Co. Ltd. manufactures two products, A and B, and sells them through two divisions— North and South. For the purpose of submission of sales budget to the budget committee, the following information has been made available:

Product	*North*	*South*
A	4,000 at ₹ 9	6,000 at ₹ 9
B	3,000 at ₹ 21	5,000 at ₹ 21

Actual sales of the current year were:

Product	*North*	*South*
A	5,000 at ₹ 9	6,000 at ₹ 9
B	2000 at ₹ 21	4,000 at ₹ 21

Market studies reveal that the product, A, is popular but under-priced. It is observed that if the price of A is increased by ₹ 1 it will still find E ready market. On the other hand, B is over-priced to customers and the market could absorb more if the sales price of B is reduced by ₹ 1. The management has agreed to give effect to the above price changes.

From the information relating to these price changes and reports from salesman, the following estimates have been prepared by divisional managers.

Solution

Sales Budget
AB Co. Ltd.

Prepared by.... For the Year 20.........
Checked by......
Submitted on...

Division	*Product*	*Budget for future period*			*Budget for current period*			*Actual sales for current period*		
		Unit	*Price*	*Value*	*Unit*	*Price*	*Value*	*Unit*		*Price value*
North	A	5,000	10	50,000	4,000					
	B	4,000	20	80,000	3,000	21	63,000	2,000	21	42,000
Total		9,000		1,30,000	7,000		99,000	7,000		87,000
South	A	7,000	10	70,000	6,000	9	54,000	7,000	9	63,000
	B	6,000	20	1,20,000	5,000	21	1,05.000	4,000	21	84,000
Total		13,000		1.20,000	11,000		1,59,00	11,000		1.47000
Total	A	12,000	10	1,20,000	10,000	9	90,000	12,000	9	1.08.000
(Summary)	B	10,000	20	2,00,000	8,000	21	1,68,000	6,000	21	1.26,000
Total		22,000		3,20,000	18,000		2,58,000	18,000		2,34,000

Percentage increase in sales over current budget is:

Product	*North*	*South*
A	+10%	+ 5%
B	+20%	+10%

With the help of an intensive advertisement campaign the following additional sales over the estimated sales of divisional managers are possible:

Additional sales above the estimated sales of divisional managers

Product	*North (Units)*	*South (Units)*
A	600	700
B	400`	500

You are required to prepare a budget for sales incorporating the above estimates and also show the budgeted and actual sales of current year.

This budget may be modified according to salesmen, or period such as months, quarters, etc.

Illustration 2

In the Stansales Co Ltd., there are four sales divisions, each consisting of four areas — North South, East and West. The company sells two products, X and Y. Budgeted sales for the six months ended on June 30, 2019 area of division 1 were as follows:

North	X	10,000	units at	₹	10 each
	Y	6,000	units at	₹	5 each
South	Y	12.000	units at	₹	5 each
East	X	15,000	units at	₹	10 each
West	X	8,000	units at	₹	10 each
	Y	5,000	units at	₹	5 each
Actual sales for the same period in division 1 were as follows:					
North	X	11,500	units at	₹	10 each
	Y	7,000	units at	₹	5 each
	Y	12,500	units at	₹	5 each
East	X	16,500	units at	₹	10 each
West	X	9,500	units at	₹	10 each

From the salesman's report and observations of the area sales managers, it is thought that sales could be budgeted for the six months ended on June 30, 2020, as follows:

Illustration 3

Division Area	*No.1 Product*		*Sales Budget* *Budget June 30, 2018*			*Budget June 30, 2019*			*Six Months to June 30, 2019* *Actual June 30, 2019*		
North	X		12,000	10	120,000	10,000	10	100,000	11,500	10	115,000
	Y		6,500	5	32,500	6,000	5	30,000	7,000	5	35,000
		Total	18,500		152,000	16,000		130,000	18,500		150,000
South	X		3,000	10	30,000	-	-	-	-	-	-
	Y		13,000	5	65,000	12,000	5	60,000	12,500	5	62,500
		Total	16,000		95,000	12,000	5	60,000	12,500	5	62,500
East	X		17,000	10	170,000	15,000	10	150,000	16,500	10	165,000
	Y		5,000	5	25,000	-	-	-	-	-	-
		Total	22,000		195,000	15,000		150,000	16,500		165,000
West	X		9,000	10	90,000	8,000	10	80,000	9,500	10	95,000
	Y		5,500	5	27,500	5,000	5	25,000	5,250	5	26,250
	Total		14,500		117,500	13,000		105	14,750		121,250
Total	X		41,000	10	410,000	33,000	10	330,000	37,500	10	375,000
	Y		30,000	5	150,000	23,000	5	115,000	24,750	5	123,750
	Total		71,000		560,000			445,000	62,250		498,750

Similar budgets will be prepared for each division, then a sales budget prepared for the company as a whole showing sales by divisions rather than areas. Sales in the division will be further analyse to show sales by salesmen and by customer.

North	X	Budgeted increase of 2,000 units on June 2018 budget
	Y	Budgeted increase of 500 units on June 2018 budget
South	Y	Budgeted increase of 1,000 units on June 2018 budget
East	X	Budgeted increase of 2,000 units on June 2018 budget
West	X	Budgeted increase of 1,000 units on June 2018 budget
	Y	Budgeted increase of 500 units on June 2018 budget

At a meeting of area sales manager with the divisional sales manager it is decided that sales campaigns will be undertaken in areas of South and East. It is anticipated that these campaigns will result in additional sales of 3,000 units of X in the South area, and 5,000 units of Y in the East area.

Prepare for presentation to top management the sales budget for the six months ended June 30, 2019 showing also the budgeted and actual sales for June 30, 2020 which are to be provided as a guideline in fixing the sales budget.

PRODUCTION BUDGET

Like the sales budget, the production budget is built up in terms of quantities and money. The quantities are entered at the beginning and, when the remainder of the budgets have been built up and the costs of production calculated, the costs are entered to compile a production cost budget. In preparing the production budget, consideration should be given to the following:

1. Principal budget factor, e.g., if sales be the budget factor then it should be the sales budget; otherwise other budgets.
2. Production planning and determination of optimum factory capacity.
3. The opening stocks, and stocks required to be carried at the end of the period.
4. The policy of the management regarding manufacture or purchase of components.

The production budget may be classified under the following heads:

(*a*) Products

(*b*) Manufacturing department

(*c*) Months, quarters, etc.

Illustration 4

Production budget, of AB' Co. Ltd. based on the sales budget of Illustration 1, and the following estimated stocks at the beginning and end of the future budget period:

Product	*Estimated stock 1st January Units*	*31st December Units*	*Sales as per sales budget Units*
A	1,000	1,000	12,000
B	1,000	2,000	10,000

Solution

ABC Co. Ltd.
Production Budget (in units)

Items	A	B	Remarks
Sales during the period	12,000	10,000	
Required stock on 31st Dec.	1,000	2,000	
Total	13,000	12,000	
Less Estimated opening stock	1,000	1,000	
Estimated production	12,000	11,000	

In case of normal loss on distribution, the quantity to be produced will be correspondingly increased. The total yearly production may be segregated to show monthly or quarterly production.

PRODUCTION COST BUDGET

A production cost budget summarises the materials budget, labour budget, and factory overhead budget, and may be expressed and analysed by departments and/or products. A production cost budget shows the estimated cost of carrying out the production plans and programmes set out in production budget. It shows the following:

1. Material cost from materials budget.
2. Labour cost from labour budget.
3. Factory overhead-subdivided into fixed, variable and semi-variable costs, from factory overhead budget.

These costs are analysed by departments and/or products according to convenience.

Items	For the Year....		
	A ₹	B ₹	Total . ₹
Units to be produced Elements of cost Material cost (from material budget) Labour cost (from labour budget) Factory overhead (from factory overhead budget)			
		Total	

MATERIALS BUDGET

A Materials Budget shows the estimated quantities as well as cost of raw materials and components required for producing goods as per production budget. At the first stage of preparation of the materials budget only quantities are incorporated. Later on the prices from the purchases budget are used to obtain the cost of each material consumed.

Illustration 5

Prepare a Materials Budget of XYZ Co., based on Production budget as given above. The production orders of the products show the following consumption.

Consumption for a batch of 100 units of

Material No.	*Product X* *kg*	*Product Y* *kg*
01	50	80
02	10	5
03	–	30
04	6	10
05	4	4
Total	70	129

Solution

XYZ Co. Ltd.
Materials Budget
For the year 2018

Product	*Qty. to be produced*	*Mat 1*	*Mat 2*	*Mat 3*	*Mat 4*	*Mat 5*
X	12,000	600	1200	–	720	480
Y	11,000	880	550	3500	110	440
Total quantity		1,4800	1750	3500	1820	920
Rate per kg.		₹ 60	₹ 60	₹ 10	₹ 50	₹ 25
Cost of each material		₹ 88,800	₹ 10,500	₹ 3,500	₹ 9,100	₹ 2,300

Note: Cost of Material = Qty. × Rate per kg.

PURCHASE BUDGET

A purchase Budget gives the details of the purchase which must be made to meet the needs of the business. It includes all items of purchase, such as raw materials, indirect materials and other equipments. The purchase budget for raw materials is the most important and the following factors are required to be considered in preparing this budget:

1. Opening and closing stocks.
2. Unfulfilled orders at the beginning of the budget period.
3. Storage space, economic buying quantity, and financial resources.
4. The prices to be paid.

Illustration 6

The following information regarding the stocks of materials required for the production programme of Ramesh Limited is available.

Materials	*Estimated Consumption during 2019-2020*	*On Ist July 2019*	*Estimated stocks (in kg) on 30th June 2020*
AB	90,30,00	20,000	17,000
GH	69,00,00	10,000	20,000
XY	54,70,00	30,000	33,000

Collating the details given above with the information contained in the Materials Budget, prepare the Purchase Budget of Ramesh Limited.

Particulars	*AB kg*	*GH kg*	*XY kg*
Estimated Consumption	9,03,000	6,90,000	5,47,000
Add: Stock required on 30-6-2020	17,000	20,000	33,000
Total requirements	9,20,000	7,10,000	5,80,000
Less: Estimated stock on 1st July 2019	20,000	10,000	30,000
Quantity to be purchased	9,00,000	7,00,000	5,50,000
Price per kg (Estimated)	9,00,000	50 p	40 p
Estimated cost of purchase of materials (₹)	90,00,000	3,50,000	2,20,000

Preparation of Cash Budget

A complete system of budgetary control makes the construction of cash budget easy. It is one of the functional budgets which is prepared along with other budgets. There are three recognised methods of preparing a cash budget:

(*a*) The Receipts and Payments Method;
(*b*) The Adjusted Profit and Loss Method; and
(*c*) The Balance Sheet Method.

Receipts and payments method

Under this method, all actual possible items of cash receipt and payments for the budgeted period are considered. Sources of information are the various other budgets. For example, (*a*) Sales from the sales budget (*b*) Materials, labour, overhead expenditure and captial expenditure etc., from the concerned budgets.

Steps to be adopted

Cash Receipts Forecast: Cash receipts from sales, debtors, income from sales of assets and investments, and probable borrowings should be forecast and brought into cash budget. Any lag in payment by debtors or by others shall be considered for ascertaining further cash inflows.

Cash Requirements Forecast: Total cash outflows are taken-out from operating budgets for the elements of cost, and from capital expenditure budget for the purchase of fixed assets. Adjustments are to be made for any lag in payments.

Care must be taken to ensure that outstandings or accruals are excluded from the cash budget since this method is based on the concept of actual cash flows.

Illustration 7

A newly started company Quick Co. Ltd., wishes to prepare cash budget from January. Prepare a cash budget for the first six months from the following estimated revenue and expenditure:

	Amount [₹]	Amount [₹]	Amount [₹]	Amount [₹]	Amount [₹]
Jan.	20,000	20,000	4,000.	3,200	800
Feb.	22,000	14,000	4,400	3,300	900
Mar.	24,000	14,000	4,600	3,300	800
Apl.	26,000	12,000	4,600	3,400	900
May	28,000	12,000	4,800	3,500	900
June	30,000	16,000	4,800	3,600	1,000

Cash balance on 1st January was ₹ 10,000. A new machine is to be installed at ₹ 30,000 on credit, to be repaid by two equal instalments in March and April.

Sales commission @ 5% on total sales is to be paid within the month following actual sales. ₹ 10,000 being the amount of 2nd call may be received in March. Share premium amounting to ₹ 2,000 is also obtainable with 2nd call.

Period of credit allowed by suppliers	2	months
Period of credit allowed to customers	1	month
Delay in payment of overheads	1	month
Delay in payment of wages	1/2	month

Assume cash sales to be 50% of total sales.

Quick Co. Limited—Cash Budget—For the period January to June 2020

Quick Co. Limited
Cash Budget

Details	*Jan.*	*Feb.*	*Mar.*	*April*	*May*	*June*
	Amount[₹]	*Amount*[₹]	*Amount*[₹]	*Amount*[₹]	*Amount*[₹]	*Amount*[₹]
A *Balance* B/D	10,000	18,000	29,800	20,000	6,100	8,800
B *Receipts:*						
Cash sales (50%)	10,000	11,000	12,000	13,000	14,000	15,000
Debtors	—	10,000	11,000	12,000	13,000	14,000
Capital	—	—	10,000	—	—	—
Share premium	—	—	2,000	—	—	—
(A+B) Total	20,000	39,000	64,800	45,000	33,100	37,800
C *Payments*						
Material	—	—	20,000	14,000	14,000	12,000
Wages	2,000	4,200	4,500	4,600	4,700	4,800
Production Overheads	—	3,200	3,300	3,300	3,400	3,500
Selling and Distribution Overheads	—	800	900	800	900	900
Commission	—	1,000	1,100	1,200	1,300	1,400
Machinery	—	—	15,000	15,000	—	—
(C) Total	2,000	9,200	44,800	38,900	24,300	22,600
Balance (A+B–C)	18,000	29,800	20,000	6,100	8,800	15,200

Sometimes, it is required to forecast cash or working capital and this can be computed in the usual way as described above. Further consideration is necessary in respect of lag in payments and lag in realisation.

Adjusted profit and loss method

Compared with the previous method, this method is less detailed and more difficult to comprehend. It is particularly useful for the long-term forecasts, say for a period of over three years. It is called thus, because it transforms the profit and loss account into cash forecast. The basic assumption in this method is that any increase or decrease in cash balance is due to profit or loss of the business. All non-cash items such as depreciation, write-offs or write-ups etc., are mainly adjusted to the net profit. The theory, under this method, is based on the assumption that profit is cash. If there were no credit transactions or transactions resulting in capital profits, the balance of profit on the Profit and Loss account should be equal to the balance of cash in the cash book. Such a situation however will never exist in practice in any business. Hence all adjustments with regard to the above items are to be made in the cash forecast. Sources of information are the firm's profit and loss account and balance sheet.

Illustration 8

From the following information prepare a cash budget under the adjusted profit and loss method:

Balance Sheet as on 1-1-2019

Liabilities	*Amount* [₹]	*Assets*	*Amount* [₹]
Share capital reserve	50,000	Land and building	30,000
Profit and loss a/c	5,000	Plant and machinery	20,000
Debentures creditors	9,000	Furniture and fixtures	5,000
Accrued expenses	10,000	Closing stock	4,000
	28,800	Debtors	26,000
	200	Bank	18,000
	1,03,000		1,03,000

Forecasting Trading, and Profit and Loss Account
For the Year Ending 31-12-2019

Particulars	*Amount* [₹]	*Particulars*	*Amount* [₹]
To Opening stock	4,000	By Sales Closing stock	80,000
To Purchases	60,000	By Closing stock	10,000
To Gross profit c/d	26,000		
	90,000		90,000
To Salary and wages 2,500		By Gross Profit b/d	26,000
Outstanding 500	3,000	By Interest received	100
To Depreciation:			
To Plant and machinery	2,000		
To Furniture and fixture	1,000		
To Administrative expenses	3,500		

Selling expenses Net Profit c/d	1,500 14,100	By Balance b/d	26,100
	26,100		
Dividends paid Balance c/d	10,000 13,100		9,000
	26,100		26,100

The following are the additional information for the year 2019: shares were issued for ₹ 10,000, and debentures were issued for ₹ 2,000.

On 31-12-2019 expenses were ₹ 500, Debtors ₹ 20,000, Creditors ₹ 30,000 and land and buildings, ₹ 40,000.

Cash Budget — Adjusted Profit and Loss Method

Particulars	*Amount* [₹]	*Amount* [₹]	*Amount* [₹]
Cash balance on 1-1-2019			18,000
Additions to cash:			
Income—Net profit for the year		14,100	
Depreciation:			
Plant and machinery	2,000		
Furniture and fixture	1,000	3,000	
Accrued expenses (difference)	300		
Reduction in debtors	6,000		
Increase in creditors	1,200		
Issue of share capital	10,000		
Issue of debentures	2,000		
		19,500	36,600
Cash available			54,600
Deduction from cash:			
Dividends paid	10,000		
Increase of stock	6,000		
Purchase of land and building	10,000		
			26,000
Cash balance as on 31.12.2019			28,600

Balance sheet method

The same theoretical assumption of the adjusted profit and loss method holds good in this method also. Under this method, a budgeted balance sheet is prepared showing all items of assets and liabilities except cash balance. The balancing figure is considered to represent cash balance. If there is excess of liabilities over assets, the balance is ordinary cash balance; if there is excess of assets over liabilities, the balance is assumed to be bank overdraft. Of these three methods, the first method is mostly preferred because it is a short-term forecast and in much more detailed than the other two methods which are normally used as long-term forecasts.

Illustration 9

Using the data of Illustration 8, prepare a cash forecast showing cash at bank on 31-12-2019 under balance sheet method.

Solution

The balancing figure of ₹ 28,600 represents cash at bank on 31-12-2019. This is obtained by completing the balance sheet from the information obtained from Illustration 8, as follows:

Forecast Balance Sheet as on 31-12-2019

Liabilities	*Amount*[₹]	*Assets*	*Amount*[₹]
Share capital	60,000	Land and building	40,000
Capital reserve	5,000	Plant and machinery	18,000
Profit and loss account	13,100	Furniture and fixture	4,000
Debenture	12,000	Closing stock	10,000
Creditors	30,000	Debtors	20,000
Accrued expenses	500	Bank (balancing figure)	28,600
	1,20,600		1,20,600

FLEXIBLE BUDGETS

In those industries where the pattern of demand is stable, a fixed budget may be adequate, especially where the budget period is comparatively short. In such businesses it is possible to forecast sales with a considerable degree of accuracy. There are many undertakings where stable conditions are absent. In such concerns fluctuations in output might lead to violent deviations from the budget. In such concerns it is usual to adopt the flexible budgetary technique. A flexible budget is a budget which is designed to change in accordance with the level of activity actually attained. If flexible budgeting is adopted, a series of budgets would be compiled to cover the range of levels of activity possible. In such budgets division of costs and expenses into fixed and variable is extremely important.

The need for a flexible budget can be illustrated as follows:

The owner of a car knows that the more he uses it per year the more it costs him to operate it. He also knows that the more he uses his car the less its costs per running kilometre. The reason for this lies in the nature of the expenses, some of which are fixed while others are variable or semi-variable. Insurance, taxes, registration, and garaging are fixed costs; they remain the same whether the car is operated 1,000 or 2,000 kilometres. The costs of tyres, petrol oil, and repairs are variable costs and depend largely upon the kilometres driven. Obsolescence and depreciation result in a combined type of cost that, although fluctuating to some degree upon the usage of the car, is semi-variable for it does not vary directly with the usage. The cost of operating the car per kilometre depends on the number of kilometres the car is used. The mileage constitutes the basis for judging the activity of the automobile. If the owner prepares an estimate of total costs and compares his actual expenses with the budget in keeping his expenses within the allowed limits, unless he takes the mileage factor into account.

The underlying principle of a flexible budget is that for any given volume of business there should be some norm of expenditure and that norm should be known beforehand to provide a guideline to actual expenditure. To recognize this principle is to accept the fact that every business is dynamic, and ever-changing. It is futile to expect a business to, conform to a fixed, pre-conceived pattern. Preparation of flexible budgets result in the construction of a series of formula, one for each department or cost centre. The formula for each account indicates the fixed amount and/or or variable rate. The fixed amount remains constant regardless of activity. The variable portion of the formula is a variable rate expressed in relation to a base such as direct labour hours, direct labour cost, or machine hours.

Originally, the flexible budget idea was applied principally to the control of departmental factory overhead. In recent years, however, the idea has been applied to the entire budget so that production budgets as well as selling and administrative budgets are prepared on a flexible basis. The construction of a flexible budget is identical with that of a fixed budget, except that a budget is calculated for each volume ranging from a possible 60 per cent to 100 per cent of capacity. When actual figures are available estimate previously determined for the level attained are compared with actual results, and the differences are noted. This end-of-period comparison is used to measure the performance of each department head. It is this readymade method of comparison that makes the flexible budget a valuable instrument for cost control. The flexible budget, assists in evaluating the effects of varying volumes of activity on profits and on cash position.

Illustration 10

The following data are available in a manufacturing company for the half-year period ending 30th June, 2019

	₹ (lakhs)	
Fixed expenses:		
Wages and salaries	8.4	
Rent, rates, and taxes	5.6	
Depreciation	7.0	
Sundry administrative expenses	8.9	29.9
Semi-variable expenses: @ 50% of capacity -		
Maintenance and repairs	2.5	
Indirect labour	9.9	
Sales department salaries etc.	2.9	
Sundry administrative expenses	2.6	17.9
Variable expenses: @ 50% of capacity —		
Material	24.0	
Labour 25.6		
Other expenses	3.8	53.4

It is assumed that fixed expenses remain constant for all levels of production; semi-variable expenses remain constant between 45% and 65% of capacity, increasing by 10% between 65% and 80% of capacity and 20% between 80% and 100% of capacity.

Sales at the various levels are:

60% capacity	₹ 100.00 lakhs
75% capacity	₹ 120.00 lakhs
90% capacity	₹ 150.00 lakhs
100% capacity	₹ 170.00 lakhs

Prepare a flexible budget for the half-year and forecast the profits at 60%, 75%, and 90% of capacity.

Solution

Flexible Budget for the Half-Year Ending 30th June 2019
(Showing the forecast of profit of different levels)

Particulars	*Operating capacity*				*Standard*
Elements of cost	50%	60%	75%	90%	100%
A. *Fixed expenses:*					
Wages and salaries	8.4	8.4	814	8.4	8.4
Rent, rates and taxes	5.6	5.6	5.6	5.6	5.6
Depreciation	7.0	7.0	7.0	7.0	7.0
Sundry expenses	8.9	8.9	8.9	8.9	8.9
	29.9	29.9	29.9	29.9	29.9
B. *Semi-variable exp:*					
Maintenance and repairs	2.5	2.5	2.75	3.00	3.00
Indirect labour	9.9	9.9	10.89	11.88	11.88
Sales Dept. salaries	2.9	2.9	3.19	3.48	3.48
Sundry adm. expenses	2.6	2.6	2.86	3.12	3.12
	17.9	17.9	19.69	21.48	21.48

Particulars	*Operating capacity*				*Standard*
Elements of cost	50%	60%	75%	90%	100%
C. *Variable expenses:*					
Material	24.0	28.80	36.00	43.20	48.0
Labour	25.6	30.72	38.47	46.08	51.2
Other expenses	3.8	4.56	5.70	6.84	7.6
	53.4	64.08	80.17	96.12	106.8
Total cost of production	101.2	111.88	129.76	147.50	158.18
Profit (+) or Loss (–)		–11.88	– 9.76	+2.50	+11.82
Sales		100.00	120.00	150.00	170.00

CONSOLIDATION OF BUDGETS

A coordinating authority is necessary to resolve difficulties and disputes which arise between the departmental heads in relation to the budgets. The aim of budgeting is to produce a complete forecast of how all the various sections of the business should behave. Therefore, adjustments are often necessary. Decisions of this nature are the functions of the Managing Director. He will normally appoint a committee of the departmental heads to advice him. If, however, vital matters of policy are involved, the decision must be made by the Board of Directors. The Chief Accountant should prepare statement summarising the various budgets and bring out the points which need clarification and decision by the Managing Director.

Master Budget

When the necessary decisions have been taken by the Managing Director to harmonise the different sectional budgets, a Master Budget will be prepared. This will set out, in considerable detail, the plan of operation for all departments for the budget period and will be placed before the Board of Directors, for its acceptance. After acceptance, the Master Budget becomes the authority for the necessary executive action to be taken to implement it. A Master Budget is basically a summary budget as it embodies the summarised figures, the details of which are incorporated in other principal budgets. It represents the overall plan of the enterprise. A specimen of a Master Budget is given below:

Example 1

Master Budget

1. Revenue Budget for 3 Months up to March 31, 2019

Products	*P*	*Q*	*R*	*Total*
	Amount [₹]	*Amount* [₹]	*Amount* [₹]	*Amount* [₹]
Sales	5,82,000	2,60,000	2,30,000	10,72,000
Materials	4,75,552	2,05,020	1,76,256	8,56,828
Labour	8,959	5,917	3,676	18,552
Factory overheads	26,015	18,900	8,580	53,495
	5,10,526	2,29,837	1,88,512	9,28,875
Administration				
Overheads:				
Fixed				20,000
Variable				10,000
Selling and Distribution:				
Fixed				11,000
Variable				18,000
Budget profit on production c/d				84,125
Budget profit on production b/d				10,72,000
Deduct Directors fees				84,125
Profit as per Capital Movement Budget, March 31, 2020				2,000
				82,125

2. Capital Movement Budget, 3 Months to March 31, 2019

Particulars		*Amount*[₹]
Capital expenditure		18,500
Increase in stock		50,000
Increase in debtors		36,000
Reduction in:		
Tax	2,00,000	
Dividends	60,000	2,60,000
		3,64,500
Proceeds of shares issue		1,00,000
Increase in provision for depreciation		8,110
Increase in creditors		32,915
Reduction in cash at bank		1,41,350
Budgeted profit		82,125
		3,64,500

PRACTICAL PROBLEMS

Illustration 11

P. Co. Ltd. operates a system of flexible budgetary control. A flexible budget is required to show levels of activity of 80%, 90% and 100%. The following information is available:

Sales, based on normal level of activity of 80% are 800,000 units at ₹ 10 each. If output is increased to 90%, it is thought that the selling price should be reduced by 2%, and if output reached is 100%, it would be necessary to reduce the original selling price by 5% in order to reach a wider market

Prime costs are:

Directional material	₹ 3.50
Direct labour	₹ 1.25
Direct expenses	₹ 0.25

If output reaches a 90% level of activity as above, the purchase price of raw material will be reduced by 5%.

Variable overheads. Salesmen's commission is 5% on sales value.

Semi-variable overheads at normal level of activity are:

	Amount [₹]
Supervision	80,000
Power	70,000
Heat and light	40,000
Maintenance	50,000
Indirect labour	100,000
Salesmen expenses	60,000
Transport	200,000

Semi-variable overheads are expected to increase by 5% if output reaches a level of activity of 90% and by a further 10% if it reaches the 100% level.

Fixed overheads are:

	Amount [₹]
Rent and rates	100,000
Depreciation	400,000
Administration	750,000
Sales department	200,000
Advertising	500,000
General	50,000

Solution

Flexible Budget

Particulars	*Normal level of activity 80% level of activity*		
	80% ₹	*90%* ₹	*100 %* ₹
Direct material	28,00,000	29,92,500	33,25,000
Direct labour	10,00,000	11,25,000	12,50,000
Direct expenses	2,00,000	2,25,000	2,50,000
Variable overhead	40,00,00	43,42,500	48,25,000
Salesmeǹs commission	4,00,000	4,38,750	4,75,000
Semi-variable overhead 5:			
Supervision	80,000	84,000	92,400
Power	70,000	73,500	80,350
Heat and light	40,000	42,000	46,200
Maintenance	50,000	52,500	57,750
Indirect labour	100,000	105,000	115,500
Salesmen's Expenses	60,000	63,000	69,300
Transport	200,000	210,000	231,000
	600,000	630,000	693,000

Fixed Overheads			
Rent and rates	100,000	100,000	100,000
Depreciation	400,000	400,000	400,000
Administration	750,000	750,000	750,000
Sales department	200,000	20,000	200,000
Advertising	500,000	500,000	500,000
General	50,000	50,000	50,000
	2,000.000	2,000,000	2,000,000
Total cost	7,000,000	7,411,250	7,993,000
Sales	8,000,000	8,775,000	9,500,000
Profit	1,000,000	1,363,750	1,507,000

Illustration 12

Prepare a cash budget in respect of six months upto December 31 from the information given in the table below. Cash balance on July 1 was expected to be ₹ 75,000.

Month	*Sales*	*Materials*	*Wages*	*Overheads*					
	₹	₹	₹	*Production* ₹	*Administration* ₹	*Selling* ₹	*Distribution* ₹	*Research development*
April	50,000	20,000	5,000	2,200	1,500	800	400	500
May	60,000	30,000	5,600	2,400	1,450	850	450	500
June	40,000	20,000	4,000	2,500	1,520	750	350	600
July	50,000	30,000	4,200	23,000	1,480	850	450	600
August	60,000	35,000	4,600	2,600	1,510	950	550	700
September	70,000	40,000	5,000	2,700	1,540	1,000	600	700
October	80,000	45,000	5,200	2,900	1,560	1,025	625	800
November	90,000	50,000	5,400	3,000	1,570	1,075	675	800
December	100,000	55,000	5,800	3,200	1,600	1,150	750	800

Expected capital expenditure:

Plant and machinery to be installed in August at a cost of ₹ 20,000 will be payable on September 1.

Extension to research and development department amounting to ₹ 5,000 will be completed on August 1. Payable ₹ 1000 per month from completion date. Under a hire-purchase agreement, Rs 2,000 is to be paid each month.

A sales commission of 5% on sales is to be paid within the month following actual sales.

Period of credit allowed by suppliers	3 months
Period of credit allowed to customers	2 months
Delay in payment of overheads	1 month
Delay in payment of wages	1/8 month

Tax of ₹ 50,000 is due for payment on October 1.

Preference shares dividend of 10% on capital of ₹ 1,000,000 is to be paid on November 1. 10% calls on ordinary share capital of ₹ 200,00 CWs due on July 1, and September 1. Dividend from investments amounting to ₹ 15,000 expected on November 1. Cash sales of ₹ 1,000 per month are expected; no commission payable.

Illustration 13

The following, data are available in a manufacturing company for the period of a year.

	₹ in (Lakhs)
Fixed expenses:	
Wages and salaries	9.5
Rent, rates and taxes	6.6
Depreciation	7.4
Sundry administrative expenses	6.5
Semi-variable expenses:	
(at 30% of capacity)	
Maintenance and repairs	3.5
Indirect labour	7.9
Sales department salaries etc.	3.8
Sundry administrative expenses	2.8
Variable expenses: (at 50% of capacity)	
Materials	21.7
Labour	20.4
Other expenses	7.9
	98.0

Assume that the fixed expenses remain constant for all levels of production; semi-variable expenses remain constant between 45% and 65% of capacity, increasing by 10% between 65% and 80% capacity, and by 20% between 80% and 100% capacity.

Sales at various levels are:

	₹ (lakhs)		₹ (lakhs)
50% capacity	100	90% capacity	180
60% capacity	120	100% capacity	200
75% capacity	150		

Prepare the flexible budget for the year and forecast the profits at 60%, 75%, 90% and 100% of capacity.

Illustration 12 Answers

Details	*July*	*August*	*September*	*October*	*November*	*December*
Receipts	₹	₹	₹	₹	₹	₹
Balance b/d	75,000	1,22,105	1,17,375	1,31,115	93,900	25,615
Debtors	60,000	40,000	50,000	60,000	70,000	80,000
Cash sales	1,000	1,000	1,000	1,000	1,000	1,000
Capital	20,000	—	20,000	—	—	—
Dividend	—	—	—	—	15,000	—
Total	₹ 1,56,000	1,63,105	1,88,375	1,92,115	1,79,900	1,06,615
Payments						
Materials	20,000	30,000	70,000	30,000	35,000	40,000
Wages	4,175	4,550	4,950	5,175	5,375	5,750
Production overhead	2,500	2,300	2,600	2,700	2,900	3,000
Administration overhead	1,520	1,480	1,5190	1,540	1,560	1,570
Selling overhead	750	850	950	1,000	1,025	1,075
Distribution overhead	350	450	550	600	625	675
Research overhead	600	600	700	700	800	500
Commission	2,000	2,500	3,000	3,500	4,000	4,500
Capital	2,000	3,000	23,000	3,000	3,000	3,000
Taxes	—	—	—	50,000	—	—
Dividend	—	—	—	—	1,00,000	—
Total	33,895	45,730	57,260	98,215	1,54,285	60,370
Balance c/d	1,22,105	1,17,375	1,31,115	93,900	25,615	46,245

Flexible Budget

Particulars	Capacity				
	50% ₹ (lakhs)	60% ₹ (lakhs)	75% ₹ (lakhs)	90% ₹ (lakhs)	100% ₹ (lakhs)
Sales	100	120	150	180	200
Variable expenses:					
Materials	21.70	2,604	32.55	39.06	43.40
Labour	20.40	24.48	30.60	36.72	40.80
Other expenses	7.90	9.48	11.85	14.22	15.80
Semi variable expenses:					
Maintenance and Repairs	3.50	3.50	3.85	4.20	4.20
Indirect labour	7.90	7.90	8.69	9.48	9.48
Sales department salaries etc.	3.80	3.80	4.18	.4.56	4.56
Sundry administrative expenses	2.80	2.80	3.08	3.36	3.36
Fixed expenses:					
Wages and salaries	9.50	9.50	9.50	9.50	9.50
Rent, rates and Taxes	6.60	6.60	6.60	6.60	6.6
Depreciation	7.40	7.40	7.40	7.40	7.40
Sundry administrative Expenses	6.50	6.50	6.50	6.50	6.50
Total cost	98.0	108.0	124.8	141.6	152.6
Estimated profit		12.0		38.4	47.4

Illustration 14

The books of a Ltd., company show the final position as follows:

Profit and Loss Account for the Year Ending 31st December 2018

Dr. *Cr.*

Particulars	*Amount* [₹]	*Particulars*	*Amount* [₹]
To Material consumed	36,000	By Sales	
To Wages	12,000		
To Manufacture overhead			
To Variable expenses	4,200		
To Fixed expense	3,000		
To Depreciation	3,000		
To Administration overhead	4,000		
To Selling and distribution overheads	6,000		
To variable expenses			
To Fixed expenses	2,000		
To Net profit c/d	55,800		
	1,26,000		1,26,000
To Income – Tax	23,000	By Net profit	55,800
To Dividend	12,000		
To Balance c/d	20,800		
	55,800		55,800

Liabilities	*Amount*[₹]	*Assets*	*Amount*[₹]
Share capital	2,00,000	Fixed assets (written down)	2,00,000
Reserve and surplus	19,000	Stock of materials	20,000
Sundry creditors	20,000	Sundry debtors	29,000
Provision:		Cash	25,000
Tax	23,000		
Dividend	12,000		
	2,74,000		2,74,000

With the help of the following additional information, you are required to prepare a Forecast Profit and Loss Account for the year 2018, and a Forecast Balance Sheet as on 31st December 2018.

Particulars	*Present* 2018	*Future* 2019
Capacity utilized	60%	80%
Units produced	60,000	
Sale price per unit	2.10	2.30
Material		Price increase of 25% expected 10% increase in rates expected
Manufacturing overheads Administration overheads Selling and distribution overheads Capital expenditure Depreciation ₹ 3,000 per year Income tax Dividend		10% increase in cost expected 5% increase in cost expected 10% increase in cost expected ₹ 60,000, ₹ 3,000 per year ₹ 50,000 – ₹ 0,000

Period allowed: To debtors – one month by creditors – two months

Stock of raw materials maintained: 3 months requirement. The time-lag in payment of wages and expenses being insignificant, may be ignored.

There is no stock of finished goods at year-end.

Solution

Working Notes

1. Sales budget:

$$\text{Units} = \frac{80}{60} \times 60{,}000 = 80{,}000 \text{ at ₹ } 2.30$$

Sale Value = ₹ 1,84,000

2. Purchase budget (Materials):

Particulars	*Amount* [₹]
Consumption during 2019	36,000
Add 33 1/3% for increase in capacity	12,000
	48,000
	12,000
Add 3 months stock to be held	
	60,000
Less opening stock	20,000

3. Consumption during 2019

Price increase of 25%			40,000
	Total requirement		10,000
(3)	Consumption during 2019		
	Opening stock	20,000	
	Add Purchases	50,000	
	Less Closing stock	70,000	
		15,000	₹ 55,000
	Including price rise 12,000 × $\frac{25}{100}$		
(4)	Wages budget	12,000	
	Wages paid in 2018	4,000	
	Add 33 1/3% for capacity increase	16,000	
		1,600	
		17,600	
(5)	Overhead budget	4,200	
	Manufacturing overhead	1,400	
	Variables expenses	5,600	
		560	
	Add 33 1/3% for volume increase	6,160	
(6)	Fixed expenses	3,000	
	Add 10% for cost increase	300	
		3,300	

(7)	Depreciation	3,000	
(8)	Administration overheads		
	Expenditure during 2018	4,000	
	Add 5% for cost increase	200	
		4,200	
(9)	Selling and distribution overheads	6,000	
	Add 331/3% for volume increase	2,000	
		8,000	
	Add 10% for cost increases	800	
		8,800	
	Fixed expenses	2,200	
	Add 10% for cost increase	200	
		2,200	
(10)	Cash budget		
	Receipts		
	Opening balance		25,000
	Debtors		
	Opening balance	29,000	
	Sales	1,84,000	
	Less Closing balance	15,333	1,97,677
	(1 × 12 × ₹ 1,84,000)		
			2,22,667
	Payments:		
	Creditors (Purchases):		
	Opening balance	20,000	
	Purchases	50,000	
	Less Closing balance	8,333	
	Wages		61,667
	Overheads	20,000	17,600
	Manufacturing	50,000	
	Less Closing balance	8,333	
	Wages		61,667
	Overheads		17,600
	Manufacturing		9,460
	Administration		4,200
	Selling and distribution		11,000
	Income tax		23,000
	Dividend		12,000
	Capital expenditure		60,000
			1,98,927
	Closing balance		**23,740**

Forecast Profit and Loss Account
For the Year Ending 31st December 2019

Dr. *Cr.*

Particulars	*Amount*[₹]	*Particulars*	*Amount*[₹]
To Material consumed	55,000	By Sales	1,84,000
Wages	17,600		
Overheads			
Variables expenses	6,160		
Fixed expenses	3,300		
Depreciation	3,000		
Administration overhead	4,200		
Selling and distribution overheads			
Variable expenses	8,800		
Fixed expenses	2,200		
Net profit	83,740		
	1,84,000		1,84,000
Income Tax	50,000	By Net profit	83,740
Dividend	20,000		
Balance c/d	13,740		
	83,740		83,740

Liabilities		*Amount*[₹]	*Assets*	*Amount*[₹]
Share capital		2,00,000	Fixed Assets	2,00,000
Balance	19,000		Less Depreciation	3,000
Profit this year	13,470	32,740		1,97,000
			Addition	60,000
			Closing stock (materials)	15,000
Sundry creditors		8,333	Sundry debtors	15,333
Provision			Cash	23,740
Tax		50,000		
Dividend		20,000		
		3,11,073		3,11,073

Meaning of PB

Performance budget may be defined as a budget based on functions, activities and projects. Performance budgeting may be described as a budgeting system, where under input costs are related to the end results, i.e., performance. According to the National Institute of Bank Management, Mumbai, the PB is the process of analyzing, identifying, simplifying, and crystallizing specific performance objectives of a job to be completed over a period, in the framework of the organizational objectives, the purpose and objectives of the job. It involves the evaluation of the performance of the organization in the context of both specific as well as overall objectives of the organization.

Purpose of PB

The performance budget is an instrument through which financial resources are allocated according to purposes and objectives. The cost of various programmes proposed for achieving these objectives are clearly indicated. It also presents data for measuring worth performance or the accomplishment of objectives set under each programme. The focus of attention is not only on expenditure but also on achievement. Both are integral parts of financial planning and expenditure authorization.

Process of PB

PB is a technique or a method employed by any agency/department. The first stage is to decide what its goal or objective should be, the next stage is to decide on a set of programmes in order to achieve the goal and then to implement the programme. Final stage is to evaluate the actual performance of each segment and its contribution towards achievement of its goal.

Operational Steps in PB

(*a*) Formulation of objectives of the agency/department.

(*b*) Identification of various programmes or projects, which will help the agency to achieve its objective.

(*c*) Evaluation of the programmes in terms of benefits that they produce compared to the resources that they consume.

(*d*) Selection of the programmes on the basis of cost benefit analysis in order to utilize the funds in the optimal manner.

(*e*) Development of performance criteria for the various programmes [suitable work measurement units, norms, yardsticks, standards, and other performance indicators].

(*f*) Preparation of long-term physical as well as financial plans.

(*g*) Preparation of the annual budget.

(*h*) Assessment of performance of each programme and by each responsibility unit and comparison of the same with the budget.

(*i*) Undertaking periodical review of programmes with a view to assess the strengths and weaknesses and make modification, if necessary.

Programme Budgeting

Programme budgeting was first evolved in United States. In Britain it is referred to as-Output Budgeting. It is mainly useful to government departments and non-profit organizations. In programme budgeting special emphasis is laid on formulation of different budgets for different programmes. It utilizes a planning and budgeting process in an output oriented programme format;

which is oriented to its objectives to facilitate developing and evaluating alternatives. It leads to the allocation of resources over a planning period. Programme budgeting integrates all the organizations planning activities and budgeting into a total system.

Programme Budgeting Process

First, programmes are identified for achieving different goals of the organization. Then each programme is divided into different elements. Resources such as materials, men, machines, utilities, etc., are allocated to various programmes over the period. The emphasis is continuously placed on analysis of alternatives [including existing programmes] and estimating cost of accomplishing objectives and fulfilling purposes and needs. The steps involved in the programming budgeting may be listed as follows:

(*a*) Identification of programmes required fulfilling the mission.

(*b*) Identification of programme elements.

(*c*) Allocation of resources to programmes.

(*d*) Utilizing forecast studies analysis—mostly multi-year forecasts are considered in programmed budgeting.

(*e*) Measuring the actual performance of approved programmes and comparing with budget performance.

In the case of non-profit organizations, output indicators are to be developed because output cannot be measured in monetary terms. For example, for training programmes the output indicator may be in terms of number of employees trained. For health programmes, output indicator may be reduction in disease. The programme budget, however, does not eliminate the need for traditional budget. It adds only a new dimension to planning and budgeting system. A traditional budget can be divided into a number of programme budgets.

Traditional Budgeting vs. Programme Budgeting

Traditional budgeting involves establishment of functional budgets and their integration into a master budget. It works well in profit-oriented organizations. While it emphasizes the method and means used, the programme budgeting stresses the purpose and objectives of the programme. Programme budgeting is not only a linkage system for planning and budgeting but also a strategic decision-making tool for allocating resources. It provides the decision-makers with relevant data appropriately structured into object-oriented format and analysis into decision-making mode.

Performance Budgeting vs. Programme Budgeting

1. Performance budgeting is a backward-looking approach and is based on past information and prior accomplishment whereas programme budgeting is a forward-looking approach. Programme budgeting is useful for review and decision-making at and above the departmental level it is adapted to the requirement by overall budgetary planning.
2. Performance budget has drawn much of its form from cost accounting and scientific management. In contrast, programme budgeting has drawn its core of ideas from economic analysis and systems analysis.

3. A performance budget is normally considered as a work programme and as a tool of management. But, a programme budget is considered as a statement and allocation process among competitive claims.

ZERO-BASE BUDGETING [ZBB]

Traditional budgeting starts with previous year expenditure level as a base and discussion is focused on certain additions and cuts to be made in the previous year spending. The top management finally gives its approval after hearing the arguments for and against the additions and cuts. In ZBB reference is not made to previous level of spending. A convincing case is made for each decision unit to justify the budget allotment for that unit during that period.

Meaning of ZBB

ZBB is a new approach to budgeting. It is defined by Peter A. Pyhor as an operating planning and budgeting process, which requires each manager to justify his entire budget in detail from scratch (hence zero-base) and shifts the burden of proof to each manager to justify why he should spend any money at all.

This approach requires that all activities should be identified in decision packages, which should be evaluated by systematic analysis and ranked in order of importance. Leonard Mereunit and Stephen Sosmick define, ZBB as a technique, which complements and links the existing planning, budgeting and review processes. It identifies alternative efficient methods of utilizing limited resources in effective attainment of selected benefits. It is a flexible management approach, which provides credible rationale for reallocating resources by focusing on the systematic review and justification of the funding and performance levels of current programmes or activities.

ZBB thus examines a programme or activity from scratch (i.e., zero-base). The manager proposing the activity should prove that the activity is essential and his budgeting request for funds is reasonable. Nothing can be taken for granted, for it was being done or allowed in the past. Hence, ZBB is a technique whereby each programmes, whether new or existing must be justified in its entirety each time a new budget is formulated.

Features of ZBB

The essential features of ZBB are as follows:

(*a*) The budget allotment to any decision unit should be first justified by the manager of that decision unit. He should justify his request without making any reference to previous level of spending in his decision unit.

(*b*) Activities are identified as decision packages and then the latter are ranked in order of priority.

(*c*) Decision packages are evaluated by systematic analysis linking them with clearly laid down corporate objectives.

(*d*) A frank relationship exists between superiors and subordinates.

(*e*) Available resources are directed towards alternatives in order of priority to ensure optimum results.

Process of ZBB

The following steps are implied in ZBB: The managers at all levels have to determine the objective of each programme of activity that they supervise and prepare alternative spending plans as decision packages. There should be at least three, if not more, of such packages; one involving expenditure, or the minimum expenditure, which will permit the programme to continued meaningfully; another package indicating resources in men, materials and money, which will be needed to continue the present levels of performance and objectives; and a third package to indicate what more could be achieved if additional funds were available to the extent of say 10% or more.

The executives at the next higher level have then to consolidate these decision packages and rank them in order of priorities, keeping in view the cost benefit analysis and available funds.

ZBB differs from traditional budgeting on many points and following are a few points of difference between the two systems of budgeting:

Traditional Budgeting vs. ZBB

1. Traditional budgeting is accounting-oriented and mainly lays its emphasis on previous year expenditure. ZBB is decision-oriented and makes all projects and programmes old and new programmes to compete for scarce resources.
2. In traditional budgeting, past expenditure forms the basis for future demand for inflation and new programmes. In ZBB, a decision unit is broken down into decision packages, which are ranked on priority basis.
3. In traditional budgeting, the top management takes decisions as regards the amount to be spent on a decision unit. But in ZBB this responsibility is shifted to the manager of a decision unit.
4. In traditional budgeting, deliberate manipulation of budget proposals is possible. But in ZBB, a rational analysis of budget proposals is made. Management approves only those carefully devised result-oriented decision packages.
5. Traditional budgeting makes a routine approach and is not clear and distinctive. ZBB makes each decision on budget proposals very distinctive and clear. It is a straightforward approach and highlights priority projects distinctively.

Advantages of ZBB

1. ZBB provides the organization with a systematic way to evaluate operations and programmes of activity, and allows management to allocate resources according to the priority of programmes.
2. It ensures through examination of every function. Managers are required to evaluate the need for every programme, and to consider different levels of effort and alternative ways of performing the operations.

3. It enables departmental budgets to be approved on the basis of cost-benefit comparison rather than be open to any arbitrary cuts or increases in budget estimates.
4. If decision packages are ranked in order of priority, subsequent budget cycles do not have to be based on a complete recycling of budget inputs.
5. If available resources vary from the budgeted estimates during the budget year, decision packages can be reduced or expanded on the basis of priority ranking of packages.
6. Long-range goals and plans can be linked with the annual budgets through the zero-base budget. Not only does it facilitate quantification of costs and benefits of contemplated decisions, it also enables managers to communicate problems and opportunities to the higher management.
7. The performance of line managers can be judged against their commitments in terms of the approved decision packages and their budgets.

Limitations of ZBB

The limitations of ZBB, which arise due to certain operational problems, are as follows:

1. Implementation Problems: Successful implementation of ZBB may require wholehearted support from the top management, which may not readily be available owing to fear and problems in the minds of top management. The concerned managers should continue in the same decision units. If they are transferred frequently to other departments, it may lead to waste of time and resources in training and developing new managers.
2. Formulation Problems: Considerable problems may arise while formulating decision packages. For example, problems may arise in the fixation of minimum level of effort. Managers may not like to fix the minimum level below the current levels. Similarly problems may arise in formulating meaningful performance evaluation measures.
3. Ranking Problems: Problems may arise in ranking of decision packages. General managers may like to continue their favourable projects for the reasons best known to them. Ranking may also become difficult when there are a large number of decision packages, particularly in a multi-product manufacturing firm.
4. Cost Problems: ZBB needs properly trained managerial personnel to do the required job. This involves time as well as cost.

All these operational problems can, however, be overcome by consistent efforts. They may arise only in initial stages and once a system is created and methodology is clear, ZBB becomes a routine task for the managers. It may be time consuming at the beginning. But if it is done systematically it can help top management in solving a number of managerial, administrative and other problems.

ADDITIONAL PROBLEMS

Illustration 15

The MNO company expects the following sales by month in units for the first six months of next year.

January	5,400	April	5,700
February	5,700	May	6,000
March	7,500	June	4,500

The company has a policy of maintaining an inventory equal to budgeted sales for the following two months. The beginning inventory reflects this policy. Each units costs ₹ 10.

You are required to prepare purchase budget for as many months as you can both in units and Rupees. Explain also why you had to stop where you did.

Solution

Purchase Budget (January to April, next year) in units and rupees of MNO Company)

Month	*Sales (units)*	*Planned inventory in units*		*Estimated Purchases in units (Col. 2 + 3 – 4)*	*Estimated Purchases in Rupees (Col. 5 × ₹ 10)*
		Closing	*Opening*		
1	2	3	4	5	6
January	5,400	13,200	11,100	7,500	75,000
February	5,700	13,200	13,200	5,700	57,000
March	7,500	11,700	13,200	6,000	60,000
April	5,700	10,500	11,700	4,500	45,000

Month	*Sales (units)*	*Planned inventory in units*		*Estimated Purchases in units (Col. 2 + 3 – 4)*	*Estimated Purchases in Rupees (Col. 5 × ₹ 10)*
		Closing	*Opening*		
1	2	3	4	5	6
January	5,400	13,200	11,100	7,500	75,000
February	5,700	13,200	13,200	5,700	57,000
March	7,500	11,700	13,200	6,000	60,000
April	5,700	10,500	11,700	4,500	45,000

It was not possible to go beyond April because we must know budgeted sales for two months in advance. To budget purchases for May requires the sales forecast for July (information for which is not available).

Illustration 16

A Ltd. manufactures products X and Y. During January 2019 expects to sell 1000 kg. of X and 40,000 kg of Y at ₹ 20 and ₹ 10 respectively. Direct materials P, Q and S, are mixed in equal proportions to produce X and materials Q, R and S are mixed in the ratio of 3:5:2 to produce Y. There is no loss of weight in production.

Actual and Budgeted stocks in quantities and costs for the month are as follows:

Particulars		*Opening stock (kg)*	*Desired closing Stock (kg)*	*Anticipated cost (Per kg) ₹*
Material	P	3,000	2,000	5.5
	Q	2,000	4,000	5.0
	R	20,000	6,000	1.0
	S	10,000	12,000	3.5
Product	X	2,000	1,000	-
	Y	10,000	12,000	-

You are required to prepare (*a*) the Production Budget and (*b*) the Materials Purchase Budget including the expenditure on raw materials for January.

Solution

(*a*) Production Budget for the Month of January, 2018

Sales Budget Add.	10,000	40,000
Closing stock	1,000	2,000
Less: Opening Stock	11,000	42,000
Production	2,000	10,000
	9,000	32,000

(*b*) Materials Purchase Budget for the Month of January, 2018

Particulars	*P (kg)*	*Q (kg)*	*R (kg)*	*S (kg)*
Materials required for production X	3,000	3,000		3,000
Y		12,600	-	8,400
	3,000	15,600	21,000	11,400
Material required for closing stock	2,000	4,000	6000	12,000
	5,000	19,600	27,000	23,400
Opening stock	3,000			
Cost per kg (₹)	2,000	2,000	20,000	10,000
Purchase price (₹)	5.5	17,600	7,000	13,400
	11,000	5	1	3.5

Illustration 17

The Fareal Cômpany uses single raw material to make its product; for each unit of product three pounds of this material are required. The price of this material is 10 per pound. The Company follows a purchasing policy of placing orders on or before the 5th of each month to cover that month's requirements. It plans its inventory position in advance to cover expected situations.

The inventory of material at Dec. 31, 2018 was 9,000 pounds

The inventory level planned for Jan. 2019 was 15,000 pounds

The inventory level planned for Feb. 2019 was 30,000 pounds

The inventory level planned for March 2019 was 20,000 pounds. Production scheduled for the three months period was;

During Jan. 2019 10,000 units

During Feb. 2019 12,000 units

During March 2019 units

Assume that this set of plans is carried out. Prepare Material Purchase Budget for the three months ending on 31st March 2019.

	Jan.	*Feb.*	*March*
Estimated output (in units)	10,000	12,000	14,000
Production requirements (in IBS)	30,000	36,000	42,000
	15,000	30,000	20,000
Less inventory at the beginning of the month	45,000	66,000	62,000
	9,00	15,000	30,000
Purchase required (in Ibs)	36,000	51,000	32,000
Price per IB.	10	10	10
Estimated cost of purchase (in ₹)	3,60,000	5,10,000	3,20,000

Illustration 18

The production manager of the ABC Company desires to maintain an inventory of raw material equal to the budgeted production needs for the next 2 months. Each unit of product takes 10 kg of raw material. Inventory of finished goods is usually maintained at one and half times of the following month's sales; the forecast sales of 6 months of next year, in units are as follows:

January	3,600	April	4,800
February	4,200	May	5,600
March	3,200	June	3,800

On 31st December of last year, there were 80,000 kg of raw material on hand and 5,600 units on finished goods.

You are required, to prepare (*i*) budget for production and (*ii*) budget for purchases of raw materials in units for as many months as possible.

Solution

(*i*) Production budget (January to May next year) in units of ABC Company.

Months	*Sales* (*Units*)	*Desired inventory* Closing	Opening	*Desired production* (*Col. 2 + 3 – 4*)
1	2	3	4	5
January	3,600	6,300	– 5,600	4,300
February	4,200	4,800	6,300	2,700
March	3,200	7,200	4,800	5,600
April	4,800	8,400	7,200	6,000
May	5,600	5,700	8,400	2,900

(*ii*) Purchase budget (January to March next year) in unit

Months	*Raw material required for (production × 10)*	*Planned inventory* Closing	Opening	*Desired purchases of raw material (Col. 2 + 3 – 4)*
1	2	3	4	5
January	43,000	83,000	80,000	46,000
February	27,000	1,16,000	83,000	60,000
March	56,000	89,000	1,16,000	29,000

Illustration 19

Production costs of a factory for a year are as follows:

	Amount [₹]
Direct wages	80,000
Direct materials	1,20,000
Product overheads	40,000
Fixed Variable	60,000

During the forthcoming year it is anticipated that:

(*a*) The average rate for direct labour remuneration will fall from ₹ 0.80 per hour to ₹ 0.75 per hour.

(*b*) Production efficiency will be reduced by 5%.

(*c*) Price per unit of direct material and of other materials and services which comprise overheads will remain unchanged, and (*d*) Production in the coming year will increase by 331/3%. Draw up a production cost budget.

Solution

Production Cost Budget for the Next Year

		Amount [₹]
Direct wages (1,40,000 hours × ₹ 0.75)		1,05,000
Direct materials: Present	₹ 1,20,000	
Add additional expenses		
(increase in 1/3 capacity)	40,006	
		1,60,000
Product overheads: Fixed		40,000
Variable (1,40,000 × ₹ 0.60)		84,000
Total production cost		**3,89,000**

Working Notes

Determination of direct wages

Direct labour hours (last year)

(Total wage bill + Labour rate per hour)

(₹ 80,000 + ₹ 0.80) 1,00,000

Due to decline in efficiency labour hours to carry out the present volume of production will be more by 5% i.e., 1,05,000 hours. Since there is an increase in one-third capacity, total direct labour hours required during the year would be 1,05,000 + 33 1/3% = 1,40,000 hours.

Determination of variable overheads

Existing variable overhead rate per hour

(Total variable overhead + 1,00,000) = ₹ 0.60 per hour.

Illustration 20

You are required to construct a selling overhead budget from the indication given below:

	Amount [₹]
Establishment expenses of Sales department	10,000
Other expenses of Sales department	4,000
Advertisement	3,000
Salaries to counter salesmen	10,000

Commission to counter salesmen @ 2% on their Sales Commission to Travelling salesmen @5% on their sales and out of pocket expenses @ 3% on their sales. The following are the likely sales range for a year:

Sales at counter	*Sales by travelling salesmen*
₹	₹
1,50,000	15,000
2,00,000	20,000
2,50,000	25,000

Solution

Selling Overhead Budget

Particulars	*Amount*[₹]	*Amount*[₹]	*Amount*[₹]
Counter sales	1,50,000	2,00,000	2,50,000
Travelling salesman's sales	15,000	20,000	25,000
Total estimated sales	1,65,000	2,20,000	2,75,000
Variable expenses:			
Commission to counter salesman @2% of their sales	3,000	4,000	5,000
Commission to travelling salesman @ *5%* on their sales	750	1,000	1,250
Out of pocket expenses @ 3% on their sales	450	600	750
	4,200	5,600	7,000
Fixed expenses:			
Establishment expenses	10,000	10,000	10,000
Other expenses	4,000	4,000	4,000
Advertisement	3,000	3,000	3,000
Salaries to counter salesman	10,000	10,000	10,000
	27,000	27,000	27,000
Total	31,200	32,600	34,000

Illustration 21

The projected sales of ABC Limited for the months of July to November 2019 are:

Months	*Year*	*Amount* [₹]
July	2019	6,20,000
August	2019	6,20,000
September	2019	5,80,000
October	2019	5,60,000
November	2019	6,00,000

The anticipated purchases are:

July	2019	3,80,000
August	2019	3,33,000
September	2019	3,50,000
October	2019	3,90,000
November	2019	3,40,000

The wages are expected to be ₹ 1,00,000 per month. The management, is expected to pay two months wages as bonus during October 2019. The company-expected to pay an advance tax ₹ 90,000 before 15th September 2019. The company has ordered in June 2019, a machine costing ₹ 16,00,000. IDBI has agreed to finance the purchase of machine which is expected to be delivered in January 2020. The company has advanced 5% in June 2019 with order, and they have agreed to pay another 10% advance after 3 months. The company extends 2 month's credit for the customers and the company enjoys one month credit from the suppliers. The general expenses for the company is ₹ 60,000 per month payable at the end of each month. The company anticipates to receive interim dividend of 10% for the investment of 90,000 shares of ₹ 10 each during, October 2019. The company anticipates to have an overdraft of ₹ 40,000 on 1st September, 2019 (sanctioned is ₹ 55,000). Draw a cash budget for September–November 2019 for approaching your bankers for a short-term further credit.

Solution

ABC Limited

Cash Budget for September–November 2019

Particulars	*September*	*October*	*November*	*Total*
	₹	₹	₹	₹
Cash Receipts:				
Cash balance in the beginning				
Collection from debtors	6,20,000	6,40,000	5,80,000	18,40,000
Interim dividends	–	90,000	–	90,000
Total cash available before current financing (A)	6,20,000	7,30,000	5,80,000	19,30,000

Payment:

Cash Payments:	Amount[₹]	Amount[₹]	Amount[₹]	Amount[₹]
Payments to creditors for purchases	3,33,000	3,50,000	3,90,000	10,73,000
Wages	1,00,000	1,00,000	1,00,000	3,00,000
Bonus to workers	—	2,00,000	—	2,00,000
Advance-tax for income-tax	90,000	—	—	90,000
Advance for the purchase of machine	1,60,000	—	—	1,60,000
General expenses	60,000	60,000	60,000	1,80,000
Total payments (B)	7,43,000	7,10,000	5,50,000	20,03,000
Surplus (Deficit) A–B	(1,23,000)	20,000	30,000	(73,000)
Financing required:				
Borrowings	1,23,000	—	—	1,23,000
Repayments	—	(20,000)	(30,000)	(50,000)
Total effect of financing (C)	—	(20,000)	(30,000)	73,000
Closing cash balance	—	—	—	—
(A + C – B)	—	—	—	—

The company is likely to make up deficit by raising ₹ 40,000 as bank overdraft and will have unutilized bank overdraft limit of ₹ 15,000. It should, therefore, approach the bankers for a further short-term credit of ₹ 1,08,000 in September. The company will be able to repay ₹ 20,000 in October, ₹ 30,000 in November and the balance up to January 2018; particularly when funds are received from IDBI on delivery of machine for which it agreed to finance.

Illustration 22

A limited company is to be incorporated to take over a running business. It is proposed to raise ₹ 50 lakhs by issuing equity shares and balance of capital required in first six months is to be financed by a financial institution. The latter is to be given 8 per cent debenture to the nearest ₹ 1 lakh above the amount required, secured on fixed assets. Initial investment consists of:

Freehold premises	₹ 20 lakhs
Plant	₹ 8 lakhs
Stock	₹ 5 lakhs
Motor vans and other items	₹ 6 lakhs

Payment on account of above items are to be made in the month of incorporation.

Estimates of transactions for the first 6 months commencing from July are given below:

Sales: July ₹ 12.50 lakhs, August ₹ 15.00 lakhs, September ₹ 18.00 lakhs, October ₹ 22.00 lakhs, November ₹ 23.00 lakhs and for each of the next three months ₹ 24.00 lakhs. Gross profit on sales to be at the rate of 20 per cent.

Debtors: to get two months credit.

Creditors: to be paid at the end of the month following the month of purchase.

Expenses:

1. Preliminary expenses ₹ 50,000 to be paid in August
2. General expenses ₹ 40,000 per month payable at the end of each month
3. Wages and Salaries payable on the first day of next month. ₹ 70,000 for first three months and ₹ 85,000 thereafter.

Assume that shares and debentures are issued on 1st July. Draw up a cash budget and budgeted final accounts and balance sheet as on 31st Decc nber.

Solution

Cash Budget

Period Six Months Ending: 31st December

(Amount in lakhs ₹)

Details	*July*	*Aug.*	*Sept.*	*Oct.*	*Nov.*	*Dec.*
Cash Receipts :						
Opening balance	-	11.6	0.7	0.8	1.0	1.0
Equity shares	50	-	-	-	-	-
Debentures	1	-	-	-	-	-
Cash from debtors	-	-	12.5	15.0	18.0	22.0
Cash Payment :						
Initial investment (including initial stock)	39	-	-	-	-	-
Accounts payable	-	9.3	11.3	13.7	16.75	17.55
Preliminary expenses	-	.5	-	-	-	-
General expenses	.4	.4	.4	.4	.40	.40
Wages and salaries	-	.7	.7	.7	.85	.85
Cash required	39.4	10.9	12.4	14.8	18.00	18.80
Closing balance	11.6	0.7	0.8	1.0	1.0	4.20

Working

(1) Computation of Debenture Finance

(Amount in lakhs ₹)

Details	*July*	*Aug.*	*Sept.*	*Oct.*	*Nov.*	*Dec.*
Receipts						
Opening balance	-	+ 10.6	-0.3	0.2	-	-
Equity shares	50	-	-	-	-	-
Cash from debtors	-	-	12.5	15.0	18.0	22.0
Cash available	50	10.6	12.2	14.8	18.0	22.0
Cash available	50	10.6	12.2	14.8	18.0	22.0
Cash required	39.4	10.9	12.4	14.8	18.0	18.8
Closing balance	10.6	-0.3	-0.2	-	-	+3.2

Thus, the maximum deficiency is ₹ 30,000. This could be made up by the issue of debentures of ₹ 1 Lakh.

(2) Disbursements on Accounts Payable

Assuming that the stock is maintained at a constant level of ₹ 5 lakhs throughout the period and that the rate of gross profit is based on cost comprising both materials and wages, disbursements on accounts payable will be as follows:

(Amount in lakhs ₹)

Particulars	*July*	*Aug.*	*Sept.*	*Oct.*	*Nov.*	*Dec.*
Opening Balance	-	+10.6	– 0.3	– 0.2	-	-
Equity shares	50	-	-	-	-	-
Cash from debtors	-		12.5	15.0	18.0	22.0
Cash Available	50	10.6	12.2	14.8	18.0	22.0
Cash Required	39.4	10.9	12.4	14.8	18.0	18.8
Closing Balance	10.6	–0.3	– 0.2	-	-	+3.2

Thus, the maximum deficiency is ₹ 30,000. This could be made up by the issue of debentures of ₹ 1 Lakh.

(2) Disbursements on Accounts Payable

Assuming that the stock is maintained at a constant level of ₹ 5 lakhs throughout the period and that the rate of gross profit is based on cost comprising both materials and wages, disbursements on accounts payable will be as follows:

(Amount in lakhs ₹)

Particulars	*July*	*Aug.*	*Sept.*	*Oct.*	*Nov.*	*Dec*
Sales	12.5	15.0	18.0	22.0	23.0	24.0
Less G.P. (20%)	2.5	3.0	3.6	4.4	4.6	4.8
Cost of Goods sold *Less*	10.0	12.0	14.4	17.60	18.40	19.2
Wages	0.7	0.7	0.7	0.85	0.85	0.85
Cost of Purchase	9.3	11.3	13.7	16.75	17.55	13.35

Disbursements on accounts payable is in the following month of purchase.

Budgeted Trading and Profit and Loss A/c for Six Months Ending 31st December

Equity share capital	50,00,000	Freehold premises	20,00,000
P & L balance	20,46,000	Plant	8,00,000
8% Debentures	1,00,000	Motor van	6,00,000
Outstanding interest	4,000	Stock	5,00,000
Outstanding wages	85,000	Sundry debtors	47,00,000
Creditors	18,35,000	Cash	4,20,000
		Preliminary exps.	50,000

Illustration 23

Ram and Mohan doing business in partnership have developed a new technique to manufacture a particular product. The cost of the factory is estimated at ₹ 80,000 and that of plant and machinery at ₹ 1,00,000. The firm will be converted into a limited company to which each partner will contribute ₹ 50,000 as capital. The production will start on January 1, 2019. The other relevant information is the following: (*a*) *Cost:* The prime cost is estimated at ₹ 40 being ₹ 20 for direct labour and ₹ 20 box direct materials. Factory and administrative expenses are estimated for each month to be ₹ 2,000. A publicity campaign is to be launched from February 2019 which is to cost ₹ 2,000 for the first month and ₹ 400 for each subsequent month. Selling expenses are expected to amount to ₹ 3,000 per month commencing from February l, 2019. Preliminary expenses have been estimated at ₹ 4,000 and initial contingencies at ₹ 25,000.

(*b*) *Sales:* These have been estimated as follows; January 200 units, February 300 units, March to December 400 units per month. The selling price is fixed at ₹ 100 per unit.

(*c*) *Stocks:* Raw materials costing ₹ 12,000 are to be purchased and to be paid for within one month. 20% of sales will be for cash and the balance on credit receivables within one month. Approximately a quarter of these credit sales will be payable within the month in which they are incurred.

You are required to prepare an initial cash forecast for the first four months up to April, 2019 divided to show working capital and permanent capital.

Cash Forecast of Working Capital

Period 4 Months Ending: April 30, 2019

Details	*Jan.* ₹	*Feb* ₹	*March* ₹	*April* ₹
Cash Receipts:				
Opening balance		2,000	2,800	15,100
Cash sales	4,000	6,000	8,000	8,000
Cash from debtors	-	15,800	23,700	31,600
Cash available	4,000	23,800	34,500	54,700
Cash Payment:				
Direct materials	-	4,000	6,000	8,000
Direct Labour	4,000	6,000	8,000	8,000
Factory and administrative overheads	2,000	2,000	2,000	2,000
Advertising	-	2,000	400	400
Selling and distribution overheads	-	3,000	3,000	3,000
Cash required	6,000	17,000	19,400	22,400
Closing balance c/fd	– 2,000	6,800	15,100	323,400

As is clear from above, there will be a cash deficit of ₹ 2,000 in the month of January. This deficit will be financed by the initial permanent capital.

Cash Forecast of Permanent Capital

Fixed Assets Requirements:	*Amount*[₹]
Cost of factory	80,000
Plant and machinery	1,00,000
Preliminary expenses	4,000
Minimum Stock Requirements:	
Raw materials	12,000
Finished goods (50 units @ ₹ 45)	2,250
Working Capital Requirement:	
Reserve for initial contingencies	25,000
Working capital deficiency in January	2,000
Permanent capital required	2,25,250

As regards financing of the permanent capital, it may be pointed out that the company's requirements are of the order of ₹ 2,25,250 and the amount available from the partners is only ₹ 1,00,000 thereby necessitating the issue of shares or resort to long-term borrowings.

The value of 50 units of finished goods has been calculated thus on the assumption of production level of 400 units per month.

$$\frac{(400 \times 400) + 2{,}000}{4{,}000} = 45 \text{ per unit}$$

Illustration 24

Premier Ltd. has ₹ 50,000 share capital and ₹ 6,000 Reserve against ₹ 40,000 invested in Fixed Assets. Stock and debtors were ₹ 4,000 and 13,000 and Trade Creditors were ₹ 2,000. To sustain the increase in activity, stock level is proposed to be increased by 100% by the end of the year. Machinery worth ₹ 2,000 is proposed to be acquired during the year as per Capital Expenditure budget. Estimated profit for the year is ₹ 7,000 after charging ₹ 4,000 depreciation and 50% of profit for taxation. Advance income tax payment is estimated at ₹ 6,000. Trade creditors are likely to be doubled. A 5% dividend is to be paid and provision for 10% dividend for next year is to be made. Debtors are estimated to be outstanding for 2 months/Sales budget shows ₹ 1,50,000 sales.

Make an estimate of cash position as at the end of the budget period.

Solution

Budgeted Balance Sheet as on....

Liability		*Amount* [₹]	*Assets*		*Amount* [₹]
Share capital		50,000	Fixed assets	40,000	
Reserves and surplus			Additions	2,000	
Reserve ₹	6,000			42,000	
Profit for the year	7,000		*Less*: Depreciation	4,000	38,000
Less: Last year loss	13,000				
	1,000				
			Current assets:		
			Stock		8,000
	12,000		Debtors		25,000
Less: Dividend	2,500		Advance tax		6,000
Less: Provision for dividend	5,000	4,500			
Current Liabilities:					
Trade creditors		4,000			
Provision for tax		7,000			
Provision for dividend		5,000			
Bank overdraft (Balancing figure)		6,500			
		77,000			77,000

Illustration 25

Prepare a flexible budget from the following data made available in respect of a half-yearly period and forecast the working results at 70%, 85% and 100% of capacity when the respective sales are ₹ 50 lakhs, ₹ 60 lakhs and ₹ 85 lakhs. While fixed expenses remain constant, semi-variable expenses are constant between 55% and 75% of capacity, increasing by 10% between 75% and 85% of capacity and by 20% between 90% and 100% of capacity. The expenses at 60% capacity are as follows:

Particulars	*(Amount in lakhs)*
Maintenance and repairs	1.25
Indirect labour	5.00
Sales department expenses	1.50
Sundry overheads	1.25
Material	12.00
Labour	13.00
Other expenses	2.00
Wages and salaries	4.20
Rent, rates and taxes	2.80
Depreciation	3.50
Sundry overheads	4.50
	51.00

Solution

Flexible Budget

Particulars	70% ₹	85% ₹	100% ₹
(A) Material	14.00	17.00	20.00
Labour	15.17	18.42	21.67
Other expenses	2.33	2.83	3.33
	31.50	38.25	45.00
(B) Semi-variable expenses			
Maintenance and repairs	1.25	1.38	1.50
Indirect labour	5.00	5.50	6.00
Sales department salaries	1.50	1.65	1.80
Administrative salaries	1.25	1.37	1.50
Total semi-variable expenses	9.00	9.90	10.80
(C) Fixed expenses			
Wages and salaries	4.20	4.20	4.20
Rent, rates and taxes	2.80	2.80	2.80
Depreciation	3.50	3.50	3.50
Sundry and other overheads	4.50	4.50	4.50
	15.00	15.00	15.00
Total Costs (A+B+C)	55.50	63.15	70.80
Budget profit (loss)	(–5.50)	(3.15)	14.20

Illustration 26

Prepare a Flexible Budget for the year from the following data made available in respect of half-yearly period and forecast the results at 70%, 85% and 100% of capacity. When the respective sales are ₹ 110 lakhs, ₹ 134 lakhs and ₹ 150 lakhs. While fixed costs remain constant semi-variable expenses are constant between 60% and 75% capacity, increasing by 10% between 75% and 90% capacity, and by 20% between 90% and 100% capacity. The expenses at 60% capacity are as follows:

Expenses	*Particulars*	*₹ in Lacs*
Variable	Materials	30.00
	Labour	18.00
	Other expenses	3.60
Semi-variable	Repairs & maintenance	3.00
	Indirect labour	10.00
	Selling overheads	2.00
	Sundry other overheads	2.00
Fixed	Salaries & wages	8.40
	Rent, taxes & rates	5.00
	Depreciation	6.00
	Sundry overheads	8.00
		96.00

Solution

Flexible Budget for the Year

Capacity Utilisation / Particulars	*Existing 60% Remarks*	*70% Remarks*	*85% Remarks*	*100% Remarks*
Variables costs:				
Materials	30.00	35.00	42.50	50.00
Labour	18.00	21.00	25.50	30.00
Other expenses	3.60	4.20	5.10	6.00
Semivariable costs:				
Repairs and maintenance	3.00	3.00	3.30	3.60
Indirect labour	10.00	10.00	11.00	12.00
Selling overheads	2.00	2.00	2.20	2.40
Sundry other overheads	2.00	2.00	2.00	2.50
Fixed cost:				
Salaries and wages	8.40	8.40	8.40	8.40
Rent, rates and taxes	5.00	5.00	5.00	5.00
Depreciation	6.00	6.00	6.00	6.00
Sundry overheads	8.00	8.00	8.00	8.00
Total Costs	96.00	104.60	119.20	133.80
Sales		110.00	134.00	150.00
Profit		5.40	14.80	16.20

Illustration 27

A glass manufacturing company requires you to calculate and present the budget for the year from the following information:

Toughened glass	₹ 3,60,000
Bent toughened glass	₹ 5,40,000
Direct material cost	60% of sales

Direct wages of 20 workers at the rate of ₹ 200 per month.

Factory overheads:	
Works Manager	₹ 600 per month
Foreman	₹ 500 per month
Stores and spares	2% on sales
Depreciation on machinery	₹ 12,500
Light and power	₹ 5,000
Repairs and maintenance	₹ 8,000
Other sundries	10% on direct wages
Administration, selling and distribution expenses	₹ 16,000 per year

Solution

Budgeted Income Statement of a Glass Manufacturing Company for the next year

Sales revenue: Toughened glass		₹ 3,60,000	
Bent toughened glass		5,40,000	9,00,000
Less costs:			
Direct material cost (60% × ₹ 9,00,000)		5,40,000	
Direct wages (20 × ₹ 200 × 12 months)		48,000	
Factory overheads	₹		
Works Manager Salary (600 × 12)	7,200		
Foreman salary (₹ 500 × 12)	6,000		
Stores and spares $\frac{(2.5 \times ₹\ 9,00,000)}{100}$	22,500		
Depreciation on machinery	12,500		
Light and power	5,000		
Repairs and Maintenance	8,000		
Sundries (10% × ₹ 48,000)	4,800	66,000	
Administration, selling and Distribution expenses		16,000	6,70,000
Budgeted net income			2,30,000

REVIEW QUESTIONS

1. Define the following terms:
   (*a*) Budget.
   (*b*) Budgetary control.
   (*c*) Budgeting.
2. State the essentials of a budget.
3. What is "Master Budget"?
4. Briefly explain the following:
   (*a*) Sales budget.
   (*b*) Selling and distribution budget.
   (*c*) Capital expenditure budget.
5. List out the various important budgets.
6. Define and explain the term "flexible budget".
7. Enumerate the advantages of budgetary control.
8. Define and explain the term "flexible budget".
9. Define the following terms:
   (*a*) Principal budget factor.
   (*b*) Budget centre.
   (*c*) Fixed budget.
10. Write short notes on:
    (*a*) Budget period.
    (*b*) Budget committee.
11. Explain the term "Master Budget". What are its components?
12. State briefly the points to be considered while preparing:
    (*a*) Sales budget.
    (*b*) Purchase budget.
    (*c*) Research and development expenditure budget.
13. What is budgetary control? What are the major objectives of budgetary control?
14. Briefly discuss the importance of cash budget in a manufacturing concern.
15. State the advantages of a "flexible budget" system.
16. Briefly explain the various types of budgets.
17. Summarise the details and responsibilities of a budget officer.
18. What is a flexible budget? How does it differ from a fixed budget?
19. Define "budget" and budgetary control. Discuss the objectives and limitations of budgetary control in an organisation?
20. Define and explain the term "cash budget". How and why are cash budgets prepared?
21. Describe the various preliminaries required for the adoption of an effective system of budgetary control.

22. Explain the term flexible budget. How is a flexible budget constructed? What advantages if any, does a flexible budget have over an ordinary budget?

23. "Mere contribution of a master budget and the existence of a budget committee will not ensure the success of a budgetary control system." Do you agree?

24. (*a*) Discuss the various steps involved in framing a budgetary control method.

(*b*) Draft with imaginary figures a budgetary control report in respect of any service department

25. Chajju Bros, sell two products which are manufactured in one plant. During the year 2018 they plan to sell the following quantities of each product.

SALES BUDGET (UNITS)

	First quarter	*Second quarter*	*Third quarter*	*Fourth quarter*	*Total quarter*
Product 1	90,000	2,30,000	3,00,000	80,000	7,00,000
Product 2	85,000	75,000	55,000	85,000	3,00,000

Each of these two products is sold on a seasonal basis. Product 1 tends to sell better in the summer months, while Product 2 sells better during the winter. Chajju Bros, plan to sell Product 1 throughout the year at a price of ₹ 10 a unit, and Product 2 at a price of ₹ 20 a unit.

A study of the past experiences reveals that Chajju Bros, have lost about 3% of their billed revenue each year because of returns (constituting 2% of loss of revenue) allowances and bad debts (1% loss). Prepare a budget incorporating the given information.

25. The Golden Company plans to sell 1,08,000 units of a certain product line in the first fiscal quarter, 1,20,000 units in the second quarter, 1,32,000 units in the third quarter, 1,56,000 units in the fourth quarter, and 1,38,000 units in the first quarter of the following year. At the beginning of the first quarter of the current year, there are 18,000 units of the product in stock. At the end of each quarter, the company plans to have an inventory equal to one-sixth of the sales for the next fiscal quarter.

How many units must be manufactured in each quarter of the current year?

26. ABC Co., wishes to arrange overdraft facilities with its bankers during the period April to June, 2018 when it will be manufacturing mostly for stock. Prepare a cash budget for the above period from the following data, indicating the extent of the bank facilities the company will require at the end of each month:

(*a*)

Months	*Sales* ₹	*Purchases* ₹	*Wages* ₹
February 2018	1,80,000	1,24,800	12,000
March 2018	1,92,000	1,44,000	14,000
April 2018	1,08,000	2,43,000	11,000
May 2018	1,74,000	2,46,000	10,000
June 2018	1,26,000	2,68,000	15,000

(*b*) 50 per cent of credit sales are realised in the month following the sales, and the remaining 50 per cent in the second month following. Creditors are paid in the month following the month of purchase.

Cash at bank on 1.4.2018 (estimated) is ₹ 25,000.

27. For production of 10,000 electrical automatic irons, the following are the budgeted expenses:

	Per Unit ₹
Direct materials	60
Direct labour	30
Variable overheads	25
Fixed overheads (₹ 1,50,000)	15
Variable expenses (direct)	5
Selling expenses (10% fixed)	15
Administration expenses (₹ 50,000 rigid for all levels of production)	5
Distribution expenses (20% fixed)	5
Total cost of sales per unit	160

Prepare a budget for production of 6,000, 7,000 and 8,000 irons, showing distinctly marginal cost and total cost.

28. A glass manufacturing company requires you to calculate and present the budget for the next year from the following information:

Sales:

Bent toughened glass	₹ 3,00,000
Toughened glass	₹ 5,00,000
Direct material cost	60% sales
Direct wages	20 workers @ ₹ 150 pm.

Factory overheads:

Indirect labour:

Works manager ₹ 500 per month

Foreman ₹ 400 per month

Stores and spares	$2\frac{1}{2}$% on sales
Depreciation on machinery	₹ 12,600
Light and power	₹ 5,000
Repairs and maintenance	₹ 8,000
Other Sundries	10% on direct wages

Administration, selling and distribution expenses ₹ 14,000 per year.

29. The selling expenses of a business for a particular budget period are:

	Amount [₹]
Sales office salaries	4,000
Fixed expenses of sales office	3,000
Amount allocated for advertising	4,000
Fixed salaries and car allowances	12,000
Traveller's remuneration and Commission 1% on sales effected	
Outward carriage estimated @ 5% on sales	
Agent's commission 7½% on sales	

Prepare selling overheads budget for the following levels of sales for the period:

₹ 2,80,000 including agents sales	₹ 30,000
₹ 3,20,000 including agents sales	₹ 35,000
₹ 3,60,000 including agents sales	₹ 35,000

[**Ans.** ₹ 41,750, ₹ 44,475, ₹ 46,875]

30. A manufacturing company submits the following figures for the first quarter of 2019:

Particulars	*Product* X	*Product* Y	*Product* Z
Sales (in Units) Jan.	25,000	30,000	10,000
Feb.	20,000	25,000	10,000
March	30,000	35,000	10,000
Selling price per unit	₹ 10	₹ 20	₹ 40
Targets for 1st Quarter 2018			
Sales quantity increase	20%	10%	10%
Sales price increase	Nil	10%	25%
Stock position 1st Jan. 2019			
Percentage of Jan. + 2018 sales 50%	50%	50%	50%
Stock position 31st March 2018	20,000	25,000	5,000
Stock positioned end Jan.+ 2018 sales 50%	50%	50%	50%

You are required to prepare the sales and production budgets for the 1st quarter of 2019. Show, working clearly.

[**Ans.:** Sales Budget]

Particulars	X *Amount*[₹]	Y *Amount*[₹]	Z *Amount*[₹]
Jan.	3,00,000	7,26,000	5,50,000
Feb.	2,40,000	6,05,000	5,50,000
March	3,60,000	8,47,000	5,50,000
Production budget	(Units)	(Units)	(Units)
Jan.	27,000	30,250	11,000
Feb.	30,000	33,000	11,000
March	38,000	44,250	10,500

31. In May 2016 Sri Ananth got ₹ 20,000 in a Delhi Lottery and started a business to manufacture a certain component for BHEL. During the same month, he purchased machineries for ₹ 5,00,000 out of a gift of ₹ 1,00,000 from his father-in-law and a loan of ₹ 4,00,000 from a bank. Interest at 9% per annum is payable quarterly in arrears from the month of borrowing. The principal is repayable at ₹ 20,000 every half year. He commenced manufacturing on 16.9.2016 and his production delivery schedule is as under:

30-6-2018	1,000 units
31-7-2018	1,500 units
31-8-2018	2,000 units
30-9-2018	32,500 units
31-10-2018	3,000 units

and thereafter 3,000 units every month.

He gets ₹ 10 per unit-from BHEL. His variable cost is ₹ 6 per unit. He has fixed expenses to the extent of ₹ 1,000 per month. He also wants to draw ₹ 1,000 per month for his maintenance. His bills are settled after 30 days from the date of supply. His variable cost is to be met by actual payment every month. The fixed cost and his drawings are met on the 1st day of the next month. He desires always to carry a minimum cash balance of ₹ 2,000 and a maximum one of ₹ 10,000.

You are required to prepare a cash budget for each of the 9 months from May 2018 to January 2019. Assume a temporary overdraft from the Bank, whenever required within the above-mentioned minimum and maximum cash balance requirements. Ignore interest on the overdraft.

[**Ans.** balance of cash on Jan. 31, 2019 ₹ 4,000]

32. (*a*) What is a Flexible Budget? What are its advantages?

(*b*) Excellent Engineering works had prepared its budget for 2018 based on the production of 1 lakh units of their only product as follows:

(*i*) Raw materials	252
(*ii*) Direct labour	75
(*iii*) Direct expenses	10
(*iv*) Works overhead (60% fixed)	225
(*v*) Administrative overheads	40
(*vi*) Selling overheads (50% fixed)	20

For want of demand the actual production for that period was only 60,000 untis.

33. Calculate the budgeted cost per unit under both the original plan and under actual performance.

34. Laxmi Enterprises Ltd., ended with the following profit/loss during the year 2018 (All figures in ₹ lakhs).

Sales		35.58
Less Expenses: Raw materials	7.42	
Stores	4.88	
Expenses	20.40	
Interest	2.00	
Depreciation	2.00	
		36.70
Loss for the year		1.12

The company had been working at 60% of capacity during the year and of the expenses of ₹ 20.40 lakhs 25% is variable.

Production/sale volume at 80% of capacity is expected to be achieved next year. Fixed cost is however expected to increase by ₹ 1.20 lakhs.

Draw up a budget for next year.

■ ■ ■

14

Capital Budgeting

CONCEPT OF CAPITAL INVESTMENT DECISION

Capital Investment Decision or Simply Investment Decision involves a largely irreversible commitment of resources that is generally subject to significant degree of risk. Such decisions have far-reaching efforts on a firm's profitability and flexibility over the long term. The investment proposals need to be related to the underlying corporate objective i.e., creation of wealth for the organization. Investments are normally termed as capital expenditures. Capital expenditure is one, which is intended for future periods and normally includes investment in fixed assets and other development projects. Every business concern has to face the problem of capital expenditure decisions some time or the other. Hence, planning for capital expenditure has become an integral part of policy-making management and budgetary control. It is essentially a long-term function and such a decision to buy land, buildings or plant and machinery, etc., would influence the activity of business for a considerable period of time. Hence, it is essential to keep a close watch on capital expenditure at all times. Further, the mechanization and automation has resulted in management being confronted with ever more frequent and difficult problems. Despite the fact that various techniques have been developed to assist management in its task of decision-making more effectively, the ultimate decision depends on the availability of relevant information, which can be generated by a well-established capital expenditure budgeting system.

CONCEPT OF CAPITAL BUDGETING

Capital budgeting normally refers to long-term planning for proposed capital outlays and their financing. It is the decision-making process by which firms evaluate the acquisition of major fixed assets whose benefits would spread over several time periods. Succinctly, it involves current investment in which the benefits are expected to be received beyond one year in future. The use of one year as a line of demarcation is, however, somewhat arbitrary. The main exercise in capital budgeting is to judge whether or not an investment proposal provides a reasonable return to business. Hence, capital budgeting involves generation of investment proposals, estimating costs and benefits (cash flows) for the investment proposals and estimation of net benefits and selection of projects based upon an acceptance criterion.

Importance of Capital Budgeting

1. **Commitment of huge financial resources:** The capital investment involved is usually very large. It will have several far-reaching implications on the activities of business and may seriously affect the very financial stability or flexibility of the business. It is these implications, which make capital budgeting so important.
2. **Wrong decisions may lead to over or under-investment of financial resources.** For example, wrong sales forecast may result in over or under-investment in fixed assets, i.e., excess production capacity or inadequate capacity. It also enables the cash forecast to be completed.
3. **Better timing of assets:** Capital budgeting may allow alternative forms of assets to be considered as replacements for assets, which are wearing out or in danger of becoming obsolete. In other words, it would lead to better timing of assets purchases and improvement in quality of assets purchased. It helps to match efficiently the need for capital goods and their availability. It also assists in formulating a sound depreciation and asset replacement policy.
4. **It ensures the selection of right source of finance at the right time.** Capital expenditure decisions involve substantial funds, which may not be immediately, and automatically available. A well-established capital budgeting system would enable management to decide in advance the sources of finance and ensure their availability at the right time.

Objectives of Capital Budgeting

1. **Selection of the right mix of profitable projects.** The overall objective of capital budgeting is to allocate the available resources among the competing projects in order to maximize the total profitability. This is made possible by employing the various evaluation techniques for the selection of investment projects, which contribute the maximum towards the overall investment objective. In the case of public enterprises, capital budgeting may also assure fulfillment of other objectives such as promotion of employment, development of backward region, etc.
2. **Capital expenditure control.** Control of capital expenditure is the next important objective of capital budgeting. Forecasting the long-term financial requirements and thereby enabling the management to plan in advance to raise the funds at the right time achieve this. The objective of preparing capital budget is to plan and then compare the actual capital expenditure with the budgeted figure for controlling costs.

3. Determining the required quantum and the right source of funds for investments. The next important objective is to determine the funds required for long-term projects and to see that such estimates fall in line with the company financial policies. It also aims to compromise between availability of funds and needs of the capital projects.

TYPES OF CAPITAL INVESTMENT PROJECTS

Investment projects may be classified in a number of ways. Both private and public sector business units in their capital expenditure forecasts commonly use the following types of investment projects:

(*a*) Expansion of existing product lines,

(*b*) Expansion into new product lines,

(*c*) Replacement and Modernization Schemes,

(*d*) Projects for the utilization of scraps, and also of surplus installed capacity, and

(*e*) Cost Reduction Projects.

The projects listed above are generally profit-oriented and therefore, they may be evaluated on the basis of their cost and benefits. But there are investments, which are undertaken by all business units and on which it would be difficult to measure returns, such as the following:

(*i*) **Safety Precautions:** Provision of safety devices and equipment may be demanded by various legal requirements.

(*ii*) **Welfare Projects:** Provision of sport facilities for employees may boost employees' morale. This cannot be evaluated financially.

(*iii*) **Service Projects:** Provision of buildings and equipments for non-manufacturing departments may be essential, but the return from investment on them cannot be evaluated.

(*iv*) **Research and Development:** This may be initiated to improve the company.

(*v*) **Educational Projects:** Provision of company training course may be instrumental in improving the efficiency of employees but the returns from investment on such programmes may be difficult to evaluate.

CONCEPT OF PROJECT APPRAISAL

Project appraisal is the analysis of costs and benefits of a proposed project with the goal of assuring a rational allocation of limited funds among alternative investment opportunities in view of achieving certain specified goals. Project appraisal is necessary as the number of projects to satisfy the identified needs always exceeds the availability of resources and a choice among alternative projects is to be made.

Project appraisal is ex-ante analysis. It identifies and values the expected costs and benefits of a project. Project evaluation is ex-post analysis of an executed project. It determines the real cost and benefits of the project. By comparing the real costs and benefits, the project's real profitability is ascertained at the evaluation stage. However, sometimes the concepts of project appraisal and evaluation are used interchangeably.

PROJECT APPRAISAL METHODS

Project appraisal is a process of transmitting information accumulated through feasibility studies into a comprehensive form in order to enable the decision-maker undertake a comparative appraisal of various projects and embark on a particular project or projects for allocating scarce resources. Keeping the overall objective of the enterprise in view, the appraisal is carried out employing certain decision criteria, viz., profitability or social profitability. Commonly used appraisal methods are as follows:

(*a*) Payback Period

(*b*) Average Rate of Return

(*c*) Discounted Cash Flow Techniques:

- (*i*) Net Present Value
- (*ii*) Benefit Cost Ratio
- (*iii*) Internal Rate of Return.

Apart from these, a public sector project may be appraised by employing Social Cost Benefit Analysis so as to highlight its significance to nation's economy or society.

PAYBACK PERIOD METHOD OF INVESTMENT APPRAISAL

The payback (PB) period is the length of time required to recover the initial cash outlay incurred on the project. For example, if a project involves a cash outlay of ₹ 2,00,000 and the annual cash inflows are ₹ 50,000, ₹ 80,000, ₹ 60,000, and ₹ 40,000 during its economic life of four years, the payback period is 3.25 years. During 3 years and three months, the project cost can be recovered with the cash inflows. Hence, it is the payback period. If the above-mentioned project returns constant annual cash inflows of ₹ 80,000 for four years, then the payback period is 2.5 years (₹ 2,00,000/₹ 80,000).

Formula

$$\text{Payback period} = \frac{\text{Original cost of Investment}}{\text{Annual cash inflows or savings}}$$

Selection Criteria: Among the mutually exclusive or alternative projects, whose PB periods are lower than the cut-off period, the project with the shortest PB period would be selected. In case, there is funds scarcity or budget constraints the procedure would be to rank the projects in the ascending of PB periods and select the first 'x' number of projects, which the funds position permits. However, with a view to make the selection process more realistic, a cut-off period or minimum payback ratio could be set up and all investment proposals for which the PB is greater than the cut-off period be rejected. PB ratio is the inverse of the PB period. For a PB period of 4 years, the PB ratio is 1/4. Thus, the project with larger the PB ratio would be a better project.

Suitability of PB method

1. The PB method is suitable when the project has shorter gestation period and the project cost is small.
2. When a firm suffers from shortage of cash and depends on internal generation of cash, this method will prove to be the best method of appraisal.
3. It is also suitable when the project belongs to high-risk category and is susceptible to rapid technological changes.
4. It is the most suitable method for deciding upon overseas investments, when there is political uncertainty in such countries.

Example 1

From the following information advice the management as to which project is preferable based on Payback Period. The cut-off period for the company is 3 years.

Particulars	Project A (₹)	Project B (₹)
Initial capital investment	45,000	50,000
Cash Inflows (profit before depreciation but after taxes)		
Year I	15,000	12,000
II	15,000	13,000
III	15,000	15,000
IV	9,000	10,000
V	6,000	21,000
VI	6,000	26,000
	66,000	97,000

Solution

Payback Period for Project A = (₹ 15,000 + 15,000 + 15,000 = 45,000) = 3 years

Payback Period for Project B = (₹ 12,000 + 13,000 + 15,000 + 10,000 = 50,000) = 4 years

Since the project B does not qualify for the cut-off period, it will be rejected outright. Project A will be selected for two reasons–(1) its payback period is shorter than the cut-off period and therefore it qualifies for the selection. (2) Its payback period is shorter than that of Project B. Hence, Project A will be recommended for selection.

Example 2

XY Ltd. is producing products mostly by manual labor and planning to replace it by a new machine. There are two alternative models A and B of the new machine. From the following information, prepare a Statement of profitability showing the payback period and suggest which model is preferable.

Particulars	*Machine A*	*Machine B*
Estimated life of the machine	4 years	5 years
Cost of machine	₹ 18,000	₹ 36,000
Estimated savings in scrap p.a.	1,000	1,600
Estimated savings in wages p.a.	12,000	16,000
Additional cost maintenance p.a.	1,600	2,000
Additional cost of supervision p.a.	2,400	3,600
Ignore taxation.		

Solution

Statement showing Annual cash inflows

Particulars	*Machine A (₹)*	*Machine B (₹)*
Estimated savings in scrap p.a.	1,000	1,600
Estimated savings in wages p.a.	12,000	16,000
Total savings (a) p.a.	13,000	17,600
Additional cost of maintenance p.a.	1,600	2,000
Additional cost of supervision p.a.	2,400	3,600
Total additional cost (b) p.a.	4,000	5,600
Net Cash Inflow (a – b) p.a.	9,000	12,000

Payback Period

For Machine A = 2 years

For Machine B = 3 years

Since Machine A has shorter payback period than Machine B, it is preferable.

Bailout Approach

Bailout Factor refers to the possibility of scrapping an asset or a project within the payback period if it becomes necessary. In that case it may be expected to receive certain salvage or scrap value appropriate to the age of the asset. Considering the bailout factor, a bailout payback period may be calculated and it may be used for the selection of the asset. This approach is preferable if a firm wants to avoid loss due to current financial position.

Example 3

A firm has two projects A and B under consideration. Project A costs ₹ 30,000 and B costs ₹ 48,000. Both have an eight years life with uniform cash flows of ₹ 6,000 and ₹ 12,000 per annum from A and B respectively. Expected scrap values are A ₹ 21,000 declining at an annual rate of ₹ 3,000 and B ₹ 24,000 declining at an annual rate of ₹ 6,000. Calculate the Payback Period under Traditional Approach and Bailout Approach.

Solution

Computation of Payback Period under Traditional Approach

Project A = 5 years

Project B = 4 years

Project B is preferable as it has shorter payback period.

Bailout Approach

Project A

Year	*Cumulative Cash flows (₹)*	+	*Scrap Value (₹)*	*Total (₹)*
End of year 1	6,000		21,000	27,000
End of year 2	12,000		18,000	30,000

Bailout Payback period is 2 years.

Project B

Year	*Cumulative Cash flows (₹)*	+	*Scrap Value (₹)*	*Total (₹)*
End of year 1	12,000		24,000	36,000
End of year 2	24,000		18,000	42,000
End of year 3	26,000		12,000	38,000

Bailout Payback period is 3 years.

Since the bailout payback period is shorter for Project A, it is preferable under Bailout Approach.

MERITS AND DEMERITS OF PAYBACK METHOD

Merits of PB Method

1. It is easy to operate and simple to understand.
2. This method is preferred on the ground that returns beyond three or four years are so uncertain that it is better to disregard them altogether in a planning decision.
3. It is appropriate for industries with high rate of technological obsolescence in which the receipts beyond PB are regarded as totally uncertain.
4. This method is also useful to a concern, which is short of cash and eager to get back the cash invested in project.
5. As the method considers the cash flows during the PB period of the project, the estimates would be reliable and the results may be comparatively more accurate.

Despite the simplicity and ease of operation, this method suffers from several drawbacks.

Demerits of PB Method

1. The PB is more a liquidity concept. It is not a profitability concept as it is based on the recovery of cash outlays. And it stresses the importance of liquidity that is recovery, at the cost of profitability.
2. It does not consider the earnings beyond the payback period. This may lead to wrong selection of investment projects. Profitable projects with long gestation periods or projects, which generate high returns only after a certain period of time, may be rejected under this method.
3. The most serious limitation of this method is that it ignores time value of money. In other words, it provides only for the recovery of the original investment and not for the cost of funds committed to such investments. But in practice, the investible funds of a business are not free of cost.

ACCOUNTING OR AVERAGE RATE OF RETURN METHOD

Average Rate of Return (ARR) method is considered an improvement over the PB method for it considers the earnings of a project during its entire economic life. It is also known as 'Return on Investment method'. Return on Investment is the ratio of earnings after depreciation to original cost of investment. It may be calculated using any of the following methods:

1. $$\text{ARR} = \frac{\text{Average net annual earnings}}{\text{Original investment}} \times 100$$

2. $$\text{ARR} = \frac{\text{Average net annual earnings}}{\text{Average investment}} \times 100$$

Note. The term average net annual earnings are the average of the net earnings after depreciation and tax over the entire economic life of the project.

3. $$\text{ARR} = \frac{\text{Increase in expected future annual net earnings}}{\text{Initial increase in required investment}} \times 100$$

The amount of 'average investment' can be calculated according to any of the following methods:

$$[a] = \frac{\text{Original investment}}{2}$$

$$[b] = \frac{\text{Original investment} - \text{Scrap value of the asset}}{2}$$

$$[c] = \frac{\text{Original investment} + \text{Scrap value of the asset}}{2}$$

$$[d] = \frac{\text{Original investment} + \text{Scrap value} + \text{Additional working Capital}}{2}$$

Adding all the earnings after depreciation, and dividing them by the economic life of the project compute the average return. Average investment is the simple average of the values of asset at the beginning and at the end of the useful life of the asset, which in most cases is zero. Though sometimes-initial investment is used, average investment is more logical.

Selection Criteria. The decision rule is that a project with the highest rate of return on investment is selected on condition that such rate is above the standard rate set or the cut-off rate. In the case of replacement or expansion, the return on investment on additional investment should be above the cut-off or minimum required rate. The company's cost of capital or any other desired rate might be set as the cut-off rate. Adding certain percentage to the desired rate of return could provide for risk and inflation. In case of alternative projects, one with the highest ARR is to be selected.

Example 4

From the following information calculate the Average Rate of Return for Project A and B:

Particulars	*Project A*	*Project B*
Investment (₹)	50,000	75,000
Estimated life (in years)	4	5
Net earnings (after depreciation and taxes)	₹	₹
Year 1	5,000	7,500
2	3,750	7,500
3	3,750	5,000
4	2,500	2,500
5	—	2,500

Assuming a desired rate of return of 12% suggest as to which project should be selected?

Solution

Total earnings for Project A = (₹ 5,000 + 3,750 + 3,750 + 2,500) = 15,000

Average earnings or return = ₹ 15,000/4 = 3,750

Average Investment = (₹ 50,000 + 0)/2 = ₹ 25,000

Average Rate of Return = (₹ 3,750/ 25,000) × 100 = 15%

Total earnings for Project B = (₹ 7,500 + 7,500 + 5,000 + 2,500 + 2,500)
= ₹ 25,000

Average Return or earnings = ₹ 25,000/5 = ₹ 5,000

Average Investment = (₹ 75 000 + 0)/12 = ₹ 37,500

Average Rate of Return = (₹ 5,000/37,500) × 100 = 13.33%

Suggestion: Both the projects satisfy the minimum desired rate of return of 12%. Hence, both qualify for selection. However, the average rate of return of Project A is higher than that of Project B. Therefore, it is recommended that Project A should be selected.

Example 5

A Ltd., decided to purchase a new plant to replace the old plant, which is in operation for the last 5 years. Ignore interest but consider tax at 50% of net earnings. From the following particulars, suggest which of the two alternatives should be preferred.

Particulars	*Old Plant*	*New Plant*
Cost of the Plant (₹)	2,00,000	3,00,000
Estimated life (years)	10	10
Plant running hours p.a.	2,000	2,000
Production units per hour	120	180
Wages per running hour	15	25
Power p.a.	10,000	22,500
Consumable stores p.a.	30,000	37,500
All other charges p.a.	40,000	45,000
Material cost per unit (₹)	0.50	0.50
Selling Price per unit (₹)	1.25	1.25

You may assume that the above information regarding sales and cost of sales will hold well throughout the economic life of each of the plants. Depreciation is to be charged as per straight-line method. You may make any other assumptions if necessary.

Solution

Profitability Statement

Particulars		*Old Plant*		*New Plant*
Cost of the Plant (₹)		2,00,000		3,00,000
Life of Plants (years)		10		10
Output (units)		2,40,000		3,60,000
Sales Value (₹)		3,00,000		4,50,000
Less: Cost of sales (₹)				
Direct materials	1,20,000		1,80,000	
Wages	30,000		50,000	
Power	10,000		22,500	
Consumable stores	30,000		37,500	
Other charges	40,000		45,000	
Depreciation	20,000	2,50,000	30,000	3,65,000
Profit before tax	—	50,000		85,000
Less: Tax @ 50%		25,000		42,500
Profit after tax		25,000		42,500

Accounting Rate of Return of Old Plant is 25% and of New Plant is 28.33%.

Thus replacement of old plant by a new plant (ignoring interest) is profitable.

Note: Incremental Investment = Cost of new plant – Depreciated value of old plant

₹ 3,00,000 – 1,00,000 = ₹ 2,00,000

MERITS AND DEMERITS OF ARR METHOD

Merits

1. ARR method is easy to understand and simple to operate.
2. This method takes into account the earnings over the entire economic life of the project even though estimates of the distant future may be subject to a wide margin of errors.
3. It is really a profitability concept since it considers net earnings after depreciation, i.e., excess of earnings over original cost of investment.
4. Another advantage is that projects, which differ widely in character, could be compared under this method. For example, investment in new projects could be compared with a cost reduction project or a current investment proposal could be compared with a future project.
5. This method is inconsistent with the conventional accounting system and easy to comprehend as it is based on percentages.

Demerits

1. The most severe criticism of this method is that it ignores the time value of money.
2. This method ignores the risk and uncertainty factors also.
3. This method, which is based on conventional accounting system, is subject to the limitations of that system.
4. Normally, a host of variants are to be resolved relating to its components, viz., earnings and investment cost. For example, it may be the gross, net, or average investment that should be considered for computation. This may produce different rates of return for any investment on proposal.
5. Another problem is with regard to a reasonable rate of return on investments. Some stipulate a minimum rate so that if projects do not satisfy this rate they may be summarily excluded from consideration.

DISCOUNTED CASH FLOW TECHNIQUES (DCF)

Investments are essentially current capital expenditures incurred at present in anticipation of future returns. Hence, the timing of expected future cash flows is important in the investment decision. In any economy, capital or funds invested have value and therefore, time value of money is an important concept. For example, investors place a higher value on recent returns than on future ones. Hence, the technique that discounts (or reduces) the future values into their present values at a specified time value (discount rate) is called as DCF technique. It is considered that DCF techniques provide a more objective basis for evaluating and selecting investment projects. Also they enable one to isolate differences in the timing of cash flows for various projects by discounting the cash flows to their present values. Because these techniques take account of both the magnitude and the timing of expected cash flows in each period of a project's life. Generally, these techniques consider the net cash flows as representing the recovery of original investment plus a return on capital invested. There are mainly two types of DCF techniques viz., Net Present Value (NPV) and Internal Rate of Return (IRR).

Meaning of Discounting

Discounting is reducing the values of future cash flows or returns to make it directly comparable to the values at present. It is the basic operation of any DCF method. The problem is that a rupee today is worth more than the same rupee in a year's time regardless of inflation, because the rupee one has invested can grow to a larger sum in the future. The rate at which the future cash flows are reduced to their present value is termed as discount rate. Discount rate, otherwise called as the time value of money, is some interest rate that expresses the time preference for a particular future cash flow. Realistic capital investment appraisal depends on two factors, viz., discounting period and a suitable discount rate.

Normally, the economic life of a project is used as the discounting period. However, the length of discounting period depends on factors such as the life of equipment with the largest life span, technological change, availability of raw materials, market stability, etc. The market rate of interest is normally considered for discounting. But the cost of capital computed based on the overall capital structure of the company or on the basis of financial pattern would be an appropriate discount rate.

DEFINITION OF NET PRESENT VALUE TECHNIQUES (NPV)

Net Present Value may be defined as the excess of present value of project cash inflows (stream of benefits) over that of outflows (cash outlays). The cash flows of a project are discounted at some desired rate of return, which is mostly equivalent to the cost of capital. For a conventional investment where all cash outflows take place in the base year, NPV may be represented as follows:

$$\text{NPV} = \frac{B_1}{(1+k)} + \frac{B_2}{(1+k)} + \frac{B_3}{(1+k)} + \text{.........} + \frac{B_n}{(1+k)} - C_o$$

$$\text{NPV} = \sum_{t=1}^{n} \frac{Bt}{(1+k)} - C_o$$

Where $B_t = B_1, B_2, B_3, \ldots B_n$ represents the cash inflows in periods 1, 2, 3, ... *n*.

C_o represents the cash outlays in time period 0.

'*k*' represents the discount rate, which is equal to firm's cost of capital.

For a non-conventional investment where the cash outflows take place over more than one year.

$$\text{NPV} = \frac{B_1}{(1+k)} + \frac{B_2}{(1+k)} + \frac{B_3}{(1+k)} + \ldots\ldots\ldots \frac{B_n}{(1+k)} - C_o + \frac{C_1}{(1+k)} + \frac{C_2}{(1+k)} + \frac{C_3}{(1+k)} \ldots\ldots \frac{C_n}{(1+k)}$$

$$\text{NPV} = \sum_{t=1}^{n} \frac{Bt}{(1+k)^t} - \sum_{t=0}^{n} \frac{Ct}{(1+k)^t}$$

where 'B' represents cash inflows in periods 0, 1, 2, 3, ...*n*.

'C' represents cash outlays in periods 0, 1, 2, 3, ... *n*,

'*k*' represents the firm's cost of capital or desired rate of return.

Selection Criteria. In the case of mutually exclusive projects or alternative projects (where only one project is to be selected) accept a project that has the highest NPV. In the case of independent investment projects, accept a project if its NPV is greater than or equal to zero; reject if its NPV is negative.

In the case budget constraints or capital rationing, project selection could be done by ranking projects having positive NPV in the descending order of their NPVs and then choosing the first 'x' number of projects that the budget provision permits.

Example 6 (Independent Investment)

X Ltd., is planning to buy a new machine costing ₹ 80,000. Cash flows are expected to be as follows:

Years:	1	2	3	4	5
Cash Flows (₹):	8,000	24,000	32,000	48,000	32,000

The company expects a minimum return of 10 per cent. On this basis, find the profitability of the machine and state if it is financially preferable.

Solution

Year	*Cash Flows*	*Discount Factor @10%*	*Present Value of Cash flows*
1	8,000	0.909	7,272
2	24,000	0.826	19,824
3	32,000	0.751	24,032
4	48,000	0.683	32,784
5	32,000	0.621	19,872
Total	1,44,000		1,03,784
Less Cost	80,000		80,000
		Net Present Value	23,784

Since the NPV is positive (i.e., the PV of cash inflows is greater than the PV of cash outflows or cost), the new machine would be profitable and therefore, may be purchased.

Example 7 (Mutually Exclusive or Alternative Investments)

Nancy Ltd., is planning to buy a new machine. Two alternative machines (A and B) each costing ₹ 4,00,000 and requiring an additional working capital of ₹ 20,000 at the end of the first year.

Earnings after taxation are expected to be as follows:

Year	*1*	*2*	*3*	*4*	*5*
Cash flows (₹)					
Machine A	40,000	1,20,000	1,60,000	2,40,000	1,60,000
Machine B	1,20,000	1,60,000	2,00,000	1,20,000	80,000

The company has a target return on capital at 10% and on this basis you are requested to ascertain the profitability of the machines and suggest which alternative you consider financially feasible.

Note: The following table gives the present value of Re. 1 due in 'n' number of years.

Year:	1	2	3	4	5
P.V. @ 10%:	0.91	0.83	0.75	0.68	0.62

Solution

Year	*Discount Factor*	*Machine A* Cash Inflows Amount [₹]	*Machine A* Present Value Amount [₹]	*Machine B* Cash Inflows Amount [₹]	*Machine B* Present Value Amount [₹]
1.	0.91	40,000	36,400	1,20,000	1,09,200
2.	0.83	1,20,000	99,600	1,60,000	1,32,800
3.	0.75	1,60,000	1,20,000	2,00,000	1,50,000
4.	0.68	2,40,000	1,63,200	1,20,000	81,600
5.	0.62	1,60,000	99,200	80,000	49,600
	Total	7,20,000	5,18,400	6,80,000	5,23,200
	Less Cash outflows	4,20,000	4,18,200	4,20,000	4,18,200

Workings: Present value of cash outflows = Cost of machine (₹ 4,00,000) plus working capital introduced at the end of 1st year (₹ 20,000 × 0.91 = 18,200) = ₹ 4,18,200.

Recommendation: Since the NPV of Machine B is greater than that of Machine A by ₹ 4,800, it is preferable. Though the total cash inflows of Machine A is more than that of Machine B by ₹ 40,000, the NPV of Machine B is greater, for its cash inflows in the earlier years are comparatively higher than those of Machine A.

MERITS AND DEMERITS OF NPV METHOD

Merits

1. The salient feature of NPV technique is that it indicates the value added to the total assets of the firm by taking up the proposed investment at a particular rate of discount.
2. The NPV criterion automatically allows for the recovery of the initial investment and the cost of funds invested in such investments. For example, if the gross PV of a project costing ₹ 50,000 is ₹ 58,645 at 10% discount rate, it means that the value added to the total assets in present value terms is ₹ 8,645 (i.e., NPV = ₹ 58,645 – 50,000). This is after providing for the initial investment of ₹ 50,000 and for interest cost at 10% p.a.
3. The most significant advantage of NPV method is that it recognizes the time value of money and considers all cash flows over the entire economic life of the project.
4. It is in consistent with the objective of maximizing the welfare of the owners of the firm.

Demerits

1. It is difficult to understand and use. Since it requires accurate cash flows, accurate life of the project and discount rate.
2. It may not give satisfactory answer when the projects being compared involve different amounts of investments. For example, a project with high NPV may not be desirable if it also requires a large investment.
3. Selection of an appropriate discount rate is very difficult.
4. This technique is based on compound interest principle. Under this method, it is assumed that the cash flows could be reinvested at the same rate of interest (discount rate), which is not practically feasible.
5. Under the NPV criterion, profitability is not related to the capital outlay required for it. A project may have a high NPV but it can still be unattractive, for it requires a very high capital outlay. For example, two projects costing ₹ 50,000 and ₹ 80,000 respectively generate NPVs of ₹ 11,500 and ₹ 12,500. Of these two, Project would be recommended by NPV criterion since its NPV is higher by ₹ 1,000. However, the profitability is not attractive compared to the additional investment required for Project B.

MEANING OF BENEFIT/COST RATIO (BCR)

With a view to establishing the profitability of projects relating to the investment required, the NPV criterion is usually supplemented with an additional tool called 'Benefit/Cost Ratio' or 'Profitability Index'. BCR may be defined as the ratio of gross discounted benefits to gross discounted costs. It is expressed in coefficient, or in percentage. Symbolically this could be expressed as follows:

BCR = B/C or B/C × 100

Or Profitability Index (PI) = (B – C)/C × 100

Where B = Gross discounted benefits, and

C = Gross discounted costs.

Example: Suppose the gross discounted value of benefits is ₹ 1,03,784 and gross discounted value of costs is ₹ 80,000, and then the BCR and PI would be as follows:

BCR = ₹ 1,03,784/80,000 = 1.297 (approx.)

PI = (₹ 1,03,784 – ₹ 80,000)/₹ 80,000

= ₹ 23,784/80,000 = 0.297 (approx.)

The salient feature of BCR is that it can also explain the NPV position of an investment. If BCR is equal to ONE then NPV will be equal to ZERO. If it is greater than ONE, then NPV will be positive; if it is lesser than ONE then NPV will be negative.

Decision Criteria. In the case of independent investments, accept a project if the BCR is greater than one and reject it otherwise. In the case mutually exclusive or alternative investments, accept the project with the largest BCR, provided it is greater than one; reject others. Under conditions of capital rationing or budget constraints, rank the projects in the descending order of their BCRs and choose the first 'x' number of projects that the budget provision permits.

BCR is particularly useful for ranking the projects on the basis of their profitability. However, it suffers from the same limitations as the NPV technique. In other words, all the merits and demerits of NPV technique are attributable to this technique also.

Example 8

From the following information calculate the NPV and BCRs for the Machines A and B:

Particulars		*Machine A*	*Machine B*
Initial Investment (₹)		40,000	60,000
Expected life (years)		5	5
Salvage value (₹)		2,000	3,000
Cash Inflows (₹)			
	Year 1	10,000	40,000
	Year 2	20,000	20,000
	Year 3	20,000	10,000
	Year 4	5,000	6,000
	Year 5	5,000	4,000

The management fixes 10% as the required rate of return for the proposed investment project. Discount factors at this rate are given below:

Solution

Particulars	*D.F.*	*Machine A*		*Machine B*	
		Cash Flow (₹)	*P.V. of Cash Flow*	*Cash Flow (₹)*	*P.V. of Cash Flow*
Investment	1.000	40,000	40,000	60,000	60,000
Cash Inflows (₹)					
Year 1	0.909	10,000	9,090	40,000	36,360
Year 2	0.826	20,000	16,520	20,000	16,520
Year 3	0.751	20,000	15,020	10,000	7,510
Year 4	0.683	5,000	3,415	6,000	4,098
Year 5	0.621	5,000	3,105	4,000	2,484
Salvage value	0.621	2,000	1,242	3,000	1,863
Total present value			48,392		68,835
NPV			8,932		8,835

Computation of BCR

$$\text{BCR} = \frac{\text{Gross PV of Cash Inflow}}{\text{Gross PV of Cash Outflow}}$$

$$\text{BCR} = \frac{48{,}392}{40{,}000} = 1.21 \text{ (approx.)}$$

Machine A $= 1.21$ (approx.)

Machine $= \text{BCR} = 1.15$ (approx.)

Profitability Index $$\text{PI} = \frac{\text{Net present value}}{\text{Gross PV of cash outflows}}$$

Machine A $$\text{PI} = \frac{8{,}392}{40{,}000} = 0.21 \text{ (approx.)}$$

Machine B $$\text{PI} = \frac{8{,}835}{60{,}000} = 0.15 \text{ (approx.)}$$

Comments: As per NPV method, Machine B is preferable. As per BCR method, Machine A is preferable.

DEFINITION OF INTERNAL RATE OF RETURN (IRR)

The Internal Rate of Return may be defined as that rate of interest when used to discount the cash flows of an investment, reduce its NPV to zero. Or it is the rate of discount, which equates the aggregate discounted benefits with aggregate discounted costs. IRR is also called as 'Discounted Cash Flow Method' or 'Yield Method' or 'Time Adjusted Rate of Return Method'. This method is used when the cost of investment and the annual cash inflows are known but the discount rate (rate of return) is not known and is to be calculated. Symbolically, the IRR may be expressed as follows:

For a conventional investment,

$$\text{NPV} = \sum_{t=1}^{n} \frac{B_t}{(1+r)^t} = C_o = 0$$

(Aggregate discounted cash inflows) = (Aggregate initial investment)

Where the discount rate 'r' is the IRR. B_t represents cash inflows during the time period 1, 2, 3 , ...n, and C_o is the initial cash outflows.

IRR indicates the maximum rate of return that a project can contribute and is mainly based on the internal cash inflows generated by it. In other words it is the break-even interest showing the highest interest rate consistent with the project not making any loss. However, in order to judge the profitability of the project, IRR should be compared with a cut-off rate of return, which might be the company's cost of capital.

Decision Criteria. In the case of an independent project, accept the project if it's IRR is greater than the cut-off rate; if lower, reject it. In the case of mutually exclusive projects, accept the project with the largest IRR, provided it is greater than the cut-off rate; reject others. In case there are budget constraints, rank the projects in the descending order of their IRRs and choose the first 'x' number of projects, which the budget provision permits.

Method of Calculating IRR

Trial and Error Yield Method: As the name suggests, the object is to find the expected yield from the investment. The procedure involved may be summarized as follows:

(*a*) List the annual sales and cost other than depreciation and reducing the latter from the former obtain the net cash flow.

(*b*) Obtain the capital investment cost. Often this will be at present value because the amount spent is invested in the base year.

(*c*) Calculate the present value of the net cash inflows by using an appropriate discount rate. This rate is found by trial and error method from the present value tables. The object is to make the present value of cash inflows equal to the capital investment cost.

(*d*) Carry out this procedure for each project being considered and then rank them in the order of preference.

Merits of IRR Method

1. Like NPV method, IRR method also recognizes the time value of money and considers cash flows over the entire life of the project.

2. It has a psychological appeal to the user as it is expressed in percentage figure.
3. Unlike NPV method, it does not require any discount rate. IRR is itself a break-even rate (discount rate), which makes the present values of all cash inflows equal to those of cash outflows.
4. It is also in consistent with the firm's objective of maximizing owners' welfare.

Limitations of IRR Method

1. It is very difficult to use in practice as it involves complicated computational problems.
2. It assumes that the reinvestment rate of cash flows is at IRR, but it may be different for different projects considered by a firm. Under NPV method, the reinvestment rate (discount rate) is assumed to be the same for all projects, which seems a more appropriate assumption.
3. The IRR method may yield multiple rates for a project when cash flows take place at different time periods. This will make the decision-making more complicated.
4. It may give inconsistent results with NPV if the projects differ in their expected lives, or cash flows, or timing of cash flows.

Example 9

PQR Ltd., is planning to increase its present capacity and is considering purchase of a new machine. Machine X is available for a price of ₹ 40,000. Earnings before tax have been estimated as follows:

Year:	1	2	3	4	5
Cash inflows (₹):	11,000	15,000	20,000	16,000	8,000

Compute IRR and ascertain the profitability of the new machine.

Solution

Trial and Error Method

Year	*Cash flows*	*I trial DF (20%)*	*PV of I trial*	*II trial rate (24%)*	*PV of II rate*	*III trial rate (22%)*	*PV of III rate*
0	[40,000]	1.000	[40,000]	1.000	[40,000]	1.000	[40,000]
1	11,000	0.833	9,163	0.806	8,866	0.820	9,020
2	15,000	0.694	10,410	0.650	9,750	0.672	10,080
3	20,000	0.579	11,580	0.524	10,840	0.551	11,020
4	16,000	0.482	7,712	0.423	6,768	0.451	7,216
5	8,000	0.402	3,216	0.341	2,728	0.370	2,960
NPV			2,081		(1,048)		296

From the above statement it is ascertained that in the first trial at 20% the present value of cash inflows exceeds the present value of cash outflows by ₹ 2,081 (i.e., NPV = ₹ 2,081). On the second trial at 24%, the NPV is negative by ₹ 1,048. The IRR must lie between these two rates. Hence, the third trial rate is taken as 22%. At this rate the NPV is positive by ₹ 296. It may, therefore, be concluded that the IRR is approximately 22% where the PV of cash inflows approximately equals the PV of cash outflows. If greater accuracy is required interpolation may be used to find the required discount rate, rather than making calculations of unlimited trial rates. By applying interpolation technique the correct rate may be computed as follows:

$$\text{IRR} = 22\% + \left[\frac{296}{296 - 1048}\right] \times 2\% = 22.44\%$$

Formula for Interpolation

$$\text{IRR} = A + \left[\frac{C}{C - D}\right] \times [B - A]$$

Where A = Discount factor of the lower trial

B = Discount factor of the higher trial

C = NPV of cash flows of the lower trial

D = NPV of cash flows of the higher trial

Establishing the Trial Rates

In the Trial and Error method, difficulty is often experienced in the selection of the first trial rate. Once the first rate is established, the second trial rate is determined by considering the value of NPV. If the NPV is negative, the second trial rate will be higher than the first rate. If the NPV is positive, the second rate should be lower than the first rate. However, the problem is to select the first trial rate. As an aid to this selection, a rough guide is as follows:

$$\text{1st Trial Rate} = \frac{\text{Average Earnings or Saving}}{\text{Investment}}$$

Another better method is to divide the investment cost by average earnings per year and get a coefficient. Then refer the annuity table to find out at what percentage, one rupee grows into the calculated value (coefficient) in the given number of years. The percentage so ascertained may be taken as the first trial rate.

For example, the initial investment is ₹ 6,00,000 and the average annual earnings or cash flows for 4 years (i.e., life of the asset) is ₹ 2,12,500. If you divide ₹ 6,00,000 by ₹ 2,12, 500, you get 2.824. By referring to the annuity table, you may find that ₹ 1 grows into 2.824 in 4 years at 15% (2.824 may be the nearest value). Then 15% may be taken as the first trial rate.

ADVANTAGES OF DCF TECHNIQUES

Advantages

1. DCF techniques are superior to other methods since they consider the earnings of a project over its entire economic life, and also the time value of money flows.

2. They are more objective, for their conclusions are not directly influenced by decisions regarding depreciation methods, capitalization versus and expense decisions and consideration.
3. The DCF method automatically gives more weight to units of money, which are nearer than those, which are distant. But other methods treat distant units of money unrealistically with the same weight as present units.
4. The DCF method allows a ready comparison to be made between projects having different lives and different timings of each flow by facilitating comparison at the same point of time.
5. By comparing the rates of return of projects with the cost of capital ratios, decisions can be taken quickly and safely.

GENERAL CRITICISMS AGAINST DCF TECHNIQUES

1. DCF methods are considered difficult to understand and operate. However, compared to the complexities associated with some modern statistical and mathematical tools, which have gained acceptance in recent times, DCF techniques are simple to understand. Further with the development of mechanized accounting and computer technology it has become very easy to operate.
2. The second assumption is against the assumption of a fixed investment rate throughout the life of the project. This assumption arises mainly because of the use of compound interest principle as the basis of these methods.
3. The third criticism is that they fail to take account of risks and uncertainties. However, recent developments in risk analysis, which could be incorporated into DCF methods, have made this criticism somewhat irrelevant.
4. It is said that the IRR and NPV methods give rise to conflicting issues while decisions are taken. Recent theoretical refinements have mitigated most of the weaknesses of these methods.

NPV AND IRR METHODS — A COMPARISON

NPV and IRR are the species of the same genus, i.e., DCF technique. They are based on the fundamental concept that money has a time value. However, there are certain fundamental differences between these two techniques.

First, the NPV treats the discount rate as a known factor while the IRR treats it as an unknown factor. In most cases the business known cost of capital is used for discounting under NPV method.

Secondly, the IRR method seeks to find the maximum rate of return at which funds invested in any given project could be repaid with earnings generated by the project. But the present value method arrives at the amount to be invested in a given project so that its anticipated earnings could recoup the amount with the interest at the market rate.

Thirdly, at a particular discount rate, there can be only one NPV, and not multiple net present values of a project. But in the case of unconventional investments, where capital outlays are incurred at different time periods, a project may have more than one IRR, which may lead to baffling contradictions.

Fourthly, the present value method explicitly recognizes availability of a market for funds and assumes that business will use the market rationally to enhance its earnings; but IRR method does not recognize the existence of such a capital market. In other words, the NPV method assumes mostly the cost of capital, which is based on the market rate of interest, as the discount rate. But the IRR method tries to find out a discount rate, which has no direct bearing on the market rate of interest.

TERMINAL VALUE METHOD

Under the Terminal value method, it is assumed that each cash inflow is reinvested immediately in some other project elsewhere at a certain rate of interest until the project terminates. The sum total of the compounded reinvested cash inflows is discounted at the desired rate of return or at the company's cost of capital. If the present value of the cash inflows is greater than that of the cash outflows, the proposed project is accepted, otherwise rejected. The following example illustrates the above points.

Example 10

From the following particulars suggest whether the project should be accepted under the Terminal Value Method.

Project Cost	₹ 40,000
Estimated life of the project	3 years

Cash inflows ₹ 20,000 per annum for 3 years

Required rate of return 10% per annum

Expected interest rate at which the cash inflows will be reinvested is 8% for all the three years.

Solution

Year	*Cash inflows* ₹	*Interest rate* %	*Years for investment*	*Compounded value*	*Total sum compounded value* (₹)
1	20,000	8	2	1.166	23,320
2	20,000	8	1	1.080	21,600
3	20,000	8	0	1.000	20,000

Present value of Total sum of compounded reinvested cash inflows should be calculated by using the desired rate of return. The PV of ₹ 1 for the third year at 10% (desired rate of return) is 0.751.

PV of total sum of compounded cash inflows = ₹ 64,920 × 0.751 = ₹ 48,755

Since the present value of the compounded reinvested cash inflows (i.e., ₹ 48,755) is more than the original project cost (i.e., ₹ 40,000), the project should be accepted.

PROJECT APPRAISAL UNDER RISK AND UNCERTAINTY

NEED FOR RISK ANALYSIS

Project cost estimates, life of the project and the estimates of demand, production, sales and prices, etc., may contain errors because of uncertainty about the future. Project decisions underlie many political and social developments as well as changes in technology, prices, and productivity. Hence, while deciding about the desirability of a project, all these factors have to be taken into account in the form of foreseeable risk, which the project proposal either can or cannot carry. This is probably the most difficult decision to be made during the entire process of project preparation. The size of allowance provided for this purpose will have a decisive impact on the profitability of the project and may, in the case of marginal proposal tilt the balance against the implementation of the project. Hence, it is essential to incorporate measures at the appraisal stage to identify the risk factors and provide for the same.

MEANING OF THE CONCEPTS OF RISK AND UNCERTAINTY

The decision situations are generally classified into three types, viz., certainty, risk and uncertainty. Certainty situation is one where the future occurrence of a particular outcome such as future cash flow or discount rate could be expressed with certitude. But in practice, all investment decisions are undertaken under conditions of risk and uncertainty. Risk refers to a situation where the probability distribution of a particular outcome could be objectively known in advance, while uncertainty refers to a situation where such probability distribution cannot be objectively known, but only guessed. However, in the case of investment decisions, such a theoretical distinction is hypothetical and may not serve much useful purpose in practice. Even the best estimates of the project manager regarding the probability of the expected cash flows materializing, and their magnitude are only subjective guesses. Hence, both risk and uncertainty are used interchangeably to mean the same thing.

Some of the factors, which add to the degree of risk or uncertainty of an investment are the possibilities of (*a*) the process or product becoming obsolete, (*b*) declining demand for the product, (*c*) change in government policy on business, (*d*) price fluctuations, (*e*) foreign exchange restrictions, and (*f*) inflationary tendencies, etc.

MODERN QUANTITATIVE TECHNIQUES THAT MAY BE USED IN RISK MANAGEMENT

Systems Analysis: Systems analysis refers to the set of techniques concerned with the analysis, procedures, and other methods of doing things, and with the design and implementation of new and superior systems. Its principal objective is to evaluate alternatives in a consistent unarbitrary manner. Growth in size and complexity of business operations need a systematic examination of a problem of choice in which each step of the analysis is made explicit. This enables business units derive the benefits of computer technology.

Marketing Research: Marketing Research is used to forecast objectively the demand potential for goods and services of the prospective project. Demand appraisal is, in fact, the starting of point of feasibility analysis. The objective is to assess the available opportunities and study the future trends of these opportunities so that the investment decision could be taken with a degree of confidence. This would help to reduce the degree of risk.

Operations Research (O.R.): O.R. enables a decision-maker to be more objective in choosing among alternatives. It surrogates mathematical reasoning for verbal arguments. Some well known O.R. techniques are: (*a*) Linear Programming or Integer Programming — under conditions of capital rationing, integer or linear programming models could be used to determine the right project mix to commit scarce resources; (*b*) Game theory, for instance, would be an effective tool to predict to a certain extent the strategies of competing firms and counteract them; and (*c*) Inventory control techniques such as ABC analysis, EOQ models, etc.

Network Analysis (PERT/CPM): The gestation period is the time lag, which will elapse between the commencement of investment and the start of the return on investment — a vital determinant in establishing the acceptability of the project. The longer the gestation period is, higher would be the cost escalations and the risks associated with the project resulting in low returns. PERT and CPM provide the project formulation team with one of the most effective analytical aids. Network analysis is useful in (*a*) developing the project, (*b*) controlling the project implementation delays and project cost, and (*c*) determining the gestation period realistically.

Cost-Volume-Profit Analysis: This analysis indicates the operating characteristics of a project. Under this analysis, first the break-even point i.e., no profit-no loss sales volume, is determined in terms of the project and may even be expressed as a percentage of the project capacity. It helps to identify the operating sensitivity of the project in terms of changes in the cost of raw materials, wages, and other project inputs.

Ratio Analysis: While comparing two or more investment proposals for resource allocation, costs, benefits and profits measured in absolute figures do not give information clearly. Hence, ratio analysis could be used for better, easy and useful comparisons.

All these management aids, when used at the project formulation stage, would minimize the degree of risk involved in different types of investment decisions. However, these tools cannot eliminate risk completely. Hence, risk analysis becomes an integral part of any investment analysis.

Techniques of Risk Analysis

The techniques used to handle risk in project appraisal may be classified into two groups as follows:

(*a*) Conservative Methods — such as Shorter Payback Period, Risk-adjusted Discount Rate, and Conservative Forecasts or Certainty Equivalents, etc.

(*b*) Modern Methods — such as Sensitivity Analysis, Probability Analysis, Decision Tree Analysis, etc.

CONSERVATIVE METHODS OR TOOLS OF RISK ANALYSIS

Shorter Payback Period: According to this method, projects with shorter payback periods are normally preferred to those with longer payback periods. It would be more effective when it is combined with a 'cut off period'. Cut off period denotes the risk tolerance level in the firm. For example, a firm has three projects, A, B, C for consideration with different economic lives, say 15, 16 and 7 years respectively, and with payback periods of say 6, 7, and 5 years. Of these three, project C will be preferred because its payback period is the shortest. Suppose, the firm's cut off period is 4 years, then all the three projects will be rejected.

Risk-adjusted Discount Rate: Under this method, the cut off rate or minimum required rate of return (mostly the firm's cost of capital) is raised by adding what is called 'risk premium' to it. When the risk is greater, the premium to be added would be greater. For example, if the risk free discount rate (say, cost of capital) is 10%, and the project under consideration is a riskier one, then the premium of, say 5% is added to the above risk-free rate. The risk-adjusted discount rate would be 15%, which may be used either for discounting purposes under NPV, or as a cut off rate under IRR.

Merits of Risk-adjusted Discount Rate

1. It is easy to understand and simple to operate.
2. It has a great deal of intuitive appeal for risk adverse decision-makers.
3. It incorporates an attitude towards uncertainty.

Demerits

1. There is no easy way to derive a risk-adjusted discount rate.
2. A uniform risk discount factor used for discounting all future returns is unscientific as the degree of risk may vary over the years in future.
3. It assumes that investors are risk averse. Though it is generally true, there do exist risk-seekers in real world situation that may demand premium for assuming risk.

Conservative Forecasts: Under this method, employing intuitive correction factor or certainty equivalent coefficient, which is calculated by the decision-maker subjectively or objectively, reduces the estimated risks from cash flows. Normally, this coefficient reflects the decision-maker's confidence in obtaining a particular cash flow in a particular period. For example, the decision-maker estimates a net cash flow of ₹ 60,000 next year but if he feels (subjectively) that only 60% of such cash flow is a definite sum, and then the said coefficient would be 0.6. This may also be determined (objectively) by relating the desirable cash flows with estimated cash flows as follows:

$$\text{Certainty Equivalent Coefficient} = \frac{\text{Desirable Cash Flow}}{\text{Estimated Cash Flow}}$$

For Example, if the estimated cash flow is ₹ 80,000 in period 't' and an equally desirable cash flow for the same period is ₹ 60,000, then the certainty equivalent is 0.75 (60,000/80,000). Besides the computations of certain cash flows in order to provide for more risk, the economic life over which cash flows are estimated may be reduced simultaneously.

MODERN METHODS OF RISK ANALYSIS

Sensitivity Analysis: Sensitivity analysis is a simulation technique in which key variables are changed and the resulting change in the rate of return or (the NPV) is observed. Some of the key variables are cost, prices, project life, market share, etc. The most practical way to do this is to select those variables whose estimated values may contain some significant errors or an element of uncertainty, and then to calculate the effect of errors of different sizes on the present value of the project. The common operating mechanism would be to vary each strategic variable by certain fixed percentages in both positive as well as negative directions in turn, say plus or minus 10% or plus or minus 5% etc., and study the effect of change on the rate of return (or on NPV).

It is an effective tool to handle risk in project appraisal. However, there are certain limitations in using this tool. They are:

(*a*) Unless the combined effect of change in a set of Inter-correlated variables is examined, single variable sensitivity testing could be worse than useless. It may lead to wrong conclusions. Hence, it is a very difficult task.

(*b*) The second limitation lies in the fact that the values of the variables (components) are generally changed in an arbitrary manner by say 5% or 10% to examine the effect on the returns. Unless it is done in a meaningful manner, it might mislead the investor.

(*c*) The third one is that it ignores the chances associated with the different possible values of the components.

Probability Analysis: Probability may be defined as a measure of some one's opinion about the likelihood that an event (cash flow) will occur. The likelihood of occurrence normally ranges from 1 to 0 i.e., 100 per cent certainty to 100 per cent uncertainty. In this analysis, in the place of one single estimate a range of estimates and their associated probabilities are calculated. A probability distribution in its simplest form could be with a few estimates such as "optimistic", "pessimistic", and "most likely". The real problem, however, is how this probability distribution can be obtained. Two types of probabilities—objective and subjective—are normally used for decision-making under uncertainty. The objective probability is the probability estimate, which is based on a very large number of observations, say, for example, on the objective evidence of 100 trials conducted repeatedly under independent identical situations. Subjective probabilities are those probability measures, which are based on the state of belief of a person rather than the objective evidence of a large number of trials. As the capital expenditure decisions are mostly non-repetitive and not made under identical situations, only subjective probabilities are useful.

Expected Values (EV): EV is the sum of products of estimated outcomes and their respective probabilities. For example, if the possible yields for an investment are 8%, 12%, and 16% and the probabilities that any one of these will be achieved is 0.25, 0.50, and 0.25 respectively, the EV of the yield is as follows:

$$EV = (0.25 \times 8) + (0.50 \times 12) + (0.25 \times 16) = 12\%$$

In the case of alternative projects, one with the highest EV is considered for selection. EVs may be used for computation of IRR and NPV. However, EVs fail to articulate the degree of risk involved.

Decision Tree Analysis: A decision may be taken by comparing various alternative courses at present with the decision-maker, each alternative course being studied in the light of the future possible conditions followed by future alternative decisions. The group of all these decisions present as well as future, viewed in relation to one another is called a 'decision tree'. It is a graphic display of the relationship between a present decision and future events, and future decisions and their consequences. The sequence of events is normally represented over time in a format similar to the branches of a tree. The major steps in a decision tree process are:

(*a*) The investment decision is defined clearly.

(*b*) The decision alternatives are identified.

(*c*) The decision tree graph indicates decision points, chance events, and other data.

(*d*) It presents the relevant data such as the projected cash flow, probability distribution, expected present value, etc., on the decision tree branches.

(*e*) Choosing the best alternative by analysis from the results displayed.

Example 11

MNM Ltd. is considering purchase of a new machine at a cost of ₹ 20,000. The cash inflows for the three years of its life are forecast as follows:

Year	*Cash Inflows* (₹)	*Probability*	*Cash Inflows* (₹)	*Probability*
1	8,000	0.4	12,000	0.6
2	16,000	0.2	20,000	0.8
3	6,000	0.7	8,000	0.3

The desired rate of return for NPV purposes is 20 per cent. Calculate the probability of the machine. Also draw a Decision Tree Diagram.

Solution

See the diagram in the annexed sheet

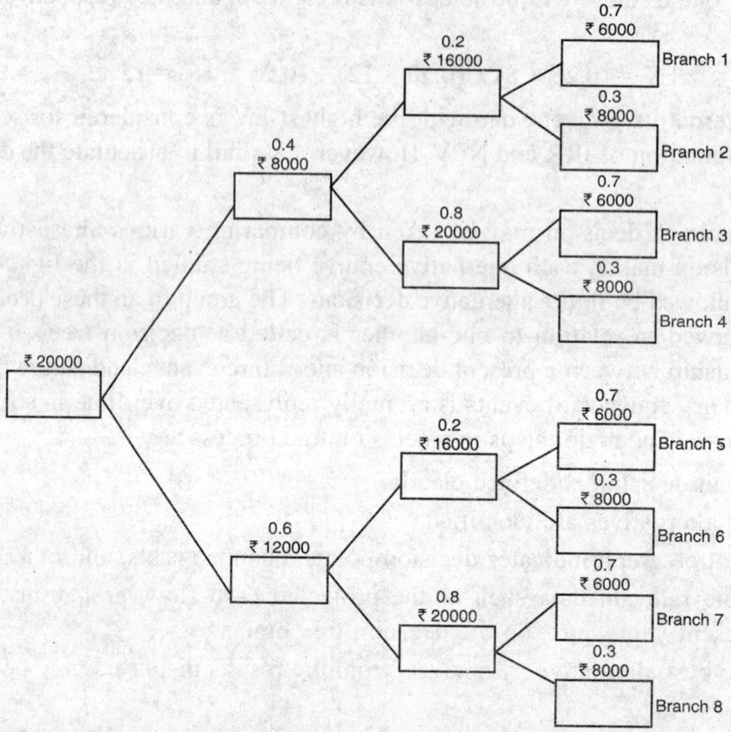

Net Present Values (at 20 per cent discount)

Branch	*Year*	*Cash flow (₹)*	*Discount factor*	*NPV (₹)*
1	0	[20,000]	1,000	[20,000]
	1	8.000	0.833	6,664
	2	16,000	0.694	11,104
	3	6,000	0.579	3,474
				1,242
2	0	[20,000]	1.000	[20,000]
	1	8,000	0.833	6,664
	2	16,000	0.694	11,104
	3	8,000	0.579	4,632
				2,400
3	0	[20,000]	1.000	[20,000]
	1	8,000	0.833	6,664
	2	20,000	0.694	13.880
	3	6,000	0.579	3,474
				4.018

Contd...

4	0	[20,000]	1.000	[20,000]
	1	8,000	0.833	6,664
	2	20,000	0.694	13,880
	3	8,000	0.579	4,632
				5,176
5	0	[20,000]	1.000	[20,000]
	1	12,000	0.833	9,996
	2	16,000	0.694	11,104
	3	6.000	0.579	3,474
				4,574
6	0	[20,000]	1.000	[20,000]
	1	12,000	0.833	9,996
	2	16,000	0.694	11,104
	3	8,000	0.579	4,632
				5,732
7	0	[20,000]	1.000	[20,000]
	1	12,000	0.833	9,996
	2	20,000	0.694	13,880
	3	6,000	0.579	3,474
				7,350
8	0	[20,000]	1.000	[20,000]
	1	12,000	0.833	9,996
	2	20,000	0.694	13,880
	3	8,000	0.579	4,632
				8,508

Probability Calculations

Branch 1 $0.4 \times 0.2 \times 0.7 = 0.056$

Branch 2 $0.4 \times 0.2 \times 0.3 = 0.024$

Branch 3 $0.4 \times 0.8 \times 0.7 = 0.224$

Branch 4 $0.4 \times 0.8 \times 0.3 = 0.096$

Branch 5 $0.6 \times 0.2 \times 0.7 = 0.084$

Branch 6 $0.6 \times 0.2 \times 0.3 = 0.036$

Branch 7 $0.6 \times 0.8 \times 0.7 = 0.336$

Branch 8 $0.6 \times 0.8 \times 0.3 = 0.144$

PRACTICAL PROBLEMS

Illustration 1

A Ltd., is planning to buy a new machine. Two alternative models—Model L and Model H are available. From the following particulars, prepare a profitability statement for submission to the management.

Particulars	*Model L* (₹)	*Model H* (₹)
Cost of Machine	90,000	1,50,000
Estimated life (in years)	10	10
Estimated savings in scrap p.a.,	6,000	9,000
Additional cost of supervision p.a.,	7,200	9,600
Additional cost of maintenance p.a.,	4,200	6,600
Cost of indirect materials p.a.,	3,600	4,800
Estimated savings in wages:		
Wages per worker p.a.,	360	360
Workers not required	150	150

Assume the taxation rate to be 50% of profits. Suggest which model should be purchased based on Payback period method of appraisal, giving reasons for your answer.

Solution

Profitability Statement

Particulars	*Model L* ₹	₹	*Model H* ₹	₹
Estimated savings p.a.				
Scrap	6,000		9,000	
Wages	54,000	60,000	72,000	81,000
Less: Additional cost p.a.				
Cost of supervision	7,200		9,600	
Cost of maintenance	4,200		6,600	
Indirect materials	3,600	15,000	4,800	21,000
Savings before depreciation		45,000		60,000
Less: Depreciation		9,000		10,000
Savings after depreciation		36,000		50,000
Less: Tax at 50%		18,000		25,000
Net savings p.a.		18,000		25,000
Annual cash flow:				
Net savings	18,000		25,000	
Depreciation	9,000	27,000	10,000	35,000

Payback period =

	Model L	Model H
Payback period before tax	= 2 years	= 2.5 years
Payback period after tax	= 3.33 years	= 4.3 years

Model L is recommended, as its payback period is shorter than that of Model H. However, the recommendation may be supplemented with some additional information as regards profitability beyond payback period.

Particulars	*Model L*	*Model H*
Profitability beyond PB before tax:		
Estimated life beyond PB period	8 years	12.5 years
Savings per annum	₹ 45,000	₹ 60,000
Total savings	₹ 3,60,000	₹ 7,50,000
Profitability after tax:		
Estimated life beyond PB period	6.67 years	10.7 years
Savings per annum	₹ 27,000	₹ 35,000
Total savings	₹ 1,80,000	₹ 3,75,000

Based on profitability beyond PB period, Model H looks attractive.

Illustration 2

A company is planning to expand its production capacity. It can go in for an automatic machine costing ₹ 2,24,000 with an estimated life of 5.5 years or an ordinary machine costing ₹ 60,000 having an estimated life of 8 years. The annual sales and costs are estimated as follows:

Particulars	*Automatic Machine* (₹)	*Ordinary Machine* (₹)
Sales	1,50,000	1,50,000
Costs: Materials	50,000	50,000
Wages	12,000	12,000
Variable overheads	24,000	20,000

Compute a comparative profitability of the proposals under the Payback period and Return on Investment methods.

Solution

Comparative Profitability Statement

Particulars		Automatic Machine (₹)		Ordinary Machine (₹)
Investment cost		2,24,000		60,000
Sales		1,50,000		1,50,000
Less: Variable costs: Materials	50,000		50,000	
Wages	12,000		60,000	
Overheads	24,000	86,000	20,000	1,30,000
Contribution		64,000		20,000

Payback Period =

Automatic Machine = ₹ 2,24,000/64,000 = 3.5 years
Ordinary Machine = ₹ 60,000/20,000 = 3 years.

Post Payback Profitability

Automatic machine = ₹ 64,000 × 2 (5.5 – 3.5) = ₹ 1,28,000
Ordinary machine = ₹ 20,000 × 5 (8 – 3) = ₹ 1,00,000

Since the PB period of Ordinary machine is shorter, it is preferable. However, the post payback profitability is more in the case of Automatic machine (i.e., ₹ 1,28,000) than the Ordinary machine (i.e., ₹ 1,00,000). Further, the working capital requirement is less in the case of Automatic machine (i.e., ₹ 86,000) when compared to Ordinary machine (i.e., ₹ 1,30,000). Liquidity is very high in the case of Automatic machine because ₹ 1,28,000 is earned in two years when compared to Ordinary machine which takes 5 years to return ₹ 1,00,000. Based on these facts, it is better to select Automatic machine.

Return on Investment Method

Particulars	Automatic machine (₹)	Ordinary machine (₹)
Contribution	64,000	20,000
Less: Depreciation [Original cost/Estimated life]	40,725	7,500
Net Profit	23,275	12,500

Return on Investment

Automatic Machine = ₹ 23,275/2,24,000 × 100 = 10.4%
₹ 23,275/1,12,000 × 100 = 20.83%

Ordinary Machine = ₹ 12,500/60,000 × 100 = 20.83%
₹ 12,500/30,000 × 100 = 41.67

Since the ROI of the Ordinary machine is higher, it is preferable.

Illustration 3

A Ltd., is considering a project costing ₹ 1,00,000 with a scrap value of ₹ 20,000. The project returns a stream of income before depreciation and taxes during its live of five years as follows:

Period:	1	2	3	4	5
Income (₹)	20,000	24,000	28,000	32,000	40,000

Assume a tax rate at 50 per cent and depreciation on straight-line basis. Compute the Accounting Rate of Return for the project.

Solution

Profitability Statement

Period	*1*	*2*	*3*	*4*	*5*	*Average*
Income before Dep. & tax (₹)	20,000	24,000	28,000	32,000	40,000	28,800
Less: Dep.	16,000	16,000	16,000	16,000	16,000	16,000
Income before Tax	4,000	8,000	12,000	16,000	24,000	12,800
Less: Tax @ 50%	2,000	4,000	6,000	8,000	12,000	6,400
Income after Tax	2,000	4,000	6,000	8,000	12,000	6,400
Investment						
Opening	1,00,000	84,000	68,000	52,000	36,000	
Ending	84,000	68,000	52,000	36,000	20,000	
Average	92,000	76,000	60,000	44,000	40,000	

Average Investment = (Original investment – Scrap value)/2

= (₹ 1,00,000 – 20,000)/2 = ₹ 40,000

Accounting Rate of Return = (Average Return/Average Investment) × 100

(₹ 6,400/40,000) × 100 = 16 %

Illustration 4

A choice is to be made between two competing proposals requiring an equal investment of ₹ 50,000 and expected to generate net cash flows as under:

End of year	1	2	3	4	5	6
Project I (₹)	25,000	15,000	10,000	Zero	12,000	6,000
Project II (₹)	10,000	12,000	18,000	25,000	8,000	4,000

The cost of capital of the company is 10%. The following are the present value factors at 10% p.a.

Year:	1	2	3	4	5	6
PV factors:	0.909	0.826	0.751	0.686	0.621	0.564

Evaluate the project proposals under (*a*) Payback period and (*b*) Net Present Value method. Suggest which project proposal should be chosen and why?

Solution

Computation of Payback Period

Year	*Project I*		*Project II*	
	Cash flows	*Cumulative CFs*	*Cash flows*	*Cumulative CFs*
1	25,000	25,000	10,000	10,000
2	15,000	40,000	12,000	40,000
3	10,000	50,000	18,000	40,000
4			25,000	65,000

The cost of the investment is ₹ 50,000. Project I returns the investment cost in 3 years, which is its Payback period. Project II takes 3 years and (10,000/25,000) 2/5 years or 3.4 years, which is its Payback period. Project I is preferred since it has shorter payback period.

Computation of Net Present Value

Year	*DF @10%*	*Project I Cash flows (₹)*	*Project I PV of cash (₹)*	*Project II Cash flows flows (₹)*	*Project II PV of cash flows (₹)*
1	0.909	25,000	22,725	10,000	9,090
2	0.826	15,000	12,390	12,000	9,912
3	0.751	10,000	7,510	18,000	13,518
4	0.683	0	0	25,000	17,075
5	0.621	12,000	7,452	8,000	4,968
6	0.564	6,000	3,384	6 ,000	2,256
			53,461		56,819
	Less: Initial Investment		50,000		50,000
	Net Present Value	[NPV]	3,461		6,819

Project II is profitable since its NPV is higher than that of Project I.

Illustration 5

P Ltd., is planning to take up a project. Two alternative projects A and B are available. The details of which is given below:

Particulars	*Project A (₹)*	*Project B (₹)*
Investment outlay	40,000	60,000
Estimated life	4 years	5 years
Expected annual cash flows before tax:		
Year 1	18,000	24,000
2	16,000	24,000
3	16,000	20,000
4	14,000	18,000
5	—	16,000

The corporate tax rate is 50 per cent. Calculate the average rate of return and advice the management as to which project should be selected if the minimum required rate of return is 12 per cent.

Solution

Project A

Calculation of Return after Depreciation and Tax and ARR

Year	*Cash inflows (₹)*	*Depreciation (₹)*	*Tax @50% (₹)*	*Net income*
1	18,000	10,000	4,000	4,000
2	16,000	10,000	3,000	3,000
3	16,000	10,000	3,000	3,000
4	14,000	10,000	2,000	2,000
			Total income	12,000

Average Return ₹ 12,000/4 = ₹ 3,000

Average Rate of Return on Original Investment

$$\text{ARR} = \frac{3,000}{40,000} \times 100 = 7.5\%$$

$$\text{ARR on Average Investment} = \frac{3,000}{20,000} \times 100 = 15\%$$

Project B

Calculation of Return after Depreciation and Tax and ARR

Year	*Cash inflows (₹)*	*Depreciation (₹)*	*Tax @50% (₹)*	*Net income*
1	24,000	12,000	6,000	6,000
2	24,000	12,000	6,000	6,000
3	20,000	12,000	4,000	4,000
4	18,000	12,000	3,000	3,000
5	16,000	12,000	2,000	2,000
			Total income	21,000

Average Income = 21,000/5 = ₹ 4,200

ARR on original investment

$$\text{ARR} = \frac{4,200}{60,000} \times 100 = 7\%$$

ARR on average investment

$$\text{ARR} = \frac{4,200}{30,000} \times 100 = 14\%$$

Both the projects qualify for selection, as their ARRs on average investments are higher than the required rate of return. However, they are alternative projects and the company can choose Project A since its ARR is higher than that of Project B.

Illustration 6

S Ltd., has ₹ 10 lakhs allocated for capital budgeting purposes. The following proposals and associated profitability indices have been determined:

Project	*Investment Cost (₹)*	*Profitability index*
1	3,00,000	1.22
2	1,50,000	0.95
3	3,50,000	1.20
4	4,50,000	1.18
5	2,00,000	1.20
6	4,00,000	1.05

Which of the above investments should be undertaken? Assume that the projects are indivisible and there is no alternative use of money allocated for capital budgeting.

Solution

Ranking of Projects based on Profitability Indices

Project	*Investment cost (₹)*	*Profitability Index*	*Rank*
1	3,00,000	1.22	1
2	1,50,000	0.95	5
3	3,50,000	1.20	2
4	4,50,000	1.18	3
5	2,00,000	1.20	2
6	4,00,000	1.05	4

Projects are indivisible and there is no alternative use of money allocated for capital budgeting on the basis of profitability index. Hence, A Ltd., is advised to take up projects 1, 3, and 5, as their indices are higher than others. The company can invest only ₹ 8,50,000. The remaining ₹ 1,50,000 may be used for working capital purposes.

Suppose the company wants to maximize shareholders' wealth and the projects are alternative in nature, the allocation should be made on the basis of NPVs of the projects. The following table will explain the point.

Project	*Investment (₹)*	*P I (₹)*	*PV of cash flows (₹)*	*NPV of project*
1	3,00,000	1.22	3,66,000	66,000
2	1,50,000	0.95	1,42,500	(–) 7,500
3	3,50,000	1.20	4,20,000	70,000
4	4,50,000	1.18	5,31,000	81,000
5	2,00,000	1.20	2,40,000	40,000
6	4,00,000	1.05	4,20,000	20,000

Considering the indivisibility factor and based on NPVs, projects 3, 4, and 5 should be selected. Their total NPV (i.e., wealth) is ₹ 1,91,000, which is more than that of projects 1, 3, and 5 (i.e., ₹ 1,76,000). Hence, the company should adopt projects 3, 4, and 5.

Illustration 7

A Ltd., is evaluating a proposal for new capital investment. The following information is available:

Particulars	*Proposal B*
Investment cost (₹)	1,00,000
Economic life (years)	5
Earnings before depreciation and taxes (₹):	
Year 1	28,000
2	32,000
3	36,000
4	44,000
5	40,000

The company's cost of capital is 10% and tax rate is 50%. Using DCF techniques, advice the management on the profitability of the proposal.

Solution

Computation of Cash Flows

Year	*1*	*2*	*3*	*4*	*5*
Earnings (₹)	28,000	32,000	36,000	44,000	40,000
Less: Depreciation	20,000	20,000	20,000	20,000	20,000
Earnings after depreciation	8,000	12,000	16,000	24,000	20,000
Less Tax at 50 %	4,000	6,000	8,000	12,000	10,000
Earnings after tax	4,000	6,000	8,000	12,000	10,000
Add: Depreciation	20,000	20,000	20,000	20,000	20,000

Computation of NPV and BCR

Profitability Statement

Year	*Cash Flows (₹)*	*DF at 10%*	*Present Value of Cash flows (₹)*
0	(1,00,000)	1.000	(1,00,000)
1	24,000	0.909	21,816
2	26,000	0.826	21,476
3	28,000	0.751	21,028
4	32,000	0.683	21,856
5	30,000	0.621	18,630

NPV of the Project = ₹ 4,806.

$$\textbf{Profitability Index} = \frac{\text{NVP of Cash Inflow}}{\text{PV of Cash Outflow}} = \frac{4,806}{1,00,000} = 0.048$$

$$\textbf{Benefit /Cost Ratio} = \frac{\text{Gross PV of Cash Inflow}}{\text{Gross PV of Cash Outflow}} = \frac{1,04,806}{1,00,000} = 1.048$$

Computation of Internal Rate of Return

The first trial rate may be taken as 10% since it has been used for the calculation of NPV. The NPV is positive and therefore, a higher discount rate could be tried. The second trial rate may be 12% for computing NPV. The following table explains the same.

Profitability Statement

Year	Cash Flows (₹)	DF at 2%	Present Value of Cash flows (₹)
0	(1,00,000)	1.000	(1,00,000)
1	24,000	0.893	21,432
2	26,000	0.797	20,722
3	28,000	0.712	19,936
4	32,000	0.636	20,352
5	30,000	0.567	17,010
		NPV	[548]

At 12% discount rate the NPV is negative. Hence, the actual rate should be below 12% but above 10%. The correct rate may be ascertained by interpolation.

$$\text{IRR of Proposal B} = 10\% \frac{4{,}806}{5{,}354} = 11.8\%$$

Under all three DCF methods the profitability of the Proposal B is satisfactory. Hence, it may be adopted.

Illustration 8

An investment of ₹ 1,20,000 was made in a capital project two years ago. Following estimates were made at the time of investment:

(*a*) The effective life of the project was to be 5 years.

(*b*) The scrap value at the end of 5th year is to be ₹ 4,000.

(*c*) The expected cash inflows for 5 years were as follows: Year 1 ₹ 60,000; Year 2 ₹ 50,000; Year 3 ₹ 40,000; Year 4 ₹ 30,000; Year 5 ₹ 20,000.

(*d*) The required rate was to be 10%. However, the past two years' results have not been promising. The net cash inflows for the last two years have been only ₹ 50,000 and ₹ 30,000 respectively. In view of the last two years' poor results, the cash inflows for the remaining three years are expected to be only ₹ 24,000, ₹ 18,000, and ₹ 8,000 respectively. However, the investment has a present abandonment value of ₹ 48,000. Would you advise the management for abandoning the investment? Substantiate your answer.

Solution

Investment project with 5 years estimated life has been taken up two years ago. Cash flows have been estimated for 5 years with a scrap value of ₹ 4,000 at the end of the 5th year. But last two years' results are poor. Hence, cash flows have been revised for the remaining three years as follows:

Year 3 (current year)	₹ 24,000
Year 4 (next year)	₹ 18,000
Year 5 (third year)	₹ 4,000
Year 5 (Scrap value)	₹ 4,000

If the project is abandoned now, that is in the third year, it will fetch ₹ 48,000. In order to take a decision as to abandonment, the present value of cash flows of the remaining three years and scrap value should be calculated and compared with the abandonment value.

Computation of PV of Revised Estimates of Cash Flows

Year	*DF at 10%*	*Revised cash flows (₹)*	*PV of Cash flows*
Current year (original year 3)	0.909	24,000	21,816
Second year (original year 4)	0.826	18,000	14,868
Third year (original year 5)	0.751	8,000	6,008
Scrap value	0.751	4,000	3,004
		Total Present Value	45,696

Present value of future cash flows = ₹ 45,696

Abandonment value = ₹ 48,000

Since the abandonment value is more than the present value of future cash flows, it is advisable to abandon the project now.

Illustration 9

A Ltd., is considering a proposal to invest ₹ 70,000 in a project. The expected cash flows after taxes (CFAT) from the project for a period of three consecutive years are ₹ 40,000 each. The estimated salvage value of the project is ₹ 2,000. The company's cost of capital is 10% and a risk premium of 8% is considered necessary for undertaking the project. Advise the management as to the acceptance of the proposal. (P.V. of annuity of ₹ 1 at 18% for three years 2.174 and P.V. of ₹ 1 at 10% for the third year 0.751).

Solution

Risk free rate = 10%

Risk premium = 8%

Risk adjusted discount rate = 18%

Profitability Statement

Proposal A

Year	*CFAT (₹)*	*PV factor at 18%*	*PV of CFAT (₹)*
1 – 3	40,000	2.174	86,960
3	2,000	0.751	1,502
		Total	88,462
		Less: Capital Investment Outlay	70,000
		NPV	18,462

The company may undertake the investment proposal.

(As the salvage value is a certainty factor, the risk free rate is used for discounting.)

Illustration 10

B Ltd., is examining two mutually exclusive investment proposals. The management wants to use certainty equivalents (CE) for evaluation of new proposals. From the following information relating to these projects advice the management as to which project should be undertaken by it.

Year	*Proposal A*		*Proposal B*	
	Cash Flows	*CE*	*Cash Flows*	*CE*
0	[₹ 50,000]	1.0	[₹ 50,000]	1.0
1	30,300	0.8	20,000	0.9
2	35,000	0.7	35,000	0.8
3	30,000	0.6	25,000	0.7
4	25,000	0.5	30,000	0.5

The company's cost of capital is 12% and the risk free borrowing rate is 10%.

Solution

Profitability Statement

Year	*Risky Cash Flows*	*CE*	*Risk Adjusted CF*	*PV Factor @ 10%*	*Total PV*
0	[50,000]	1.00	[50,000]	1.000	[50,000]
1	30,300	0.80	24,240	0.909	22,034
2	35,000	0.70	24,500	0.826	20,237
3	30,000	0.60	18,000	0.751	13,518
4	25,000	0.50	12,500	0.683	8,538
				NPV	14,327

Proposal B

Year	Risky Cash Flows	CE	Risk Adjusted CF	PV Factor @ 10%	Total PV
0	[50,000]	1.00	[50,000]	1.000	[50,000]
1	20,000	0.90	18,000	0.909	16,362
2	35,000	0.80	28,000	0.826	23,128
3	25,000	0.70	17,500	0.751	13,143
4	30,000	0.50	15,000	0.683	10,245
				NPV	12,878

Recommendation: Project A should be accepted.

Illustration 11

A company is considering two mutually exclusive projects. Both require initial cash out lay of ₹ 10,000 each and have a life of 5 years. The company's required rate of return is 10% and pays tax at a 50% rate. The projects will be depreciated on straight-line basis. The before tax cash flows expected to be generated by the projects are as follows:

Before Tax Cash Flows [₹]

Year	1	2	3	4	5
Project A	4,000	4,000	4,000	4,000	4,000
Project B	6,000	3,000	2,000	5,000	5,000

Calculate for each project:

(*i*) The payback,

(*ii*) The accounting rate of return,

(*iii*) The net present value and profitability index, and

(*iv*) The internal rate of return,

Which project should be accepted and why?

Computation of Cash Flows after Tax for Project A **[₹]**

Year	CFBT	Dep.	PBT	Tax	PAT	+ Dep.	CFAT
1	4,000	2,000	2,000	1,000	1,000	2,000	3,000
2	4,000	2,000	2,000	1,000	1,000	2,000	3,000
3	4,000	2,000	2,000	1,000	1,000	2,000	3,000
4	4,000	2,000	2,000	1,000	1,000	2,000	3,000
5	4,000	2,000	2,000	1,000	1,000	2,000	3,000

Computation of Cash Flows After Tax for Project B [₹]

Year	*CFBT*	*Dep.*	*PBT*	*Tax @50%*	*PAT*	*+ Dep.*	*CFAT*
1	6,000	2,000	4,000	2,000	2,000	2,000	4,000
2	3,000	2,000	1,000	500	500	2,000	2,500
3	2,000	2,000	0	0	0	2,000	2,000
4	5,000	2,000	3,000	1,500	1,500	2,000	3,500
5	5,000	2,000	3,000	1,500	1,500	2,000	3,500

Computation of Payback Period

Project A = Investment/ Annual cash flows = ₹ 10,000/3,000 = $3\frac{1}{3}$ years

Project B = Annual cash flows for 3 years i.e., ₹ 8,500 plus ₹ 1,500/3,500 (4th year cash flow) = $3\frac{3}{7}$ years

Based on Payback Project A is preferable, since its payback is shorter than that of Project B.

Computation of Accounting rate of Return

Project A = Average Return/Original Investment or Average Investment

= (₹ 1,000/ ₹ 10,000) × 100 = 10% OR ₹ 1,000/₹ 5,000 = 20%

Average Investment = (Original cost + Scrap Value)/2 = (₹ 10,000 + 0)/2 = ₹ 5,000

Project B: Average Return = ₹ 5,500/5 = ₹ 1,100

ARR = (₹ 1,100/₹ 10,000) × 100 = 11% OR (₹ 1,100/₹ 5,000) × 100 = 22%

Based on Accounting Rate of Return, Project B is preferable since its ARR is higher than that of Project A.

Computation of Net Present Value and Profitability Index for Project A

Project A has uniform cash inflows for all the five years, i.e., ₹ 3,000 per year. Hence by referring to the annuity table for ₹ 1 received annually for 5 years we may find the present value is ₹ 3.791. The present value of ₹ 3,000 received annually for 5 years is ₹ 3,000 × 3.791 = ₹ 11,373.

NPV = ₹ 11,373 – ₹ 10,000 = ₹ 1,373

Profitability Index = NPV/Original cost

= ₹ 1,373/₹ 10,000 = 0.1373

Computation of NPV and Profitability Index for Project B

Year	*CFAT (₹)*	*Discount Factor (10%)*	*Present Value (₹)*
1	4,000	0.909	3,636
2	2,500	0.826	2,065
3	2,000	0.751	1,502
4	3,500	0.683	2,390.5
5	3,500	0.621	2,173.5
		Total	11,767
		Less: Investment Cost	10,000

Profitability Index = ₹ 1,767/₹ 10,000 = 0.1767

Based on NPV and PI, Project B is preferable since its NPV and PI are higher than those of Project A.

Computation of Internal Rate of Return (IRR) for Project A

The first trial rate may be taken as 10% and the NPV is ₹ 1,373 positive. Hence the second rate should be above 10%, which may be, say 15%. At 15% the annuity of Re. 1 received for 5 years is 3.352.

Present Value of ₹ 3,000 = 3.352 × 3,000 = 10,056 which is very close to ₹ 10,000 or NPV is ₹ 56. IRR may be taken as 15%. In order to ascertain the exact rate method of interpolation may be applied and the correct value may be ascertained as follows:

$$\text{IRR} = \text{Lower rate} + \frac{\text{NVP lower trial} \times [\text{Higher rate} - \text{lower rate}]}{\text{NPV of lower rate} - \text{NVP of higher rate}}$$

$$\text{IRR} = 10\% \; \frac{1373 \times (15\% - 10\%)}{(1373 - 56)} = 10\% \; \frac{6868}{1371} = 15.01\%$$

Computation of Internal Rate of Return for Project B

The first rate may be taken as 10% and its NPV is ₹ 1,767 positive. Hence, the second rate should be higher than 10%, which may be, say 16%.

Year	*CFAT (₹)*	*Discount Factor at (10%)*	*PV of Cash Flows (₹)*
1	4,000	0.862	3,448.00
2	2,500	0.743	1,857.50
3	2,000	0.641	1,262.00
4	3,500	0.552	1,932.00
5	3,500	0.476	1,666.00
		Total	10,165.50
		Less: Cost	10,000.00
		NPV	165.50

$$IRR = 10\% \frac{1767 \times 46\% - 10\%}{1767 - 165.5} = 10\% \frac{10602}{1601.5} = 16.62\%$$

Based on IRR criterion, Project B is preferable, since its IRR value is more than that of Project A. On the whole Project B is better than Project A because it stands superior to Project A under ARR, NPV, PI and IRR.

Illustration 12

Project P has the following cash flows:

	Cash Flows (₹)	
C_0	C_1	C_2
– 800	1,200	– 400

Calculate the project's Internal rate Return(s). If the required rate of return is 25% would you accept the project? Why?

Solution

Total cash outflows are equal to total cash inflows. Hence the project is not profitable. If the required rate of return is 25%, the NPV will be as follows:

Year	*Discount Factor*	*Cash Flows (₹)*	*PV of Cash Flows (₹)*
0	1.000	[800]	[800]
1	0.800	1,200	960
2	0.640	[400]	[256]
		NPV	[96]

If the required rate of return is 25% the project should not be accepted, since the NPV is negative.

At Zero per cent the cash inflows will be equal to cash outflows. Or the IRR will be negative. Hence, the project should be rejected.

REVIEW QUESTIONS AND PROBLEMS

1. Define the concept of Investment Decision.
2. Define the concept of Capital Budgeting.
3. State the objectives of Capital Budgeting.
4. Discuss the importance of Capital Budgeting.
5. Mention the various types of capital investment projects.
6. Define the concept of project appraisal.
7. Describe the Payback Method and enumerate its merits and demerits.
8. Describe the Average Rate of Return Method. What are its merits and demerits?

9. What are DCF techniques? State the advantages and criticisms of DCF techniques.
10. Define Net Present Value technique.
11. What is Benefit-Cost ratio?
12. What is Profitability Index? Which is a superior ranking criterion, Profitability Index or Net Present Value?
13. Under what circumstances do the NPV and the IRR methods differ? Which method would you prefer and why?
14. What are mutually exclusive projects? Discuss the decision criteria, when conflicting ranking would be given by the IRR and NPV to such projects.
15. Explain the meaning, merits, and limitations of IRR method.
16. Compare the advantages and limitations of various investment analysis techniques with a simple example for each.
17. Explain the concepts of Risk and Uncertainty.
18. Describe the various modern Quantitative techniques used in Risk analysis.
19. Discuss the various conservative methods of risk analysis.
20. Describe a few modern methods of Risk Analysis.
21. Describe Decision Tree Analysis giving one illustration.
22. A Ltd., is considering two projects Exe and Wye each costing ₹ 20,000. The net cash flows from the projects are as follows:

Year	1	2	3	4	5	6
Exe (₹)	10,000	8,000	6,000	2,000	—	—
Wye (₹)	2,000	4,000	6,000	8,000	8,000	9,000

The company has fixed three years as the cut-off period. Based on Payback period method, state which project should be accepted?

[**Ans.** PB for Exe 2 yrs 4 months and Wye 4 yrs. Project Exe should be accepted.]

23. Excel Ltd., is considering the purchase of a new machine, which would carry out some operations at present performed by Manual labour. Two models are available. Experts make the following estimates:

	Machine A	*Machine B*
Estimated working life (years)	5	6
	₹	₹
Cost of machine	1,00,000	1,50,000
Savings in scrap per annum	5,000	6,000
Indirect materials per annum	3,000	3,500
Savings in labour per annum	50,000	60,000
Cost of maintenance per annum	11,500	7,500

The tax rate may be regarded at 40 per cent of profits. Which model can be recommended for purchase? Use Payback Period and Average Rate of Return methods of projects appraisal.

[**Ans.** PB period A 3.1 yrs and B 3.49 yrs (approx) and ARR (on average investment) A 24.6% and B 24%. Machine A can be recommended]

24. A Ltd., is considering a project costing ₹ 80,000. The net income before depreciation and tax is estimated as follows:

Year	1	2	3	4	5
Net Income (₹)	20,000	24,000	28,000	32,000	40,000

Depreciation is charged at 20 per cent per annum. Corporate tax rate is 40%. Calculate the ARR on average investment.

[**Ans.** ARR = (₹ 7,680/40,000) × 100 = 19.2%]

25. The initial cash outlay of a project is ₹ 50,000 and it generates cash inflows of ₹ 20,000, ₹ 15,000, ₹ 25,000, and ₹ 10,000 in four years. Using the net present value method appraise the profitability of the proposed investment using 10% rate of discount.

[**Ans.** NPV = ₹ 6,175]

26. NP Ltd., is considering purchase of a machine, which will have a working life of 5 years. The machine is expected to earn ₹ 15,000 per annum, before taxes for the first three years, and ₹ 12,000 and ₹ 8,000 for the fourth and fifth years respectively. The company considers a yield of 20% necessary before investment is made in a project. How much can be spent in purchasing the machine?

[**Ans.** Gross Present Value ₹ 40,590 would be amount that can be spent.]

27. Your company is considering investing in a project for which the investment data are as follows:

Capital outlay: ₹ 2,00,000; Depreciation charge: 20% per annum

Forecasted annual income before charging depreciation but all other charges was as follows:

Year	1	2	3	4	5
Annual Income (₹)	1,00,000	1,00,000	80,000	80,000	40,000

On the basis of figures given above, set out calculations illustrating and comparing the following methods of evaluating the return on capital employed:

(a) Payback Period (b) Average Rate of Return (c) NPV at 10% and (d) BCR

[**Ans.** (a) 2 years (b) 40% (c) ₹ 1,25,480 (d) 1.63 (approx.)]

28. An investor who must have a minimum rate of return of 12% p.a., has two projects in view, both requiring initial outlay of ₹ 30,000. Project A gives an annual net income of ₹ 6,000 with a salvage value of ₹ 10,000 at the end of 10 years. Project B gives an annual net income of ₹ 5,000 with a salvage value of ₹ 2,000 at the end of 10 years. Which project should he prefer? (Note: PV of ₹ 1 at 12% received annually for 10 years = 5.65 and at the end of 10th year = 0.322)

[**Ans.** NPV of Project A = ₹ 7,120 and NPV of B = ₹ 4,690]

29. The initial cost of equipment is ₹ 3,00,000. Cash flows for 5 years are estimated to be ₹ 2,00,000 per year. Desired rate of return is 15%. Calculate the net present value and excess present value index.

[**Ans.** NPV (₹ 2,00,000 × 3.352) – ₹ 3,00,000 = ₹ 3,70,400; PI = 1.235]

30. An investment of ₹ 6,00,000 was made in a capital project two years ago. Following estimates were made at that time of investment:

(*a*) The effective life of the project was to be 5 years.

(*b*) The scrap value at the end of 5th year is to be ₹ 20,000.

(*c*) The expected cash inflows for 5 years were as follows: Year 1 ₹ 3,00,000; Year 2 ₹ 2,50,000; Year 3 ₹ 2,00,000; Year 4 ₹ 1,50,000; Year 5 ₹ 1,00,000

(*d*) The required rate was to be 10%. However, the past two years' results have not been promising. The net cash inflows for the last two years have been only ₹ 2,50,000 and ₹ 1,50,000 respectively. In view of the last two years' poor results, the cash inflows for the remaining three years are expected to be only ₹ 1,20,000, ₹ 90,000, and ₹ 40,000 respectively. However, the investment has a present abandonment value of ₹ 2,40,000. Would you advise the management for abandoning the investment? Substantiate your answer.

[**Ans.** PV of new cash inflows is ₹ 2,28,480, which is lower than the abandonment value. Hence, the management is advised to abandon the project.]

31. From the following data, state which project is better?

Year	Project A Cash Flows (₹)	Project B Cash Flows (₹)
0	[10,000]	[10,000]
1	4,000	5,000
2	4,000	6,000
3	2,000	3,000

Risk less discount rate is 5%. Project A is less risky as compared to Project B. The management considers risk premium rates at 5% and 10% respectively appropriate for discounting the cash flows.

[**Ans.** Risk-adjusted discount rate, Project A 10%, and Project B 15%; NPV for A (₹ 1,558), and that of B ₹ 860, hence B is better.]

32. A project needs an investment of ₹ 1,38,500. The cost of capital is 12%. The net cash inflows are as under:

Year	1	2	3	4	5
Cash inflows (₹):	30,000	40,000	60,000	30,000	20,000

Calculate the Internal Rate of Return and suggest whether the project should be accepted or not?

[**Ans.** IRR 10%, the project should not be accepted]

33. The following data is pertaining to a capital investment: Initial Investment = ₹ 6,00,000. Life of the asset = 4 years. Estimated annual cash flows:

Year:	1	2	3	4
Cash inflows (₹):	1,50,000	2,00,000	3,00,000	2,00,000

Calculate internal rate of return.

[**Ans.** IRR = 14.45%]

34. B Ltd., has a machine having an additional life of 5 years, cost ₹ 50,000. Its book value is ₹ 20,000, market value ₹ 5,000. A new machine costing ₹ 1,00,000 is available. The new machine will have a variable cost saving of ₹ 40,000 per annum. Life of the new machine is 5 years and its scrap value will be ₹ 10,000. Income tax rate is 50%. Interest rate is 12%. Advise B Ltd. whether the old machine should be replaced or not.

[**Ans.** Yes. NPV ₹ 22,715; Annual cash inflows ₹ 29,000]

35. A company has to choose one of the following two mutually exclusive projects. Both the projects will be depreciated on a straight-line method. The firm's cost of capital is 10% and the tax rate is 43%. The before tax cash flows are as follows:

Project	C_0	C_1	C_2	C_3	C_4	C_5
X (₹)	– 20,000	4,200	4,800	7,000	8,000	2,000
Y (₹)	– 15,000	4,200	4,500	4,000	5,000	1,000

Which should the firm accept if the following criteria are used?

(1) Payback Period (2) Internal Rate of Return

(3) Net Present Value (4) Profitability Index

[**Ans.** Project X (1) 3.91 years (2) 6% (3) [1226.20] (4) 0.89; Project Y (1) 3.94 years (2) 5% (3) [1802.26] (4) 0.88]

36. A finance executive has calculated the profitability index for a new proposal to be 1.12. The proposal's initial cash outlay is ₹ 5,00,000. Find out the proposal's annual cash inflow if it has a life of 5 years and the required rate of return is 8%.

[**Ans.** ₹ 1,40,245]

37. Original cost of a project is ₹ 16,000. Estimated life of the project is 3 years. Cash inflows for three years are ₹ 8,000 per annum. The company's cost of capital is 10%. Expected interest rate at which the cash inflows will be reinvested is 8% for all the three years.

Whether the project should be accepted or not? Why?

[**Ans.** Total sum of compounded reinvested cash inflows = ₹ 25,968. PV of compounded cash inflows = ₹ 19,502. Project should be accepted.]

■■■

15

Responsibility Accounting

The modern approach to accounting and reporting is the development of an accounting system to control expenditures by directly relating the reporting of expenditures to individuals in the organization who are responsible for cost control. This system leads to preparation of accounting statements for all levels of management which can be effectively used by the operating staff in controlling operations and costs. In other words, this system places special emphasis on information that is useful to the operating management level relegating the accounting and book-keeping aspects to a secondary position. It makes possible the operation of a good budget system, i.e. it creates a feeling in each responsible individual in an organization that the budget is his budget and not something forced upon him. Only this type of feeling will make him live within it, and use the information as means of controlling his operations. Under this system, expenditures must be reported on the basis of where they were incurred and who had the responsibility for incurring them. This system is referred to as responsibility accounting or reporting.

THE CONCEPT OF RESPONSIBILITY ACCOUNTING

Responsibility accounting is a system under which managers are given decision-making authority and responsibility for each activity occurring within a specific area of the company. Under this system managers are made responsible for activities of segments. These segments may be called departments, or divisions, etc.

According to Charles T. Horngren, Responsibility Accounting or Profitability Accounting or Activity Accounting means the same thing. It is a system that recognizes various decisions or responsibility centres throughout the organization and traces costs (and revenue, assets and liabilities where pertinent) to the individual managers who are primarily responsible for making decisions about the cost in question.

Robert N. Antony defines Responsibility Accounting as that type of management accounting which collects and reports both planned and actual accounting information in terms of responsibility centre. Another definition of responsibility accounting is that it is a system of accounting which is tailored to an organization so that costs are accumulated and reported by levels of responsibility within the organization. Each supervisory area in the organization is charged only with the cost for which it is responsible and over which it has control.

Steps Involved. From the above definitions, it is clear that organizations should be classified into suitable responsibility centres. The authority and responsibility of each individual should be defined clearly. Each executive must know about what he is expected to do, and what his present level of performance is. For this purpose, the reporting system should be so designed that the executive obtains the information needed. The budget system should be given a personal touch, that is, the executive should feel that it is his budget and he has a responsibility to achieve the budgeted targets. In this regard, the target set should be communicated to the concerned executives and there should be a continuous appraisal system for evaluating the actual results with the budget estimates. The variances are reported to the top management and corrective measures taken are intimated to the responsibility centre concerned. In short, communication should be effective and executives should participate in the system wholeheartedly.

RESPONSIBILITY CENTRES

The most important point in Responsibility Accounting is that the manager is responsible for a segment of an organization which is normally referred to as a responsibility centre. There are three types of responsibility centres, viz., cost centres, profit centres, and investment centres.

A cost centre is a responsibility centre whose manager is responsible for costs incurred by the segment. Cost centres do not generate revenue directly. This type of responsibility centre is found in manufacturing firms. For example, the foreman of a painting department in a factory is responsible for the amount of paint used, labour costs and perhaps for some of the variable overheads incurred by the department. When actual costs of the department differ from budgeted costs the foreman must explain the significant variances.

A profit centre usually refers to a segment of an organization that generates revenue. It is responsibility centre, the manager of which is responsible for the amount of profits earned. The managers in the profit centre are, therefore, responsible for both revenue and costs. For example, the manager of a furniture department of a departmental store is responsible for earning profit on the furniture sold.

An investment centre is a responsibility centre whose manager is responsible for earning a rate of return on assets used in his responsibility centre. Major segments of companies are normally investment centres. For example, a segment in an automobile manufacturing company, individual departments of a departmental store, and individual branches of a multiple shop are investment centres.

An investment centre differs from a profit centre in that as investment centre is evaluated on the basis of the rate of return earned on assets invested in the segment, while a profit centre is evaluated on the basis of excess revenue over expenses for the period. However, it is better to designate a segment as an investment centre rather than a profit centre in order to enhance the utility of responsibility accounting. A segment may earn greater profits than others not because of better performance but by using more assets to earn such profits.

ILLUSTRATION OF RESPONSIBILITY ACCOUNTING

A system of Responsibility Accounting uses the management by exception concept under which management concentrates its time and efforts in exceptional or problem situations. In other words, in evaluating performance, management is concerned only with significant deviations from the budgets, or standards. Responsibility Accounting and the management by exception concept is explained through a simple illustration here.

Stores Operations

Table 15.1: Operating Income Performance Report for the month ended on May 31, 2019

	Budget (₹)	*Actual (₹)*	*Variance (₹)*	*Per cent Variance (%)*
Madurai	2,40,000	2,50,000	10,000 (F)	+ 4.2
Coimbatore	3,00,000	3,07,800	7,800 (F)	+ 2.6
Madras	2,00,000	1,96,000	4,000 (A)	– 2.0
Total	7,40,000	7,53,800	21,800 (F)	+ 2.9

Coimbatore Operations Operating Income Performance Report for the month ended on May 31, 2019

	Budget (₹)	*Actual (₹)*	*Variance (₹)*	*Per cent Variance %*
Northern Region	60,000	61,800	1,800 (F)	+ 3.0
Southern Region	1,90,000	1,99,000	9,000 (F)	+ 4,7
Central Region	50,000	47,000	3,000 (A)	– 6.0
Total	3,00,000	3,07,800	7,800 (F)	+ 2.6

Northern Region Operations Operating Income Performance Report for the month ended May 31, 2019

Particulars	*Budget* (₹)	*Actual* (₹)	*Variance* (₹)		*Per cent Variance* %
Store number 1	10,000	10,400	400	(F)	+ 4.0
Store number 2	16,000	15,000	1,000	(A)	– 6.3
Store number 3	8,000	7,800	200	(A)	– 2.5
Store number 4	14,000	16,000	2,000	(F)	+ 14.3
Store number 5	12,000	12,600	600	(F)	+ 5.0
Total	60,000	61,800	1,800	(F)»	+ 5.0

The Area Operations Manager for the Northern Region receives the operation income figures for each of the five stores in his area. The firm believes that actual operating income should generally be within 5 per cent of the budget. The performance report shows that store 2 is 0.3 per cent below the budget. The Area Operations Manager may ask the concerned stores manager for more details on operations in an effort to determine why actual income is less than budgeted income by more than 5 per cent. Each store manager would have received a performance report on his or her individual store. Therefore, the store managers should already be aware of the problems pointed out by the report. The store performance reports may have included detailed information regarding each of the departments.

Store 4 has exceeded the budget by 14.3 per cent. This performance is probably regarded as favourable. Nevertheless, the Area Operation Manager will be interested in knowing how store 4 has managed to out perform the other stores. It may be a sign of efficient management. Or, it is possible that the original budget for store 4 was unrealistically low.

Typically, performance reports show the year-to-date information along with the current month's status and provide management with, an insight into how the segments are doing for the whole year. In some, instances, unfavourable variances in one month may be more than offset by favourable variances in another month. Therefore, year-to-date information provides a perspective on operations throughout the whole year. Under the management by exception concept the Northern Region manager may not enquire too much into the operations of stores 1, 4, and 5, since they are with content 5 per cent tolerance set by the management.

The manager of Coimbatore area operations receives a performance report (middle portion) for all the regional operations under his supervision.

The performance report shows that Coimbatore area exceeded its operating income budget by 2.0 per cent. In looking at the three areas, the manager notes that the central region failed to meet its budget by 6%. The Coimbatore area manager would naturally enquire more into the central region than those operations of other regions that have smaller deviations. This illustrates the meaning of the concept of management by exception. Without a performance report, the area manager might spend equal time on all areas, which might mean watching two regions and not spending enough time on the central region.

The Regional Sales Manager receives a performance report (top portion) showing that all districts under his control exceeded the budgeted income by 2.9 per cent. Looking at the performance report he can see that Madurai and Coimbatore exceeded the budget by 4.2 per cent and 2.6 per cent respectively, while Madras failed to meet the budget by 2 per cent. In no case was the variance more than 5 per cent of the budget. Therefore, under management by exception, it appears that no area requires attention.

The Sales Manager of the company receives a performance report (not shown) from the Regional Managers of Stores Operations showing that stores have exceeded the profit goals by 2.9 per cent.

Since this is within the 5% range it is unlikely that the Stores Manager will make any specific inquiries into store operations. The Sales Manager also receives performance reports from the other Regional Managers. The nature of these performance reports however differs from those received from the other Regional Managers of stores operations.

The responsibility accounting system presented in Table No. I shows only operating income performance. However, performance reports may include more details regarding revenues and costs as well. In some instances, the departments may be investment centres. Management might be interested in the total number of customers as well. The point is that under the concept of management by exception, management can get whatever information it needs in order to make decisions about operations and can look most closely at operations that significantly deviate from standards.

MANAGEMENT OF SEGMENT PERFORMANCE

Responsibility Accounting requires a knowledge about how well a segment has performed. This section illustrates how segment data should be presented so that meaningful decisions regarding segment performacne can be taken.

Cost Allocation. A manager's performance is evaluated to a large extent on the basis of comparison of costs incurred with costs budgeted. It is therefore important to determine the appropriate costs to be charged to the segments being measured. Problems often arise in this process because of the way costs are allocated to segments.

Segments Margin. One way of measuring a segment's performance is to determine its profitability based on "segment margin" excess of segment's revenue over its direct costs. Segment margin represents the amount of income that has been earned by the particular segment. An illustration of segment performance is shown for Seamens Stores in Table II. Branch A has a rate of return on sales of 8.3% (₹ 25,000 - 3,00,000) and Branch B that of 8.8% (₹ 35,000 - ₹ 4,00,000). It is important to note that only those costs incurred by the branch are deducted for determining segment margin. Head office expenses are deducted only from the total margin.

Table 15.2: Segment Performance
Seamens Stores Income Statement of the Year Ended 31-12-2016

Particulars	*Branch A* (₹)	*Branch B* (₹)	*Company total* (₹)
Sales	3,00,000	4,00,000	7,00,000
Less: Cost of sales (direct cost)	2,10,000	2,85,000	4,95,000
Contribution	90,000	1,15,000	2,05,000
Less: Fixed cost	65,000	80,000	1,45,000
Segment margin	25,000	35,000	60,000
Less: Head office expenses			21,000
Net income			39,000

Frequently, head office expenses are allocated to branches. It is illogical, and therefore the head office expenses should not be allocated to branches on the basis of sales. Head office expenses may remain constant irrespective of the volume of sales effected by each branch. Hence, it is not a good policy to charge head office expenses against the segment margin.

CONTRIBUTION BY SEGMENTS

The primary purpose of a responsibility accounting system is to determine how well or how poorly individual segment managers are doing. This determination is based on the type of responsibility the centre is being considered. Managers of cost centres are responsible for controlling costs, which means that they must ensure that costs do not exceed the budget by a significant amount. Managers of profit centres are responsible for earning an acceptable profit, measured in terms of segment margin, or rate of return on sales for the profit centre. An investment centre's manager is responsible for earning a rate of return on the segment's investment in assets.

ROI AND DIVISIONAL CONTROL

Top management establishes a minimum rate of return which is considered minimum acceptable performance. Many firms set the minimum rate of return at their cost of capital. A firm should not invest in a project that earns the cost of funds used for the investment. Therefore, cost of capital becomes the desired rate of return. Firms may require a rate of return higher than the minimum for their investments. It is used as the basis for evaluating managerial performance.

Return of Investment (ROI): One way of evaluating managerial performance is to calculate the ROI for the segment, The calculation for ROI is:

ROI = Income/Investment = (Income/Sales) × (Sales/Investment)

In the equation, income is the segment margin of the segment being measured. Investment is the amount of average assets used by the segment. In the second equation, the first component is called the Return on Sale or Sales Margin as a percentage of sales, if it represents segment margin as a percentage of sales. The second component (sales investment) is called the Investment Turnover or Assets Turnover or Capital Turnover. To improve the return on investment, a segment can increase its return on sales, increase its investment turnover or do both. A low rate of return on sales requires a greater amount of sales in order to make the profit high. By the same token, a firm with a high investment turnover may accept a low return on sales; an increasing sales will increase ROI because it increases income. Two other ways of improving ROI are to reduce expenses, thereby increasing incomes, or to reduce investment. If a segment can reduce its investment in assets without reducing sales, its ROI will increase. This encourages management to reduce funds invested in assets that are not productive.

ROI for the firm, as a whole, must not fail to meet the goals of top management. Therefore, the ROI required by the operating segments must be high enough to provide an adequate rate of return for the firm as a whole. It is better to require a segment to earn a higher minimum rate of return than to make segment managers "aware" of their responsibilities by charging them with expenses over which they have no control.

Residual Income: Residual income is the difference between actual income (segment margin) earned on an investment and the desired income on the investment as specified by minimum desired rate of return. It is calculated as follows:

Residual Income (RI) = Income – Investment × Minimum desired rate of return.

In effect, RI is the excess the earnings above the minimum desired rate of return. If the firm sets its minimum rate of return at its cost of capital, it must earn an ROI that is at least equal to the cost of funds used in making the investment. Any amount of income earned above the cost of capital is profit to the firm. More is the income earned above the cost of capital, it will be better for the firm. In short, a firm has to maximise its RI.

RI is used often as a substitute for, or along with, ROI, as means of evaluating managerial performance. The problem with using ROI as the sole criterion for evaluating performance is that it can cause managers to avoid investing in any project that might lower the rate of return. The use of RI as a criterion in the evaluation of management of performance helps to foster 'goal congruency'—that is, to make the goal of the segment managers conform with the goal of the company. The firm is interested in maximising its income above the cost of capital. If the segment managers are measured only on the basis of ROI, they will not necessarily maximise RI. Thus, the manager's goal of maximising ROI and the firm's goal of maximising income are incongruent. Using RI in evaluating the segment performance reduces this problem.

TRANSFER PRICING

In many firms, a product is transferred from one segment to another. To account for the transfer properly a price (rupee amount) must be recorded. The question is: which price is to be used for making the transfer price? The price is important because it has a direct effect on the ROI of both the selling segment and the buying segments. Transfer price is typically based on cost, market price, variable cost, or a price negotiated between the segment managers. To some extent, transfer price determination is based on the type of segment, the type of product, the type of firm, and the degree of decentralisation within the firm.

Cost: Transfers between cost centres are typically based on cost. Normally, this should be standard cost and should include both variable and fixed costs. Since managers of cost centres are evaluated on their conformity to standard cost, transfer price does not normally present any problem.

If a firm transfers actual costs rather than standard costs, problems may develop. The transfer rate of actual costs provides no incentive for efficiency in the division transferring the costs because if it incurs excess costs, it merely transfers them. In addition, the segment receiving costs is unfairly charged with the cost of inefficiencies of the segment that transferred them. If the receiving segment is an investment centre, the rate of return is affected by the inefficiency of the cost centre. For the reason, the use of standard cost not actual cost, is encouraged when cost centres transfer costs.

Cost Plus Profit: If the selling segment is a profit or investment centre. It will want to sell its product to the buying segment at some amount greater than cost. It would like to earn profit on its sale that is in line with what is required to earn an adequate profit or rate of return for the segment. In some instances, the transfer price, and therefore the profit, may be based on the outside market price. If no outside market price exists, the question of how much to charge above cost is sometimes difficult to determine. If the selling segment sells other products, it may calculate its profit on the internal transfer in the same way as it calculates its profit on the other products—a percentage of cost, for example. As described below, the transfer price may also be based on negotiations between the buying and selling segments.

Market Price: If there is an outside market for the product being transferred between segments of a firm, then that price often serves as the basis for the transfer price. Many times, the outside market price is the ideal transfer price, because it is considered to objectively determine the amount that was arrived at by factors outside the firm and therefore no one within the firm was able to influence it. The market price is usually considered an ideal price to use for profit centres and investment centres.

Since investment centres are interested in maximising their rate of return (or residual income) the selling segment wants to transfer the product to the buying segment at the highest possible price. By the same token, the buying segment wants to buy the product from the selling segment at the lowest possible price. Therefore, disputes often arise. The use of outside market prices settles disputes in many cases.

REVIEW QUESTIONS

1. Define 'Responsibility Accounting'.
2. Explain the following concepts: (*a*) Cost Centre (*b*) Profit Centre (*c*) Investment Centre (*d*) Responsibility Centre.
3. Explain Responsibility Accounting with an illustration.
4. Write a note on 'measuring segment performance.'
5. Explain the following concepts: Segment margin, Contribution Margin, ROI, RI.

6. What do you mean by Transfer Pricing?
7. Briefly describe the problems involved in determining Transfer Price.
8. What is Management by Exception?
9. Distinguish between a Cost Centre, an Investment Centre and a Profit Centre.
10. What are the base normally used for arriving at transfer prices?
11. Why is market price generally considered an ideal basis for a transfer price?

■ ■ ■

16

Management Reporting

Information is the basis for decision making in an organisation. The efficiency of management depends, to a larger extent, upon the availability of regular and relevant information to those who exercise the managerial functions. No planning and control procedure is complete without prompt and accurate feedback of operating results and availability of other information. For example, management must know how the actual profit performance collates with that of budgeted or standard or with past performances and to what extent variations have been caused by various influencing factors. A regular system of reporting is considered as a better guarantee of efficiency and operation than reliance on personal qualities. Hence, it is essential that an effective and efficient reporting system is developed as part of accounting methods.

MEANING

The term 'reporting' connotes different meanings as under:

1. Narrating some facts.
2. Reviewing certain matter with its merits and demerits and offering comments.
3. Furnishing data at regular intervals in standardised forms.
4. Submitting specific information for particular purpose upon specific request instruction.

Management reporting refers to the formal system whereby relevant required information is furnished to management by means of reports constantly. Thus, 'report' is the essence of any management reporting system.

The term 'Report' normally refers to a formal communication which moves upward, i.e., for factual communication by a lower level to a higher level of authority in response to orders received from higher level. Reports provide means of checking the performance. A person, who is issued with orders or instructions to do certain things should report back what he has done in compliance thereof. Reports may be oral or written and also routine or special.

OBJECTS OF REPORTING

The primary object of management reporting is to obtain the required information about the operating results of the organisation regularly in order to use them for future planning and control. Another object is to secure understanding and approval of the judgement by the people engaged in various aspects of the work of enterprise. The second object is closely related to the first one and is important in terms of efficiency, morale and motivation.

ESSENTIALS OF A GOOD REPORTING SYSTEM

Reporting system enables management at all levels to keep itself abreast of past performance as well as developments and it facilitates a check on individual operating levels. Based on reports, management takes crucial decisions. Hence, essentials of good reporting system are as follows:

1. *Proper Form:* In order to facilitate decision-making the information should be supplied in proper form. The style and layout of a report depends on the needs of the individual who will use the same. The report may be submitted in the form of narration (written statement of facts), statistical tabulations, graphs, charts, etc.
2. *Proper Time:* Promptness is very important because information delayed is information denied. Reports are meant for action and when adverse tendencies or events are noticed, action should follow forthwith. The sooner the report is made, the quicker can be the corrective action taken.
3. *Proper Flow of Information:* The information should flow from the right level of authority to the level of authority where decisions are to be made. Further, a complete and consistent information should flow in a systematic manner.
4. *Flexibility:* The system should be capable of being adjusted according to the requirements of the user. For example, production manager should be provided with information relating to his division or area of control only.
5. *Facilitation of Evaluation:* The system should distinctively report deviations from standards or estimates. Controllable factors should be distinguished from non-controllable factors and reported separately. A good reporting system should give information required for the evaluation of each manager's area of responsibility in relation to the goal of the organisation.
6. *Economy:* There is a cost for rendering information and such cost should be compared with benefits derived from the report or loss sustained by not having the report. Economy is an information aspect to be considered while developing the reporting system.

MODES OF REPORTING

Reports may be presented in the form of written statements, graphs, and/or oral.

1. *Written Statements*

(*a*) *Formal Financial Statements:* These statements may deal with any one or more of the following:

(*i*) Actuals against the budgeted figures.

(*ii*) Comparative statements over a period of time.

(*b*) *Tabulated Statistics:* This statement may deal with statistical analysis of a particular type of expenditure over a period of time or sales of a product over a period in different regions, etc.

(*c*) *Accounting Ratios:* Ratios may either form part of the formal financial statements or be given in the form of separate statements. Information is also given to throw the light on certain aspects of operations of business, especially the following: (*i*) Return on capital employed; (*ii*) Profit/Volume Ratio; (*iii*) Break-even point, etc.

2. *Graphic Reports*

The information may be presented by means of graphic reports, which give a better visual view of the data than the long array of figures given in statements. Charts, diagrams and pictures are the usual forms of graphic reports. They have the advantage of facilitating quick grasp of significant trends by receivers of information.

3. *Oral Reports*

Oral reports are mostly presented at group meetings and conferences with individuals.

However, a written report is always considered as the most appropriate basis for important managerial decisions.

BASIC REQUISITES OF A GOOD REPORT

A report is a vehicle carrying information to different levels of administration. Quality of decision-making depends, to a large extent, on the quality of information supplied and on the promptness and consistency of reporting. Good reporting is necessary for effective communication. Hence, a good report should possess the following basic requisites.

1. *Promptness:* It means that report must be prepared and presented on time. Reports are meant for action. Business executives may need quick reports for day-to-day decision making. In such cases, accuracy may be sacrificed for speed and timely need. In order to achieve promptness accounting executives may improve the methods of collecting data, and employ modern mechanical accounting devices.

2. *Form and Content:* A good report should have a suggestive title, headings, sub-headings, paragraph divisions, statistical figures, facts, data, etc. Further, contents should follow a logical sequence: (*a*) the summary of present position; (*b*) the course and expected results; and (*c*) recommendations and reasons for their submission.

3. *Comparability:* Reports are also meant for comparison. Hence, the information is placed in some perspectives. Comparisons are generally effected over time as well as with a norm of performance. Figures should be given for some previous period, such as "last month or same month for the last year", etc. Actual figures may also be placed side by side with corresponding budgets, standards or estimates. The objective is to highlight significant variances.
4. *Consistency:* Consistency envisages the presentation of the same type of information as between different reporting periods. Uniform procedure should be followed over a period of time for collection, classification and presentation of the accounting information. It is also important to present information in a consistent manner to the various operating levels of management.
5. *Simplicity:* The report should be in a simple unambiguous and concise form. In other words, the report should avoid technical jargons and be presented in simple style. Use of suitable units of measurement, such as quantity, value, weight, machine hours, man hours, percentages, ratio, index numbers, etc., would greatly enhance the utility of the report.
6. *Controllability:* It is necessary that every report should be addressed to a responsibility centre and present controllable and uncontrollable factors separately, so that while reporting performances against plans and targets, variances which are controllable could' be analysed in depth, and details are interpreted in an objective manner to help him for taking corrective action.
7. *Appropriateness:* Reports are sent to different levels of management and forms should be designed to suit the respective levels. While reporting to top management, broad trends and significant exceptions are to be presented in summarised form with brevity, clarity and should have comprehensive coverage. Reports to departmental managers are to be more detailed, covering all aspects about their departments. Reports to sectional supervisors must be still more detailed, with full information about their sections.
8. *Cost Considerations:* The cost of maintaining the reporting system should commensurate with benefits derived therefrom. Hence, it may not be an unnecessary burden on the resources of an enterprise.
9. *Accuracy:* The report should be reasonably accurate. This means that the report should be correct and be within be margin of error allowed; otherwise management may lose faith in reports.

Classification of Reports

Reports may be classified in a number of ways and some of the important ways are as follows:

1. According to object—(*a*) External Reports, (*b*) Internal Reports
2. According to period—(*a*) Routine Reports, (*b*) Special Reports.
3. According to function—(*a*) Operating Reports, (*b*) Financial Reports.

External Reports: These reports are meant for external parties, such as government, shareholders, bankers, financial institutions, etc., for example, published financial statements of companies. Copies of such reports are also to be Filed with the Registrar of Joint Stock Companies and with the stock exchange. In the interest of general understanding these reports are expected to conform to certain minimum standards of disclosure and disclose certain basic details under the Companies Act, 1956.

Internal Reports: These reports are meant for internal uses of different levels of management such as top level, middle level and junior level managements. Hence, the approach to the reporting problem would vary according to the reporting level. These reports do not have to conform to any statutory standards. While reports meant for top management have to be comprehensive and concise, those for operating supervisors should be specific and detailed.

NEEDS OF REPORTING DIFFERENT MANAGEMENT LEVELS

Generally, the reporting levels in the internal management fall in the following three broad categories:

Top Management Level

The top management is primarily concerned with the policy formulations, planning and organising. Hence, their function is to evolve proper plans, to carry out proper delegation of responsibility to subordinates with a view to obtain an effective and efficient utilisation of resources and to promote appropriate development schemes. For this purpose, they should rather be supplied with information in summary form covering all aspects of operating performance together with a comparison of actuals with budgeted performance.

Generally, the top management should receive the following reports at different intervals:

Board of Directors—Quarterly statements on production costs, machine and labour utilisation, Cash Flow Statements, Income Statement on a quarterly basis and Balance Sheet.

Finance Director—Monthly abstract of receipts & payments and monthly cash flow statements.

Production Director—Production Cost Statement, department wise machine & labour utilisation statements, material scrap statement, overheads cost and production statements are to be presented to the Production Director on a monthly basis.

Sales Director—He is to receive the following reports on monthly basis: Report on the status of orders received, orders executed, orders kept pending—divisionwise; Reports on finished goods stock position; Reports on selling and distribution cost-divisionwise; Reports on credit collections balances and bad debts—divisionwise.

Middle Management

The middle management—Departmental managers such as production, sales, etc., are always concerned with the execution of plans formulated by top management. They act mainly as coordinating executives to administer policies, direct operating supervisors and evaluate their performance. Hence, reports submitted to them should enable them to exercise their functions more effectively. They may require reports at shorter intervals, say, weekly or fortnightly basis. For example, the works manager requires weekly reports on idle time, idle capacity, scrap production costs, quantity produced, etc. The sales manager needs fortnightly reports on budgeted and actual sales, credit collection, orders booked, executed and pending, and stock positions—product-wise and area-wise.

Junior Management

Foremen, superintendents, etc. constitute this level of management. They are interested in reports which will appraise them of progress of various jobs under their control. Some of these various reports are almost in the form of scrap paper having no proper format. They may need reports on daily or weekly basis. For example, the shop foreman requires daily reports on idle time and machine utilisation, daily scrap reports and daily report of production—actual and budgeted. Sales area supervisor needs weekly reports on sales—salesman-wise, orders booked, executed and outstanding, credit collections and outstanding, etc.

Routine Reports

Reports, which are submitted at periodical intervals on a regular basis covering routine matters e.g., variance analysis, financial statements, budgetary control statements, are routine reports. They are submitted to different levels of management as per a fixed time schedule. Routine reports are usually printed or cyclostyled forms with blank spaces to be filled in. Most of the internal reports explained above are of the nature of routine reports.

Special Reports

Reports which are submitted on particular occasions on specific request or instruction are special reports. When problems arise in a business, they are to be investigated. The result of investigations and recommendations are submitted by way of special reports. The form and contents of special reports will vary according to the nature of problem investigated. Usually, a special report contains terms of reference, i.e., the problem to be studied, investigations made, findings and observation and, finally, conclusions and recommendations. Examples of some of the special reports are: (*i*) Reports of information about competitive products, (*ii*) Reports by the cost accountants on the implications of price changes on the cost of products, (*iii*) Report regarding choice of products or selection of a production method, etc.

Operating Reports

These reports may be classified into control report information-cum-venture measurement report.

Control Report

It is an important ingredient of control process and helps in controlling different activities of an enterprise. It provides information properly collected and analysed to different levels of management.

The framework of this report is determined by the needs of the undertaking. It is prepared on the basis of company developed budgets or standards, vouched in its own terminology, related to responsibility centres and observes decisional needs. This report may be prepared on weekly, fortnightly, monthly or yearly basis, depending upon the urgency of the matter reported. Most of the internal reports explained before are examples of control reports. They are also a sort of routine reports.

Information Report: These reports provide information which are very useful for future planning and policy formulation. They may take the form of trend reports and analytical reports. Trend reports provide information in a comparative form over a period of time. On the other hand, analytical reports provide information in a classified manner. Sometimes, these reports provide information in a summarised form, the results of operation of a specific venture or of the organisation as a whole for a specific period. In such cases, they may be called venture measurement reports.

Financial Reports

These reports contain information about the financial position of the business. They may be classified into Static Reports and Dynamic Reports. Static Report reveals the financial position on a particular data e.g., Balance Sheet of a company. On the other hand, the dynamic report reveals the movement of funds during a specified period, e.g., Fund Flow Statement, Cash Flow Statement.

Preparation of Reports

Management reporting is a difficult task therefore, the report writer must possess special skill for this job. He must be a, financial analyst so in that capacity, must be well trained in the areas of accounting, finance and management. He must be able to make the analysis objectively by putting his ideas cogently, clearly and communicate results in a readable form for effective action.

Effective and efficient reporting requires the following steps to be followed:

(*i*) Reporting requires detailed planning of flow of paper work and its analysis. It should be the logical outcome of accounting and operations.

(*ii*) Duplication of work should be avoided. Accounting records should be designed in such a way as to obtain "control data" without additional analysis.

(*iii*) Codification and mechanisation should be used for processing accounting data. They will help in speeding up of reports.

(*iv*) Accounting records should be closed before time. This will facilitate the preparation of reports in time.

(*v*) When actual data are not readily available, certain estimates may be used in their place in order to avoid unnecessary delays. However, the actuals may be compared with the estimate of a later data and deviations, if any, may be found out and analysed. Such an analysis of deviations will help in making better estimates in future.

Usefulness of Reporting

The Reporting system enables management to understand the functioning of the undertaking. When a particular reporting system fails to meet the requirement, it is either scrapped or readjusted to the needs. Hence, it is in a state of continuous development.

A good reporting system is a handy instrument of management to identify the areas of weaknesses and any untoward or unusual occurrence. Employees are put under constant control and management is free to devote fully on policy formulation and future development. Reports deal with forecast of conditions under which planned operations would be carried out. This applies to budget estimates on product lines and forecast of business conditions in general.

Reports deal with forecast of conditions under which planned operations would be carried. This applies to budget estimates of product lines and forecast of business conditions in general.

Reports also provide a useful basis for deciding operating policy, volume of sales or production, stock policy, quality production, product design, etc.

Current reports enable management at different needs of levels to keep itself abreast of past performance as well as development and it can keep a check on individual operating levels.

Reports and reporting methods provide executives with factual information for the execution of their duties. This forms the basis for developing policies by operating executives.

REVIEW QUESTIONS

1. What is meant by Management Reporting?
2. What is Reporting? Explain the various types of reports submitted to management.
3. What are the essentials of a good Reporting System?
4. Distinguish between (*a*) Routine Report and Special Report, and (*b*) Operating Reports and Financial Reports.
5. Describe briefly the informational needs of different levels of management.
6. Explain the basic requisites of a good report.
7. Explain the different types of reports that are used for the internal management of an enterprise.
8. Explain the steps involved in the preparation of reports.
9. Discuss the importance of a proper system of reporting.
10. What is the role of Management Accountant in the preparation of reports?
11. "Reporting is one of the main duties of a Management Accountant". Explain.
12. Explain the usefulness of reporting to management.
13. What are the objects of reporting?
14. Describe the various modes of reporting.
15. How can reports be classified? Explain giving suitable examples.

■ ■ ■

Index